INTRODUCTION TO
INTERNATIONAL
RELATIONS

Enduring Questions and Contemporary Perspectives

Joseph
Grieco
Duke University

G. John
Ikenberry
Princeton University

Michael
Mastanduno
Dartmouth College

macmillan
education   palgrave

First published 2015 by
PALGRAVE

Palgrave in the UK is an imprint of Macmillan Publishers Limited,
registered in England, company number 785998, of 4 Crinan Street, London N1 9XW.

Palgrave Macmillan in the US is a division of St Martin's Press LLC,
175 Fifth Avenue, New York, NY 10010.

Palgrave is the global imprint of the above companies and is represented
throughout the world.

Palgrave® and Macmillan® are registered trademarks in the United States,
the United Kingdom, Europe and other countries

ISBN 978-1-137-39880-2

This book is printed on paper suitable for recycling and made from fully
managed and sustained forest sources. Logging, pulping and manufacturing
processes are expected to conform to the environmental regulations of the
country of origin.

A catalogue record for this book is available from the British Library.

A catalog record for this book is available from the Library of Congress.

Printed and bound in Lebanon

Contents in Brief

1. Understanding International Relations   2

I. FOUNDATIONS OF INTERNATIONAL RELATIONS   31

2. The Emergence of a Global System of States, 1500–Today   32
3. Theories of International Relations   70
4. The Analysis of Foreign Policy   104

II. WAR AND PEACE: AN INTRODUCTION TO SECURITY STUDIES   137

5. War and its Causes   138
6. Pathways to Interstate Peace   174
7. Weapons of Mass Destruction   206

III. WEALTH AND POWER: AN INTRODUCTION TO INTERNATIONAL POLITICAL ECONOMY   245

8. International Economics: Basic Theory and Core Institutions   246
9. Power, Politics, and the World Economy   286
10. Dilemmas of Development   318

IV. CONTEMPORARY CHALLENGES AND THE FUTURE OF INTERNATIONAL RELATIONS   355

11. Non-State Actors and Challenges to Sovereignty   356
12. The Environment and International Relations   388
13. Facing the Future: Six Visions of an Emerging International Order   416

Contents

List of Features xv

List of Illustrative Matter xviii

About the Authors xxiii

Preface xxv

Online Teaching and Learning Resources xxxiv

Author Acknowledgements xxxvi

Copyright Acknowledgements xxxvii

1. Understanding International Relations 2

International Relations are Part of Everyday Life 4

Building Blocks for the Study of International Relations ... 6

   Basic Concepts for International Relations 6

   Levels of Analysis in International Relations 8

Recognizing Enduring Questions 12

   Examples of Enduring Questions 14

Making Connections 16

   Connecting Theory and Practice 16

   Connecting Past and Present 20

   Connecting Aspiration and Reality 23

Viewing the World from Different Perspectives 24

   Recognizing Great-Power Centrism 25

   Recognizing Cleavages within the International System ... 26

Looking Ahead 28

I. FOUNDATIONS OF INTERNATIONAL RELATIONS ... 31

2. The Emergence of a Global System of States, 1500–Today ... 32

ENDURING QUESTION:

How did a fragmented world become a global, integrated system of states for which order is an ongoing problem?

Starting Point: The World in 1500 34

The Formation of the International Political System,
1500–1900   36
   A State System Emerges in Western Europe   36
   European Pursuit of Foreign Empire   39
   Why were European States Successful Imperialists? 41
World War I and World War II, 1900–1945   43
   World War I: Origins, Conduct, and Aftermath   43
   The Versailles Treaty and the League of Nations 45
   Failed Global Reconstruction and the March to World War II,
   1920–1939   46
   War Comes Again to Europe and the World, 1939–1945 49
The Global Struggle of the Cold War, 1945–1989   51
   The World in 1945   51
   Explaining the Origins of the Cold War   52
   The Cold War as an International Order   55
The View from the South: Decolonization, the
Non-Aligned Movement, and the Quest for a New
International Economic Order   58
   Decolonization   58
   The Non-Aligned Movement and Third-World Pressure for
   a New International Economic Order   59
The End of the Cold War and the Collapse of the
Soviet Union   61
   Soviet Economic Reform and its Unintended Political Consequences 61
   Reagan Made Them Do It   63
   The Power of the People, Not the Leaders   64
The Contemporary International Order   65
Revisiting the Enduring Question and Looking Ahead   67

3.   Theories of International Relations   70
   ENDURING QUESTION:
   How do theoretical traditions in international relations
   differ on how to understand actors and their behavior on
   the global stage?
   The Realist Tradition   72
   Realist Assumptions   72
   Realist Propositions   74
   The English School of International Relations   77
   The Liberal Tradition   79
   Liberal Assumptions   79
   Liberal Propositions   82
   The Marxist Tradition   86
   Marxist Assumptions   88
   Marxist Propositions   90
   The Constructivist Tradition   92
   Constructivist Assumptions   93
   Constructivist Propositions   93

The Feminist Tradition   96
   Feminist Assumptions   96
   Feminist Propositions   97
Comparing Traditions   99
Revisiting the Enduring Question and Looking Ahead   102

4. The Analysis of Foreign Policy   104
   ENDURING QUESTION:
   What factors most influence the foreign policies of states?
Foreign Policy Analysis: Connections to International
Relations and Core Concepts   106
   The Study of International Relations and the Analysis of
   Foreign Policy   106
   Foreign Policy Interests   107
   Foreign Policy Strategy   107
The Sources of Foreign Policy   112
   Sources of Foreign Policy at the Individual Level of Analysis   113
   Sources of Foreign Policy at the State Level of Analysis   114
   Sources of Foreign Policy at the International Level of Analysis 123
How and Why States Change Their Foreign Policy   126
   Sources of Foreign Policy Change at the Individual Level of
   Analysis   126
   Sources of Foreign Policy Change at the State Level of Analysis 129
   Sources of Foreign Policy Change at the International Level
   of Analysis   132
Revisiting the Enduring Question and Looking Ahead   133

II. WAR AND PEACE: AN INTRODUCTION TO
SECURITY STUDIES   137

5. War and Its Causes   138
   ENDURING QUESTION:
   Why is war a persistent feature of international relations?
Wars between Countries   140
   Types of Military Conflicts between Countries   140
   Incidence of International Military Conflicts   142
   Lethality of International Wars   144
Immediate Causes of War   147
Underlying Causes of War: the Individual Level of Analysis   151
   Misperception, Crisis Escalation, and War: the Role of Stress
   and 'Motivated Biases'   152
   Social Psychology of Small Groups: Groupthink   153
   Personality Traits of Leaders: Over-Optimism   155
Underlying Causes of War: the State Level of Analysis   157
   Domestic Economic Systems and War   157
   Domestic Political Institutions and Governmental Processes 157

Underlying Causes of War: the International Level of
Analysis   160
   Anarchy as a Permissive Condition for War   160
   Anarchy as a Propellant of International Conflict   160
Internal Wars and their Causes   163
   Internal Wars and International Peace and Security   163
   Internal Wars: Types and Trends   164
   Causes of Internal Wars   168
Revisiting the Enduring Question and Looking Ahead   171

6. Pathways to Interstate Peace   174
ENDURING QUESTION:
What factors make it more likely that states will resolve their differences and avoid war?
The International Distribution of Power as a Condition for Peace   176
   Balance of Power   176
   Hegemony   177
State Strategies for Achieving Interstate Peace   178
   Diplomacy   178
   Power Balancing   182
International Law and Institutions as Mechanisms for Peace   185
   Essential Features of International Law and Institutions   185
   Three Experiences with International Law and Institutions: the League of Nations, the United Nations, and the European Union   188
Transnational Mechanisms for Peace   196
   Economic Interdependence   196
   A Possible International Community of Democratic Nations   199
   Peace Movements and Global Civil Society   202
Revisiting the Enduring Question and Looking Ahead   204

7. Weapons of Mass Destruction   206
ENDURING QUESTION:
How have weapons of mass destruction, and in particular nuclear weapons, changed the practice of international relations?
Nuclear Weapons   208
The Nuclear Revolution   213
   Assured Destruction and the Peculiar Logic of MAD   213
   Should Governments Prepare to Fight Nuclear War?   217
   Living with MAD: Arms Control Efforts   220
   Does MAD Still Exist Today?   222
Nuclear Proliferation and Efforts to Halt it   223
   Obtaining Nuclear Capability: Difficult But Not Impossible   224
   Why do States Want Nuclear Weapons?   226

How Dangerous is Nuclear Proliferation?		228
Efforts to Halt Proliferation: The Grand Bargain		230
Chemical and Biological Weapons		235
How They Work and Efforts to Control Them		235
Comparing Nuclear, Biological, and Chemical Weapons		238
Weapons of Mass Destruction and Terrorism		240
The Emergence of Cyber-Warfare		241
Revisiting the Enduring Question and Looking Ahead		242

III. WEALTH AND POWER: AN INTRODUCTION TO INTERNATIONAL POLITICAL ECONOMY
245

8. International Economics: Basic Theory and Core Institutions — 246

ENDURING QUESTION:
How do politics shape the global economy?

Basic Elements of International Trade Theory and Policy		248
Building Blocks for Analysis: Consumption and Production		248
Comparative Advantage		249
The Gains from Trade		251
Why do Countries Protect Themselves from Trade?		253
Basic Elements of International Money		257
National Exchange-Rate Systems		258
Fixed Exchange-Rate Systems: Benefits and Problems		263
Multinational Enterprises and International Political Economy		265
Definition and Characteristics of Multinational Enterprises		265
Importance of MNEs to the World Economy		267
Political Issues Surrounding MNEs		268
The Institutions of the World Economy		272
International Trade: From ITO to GATT to WTO		272
International Finance: Why is the IMF so Controversial?		277
Global Governance: From the G-7 and G-8 to the G-20		281
Revisiting the Enduring Question and Looking Ahead		284

9. Power, Politics, and the World Economy — 286

ENDURING QUESTION:
How do governments use international economic relations to further national political objectives?

Two Great Eras of Economic Globalization		288
States and Markets: Three Great Traditions of Thought		292
Economic Liberalism		292
Economic Nationalism		294
Marxism		295

States and Markets in a World of Anarchy   296

The Two-Sided Government: Managing Domestic and
International Relations   297

State Building, War, and Markets   307

Great Powers and the World Economy   310

Leadership and the Liberal World Economy   312

The Contemporary World Economy: Globalization
and its Challenges   314

Revisiting the Enduring Question and Looking Ahead   316

10. Dilemmas of Development   318

ENDURING QUESTION:

How does participation in the world economy help or
hinder the economic development of poorer countries?

What, and Where Are the Developing Countries?   320

What is Economic Development?   320

Growth Experiences of Different Groups of Developing Countries   321

International Relations and Challenges to Developing
Countries   323

Failure to Develop: A Legacy of Colonialism?   323

Difficulties in Development   324

Is International Trade a Path to Development?   326

Developing Countries and Market-Controlling Trade Strategies   327

Developing Countries and Market-Accepting Trade Strategies   329

Is International Finance a Path to Development?   332

International Financial Flows: Meaning, Types, and Magnitudes   332

Financial Flows: Opportunities and Challenges for Developing
Countries   335

Development Strategies and Emerging Great Powers –
the BRICS   342

China   343

India   345

Brazil   347

Russia   348

South Africa   350

Revisiting the Enduring Question and Looking Ahead   351

IV. CONTEMPORARY CHALLENGES AND THE
FUTURE OF INTERNATIONAL RELATIONS   355

11. Non-state Actors and Challenges to Sovereignty   356

ENDURING QUESTION:

Can the State Continue to Overcome Challenges to its
Authority?

States, Sovereignty, and the Westphalian System   358

Challenges to Sovereign States   360

Piracy   362

Weak/Failed States	364
Terrorism	371
Technology and the Privatization of War	374
International Responses to Non-State Actors	377
Global Response to Failed States	379
Whither the State?	384
Revisiting the Enduring Question and Looking Ahead	386

12. The Environment and International Relations   388

ENDURING QUESTION:

How does the natural environment influence international relations?

Sources of Problems for the Global Environment and Natural Resources	390
Negative Externalities	390
The Tragedy of the Commons	391
Challenges for the World's Environment and Natural Resources	394
Problems with the Atmosphere	394
Damage to the World's Water Resources	399
Damage to the Land	403
Management of International Environmental Problems	406
Unilateral Responses	406
Bilateral Efforts	407
Multilateral Approaches	407
Revisiting the Enduring Question and Looking Ahead	413

13. Facing the Future: Six Visions of an Emerging International Order   416

ENDURING QUESTION:

Will the international system undergo fundamental change in the future?

Model 1: A World of Geo-Economic Competition	418
Characteristics of Geo-Economic Competition	418
International Trends	422
Contrary Evidence and Questions	424
Model 2: A Return to Multipolarity	426
Characteristics of Multipolarity	428
International Trends	428
Contrary Evidence and Questions	430
Model 3: A New Bipolarity	432
Characteristics of a New Bipolarity	433
International Trends	434
Contrary Evidence and Questions	435
Model 4: A Democratic Peace	436
Characteristics of Democratic Peace	436

International Trends 438

Contrary Evidence and Questions 439

Model 5: A Clash of Civilizations 442

Characteristics of a Clash of Civilizations 442

International Trends 443

Contrary Evidence and Questions 444

**Model 6: Global Fracture: Pre-modern, Modern, and
Post-Modern Zones** 446

Characteristics of Global Fracture 446

International Trends 449

Contrary Evidence and Questions 450

**Looking Back: A Reminder to Focus on Enduring
Questions** 451

Glossary 454

References 475

Index 495

List of Features

Box 1.1 *Enduring Questions in International Relations*   14

Making Connections, Theory and Practice

Box 2.1 *Religious Identity and the Franco-Ottoman Military Alliance*   38

Box 3.1 *Realism and State Rationality – the Issue of State Self-Defeatism*   73

Box 4.4 *The Influence of Bankers on Foreign Policy across Countries*   125

Box 5.5 *Institutional Politics and War: The US Oil Embargo Against Japan, 1941*   158

Box 6.2 *Realist Theory on International Law, Institutions and Government Actions*   187

Box 7.2 *The Logic of MAD versus the Cold War Nuclear Strategies of the United States and Soviet Union*   216

Box 8.2 *The Economic Logic of Specialization and Trade versus the Political Power of Domestic Interest Groups*   256

Box 9.3 *The Trade Dispute over China's 'Rare Earth' Mineral Exports*   305

Box 10.3 *Foreign Aid and Economic Development in Africa*   338

Box 11.3 *State Sovereignty*   375

Box 12.1 *The Tragedy of the Commons and Deforestation of Tropical Forests*   393

Box 13.3 *The Future of NATO under Multipolarity*   431

Making Connections, Then and Now

Box 2.2 *The Persistence of the Munich Analogy*   49

Box 3.3 *Changing Character of Economic Doctrines*   81

Box 4.3 *Presidents Woodrow Wilson, Harry Truman, and Barack Obama on Working with Congress on Foreign Policy*   122

Box 5.1 *Conflict of Interest over Domestic Political Regimes: the French Revolutionary Period in the 1790s and the Build-up to the US Invasion of Iraq in 2003*   148

Box 6.1	*The Growth of Modern International Diplomacy*	179
Box 7.5	*Proposals from US Political Elites for a Nuclear-Free World*	234
Box 8.4	*Trade-Dispute Settlement in the GATT and WTO*	275
Box 9.1	*The Rise of a Liberal World Economy*	289
Box 10.1	*State Leaders Describe the Importance of National Economic Self-Sufficiency*	325
Box 11.1	*Pirates in the Seventeenth and Twenty-first Centuries*	365
Box 12.2	*From Sporadic Over-Fishing to Possible Collapse of Vital Marine Life*	402
Box 13.2	*Regional Economic Blocs*	426

Making Connections, Aspiration versus Reality

Box 2.3	*The United States and Support for Democracy during the Cold War*	55
Box 3.4	*Liberal Visions of Shared Benefits of Economic Growth*	87
Box 4.1	*US Foreign Policy toward China, 2009*	108
Box 5.4	*Pre-Conflict Aspirations of Leaders and the Realities of War*	155
Box 6.3	*Collective Security versus Britain's Abandonment of Czechoslovakia*	191
Box 7.3	*Government Advice on Preparing for Nuclear War versus Government Response to Hurricane Katrina*	218
Box 8.3	*Dollarization in Central and South America*	262
Box 9.4	*Free Trade in Principle, Not Practice*	308
Box 10.4	*Developed Countries' Pledges and Performance on Official Development Assistance*	340
Box 11.2	*Building the Afghanistan State*	368
Box 12.3	*Compliance with the Kyoto Protocol*	409
Box 13.4	*Revolutionary Upheaval in the Middle East*	440

Differing Perspectives

Box 2.4	*The Cuban Missile Crisis of October 1962*	57
Box 3.2	*China, Southeast Asia, and the Security Dilemma*	76
Box 4.2	*Explaining Iraq's Foreign Policy and Decision to Go to War in 1991*	115
Box 5.2	*Conflict of Interest over Territory: Taiwan, China, and the Risk of Military Conflict in East Asia*	150
Box 6.5	*Liberals and Realists on Interdependence and the Rise of China*	202
Box 7.1	*Were Nuclear Attacks on Japan Needed to End World War II?*	209
Box 8.1	*Infant-Industry Protection in Developing Countries*	255
Box 9.2	*The Chinese Government and Google*	291
Box 10.2	*Fernando Henrique Cardoso on the Benefits of International Economic Integration*	331
Box 11.4	*How to Cope with the Threat of International Terrorism*	379
Box 12.4	*The United States, India, and Greenhouse Gas Emissions*	410
Box 13.5	*The Clash of Civilizations*	445

Differing Theoretical Approaches

Box 3.5	*Sources of Change in International Relations*	100
Box 4.5	*Why Did the United States and the European Community Impose Economic Sanctions against South Africa?*	130
Box 5.3	*Constructivist and Feminist Interpretations of Groupthink and the Bay of Pigs*	154
Box 6.4	*The Role and Significance of the United Nations*	194
Box 7.4	*Why Don't More States Pursue Nuclear Weapons?*	229
Box 8.5	*Realist, Liberal, and Constructivist Views on the Prospects for an Ambitious G-20 Agenda*	282
Box 9.5	*Why has China Embraced International Institutions?*	312
Box 10.5	*The Future of the BRICS*	343
Box 11.5	*The Future of the Nation-State*	385
Box 12.5	*Factors Affecting the Likelihood of a Comprehensive Climate-Change Agreement*	412
Box 13.1	*Explaining the End of the Cold War*	421

List of Illustrative Material

Figures

3.1	World Trends in Governance, 1800–2010	84
5.1	Incidence of Interstate Wars, 1816–2007, and During and After the Cold War	142
5.2	Incidence of Militarized Interstate Disputes, 1816–2010, and During and After the Cold War	143
5.3	Severity of Militarized Interstate Disputes, 1900–2010	144
5.4	Incidence of Extra-state Wars, 1816–2007, and During and After the Cold War	145
5.5	Battlefield Deaths in Interstate and Extra-state Wars, 1816–2007, and During and After the Cold War	146
5.6	The Prisoner's Dilemma	162
5.7	Incidence of Internal Wars, 1816–2007, and During and After the Cold War	165
5.8	Lethality of Internal Wars, 1816–2007, and During and After the Cold War	166
5.9	International Interventions in Internal Wars, 1816–2007, and During and After the Cold War	167
6.1	International Organizations by Year and Type, 1909–99	179
7.1	Timeline of Nuclear Arms Control Agreements and Treaties	221
7.2	A Schematic Diagram of an Implosion Bomb	224
8.1	Hypothetical US Production Possibilities Frontier	249
8.2	Specialization and Trade: the United Kingdom and Vietnam	251
8.3	Determination of Exchange Rates: Canadian Dollar and Swiss franc	259
8.4	US Dollar/Chinese Renminbi Exchange Rate, 2000–12	264
8.5	Global Economic Significance of MNEs, 1990–2011	268
8.6	The Kindleberger Spiral of Declining World Trade	273
9.1	Merchandise Exports as Per Cent of GDP in 1990 Prices, 5 Countries and World, 1870–2007	289
9.2	Top 20 Foreign Holders of US Treasury Securities, end January 2014	303

10.1	Annual Rates of Growth in Per Capita GDP, by Region and Decade, 1980–2010	322
10.2	Global Oil Production and Proven Reserves, 2012	328
10.3	Total Private and Official Financial Flows to Developing Countries, 1980–2010	333
10.4	Composition of Private Financial Flows to Developing Countries, 2000–10	333
10.5	Official Financial Flows to Developing Countries, by Type, 1980–2010	334
10.6	Private and Official Financial Flows to Countries in Sub-Saharan Africa, 2010	334
10.7	Foreign Assistance and Economic Growth in Africa, 1970–99	338
10.8	Official Development Assistance as Percent of National Income, Major Donors, Five-Year Average, 2008–12	341
10.9	Shares of World GDP 2011 and Projection for 2030	345
12.1	Increasing Concentration of CO_2 in the Atmosphere, 1958–2013	395
12.2	Responsibility for Addressing the Problem of Global Warming: Developed and Developing Countries and CO_2 Emissions	397
12.3	Utilization of World Marine Fish Stocks, 1974–2009	403
12.4	Meeting Kyoto Protocol Commitments to Cut Greenhouse Gases	409
13.1	Evolution of Regional Trade Agreements (RTAs), 1948—2014	424
13.2	Chinese FDI Flows to Asia and Africa, 2003–12	425

Maps

1.1	A National Interest: China and its Claims to the South China Sea	8
1.2	Greece in the Era of the Peloponnesian War	13
1.3	Imperialism and Colonialism in Africa on the Eve of World War I	18
1.4	Africa Today	19
2.1	The Eastern Hemisphere in 1500	34
2.2	Inca, Mayas, and Aztec Empires in the Western Hemisphere in 1500	35
2.3	The British Empire, Early 1900s	40
2.4	Atlantic Basin Triangle Trade in the Seventeenth and Eighteenth Centuries	42
2.5	The Schlieffen Plan of 1905 and the Western Front in Late 1914	45
2.6	Postwar Occupation Zones for Germany	52
2.7	Patterns of Decolonization	59
2.8	The Territory of the Former Soviet Union after its Collapse into 15 Sovereign States	62
4.1	Critical Waterway for Oil Exports: the Strait of Hormuz	110
4.2	Covert Operation: the Killing of Osama bin Laden	111
6.1	The Roman Empire in 116 CE	176
6.2	The Han Empire in 100 BCE	177
6.3	The Wars of German Unification, 1866–1871	183
7.1	Israel, Iran and the Middle East	215
8.1	Members of the European Union Using the Euro, 2014	261

8.2	A Multinational Enterprise: Ford Motor Company's Worldwide Operations	266
9.1	The Dutch East India Company	288
9.2	European Gas Pipelines	301
9.3	East China Sea	302
9.4	China and East Asia	304
10.1	A World of Different Life Opportunities	321
11.1	The Failed State Index 2013	366
12.1	Possible Sign of Global Warming: Retreat of Arctic Summer Ice, 2012	394
12.2	Exposure of Bangladesh to Risk of Rising Seas	396
12.3	Gulf of Mexico Oil Spill, 2010	401
12.4	Worldwide Distribution of Tropical Forests	404
13.1	The Soviet Union and Eastern Europe during the Cold War	419
13.2	Russia and the Eastward Expansion of NATO	420
13.3	Regional Economic Blocs: NAFTA, European Union, and APEC	423
13.4	Syria and its Neighbors	449

Tables

3.1	European Union Member States	80
4.1	China's New Top Leaders: The Politburo Standing Committee, 2012	117
7.1	Ten Bombs on Ten South Asian Cities	211
7.2	World Nuclear forces, January 2013	212
8.1	Hypothetical Output and Opportunity Costs, Bottles of Medications and Pairs of Shoes, UK and Vietnam	251
8.2	UK–Vietnam Trade: Gains in Consumption	253
8.3	Selected Currency Rates	259
8.4	Largest Voting Shares in the IMF by Individual Country, 2014	279
8.5	The Group of 20	281
13.1	Intraregional Trade as a Share of Total Trade of Each Region, 1962–94	427

Photos

1.1	The Berlin Wall, 1961	5
1.2	The Berlin Wall, 1989	6
1.3	Adolf Hitler	11
1.4	Vietnam War Memorial	20
1.5	Tragedy in Srebrenica	22
2.1	Trench Warfare during World War I	45
2.2	Emergency Aid in New York City during the Great Depression	48
2.3	Hiroshima after the Atomic Blast	50
2.4	Churchill, Roosevelt, and Stalin at Yalta	53
2.5	Founders of the Non-Aligned Movement	60
3.1	Secretary of State Dean Acheson Signs the NATO Alliance Pact	75

3.2   Serbian Nationalist Rally   78
3.3 and 3.4   Trials for Crimes Against Humanity   82
3.5   Cosmopolitanism   85
3.6   NATO Soldiers on a Humanitarian Mission in Afghanistan, 2007   94
3.7   Secretary of State Hillary Clinton visits Sarajevo, October 2010   98
4.1   Chinese Administrative Facility, Paracel Islands, 2012   112
4.2   A Difficult Partnership   116
4.3   Romney–Obama Presidential Debate on Foreign Policy,
        October 22, 2012   119
4.4   War Zones   121
4.5   Greenpeace Protests   132
5.1   The Holocaust in Europe During World War II   147
5.2   Strategically Important Territory: The Golan Heights   149
5.3   Child Soldier in Civil War in Liberia, 2003   164
5.4 and 5.5   Genocide in Cambodia and Rwanda   167
5.6   Janjaweed Militia Fighters, October 2004   169
6.1   The Embassies of Greece and Georgia on Embassy Row in
        Washington, DC   181
6.2   UN Peacekeeping Operations   193
6.3   The European Court of Justice in Luxembourg   195
6.4   American Poster from World War II   201
6.5   A Vietnam War Protest in Washington, DC   203
7.1   'Ivy Mike' Thermonuclear Explosion in the Marshall Islands   210
7.2   Iran's Nuclear Power Plant at Bushehr   225
7.3   The International Atomic Energy Agency at Work   231
7.4   The Trial of 'Chemical Ali'   236
7.5   Syrian Victims of Chemical Weapons Attack, 2013   237
7.6   Israeli Citizens Prepare for Possible Chemical Attack from Iraq
        during 1990–91 Gulf War   239
8.1   Multinational Enterprises at Work   267
8.2   The Bretton Woods Conference   274
8.3   Anti-WTO Protest, Hong Kong, December 2005   277
8.4   IMF Headquarters in Washington, DC   278
8.5   Greek Citizens Protest Austerity Imposed by IMF and EU   280
9.1   Witnessing the Effects of the 2008 Financial Crisis   290
9.2   Adam Smith   292
9.3   Beijing 2008 Olympic Games   298
9.4   Twenty-First-Century Greece   299
9.5   Free Trade Creates Greater Consumer Choice   309
10.1   4th OPEC International Seminar, 2009   329
10.2   Child Labor in Developing Countries   336
10.3   National Leaders at the Fifth BRICS meeting   342
10.4   Slums and Skyscrapers: Two Faces of India   346
10.5   Brazil's Agricultural Miracle   348
11.1   The Assassination of Paolo Borsellino, 1992   359
11.2   Airport Body Scanners   361
11.3   The Use of Unmanned Drones   362
11.4   Pirates off the Coast of Somalia   363

11.5	The Kashirskoye Shosse Apartment Bombing, Moscow, Russia 1999	367
11.6	Mural Idolizing the IRA in Belfast, North Ireland	373
11.7	NATO Bombing of Belgrade, 1999	380
12.1	Effects of Acid Rain on Forests	391
12.2	Deforestation	392
12.3	Water Pollution, The River Ganges, India	400
12.4	Norwegian Minke Whale Hunting	403
12.5	Biodiversity in the Forest	405
13.1	Leaders Pose at an SCO Summit, 2012	429
13.2	Taiwanese Protesters in 2010	433
13.3	Energy resources of the Middle East	434
13.4	Arab Spring	439
13.5	Women in Somalia	448

About the Authors

Joseph Grieco is Professor in the Department of Political Science at Duke University. He is the co-author (with G. John Ikenberry) of *State Power and World Markets: the International Political Economy*, and is the author of *Cooperation among Nations: Europe, America, and Non-Tariff Barriers to Trade* and *Between Dependency and Autonomy: India's Experience with the International Computer Industry*. He is the author or co-author of articles and notes that have appeared in *American Journal of Political Science, International Organization, Journal of Peace Research, Journal of Conflict Resolution, International Studies Quarterly, British Journal of Politics and International Relations, Korean Journal of International Studies, Security Studies, Review of International Studies, American Political Science Review, Journal of Politics,* and *World Politics.* He has had research fellowships at Princeton, Harvard, and the Social Science Center in Berlin, and his research has been supported by the US National Science Foundation, the John D. and Catherine T. MacArthur Foundation, and the German–Marshall Foundation. As an International Affairs fellow with the Council on Foreign Relations he served at the Office of the US Trade Representative and the International Monetary Fund. He has taught in the International Relations program at the University of Bologna at Forli, and since 1996 he has been a Visiting Professor at the Post-Graduate School of Economics and International Relations at the Catholic University of Milan.

G. John Ikenberry is the Albert G. Milbank Professor of Politics and International Affairs at Princeton University in the Department of Politics and the Woodrow Wilson School of Public and International Affairs. He is also Co-Director of Princeton's Center for International Security Studies. Ikenberry is also a Global Eminence Scholar at Kyung Hee University in Seoul, Korea. In 2013–14, he was the 72nd Eastman Visiting Professor at Balliol College, Oxford. Professor Ikenberry is the author of many books, including *Liberal Leviathan: The Origins, Crisis, and Transformation of the*

American System. His book *After Victory: Institutions, Strategic Restraint, and the Rebuilding of Order after Major Wars* won the 2002 Schroeder-Jervis Award presented by the American Political Science Association for the best book in international history and politics. Professor Ikenberry is the co-director of the Princeton Project on National Security. Among his many activities, he served as a member of the Policy Planning Staff in 1991–92, and as a member of an advisory group at the State Department in 2003–04, and as a member of the Council on Foreign Relations Task Force on US–European relations, the so-called Kissinger-Summers commission. He is also a reviewer of books on political and legal affairs for *Foreign Affairs*.

 Michael Mastanduno is the Nelson A. Rockefeller Professor of Government and Dean of the Faculty of Arts and Sciences at Dartmouth College in Hanover, NH. He has taught at Dartmouth since 1987, and his areas of research and teaching specialization include international relations theory, US foreign policy, and the politics of the world economy. His current research concerns the rise of China and its implications for international economics and security. His articles have appeared in many journals including *World Politics, International Organization, International Studies Quarterly*, and *International Security*. He is author or editor of numerous books including *Economic Containment, Beyond Westphalia?, International Relations Theory and the Asia-Pacific, Unipolar Politics, US Hegemony and International Organizations*, and *International Relations Theory and the Consequences of Unipolarity*. Professor Mastanduno lectures frequently in Europe and Asia and has been a guest faculty member at the University of Tokyo, the Graduate School of Economics and International Relations at Milan, and the Geneva Center for Security Policy. He has been awarded fellowships from the Brookings Institution, the Salzburg Seminar, the Council on Foreign Relations, and the East–West Center. He served during sabbatical from Dartmouth as an assistant in the Office of the US Trade Representative, and he is a member of the Council on Foreign Relations.

Preface

Why does our field need yet another introductory textbook? We three authors have arrived at an answer through a long series of conversations based on our three decades of experience teaching International Relations to interested and always interesting undergraduates. We recognize that students new to the discipline seek to understand what is happening *now* in a complex world that excites them intellectually but is difficult to fully comprehend. The problem is that courses which place too much emphasis on current events may engage for the moment, but leave students short of the tools needed for sound analysis when, inevitably, the headlines change. On the other hand, courses that focus too heavily on disciplinary or scholastic debates risk leaving new students feeling like outsiders, lacking the context and background to appreciate what is at stake. Professional scholars make sense of the complexity of the world through international relations theories; their natural inclination is to impart knowledge of those theories and their specialized jargon at ever increasing levels of nuance and specificity to initiate even our newest students. Yet, we know that dosage matters: too much theory leaves a new student of international relations overwhelmed and wondering how these debates and typologies matter for the real world, while too little leaves a student unprepared to navigate a complicated and confusing substantive terrain.

We take a different approach to these dilemmas. We begin with the premise that the essentials of international relations are animated less by the news of the day or by the latest twist in theoretical paradigms, and more by a set of long-standing questions that have engaged and challenged generations of international relations scholars and students. We call these *enduring questions* and we motivate each chapter around one of them. Instructors using our book will immediately recognize a familiar organizational structure build around theories and approaches, security studies, international political economy, the role of international organizations and non-state actors, and the future of the international system. But students will be invited to engage with the material in a different way. Once students appreciate that international relations is about grappling with large, challenging questions that have stood the test of time, we believe they will demand the tools necessary to make their own attempt to answer them. Our text provides those tools and offers a variety of approaches and answers to these questions, reflecting differences in the scholarly field of international relations and, in some cases, among ourselves.

We have tried to convey the material of our field in language that is clear and intuitive to undergraduates. We believe it is possible, indeed necessary, to be both comprehensive in coverage and accessible in style. Our intention has not been to make the material artificially easy, but to employ a direct style of writing so that our text welcomes new participants into the enduring conversations of our field, rather than treat them as visitors who need passports and phrase books as they tour a foreign land with exotic customs and language. We aim to inspire students, who are also citizens, to join and remain engaged in those conversations. By developing an appreciation of the enduring questions of our field, and the political, economic and social dynamics that underlie those questions, student-citizens will be more capable not only of understanding today's headlines but also those international issues and problems that will arise long after they have completed their introductory course.

Thematic Framework

We believe the best way for students to attain a firm understanding of international relations is to be able to recognize *enduring questions* in the unfolding of international relations; to grasp the analytical utility of the *levels of analysis;* to understand the interplay of *theory and history;* to *make connections* between the past and present, theory and practice, and political aspirations and practical realities; and to view the world from *different perspectives*.

Enduring Questions

Each chapter following the introduction is organized around an enduring question of international relations. Such questions about relations among countries recur throughout history, have important consequences and are the subject of considerable policy and scholarly debate. For example, consider the question 'In what ways does participation in the world economy help or hinder the development of poorer countries?' America's founding fathers debated that question in the late eighteenth century, the leaders of a newly unified Germany debated it at the end of the nineteenth century, and politicians in China, Brazil, and India struggle with it today. Political scientists and economists have joined that debate over the centuries, often putting forward radically differing answers. Those answers are profoundly consequential for countries seeking to free millions of people from the grip of poverty, and for ambitious leaders seeking to promote national economic strength in order to compete more effectively in the international arena.

As we progress through the chapters that follow, each focusing on an important area of international relations, we begin with a broad, enduring question of international relations to frame the substance of each chapter and to help students recognize that, notwithstanding the presumed novelty of today's fast-paced world, many of the critical issues of contemporary international politics have recurred in one form or another across time. The enduring questions that we address on a chapter-by-chapter basis are summarized in Box 1.1 in Chapter 1. We weave enduring questions throughout the chapters, and at the end of each we revisit that chapter's enduring question and its significance.

Levels of Analysis

The levels-of-analysis framework is a long-standing and battle-tested device for categorizing theories, arguments and insights about international relations. It is valuable both to instructors seeking to organize and teach our field and to students making their initial attempts to understand it. In this text we employ and systematically highlight the individual, state, and international system levels of analysis. For example, our discussion of why the Cold War ended invites students to debate the relative explanatory weight of the role of great leaders and social movements, the calculations of state interest on the part of the United States and Soviet Union, and the shifting balance of economic and technological power between these two superpowers. Our chapters on international political economy go beyond the standard 'trade, money, and investment' format and encourage students to view economic interactions and outcomes from the perspective of the world economy as a whole as well as through the ambitions and strategies of nation-states at different stages of development.

Our goal is for students to move easily across the different levels, yet to be aware of the analytical and theoretical implications of making those moves. At the end of each major section in a chapter, we offer a boxed summary feature prompting students to reflect on the substantive material just presented at one or more relevant levels of analysis. These boxes use icons to represent the different levels of analysis so that instructors and students have an easily identifiable point of reference.

Theory and History

Theoretical frameworks are vital in the study of international relations; they allow us to make sense of the past and anticipate possible patterns in the future. Most beginning students, however, have minimal knowledge of the history of the international system and that constrains their capacity to appreciate either the context in which international relations theories developed or the reason why theories are so important. Our text addresses this problem by providing a comprehensive chapter on the history of international relations and placing it *before* introducing students to the theoretical frameworks and traditions of the field. Scholars have often put forward theories of international relations as a reaction to developments in the world; one must have some baseline knowledge of that world in order to appreciate what has motivated theoretical debates and is at stake within them. We also emphasize that theory and history interact at different levels of analysis, for example by following the chapter on broad theoretical traditions with one on the analysis of state-level foreign policies.

Making Connections

The ability of students to identify and discuss connections across ideas, themes, and issues is an important skill in the development of critical thinking. In the study of international relations, it is obviously critical to appreciate the links between domestic and international politics and between international politics and economics. Other types of important connections may be less obvious to students, so in each chapter we have provided special boxed features that enable students to make connections between theory and practice, between past and present, and between aspirations and reality.

- *Making Connections, Theory and Practice:* By highlighting this connection we help students appreciate both the value and the limits of the standard theories of international relations as devices for organizing and explaining international events. In Chapter 6, for example, we include a box that highlights 'Realist Theory on International Law, Institutions, and Government Actions.' We explain that realism generally places very little weight on the value of international law and institutions; yet, even powerful governments like that of the United States seem to place great emphasis in their diplomacy on the workings of these institutions. We encourage students to unravel this puzzle by considering and discussing why governments feel the need to adhere to international law and organizations even when they are not forced to do so, and whether realist theory can account for that seemingly puzzling behaviour.
- *Making Connections, Then and Now:* The boxes that focus on these connections help students to gain insight by uncovering the historical sources of contemporary international initiatives. In Chapter 2, for example, we provide a box on 'The Persistence of the Munich-Appeasement Analogy,' showing how that pre-World World II episode shaped the thinking of President Lyndon Johnson about the Vietnam War in 1965 and the calculations of President George W. Bush on the eve of the Iraq War of 2003. We ask students to consider why this type of analogy is so appealing to policy makers, and also to explore whether the logic of the Munich analogy would be persuasive in the event a future American president contemplated military conflict with Iran or North Korea.
- *Making Connections, Aspiration versus Reality:* The boxes that make explicit connections between aspiration and reality remind students of the often profound differences between how the world is and how students, teachers and national leaders might like it to be. For example, in Chapter 12 we provide a feature entitled 'Compliance with the Kyoto Protocol.' We show students that among the countries that committed to a treaty to reduce greenhouse gas emissions, some countries met their stated targets while others did not. Why are governments often unable to follow through on commitments they make to improve the global environment? Students may use this feature to debate the role of domestic politics in international behavior, and even to consider the fairness of treaties that hold different countries to different standards in pursuit of a common objective.

Differing Perspectives and Differing Theoretical Approaches

We display two other boxed features chapter by chapter to emphasize to students the importance of viewing the world, and international relations theories about it, from multiple perspectives. First, we use a box labeled Differing Perspectives to help students appreciate that how an individual, group or indeed a political community views a particular international relations issue depends significantly on, among other factors, whether the actor in question is weak or powerful, secure or insecure, or wealthy or poor. For example, countries that already possess nuclear weapons tend to think differently about the dangers of the further spread of nuclear weapons than do countries that do not have those weapons and perceive threats from their neighbors. Our emphasis on multiple perspectives will help students grasp the variety and complexity of the motivations, interests and goals among the many actors on the international stage. In Chapter 10, we feature Fernando Henrique Cardoso on the Benefits of International Economic Integration, 1970s versus the 1990s and early 2000s. As a Latin American scholar writing in the 1970s, Cardoso counseled developing countries to minimize their links to the world economy. Later, as president of Brazil during the 1990s, he fully embraced his country's global economic integration. Did Cardoso simply change his mind, did Brazil change its economic position, or did the world economy itself change? We encourage students to consider, discuss and debate how differing perspectives affect the nature of international relations, and how developments in international politics, in turn, change the perspectives of actors.

Second, and beginning in Chapter 3, we include a box labeled Differing Theoretical Approaches. These boxes each pick a particular outcome or decision of relevance to the chapter and describe, in a simple and intuitive way, how scholars working from the perspective of different theoretical traditions (such as liberalism, constructivism, realism, Marxism and feminism) might explain that outcome or decision. For example, in Chapter 4, which focuses on explanations of foreign policy and foreign policy change, we discuss how constructivists, realists and Marxists might account for why Great Britain and the United States long supported South Africa's apartheid regime, yet in the mid-1980s shifted to a strategy of economic sanctions designed to isolate the regime and pressure it to make domestic changes.

Organization of the Book: Integrating Theory, History, and Contemporary International Relations

Chapter 1 serves as our introduction to the study of global politics. We describe how and why international relations are part of the everyday lives of people around the world, including the students reading this book and probably taking their first class in international relations. We provide some basic terms and concepts, elaborate upon the thematic framework of the book, and provide a rationale for our emphasis on recognizing enduring questions, utilizing levels of analysis, making connections, and viewing international relations from differing perspectives.

Beyond the introductory chapter, the book is divided into four parts:

- Part I: Foundations of International Relations (Chapters 2, 3, and 4).
- Part II: War and Peace: An Introduction to Security Studies (Chapters 5, 6, and 7).
- Part III: Wealth and Power: An Introduction to International Political Economy (Chapters 8, 9, and 10).
- Part IV: Contemporary Challenges and the Future of International Relations (Chapters 11, 12, and 13).

Part I: Foundations of International Relations

Part I provides the analytical tools that are integral to the study of international relations. We begin by tracing the evolution of the international system. World politics did not begin in 1945, much less in 1990. Thus, Chapter 2 examines – in broad thematic strokes – global history between 1500 and 2012, covering both the non-Western and the Western origins of the international system. In this chapter we introduce students to key moments in the development of states and the international system up to 1900; then we examine the origins, conduct and consequences during the twentieth century of World War I and World War II, as well as the origins and ending of the

Cold War; and finally we present the key features of the contemporary international order, including the problem of global terrorism.

In Chapter 3, we offer a comprehensive introduction to the primary theoretical frameworks of international relations. We explain why it is important to think theoretically about international relations, and we explore in detail the theoretical traditions of liberalism, realism, constructivism, Marxism, and feminism. Chapter 4 moves from the level of the international system to that of the individual country and provides an overview of foreign policy analysis. Interests and strategies are core concepts in the study of international relations; we examine their internal and external sources, and discuss how and why interests and strategies change over time.

Part II: War and Peace: An Introduction to Security Studies

Part II of the book introduces the subfield of security studies. In Chapter 5 we examine the pathways and mechanisms that sometimes lead states to war. We describe the main characteristics and frequency of international wars and explore the types of issues over which states sometimes fight wars. We also examine wars within states, or civil wars, which are intrinsically important and can have a variety of weighty implications for international relations. In Chapter 6 we explore the parallel issue of the pathways leading states to peace. We examine the importance that leaders and especially ordinary people have assigned to peace, and identify various mechanisms that governments and citizens have used to promote peace. Peace-building efforts are lodged at different levels of analysis, and thus we explore international mechanisms (for example, international law and institutions, and hegemony), transnational mechanisms (for example, peace movements and economic interdependence) and state-level mechanisms (for example, diplomacy and power balancing) to provide students with a comprehensive understanding.

We turn in Chapter 7 to the issues and problems pertaining to weapons of mass destruction (WMD), as well as their effects on international relations. We devote an entire chapter to this topic because students must appreciate the profound effects that WMD and, most importantly, nuclear weapons have had on war-making and peace-making in international relations. This chapter describes the unprecedented destructive capacity of nuclear weapons, explains the peculiar logic of nuclear deterrence, examines the problem of nuclear proliferation and the dangers posed by the possession and spread of chemical and biological weapons, and offers a detailed discussion of the dangerous liaisons that may be bringing together non-state actors, terrorism, and weapons of mass destruction.

Part III: Wealth and Power: An Introduction to International Political Economy

Part III introduces students to the subfield of international political economy, or IPE. We seek to highlight and identify connections between wealth and power by shifting our focus back and forth between international relationships and the foreign policies of states. Chapter 8 begins with the premise that students new to International Relations need to be familiar with the basic concepts of international economics (for example, comparative advantage, or the movement of exchange rates) to appreciate how international politics and economics interact. We focus in Chapter 8 on trade, money, and investment. We draw upon both economics and political science to analyze the reasons for and consequences of trade, and explain why some states nevertheless choose strategies of protection. We also introduce the types and dynamics of international financial transactions, including the role of exchange rates and the activities of multinational corporations. We explore the institutionalized mechanisms through which states manage their economic relationships, and we concentrate on how states have learned to promote and manage economic globalization in part through forming and working through such international institutions as the World Trade Organization (WTO) and the International Monetary Fund (IMF).

Once students have a basic grasp of economic concepts and of the substance and workings of the world economy, we move in Chapter 9 to the state level and examine how states seek to shape the global economy to promote their influence, defend their national interests, and maintain when possible their national economic autonomy. We explore the major perspectives on the relationships between states and markets as they inform the economic choices of states in a competitive geopolitical world; the relationships among state-building, war, and markets; the role of powerful states in the creation of open markets; the relationship between economic interdependence and interstate conflict; and the use of economic relations as political tools. Chapter 10 focuses in particular on developing and emerging economies. We provide perspectives on the meaning of economic development and review the economic experiences over recent decades of different groups of developing countries. We also introduce students to the structural challenges that past linkages to the global economy pose for poorer countries as they have sought to achieve economic development, and explore opportunities and problems that contemporary globalization in trade and finance may present to developing countries. We devote a section of this chapter to the particular opportunities and challenges facing prominent emerging economies such as Brazil, China, India, Russia and South Africa.

Part IV: Contemporary Challenges and the Future of International Relations

Part IV focuses on contemporary versions of recurring challenges to the international system. Chapter 11 analyzes terrorism as both an old and new problem in international relations. We consider the problems that drug cartels and pirates on the high seas pose for state authority; and we discuss the special problems associated with failed states. We probe the issue of human rights, and in particular whether the international community has a responsibility to protect individuals in failed states who are being harmed by their home governments, even if doing so violates the sovereignty of those states. Chapter 12 takes up the international environment and natural resources as international political issues. We describe key global environmental and resource issues involving the atmosphere, the oceans, and the land, and we investigate why such problems arise, how governments try to address them, and what helps or hinders those efforts. We also explore links between environmental and resource problems on the one hand and civil and international conflict on the other.

Chapter 13 serves as the conclusion to the textbook. Here we invite students to draw on the enduring questions, connections and perspectives they have absorbed throughout the course to think systematically about the future. We assist that effort by laying out several visions of the future of world politics. We draw contrasts between those who believe that the distribution of global power will be important in shaping the future of world politics and those who do not, and in particular we explore the implications of international systems characterized by one or multiple great powers. We juxtapose the ideas of globalization optimists, who focus on the beneficent effects on world politics of the global spread of the democratic peace, with the views of globalization pessimists, who worry about the clash of civilizations and the renewed significance of religion. We also engage with the possibility that the international system might be moving toward a period of global fracture, that is, an uneasy world of interacting pre-modern, modern and post-modern zones of world politics.

Distinguishing Emphases and Components of the Book

In summary, instructors and students will find the following distinguishing features in our text:

- Each chapter begins with an enduring question that frames the substance of the chapter and helps students recognize key issues in the field of international relations.
- Each chapter begins with a clear specification of learning objectives and ends with a list of further reading and suggested study questions.
- Each chapter utilizes the levels-of-analysis framework and connects it to our enduring question using boxed features and easy-to-recognize icons.
- Each chapter contains five text boxes to help students make the critical connections between theory and practice, between past and present, between aspiration and reality, and to highlight differing perspectives, both in general and in terms of international relations theories.
- A chapter (Chapter 2) that analyzes the key themes in the formation and evolution of the international system from 1500 to the present.
- A separate chapter (Chapter 4) that is devoted to the concepts needed to analyze the foreign policies of particular states and that allows instructors and students to move back and forth across the international and national levels of analysis.
- Sustained attention to both economic and security issues, and to their interaction in the past and current international systems.
- Systematic treatment of important issues in contemporary international relations, such as the rise of non-state and transnational actors and the role of the environment in world politics.
- A chapter (Chapter 7) dedicated to the special problems posed by nuclear and other weapons of mass destruction.
- An extended discussion of rising powers – China, Brazil, India, Russia and South Africa – in the current international system.
- An innovative concluding chapter that draws upon enduring questions and multiple perspectives to encourage students to think creatively yet systematically about alternative futures for world politics.

A Note to Students

Your world appears to be in a constant state of rapid change. Things that seemed important ten or even five years ago – especially if they involve technology, mobile phones or social networking – today seem out of date. You will find that change is also a salient feature of international relations; this book will help you to recognize the profound transformations that have taken place over the space of several decades and even several centuries.

Yet there is some truth to the nineteenth-century French proverb (and the twenty-first-century popular song) that 'the more things change, the more they stay the same.' It is critical, especially when change appears to be the normal state of affairs, to grasp the enduring continuities that help define and shape international relations. This book will enable you to appreciate both continuity and change in the fascinating international landscape, and to recognize that not everyone sees the international landscape in the same way. We invite you to use this book as a starting point to explore the terrain of international relations yourself, with your fellow students and friends, and over the course of your life.

Online Teaching and Learning Resources

www.palgrave.com/politics/grieco is a freely-accessible website containing an array of comprehensive and innovative resources for both instructors and students.

Author Video Debates

The website offers eight videos in which the authors engage in lively debate. These videos demonstrate different viewpoints in International Relations and are intended to inspire students to engage in further debate.

There are two videos relating to each part in the book; these can be viewed at the start of each new part as an introduction to what topics will be covered. The questions debated have been chosen both to expand upon the issues raised in the book and to highlight key questions in world politics.

- Part I: Foundations of International Relations
  Q1: Is the history of international relations characterized by progress or continuity?
  Q2: Why do we have so many theories of international relations?

- Part II: War and Peace: An Introduction to Security Studies
  Q1: Are China and Russia 'revisionist states'?
  Q2: Is war between great powers a thing of the past?

- Part III: Wealth and Power: An Introduction to International Political Economy
  Q1: What does globalization mean and what are its effects?
  Q2: Do international organizations promote peace, prosperity and justice?

- Part IV: Contemporary Challenges and the Future of International Relations
  Q1: What are the main global challenges facing the international community?
  Q2: What might the future hold for international relations?

Resources for Students

The website also offers a range of useful resources for students to aid revision and critical thinking.

- A comprehensive study guide for each chapter including:
  Chapter summaries
  Multiple choice and discussion questions
  Flashcards of key terms in international relations
- Pivotal decisions. In these interactive games, students must consider the pros and cons of a complicated decision with grave consequences. Some of these decisions are genuine historical dilemmas that world leaders have faced. Others are possible dilemmas that can the student can grapple with using the tools they have acquired by studying this book.
- Interactive simulations. In these exercises, students again play the part of a world leader at a crucial political juncture. However, instead of considering the pros and cons of a particular decision, they must simulate the entire decision-making process. Each decision they make leads to new circumstances.
- Outside resources, including links to contemporary articles, videos and games, which have been selected to illustrate the continuing relevance of the enduring question in each chapter.

Resources for Instructors

A selection of resources has been provided to help instructors plan and deliver their courses.

- A testbank containing multiple choice and essay questions for every chapter
- Lecture slides to aid teaching
- Class discussion questions
- Lecture notes that outline the key points in every chapter
- A sample syllabus

Author Acknowledgements

First and foremost, we thank our undergraduate students at Dartmouth, Duke, and Princeton; from them we have gained inspiration and learned that the enduring questions in international relations can be addressed most effectively by way of reasoned and respectful debate. We also wish to thank the many anonymous reviewers who provided thoughtful criticisms and helpful suggestions across the manuscript. Finally, we offer a special thank you to Henry Frost, Dartmouth class of 2015, who prepared the materials for this book's accompanying website thoughtfully and creatively.

JOSEPH GRIECO
G. JOHN IKENBERRY
MICHAEL MASTANDUNO

Copyright Acknowledgements

The authors and publishers are grateful for permission to reproduce the following copyright material:

The Brookings Institution for Table 4.1 China's New Top Leaders: The Politburo Standing Committee, 2012 from Li, Cheng. Table 1: China's Top Seven Leaders: The New Politburo Standing Committee 2012. © 2012 The Brookings Institution. Reprinted with permission.

The Centre for Systemic Peace, Polity IV Project for Figure 3.1 World Trends in Governance, 1800–2010.

Correlates of War for data in Figures 5.1, 5.2, 5.3, 5.4, 5.5, 5.7, 5.8 and 5.9.

Fetterer, F., K. Knowles, W. Meier, and M. Savoie. 2002, updated daily. *Sea Ice Index*. Boulder, Colorado USA: National Snow and Ice Data Center for Map 12.1 Possible Sign of Global Warming: Retreat of Arctic Summer Ice, 2012.

Food and Agriculture Organization of the United Nations for Figure 12.3 Utilization of World Marine Fish Stocks, 1974–2009.

Fund for Peace for Map 11.1: The Failed State Index 2013.

Graham Holdings for Figure 10.7 from William Easterly, 'The Cartel of Good Intentions', *Foreign Policy* 131 (July–August 2002), p. 45.

Guardian News and Media for Figure 12.4 Meeting Kyoto Protocol Commitments to Cut Greenhouse Gases from Duncan Clark, 'Has the Kyoto Protocol Made Any Difference to Carbon Emissions?', Guardian, November 26, 2012.

Jean-Paul Rodrigue for Map 9.1: The Dutch East India Company.

OECD Publishing for Figure 10.9 Shares of World GDP, 2011 and Projection for 2030 from Johansson, Å. *et al.* (2012) 'Looking to 2060: Long-Term Global Growth Prospects: A Going for Growth Report', *OECD Economic Policy Papers*, No. 3, OECD Publishing, p.23.

Institute for International Economics for Table 13.1 Intraregional Trade as a Share of Total Trade of Each Region, 1962–94 from Jeffrey A. Frankel (1997) *Regional Trading*

Blocs in the World Economic System (Washington, DC: Institute for International Economics), p. 22.

Natural Resources Defense Council for Table 7.1 Ten Bombs on Ten South Asian Cities.

Petroleum Economist for Map 9.2 European Gas Pipelines.

Scripps Institution of Oceanography for Figure 12.1 Increasing Concentration of CO2 in the Atmosphere, 1958–2013.

Stockholm International Peace Research Institute for Table 7.2 World Nuclear forces, January 2013 from *SIPRI Yearbook 2013: Armaments, Disarmament and International Security*.

United Nations Publications for data in Figure 8.5 Global Economic Significance of MNEs, 1990–2011 and Figure 10.8 Official Development Assistance, Major Donors 2008–12.

US Energy Information Administration for Map 1.1 A National Interest: China and its Claims to the South China Sea from 'Country Analysis Brief: South China Sea,' February 2013; data in Figure 10.2 Global Oil Production and Proven Reserves, 2012 from International Energy Statistics; data in Figure 12.2 Responsibility for Addressing the Problem of Global Warming: Developed and Developing Countries and CO2 Emissions, data in Panels A and B from 'Energy-Related Carbon Dioxide Emissions', in *International Energy Outlook* 2013, available at http://www.eia.gov/forecasts/ieo/emissions.cfm, historical data in Panel C from International Energy Statistics database (as of November 2012), www.eia.gov/ies , projected data from Annual Energy Outlook 2013, DOE/EIA-0383(2013) (Washington, DC: April 2013), AEO2013 National Energy Modeling System, run REF2013.D102312A, www.eia.gov/aeo , and World Energy Projection System Plus (2013).

The publishers are also grateful to the following suppliers of images in the book:

Corbis, Court of Justice of the European Union, David Hunt, Defence Imagery (Ministry of Defence), Fotolia, Greenpeace, Harvard Law School Library, IAEA, IMF, iStockphoto, NATO, OPEC Secretariat, Photoalto, PA Images, Science Photo Library, UN Photo, US State Department.

1

Understanding International Relations

International relations are concerned with the political, economic, social, and cultural relations between two countries or among many countries. We also include in this definition relations countries have with other important actors such as global corporations or international organizations. Did you know that what we currently consider international relations can be traced back at least 2,500 years? During the fifth BCE, the relevant political groups were Greek city-states rather than modern nation-states. City-states such as Athens and Sparta traded with each other, participated in cross-border sports competitions, practiced diplomacy, formed alliances, and fought wars against each other as enemies and as allies against the Persian Empire. International relations in that period in some ways looks similar to what it is today, but, of course, the modern international system also looks very different. Today's nation-states operate in a global system of interaction. Goods, technology, and money change hands with the click of a mouse rather than with the launch of a sailing ship. States still fight wars, but the destructive capacity of modern weapons, especially nuclear weapons, introduces a strong element of caution into how states resolve conflicts with each other. Non-state actors, such as global corporations, environmental advocacy groups, and criminal and terrorist networks cross borders and share the stage with countries and their governments.

This book introduces you to the fascinating and complex world of international relations. The best way to begin to acquire a solid knowledge of this field is to master some basic terms and concepts that are used to describe international relations and foreign policy and to learn how to employ the levels-of-analysis framework for organizing and understanding arguments and ideas about international relations. Second and most importantly, we believe you can begin to master the complexity of international relations by exploring what we call enduring questions. These are questions which have engaged and challenged generations of international relations scholars and students – large, challenging questions that have stood the test of time. Finally, we believe it is critically important that you be able to make connections about international relations that relate the past and the present, theory and practice, and aspiration and reality, and be able to view the world from multiple perspectives. We will explain what we mean by each of these defining features of our book as we introduce you in this chapter to the field of international relations.

Source: © Cousin_Avi–Fotolia.com.

Learning Objectives

By the end of this chapter you will be able to:

→ Understand why international relations matter.

→ Apply a basic vocabulary and the levels-of-analysis analytical device in international relations and foreign policy.

→ Analyze the use of enduring questions in international relations.

→ Recognize the need to make connections between international relations theory and practice, the past and present, and aspirations and reality in order to develop a better understanding of international relations.

→ Evaluate the significance of viewing world politics from multiple perspectives.

Chapter Contents

- International Relations are Part of Everyday Life
- Building Blocks for the Study of International Relations
- Recognizing Enduring Questions
- Making Connections
- Viewing the World from Different Perspectives
- Looking Ahead

International Relations are Part of Everyday Life

If you happen to be one of the many people – over one billion worldwide as of 2013 – to own an iPhone, you are probably familiar with Apple, the famous American computer company. Although the iPhone was designed by Apple in California, its components are produced all over the world. A South Korean company, Samsung, manufactures the applications processor. The display module and touch screen come from Japan. Infineon, a German-based company, produces the camera module. The various components are sent to China, where a company named Foxconn assembles and ships phones to customers around the globe (Xing and Detert 2010). As a consumer, you benefit directly from this global network of trade: the mobile phone you buy and the service you receive are more affordable than if your phone had been built and serviced all in one country. Some East Asian, European, and American workers share in the benefits of this trade as well, since the more phones that are sold, the more US-, European-, and East Asian-based jobs are created to produce and service them.

The stakes in international relations sometimes involve conflict and war rather than, or alongside, trade and mutual economic benefit. On September 11, 2001, members of the Al Qaeda transnational terrorist organization hijacked two airliners and crashed them into the Twin Towers of the World Trade Center in New York City. Al Qaeda hijackers flew a third plane into the Pentagon in the nation's capital. They commandeered a fourth plane that was also headed for Washington, but due to a passenger uprising failed to keep control of the plane and crashed it in a field in Pennsylvania. Over 3,000 people died during the September 11 attacks, including several hundred police and fire workers who tried to save the initial victims in the Twin Towers. These attacks prompted a US invasion of Afghanistan, whose Taliban government had been giving refuge to Al Qaeda, and served as one justification for a second US war, against Iraq, in 2003. It also prompted US special-forces and spy operations against Al Qaeda in numerous countries, including one in Pakistan in May 2011 in which its leader, Osama bin Laden, was killed. The conflict between the United States and Al Qaeda has continued, and in 2012 Al Qaeda operatives attacked the US consulate in Bengazi, Libya, killing four Americans including the US ambassador to that North African country.

The war on terrorism has been a prominent part of America's recent engagement with international relations. But taking a longer view, we should recognize that in relative terms Americans have been among the peoples of the world least affected by foreign wars. Consider that, for example, in the Vietnam War, one of the longest and costliest wars fought by the United States, 58,000 Americans were killed and about 300,000 were wounded. However America's adversary, North Vietnam, suffered 1.1 million dead and 600,000 wounded. In 1995, the Vietnamese government estimated that 2 million civilians in the North and another 2 million in the South also died during the war. Vietnamese casualties represented a shocking 13 percent of the total population of that country.

Consider that the citizens of France and Germany treated each other as adversaries for almost 100 years. These two countries fought a major war against each other in 1870, and were the principal combatants in two devastating world wars, between 1914 and 1918 and again between 1939 and 1945. It is not surprising that, for many decades, the French and German people regarded each other with suspicion and resentment and considered each other mortal enemies. But, since 1945, the French and German governments have cooperated with each other politically and economically in what is today called the **European Union** (EU) – a group of 28 European countries that abide by common laws and practices – and militarily in an alliance called the **North Atlantic Treaty Organization** (NATO), which requires the United States and its European partners to come to the defense of each other in the event of a military attack against one of them. Today, war between France and Germany is almost unthinkable, and in 2012 the European Union was awarded the Nobel Peace Prize in recognition of its historical accomplishments. French and German citizens freely cross each other's borders and work in each other's factories and offices. The Germans and French even gave up their long-standing national currencies, the Deutschmark and the French franc; beginning in 2002, they have shared, along with fifteen other European Union members, a common currency called the **euro**. Today, members of the European Union worry very little about war with each other and very much about economic instability as they struggle to recover from a financial crisis that has threatened their own prosperity and that of the global economy.

International relations involve not just war and the movement of goods and money across borders, but also the ability of people themselves to move across those borders. If you are not a citizen, national governments require you to have special permission (for example, in Australia an employer-sponsored 457 visa, or in the United States, an identification document commonly known as a green card) before you may legally work in their country. Even visiting different countries simply as a tourist often requires you to request permission in the form of a visa from the respective governments of those countries. The citizens of some countries have an easier time crossing borders than do the citizens of others; in 2012, for example, citizens of Sweden and Finland could enter 168 other countries without needing a visa, while Chinese citizens could only enter 41 countries and Pakistani citizens only 32 countries visa-free (Henley 2012). Today many Americans with sufficient means take for granted their ability to travel just about anywhere outside the United States. But one country they cannot visit without special permission from their own government is Cuba, because the US government has long attempted to punish Cuba's communist regime by isolating it. This is a relatively small inconvenience

Euro: the common currency of the Euro zone.

European Union: A group of 28 European countries that abide by common laws and practices.

North Atlantic Treaty Organization (NATO): A defense pact formed in 1949 between the US, Britain, and several other western European states. It has since expanded and is still very active today.

◀ **Photo 1.1 The Berlin Wall, 1961**

East German policemen heightening the Berlin Wall, September 9, 1961. Armed forces erected the Wall on August 13, 1961 to stop people fleeing from East to West Berlin.

Source: PA Images.

Iron Curtain: A term coined by British leader Winston Churchill to capture the profound political and human divisions separating the western and eastern parts of Europe.

Berlin Wall: The wall that divided Soviet East Berlin from American, French, and British West Berlin during the Cold War, until its fall in 1989.

International governmental organizations (IGOs): Organizations that states join to further their political or economic interests.

National leaders: Individuals who hold executive offices as a result of which they are entitled to make foreign policy and military decisions on behalf of their countries.

▼ **Photo 1.2 The Berlin Wall, 1989**

Germans from East and West standing on the Berlin Wall in front of the Brandenburg Gate, November 10, 1989, one day after the wall opened.

Source: PA Images.

compared to what international relations imposed on people living in Eastern Europe between the late 1940s and late 1980s. During that time an iron curtain, a term coined by British leader Winston Churchill to capture the profound political and human divisions, separated the western and eastern parts of Europe. The communist governments of Eastern European countries tried to prevent their citizens from traveling to the West because they feared people would find freedom so attractive that they would not return home. The eastern and western parts of today's German capital city, Berlin, were divided by the Berlin Wall. East Berliners trying to escape across the wall to West Berlin were routinely shot by East German guards.

International relations powerfully affect our everyday lives. There are 196 countries in the world today (that includes Taiwan, which operates as a country but which is also claimed by the People's Republic of China as a part of its own country) and they interact with each other over a wide variety of political, economic, social, cultural, and scientific issues. They also interact with an array of international governmental organizations (IGOs) – organizations that states join to further their political or economic interests – such as the United Nations (UN), International Monetary Fund (IMF), World Health Organization (WHO), World Trade Organization (WTO), and Organization of Petroleum Exporting Countries (OPEC). Countries also deal regularly with private actors whose work crosses borders, such as the US-based conglomerate General Electric, the Chinese-based computer company Lenovo, the international health crisis response team Médecins Sans Frontières (Doctors Without Borders), and transnational political and social movements such as the Muslim Brotherhood and the World Social Forum. Your task is to gain an understanding of those relationships, and so we begin by laying some of the necessary foundations.

Building Blocks for the Study of International Relations

In this section we provide you with some foundational material for the study of international relations. We start with some basic terminology that will help you become familiar with discussions in the field. Then we introduce the levels-of-analysis device which helps scholars and students organize their ideas and arguments about international relations.

Basic Concepts for International Relations

The initial step is to identify the fundamental actors in international relations. While the question of which actors in international relations are most important is controversial and will be taken up in many of the chapters that follow, for now we can identify at least three important classes of key actors in international relations.

First, we are interested in individual **national leaders**. By national leaders we mean individuals, like the President of the United States, the Prime Minister of Pakistan, or the Chancellor of Germany, who hold executive offices as a result of which they are entitled to make foreign policy and military decisions on behalf of their countries. We also include those individuals, such as the Russian Defense Minister or the Brazilian Minister of Agriculture, who as a result of the offices they hold give counsel to and implement the decisions of their respective core executive leaders, like the Russian or Brazilian President.

Second, we are interested in states. In international relations we often say 'India' has this or that foreign policy interest, or that 'China' has this or that strategy toward 'Russia,' or that 'Venezuela' is making use of this or that foreign policy instrument to attain some goal. India, China, Russia, and Venezuela are among the 196 states in the current international system. But what, in general, is a state? It is a political entity with two key features: a piece of territory with reasonably well defined borders, and political authorities who enjoy **sovereignty**, that is, they have an effective and recognized capacity to govern residents within the territory and an ability to establish relationships with governments that control other states.

The state should be distinguished from another key international relations actor, the **nation**. States are political units, while nations are collections of people who share a common culture, history, or language. The term **nation-state** refers to a political unit inhabited by people sharing common culture, history, or language. Although nation-state is used frequently in international relations literature, often as a synonym for country, pure nation-states are rare: possible examples might include Albania, where over 95 percent of the population consists of ethnic Albanians, or Iceland, which has a language and culture found only on that island. Nations often transcend the boundary of any single state; members of the Chinese nation, for example, are found in mainland China and in Taiwan, but also in Singapore, Malaysia, and other parts of Southeast Asia. Similarly, states often contain more than one nation. The former Soviet Union included not only Russians but Armenians, Ukrainians, Georgians, Latvians, and Lithuanians, among others.

Third, to understand international relations we often want to analyze **non-state actors**. These are actors others than states that operate within or across state borders with important consequences for international relations. Multinational enterprises such as the US-based soft drink company Coca Cola, the Netherlands-based electronics firm Phillips, and the Japan-based conglomerate Mitsubishi are non-state actors with important business operations all across the globe. The Catholic Church and the US National Council of Churches are both active around the world and are thus important non-state actors; and, with radically different aims and methods, several criminal and terrorist organizations, such as mafias or Al Qaeda, are consequential non-state actors.

What do these actors want and how do they get what they want in international relations? Here it is useful to distinguish interests, strategies, objectives (or goals), and policy instruments.

When we say that a state (or nation-state) has a particular **interest**, we mean that the state wishes either to maintain or attain some condition of the world sufficiently important that it is willing to pay meaningful costs. For example, in recent years, the Chinese government has revealed that it has an interest in attaining sovereignty over the South China Sea, perhaps because that area may be rich in oil and natural gas. In making that claim it has come into conflict with numerous neighbors such as Indonesia, Malaysia, the Philippines, and Vietnam, for they too claim sovereignty over parts of that sea space (see Map 1.1). Not surprisingly, the South China Sea has become a potential flash-point in world politics.

State: A political entity with two key features: a piece of territory with reasonably well-defined borders, and political authorities who enjoy sovereignty.

Sovereignty: The effective and recognized capacity to govern residents within a given territory and an ability to establish relationships with governments that control other states.

Nation: Collections of people who share a common culture, history, or language.

Nation-state: A political unit inhabited by people sharing common culture, history, or language.

Non-state actors: Actors others than states that operate within or across state borders with important consequences for international relations..

Interest: Some condition of the world sufficiently important that a state is willing to pay meaningful costs to attain or maintain it.

► **Map 1.1 A National Interest: China and its Claims to the South China Sea**

This map shows why the South China Sea is an area of geopolitical dispute in the current international system. The region is potentially rich in energy resources and several countries, including China, Malaysia, Vietnam, Indonesia and the Philippines, claim that the territory falls within their jurisdiction. In recent years China has employed a variety of diplomatic and coercive tactics to try to convince other countries that they should recognize China's claim.

Source: US State Department. See also US Energy Information Administration, 'Country Analysis Brief: South China Sea', February 2013.

Agreed maritime boundaries

1. ——— China–Vietnam Gulf of Tonkin boundary (2000)
2. ——— Indonesia–Malaysia continental shelf boundary (1969)
3. ——— Indonesia–Vietnam continental shelf boundary (2003)
4. ——— Brunei–Malaysia Orders of Council boundary (1959)
5. ——— Malaysian oil blocks ceded to Brunei (2010)
6. ——— Thailand–Vietnam EEZ/continental shelf boundary (1996)

Pratas Island: administered by Taiwan
Paracel Islands: occupied by China, claimed by Vietnam
Spratly Islands: claimed entirely by China, Taiwan and Vietnam
Scarborough Reef: claimed by Philippines, China and Taiwan

Declared limits

8. ——— China/Taiwan undefined claim (1946)
9. ——— Philippine Malayaan Island Group limits (1978)
10. ——— Malaysia continental shelf limits (1979)
11. ——— Brunei limits (1988)
12. ——— Malaysia–Vietnam joint extended continental shelf (ECS) submission (2009)

Areas

14. ▨ Malaysia–Vietnam continental shelf Defined Area (1992)
15. ▨ Malaysia–Thailand Joint Development Area (1979)

How do states promote or defend an interest? They do so by the development and implementation of a **strategy**. A strategy essentially connects means to an end. If China's ultimate **objective** or goal is to attain sovereignty over the South China Sea, part of its strategy might be to induce such countries as Vietnam and the Philippines to renounce their own claims over the South China Sea, and to recognize Chinese sovereignty over the area. China will rely on **policy instruments** to help it obtain that goal. Policy instruments can take a variety of forms, and we will examine some in detail in Chapter 4. In the South China Sea case, China thus far has used multiple policy instruments, including diplomacy, propaganda, and low levels of military force.

Levels of Analysis in International Relations

We now have a basic language for the description of the actions and interactions of states. Many more important terms will be introduced in the chapters that follow. You will also encounter many different arguments, ideas and theories about international relations. **Theories** help us understand *why* something occurred in international relations, and the likelihood that it will happen again. As you will see in subsequent chapters, there are many such theories, and debates over how useful or valid particular theories are. How do we keep track of these different arguments, ideas, and theories? How do we compare and contrast them to one another so that we can get a better sense of each and assess their relative strengths and weaknesses?

We employ a particular and well regarded analytical device for the classification of arguments about international relations. This device is called the **levels-of-analysis** framework. It emerged from the writings of two scholars, Kenneth Waltz and J. David Singer (Waltz 1959; Singer 1961). It is based on the view that a writer who puts forward any theory or explanation about international relations has had to make choices about which actors and causal processes are to be emphasized. Put differently, analysts of international relations have to decide *where to look* for explanations. The choices usually lead them to concentrate on actors and processes that are principally situated in one of three different categories, or levels of analysis.

Many explanations and arguments in international relations focus on actors and processes that are situated at the **individual level of analysis**. Scholars who work at this level focus their attention on the impact of individual decision makers (like Presidents and their main advisors) on international relations and foreign policy. There are several classes of individual-level theories about foreign policy and the causes of war, which we will discuss in detail in Chapters 3, 4, and 5. Some scholars believe, for example, that to understand the causes of World War II requires you to focus on the personal experiences and ambitions of Adolf Hitler, the dictator who led Germany into war.

Other studies at the individual level of analysis have focused on the psychological capacity of national leaders and their top officials, and in particular on how limitations on how human beings process information, especially in moments of stress and crisis, can lead to errors in judgment. When national leaders make these types of errors, it could lead to diplomatic crises and even war. We will also see that most feminist theories of international relations are cast at the individual level of analysis: these works, we will see in Chapters 3 and 5, propose that the biochemistry or upbringing of males often leads them to be more prone to risk taking and violence, including the choosing of military solutions to diplomatic conflicts of interest.

Strategy: The overarching connection of means to an end for a state. A strategy aims at a policy objective, and outlines what policy instruments will be used to attain that objective.

Objective: A state's goal in IR, generally the attainment or maintenance of some interest.

Policy instrument: A tool used by a state's government to attain its interests. Policy instruments come in many forms, divided into persuasive and coercive forms.

Theory: A group of ideas intended to explain some empirical phenomenon.

Levels of analysis: Different ways of looking for answers to questions in international relations, generally grouped into the individual, state, and international levels.

Individual level of analysis: A level of analysis focusing on the impact of individual decision makers (like presidents and their main advisors) on international relations and foreign policy.

State level of analysis: A level of analysis focusing on the particular political or economic characteristics of countries or states.

Democratic peace theory: The theory that democracies are unusually peaceful toward each other. Democracies, or republics, are understood as states that have elected governments, a free press, private property, and the rule of law.

The **state level of analysis** comprises arguments that focus on the particular political or economic characteristics of countries or states. A good example of a state level-of-analysis argument is **democratic peace theory**, a set of ideas developed by many international relations scholars including Michael Doyle and Bruce Russett (Doyle 1997; Russett 1993). That argument suggests that what states do abroad, including whether they get into conflict with one another, is heavily influenced by the domestic political institutions of the country. States with democratic governments, the theory suggests, are very unlikely to fight wars with one another, for reasons we will explore in Chapters 3 and 5. Another state level-of-analysis theory we will examine later in this chapter concerns economic systems: a long-standing argument by critics of capitalism is that states with capitalist economic systems at home are more likely to get into wars with one another than would be true if those same states were organized according to different principles. We will also encounter other types of argument about economic policy at the state level of analysis. The governments of countries in which multinational businesses exert a lot of influence, for example, might pursue strategies of open trade and investment because those policies support the financial interests of powerful companies.

International level of analysis: A level of analysis focusing on the international system

International system: States and non-state actors, taken collectively, co-existing and interacting at some point in history.

Anarchy: The fact that in international relations there is no centralized authority, no government of the whole world to adjudicate disputes among states and protect weak ones from strong ones.

Finally, many arguments about world politics emphasize the **international level of analysis**. Countries do not exist in isolation; they interact with each other. Taken collectively, states and non-state actors co-existing and interacting at any point in history form an **international system**. That system has its own features and characteristics which themselves might strongly influence how countries behave. For example, many political scientists emphasize anarchy, or the fact that in international relations there is no centralized authority, no government of the whole world to adjudicate disputes among states and protect weak ones from strong ones. As we will discuss later, the United Nations might be seen as an imperfect attempt to take on some of the functions of the non-existent world government.

Here is a simple way to remember the differences across levels of analysis. Ask yourself this fundamental question about international relations: what causes war? Scholars working at the individual level might answer that war is caused by overly aggressive or ambitious leaders. Some analysts place the blame (or give credit) for the 2003 Iraq War on the personal calculations of US President George W. Bush. Scholars who place their 'analytical bets' at the second level provide a different answer; they argue that wars are caused by certain types of states, or by powerful groups within states (like oil companies), regardless of the particular personal ambitions or characteristics of their leaders. Scholars working at the international system level might say that it doesn't matter whether leaders are good or bad, whether states are democratic or non-democratic, or whether big companies are politically powerful or not. What matters for these scholars is the international situation in which states find themselves. Lacking any centralized governing authority, any state at any time could start a war because it feels threatened by other states, needs more resources or territory than it already has, or has some other particular reason to use force against some other state in the system.

None of these arguments or theories is necessarily right or wrong. Each would need to be tested logically and against the evidence that the past and present of international relations offers to us. The important first step, aided by the levels of analysis, is to categorize arguments and understand where they are coming from. For that reason, in each chapter that follows we employ special features to remind you to think about arguments, theories, and ideas with the aid of the levels-of-analysis framework. After every major section of each chapter, we use a box to summarize the material you have just learned from the perspective of different levels. We use simple icons in these boxes to represent the different levels visually. In some cases these boxes will display information at each of the three levels; in other cases, depending on the nature of the material covered, we will display information only with regard to one or two of the levels.

It is also important to recognize that the levels of analysis are not isolated from each other. Often a good explanation will combine or integrate ideas from different levels. For example, why do the United States and European Union have such close economic ties to each other? Part of the answer might be found at the international level: the trans-Atlantic partners are military allies, and close military cooperation encourages and reinforces close economic cooperation. Part of the explanation may be found at the state level as well: the United States and countries of the European Union are capitalist democracies with strong business sectors that operate across borders and thus have a mutual interest in open trade and investment.

Although in this text we focus on three basic levels of analysis, scholars sometimes make finer distinctions that incorporate additional levels. Some, for example, highlight a regional level situated analytically between the state level and the international level (Tow 2009). Regional characteristics – for example, the existence or absence of well-established regional institutions like the EU – might help us to understand why some parts of the world are more prone to conflict than are others.

International relations are complicated, and what actually happens within them often blurs or cross-cuts the neat dividing lines between different levels. The levels-of-analysis framework can never fully capture the complexity of activity on the world stage. However it is a useful analytical tool and a starting point for helping us to make sense of that complexity.

The question 'what causes war?' is a large and important one in the study of international relations. In fact, it is what we call an **enduring question**. Enduring questions cast powerful light on some of the most important subjects in our field. In the next section, we introduce this additional and crucial analytical tool that we use to organize the material of this book.

Recognizing Enduring Questions

It is natural to associate the study of international relations with current events. Daily and weekly news outlets bombard us all with reports on whether Israelis and Palestinians will be able to make peace, whether Iran will acquire nuclear weapons and how the international community will react if it does, whether the United States and China will maintain harmonious relations with each other, whether African countries

▲ **Photo 1.3 Adolf Hitler**

Adolf Hitler, the head of Germany's Nazi Party, was appointed Chancellor of Germany in 1933 and quickly transformed German's Weimar Republic into a dictatorship. Hitler felt Germany had been humiliated by the victorious Western powers after World War I, and he believed the German people were a superior breed that required 'living space' through territorial conquest. Many view his aggressive foreign policy as the key cause of World War II.

Source: PA Images.

will prosper or face food shortages, and numerous other issues. This textbook will help you make sense of current international events. But international relations, and the effort to understand them, range far beyond analyses of the politics of the moment.

The *modern* international system dates from the creation of nation-states and the Peace of Westphalia of 1648, which we will discuss in greater detail in Chapter 2. But we can trace the systematic attempt to study international politics back considerably further, at least to the writings of a classic Greek thinker named Thucydides. Thucydides was an Athenian general who fought in the great Peloponnesian War, a conflict between two powerful Greek city-states, Athens and Sparta, and their respective allies, between 431 and 404 BCE.

But Thucydides was far more important as an observer and reporter than as a participant. He wrote a detailed account of this great war, and in addition to examining how it was fought and ended, he sought to understand why the war began, and what were its consequences. In writing this analysis, he said, 'My work is not a piece of writing designed to meet the taste of an immediate public, but was done to last forever' (Thucydides, 1954 edition: 48). Although the term was not used commonly back then, Thucydides was in fact acting as a political scientist. He was interested not just in reporting on the war of his day, but in understanding more generally the problem of warfare, or why humans organize themselves into groups and engage in armed conflicts. He wanted to understand not just the Delian League, an alliance of city-states led by Athens, but why states enter into agreements with each other and why those agreements break down. Thucydides used the experience of the Greek city-states to ponder the ethical issue of whether 'might makes right,' or whether the more powerful groups in human society have the right to govern the weaker. He drew upon Athens' failed expedition to Sicily near the end of the war to question why powerful states make foolish errors in international relations, overextending themselves in ways that ultimately lead to the collapse of their own position of power. Thucydides wrote about a particular set of events at a particular time, but his larger goal was to illuminate what he considered to be the core problems of international relations.

Our book proceeds in a similar spirit. We believe that the best way to unravel the complexity of international relations is to focus on what we call enduring questions. Enduring questions in international relations are those questions that share the common characteristics of being recurring, unresolved, and consequential. Take, for example, the question we noted earlier, 'what causes war?' That question is *recurring*: it was as relevant in the city-state politics of ancient Greece, the dynastic struggles of early modern Europe, and the colonial wars of nineteenth-century Africa as it is in the politics of the contemporary global system. It is also an *unresolved* question. Some scholars believe wars occur because human beings are inherently evil. Some think war results because there are not enough scarce resources (like oil) to satisfy everyone's desires. Others argue that certain kinds of states are more war prone than others. There are many other reasonable answers, as you will find in Chapters 3 and 5. Scholars have made good progress addressing this enduring question, but have not resolved it to everyone's satisfaction. Finally, enduring questions are *consequential*. They matter greatly to people, states, and the international system as a whole. Solving the problem of why war occurs would potentially affect the lives of tens of millions of people.

We focus on enduring questions for several reasons. First, enduring questions allow us to separate what is significant and foundational in the study of global politics from

◀ **Map 1.2 Greece in the Era of the Peloponnesian War**

Four hundred years before Christ, Greek city-states interacted with each other as members of a local international system. Sparta was a powerful city-state on land, and Athens was a seafaring city-state. The Greek city-states also interacted and battled with outsiders, most importantly the Persian Empire, which was organized on the eastern side of the Aegean Sea.

what is trendy or simply the 'news of the day.' The insights you gain in an international relations class should remain relevant over long periods of time, rather than expiring when the issues that were hot topics when you took the class are no longer in the news. By now you are aware that there are dozens or even hundreds of particular events unfolding in the international arena at any given time. The enduring question approach offers a navigational strategy, a series of well-worn paths to help you make your way through the maze of information and events.

The second reason we focus on enduring questions is that it helps us more effectively understand the development and current status of the study of international relations. Focusing on the core problems in the field reveals what we know and do not know about international relations. In Chapter 3, we introduce the major schools of thought in the study of international relations. Each of these schools, or paradigms, is based on different assumptions about how the world works, and offers different interpretations and explanations of the knottiest problems in international politics.

Examples of Enduring Questions

There is no set number of enduring questions and no standard list on which everyone might agree. Different scholars would likely vary to some degree in the questions they consider to be the most enduring in the study of international relations. We have already mentioned what we consider to be one enduring question, the question of why states fight wars. Here are several other examples of enduring questions you will encounter in the chapters that follow. Box 1.1 provides a list of the particular enduring

1.1

**Enduring
Questions in
International
Relations**

Chapter 2	How did a fragmented world become a global, integrated system of states for which order is an ongoing problem?
Chapter 3	How do theoretical traditions in international relations differ on how to understand actors and their behavior on the global stage?
Chapter 4	What factors most influence the foreign policies of states?
Chapter 5	Why is war a persistent feature of international relations?
Chapter 6	What factors make it more likely that states will resolve their differences and avoid war?
Chapter 7	How have weapons of mass destruction, and in particular nuclear weapons, changed the practice of international relations?
Chapter 8	How do politics shape the global economy?
Chapter 9	How do governments use international economic relations to further national political objectives?
Chapter 10	How does participation in the world economy help or hinder the economic development of poorer countries?
Chapter 11	Can the state continue to overcome challenges to its authority?
Chapter 12	How does the natural environment influence international relations?
Chapter 13	Will the international system undergo fundamental change in the future?

questions that we use to organize and motivate the study of international relations chapter by chapter.

How is a stable order among countries – one in which they avoid major conflict with each other – maintained in international relations? Thucydides observed that a key cause of the Peloponnesian War was the rise of Athenian power and the fear it caused in Sparta. As we discuss in Chapter 2, in the latter part of the nineteenth century, a set of German city-states unified into a single powerful German nation-state which, in turn, challenged the dominant international position of Great Britain. The competition between these two countries contributed to the outbreak of World War I. But challenges to the great powers do not always end in war. Between 1880 and 1950, the United States increased its power and eventually overtook Great Britain. Did the two change positions peacefully because they were like-minded democratic allies, or because they perceived greater threats than each other? Today, new powers are rising, including China, India, and Brazil. We consider their prospects in Chapter 10. An understanding of why new powers rise and why existing powers accommodate them, restrain them, or fight wars with them is critical for assessing the prospects for peace and stability in the current and emerging international system.

To what extent have nuclear weapons fundamentally changed international politics? Before the nuclear era, pre-1945, the most powerful states settled their fundamental differences by fighting major, costly wars like World Wars I and II. But, as we will discuss in Chapter 7, nuclear weapons are so destructive that if two well-armed powers used them, they would likely destroy each other so thoroughly that no one could claim victory in a meaningful sense. It is remarkable that since 1945, the world's great powers have not fought each other in a major war. Is this because of nuclear weapons, or some other reason? What about conflicting states with smaller nuclear arsenals, or two states with nuclear arsenals of radically different sizes; are they more likely to be tempted to use them against each other? Even if countries with well-established governments do not use nuclear weapons, we might be concerned that non-state actors, such as terrorist groups, might be more prone to use them if they managed to acquire them. It is harder to retaliate against a shadowy terrorist group than a country with an obvious population and territory. The existence of nuclear weapons and other weapons of mass destruction pose an enduring problem for international politics, and the significance and implications of such weapons for diplomacy and warfare constitute enduring questions for students of international politics.

In later chapters we introduce you to **international political economy (IPE)**, which is the subfield of international relations that seeks to understand how politics and economics interact and shape one another in the international domain. In particular, we introduce you to enduring questions in the field of IPE, such as: Why are global economic relations sometimes characterized by cooperation and prosperity and, at other times, by conflict and economic deprivation? For about 200 years (1650–1850), the governments of European great powers tried to protect their own economies from what they viewed as the disruptive effects of international trade. By the latter part of the nineteenth century, these same governments were cooperating economically, trading more intensely with each other, investing in each other's economies, and connecting the European economies with economies in other parts of the world. The result was an increase in global prosperity, yet one in which some countries and groups within them benefited far more than others. But this first great age of **globalization**, or the process and attainment of heightened cross-border contacts through the movement of trade, money, and people, was brought to an end by the onset of World War I, between 1914 and 1918. After World War I, the leading states tried to resuscitate the global economy, and made some progress toward that end during the mid-to-late 1920s. But the era of global economic recovery was aborted by what came to be known as the Great Depression of 1929–33, during which there was a sharp, sustained contraction of economic activity, and a corresponding increase in unemployment. With major countries like the United States, Britain, France, and Germany closing their national markets to international competitors in a failed attempt to ward off the Great Depression, international economic relations became a source of conflict that eventually contributed to the outbreak of World War II.

Today, the world economy is in the midst of a second great era of globalization, as goods, capital, technology, and ideas move relatively freely across international borders. The modern era of globalization has contributed to unprecedented levels of economic wealth but has also raised serious problems of inequality in developing nations and older industrial countries like the United States and Britain. The rapid movement of money across borders has contributed to financial crises such as the one that began in 2008. Some observers believe that globalization has a momentum that cannot be stopped, making a return to a world of economic conflicts and depression highly unlikely. Others see a prosperous but troubled world economy, whose political foundations are sufficiently fragile to make a global economic collapse a cause for concern. In Chapters 8, 9, and 10 we will explain how the world economy works and why global economic cooperation is important to achieve, yet difficult to sustain.

Why are states the central actors in world politics, and will they remain so? In Chapter 2, we will explain how the state and the nation-state system came into existence, and how it has preserved itself and expanded over time. Later, in Chapters 11 and 13, we will take up the question of whether and how the state system will persist as it faces challenges from non-state actors utilizing modern technology and communications.

International Political Economy (IPE): The subfield of international relations that seeks to understand how politics and economics interact and shape one another in the international domain.

Globalization: The ongoing process of international economic and technological integration, made possible by advances in transportation and communication.

Using enduring questions, along with the levels of analysis, as organizing frameworks will help to provide a path through the maze of modern global issues. In the next section, we introduce another important device to guide you through international relations – the ability to make a variety of analytical connections.

Making Connections

A thorough understanding of international relations includes the exploration of regional and global context, common and differing interests among actors, and causal relationships that can affect outcomes. This kind of critical thinking requires that you make three types of connections in your study of the issues: between *theory and practice*, *past and present*, and *aspiration and reality*. You also must be able to identify and appreciate how different leaders, governments, and perhaps even whole nations can have differing perspectives on the same question.

Because we believe these two organizing themes, making connections and recognizing different perspectives, are so important to an understanding of international relations, we emphasize them consistently throughout this book. In each subsequent chapter you will find five boxed features. Three of these features will help you make connections between theory and practice, past and present, and aspiration and reality. Two of them highlight different perspectives across individuals, groups, or countries on an important historical or contemporary international issue, and across theories of international relations which differ over how best to explain a significant international event.

Connecting Theory and Practice

All students of international relations need to appreciate the links between theory and practice. As we suggested earlier, theories help us to describe and explain the world. They are analytical devices that make assumptions, put forward causal arguments, and offer predictions about the workings of the international arena. Theories are usually not completely right or wrong, but may be more or less useful. Any particular theory might be useful for some time, until it is disproved by new evidence or overtaken by a better theory that someone develops. In the sixteenth century, the Polish-born scientist Copernicus gave us a new and (after some of his supporters had the misfortune of being burned at the stake) better theory of astronomy. Using observations and mathematical calculations, he theorized that the sun was the center of the universe and the earth moved around it, challenging the long-standing geocentric theory that placed the earth and, by implication, human beings at the center of the universe.

The creation and testing of theories is an important part of any scientific enterprise. As discussed in detail in Chapter 3, theories designed to explain how world politics works are usually grouped within broad schools of thought such as realism, liberalism, Marxism, and constructivism. Proponents within each school make a set of assumptions about what is really important, or what matters most, in international relations. Realists, for example, tend to emphasize that states use their power to pursue interests within a context of anarchy, in which no authoritative world government resolves disputes or compels the redistribution of resources from rich to poor states. Nation-states are ultimately on their own. Liberal thinkers see certain types of states as more conflict-prone than others, and also emphasize that economic interdependence brings states together and encourages peace and cooperation. Marxist thinkers view a state's economic system as the ultimate engine of its foreign relations, believing that the behavior of a capitalist state in the world arena is driven by the needs of its economic actors for markets and resources. Constructivist thinkers stress that ideas about how the world works shape or 'construct' international politics as much as money or armies do.

None of these approaches or the theories associated with them is a clear winner in explaining the complicated world of international relations. Each approach has its strengths and weaknesses, and its scholarly proponents and detractors. Although the realist approach became dominant after World War II, today many scholars find its assumptions and theories unsatisfying. Scholars of international relations approach their field from a wide variety of perspectives (Lebow and Risse-Kappen 1995). Part of the excitement of studying international relations is to participate in this ongoing contest of arguments and theories as we try to make sense of the world around us. As a student, you should be intellectually open to, but critical of, all theories, including those seemingly favored by your text book authors (who in their professional writings frequently disagree with each other!). Beginning in Chapter 3, in each chapter we use a boxed feature to showcase the ongoing conversation among different theoretical traditions in international relations.

One nice example of an international relations theory is Vladimir Lenin's theory of imperialism and war. We wouldn't normally consider Lenin a political scientist; he was the revolutionary leader of the Bolshevik movement that brought communists to power in Russia in 1917, beginning its transformation to the multinational empire of the Soviet Union. But Lenin, like Thucydides, analyzed international relations systematically, as a political scientist. He wrote a short book, *Imperialism: The Highest Stage of Capitalism*, that contains an elegant theory of international relations.

Lenin was trying to understand **imperialism** – the political domination of weaker countries by stronger ones. He argued that large banks and corporations in Europe and America at the end of the nineteenth century needed new markets to maintain their economic profits. After a while, profits declined at home so they had to look abroad, where capital was scarce and investments were more profitable. In order to capture new markets in places like Africa, the capitalists in Germany prodded the German government to conquer some African territories, giving them exclusive colonial control over the people and resources in these territories. The British banks and corporations got their government to take similar steps, and so did the American, French, and other capitalist powers. Lenin thereby explains the **scramble for Africa**, or the carving up of that continent by colonial powers after 1870, as a function of the simultaneous need of various capitalist countries to expand. When all the existing territory was taken, capitalist countries had no choice but to fight each other in order to redistribute the territory. This is how Lenin explained World War I, which was being fought when the Bolshevik revolution was carried out. Lenin also argued that capitalist countries would keep fighting each other until they exhausted themselves, allowing nation-states with economies that were less profit-driven (that is, socialist states) to take over.

Lenin's theory is important because it tries to make sense of two big outcomes in international relations: imperialism and great-power war. Theories are most useful

Imperialism: A state strategy in which one country conquers foreign lands to turn them into colonies.

Scramble for Africa: The carving up of Africa by colonial powers after 1870.

► Map 1.3
Imperialism and Colonialism in Africa on the Eve of World War I

During the latter part of the nineteenth century, European great powers engaged in a 'scramble for Africa'. Their motives were political, strategic and economic; Lenin emphasized the economic motive in crafting his theory of imperialism.

when they are connected to practice, or when they help us understand otherwise puzzling things about the world we observe. In this text, we will not ask you to learn and debate theories for their own sake, even though some political scientists may do that. We are interested in theories in so far as they illuminate the complex world of international relations.

So, how useful is Lenin's theory? Evidence accumulated over time suggests strengths and weaknesses. Many of the overseas investments of the capitalist powers during his era were directed to other capitalist powers, rather than to capital-scarce areas like Africa. This is puzzling for a theory that emphasizes the economic incentives of conquest. Also, historians have come up with a variety of non-economic reasons for late nineteenth-century imperialism, including the propositions that colonies were a source of prestige in a great-power competition and some governments believed they had a civilized obligation to control and modernize what they considered to be backward parts of the world. In other words, there are other reasonable ways to explain what Lenin was trying to explain. Lenin's supporters could say capitalist powers did fight each other in World Wars I and II, as he expected. However, at least thus far they have not exhausted themselves in a series of wars, but have found ways to cooperate with each other – something that Lenin did not expect.

On the other hand, Lenin's theory provided crucial insights that shaped the subsequent study of our field. It has led scholars to explore the 'law of uneven develop-

Today's Africa is composed of sovereign states – there are no longer any colonial powers formally in charge of African territories, as there were in 1914. The impact of colonialism remains, however, in the location of borders, politics and administration, and patterns of economic dependence between African and more powerful countries in Europe and North America.

ment,' or the tendency for countries to grow their power at different rates, thereby putting pressure for change on the international system (Gilpin 1981). It has sparked ongoing debates about the influence of corporations over the foreign policies of capitalist states. And it reminds us that global capitalism is both an engine of growth and its own worst enemy in that it creates periodic crises that threaten international prosperity and peace. Subsequent chapters will explore these themes in more detail; the point for now is that theories need not be completely correct in order to be useful.

Connecting Past and Present

Why should you care about history? Why seek connections between the past and the present? An understanding of the past affects how people, including policy makers in different countries, think about and act in world politics. For example, in 1930 the United States passed a piece of international trade legislation popularly known as the Smoot-Hawley Tariff Act (after its sponsors, Senator Reed Smoot and Representative Willis Hawley). The act raised US tariffs, or taxes, on about 20,000 goods coming into the United States from other countries. This legislation outraged other governments, many of which responded by increasing their own tariff levels. This all happened on the eve of the Great Depression, and many economists believe that the Smoot-Hawley tariff was an important reason why the depression of the 1930s was so deep and catastrophic for the global economy.

After World War II, policy makers in the United States and Western Europe learned the lesson of Smoot-Hawley. They sought freer trade, or lower taxes on goods coming into their countries from abroad. As we shall see in Chapter 8, in difficult economic times countries are often tempted to raise barriers to imported goods in order to protect jobs at home. In the United States and elsewhere, even today, the specter of Smoot-Hawley and the Great Depression is raised in political debates as a warning to resist that temptation because in a global economy, any effort to protect one market usually leads to efforts to protect others, leaving all countries worse off than when they began. In short, understanding the past experience of trade policy, and how it has been interpreted by leaders over the decades, helps give us the proper context for understanding contemporary debates about foreign economic policy and global trade.

Consider a second example. The international relations thinking of a generation of American leaders was shaped by the experience of the Vietnam War of 1965–73. Before that war, the United States seemed willing, in the words of President John F. Kennedy, to 'pay any price, and bear any burden' to defend freedom worldwide. But for almost three decades after Vietnam, the memory of that protracted and costly conflict shaped the reluctance of US policy makers to intervene militarily around the world. The lessons American policy makers drew from the failure in Vietnam included 'don't get bogged down in other people's civil wars,' 'don't fight a war without an exit strategy,' and 'don't fight without the clear support of the American people.' The wars in Afghanistan and Iraq that began in 2002 and 2003 were the first since Vietnam in which the United States made a sustained commitment of military force over several years, despite suffering significant casualties. Future historians will almost certainly point to the tragic experience of September 11, 2001 as having created a new historical memory for a generation of Americans, with profound effects on the thinking and behavior of American foreign policy makers.

Different people may draw different lessons from major historical experiences. For some Europeans, the key lesson of fascism's rise during the 1930s was that dictators like Germany's Hitler or Italy's Mussolini needed to be confronted with military force rather than appeased though diplomacy. For other Europeans, the lesson is that economic distress leads to political extremism. Far-left and far-right political movements take power when economic cooperation breaks down and jobs vanish. For some Americans, the lesson of September 11 may be 'better safe than sorry' – it is better to pre-emptively attack a potential enemy now than wait and risk a more costly conflict in the future. This kind of thinking influenced American policy makers who argued in 2002 that the

▼ **Photo 1.4 Vietnam War Memorial**

The Vietnam Veterans Memorial was completed in 1982 and declared a national monument in 1984. 'The wall,' as it is commonly known, contains in chronological order the names of over 58,000 US service personnel who gave their lives during the Vietnam War.

Source: © vmbfoto – istockphoto.com.

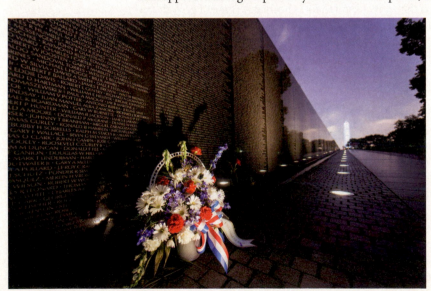

United States should invade Iraq and overthrow Saddam Hussein before he developed a nuclear weapons capability. For other Americans, the lesson of September 11 might be 'come home America' – the idea that the United States is overextended and its global military presence is creating a target for terrorists worldwide. The point is not to debate the correct lesson, but to appreciate that different understandings of the experiences of the past give us insights into why states behave as they do in the present.

History gives us perspective not only on a particular country's behavior, but on the nature and evolution of the international system as a whole. An understanding of the past helps reveal which features of the present international order are truly novel. However, an appreciation of the past may also reveal remarkable continuities in the practice of international relations alongside large-scale changes. Consider the following news account provided by a contemporary observer of the events:

> The Athenians also made an expedition against the island of Melos. They had thirty of their own ships … The Melians are a colony from Sparta. They had refused to join the Athenian empire like the other islanders, and at first had remained neutral without helping either side … Now [the Athenians], encamped with the above force in Melian territory and, before doing any harm to the land, first of all sent representatives to negotiate.

> *Athenians*: We do not want any trouble in bringing you into our empire and we want you to be spared for the good both of yourselves and of ourselves.
> *Melians*: And how could it be just as good for us to be the slaves as for you to be the masters?
> *Athenians*: You, by giving in, would save yourselves from disaster; we, by not destroying you, would be able to profit from you.

> The Melians, left to themselves, reached a conclusion … 'We are not prepared to give up in a short moment the liberty which our city has enjoyed from its foundations for 700 years.' … The Athenian representatives then went back to the army and the Athenian generals, finding that the Melians would not submit, immediately commenced hostilities … Siege operations were carried on vigorously, and the Melians surrendered unconditionally to the Athenians, who put to death all the men of military age whom they took, and sold the women and children as slaves. Melos itself they took over for themselves, sending out later a colony of 500 men.

The observer, of course, was Thucydides, and the events took place around 416 BCE (Thucydides, 1954 edition: 400–08). By today's standards, the diplomacy in this famous 'Melian dialogue' is brutally frank and the resolution – separating the men from women and children, then killing all the men and enslaving the women and children – is a form of barbarism that we associate with the distant past in human civilization. No one came to help the Melians, and Thucydides leads us to believe that what happened over Melos was not out of the ordinary.

Today, slavery and genocide are outlawed by international agreements. Colonialism is a thing of the past. We would expect that other states would react to the kind of raw aggression exhibited by the Athenians with outrage, and victims could reasonably count on members of the international community to try to deter the aggressor and come to the aid of victims if aggression took place.

But, before proclaiming our modernity and moral superiority too hastily, consider this second news account:

> Bosnian Serb forces had laid siege to the Srebrenica enclave, where tens of thousands of civilians had taken refuge from earlier Serb offensives in north-eastern Bosnia …
>
> They were under the protection of about 600 lightly armed Dutch infantry forces. Fuel was running out and no fresh food had been brought into the enclave since May.
>
> Serb forces began shelling Srebrenica …
>
> The Bosnian Serb commander Ratko Mladic entered Srebrenica… accompanied by Serb camera crews. In the evening, General Mladic summoned Colonel Karremans to a meeting at which he delivered an ultimatum that the Muslims must hand over their weapons to guarantee their lives …
>
> Buses arrived to take women and children to Muslim territory, while the Serbs began separating out all men from age 12 to 77 for 'interrogation for suspected war crimes.' It is estimated that 23,000 women and children were deported in the next 30 hours …
>
> Hundreds of men were held in trucks and warehouses. In the five days after Bosnian Serb forces overran Srebrenica, more than 7,000 Muslim men are thought to have been killed. (BBC News and Rohde, 1997)

▼ **Photo 1.5 Tragedy in Srebrenica**

A Bosnian woman weeps over her cousin's grave at the Memorial Center, Potocari, near Srebrenica in Bosnia. In July 2013 a mass was held for the burial of 409 newly identified victims of the 1995 Srebrenica massacre.

Source: PA Images.

As you might have known, the tragic events of Srebrenica took place not in ancient times but in 1995, during the Bosnian war that followed the collapse of the former multinational state of Yugoslavia. Neither the United Nations forces on the ground, the United States, nor members of the European Union came to the aid of the Bosnians, who were separated and slaughtered in much the same way that the Athenians dealt with the Melians more than 2,000 years earlier. Unlike their Athenian counterparts, the Serbian aggressors were put on trial and convicted of various war crimes, including genocide, at the International Criminal Tribunal for the Former Yugoslavia. On March 30, 2010, the Serbian parliament adopted a resolution that condemned and apologized for the war crimes that took place at Srebrenica, and subsequently the President of the Republic of Serbia wrote a public apology as well (Tadec 2010). The norms of the current international system certainly differ from those of the ancient Greek system; what was considered 'normal' practice back then is viewed as reprehensible and even criminal today. Nonetheless, and apology notwithstanding, the exercise of power by political actors in pursuit of their interests was tragically similar in Melos and Srebrenica.

Connecting Aspiration and Reality

The tragedy of Srebrenica reminds us that there is a profound difference between how the world is and how we might like it to be. It is natural to approach world politics with a particular set of values or aspirations. Different people have different values, and it would be difficult to identify a set of universal values upon which everyone across time, place, and culture would agree. Nonetheless, it is probably fair to assume that most people prefer peace to war and would welcome the eradication of global poverty. Many people believe in some notion of equality for the world's population. Some people believe that countries, especially wealthy or powerful ones, have an obligation not only to their own citizens, but to people living beyond their borders as well.

These values are often frustrated in world politics. War and poverty are all too common. International relationships are characterized by great inequalities in power and wealth. Some people have excellent life opportunities, while others are virtually imprisoned by the difficulty of their circumstances, depending on the country or region they inhabit. The governments of wealthy countries express good intentions to share wealth and combat oppression outside their borders, and they sometimes follow through. But all too often, as we will see in Chapter 10, they fail to meet their commitments on foreign aid to poorer countries. They also often look the other way in the face of human suffering in foreign countries, as evidenced by the world's slow reaction to the humanitarian tragedies in Bosnia and Rwanda during the 1990s, in the Darfur area of Sudan during the early 2000s, and in Syria in 2013.

International relations must, in the first instance, entail the study of the world not as it should be but as it actually is – keeping in mind that scholars and observers may not always agree on what constitutes the world 'as it is.' Our primary concern must be to describe how states actually behave and explain why they behave as they do, even if we find that behavior repulsive from our own political or moral vantage point. Explanation and prescription are separate tasks, and should be treated that way. But they are also connected; understanding why states behave the way they do is a necessary first step for anyone seeking ways to change that behavior. Consider, for example, various explanations for the problem of war. If international relations research shows that democratic states are less likely than non-democratic states to fight wars in general and with each other, then the transformation of non-democratic states into democracies is a worthwhile though potentially difficult strategy in pursuit of peace. But if wars are more likely caused by other factors, such as excessive nationalism, resource scarcities, overpopulation, or competing territorial claims, then different prescriptions are in order.

In this section, we have highlighted three types of connections: between theory and practice, past and present, and aspirations and reality. This book will prompt you to make other connections as well; you will encounter two others regularly in the chapters ahead. One is the connection between international politics and international economics. Although economics is a separate academic discipline from political science, an understanding of international relations requires a familiarity with the basic concepts of economics and the substance of international economic issues. We highlight the interplay of politics and economics in our examination of the history, theory, and practice of international relations. Another important connection is between domestic and international politics. The external or foreign policies of states are significantly affected by the internal or domestic politics of states. Domestic politics, in turn, are influenced by what happens in the international arena. Any successful student of international relations must also be a student of domestic politics. In Chapter 4, we explore the connections between domestic and international politics by focusing on the determinants and consequences of foreign policy behavior.

Recognizing enduring questions and making connections are critical analytical tools to help guide you through the maze of international relations. In the next section we discuss something equally valuable – the ability to view world politics from multiple perspectives.

Viewing the World from Different Perspectives

Do we believe the current international order is desirable, or would we like to see it changed? The answer to that question depends critically on who 'we' are. If we are the governing authority and citizens of a rich and powerful country like the United States, we might consider the contemporary international order – where we perceive our own country as at the top of the international hierarchy – as desirable and perhaps just. But from the perspective of countries that lack power or desire more influence, the international order probably looks much less attractive, and also less fair. Perspectives vary across nation-states and within them as well.

It is critical to consider world politics from multiple perspectives. The study of international relations seeks to understand the behavior of states and people across borders, and that behavior is influenced by how people – and collections of people within nation-states – view the international arena and their place within it. Some years ago, the political scientist Graham Allison captured this reality with an important phrase, 'where you stand depends on where you sit' (Allison 1971). Allison was referring to relations between different parts of the US government, but his aphorism applies more widely. In other words, how you think about a particular issue in world politics is likely affected by the particulars of your own situation: whether you are an American, Russian, Egyptian or Indonesian; rich or poor; male or female; and a member of the majority in a country or a racial or ethnic minority.

The same holds true for nation-states. The *national perspective* of a country is affected by a variety of factors, including historical experience. A former great power will view the world differently from a former colony of a great power. The Chinese, who for centuries enjoyed the position of political and cultural leader of Asia, have a different world view than their neighbors, the Vietnamese, who were occupied by and resisted occupations by the Chinese, French, and Americans. The national perspective will also be shaped by racial, ethnic, and religious characteristics; a nation-state like Japan that is relatively homogeneous ethnically will likely have a different perspective on immigration, for example, than a multi-ethnic Indonesia or a nation-state with strongly entrenched religious factions (Christian and Muslim) like Lebanon. Size and relative power shapes perspective; the larger a nation-state is and the more power it enjoys, the more likely it is to try to shape or alter its international environment, instead of simply reacting to it. Geographic position matters as well. Whether a country views the international system as benign or threatening depends at least in part on whether it is landlocked and surrounded by larger states, or situated securely behind natural barriers like oceans or mountain ranges.

In the chapters that follow we will continually remind you of the importance of viewing world politics from multiple perspectives. We begin that process here by drawing your attention to two important features of international relations.

Recognizing Great-Power Centrism

Sensitivity to multiple perspectives will help you guard against the tendency – a natural one if you happen to live in a wealthy nation such as, for example, the United States or Germany or the United Kingdom today – to view international relations solely or largely from the perspective of the relatively powerful and prosperous. Historically, the so-called great powers receive a lot of attention in the study of international relations because they wield disproportionate influence on the global stage. The United States, in possession of exceptional military and economic resources, finds itself in that position today. Although citizens from other countries do not vote in US elections, they are profoundly affected by the outcome of those elections. An American corporate presence and the influence of American popular culture can be found almost anywhere one travels around the world.

What is wrong with viewing international relations from the perspective of the powerful? Nothing – as long as it is recognized as such and juxtaposed to other perspectives. Americans, just as citizens of any powerful and wealthy country, must recognize, for example, that most of the people in today's world are not American, and the United States is only one of 196 countries in the global system. The rich variation in history, geography, identity, culture, and aspiration that characterizes the global landscape affects international relations. If we proceed from the explicit or even implicit assumption that one country's values, ideals and institutions are universal, or that the rest of the world is simply an imperfect replica of that country, then we are going to miss the critical insights that the study of international relations offers.

This point was driven home – painfully to Americans – in the aftermath of September 11, 2001. One immediate reaction of many ordinary US citizens to these tragic events was to ask 'who are these people, and why do they hate us?' Understanding the answer requires an appreciation of the differences between organized, non-state terrorist entities like Al Qaeda, the much larger group of Muslims living in the Middle East and Southwest Asia who may both admire and resent the United States, but are not drawn to violence to express their sentiment or advance their interests, and non-democratic regimes, like that in Saudi Arabia, who have cooperative relations with the United States but do not command the support of large segments of their own populations. Americans have also come to understand that the United States is resented by some simply because it is so powerful; by others because it represents an all-pervasive, modern consumer culture; or also due to the fact that US foreign policies have traditionally supported repressive governments in the region and have favored the interests of one party in a conflict in the Middle East, Israel, over the interests of other parties, such as the Palestinians.

One of the great students of international relations, Hans Morgenthau, proposed after World War II his four fundamental rules of diplomacy. One rule directed every nation-state to 'look at the political scene from the point of view of other nations' (Morgenthau 1985). His advice may be tempting to ignore if you happen to live in stable, influential, prosperous, and secure countries. But most people do not, and thus it is vital for students of international politics to recognize and analyze the subject from multiple vantage points.

Recognizing Cleavages within the International System

Developed countries:
Wealthy countries with
advanced economies.

Developing countries: Poor
countries with small
economies whose resi-
dents have not, on average,
attained the living stan-
dards typically enjoyed on
average by residents of
wealthy countries.

Sensitivity to multiple perspectives will also allow you to recognize that there are always key divisions, or cleavages, within any international system. In the current international system, for example, there persists a division between rich and poor, or **developed** and **developing countries**. Since developed countries tend to inhabit the northern hemisphere and less developed ones are generally found in the southern hemisphere, you will sometimes see references to *North–South* divisions in world politics.

There is a general difference in perspective between developed and developing countries on international economic issues. In developed states, where standards of living are higher, people worry that jobs are and will continue to be lost in international trade to developing states, where labor is much cheaper. American workers worry about competition from China, while German and French workers worry about competition from labor in Greece or Turkey. Northern countries also feel that southern countries, as they develop, should do their part to advance international economic cooperation by opening their markets to the products of the North. The view from the South is different. Southern states point out that it is difficult to develop in a world economy dominated by established, rich states. Developing economies want special exceptions in international trade and they want access to Northern markets, like agriculture, even if the Northern countries do not have symmetrical access to their markets. These debates, discussed in Chapter 10, are played out in various international forums, such as the United Nations and the World Trade Organization.

There are, of course, different perspectives within developed and developing countries as well. In the United States, people tend to believe the government should play a more modest role in influencing the international or domestic economy than is typically expected in European countries and Japan. In the less developed world, countries that are primarily agriculture exporters (like Ghana, which exports cocoa) view the world economy differently than oil producers and exporters (like Venezuela or Kuwait). Exporters of manufactured goods, like South Korea or Taiwan, will have a different perspective on trade negotiations as well.

There are also North–South divisions on environmental issues. The United States refused to ratify a global agreement on carbon emissions, the Kyoto Protocol, because it felt the burden of reducing emissions was not shared equally among all countries, including big developing countries like China. Developing countries argue that the existing rich countries developed without worrying about the natural environment, and now expect today's poorer countries to inhibit their own development due to environmental problems (which poorer countries see as caused by the more industrial North). Developing countries like India and China also demand aid and technology from the North to assist them in limiting emissions and adapting to the impact of climate change. These debates will be discussed in detail in Chapter 12.

There *used* to be an important cleavage in international relations between East and West. During the Cold War (1945–89), the world was divided between communist and non-communist countries. The Western countries viewed themselves as defending the rights of the individual and political and economic freedoms. The communist countries, generally located in the eastern part of Europe but also in Asia and Central America, viewed capitalism as exploitative and saw themselves defending social values, such as full employment and a more equitable distribution of income and wealth. As Chapter 2 states, each side in this conflict viewed the other as a threat and tried to enlist the support of neutral countries to its cause. The East–West division in world politics ended in 1991, with the collapse of the Soviet Union, the leader of the Eastern side.

The existence of cleavages or divisions among states within any international system leads us to what historically has been a vexing problem in international politics, that of **dissatisfied states**. These states may remain frustrated, patiently build their power, or become aggressive in an effort to advance their relative positions. Germany, Japan, and Italy after World War I are classic cases of dissatisfied states. Italy desired colonial possessions befitting its self-image as a great power. Germany sought respect and influence after what it considered the humiliation of the settlement that ended World War I. Japan, a vulnerable island economy, desired economic security, which its leaders believed could be best achieved by occupying its resource-rich neighbors. The dissatisfaction of these states and their determination to rectify it was an important cause of World War II.

A dissatisfied state is potentially dangerous, but it is not always easy to recognize. States may act aggressively because they are dissatisfied and intent on transforming the international system, or because they feel threatened and insecure. During the Cold War, policy makers and analysts in the Western countries continually debated whether the Soviet Union was a dissatisfied state intent on world domination, or a troubled and insecure great power that needed to control its immediate neighborhood because it felt threatened by a more technologically advanced set of Western countries. The debate was important. If the Soviet Union was primarily aggressive, it needed to be contained; if it was primarily insecure, then reassurance and cooperation might be the more appropriate foreign policy. The failure to contain an aggressive country could lead to trouble if that country believed itself free to dominate others. But an aggressive response to an insecure country could be provocative, reinforcing fear and insecurity and leading to a conflict that perhaps neither side wanted. International relations scholars refer to this general problem as the security dilemma.

Although it is not always easy to distinguish dissatisfied states from defensive states, it is important to do so because the stakes are very high. In today's international system, many analysts are debating the extent to which China is (or will become) a dissatisfied state that will eventually disrupt world order, a defensive state mainly seeking to resolve its internal problems and command a degree of international respect, or a satisfied state content to accept the current rules of the international order. A similar debate is taking place at a regional level, concerning the intentions and aspirations of Iran. To some, Iran is a disruptive force seeking weapons of mass destruction to threaten Israel and Sunni-controlled regimes (Iran is controlled by Shiites) in the Gulf region. To others, Iran is an insecure middle power that feels threatened by the world's dominant power, the United States, and its powerful regional ally, Israel. The United States today is closely associated politically and militarily with Iran's traditional enemy, Iraq. Iran and Iraq fought a costly and bloody war throughout the 1980s. The appropriate foreign policy depends, to some extent, on whether one has a clear understanding of the perspective of the country in question.

Dissatisfied states: States who feel that their influence, status, and material benefits should be higher than what they are actually achieving.

Looking Ahead

The rest of this textbook is divided into four sections. In Part I, Chapter 2, we provide the historical background necessary to appreciate enduring questions and give context to contemporary international politics. In Chapters 3 and 4, we introduce the basic theories and concepts in the study of international relations. This provides a 'toolbox' that will help you make sense of the practice of international politics described and analyzed in subsequent chapters.

Part II is devoted to an introduction to the issues of war and peace, or what is known in international relations as the subfield of security studies. In this section, Chapters 5 and 6, we discuss the causes of war, and the mechanisms in the international system that leads states to resolve disputes peacefully. In Chapter 7, we analyze the special problem of weapons of mass destruction, and their impact on the theory and practice of international relations.

Part III turns to the relationship between international politics and economics. In Chapter 8, we provide the basic building blocks of the world economy, focusing in particular on trade and money and the global institutions of the world economy. This basic background is critical for students to grasp before diving more deeply into how politics and economics interact. In Chapter 9, we examine foreign economic policy, and how governments use international economic relations to further their political objectives. Chapter 10 investigates the special problems and opportunities developing countries encounter as they seek to associate with, but not be overwhelmed by, the global economy.

Part IV looks at emerging challenges to the international system and world of nation-states. In Chapter 11, we examine the role of non-state actors, such as terrorists, war lords, and drug dealers, who have *privatized* political violence and, in some cases, challenged the authority of sovereign states. We also explore the obligation of the members of the international community to protect people whose human rights are threatened by their own governments, or who are the victims of war or natural disaster. We then turn in Chapter 12 to international environmental problems and the response of states, individually and collectively. In conclusion, Chapter 13 challenges you to draw on what you have learned and think creatively about the future of international relations. We provide summary observations and explore six alternate visions of the future world order.

Each chapter also pays particular attention to the major themes introduced above – the enduring question, the levels of analysis, making connections, and viewing world politics from multiple perspectives. We will remind you throughout each chapter of the enduring questions that anchor your understanding of global politics. We will illustrate the need to make connections and view the world from multiple perspectives with special features in each chapter. We also constantly challenge you with discussion questions, which we hope will help you structure your thinking about the material we cover in the text. As you explore the enduring problems and contemporary texture of international relations, we invite you at each step to engage the material with a critical eye. We ask you to challenge yourself by drawing your own conclusions about the problems of peace and conflict in international relations, as well as the opportunities for cooperation and the attainment of international peace in this, your twenty-first century.

Visit **www.palgrave.com/politics/Grieco** to access extra resources for this chapter, including:

- Chapter Summaries to help you review the material
- Multiple Choice Quizzes to test your understanding
- Flashcards to test your knowledge of the key terms in this chapter
- Outside resources including links to contemporary articles and videos, that add to what you have learned in this chapter.

Study Questions

1. In what ways do you think international relations affect your life?
2. What do you most want to learn about as you read this book and take what is likely to be your first and possibly only course in international relations?
3. From your viewpoint, which of the enduring questions about international relations discussed in this chapter, and pursued throughout this book, are the most interesting and important? Why?
4. What perspective do you think you are bringing to this course and the study of international relations? That is, when you think about international relations, do you do so from the viewpoint of a citizen of a particular country, as a young person, or as a male or female? What are the stakes and interests you bring to your study of international relations? How might that perspective be influencing the way you approach the field?

Further Reading

Axelrod, Robert (2006) *The Evolution of Cooperation*, rev. edn (New York: Basic Books). This is a classic social science study that has direct implications for international relations. Axelrod examines how cooperation emerges among self-interested actors – and how they resist the temptation to cheat each other – even when there is no central authority to police their behavior.

Drezner, Daniel (2011) *Theories of International Politics and Zombies* (Princeton: Princeton University Press). This is an unusual and irreverent introduction to international relations theories. Drezner goes through a variety of the leading theoretical traditions in international politics and shows how each might help us explain and react to the threat of a zombie invasion. An easy way to digest theory!

Gilpin, Robert (2001) *War and Change in World Politics* (Cambridge: Cambridge University Press). This is a recent international relations classic that examines the problem of managing international change peacefully. Gilpin uses a variety of approaches to illuminate great-power transitions from ancient Greece to the present day.

Jervis, Robert (1976) *Perception and Misperception in World Politics* (Princeton: Princeton University Press). In this classic study of foreign policy and international relations, Jervis explains when and why the perceptions of world leaders diverge from reality. The consequences of misperception may be conflict and sometimes inadvertent war.

Keck, Margaret and Kathryn Sikkink (eds) (1998) *Activists Beyond Borders: Advocacy Networks in International Politics* (Ithaca: Cornell University Press). This book nicely illustrates the importance of non-state actors in international relations. Keck and Sikkink and their contributors show how and why coalitions form across borders to address problems such as slavery, women's suffrage, human rights, and environmental degradation.

Mahbubani, Kishore (2004) *Can Asians Think?* (Singapore: Marshall Cavendish). This book of essays is a nice application of the need to view the world from multiple perspectives. Mahbubani is critical of the idea that the values of Western civilization are universal, and argues that other civilizations make important though at times underappreciated contributions to the human endeavor.

I
Foundations of International Relations

2 The Emergence of a Global System of States, 1500–Today

3 Theories of International Relations

4 The Analysis of Foreign Policy

Visit **www.palgrave.com/politics/grieco** to watch the authors debating the issues discussed in this Part.

Video 1: Is the history of international realtions characterized by progress or continuity?

Video 2: Why do we have so many theories of international relations?

2

The Emergence of a Global System of States, 1500–today

Enduring question: How did a fragmented world become a global, integrated system of states for which order is an ongoing problem **?**

Today's international system is a product of historical change. Some changes have been recent: while 51 independent states formed the United Nations in 1945, 193 states were members in 2014. Other changes have taken place over centuries: China was perhaps the most advanced state on earth in 1500, it then experienced decline and even subjugation by Japan and Western states during the 1900s, and during the past three decades it has once more become a global powerhouse.

How did we come to live in a system of states? We address this important question in this chapter. We will also highlight in this chapter the historical issue of international order, that is, a period of sustained peace and cooperation among states. We will see below that international order can be fragile and that war, while rare, is an ever-present threat to international order. Why, we ask below, do peace and order often share the stage of history with violence and disorder?

To address these questions thoroughly we need to explore different theories of international relations as well as contemporary international affairs. This we will do in the chapters to follow. But to address these questions we need in the first instance to know the essential features of international history.

There are three more specific reasons we need to understand international history. First, we are still living with its consequences, whether they are, for example, poverty and civil strife in sub-Saharan Africa, Palestinian–Israeli violence, or American debates about US activism in global affairs. Second, scholars often use historical materials to test theories of international relations, and if we know the basics of international history then we will be in a much stronger position to assess those tests. Third, leaders, officials, and media commentators often invoke historical analogies in support of their policy positions;

only if we know international history can we assess the utility of such analogies that draw from the past in dealing with issues in the present.

The first section in the chapter explores what the world was like around the year 1500, when European states started a process that, between 1500 and 1900, produced our modern system of states. In the second main section we examine that process in detail. The third section focuses on the years from 1900 to 1945, which began with Europe at the pinnacle of its power and ended, after two world wars, with the diminution of European global influence, the rise of the United States and the Soviet Union, and the birth of scores of new states and the creation of today's truly global system of states. The fourth section examines how the struggle between the Soviet Union and the United States emerged and shaped world politics between 1945 and 1990. The fifth section views the postwar world from the perspective of new and developing countries in the international system, and the last section describes the end of the Cold War and key features of today's contemporary global system.

Source: © kuzma–istockphoto.com.

Learning Objectives

By the end of this chapter, you will be able to:

→ Understand why history matters to international relations.

→ Describe how a system of states emerged in Europe and how those states came to control much of the world.

→ Know and assess the causes and global political effects of World Wars I and II, which ended Europe's rule over much of the world.

→ Recognize why the Cold War emerged after 1945, and understand its impact on international relations, including from the perspective of countries in the Third World.

→ Understand why the Cold War ended unexpectedly between 1988 and 1991.

→ Have a grasp of the key features of the contemporary international order.

Chapter Contents

- Starting Point: The World in 1500
- The Formation of the International Political System, 1500–1900
- World War I and World War II, 1900–1945
- The Global Struggle of the Cold War, 1945–1989
- The View from the South: Decolonization, the Non-Aligned Movement, and the Quest for a New International Economic Order
- The End of the Cold War and the Collapse of the Soviet Union
- The Contemporary International Order
- Revisiting the Enduring Question and Looking Ahead
- Study Questions
- Further Reading

Starting Point: The World in 1500

Empires: Political entities that contain a substantial geographical space, often many different peoples, and over which a single powerful ruler governs.

Consider the world in the year 1500. As can be seen in Map 2.1, with the exception of a nascent system of states in Europe, much of the eastern hemisphere consisted not of states, but of empires. An empire is a political entity that contains a substantial geographical space, often many different peoples, and over which a single powerful ruler governs. For example:

- **China** in 1500 possessed a population of about 300 million, and the largest and most advanced economy on earth (Maddison 2006: 261, 263). It had a relatively coherent empire by 1500, and had been ruled for some time by a succession of imperial dynasties (Roberts and Westad 2013: 437–57), that is, an order in which members of a given extended family and their associates, over a number of generations, maintain power within an empire.

- **Japan** in 1500 had a population of about 15 million and, while it had an Emperor, the country was fragmented into small political entities, led by local military leaders (Maddison 2006: 241, 263). This changed in the early 1600s: a warlord, Tokugawa Ieyasu, attained control over most of Japan, and the resulting family-based ruling dynasty, the Tokugawa Shogunate, governed Japan until 1868 (Roberts and Westad 2013: 465–68) .

- **India** in 1500 was home to a culturally and economically advanced population of about 110 million. During the first half of the 1500s, successive members of the Mughal dynasty, Muslim descendants of the Mongol conqueror Genghis Khan, conquered and politically unified most of India, and continued to rule much of the Indian sub-continent until the early 1700s (Roberts and Westad 2013: 537–44; Maddison 2006: 241, 263).

▼ Map 2.1 The Eastern Hemisphere in 1500

In 1500, much of the Eastern hemisphere, such as in China as well as in Africa, consisted of large empires; in Western Europe a nascent system of independent states was forming.

◀ Map 2.2: Inca, Mayas, and Aztec Empires in the Western Hemisphere in 1500

In the year 1500, there were two important empires in the Western hemisphere: those of the Inca and the Aztecs, and remnants of a third, the Maya.

- **The Ottoman Empire** began when Muslim Turkish tribes entered Asia Minor in the eleventh century; by the mid-1400s, they conquered Asia Minor and, in 1453, the capital city of the Byzantine Empire, Constantinople (Crowley 2005). By the 1600s, the Ottoman Empire included all of Asia Minor, the Balkans region, a good part of central Europe, the Middle East, and North Africa (Roberts and Westad 2013: 397–405).

- **Sub-Saharan Africa** in 1500 was home to perhaps 38 million people (Maddison 2006: 239). Sub-Saharan Africa and northern Africa at that time enjoyed substantial economic activity. To the west, the Mali Empire was the largest African political community during the 1300s and the 1400s; it was replaced by the Songhai Empire during the 1500s.

- **Europe** in 1500 consisted of perhaps 82 million people in Western Europe, Eastern Europe, and what is today western Russia. Dynastic families, such as the Valois in France, the Tudors in England, and the Habsburgs in a territory from Austria to Belgium and even Spain, governed these early European states, which we call **dynastic states**. Dynastic states, it should be noted, did not develop in all the main parts of Western Europe during this period. Italian city-states remained independent of one another, and some 300 independent duchies, church-ruled lands, and free cities occupied German-speaking lands in central Europe.

Dynastic states: States ruled by 'imperial dynasties' or 'dynastic families,' in which members of a given extended family, over a number of generations, maintain power within a state or empire.

- **The Americas in 1500** (see Map 2.2) was most populated in today's Mexico (perhaps 7.5 million), Peru (4 million), and Brazil (1 million); another 2 million people lived in what are now the United States and Canada, with additional populations on the Caribbean islands (Maddison 2006: 233, 243, 263). Two main empires were in existence around 1500 in the Americas: the Aztec Empire, in the central part of today's Mexico, and the Incan Empire, stretching some 2,500 miles along the Andes mountain range in the western part of South America (Roberts and Westad 2013: 475–81).

The world of 1500 was fragmented into relatively discrete regions ruled by empires or, in Europe, a complex tapestry of dynastic states, city-states, or small duchies. Yet, today we live in a world of states. What brought states into existence? How did they come into contact with one another and form the more coherent system of states that we see today? Those are the questions we take up in the next section.

Levels of Analysis
The World of 1500

👤 Individual	👥 State	🌐 International
Most individuals in 1500 played little or no role in the governance of the entities in which they lived.	Large regions of the eastern and western hemispheres in the 1500s consisted of empires.	By 1500 a nascent system of dynastically ruled states came into existence in Europe.
	Dynastic states, city states, or small duchies governed Europe in the 1500s.	
	China was a consolidated state in 1500.	

The Formation of the International Political System, 1500–1900

European states set the world in motion toward the system of states in which we all still live. To understand this process, we need to examine how a system of states emerged in Europe between 1500 and 1815. We also need to see how these European states came to control the Americas, sub-Saharan Africa, and the Indian sub-continent, and how they made similar inroads in China and the Ottoman Empire, but not Japan. Finally, we need to understand why European states were able to attain control of such a large portion of the world's space and population.

A State System Emerges in Western Europe

State system: A group of competing states.

Feudalism: A system in which individuals act as 'vassals' and receive land in exchange for swearing loyalty to specific high-ranking leaders (e.g., counts, dukes) and, at the apex of the system, the king.

From the 1400s to the 1600s, a **state system**, or a group of competing states, came into being in Europe (Dehio 1962; Tilly 1975; Tilly 1990; Kaiser 2000). It emerged from two sources. The first was European **feudalism**. Second, in German-speaking areas in Central Europe, a loose and largely symbolic association termed the Holy Roman Empire was controlled by the Habsburg dynasty by the early 1500s.

The formation of the European state system was the unintended consequence of a succession of failed efforts over three hundred years by powerful European leaders to use war to establish control over the European continent. These leaders repeatedly sought to create an imperial order in Europe. Those leaders with imperial ambitions catalyzed the historical process by which independent, interacting, and often competing states were created in Europe. The resulting states, and the state system they formed, became entrenched, producing the nucleus for today's global system of states.

The imperial efforts were made by the Habsburg Emperor Charles V between 1519 and 1556; his son Philip II during the late 1500s; the Austrian and Spanish Habsburgs during the Thirty Years War of 1618–48; France's King Louis XIV between 1667 and 1715; France again between 1789 and 1815, most spectacularly after General Napoleon Bonaparte seized power in 1799 in a military coup and made himself emperor in 1804; and Germany under Adolph Hitler between 1933 and 1945. Leaders of other European states formed alliances to counter these efforts, and these alliances ultimately defeated each bid for empire.

An example of a network of alliances that was formed to prevent the creation of an empire in Europe is what took place from the 1520s to the 1550s. At its core was France: to prevent the Habsburgs from attaining military and political hegemony in Europe, France allied on the one hand with a host of small German principalities, and on the other hand with the Ottoman Turks. This network of alliances raises interesting questions about the importance of identity – in this instance, religious identity – in foreign policy, and we pursue this issue in detail in Box 2.1. For the moment, consider this: for almost seven centuries – from the Muslim conquest of Spain in the eighth century, through the Christian crusades in the Levant in the eleventh, twelfth, and thirteenth centuries, through the subsequent rise of the Ottomans – Muslim states and rulers posed a fundamental challenge to Europe and its states and monarchs. Yet, notwithstanding that common challenge from the Muslim world, Catholic France, determined not to be dominated politically by Habsburg co-religionists, during the first half of the 1500s crafted a formal military alliance with the Muslim Ottoman Turks, and worked with that country against their mutual enemy, the Habsburgs. In the same vein, fearful that Emperor Charles V would bring Europe under Habsburg control, Catholic France supported Protestant German princes in their initial rebellion against the Habsburgs in the first half of the 1500s. Later, during the Thirty Years War of 1618–48, Catholic France again intervened on behalf of the Protestants against the Austrian and Spanish Habsburgs, at first providing subsidies to the Dutch Republic and Sweden, and later going directly to war against the Habsburgs. Thus, French monarchs demonstrated repeatedly over a period of 150 years that they were willing and able to put aside differences with two communities with which they had the most fundamental of differences in identity – Muslim Ottomans and Protestant Germans – in order to prevent the establishment of a Habsburg empire in Europe.

The Thirty Years War was brought to a conclusion in 1648 by a series of agreements that have come to be known as the **Peace of Westphalia**. Each signatory to the treaties, including the Germanic states that previously had at least a nominal duty to defer to the Habsburg Holy Roman Emperor, was now a free agent, including on such important matters as the establishment of Catholicism or Protestantism within their jurisdictions as the state-sponsored religion, and the crafting of alliances and other agreements with other states. We live in a system of sovereign states over which there is no higher political authority, and to describe this system scholars of international relations often say that we live in a **Westphalian state system**. Sovereignty, as we dis-

Peace of Westphalia: Treaties that ended the Thirty Years War and divided Europe into sovereign states independent of higher authorities, giving rise to the state system that characterizes the international order today.

Westphalian state system: A state system in which each state is sovereign, with no higher authority (such as a church or empire) to answer to. The modern state system is Westphalian.

Religious Identity and the Franco-Ottoman Military Alliance

Theory: *States with Common Identities Should Find Cooperation Easier than States with Conflicting Identities*

In Chapter 3, we will explore different theories of international relations, including constructivist theory, which suggests that belief systems influence the foreign policy decisions and actions of national leaders. We might expect then that state leaders sharing similar world views, including religious beliefs, find it easier to cooperate with each other than leaders with radically different world views.

Practice: *The Alliance between Catholic France and the Muslim Ottoman Empire*

After France lost a number of battles against Habsburg military forces, and Francis I, the French King, was taken prisoner for a time after a major defeat at the hands of the Habsburgs in 1525, the French King attained a military alliance with Suleiman the Magnificent, leader of the Ottoman Turkish Empire. In 1531, King Francis explained to the Venetian ambassador why he had aligned France with the Ottoman Turks: he said that 'I cannot deny that I wish to see the Turk all-powerful and ready for war, not for himself – for he is an infidel and we are all Christians – but to weaken the power of the emperor, to compel him to make major expenses, and to reassure all the other governments who are opposed to such a formidable enemy.'

Notwithstanding the fact that they were both largely Catholic, the drive by the Habsburgs for European domination combined with the rejection by France of such domination caused bitter enmity between the two, to the extent that even though they came from mutually hostile religious traditions, France worked with the Ottoman Empire against the Habsburgs.

Source: Crowley 2008: 66.

cussed in Chapter 1, implies that each state has political authority within its territory and each can establish its own foreign policy toward other states. The inclusion of these two provisions in the Peace of Westphalia recognized and formalized the existence of what in fact was already an inter-state system in Europe. That system of states, we will see below, gradually expanded to include the entire globe.

The Peace of Westphalia may have been a turning point in establishing the idea of sovereign states, but it did not end the quest by particular European states to establish an empire in that part of the world. In 1672, 1681, and in 1700, France's King Louis XIV launched or became involved in large European wars as a part of his strategy to establish French hegemony over the Continent. In each case, Holland played a key role in organizing a counter-coalition against France, and among other allies the Dutch were successful in recruiting and working with two of their former enemies, the Austrians and, perhaps most remarkably, their former masters (and because of that the deeply hated) Spanish. Shortly after the French Revolution of 1789, French revolutionary governments, and then France under Napoleon Bonaparte, waged a sequence of wars – the former known as the French Revolutionary Wars of 1792–1802, the latter the Napoleonic Wars of 1803–15 – as a result of which France came very close to establishing hegemony over much of Europe. However, Napoleon was defeated in 1814 and 1815 as a result of an alliance of a democratizing England and an autocratic Prussia, Russia, and Austria.

In the wake of the French Revolutionary and Napoleonic wars, Britain, France (at first under a restored monarchy), Prussia (later Germany), Austria (later Austria-Hungary), and Russia established an informal 'Concert of Europe.' These 'great powers' and other lesser states as relevant would meet in congress to address political problems that might threaten Europe's peace. They sought to create an **international order**, that is, a period of sustained peace and cooperation among the great powers. The Concert played a positive role in contributing to European stability even as late as 1878 and the Congress of Berlin, to be discussed below, but as we will also see below the Concert ultimately failed to find a sure path toward a permanent European peace.

International order: A period of sustained peace and cooperation among the great powers

European Pursuit of Foreign Empire

From the mid-1500s to the late 1800s, Europeans conquered the Americas, South Asia, and sub-Saharan Africa, largely subjugated China and the Ottoman Turks, and tried but failed to colonize Japan (Roberts and Westad 2013: 633–60, 791–845).

Mercantilism and European Imperialism

Europeans sought foreign colonies because many state leaders believed in the doctrine of **mercantilism**. According to this doctrine, military power is the central goal of states; such power rests on financial wealth; and world financial wealth is a fixed quantity. One's own state could become wealthier (and thus more powerful) only at the expense of the wealth (and power) of other states. The best way to attain wealth and power, according to the doctrine, was **imperialism**, a state strategy by which one country conquers foreign lands to turn them into **colonies**, or areas over which they have political and economic control, so the conquering country can exploit the colonized lands and the peoples inhabiting them, either through trade or by settling the conquered territories.

Mercantilism: A doctrine that states that military power is the central goal of states, such power rests on financial wealth, and the financial wealth of the world is a fixed quantity. Thus, the best way to gain wealth and thereby power is to pursue imperialism.

Imperialism: A state strategy in which one country conquers foreign lands to turn them into colonies.

European Subjugation of the Americas, Sub-Saharan Africa, and India

During the 1300s and 1400s, Chinese ships moved spices and manufactured goods to India; Muslim ships then moved these goods to Middle Eastern ports; and Venetian traders took the cargoes to Europe. By the early 1500s, Portugal broke into this lucrative business by sailing down the African coast, then north to India and the islands of today's Indonesia, as well as to China and Japan. By 1500, Portugal also discovered and began to colonize Brazil. Spain, seeking a new path to East Asia by supporting Columbus's expedition, reached the Americas instead, conquered the Aztec Empire in 1519, the Inca Empire in 1531, and soon thereafter found in those regions gold and especially silver in abundance (Kamen 2004). The Dutch, by the early 1700s, supplanted the Portuguese in much of East Asia and the East Indies (today's Indonesia), and the French established small colonies in North America and the Caribbean.

Colonies: Areas conquered by a colonizing power over which the colonizer has political and economic control. Colonizers exploit colonized lands and peoples through trade or settlement for economic and political gain.

The British established the largest overseas empire (Ferguson 2004). By 1700, they had founded colonies along the Atlantic seaboard, as well as numerous islands in the Caribbean. English trading posts were operating in the Indian ports of Bombay, Madras, and Calcutta. Britain's victory over France in wars during the first half of the 1700s left it in possession of all of Canada and in a pre-eminent position in much of India. America's successful War of Independence against Britain between 1775 and 1783 sharply constrained Britain's position in and control over the Americas. However, Britain's victory over Napoleon in 1815 gave Britain possession of the Cape of Good Hope, all of India, Malta, and a number of additional sugar-rich islands in the

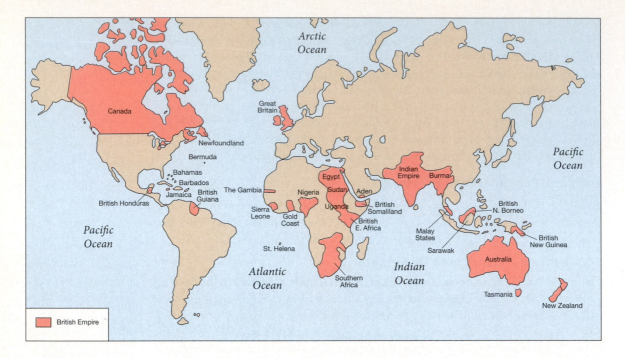

▲ Map 2.3 The British Empire, Early 1900s

Britain by 1900 possessed an empire that spanned the globe from Canada through Egypt and India and all the way to New Zealand.

Rum Triangle: A trans-Atlantic trading triangle active in the seventeenth and eighteenth centuries between Europe, West Africa, and the Americas. The Rum Triangle was the result of European imperialism, and the exploitation of West African and Native American populations by the imperialists was catastrophic to those populations (and highly beneficial to the imperialists).

Caribbean. By the early 1900s, as can be seen in Map 2.3, a popular saying at the time was that 'the sun never sets on the British Empire.'

During the nineteenth and early twentieth century, the major European imperial powers, joined by the United States, Germany, Japan, Belgium, and Italy, fortified their existing colonial holdings and extended their empires to new regions. The United States seized Texas, California, and the American Southwest by defeating Mexico in a war from 1846 to 1848; it formally annexed Hawaii in 1898; and that same year, by defeating Spain, it seized Cuba, Puerto Rico, Guam, and the Philippines. Britain undertook direct rule in India in 1857 after an attempted rebellion by Indian army units, and in 1882 took control of Egypt, which had been in the process of breaking away from the Ottoman Turkish Empire. At the same time, France seized Algeria and Tunisia, and made inroads into Morocco. By 1900, Belgium was in control of the Congo region, Portugal expanded into Angola and Mozambique, and Italy seized Libya during 1911 and 1912. Germany by 1900 gained territories in eastern, western, and southwestern Africa, and the Netherlands consolidated its control over the East Indies.

The consequences of European imperialism for the conquered peoples were catastrophic. We see this most graphically in the operation during the seventeenth and eighteenth centuries of what historians call the Atlantic Basin 'rum triangle trade,' which is depicted in Map 2.4. British traders transported British manufactured goods, such as clothing, to western African ports, and traded those goods for Africans who had been kidnapped by professional slavers or captured by other Africans during inter-tribal wars. The traders would then transport the Africans by ship under barbarous conditions to Caribbean plantations. There, the traders exchanged the Africans for sugar or rum, which they then sold in England. The Africans, isolated from their families and tribes, malnourished, and terrorized, were worked to death on slave plantations. A very similar trading triangle linked New England rum makers, West African slavers, and Caribbean sugar plantation owners.

Kidnapped slaves were also transported through this system to the British colonies in North America, where they were forced to labor in the cultivation of tobacco and cotton.

China and the Ottomans are Subdued and Japan Successfully Resists

The Chinese Empire remained the pre-eminent state in Asia from the sixteenth century until the first half of the nineteenth century. Yet, a succession of rebellions from the middle of the nineteenth century seriously weakened the Imperial government. At the same time, British firms paid for imports of Chinese tea and other products by exporting opium to China; when Chinese authorities sought to stop the drug trade, Britain launched and won the Opium Wars of 1839–42 and 1856–60. By 1900, European and American trading communities were operating in numerous Chinese ports and were immune from Chinese law, and European states and Japan seized control of portions of northeastern China (McNeill 1965: 710–11, 714–17).

By 1683, Ottoman military forces reached the outskirts of Vienna. Then, the tide turned. Various combinations of European states pushed the Ottomans south of the Danube River. By the early 1830s, Russia expelled and supplanted the Ottomans in the Ukraine, the Crimea, the Caucasus, and the Balkans. Egyptian local elites, by the early 1800s, shook off imperial Ottoman control. By the mid-1800s, Ottoman weakness was a bigger problem for the Western European states than Ottoman strength, for they feared that Russia would grow in power as it came to control ever more former Ottoman territories. Indeed, Britain and France, together with the small state of Sardinia-Piedmont (in northwestern Italy) actually banded together to defend Turkey against Russia in the Crimean War of 1853–56. By the early 1900s, the Ottoman Turks were no longer a European or North African power, but they did maintain substantial holdings in the Middle East and the Gulf region.

Japan had largely closed itself off from European contact after the Tokugawa Shogunate came to power in the early 1600s. However, in 1853 and 1854, US naval ships entered Tokyo Bay, and their commander, Commodore Perry, compelled the Japanese government to sign treaties to open itself to trade on terms highly favorable to the United States. Russia, Britain, and France soon compelled Japan to grant them comparable access. It appeared that Japan might soon suffer the same fate as China. Yet, when the traditional Shogunate governing elite failed to resist these pressures from the United States and other Western powers, a wing of the Japanese nobility seized power in 1867 and tilted the balance of influence at the pinnacle of Japanese society away from the Shogun in favor of Emperor Meiji, who ascended his throne in 1868. The new government set Japan on a course of selective adaptation of Western science, education, and industrial technology for the purposes of fostering a strong Japanese economy and, more pointedly, a strong Japanese military able to resist Western encroachments. These leaders of the modernizing element of the Japanese nobility came to be known as the Meiji Restoration. Japan soon showed that rather than becoming a target of imperialism, it could become a successful imperialist itself. It defeated China in a war of 1894–95, and seized control of Formosa, and defeated Russia in an even bigger war in 1904–05, and occupied parts of northern China and Korea.

Why were European States Successful Imperialists?

Four factors contributed to the success of the European imperialists (Diamond 1999; Jones 2003; Acemoglu and Robinson 2012). First, the European states, and later the

Opium Wars: Two wars, fought in 1839–42 and 1856–60, in which the British defeated the Chinese. The result was the opening of China to British (and eventually American) trading communities and the weakening of China as a world power.

Meiji Restoration: The leaders of a modernizing element of the Japanese nobility who, beginning with the rise of Emperor Meiji in 1868, set Japan on a course of selective adaptation of Western science, education, and industrial technology for the purposes of strengthening Japan economically and militarily.

► **Map 2.4 Atlantic Basin Triangle Trade in the Seventeenth and Eighteenth Centuries**

During the seventeenth and eighteenth centuries, the rum triangle represented both the highest levels of economic integration and the most extreme human misery.

United States, enjoyed technically superior weapons. For example, by the early 1500s, the Portuguese used large ships with multiple masts, which gave them a decisive edge in terms of the numbers of guns they could deploy. In a key naval battle in 1509 against Muslim ships, Portugal won and thereby gained control of the Arabian Sea (McNeill 1965: 571). Second, the West enjoyed stronger economic bases. By 1913, the average economic output per person in Western Europe was about $3,500; in China it was about $550, and in India it was a bit higher than $670 (Maddison 2006: 262). Third, because Europeans states for decades had been caught up in a competitive, war-prone states system, they were induced to mobilize resources and find ways to foster economic growth and technological advances, which made them more formidable foes against non-Westerners.

Finally, Western Europeans benefited from a climate, geography, and history of disease that made it easier for them to emerge as powerful forces in world history. A temperate climate enhanced Europe's ability to develop agriculture, and relatively easy transportation across Europe and further east permitted Western Europeans to develop commerce and learn of technological advances from one another and distant communities. In addition, European populations suffered from such diseases as smallpox, influenza, measles, and typhus for centuries. When the Spanish and later the Dutch and English went to the Americas, they brought those diseases with them. The result for indigenous peoples was catastrophic: for example, perhaps 75 percent of the peoples of the Aztec and Incan empires died from Western-transmitted diseases, making their conquest by European invaders all the more easy (Maddison 2006: 37; McNeill 1965: 571–2; Diamond 1999).

European states in 1900 controlled much of the world's landmass and peoples. Yet, by the mid-1940s, by virtue of their own actions, most European states were in ruins;

the United States and the Soviet Union had come to command the stage of world history; and Europe's collapse at least indirectly helped set the scene for the single greatest development of our times, the rise of China (Ferguson 2006). We examine how Europe's self-destruction occurred in the next section, which explores the sources, conduct, and aftermath of World War I and World War II.

👤 **Individual**	🛡 **State**	🌐 **International**	*Levels of Analysis*
From the 1500s to the early 1800s, leaders of major states in Europe – successive Habsburgs, Louis XIV, and Napoleon Bonaparte – tried but failed to establish control over the European continent.	European states attained sovereignty and projected power overseas from the 1500s to the early 1800s.	The European system of sovereign states was formalized by the Peace of Westphalia in 1648. No state achieved hegemony in Europe because of balancing by threatened states. The imbalance in power between European states and empires in the Americas and Asia led to the European conquest of the latter.	*Formation of the International Political System*

World War I and World War II, 1900–1945

We can see most vividly the problems of order and peace in the international system when we study the first half of the twentieth century, a period of two world wars and the collapse of European hegemony over the world (Keylor 2011). We begin our examination of this deadly epoch with a discussion of World War I. We then focus on the failed efforts by European states to re-establish a global order after that war, and finally, we study the onset and conduct of World War II.

World War I: Origins, Conduct, and Aftermath

World War I had many causes, but three in particular command our attention: European leaders established alliances that instilled mutual fear and suspicion; they harbored false beliefs about the ease of winning a war; and they lost control of a regional crisis (Clark 2012; Joll and Martel 2007; Miller *et al.* 1991).

First, consider the role of alliances. In 1870–71, the Prussian chief minister, Otto von Bismarck, led Prussia to a decisive military victory over France. In the afterglow of that victory, Bismarck pressed formerly independent German states into a new, Prussian-dominated German Empire. Also by virtue of the Prussian victory the new German empire annexed two French areas, Alsace and Lorraine. As the first Chancellor for this new, enlarged Germany, Bismarck sought to isolate France with alliances and to stabilize Europe in order to reinforce what had become a favorable European situation for Germany. As an example of seeking to stabilize European affairs, Bismarck in 1878 sponsored the **Berlin Conference** under the auspices of the Concert of Europe and there helped the major European states resolve disputes about the division of Africa into new colonies. To isolate France, Bismarck in 1879 signed a military alliance with Austria-Hungary; Italy joined this accord in 1882, and thus was founded

Berlin Conference: A conference that brought together European leaders in 1878 to solve disputes over the division of Africa into colonies. The conference was sponsored by Otto von Bismarck in an attempt to stabilize European affairs in a manner favorable to Germany.

Triple Alliance: A military alliance finalized in 1882 between Germany, Austria-Hungary, and Italy sought and signed by Germany to isolate France.

Reinsurance Treaty: A secret 1887 treaty between Germany and Russia in which the two nations promised not to be dragged into war against each other by their respective allies, Austria and France.

Triple Entente: A military alliance finalized in 1907 between France, Britain, and Russia, forming the other pole (countering the Triple Alliance) that divided early twentieth-century Europe.

Schlieffen Plan: A German military plan believed by the Germans to be foolproof in which German forces stand on the defense against Russian forces, undertake a massive sweep through Belgium and France and, after outflanking and destroying French forces, then turn east and destroy the Russian army. The plan was not foolproof; hubris about the ease of military victory was a major cause of World War 1.

the **Triple Alliance**. Bismarck also signed a secret agreement with Russia in 1887, the **Reinsurance Treaty**, in which Germany and Russia each promised they would not be dragged into a war with one another by their respective allies, Austria and France.

In 1888, a new German Emperor, William II, came to power. He dismissed Bismarck in 1890, and decided not to renew the Reinsurance Treaty. France and Russia soon began talks that led in 1894 to a formal military alliance. In addition, William II decided in 1898 to build a world-class navy. This struck fear in Britain, which had become accustomed to dominating the seas. After failing to reach a diplomatic accommodation with Germany, Britain's leaders turned to France in 1904 and settled a number of outstanding differences, and did the same with Russia in 1907. Thus, by 1907, two blocs faced off in Europe: the Triple Alliance of Germany, Austria-Hungary, and Italy; and the **Triple Entente** of France, Britain, and Russia.

The second step to major war was prompted by an illusion. In the early 1900s, many European leaders, as well as important members of European society, looked back at recent European wars – Prussia had initiated quick and successful wars against Denmark in 1864, Austria in 1866, and, as noted above, France in 1870–71 – and thought that future wars would be similarly fast and profitable. German military leaders in particular believed they had a blueprint for quick victory, the **Schlieffen Plan**, named after its author, General Alfred von Schlieffen. The plan called for German forces to stand on the defense against Russian forces, to undertake a massive sweep through Belgium and France (see Map 2.5, panel 1), and, after outflanking and destroying French forces, to then turn east and destroy the Russian army.

Finally, in 1914 the leaders of the major European states lost control of what started as a local, limited crisis in the Balkans. They had avoided clashing with each other when states in the Balkans went to war in 1912 and 1913, but 1914 was a different matter. On June 28, 1914, a Bosnian terrorist with possible ties to the Serbian government assassinated the heir to the Austrian Habsburg throne, the Archduke Franz Ferdinand. Germany on July 6 told Austria that it would back it no matter what it did to Serbia; this tendering by Germany of what historians call a 'blank check' may have emboldened the Austrians. The latter on July 23 presented a severe ultimatum to the Serbian government; on July 25, Serbia rejected elements of that ultimatum and on July 28, Austria declared war on Serbia and began military operations. The British, German, and Italian governments recommended negotiations, but Russia mobilized its army on July 30. The next day, Germany demanded that Russia stop its general mobilization and that France promise neutrality if Germany fought Russia. Both demands were rejected. Germany declared war against Russia on August 1 and against France on August 3; Italy, on August 3, announced it was neutral (it would enter on the side of Britain and France and against Germany and Austria in 1915); and Britain declared war on Germany on August 4. The home populations of these states largely accepted their leaders' decisions for war and, in some cases crowds greeted the announcement of war with cheers.

Germany defeated Russia in the East. Russia in turn experienced a revolution in 1917 that included the abdication of the Russian Czar as well as the coming to power of the Bolshevik party under Vladimir Lenin, Russia's withdrawal from the war in 1918, and the onset of a civil war in Russia that ended with the total victory of the Bolsheviks and the creation of the Soviet Union in 1922. In the West, German forces over-ran Belgium rapidly in August 1914 and moved deeply into France by early September, but they failed to outflank the British and French armies. By the end of 1914,

Panel 1: The Schlieffen Plan for the West, 1905

Panel 2: The Western Front, late 1914

the British and French had pushed German forces back from Paris and established a front line that ran through southern Belgium and northern France. A Western Front came into being (see Map 2.5, panel 2): French, British, and, from the fall of 1917, American forces faced off against German forces along a deadly trench line that ran from the English Channel to the Swiss border (see Photo 2.1). The major battles of World War I would be fought on the Western Front, although important and highly lethal military campaigns also took place along the Austrian-Italian border, over control of the Dardanelles in Ottoman Turkey, and in the Middle East.

The United States, after German submarine attacks, declared war on Germany in April 1917. Fresh American divisions allowed the allies to defeat the last German offensives in the West in 1918. In November, Kaiser William II abdicated and escaped to the Netherlands; Austria-Hungary surrendered, and the last Habsburg Emperor, Charles II, also abdicated.

German representatives requested an armistice; it went into effect on November 11. Some 8.5 million troops and sailors had been killed in combat; another 21 million had been wounded.

▲ **Map 2.5 The Schlieffen Plan of 1905 and the Western Front in Late 1914**

While the Schlieffen Plan aimed for a fast knock-out, Germany actually experienced military stalemate and, ultimately, defeat on the Western Front.

The Versailles Treaty and the League of Nations

France, Britain, and the United States essentially dictated peace terms to the Central Powers. They crafted a particularly harsh peace treaty for Germany,

◀ **Photo 2.1 Trench Warfare during World War I**

This is a photo of British infantrymen during the Battle of the Somme. One reason World War I caused so many casualties was that soldiers dug protective trenches and fired machine guns at advancing columns of troops.

Source: PA Images.

signed at Versailles, France, on June 18, 1919. By virtue of the treaty, Germany returned to France Alsace and Lorraine. Germany also lost territories to Poland, and all its overseas colonies, mostly to France and Britain. Germany was forbidden to have an air force or an army that exceeded 100,000 troops, and it had to accept occupation by Allied forces of the Rhineland, the part of Germany on either bank of the Rhine River. It was also required to pay reparations to the European victors, later set at a staggeringly high $35 billion. Finally, Germany was required to accept responsibility for starting the war.

The Versailles settlement brought into being seven new states: Finland in the far north; Estonia, Latvia, and Lithuania in the Baltic; and Poland, Czechoslovakia, and Yugoslavia in Eastern and Southeastern Europe. Poland and Yugoslavia received territories that had been a part of Austria-Hungary. Czechoslovakia was also carved out of that former empire. Austria and Hungary were separated and made small independent states. The Ottoman Empire was also disassembled: France received Syria and Lebanon, while Britain gained Iraq and Palestine.

The Allies also agreed at Versailles to establish the League of Nations. The League was designed to provide states with an ongoing international legal and institutional framework to solve their disputes and avoid war. The League was also designed to provide collective security. That is, if any state threatened or actually used military force illegally against one or a number of the members, all the members pledged to form an overwhelming coalition to defeat that aggressor. We will return to this concept of collective security in Chapter 6. The United States and Britain signed a defense treaty with France as further insurance against renewed German aggression. However, the US Senate declined to ratify either the Treaty of Versailles or the alliance with France and Britain.

Failed Global Reconstruction and the March to World War II, 1920–1939

The Versailles settlement and the League of Nations proved ineffective in maintaining global peace and stability. After grave turbulence in the immediate aftermath of World War I, that is, between 1919 and 1923, the great powers began to work together effectively and, combined with renewed global prosperity, there seemed between 1924 and 1928 to be a chance that the world might enjoy a new age of international cooperation. However, between 1929 and 1933, the global economy collapsed in the face of the Great Depression, and German Nazism (which had been anticipated by the rise of Italian Fascism in the early 1920s) and Japanese imperialism emerged and created new challenges to Western democracy (Steiner 2005). Eventually, the world entered a Second World War, which was even more deadly and consequential than the first (Taylor 1996/2005; Bell 2007; Overy 2008; Iriye 1987; Sagan 1988).

Versailles and the New Germany

In July 1919, democratically elected German delegates met at Weimar and established a democratic constitution and what came to be called the Weimar Republic. France, however, still feared Germany, and insisted on a strict implementation of the Versailles Treaty, including reparations that were crippling the German economy. When Germany failed in 1923 to meet its reparations payments, France instigated the Ruhr Crisis: it tried to compel German reparation payments by occupying Germany's highly industrialized Ruhr valley. Germans replied with work stoppages; the German government paid workers simply by printing money and the economy experienced hyper-

League of Nations: An international body established by the Treaty of Versailles at the end of World War I and designed to provide states with an ongoing international legal and institutional framework to solve their disputes and avoid war.

Collective security: Security provided by the members of an international cooperative institution in which, if any state threatened or actually used military force illegally against a member state, the other members pledged to form an overwhelming coalition to defeat the aggressor.

Military force: A form of coercive diplomacy in which a state actively uses its military to influence another state's foreign policy.

Weimar Republic: Republic formed by democratically elected German delegates in the aftermath of World War I to replace the old imperial system.

Ruhr Crisis: When Germany failed to meet its reparations payments in 1923, France occupied Germany's Ruhr valley. Germans replied with work stoppages, the German government paid its workers simply by printing more paper money, and hyperinflation ensued.

inflation, or a vast explosion of prices. Faced with an imminent German economic collapse that could spill over into the world economy, the United States in 1924 mediated an international agreement, the Dawes Plan, named for its author Charles Dawes, whereby France left the Ruhr, Germany's reparation obligations were reduced, and private international banks lent Germany money to be used for reparations payments.

Further progress toward European political reconciliation came in 1925, with the Locarno Accords. Under the terms of those agreements, Germany accepted its borders with France and Belgium, Britain and Italy promised to guarantee Germany's compliance with those commitments, and Germany agreed to resolve its border disputes with Poland and Czechoslovakia through arbitration, not military force. In 1926, Germany was admitted to the League of Nations. In 1928, the Kellogg-Briand Pact (named after its authors, US Secretary of State Frank Kellogg and French Foreign Minister Aristide Briand) outlawed war. Ultimately, 62 countries signed the Pact, including Germany, Italy, and Japan. Global trade also enjoyed revitalization during this period, and was as large relative to total world output as was the case in 1913, prior to the start of World War I (Maddison 2006: 363).

The Great Depression and Rise of the Dictators, 1929–1939

At the end of the 1920s, Europe appeared to be on the road to economic recovery and international reconciliation: in other words, the nations seemed close to establishing a reasonably peaceful order among themselves. But the road soon ended in disaster. In October 1929, the US stock market crashed, many banks collapsed, and economic activity collapsed – it was the start of the Great Depression. Many countries turned to beggar-thy-neighbor policies, through which a national government tried to shift onto neighbors the deleterious consequences (especially unemployment) of the global contraction in economic activity. As discussed in Chapter 1, the United States Congress in 1930 passed, and President Herbert Hoover signed, the Smoot-Hawley Tariff, which raised average US tariff rates above 40 percent. Other countries retaliated. Global commerce and finance collapsed, and these policies worsened the Great Depression (Frieden 2006: 127–228).

Democracy held firm during these hard years in the United States, Britain, France, and several other countries, but it failed in Germany. Adolf Hitler became Chancellor in January 1933, and was soon the unquestioned ruler of Germany. Even before the Great Depression, in 1922, Benito Mussolini and his Fascists had seized power in Italy; in Japan, a militaristic faction had seized control by the late 1920s; and in the Soviet Union, Joseph Stalin had attained complete control by the early 1930s (Mazower 1998).

The League of Nations could not provide security to its members. In 1931, Japan attacked and occupied the northern part of China, with no effective response from the League. In 1935, Italy attacked Ethiopia (then called Abyssinia): the League ruled the attack illegal, but imposed only modest sanctions. In 1936, Italy and Germany intervened in Spain to support the rebel and fellow fascist General Francisco Franco. The Soviet Union supported the government in Madrid; Britain, France, and the United States did nothing; and Franco took over the country in 1939.

While these developments were alarming, the main threat to world peace in the 1930s emanated from Germany. Hitler pulled Germany out of the League of Nations in October 1933. In March 1935, he announced that Germany would no longer be bound by the armament restrictions in the Treaty of Versailles. France, Britain, and

Dawes Plan: US-mediated 1924 plan named for author Charles Dawes to end the Ruhr crisis. The plan called for France to leave the Ruhr, Germany's reparations payments to be reduced, and private international banks to lend Germany money to use for the payments.

Locarno Accords: In a further step toward European political reconciliation, Germany accepted its borders with France and Belgium, Britain and Italy promised to guarantee Germany's compliance with those commitments, and Germany promised to resolve border disputes with Poland and Czechoslovakia via arbitration rather than force.

Kellogg-Briand Pact: A 1928 international pact outlawing war, authored by US Secretary of State Frank Kellogg and French Foreign Minister Aristide Briande.

Great Depression: An international economic disaster precipitated by the 1929 crash of the US stock market. The disaster promptly blocked Europe's path to economic recovery and political reconciliation.

Beggar-thy-neighbor policies: Policies designed to shift the negative consequences of the global economic downturn onto a state's neighbors, pursued by many countries during the Great Depression.

Smoot-Hawley Tariff: A 1930 US law that raised tariffs to high levels in an attempt to protect the US economy. The act had disastrous consequences and contributed to the Great Depression in the United States.

► Photo 2.2 Emergency Aid in New York City during the Great Depression

In this 1932 file photo, a long line of jobless and homeless men wait outside to get free dinner at New York's municipal lodging house during the Great Depression.

Source: PA Images.

Italy reached an agreement in April 1935 to resist German expansionism and in May 1935, France signed a security accord with the Soviet Union. Yet, these countries had no unified strategy toward Germany. In June 1935, Britain announced that it had reached a bilateral agreement with Germany to limit their respective navies, which surprised and angered the French. In 1936, Italy – alienated from Britain and France over Ethiopia – collaborated with Germany in Spain.

Hitler continued to extend his gains. In March 1936, in clear violation of the Versailles settlement, Hitler ordered German troops to re-occupy the Rhineland. In the ensuing **Rhineland Crisis**, Britain and France consulted, but ultimately decided to do nothing. In March 1938, Hitler sent troops into Austria and brought about the forced unification of the two countries. Neither France nor Britain resisted, and Italy, which had resisted German moves toward unification in 1934, now accepted it.

In these years, British and French leaders followed a strategy of **appeasement**, that is, an effort by one state to reduce conflict with another by accommodating the demands of the latter (Lobell 2007; Ripsman and Levy 2008). In this instance, Britain and France sought to appease Nazi Germany. The British and French pursued appeasement to its logical conclusion in 1938, in regard to the Czechoslovakia crisis. That country was a democracy, a member of the League of Nations, and a military ally of France. In the summer of 1938, Hitler claimed that 3.5 million ethnic Germans living in the eastern part of Czechoslovakia, called the Sudetenland, were being persecuted by the Czechoslovak government, and a German invasion seemed imminent. To avoid that, Britain's Prime Minister Neville Chamberlain and France's Prime Minister Edouard Daladier met with Hitler and Mussolini in Munich on September 29 and 30, where they agreed that the Sudetenland would be transferred to Germany. The Czechoslovaks were not invited to the conference, and were informed of its outcome after the meeting.

This arrangement, known as the Munich Agreement, represented the last effort by the Western democracies to avert war through appeasement. As we will see in a moment, that effort failed. As we noted in the introduction to this chapter, **Munich** has since become a powerful historical analogy that is used in policy debates about how to deal with potential aggressors, as can be observed in Making Connections Box 2.2.

Rhineland Crisis: In March 1936, in clear violation of the Versailles settlement, Hitler ordered troops to reoccupy the Rhineland. Britain and France consulted and decided to do nothing, allowing Hitler to continue to bully Europe.

Appeasement: An effort by one state to reduce conflict with another by accommodating the demands of the latter.

Munich Analogy: A reference, sometimes invoked by political leaders, to the 1938 transfer of a part of Czechoslovakia to Nazi Germany by Western European democratic leaders. It is generally invoked as a criticism of policy or strategy that resembles appeasement.

The Persistence of the Munich Analogy

Then: President Lyndon Johnson Argues for Escalation in Vietnam, August 1965

'... If we are driven from the field in Vietnam, then no nation can ever again have the same confidence in American promise or in American protection....Nor would surrender in Vietnam bring peace, because we learned from Hitler at Munich that success only feeds the appetite of aggression. The battle would be renewed in one country and then another country, bringing with it perhaps even larger and crueler conflict, as we have learned from the lessons of history.'
Source: Johnson 1964: 262.

Now: President George H. Bush's War Ultimatum to Iraq, March 2003

'We are now acting because the risks of inaction would be far greater.... The cause of peace requires all free nations to recognize new and undeniable realities. In the 20th century, some chose to appease murderous dictators whose threats were allowed to grow into genocide and global war.'
Source: Bush 2003.

The Munich-appeasement historical analogy influenced the rhetoric and possibly the decision for war of two US presidents separated by almost four decades, suggesting that the Munich analogy has a very powerful hold on the US understanding of world politics, and highlighting how important it is for students, observers, and practitioners to know whether such analogies are valid or not.

War Comes Again to Europe and the World, 1939–45

Hitler told Chamberlain at the Munich meetings that he had no more territorial ambitions in Europe. This seemed to signify the success of appeasement and possible fortification of peace in Europe. But the strategy had not worked. In March 1939, Hitler invaded the last independent part of the Czechoslovakian state, Bohemia-Moravia, which was not German in composition. On March 20, he also made territorial demands against Poland. At this point, Britain changed course: on March 31, the British cabinet promised to defend Poland, and Britain and Poland signed a military alliance on April 6. During the spring and summer of 1939, Britain and France sought to enlist the Soviet Union as an ally against Germany.

Hitler offered Stalin more than had Britain and France: in August 1939, Nazi Germany and the Soviet Union signed the Nazi–Soviet Non-Aggression Pact. While the Nazis and Soviets promised not to attack each other, they also arranged for an attack on and partition of Poland. Germany attacked Poland from the west on September 1, and the Soviet Union did so from the east on September 17. Britain and France declared war on Germany on September 3. Once more the fundamental, enduring problems of peace and order had come to the forefront of the Continent.

Attacked from two sides, Poland collapsed within a month, and was divided between Germany and the Soviet Union. In the west, France's border fortifications, the Maginot Line, named after one of its early backers, Minister of War André Maginot, at first seemed to deter a German attack. However, in April and May, Germany attacked westward, using a new strategy, *Blitzkrieg*, or lightning war, in

Nazi–Soviet Non-Aggression Pact: A pact signed between Nazi Germany and Soviet Russia in 1939 in which the two countries agreed not to attack each other and to jointly attack Poland, dividing the country between them. The pact came as a blow to Britain and France, which had sought to enlist the Soviet Union as an ally against Germany.

► Photo 2.3
Hiroshima after the Atomic Blast

On August 6, 1945, the United States dropped an atomic bomb on the Japanese city of Hiroshima. The blast killed approximately 70,000 Japanese, mostly civilians, immediately; perhaps an equal number died of radiation-related illnesses within five years. This photo was taken in early April 1946, eight months after the Hiroshima atomic attack, and underscores the hard truth that nuclear weapons cause levels of destruction from which it is very difficult to recover.

Source: PA Images.

Blitzkrieg: Lightning war, used by Germany to conquer westward at the beginning of World War II.

Battle of Britain: A campaign of air attacks starting in June 1940 by Germany against Britain intended to compel Britain, at the time Germany's only remaining opponent, to surrender. British air defenses held.

Battle of Stalingrad: A battle between September 1942 and February 1943 in which Soviet forces destroyed a massive German army. It was a major turning point of World War II's European Theater.

which rapidly moving German armored columns pushed through weak spots in enemy lines and enveloped enemy forces. By early June, Germany occupied Norway, Denmark, the Netherlands, and Luxembourg. German forces then defeated both the French army and the British expeditionary force in Belgium and France, causing the British to retreat from the port of Dunkirk in early June, and forcing the French to surrender on June 22.

Britain, led from May 1940 by Winston Churchill, stood alone against Nazi Germany. Hitler tried to compel Britain's surrender by launching air attacks in what came to be known as the **Battle of Britain**. British air defenses held. Hitler then turned east and launched in June 1941 a massive surprise attack against the Soviet Union. By late 1941, the United States was providing Britain food, fuel, and weapons, and naval escorts to protect shipping of those supplies across the Atlantic. Then, on December 7, 1941, Japan launched a surprise air strike against Pearl Harbor. America declared war on Japan on December 8; and Hitler and Mussolini, allied to Japan from September 1940, declared war on the United States.

The decisive turn in World War II's European Theatre was the **Battle of Stalingrad**, where between September 1942 and February 1943 the Soviet Union destroyed a massive German army. American and British forces defeated German and Italian forces in northern Africa by the spring of 1943, and then invaded Sicily and Italy. In June 1944, American, British, and Canadian forces landed at Normandy and liberated France by the end of the year. Soviet forces thrust into eastern Germany in early 1945, and Anglo-American-Canadian forces also moved into Germany in the spring of 1945. Soviet forces attacked Berlin in mid-April; Hitler committed suicide on April 30; and on May 7, German military commanders surrendered unconditionally.

The war in the Pacific continued for another four months. The United States had inflicted a major blow against Japan's naval forces at the Battle of Midway in June 1942; thereafter, US forces slowly made their way across the Pacific towards the Japanese homeland. On August 6, 1945, on the orders of President Harry Truman, who assumed office on the death of President Roosevelt on April 12, the United States dropped an atomic bomb on the Japanese city of Hiroshima, and on August 9 it dropped a second bomb on Nagasaki. On August 15, Emperor Hirohito announced Japan's surrender to the United States; Japan and allies signed a formal instrument of surrender aboard the American battleship Missouri on September 2, in Tokyo Bay.

Competing states that fail at peace often turn to violence: World War II showed what that could mean. Sixty million people died as a result of hostilities during that war (Ferguson 2006: 649). The Germans alone killed almost six million Jews, and tens of millions of Poles and Russians. The Soviets for their part killed hundreds of thousands of their own people, as well as tens of thousands of Poles (Snyder 2010). Europe, Japan, and Russia lay in ruins. Britain was bankrupt. One international order had died. A new world, which we take up in the next section, would come into being.

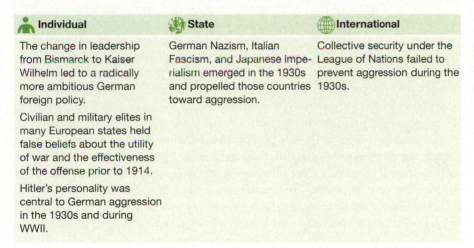

Individual	State	International
The change in leadership from Bismarck to Kaiser Wilhelm led to a radically more ambitious German foreign policy.	German Nazism, Italian Fascism, and Japanese imperialism emerged in the 1930s and propelled those countries toward aggression.	Collective security under the League of Nations failed to prevent aggression during the 1930s.
Civilian and military elites in many European states held false beliefs about the utility of war and the effectiveness of the offense prior to 1914.		
Hitler's personality was central to German aggression in the 1930s and during WWII.		

Levels of Analysis
World War I and World War II

The Global Struggle of the Cold War, 1945–1989

As collaboration between the United States and the Soviet Union began to break down at the close of World War II, and the two states became bitter rivals but avoided a full-fledged military confrontation, a number of observers, including the British writer George Orwell, the American businessperson Bernard Baruch, and the American writer Walter Lippmann, suggested that a new era had dawned, one of Soviet-American 'cold war'. The Cold War, which was in place from the mid-1940s to the late 1980s, was a time of high tension and ever-present risk of war between the United States and the Soviet Union (Gaddis 2006; LaFeber 2006; Dunbabin 2008). In this section we explore the political conditions that existed after World War II, the reasons the Cold War began, and the characteristics of the Cold War as a type of international order.

The World in 1945

Relief and optimism in 1945 co-existed with fear and exhaustion. On the one hand, Britain, the United States, and the Soviet Union had defeated Hitler's Germany. Moreover, in the fall of 1944, these three main allies agreed at Dumbarton Oaks, in Washington, DC, to create the United Nations (UN): the hope was that an ongoing association of major powers (the big three plus France and China), institutionalized through the UN, would establish and maintain the postwar peace.

Cold War: Period from the mid-1940s to the late 1980s in which there was high tension and risk of war between the United States and the Soviet Union

United Nations (UN): An international institution like the League of Nations, designed to keep international peace after World War II. Unlike the League of Nations, the UN is headed by the Security Council, an ongoing association controlled by the US, UK, France, Russia, and China.

► **Map 2.6 Postwar Occupation Zones for Germany**

Germany and its capital city of Berlin were divided into four occupation zones by the victorious allied powers of World War II. The western zones were brought together in 1949 to form the Federal Republic of Germany; the Soviet eastern zone was established that year as the German Democratic Republic.

British zone

Soviet zone

France

GB

USSR

US

The division of Berlin into zones 1945–1949

French zone

American zone

The division of Germany into zones 1945–1949

On the other hand, much of the pre-war international order lay in ruins. Germany had lost its sovereignty and was divided by the victors into four occupation zones, one each for the Soviet Union, the United States, Britain, and France (see Map 2.6). The Soviet Union had suffered stunning losses at Nazi hands: almost 24 million Soviet citizens and soldiers lost their lives during the war. Great Britain and France had suffered extensive loss of life and damage to their industrial base. The European powers lost both their capacity to rule colonies, and any claim to legitimacy for doing so. Many colonial peoples wanted their territories to become self-governing sovereign states in their own right, and in doing so appealed to the principle of **self-determination**, the idea that every people should determine and manage their own political systems. New military technologies, and in particular nuclear weapons, meant that nations could soon destroy human civilization itself. Finally, there was the question of the United States: would it take on international responsibilities commensurate with its power or would it return, as it had in 1918–19, to isolationism? The answer to that last question came quickly.

Explaining the Origins of the Cold War

Why did the Cold War begin? In engaging the debate on this question we will recognize the importance, as emphasized in Chapter 1, of viewing the world from different perspectives.

Responsibility of the Soviet Union

One view is that the Cold War started because of aggression launched by the Soviet leader, Joseph Stalin, and US responses to Stalin's aggression (Schlesinger 1967; Feis 1970; Jervis 2001). As World War II progressed, Stalin negotiated with British Prime Minister Winston Churchill to ensure that Hungary and Romania would fall within the postwar Soviet area of control, and asserted Soviet control over Bulgaria as well. When the war in Europe ended in 1945, Stalin joined the US effort in the Pacific – just long enough to claim the Northern Territories as spoils from the war with Japan. Also in February 1945, at a great power conference in Yalta, Stalin made clear that in postwar Poland, the Soviets would only tolerate a friendly government controlled by Communists rather than one organized democratically (see Photo 2.4).

The US at first seemed uncertain of the correct response to the Soviet Union's expansion. Then, in February 1946, US diplomat George Kennan penned his famous **Long Telegram** from the US embassy in Moscow (published the following year under the pseudonym of 'X') and argued that the Soviet Union could not be treated as a cooperative partner. The US soon articulated toward the USSR, in part under Kennan's influence, a strategy of **containment** that is the deployment by one state of diplomacy,

Self-determination: The idea that every people should determine and manage their own political systems. Self-determination was a popular idea among colonized people fighting for independence and decolonization.

Long Telegram: Written by US diplomat George Kennan from Moscow, the Long Telegram argued that the Soviet Union could not be treated as a cooperative partner.

Containment: a strategy by which one state employs diplomacy, economic assistance, and military power to counter and check what it believes are efforts by an adversary state to extend its global sphere of influence.

◀ **Photo 2.4
Churchill, Roosevelt,
and Stalin at Yalta**

The Yalta Conference
of February 4–11,
1945, took place in the
Crimea and was the
second of three major
postwar conferences
attended by the leaders
of the 'Big Three' – the
United States, Great
Britain and the Soviet
Union. Yalta was con-
troversial because the
three powers agreed
that postwar Poland, at
the time occupied by
the Soviet Union,
would be organized on
a broadly democratic
basis. It soon became
clear that the Soviet
Union had no inten-
tion of withdrawing its
forces from Poland or
allowing it to be ruled
by a democratic gov-
ernment.

Source: PA Images.

economic assistance, and militay power to counter and check what it believes are efforts by an adversary state to extend its global aphere of influence. In response to perceived Soviet designs on Greece and Turkey, President Harry Truman in February 1947 pledged that US. assistance would be given to 'free peoples everywhere facing external aggression or internal subversion.' This became known as the Truman Doctrine. In 1948, a coup in Czechoslovakia meant that the nations of Eastern Europe, with the exception of Yugoslavia, were under the control of the USSR. The United States responded with the Marshall Plan – named for Secretary of State George Marshall – to rebuild Western European countries economically so they might withstand Soviet pressures, and in 1949 the United States, Britain, and several Western European states formed a defense pact, the North Atlantic Treaty Organization (NATO). At the same time, the Communist party led by Mao Tse-Tung took over mainland China and allied with the Soviet Union. China and the Soviet Union supported Communist North Korea in attacking non-Communist South Korea in 1950; the United States organized an international coalition to defend the South. The Cold War, which in this narrative was mostly a US–European reaction to Soviet aggression, was in full swing.

Responsibility of the United States

Some historians and political scientists believe the United States was responsible for the onset of the Cold War. Supporters of this view argue that the United States and other capitalist states were hostile to the Soviet Union from its inception, and this hostility included an armed intervention by the United States, Great Britain, and Japan between 1918 and 1920 to try to prevent the Bolsheviks from consolidating their control over Russia. Although the Soviet Union played the major role in defeating Nazi Germany, it came out of the war in a much weaker position than the United States. Because of its vulnerable situation, and continuing fear of Germany, the Soviet Union's core postwar foreign policy objectives were to keep a formidable historical enemy weak and divided, and maintain a 'buffer zone' of

Truman Doctrine: The declaration by Harry Truman
that US assistance would
be given to 'free peoples
everywhere facing external
aggression or internal subversion.' Truman declared
this pledge in response to
perceived Soviet designs
on Greece and Turkey.

Marshall Plan: A US plan to
counteract Soviet influence
in Europe by providing economic aid to help European
nations rebuild after World
War II.

**North Atlantic Treaty
Organization (NATO)**: A
defense pact formed in
1949 between the US,
Britain, and several other
western European states.
It has since expanded and
is still very active today.

Sphere of influence: A geographic-political space, consisting of one or more countries, whose foreign and domestic policies and political institutions are greatly influenced by an external power.

friendly states – states that shared the Soviet political and economic system – in Eastern Europe. The Soviet Union simply wanted, as a matter of prudence, a **sphere of influence** in Eastern and Central Europe, that is, a geographic-political space, consisting of one or more countries, whose foreign and domestic policies and political institutions are greatly influenced by an external power.

The United States refused to accept the Soviet requirement for a sphere of influence in Eastern and Central Europe. Under the guise of self-determination, it challenged the right of the Soviet Union to impose friendly Communist regimes in that region. It did so even though the United States reserved the right to install friendly democratic governments in Japan, Italy, and the western part of Germany, not to mention to continue to maintain a sphere of influence in Latin America. In sum, according to this narrative, the United States sought to make the whole world safe for US democracy and private capitalism. Worried about its security, the natural response of the Soviet Union was to strengthen control at home, consolidate its hold over Eastern and Central Europe, look for new allies, and to maintain and strengthen its military capacity.

Tragic Mistake or Inevitable Clash?

A third perspective suggests that the Cold War was tragic and avoidable (Halle 1991). Each side assumed the worst of the other, and interpreted the behavior of the other as ominous and threatening rather than prudent and defensive. In other words, the onset of the Cold War was due to a security dilemma: each state's attempt to become more secure ended up, by the reaction it provoked, making it less secure.

For example, Stalin made a famous speech in early 1946 stressing that even though the war was over, the Soviet Union still faced many enemies and had to maintain its vigilance. Western leaders read the speech as a signal of aggressive Soviet intentions abroad, but it could be that Stalin attempted to paint for the Soviet people a frightening picture emanating from abroad to justify continued central control rather than relaxation at home. At the same time, the Truman Doctrine and Marshall Plan reflected US anxiety that Communist movements might exploit postwar instability in Europe. It was probably not intended to signal a global US crusade, but the Soviet Union feared otherwise.

Bipolarity: In an international system, the characteristic of being driven by the existence of and competition between two especially powerful states.

Superpowers: Especially powerful states with disproportionate influence in an international system.

Finally, according to a fourth view, the Cold War was an inevitable collision between two continental powers (Brzezinski 1986). The logic of **bipolarity**, or an international system driven by the existence of and competition between two especially powerful states, or **superpowers**, created incentives for each country to try to accumulate allies to join its side, and isolate the other great power in the hope that its global influence and ability to threaten might be contained. From this perspective, regardless of which particular states rose to the top of the international hierarchy, a cold war or similar conflict would have emerged as long as only two great powers defined the structure.

The onset of the Cold War reminds us once more that peace and order are difficult to attain in world politics. The debate on the origins of the Cold War also highlights the manner in which different factors influence state behavior and interstate conflict. We can see how the different levels of analysis can help provide an explanation. Claims that communist systems or capitalist systems may be prone to aggressive or expansionist foreign policies direct our attention to the state level of analysis and the relationship between domestic political systems and foreign policies. The argument about the structural causes of the Cold War, and in particular the security-dilemma thesis, directs us to the international system level. So too, the fact that

The United States and Support for Democracy during the Cold War

Aspiration

The Truman Doctrine in 1947 promised to help 'free peoples' to oppose 'totalitarian regimes.' President John Kennedy in 1961 promised that the United States would 'pay any price, bear any burden, meet any hardship, support any friend, and oppose any foe in order to assure the survival and the success of liberty.' The Reagan Doctrine of 1985 declared that America's mission was 'to nourish and defend freedom and democracy.'

Reality

American policy makers worried that leftist governments could easily be captured by anti-US communist elements, and thus preferred to support right-wing authoritarian regimes that took a pro-US and anti-communist position. President Franklin Roosevelt captured this sentiment when he said of the dictator of the Dominican Republic, Rafael Trujillo: 'He may be a son of a bitch, but he is our son of a bitch.'

For example, in 1953, the CIA helped overthrow Iran's elected government and the installation of the authoritarian Shah; in 1954, the CIA helped organize a coup against the elected government of Guatemala, and its replacement by a military regime; at different times the United States supported authoritarian rulers in the Philippines, Cuba, Nicaragua, Vietnam, and Chile (after helping overthrow the elected government), among others.

leadership perception or misperception of a potential adversary can lead to a spiral of conflict that perhaps neither side intends underscores the importance of the individual level of analysis.

The Cold War as an International Order

There were deep tensions and an over-arching risk of deadly conflict during the Cold War. Yet, the period was marked by a kind of order. That order had three distinctive features. First, the Cold War was characterized by enduring alliances. Each superpower had a set of longstanding alliance relationships with important middle-level powers. The two alliances, NATO and the Warsaw Pact, which was the multilateral alliance the Soviet Union established in 1955 between itself and the Eastern and Central European states under Soviet control, faced off against each other across the European dividing line that Winston Churchill famously called the iron curtain. Popular uprisings in East Germany in 1953, Hungary in 1956, and Czechoslovakia in 1968 sought to break free of Soviet dominance; the Soviets crushed these revolts with soldiers and tanks. In turn, the United States and other Western powers tacitly accepted the Soviet sphere of influence by refusing to intervene in support of the Soviet Union's rebellious allies.

At the same time the United States and the Soviet Union each worried that if one or two countries 'fell' to the other side, it could lead other countries to join the side of the superpower that seemed to be winning. Thus the United States worked diligently to maintain solidarity in the First World, which consisted of itself, the advanced industrial democracies of Western Europe, Canada, and Japan, while in turn the USSR sought to maintain strict obedience to its rule in the communist

Warsaw Pact: An alliance between the Soviet Union and several mid-level powers in Europe. The Warsaw Pact formed a Soviet sphere of influence in much the same way that NATO formed an American one.

Second World, which consisted of itself, the Eastern and Central European states, as well as China and North Korea. This led each superpower to compete for influence in the Third World of non-aligned and often newly independent countries in Asia, Africa, and Latin America (Westad 2005). In the United States, the image of 'falling dominoes' was a powerful one that helped justify US intervention in Vietnam. It also helped justify US support for undemocratic governments that were anti-communist, as we note in Box 2.3, including those of Ferdinand Marcos in the Philippines and that of the Shah of Iran.

Second, the Cold War was characterized by a balance of terror that prevented direct war between the two superpowers. By the 1970s, the United States and Soviet Union each possessed over 30,000 nuclear warheads and a diverse array of systems from land, sea, and air to deliver them. Once the United States and Soviet Union had sufficient weapons to destroy each other's population and territory – even after being struck first – they were essentially in a situation of mutual assured destruction, or MAD. Mutual assured destruction made the United States and Soviet Union cautious, not only about initiating nuclear war, but about fighting *any* war with each other. As will be discussed in Chapter 7, it also led to arms control negotiations, in which the United States and Soviet Union sought first to stabilize and later to reduce their nuclear arsenals.

Yet, the Cold War was not an era of peace. The United States and Soviet Union fought each other repeatedly in proxy wars. The United States and its allies fought against Chinese, but not Soviet, troops during the Korean War. The Soviet Union assisted North Vietnam in its war with the United States. Later, the United States supported rebel forces that defeated the Soviet Union in Afghanistan. Both superpowers supplied arms and financial assistance to their respective client states in the Middle East during the Arab–Israeli Wars of 1967 and 1973, and to rival sides during the Angolan civil war. The major military casualties of the Cold War were borne by populations in Asia, Africa, and the Middle East.

Moreover, while the superpowers were cautious about fighting each other, they often practiced brinksmanship – the willingness of a country to go to the brink of war to convince an adversary they are prepared to fight, even though they prefer not to fight. For example, in 1948, and again in 1958–61, the Soviet Union threatened to cut off Western access to Berlin unless the Western powers agreed to demilitarize it. The United States, supported by its NATO allies, refused to comply with Soviet ultimatums, although it accepted the building by East Germany of the Berlin Wall in 1961. Similar tests of will between the superpowers took place over the Chinese islands of Quemoy and Matsu during the 1950s, during the Arab–Israeli war of 1973, and in the Gulf region in 1979 after the Soviet invasion of Afghanistan and the collapse of the US-supported regime in Iran. By far the most dangerous episode was the Cuban Missile Crisis of 1962, examined in detail in Box 2.4, in which the United States and Soviet Union, over thirteen days, brought each other and the world to the brink of nuclear destruction until they managed a diplomatic resolution that saved face for each side and averted a direct military conflict.

Enduring alliances and a balance of terror: these were the first two main characteristics of the Cold War order. Its third characteristic was that the Cold War paralyzed the United Nations. The five permanent Security Council members each had veto power over Security Council resolutions, and during the Cold War members of one bloc would often veto important security initiatives of the other. The Security Council

Background

In October 1962, the United States discovered that the Soviet Union was placing nuclear missiles on the island of Cuba. The ensuing crisis lasted two weeks and brought the superpowers closer to nuclear war than at any other time during the Cold War.

The Soviet Perspective: Why take such a risky step?

The Soviet leaders may have placed missiles in Cuba to gain leverage over the United States in Berlin. Also, the Soviet Union faced a leadership challenge from Mao Tse-Tung, who believed China was more faithful to the Communist ideal of spreading global revolution; Soviet leaders may have believed that this bold step would reinvigorate their position as leader of the world Communist movement.

The American Perspective: Why a naval blockade?

American leaders debated various options and eventually decided to impose a naval blockade of Cuba. The blockade was intended to send a double message: the United States was willing to risk war, but was also allowing time (it would take Soviet ships several days to reach the blockade) for a possible diplomatic solution to be worked out.

The Cuban Perspective: Will we be defended?

The problem for Cuba was possible American aggression. The United States clearly opposed the Communist regime of Fidel Castro, which gained power in Cuba in 1959. The Kennedy administration tried and failed to overthrow Castro in the ill-fated Bay of Pigs invasion of April 1961. Cuba's Communist leaders wanted assurances from their Communist partner and great power patron that they would be protected. The missiles were a tangible sign of Soviet willingness to protect Cuba.

The NATO Perspective: Will we be sold out?

America's allies clearly wished to avoid nuclear war, but the US commitment to defend them from the Soviet Union included a US pledge to fight a nuclear war, if necessary, to stop a Soviet attack of Europe. NATO governments worried about the credibility of this US commitment. In a crisis, if the United States truly faced the prospect of a nuclear war that would destroy its own territory and population, would American leaders really follow through on their pledge? The Cuban crisis could not provide a definitive answer, but might offer clues to help answer this difficult question.

The Cuban Missile Crisis underscores how different leaders may view the same issue from completely different perspectives, and how those differences in perspectives can propel them to the brink of war with one another. In this instance, peace was maintained. Soviet ships did not challenge the blockade, and US President John Kennedy and Soviet leader Nikita Khrushchev crafted a mutual face-saving solution. The Soviets promised to remove their missiles from Cuba. The United States pledged not to invade Cuba. The United States also indicated it would remove its own missiles from the territory of its ally close to the border of the Soviet Union, Turkey.

acted in support of South Korea in 1950, but only because the Soviet Union's seat was absent in protest over who should occupy China's seat. In 1965, Eastern and Western powers came together to condemn the unilateral declaration of independence of the white minority regime in Rhodesia. In general, however, the ability of the Security Council to play a meaningful international role was limited by and reflective of the East–West stalemate of the Cold War.

Next, we look at the postwar world from the perspective of the many new and developing states of the global South.

Individual	State	International
Stalin's personal aggressiveness may have contributed to Western fears at the end of World War II.	The United States and the Soviet Union each believed that states in their respective spheres of influence required domestic institutions complementary to their own: democratic and capitalist in the West, authoritarian and socialist in the East.	The two world wars destroyed the European balance-of-power system that had formed the basis of international order for 300 years. As the Cold War progressed, the new bipolar structure of US–Soviet rivalry greatly influenced the character of international affairs.

The View from the South: Decolonization, the Non-Aligned Movement, and the Quest for a New International Economic Order

During the Cold War most states were a part neither of the First World nor the Second World, but instead constituted the Third World, that is, the non-aligned countries in most of Latin America, Africa, Asia, and the Middle East. The South moved through important transformations during the Cold War and, in the process, changed the international system as well.

Decolonization

Decolonization: The process by which imperial powers relinquished their overseas holdings leading to an upswell in the number of independent nations around the world. In the years following World War II, decolonization swept the globe.

One key development after 1945 was the creation of new states through the process of **decolonization**, or the achievement of independence by states formerly controlled by a colonial power (Spruyt 2005). Decolonization began long before World War II. In 1776, the original thirteen American colonies asserted their independence from Great Britain; during the early part of the nineteenth century, Brazil broke away from Portuguese control, and Argentina, Chile, Ecuador, Peru, and Bolivia achieved independence from Spain. Decolonization revived after World War I when the international community, under the auspices of the League of Nations, began a process of preparing former colonial territories for eventual self-government.

The process accelerated significantly during and after World War II. For example, Lebanon gained independence from France in 1941 and Korea from Japan in 1945. The United States granted independence to the Philippines in 1946. Soon after the war, Jordan, India, Pakistan, Burma, and Sri Lanka achieved independence from what had been the British Empire. The dismantling of the French Empire proved especially tumultuous. France fought for eight years and then finally abandoned its struggle to retain control over Vietnam in 1954. The United States, having supported France with money and advisors, would soon be deeply involved a subsequent civil and international war regarding Vietnam. Between 1954 and 1962, France fought an even more bloody and divisive war to retain Algeria, which gained independence in 1962. Great Britain and France each granted independence to numerous African countries during the 1950s and 1960s. The white minority government of Rhodesia (now Zimbabwe) declared its independence against the wishes of Great Britain in 1965. The UN imposed economic sanctions against Rhodesia, and some members of the black

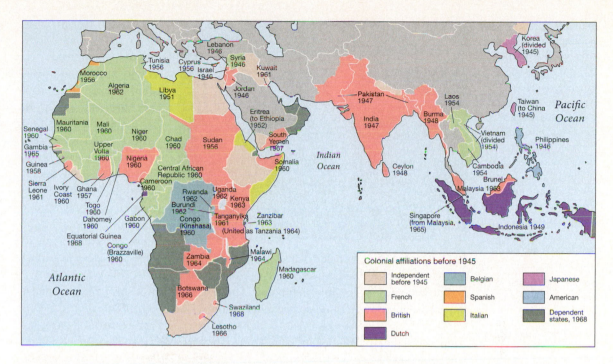

▲ Map 2.7 Patterns of Decolonization

Colonial empires were established over centuries, but collapsed relatively quickly in the aftermath of World War II.

majority population formed a guerrilla movement that fought and eventually overthrew the white-minority government in 1979. In 1975, Portugal finally succumbed to local and international pressure; its former colonies of Angola and Mozambique broke free. Decolonization was occasionally a peaceful process, but often it was a violent one involving interstate and civil war.

Decolonization had many causes. Nationalism, an intense sense of national community by a particular people in a geographically defined space, increased significantly over the two world wars, and led many people in the South to question the legitimacy of an international order in which some states were ruled formally by other states. The idea of self-determination, championed by the United States at the Versailles Peace Conference, complemented that appeal of nationalism. By 1945, both colonizing and colonized states also came to question the economic benefits of their political enmeshment. European powers also faced the mounting administrative and military costs of maintaining colonial control over populations increasingly willing to resist them.

Decolonization transformed the international system. In 1880 a handful of European great powers exercised control over much of the rest of the world. By 1980, world politics consisted of two superpowers, an array of European and Asian middle powers, and some one hundred new states that struggled simultaneously to determine their national identities and to craft a role on the international stage.

The Non-Aligned Movement and Third-World Pressure for a New International Economic Order

For some leaders of the Third World, the role of new countries was obvious: southern states needed to be non-aligned, that is, not tied to either the Eastern or Western bloc, but constituting a political entity of their own. In 1955, the leaders of India, Egypt, Yugoslavia, Ghana, and Indonesia hosted a summit meeting at which twenty-nine countries announced their formation of the **Non-Aligned**

Nationalism: A term that describes an intense political identity a people share, or a sense of collective fate as a political community.

Non-Aligned Movement: A movement founded in 1955 to create a pathway by which member states could remain aloof from the confrontations of the Cold War. The NAM now includes over 100 countries, representing over one-half of the world's population.

Movement (NAM) (see
photo 2.5). Its goal was to
provide a pathway by
which these countries
could remain aloof from
the confrontations of
the Cold War. The first
NAM summit took place
in 1961 in Belgrade,
Yugoslavia, and summit
meetings have been held
approximately every three
years since then, with the
latest hosted by Iran in
2012. The NAM now includes over 100 countries, representing nearly two-thirds
of the members of the United Nations and over half of the world's population.

The attempt to forge Southern political unity was reinforced by collective efforts
in the economic arena. In 1964, the United Nations Conference on Trade and Development (UNCTAD) was formed to highlight the special problems of developing
countries in the world economy. UNCTAD in turn spawned the Group of 77 (G-77),
which by now has grown to a group of 130 developing countries in a loose coalition
that seeks to further their economic interests through collective diplomacy at the
United Nations. UNCTAD and the G77 had marginal political clout until 1973, when
the Organization of Petroleum Exporting Countries (OPEC), a cartel of oil-producing states, decided to throw its weight behind developing countries' economic
demands for a New International Economic Order (NIEO), or changes in international rules on trade, investment, and foreign aid that would enhance the benefits that
developing countries would enjoy through their participation in the global economy.
Given the power that OPEC had demonstrated in raising prices in the wake of the
October 1973 Arab–Israeli war and the brief oil embargo that Arab OPEC members
imposed against the United States and the Netherlands, due to their support for Israel,
it seemed that an UNCTAD backed by OPEC could transform global economic rules.
This did not occur, as we will see in Chapter 10.

The NAM has held regular summits, but has never achieved the kind of political
cohesion that characterized NATO or the Warsaw Pact. Leading 'non-aligned' countries, such as Castro's Cuba, were actually quite closely aligned with one or the other
superpower. By the late 1970s, the NAM seemed to be an anti-US and anti-Western
instrument, calling on its members to struggle against imperialism, colonialism, and
Zionism (the desire and effort to create and sustain a Jewish homeland in the Middle
East, that is, today's Israel). Then, the NAM divided over the Soviet invasion of
Afghanistan in 1979: members with significant Muslim populations opposed the invasion, while members aligned with the Soviet bloc supported it. The movement with-
ered away after the end of the Cold War, although in recent years Cuba, North Korea,
and Venezuela have sought to revitalize it as a means to challenge the dominance of
the United States.

As we will see in Chapter 10, Southern states after the Cold War have been characterized more by political and economic heterogeneity than by unity. The term 'Third
World' no longer meaningfully applies. Some states, such as China, India, Brazil and

South Korea, have powerful emerging economies that have moved from primary commodity production to manufacturing and even technology-intensive activity. Others, such as Somalia and Chad, are in such bad shape in terms of domestic political and economic distress that they are termed failed states, or states in which governments are so weak and divided they cannot provide law and order for their home population. Advanced industrial countries find themselves paying attention to both the powerful emerging economies, because they are sources of markets and imports, and failed states, for humanitarian reasons and because they are a breeding ground for anti-Western resentment and, in some cases, terrorism.

The idea of a 'third world' as a prize to be captured by democracy or communism was an artifact of the Cold War. When the Cold War ended, the international system became more meaningfully a global one. We turn next to the end of the Cold War and the emergence of today's international system.

Failed states: States that lack the basic institutions and capacities of government – taxing, policing, upholding the rule of law, protecting property, providing public roads and services, and maintaining control over territory.

Individual	State	International
Leaders of a few key developing countries, such as Nehru of India and Nassar of Egypt, played a prominent role in organizing the South's Non-Aligned Movement.	The achievement of independence by states formerly controlled by a colonial power is known as decolonization.	The international system was transformed after 1945 as the 'third world' sought self-determination and brought about a vast expansion in the number of states in the system.

Levels of Analysis

Decolonization, the NAM, and the 'Third World'

The End of the Cold War and the Collapse of the Soviet Union

Two beliefs dominated scholarly thinking during the Cold War. The first was that the bipolar system of the United States and Soviet Union would last indefinitely, and the second was that if the Cold War did end, it would likely end in conflict. Both beliefs proved to be wrong. Hungary, Poland, Romania, Bulgaria, and Czechoslovakia broke free of Soviet control by the end of 1989, and the Warsaw Pact collapsed between 1989 and early 1991. The Berlin Wall was torn down at the end of 1989, and the following year East Germany joined the Federal Republic of Germany, that is, West Germany, with Berlin as the capital of the newly reunified Germany. In contrast, the Soviet Union ceased to exist at the end of 1991, and broke apart into fifteen constituent nation-states, including Russia (see Map 2.8). Leaders of the United States and the Soviet Union/Russia concluded arms control agreements that called for deep cuts in their nuclear arsenals and conventional forces in Europe.

Why did the Cold War end peacefully and on favorable terms for the West? As with the origins of the Cold War, scholars provide different answers to this question.

Soviet Economic Reform and its Unintended Political Consequences

According to this first view, the peaceful end of the Cold War resulted from multiple political processes unleashed by Soviet economic failure. By the early 1980s, Soviet economic growth had almost ceased and innovation was almost non-existent. High

► **Map 2.8 The Territory of the Former Soviet Union after its Collapse into 15 Sovereign States**

The collapse of the Soviet Union led to the formation of many new states, which have since taken different paths. Lithuania, Latvia and Estonia have become 'Western' in orientation and joined the European Union and NATO. Others, such as Belarus, have maintained close ties with the core political entity of the former Soviet Union, Russia. Others have come into direct conflict with Russia – Russia invaded and occupied Georgia in 2008.

Perestroika An economic restructuring led by Mikhail Gorbachev between 1985 and 1989 designed to keep the Soviet Union internationally competitive.

Glasnost An increase in political openness in the USSR led by Mikhail Gorbachev between 1985 and 1989 designed to keep the Soviet Union internationally competitive.

energy prices during the 1970s had hidden Soviet economic weakness, because the Soviet Union was a big oil and gas producer, but the collapse of those prices in the early 1980s made it plain that the Soviet economy had to be reformed. In 1985, Mikhail Gorbachev rose to the top of the Soviet political hierarchy with a firm conviction that the system required a fundamental shake up if the Soviet Union expected to retain its position as a superpower over the long term.

Gorbachev built his program of such reform around *perestroika*, an economic restructuring, and *glasnost*, or a political opening, that could take place in both the Soviet Union and its Eastern and Central European allies. Once it was unleashed, economic reform and political openness spread more rapidly and deeply across Eastern Europe than Gorbachev anticipated. In Poland, the Solidarity labor movement and the Catholic Church pressed the Communist government in 1989 to allow free elections, which led to an overwhelming victory for Solidarity. The Hungarian parliament followed by authorizing the formation of opposition parties and, by 1990, an anti-Communist majority asked the Soviet Union to remove its military forces from Hungarian territory. In the past, these political provocations would have been suppressed by Soviet tanks. Gorbachev seems to have believed that such repression would derail his reforms at home and that Eastern Europe, the beneficiary of Soviet aid and energy subsidies, had become more of an economic liability than a political asset. Once it became clear that Soviet repression was not forthcoming in Eastern and Central Europe, one Communist leader after another was toppled, executed, or forced to flee.

The final element in this volatile mix was nationalist discontent in the Soviet Union itself. The political opening allowed the 'Western' peoples of Latvia, Lithuania, and Estonia, the Muslims of Central Asia, the Christians of Armenia, and the nationalists of Ukraine to express their resentment at being repressed by the Russian elite. In late 1988, Estonia boldly declared itself a sovereign state within the Soviet Union, with the right to issue passports and fly its own flag. Lithuania and Latvia followed by declaring outright secession. Gorbachev tried to suppress these movements with the threat of military force. His political position was vulnerable to a larger struggle between the advocates of a return to the old order and those favoring even bolder reform. The forces of radical reform prevailed long enough for the constituent republics of the Soviet Union, including the Russian republic itself led by reformer Boris Yeltsin, to declare their independence, leading in late 1991 to the demise of the Soviet Union.

In short, the end of the Soviet Union and the Cold War were the unanticipated consequences of a bold experiment undertaken by Gorbachev in what turned out to be a remarkably fragile political environment.

Reagan Made Them Do It

A second interpretation emphasizes the role of the United States in facilitating the Soviet collapse. President Ronald Reagan in 1983 characterized the Soviet Union as the 'evil empire.' The Reagan team also pursued a $1.6 trillion defense program over five years, including an anti-missile defense system, the Strategic Defense Initiative (SDI), or what critics called 'Star Wars.' Most scientists were skeptical that such a project could ever succeed. But the very boldness of the United States' project highlighted the vast technological superiority the West enjoyed over the Soviet Union.

The Reagan administration pressured the Soviet Union in other ways. It abandoned arms control efforts and sent aid to rebel forces in countries where Soviet influence held sway but not decisively – Angola, Cambodia, Nicaragua, and most importantly Afghanistan, where Soviet forces quickly became bogged down in a Vietnam-like quagmire of their own making.

These aggressive moves forced Soviet leaders to face the weakness of their own system and their geopolitical position. It would be hard enough, with the economy shrinking, to satisfy the multiple demands of defense, consumption, and empire. The United States made it even harder by exposing the bankruptcy of the system and raising the costs of defense and empire, forcing the elite of the Soviet Union to undertake the risky reform steps that ultimately led to its demise.

Other analysts believe the United States played a prominent role in ending the Cold War but are skeptical of the interpretation just advanced. They argue that in order to undertake reform, Gorbachev needed a benign international environment. In the face of US ideological and military pressure, the Soviet military establishment would have refused to go along with a risky reform experiment. The Reagan administration was confrontational during its first term, but in its second it became more accommodating. US budget deficits slowed defense spending, and America's NATO allies refused to participate in economic embargoes intended to squeeze the Soviet economy even harder. The American people became nervous over the intensification of the superpower arms race and forced the Reagan administration to return to arms control.

These changes were taking place as Gorbachev came to power in 1985. He and Reagan unexpectedly developed a personal rapport and agreed they had a shared responsibility to minimize the danger of nuclear war. They agreed to remove intermediate-range nuclear weapons from Europe, and, at a meeting in Iceland in 1986, almost agreed to abolish all ballistic missiles. Reagan even made the impractical offer of sharing the US Star Wars initiative with the Soviet Union so that both countries could enjoy the benefits of nuclear defense.

By 1986, the United States seemed to rejoin Western Europe in emphasizing the importance of good communication and relations with the Soviet Union. In the face of these accommodating gestures, Gorbachev was able to convince hardliners within his own government that the international environment was sufficiently benign to undertake the risky steps of *perestroika* and *glasnost*.

The Power of the People, not the Leaders

According to this last perspective, while such leaders as Gorbachev and Reagan played a key role in ending the Cold War, the fundamental sources of radical international change lay not among the leaders but within the societies of the United States, Europe and the Soviet Union. In this view, Gorbachev and Reagan were only vehicles through which social change was carried out.

During the 1970s, economic interdependence began to develop between East and West. During this period of détente, or relaxation of tensions, Western businesses and farmers made profits selling factory equipment, consumer goods, and grain to the Soviet Union and Eastern Europe. The peoples of the Communist world came to appreciate the benefits of Western consumerism and began to question the popular notion in their political cultures that the West was seeking to conquer and occupy their homelands. Economic interaction and social exchanges reinforced the shared interest across the East–West divide, which relaxed rather than perpetuated the stresses of the Cold War.

By the early 1980s, as the US–Soviet conflict intensified, anxiety over a possible nuclear war spread globally. A massive peace movement emerged in Western Europe, fearful that the Reagan administration, by abandoning arms control and emphasizing rearmament, might drag Europe into an inadvertent nuclear war. In the United States, the nuclear freeze movement developed almost simultaneously, calling on the American and Soviet governments to stop building nuclear weapons of any kind. The largest demonstration ever held in New York's Central Park took place in 1982, when 500,000 people supported the nuclear freeze. The anti-nuclear movement mobilized doctors (for example, Physicians for Social Responsibility) on both sides of the East–West divide, scientists who anticipated an extended nuclear winter in the event of war, and clergy who urged governments and citizens to confront the religious and moral implications of pointing weapons of mass destruction at the innocent civilians of another country.

These social forces found a receptive hearing in the Reagan–Gorbachev partnership. The two leaders, not always with the support of their established government bureaucracies, took up the cause of anti-nuclearism. They responded to the demands of ordinary citizens in a way that led to a questioning of Cold War wisdom and, eventually, an end to the conflict.

The peaceful end of the Cold War was a remarkable international event, and it has ushered in a new international order with distinctive features. We discuss that order next.

Détente: A relaxing of tension in the middle of the Cold War in which economic interdependence began to develop between East and West.

Levels of Analysis
The End of the Cold War

🧍 Individual	👥 State	🌐 International
Leaders, especially Mikhail Gorbachev but also Ronald Reagan, played key roles in bringing the Cold War to a peaceful conclusion. Individual citizens and social groups also played important roles.	As Soviet authorities relaxed their grip on Soviet society and East European societies, opposition movements arose and pressed for more fundamental reforms and independence.	The collapse of the Soviet Union ended the bipolar structure of the international system.

The Contemporary International Order

We live today in a global system of states. That system is characterized by both conflict and cooperation, and the problems of peace, war, and order remain with us. In what kind of international order do we find ourselves at present? Some observers have suggested that the demise of the Soviet Union created, at least for a brief moment in history, **unipolarity**, that is, a distribution of world capabilities such that there is only one extraordinary power and all other countries are of markedly lesser capabilities and corresponding political influence. The United States, in this view, was after 1991 the world's single superpower and the only state that had truly global influence.

In the two decades after 1991, according to this view, the United States sought to preserve its position at the top of the international hierarchy and to fortify elements of the international order that reflect its interests and values. The United States sought to maintain its position in Europe by preserving NATO and enlarging its membership to include former members of the disbanded Warsaw Pact and even three of the new states formed after the break-up of the Soviet Union: Estonia, Latvia, and Lithuania. American officials maintained a security presence in Asia primarily by continuing and strengthening its bilateral alliance with Japan. The Clinton administration, the two Bush administrations, and the first Obama administration tried, with mixed success, to convince Russia and China to be part of an American-centered international order. They also sought to spread American values and preferred institutions globally, such as privatization, free trade, and financial liberalization on the economic side, and democracy and individual rights on the political side.

Most dramatically, through the invasion of Iraq and overthrow of Saddam Hussein, the George W. Bush administration pursued an ambitious and unsuccessful effort to impose democracy in the heart of the Middle East. The Barack Obama administration has undertaken a less forward-pressing stance on the matter of spreading of democracy in Iraq and Afghanistan, and instead has sought to wind down US wars in those two countries. The United States under President Obama has also taken a cautious stance on the **Arab Spring**, the near-simultaneous eruption of revolutions across North Africa and the Middle East that began in 2011 and was still underway in late 2014.

America's momentary supremacy in relative power resources never translated into US global political omnipotence. The United States was unable to prevent the spread of nuclear weapons to Pakistan and North Korea. It now seems unable to stop Iran from having nuclear research and production programs that may allow that country to have the capacity to build nuclear weapons. The United States became bogged down in wars in Iraq and Afghanistan and essentially has had to recognize that it will not enjoy a victory in either conflict. The United States, notwithstanding its economic might, precipitated a major global financial crisis in 2008, and played almost no role in the resolution of the European financial crisis that began the following year. In summary, the United States after the end of the Cold War was both predominant in material capabilities and tightly constrained in its ability to get its way in international affairs.

The states of Europe, in the meantime, were engaged through the European Union (EU) in an ambitious and unprecedented attempt to integrate peacefully into a political union that pools to a great degree their individual sovereignty. Twenty-eight states now belong to the European Union. Eighteen of them have gone so far as to give up

Unipolarity: In an international system, the characteristic of being driven by the existence of a single especially powerful state wielding disproportionate power.

Arab Spring: Near-simultaneous eruptions of revolutions in North Africa and the Middle East that began in 2011.

their national currencies in favor of a common European currency, the euro. Japan after the Cold War experienced sluggish economic growth, but retained great strengths in industry and technology, and as a result of renewed diplomatic tensions with China at the outset of the 2010s it seemed poised to take on a more active role in its defense, although in conjunction still with its major ally, the United States. Several countries – Brazil, India, and above all and without question China – were on a trajectory in the early post-Cold War era to become economic and possibly military great powers. Following a brief period of good relations with the West, Russia became undemocratic but slightly more prosperous, exerting influence over its weaker (former Soviet) neighbors and relying on the world's demand for its natural resources. Russia showed as well with its takeover of the Crimea region from Ukraine in March 2014 that, even in the face of political entreaties from the United States not to seize Crimea, it was prepared to use military force to defend what it considers to be core national security interests in its immediate neighborhood. In light of these developments, it is becoming clear that unipolarity as a term of analysis is unhelpful as we seek to understand the contemporary international order or international relations in the decades to come.

Politics among nations are taking on a strongly regional character. Western Europe continues to enjoy the absence of great-power conflict, remarkable in light of its long history of war. East Asia is more troubled: China and Japan are regional rivals; China and Taiwan have unresolved tensions; China has territorial disputes with Vietnam, the Philippines, and Japan; and the continuing division of the Korean peninsula presents the risk of major war. The Middle East and the Gulf region are weighed down by multiple political and military conflicts: Israel versus several neighbors; the United States against Iran; civil war within Syria; and incipient high-intensity civil conflicts in several countries, most notably Iraq and Libya. Africa and Latin America, battlegrounds of superpower competition during the Cold War, have been left to struggle with their own challenges: periodic famine, ethnic conflict, and genocide in Africa, and the struggle to control the narcotics trade and promote democracy and economic growth in Latin America. Europe, which seemed at the outset of the 2000s to be on a track toward becoming a wide-ranging zone of peace, seemed poised in 2014 to became a zone of potential conflict as the United States and its NATO partners became concerned that, after seizing Crimea, Russia might have territorial ambitions directed toward other parts of the former Soviet Union, such as Moldova, Kazakhstan, and Ukraine as a whole, and even possibly countries that now are NATO members, namely, Poland and the Baltic countries of Estonia, Latvia, and Lithuania.

Globalization: The ongoing process of international economic and technological integration, made possible by advances in transportation and communication.

Another distinctive feature of the contemporary era is **globalization**, an ongoing process of international economic and technological integration, underpinned by revolutionary advances in transportation and communication. We will pay close attention to globalization in the section on International Political Economy. Here we emphasize that well-educated individuals tend to benefit most from globalization, taking advantage of their access to information and knowledge to improve their material and social status. Those less well educated are less able to reap the benefits, and those who value traditional ways of life or means of production – such as farmers in Europe, nationalists seeking to limit immigration into the United States, religious conservatives in the Middle East – find globalization disruptive, threatening, or culturally offensive.

Some states or groups may seek ways to lash out or insulate themselves against globalization. The acquisition of weapons of mass destruction by states such as North Korea or Iran is one way weaker states attempt to neutralize the power of the strong, and we discuss this matter in Chapter 7. Terrorism is typically used by the weak to neutralize the technological advantages of the strong. Terrorism is an important feature of the contemporary era, and we explore it more fully in Chapter 11.

👤 Individual	👥 State	🌐 International
Some individuals gain from globalization through economic exchange and travel.	Europe, in the form of the European Union, is more than a collection of sovereign states, but not quite a unified sovereign state itself.	A seeming paradox: the end of the Cold War led to temporary American pre-eminence in material capabilities (unipolarity), but no appreciable or sustained increase in US global influence.
Globalization may be threatening to other individuals by challenging traditional cultural mores and creating greater economic competition.		As in previous historical periods, the inter-state system seems impervious to control by a single power.

Levels of Analysis
The End of the Cold War

Revisiting the Enduring Question and Looking Ahead

We began this chapter with a two-fold enduring question: how did the inter-state system come into being, and why is the maintenance of peace and order in that system a persistent problem? In response to the first element of the question, we showed you how European states emerged in the centuries after 1500, and why as a result of competition among themselves and conquest of others Europe acted as the catalyzing agent for the formation of the international system we inhabit today. In response to the second element of the question, we explained how the inability of European states to manage international tensions led to wars and depression, and eventually a world dominated by two continental superpowers. That world did not experience world war, but it was marked by tensions and crises. It was short-lived by historical standards, and today we have entered an international environment that is in some ways more peaceful than in previous decades, yet in some ways it is more uncertain and is still fraught with the risk of conflict.

Our exploration of international history leaves many important questions unanswered. For example, why did successive generations of European leaders, such as Germany's Kaiser Wilhelm and especially Adolf Hitler, believe they could attain hegemony in Europe, when past leaders, such as the Habsburgs or Napoleon, provided ample evidence that such efforts are almost certainly doomed to failure? Why did some leaders, such as Italy's Mussolini, elect to collaborate with Nazi Germany and its bid for European hegemony, when the broad sweep of history of Europe would argue against the chances of success of such a bid? Why is it that Germany in recent decades gives every sign that it has learned that belligerent bids for European supremacy simply do not pay, while, in recent years, China has acted on occasion as though a forceful bid for control in Asia might work to its advantage? More broadly, why is it that most of us as individuals have found it difficult to imagine ourselves as something other than citizens of states? Why, after five centuries of international strife and war, do we seem to be unable to surmount the state and the inter-state system? Why do we seem to be stuck with the inter-state system, with all its potential for conflict and war?

A sense of history is critical to any student seeking to understand the logic and dynamics of international politics. Armed with that background knowledge, we may now move ahead to examine how scholars have sought to make sense of the complexity of international politics. In the next two chapters we examine theories of international relations and foreign policy decision-making. Chapter 3 takes you through various ways international relations scholars have tried to comprehend a complicated world. We explore five different perspectives or major frameworks for thinking about international relations – liberalism, realism, constructivism, feminism, and Marxism-Leninism.

Visit **www.palgrave.com/politics/Grieco** to access extra resources for this chapter, including:

- Chapter summaries to help you review the material
- Multiple choice quizzes to test your understanding
- Flashcards to test your knowledge of the key terms in this chapter
- An interactive simulation that invites you to go through the decision-making process of a world leader at a crucial political juncture
- Pivotal decisions in which you weigh up the pros and cons of complicated decisions with grave consequences
- Outside resources, including links to contemporary articles and videos, that add to what you have learned in this chapter

Study Questions

1. What are the key benefits of having a solid knowledge of the past when thinking about international relations today? Are there any risks in framing our ideas about the present international situation in terms of the past?

2. Why do you think the medieval world ended with a system of independent, sovereign, territorial states? Why do you suppose that we don't see other modes of political organization, such as a world government?

3. China was very powerful in Asia, extending its reach as far as today's Middle East, during the fifteenth century, but by the nineteenth century it had become a target of predation by Japan and Western powers such as Great Britain. Today the United States is remarkably powerful, but if history is any guide, will America eventually be surpassed by other states, such as newly powerful China?

4. Are you surprised that the United States became an activist global power after World War II, given the isolationist traditions of America since its founding in the 1780s?

5. What kind of 'order' was established after World War II? Do you think it was a fair and just order? Can any international order be fair or just to anyone other than the state or states that dictate its major features? Who gained the most and who lost the most from the terms and conditions of the post-WWII order?

6. Do you think the onset of the Cold War between the United States and the Soviet Union, and their respective allies, was inevitable? Why or why not?

7. Are you surprised that the Cold War ended without a major Soviet–American war? Why did it end without major bloodshed?

Further Reading

Black, Jeremy (2005) *World History Atlas,* 2nd edn (London: Dorling Kindersley). A good historical atlas, almost always available at a university or public library, greatly facilitates the attainment of a strong grasp of history. This atlas has superb maps, a logical presentation of them, and informative accompanying commentary.

Clark, Christoper (2012) *The Sleepwalkers: How Europe Went to War in 1914* (New York: Harper Collins). Clark shows that the onset of war in August 1914 was due both to immediate failures of diplomacy to manage the crisis that erupted after the assassination of Archduke Ferdinand, and the build-up of domestic and international tensions in Europe from at least the 1870s.

Kennedy, Paul (1987) *The Rise and Decline of the Great Powers: Economic Change and Military Conflict from 1500 to 2000* (New York: Random House). For more than two decades Kennedy's book has provided scholars and students of international relations with one of the best one-volume historical treatments of both the internal and external relations of the major European powers, as well as the Soviet Union, Japan, and the United States.

Taylor, A.J.P. (1996/2005) *The Origins of the Second World War* (New York: Athenium). This is the most widely read (and controversial) analysis of the onset of World War II in Europe. Taylor's thesis is that the Western European democracies (and, he suggests in a preface for the American reader, at least indirectly, the United States) were as responsible for the onset of the war as Adolf Hitler.

Tuchman, Barbara (1962/2004) *The Guns of August* (New York: Ballantine Books). This is the historical work on the origins of World War I that has probably had the greatest impact on the field of international relations.

3

Theories of International Relations

Enduring question: *How do theoretical traditions in international relations differ on how to understand actors and their behavior on the global stage*

Did you know that people have tried to understand the root causes of conflict and cooperation for more than two thousand years? Over the centuries, people have watched the great dramas of international relations unfold – the emergence of nation-states, war and rivalry among great powers, the rise and decline of states, the boom and bust of global commerce, the building of alliances and political communities, the clash of cultures, religions, and ideologies – and tried to make sense of it. They have asked simple yet fundamental questions: What explains war? Why do states trade with each other? Why do states cooperate or quarrel? Do democratic states act differently than autocratic states in the conduct of foreign policy? How does the global capitalist system impact relations among states? How have international relations changed over the centuries? Are countries around the world trapped in a global system of violence and insecurity or can they cooperate to build peace? Scholars have debated these and other enduring questions for centuries and continue to debate them today.

We noted in Chapter 1 that, with so much happening across places and time, international relations may appear hopelessly complex. How do we make sense of it all? As part of their ongoing effort to understand and explain international relations, scholars have developed a set of tools called theories. A theory, we noted in Chapter 1, is a simplified picture of the patterns of actions and interactions within some domain of interest, and an account of why we see those patterns. Individual theories may be very specific, but in the study of international relations they tend to be grouped within broader categories that we may call theoretical frameworks or traditions. These frameworks allow us to focus on factors essential in organizing our thinking about international relations. Five theoretical traditions are most important in this respect: realism, liberalism, Marxism, constructivism, and feminism.

Each of these theoretical traditions places different weight on what matters most in understanding international relations. Each makes a series of assumptions and then directs you to a different set of driving forces to make sense of the complexity of world politics. Realists and constructivists, or liberals and Marxists, look out at the same world, but they each urge you to focus on very different features or, more precisely, causal mechanisms in order to understand that world. In this chapter, we explore these five theoretical traditions, highlighting the assumptions, concepts, and patterns of behavior that each school finds most important.

Source: © Image Source.

Learning Objectives

By the end of this chapter, you will be able to:

→ Recognize why the struggle for national power and security in a world of anarchy characterizes the realist tradition.

→ Analyze the interests and impulses of democratic and market-oriented states, which inform the liberal tradition.

→ Discuss the impact of the industrial revolution on theoretical frameworks, which gave rise to the class conflict of Marxism.

→ Evaluate the effects of ideas and belief systems on individuals, groups, and states; this perspective describes the constructivist tradition.

→ Illustrate the role of gender as an influence on foreign policy decision makers and international relations scholars.

Chapter Contents

- The Realist Tradition
- The Liberal Tradition
- The Marxist Tradition
- The Constructivist Tradition
- The Feminist Tradition
- Comparing Traditions
- Revisiting the Enduring Question and Looking Ahead
- Study Questions
- Further Reading

The Realist Tradition

From ancient times to the present, people have puzzled over the pervasiveness of conflict and violence among human groups, such as tribes, city-states, kingdoms, empires, and nation-states. Some of the earliest insights about conflict between political groups reflect what we call the *realist tradition* of thinking about international relations. Realism sees international relations as a struggle for power and security among competing nation-states in a dangerous world. In a world of *anarchy*, in which nation-states must provide their own security, competition and conflict is inevitable according to the realist perspective. In international politics, the resolution of conflicts between states will be shaped by the distribution of power between them. We identify the core ideas of this tradition by beginning with realism's assumptions, and then turn to its main propositions about how the world works and its predictions for the future.

Realist Assumptions

Realism is a simple vision that sees competition for power among groups or states as the central and enduring feature of international relations. It is built on five assumptions.

First, realists start with the observation that groups – currently states – exist in a world where no higher authority can enforce rules or order. That is, states operate in a world of anarchy. Anarchy does not mean chaos; instead, states are left to their own devices to protect themselves. In such a world, power is the coin of the realm, or the currency with which states do business in international relations. States achieve security or realize their interests to the extent of their power. As realists argue, in a world of anarchy the powerful prevail and the weak submit. The archetypical statement in this respect, described in Chapter 1, is Thucydides' famous observation about the Greek conquest of Melios that 'the strong do what they wish while the weak suffer what they must' (Thucydides 1954). When realists look at the long history of international relations, they see competition and the struggle for power, and sometimes even war, as the central drama. States and diplomats come and go across the global stage, but a struggle for security and power has been the recurring theme in relations among states. For realism, this *sameness* of international politics across time is due not to the character of peoples or governments, but the result of international anarchy. With no higher governing authority to protect them, states tend to be fearful of other states, and seek to increase their power in order to protect themselves and get what they want from the international system.

The second assumption for realists is that states are the main actors in international relations. Because anarchy creates insecurity, people divide themselves into conflict groups. Today, the most common form these conflict groups take is the state. Governments offer their people protection from the ravages of an insecure international system. They tax, spend, and deploy power. Citizens are tied to the state and rely on it for their well-being. Other actors in international relations, such as international organizations, churches, and private corporations, may flourish. But they are decidedly secondary in the ways and means of world politics. States command center stage as the political units that harness power and compete with other states.

Third, realists assume that states are reasonably rational actors that are able to recognize the international circumstances in which they find themselves and risks and opportunities in the international domain. When states undertake actions they can perceive the prospective benefits and losses and can adjust their behavior when the

Realism and State Rationality – the Issue of State Self-Defeatism

Theory: *Realist Theory and the Rationality of States*

Realist theory argues that states are serious and sober calculators of costs and benefits. It is generally not in a state's interest to engage in ideological crusades to remake the world or pursue self-defeating acts of hubris. Leaders will want to take steps to increase the power of the state through its economic and military capabilities. But leaders will be careful not to go to war when they are certain to be defeated or expend the wealth of the nation on fruitless military campaigns. Rationality as understood by realist theorists dictates the prudent matching up of ends to means.

Practice: *Germany and Japan in the 1930s Threatened Others and Triggered Coalitions that Brought their Complete Defeat*

In Jack Snyder's 1993 *Myths of Empire*, he describes the way in which Nazi Germany and Imperial Japan built domestic military-industrial coalitions and pursued aggression within their regions, triggering the formation of overwhelming counter-coalitions that brought the states to utter and complete defeat.

> Great powers in the industrial age have shown a striking proclivity for self-inflicted wounds. Highly advanced societies with a great deal to lose have sacrificed their blood and treasure, sometimes risking the survival of their states, as a consequence of their overly aggressive foreign policies. Germany and Japan proved so self-destructive in the first half of this century that they ended up in receivership.

In theory, states are depicted as rational decision makers. In practice, they can be loose and dysfunctional coalitions of societal interests who together pursue self-destructive foreign policy.

Source: Jack Snyder, *Myths of Empire: Domestic Politics and International Ambition* (Ithaca: Cornell University Press, 1993), p. 1.

costs of actions exceed their benefits. Assuming that states in general act rationally is not the same as saying that every state always acts this way. As we note in Box 3.1, states sometimes persist over long periods of time in behaving in ways in which the costs vastly exceed the gains. One of the challenges for the realist theoretical framework is to explain such seemingly irrational behavior.

Fourth, security is the central problem of international politics. This follows from the reality of anarchy. States operate in an international system where war and violence always lurk. Foreign policy is first and foremost an exercise in national security. Leaders must constantly scan the horizon looking for threats and dangers. States may want to spread lofty values around the world and create open trading systems, but, in the final analysis, states must worry about being exploited or attacked by other states. In certain eras of world history – as during the world wars of the twentieth century – all pretense of civility is stripped away and states struggle for survival. In these times, the bare essentials of international relations are revealed, and the bare essentials are about power and survival.

Finally, realists argue that the search for security is a competitive endeavor, so they expect competition and conflict to be inherent in world politics. There are winners and losers. Power has a relational quality. If one state grows stronger, others necessarily grow weaker. Some states are richer than others, and since power and wealth go hand in hand, to be richer is to be more secure and prosperous. Because of this logic, realists expect competition to be a natural and enduring feature of the international system. Conflict is inherent in relations among states. Peace and cooperation can be achieved at least temporarily and in specific ways, but it is not a permanent condition. States are always looking out for themselves, so they aim to exploit opportunities to gain an advantage on other states.

Realist Propositions

Balance of power: Any situation in which a rough equality of power exists between the major states in the international system at a given moment in time. Balance of power is thought by many scholars to be an important condition for peace.

Building on these assumptions about the nation-state, anarchy, and security competition, realists advance a variety of key propositions or concepts. In this discussion, we focus on the main propositions, such as those involving power balancing, alliances, security dilemmas, relative gains, power transitions, and nationalism.

For realists, a core proposition is that the **balance of power** is a basic dynamic that states have pursed across the centuries. As we discussed in Chapter 2, the balance of power is a strategy that states employ to protect themselves in a world of anarchy and danger. Faced with rising power and threats from other states, a state can attempt to protect itself by generating countervailing power. For example, if one state amasses military power by manufacturing tanks and fighter aircraft that threaten a neighboring state, that neighboring state can respond by amassing its own military power to defend itself. If the threatened state generates enough military capabilities, the threatening state is less likely to attack. In effect, power is used to neutralize or balance power.

The threatened state can also neutralize or balance power by forming a coalition of states with enough collective military power to counter-balance the threatening state. Indeed, one of the oldest tendencies in international relations is for the rise of a powerful state to trigger the formation of a coalition of states that seek protect themselves as a group through counter-balancing the rising state. For example, as discussed in Chapter 2, Napoleonic France in the late eighteenth century rose up, amassed overwhelming military capabilities, and marched its armies across Europe. The other countries in Europe, led eventually by Great Britain, formed a coalition with sufficient aggregated military power to defeat France and push it back into its borders. Likewise, during the Cold War, the United States and the Soviet Union built coalitions of states to balance against each other. Each sought to aggregate enough power through internal military mobilization and partnerships with other states to keep the other in check. Power was used to balance power.

The fact that states exist in anarchy means they can never be sure of each other's intentions. This has the potential to lead to a process we noted in Chapter 1, the security dilemma. A security dilemma exists between states when one state seeks to ensure its survivability in the international system by acquiring military power but, in doing so, triggers insecurity in another state, leading it to try to protect itself by acquiring military power – thus making both states less secure than when they started (Herz 1950; Jervis 1978). This situation can lead to a reciprocal dynamic of insecurity and an arms race. Defensive mustering of power triggers a counter-reaction which, in turn, triggers a counter-counterreaction. It is important to note that this is a dynamic driven by *defensive* steps undertaken by both states. In reality, each simply wants to protect itself, but what looks like protection or defense to one state may appear to be the means for aggression or offense in the eyes of its neighbor. Security dilemmas, then, are the result of the interplay of differences in the perspectives of states' motives, actions, and the absence of a centralized international government to which states can appeal for protection. For an example of how such differences in perspectives and understandings of states can lead to arms races and regional tension, see Box 3.2.

◀ **Photo 3.1**
Secretary of State Dean Acheson Signs the NATO Alliance Pact

The United States, from the time of its founding, had sought, in the words of President George Washington, to 'avoid entangling alliances' in its relations with other countries. US participation in the NATO alliance, which became a permanent peacetime alliance, signaled a significant shift in US foreign policy. This photo shows Secretary of State Dean Acheson signing the North Atlantic Treaty in 1949.
Source: NATO.

A companion proposition to the balance of power is that states will respond to threatening situations by forming **alliances**. Alliances, we saw in Chapter 2, are coalitions of states formed for mutual protection. The most famous and long-lasting alliance in the world is the North Atlantic Treaty Organization (NATO), which ties together the United States and its European partners. Originally established in 1949 at the beginning of the Cold War as an organization of joint protection against the Soviet Union, it has survived the end of the Cold War and remains an organization that combines American and European military capabilities to be used for various conflicts in and around Europe. For realists, alliances are the main form of cooperation among states. They are temporary associations that pool military power to guard against or deter a common foe.

The basic predicament of states operating in a world of anarchy leads realists to another important proposition: states care deeply about **relative gains** or relative position. As noted above, realists believe that it is a state's material power capacities that give it the ability to pursue its interests and protect itself in a dangerous world. The stronger a state is, the more likely it is to realize its goals and guard itself against enemies. But the critical point is that power is relative; for one state to get more of it necessarily means that other states will have less. So realists argue that states are in an ongoing and unending competitive game to enhance their power. In an anarchic world, states must be continuously making decisions on whether their actions increase power or not. That is, states care more about *relative* gains than absolute gains. Absolute gains would be the sum total of benefits that a particular agreement or action yields. Free trade, for example, may produce very large absolute gains for the system of states. But power considerations lead states to evaluate the benefits in relative terms. If free trade generates great absolute gains but leaves other potentially threatening states relatively better off, then realists believe a state will be reluctant to engage is free trade.

This question of absolute versus relative gains is very important in current debates about US policy towards China. Realists worry more than proponents of other theoretical traditions that by increasing trade with China, the United States is helping to increase China's *relative* power, and that may weigh against the national security of the United States in the future, even though the United States, in absolute terms, is gaining as well. In general, the realist worry for a state is that other states will *gain* more and, over time, this will give them power advantages. So realists argue that states

Alliances: Coalitions of states formed for mutual protection.

Relative gains: (1) The gains a state makes *relative* to other states. As opposed to absolute gains, which are simply the total materials gains made by a state, relative gains focus on the gains one state makes compared to a rival. Realists emphasize the importance of relative gains. (2) An important element of economic nationalism, relative gains is the idea that some gain more than others in economic interactions, and those who gain less lose out, even if they have positive absolute gains.

China's Perspective

Many people view China today as a powerful state rising to great power status. But Chinese leaders have reason to see the world differently. They view the United States as the most powerful state in international relations, and one that may be looking to diminish China's regional influence. The United States is allied with Japan, a neighbor of China that is technologically more advanced, and one with which China shares a history of animosity. America also has close military relationships with some Southeast Asian states, for example Singapore and Thailand, and it has a long-standing alliance relationship with Australia. For China, continuing to modernize its military capability is a prudent defensive step given the uncertainty of its region and the potential hostility of neighboring states and their great power ally.

Southeast Asian States' Perspective

States in Southeast Asia such as Singapore, Malaysia, Thailand, Vietnam, and Indonesia see it differently. They view China as a large and powerful neighbor, upon whom they are economically dependent, and who appears to have a strong interest in exercising regional influence even at the expense of smaller states. Rapid increases in Chinese defense spending, fueled by rapid economic growth, and China's claims to disputed territories in the South China Sea make the leaders of Southeast Asian states nervous. A natural and prudent response is to increase their military spending. Between 2005 and 2010, for example, Singapore and Malaysia more than doubled their defense spending. Smaller countries in the region have also enlisted the support of the United States, which has strengthened its defense relationships with Singapore, Thailand, and Vietnam and has announced plans to station more troops and ships in Australia and elsewhere in the region. These moves only reinforce China's anxieties, leading it to continue to grow its own defense spending and thereby perpetuating the action–reaction dynamic of insecurity that characterizes the security dilemma.

will exhibit a tendency to make choices based on the relative benefits that accrue to the various parties.

Realists also focus on the problem of **power transitions**. One of the great dramas of international relations is the long-term historical dynamics of the rise and decline of states. Germany rose up in the late nineteenth century to challenge Great Britain; in the current era, China is rising up to challenge the Western great powers. International change results when technological innovations and uneven economic growth lead to shifts in the relative power positions of states. The realist proposition is that power transition moments – when a rising state comes to equal or surpass an older powerful state – are fraught with danger. E.H. Carr, a British scholar, has called this the problem of **peaceful change**, or the problem of how the international system copes with the transition of order based on the domination of one state over another state (Carr 1939). Conflict is possible at these moments because as the rising state grows more powerful, it will become dissatisfied with the existing international order presided over by a dominant but declining state. It has more power and wants the international system to accommodate its interests and accord it the status and rights due to a rising state. On the other hand, the older and declining state will be threatened by the rising state and seek to preserve its declining dominance.

Power transitions do not inevitably end in war. Germany did rise up to challenge British dominance of the nineteenth-century international system. But the United States also grew more powerful than Britain during these decades; driven by indus-

Power transitions: When the relative power of two (or more) states changes, often due to technological innovations and uneven economic growth.

Peaceful change: The problem of how the international system copes with the transition of order based on the domination of one state over other states.

trialization, it became the world's leading economy and a soon to be unrivaled global power. Yet while the British–German power transition generated conflict and war, the British–American transition was peaceful. Realists argue that power transitions are moments of danger. Whether war and security competition tear the global order apart depends on how rising and declining states define their interests and the ways they decide to defend, overturn, or accommodate themselves to the existing international order.

Finally, realists offer the proposition that nationalism is a dynamic force that motivates states on the international stage. Nationalism is a term that describes the political identity a people share, or a sense of collective fate as a political community. To be part of a nation is to be part of a people with a common history and identity. Nationalism is a feeling people have that they are bound together as part of a natural political entity. The nation is a community of people who live in a world of many peoples, each with their own sense of shared identity. This sense of common identity, or a shared community of fate, gives special meaning to the nation-state. It is also what the state can rely on when it asks for sacrifices by the people on behalf of the nation, such as taxes, obedience to law, and service in the military. Realists emphasize that it is nationalism and loyalty to the nation-state which provide the foundation for dominance of the nation-state and the competitive states system. Nationalism is a potential source of conflict in that it encourages groups of people to emphasize the differences between themselves and other groups.

Nationalism: A term that describes an intense political identity a people share, or a sense of collective fate as a political community.

Within the realist tradition there are a variety of specific arguments and theories, some of which contradict each other. For example, realists agree that anarchy is important, but some realists think that anarchy tends to make states bold and aggressive, while other realists believe that anarchy tends to encourage states to be cautious and defensive. Despite these differences, however, what realists agree on is that when they look out into the world, they see international relations as a struggle for power and security among nation-states. It is a world of anarchy where competition and conflict is ever present. Law, idealism, and morality are human aspirations that make an appearance in the relations among states. But realists argue that power and the search for security are more fundamental, and they will not yield or disappear despite the best efforts of enlightened leaders.

No one can deny the influence of power and security on states' behaviors toward one another. However, states also have the tendency to build cooperative relationships in the international system. We turn next to the English School and, after this, the liberal tradition, whose scholars attempt to explain this cooperation, based on the assumptions and concepts of the theoretical framework.

The English School of International Relations

A rich body of international relations theory with links to realism is called the English School. Emerging in Great Britain in the postwar era, this tradition acknowledges the realist view that states operate within anarchy. But scholars in the English School go on to emphasize that states have organized themselves into what is called a 'society' of states. In effect, states are more 'social' than realists tend to admit. They have developed rules, norms, and institutions to manage the states system and it anarchical character. This orientation has led English School scholars to explore the historical dynamics of the modern states system – its origins, spread, and evolving political relationships.

▲ **Photo 3.2 Serbian Nationalist Rally**

People wave Serbian flags during a rally in Belgrade, Serbia, Friday, May 10, 2013. More than 3,000 nationalists have rallied in Belgrade against a deal normalizing relations with breakaway Kosovo, accusing the Serbian government of treason for accepting the agreement in order to advance the country's EU bid. According to realists, nationalism is the critical force that drives the dominance of the nation-state and the competitive international system of states. Without this collective feeling of community centered on the concept of a natural political entity, the nation-state could not exist.

Source: PA Images.

The classic statement of the English School vision is Hedley Bull's *The Anarchical Society* (Bull, 1977). Bull begins with the realist view that states are independent and competitive actors in a world of power politics. But he goes on to argue that states have shared interests in managing their anarchical circumstances. States are self-interested, but they share an interest in a stable and rule-based environment. In particular, Bull claims that states share an interest in establishing rules of the game in three areas – restraints on the use of force, sanctity of international agreements, and the security of property rights. These interests mean that states have incentives to build relations with each other, to work together to establish mutual expectations about the terms of their interaction. It is in this way that Bull sees the rise of what he calls 'international society' within the context of the modern states system. International society refers to the wide array of norms, rules, and institutions that reflect and guide relations among states. As Bull and Watson argue, an international society exists when 'a group of states (or, more generally, a group of independent political communities) which not merely form a system, in the sense that the behavior of each is a necessary factor in the calculations of the others, but also have established by dialogue and consent common rules and institutions for the conduct of their relations, and recognize their common interest in maintaining these arrangements' (Bull and Watson 1985: 1).

The focus on the rise and operation of a society of states leads English School theorists to emphasize the importance of diplomacy and dialogue in international relations. What scholars illuminate are the manifold ways in which statesmen over the centuries have worked to establish rules and understandings to manage power politics. Some scholars have focused on the rise of international law as a core institution of international society. Others have focused on the accumulation of rules and norms that regulate the states system – rules and norms relating to sovereignty, self-determination, non-discrimination, and the use of force. Others have focused on the expansion of the nation-state and the states system from Europe to the wider world. In all these areas, scholars offer accounts of the ways states have built the rules and institutions of order and established common norms and expectations about power, property, and rights. The result is a portrait of the modern international system, illuminating the remarkable spread of the system of states and the deepening of its shared norms and rules. (Dunne 1998; Buzan 2004)

English School scholars do differ on how 'social' the system of states actually is. Some scholars emphasize the 'pluralistic' character of international society, where realist dynamics of power and competition remain central, while others emphasize the 'solidaristic' character of international society, arguing that shared rules and norms have progressively weakened the role of power and coercion in world politics, or at least made it less legitimate and tolerable by states. In these various ways, the English School tradition blends realist assumptions and ideas with other international relations traditions, particularly the liberal and constructivist traditions, which we now turn to.

The Liberal Tradition

War and conflict have been pervasive features of international relations. But so too has been the tendency of states to trade, settle disputes, and build cooperative relationships. The liberal tradition offers a variety of ideas about how and why such cooperation takes place in the global system. Liberalism, like realism, is a body of thought that reaches back into the distant past with assumptions and arguments about international relations. While realism sees anarchy and the struggle for power as the defining features of international relations, liberalism sees the internal character of states, particularly the interests and impulses of democratic and market-oriented states, as the most important feature of international relations.

Liberal international theory has three intellectual branches. The first focuses on trade and its impact on international relations. Liberals believe that the spread of capitalism and market relations creates economic interdependence, joint gains, shared interests, and incentives for international cooperation. A second branch focuses on democratic states and their interaction. Here, the view is that democratic polities have a tendency to seek affiliation with other democracies and build peaceful relations. The third branch focuses on the pacifying effects of law and institutions. Liberals view international law and institutions as outgrowths of liberal societies as they seek to establish rule-based relations between them (Doyle 1997). Wielding these ideas, liberal international theory foresees the spread and development of democracy and market relations that transform and soften, even if they do not fully eliminate, the anarchic struggle for power of importance to realism.

Liberal Assumptions

Liberal theory is based on a series of five important assumptions. First is the view that the world is in an ongoing process of modernization. That is, humankind is constantly inventing, innovating, improving, and creating. Out of this constant process, people and groups advance – they modernize. The process of modernization is pushed forward by the forces of science and technology, which people are constantly using to enhance human capabilities. These transforming human capabilities have vast implications for the ways in which power, communication, relationships, interests, community, and political possibilities are arrayed. For example, innovations and discoveries in the last two centuries in telegraph, telephone, and computer technologies have transformed the way people in distant places can communicate and cooperate, and new commercial possibilities and political relationships have followed as well. This vision of human development can be contrasted with realist thinking. Realists tend to view history in cyclical terms, seeing humans making the same mistakes over and over again. Liberals are more inclined to see progress in which political, eco-

Modernization: The idea that mankind is constantly inventing, innovating, improving, and creating.

► Table 3.1 European Union Member States

As you can see from this table, the EU currently consists of 28 members. The European Union demonstrates the principles of liberal theorists, as the EU is a political community that attempts to transcend the nationalism and sovereignty of the old European states. The EU still faces issues of coordination, but the organization has learned from these past internal conflicts.

Source: © European Union.

Member Country	Year of EU Entry	Member Country	Year of EU Entry
Austria	1995	Italy	1952 (Founding Member)
Belgium	1952 (Founding Member)	Latvia	2004
Bulgaria	2007	Lithuania	2004
Croatia	2013	Luxembourg	1952 (Founding Member)
Cyprus	2004	Malta	2004
Czech Republic	2004	Netherlands	1952 (Founding Member)
Denmark	1973	Poland	2004
Estonia	2004	Portugal	1986
Finland	1995	Romania	2007
France	1952 (Founding Member)	Slovakia	2004
Germany	1952 (Founding Member)	Slovenia	2004
Greece	1981	Spain	1986
Hungary	2004	Sweden	1995
Ireland	1973	United Kingdom	1973

nomic, and social circumstances of people improve over time. Realists stress the reoccurrence of war; liberals try to find ways to transcend it.

Second, liberals believe that individuals and groups, not states, are the basic actors in international relations. Individuals, societal groups, firms, associations, and other types of groups operate in and across nation-states. Depending on their interests and inclinations, they can also be found building communities and political orders above and below the level of the nation-state. The specific size and character of human communities evolve and change over the eras. For example, liberals are not surprised to see the rise of the European Union in the decades after World War II – a project to build a political community within Europe that transcends the nationalism and sovereignty of the old European states.

Importantly, while liberals see individuals and groups as the building blocks of their theories, they also see nation-states and the states system as important. Individuals and groups build larger political groups – such as nation-states – and these larger political groups matter as well. The rise of modern liberal democracies that are based on popular sovereignty and the rule of law is an important historical breakthrough for liberal theory. It is the rise and spread of liberal democracy that has allowed individuals and groups to go beyond old forms of nationalism and empire to strengthen the rule of law and cooperation among nation-states. So individuals and groups are important to liberals, but precisely because they have the potential ability to transcend old forms of war and hostility between peoples to establish more peaceful and cooperative forms of world politics.

A third liberal assumption is that individuals have incentives and impulses embedded in the deep structures of society to trade, bargain, negotiate, and seek cooperation for joint gain. Liberals argue that individuals can move beyond 'relative gains' thinking and seize possibilities for 'joint gains' based on trade, exchange, and cooperation. Relations among states are not inherently peaceful. But, there is always ample room for individuals and groups to look for ways to advance their interests through cooperation with others within their society and across the global system.

A fourth assumption that liberals make is that modernization and advancement tend to take societies down a common path toward democracy and market society. Modernization across societies and cultures tends to produce similar sorts of chal-

Changing Character of Economic Doctrines

Then: *Diversity of Economic Systems in the 1930s*

In the first half of the twentieth century, the industrial and developing states exhibited a wide diversity of types of economic systems. As the Great Depression took hold and the world economy collapsed, countries went their own way. Germany under the Nazis became an authoritarian industrial state, Britain and France experimented with various sorts of social democracy, the United States remained more market oriented, and the Soviet Union under Stalin consolidated its state socialism system. No consensus existed on economic doctrine or the best model of economic development.'

Now: *The Washington Consensus of the 1990s*

By the 1990s, there was a widespread consensus among capitalist countries, particularly in the West and the developing world, that decontrol, deregulation, and open markets were the best way to promote growth and development. Here is Harvard University scholar Dani Rodrik's description of this consensus:

> Stabilize, privatize, and liberalize' became the mantra of a generation of technocrats who cut their teeth in the developing world and of the political leaders they counseled ... [T]his advice inspired a wave of reforms in Latin America and sub-Saharan Africa that fundamentally transformed the policy landscape in these developing areas. With the fall of the Berlin Wall and the collapse of the Soviet Union, former socialist countries similarly made a bold leap toward markets. There was more privatization, deregulation, and trade liberalization in Latin America and Eastern Europe than probably anywhere else at any point in economic history. In Sub-Saharan Africa, governments moved with less conviction and speed, but there too a substantial portion of the new policy agenda was adopted: state marketing boards were dismantled, inflation reduced, trade opened up, and significant amounts of privatization undertaken.

The financial crisis that began in 2008, however, has called the Washington Consensus into question. The crisis began in the United States, the epicenter of the Consensus, and quickly spread around the world. To many observers and participants, the crisis resulted at least in part from the policies of deregulation and liberalization championed by the proponents of the Washington Consensus.

Source: Dani Rodrik, 'Goodbye Washington Consensus, Hello Washington Confusion? A Review of the World Bank's Economic Growth in the 1990s: Learning from a Decade of Reform', *Journal of Economic Literature*, XLIV (December 2006): 973–4.

lenges and responses; the most general movement is toward loosely convergent sorts of political-economic institutions. That is, liberals see the movement of history as more or less linear, with a pathway that takes developing and advanced societies in the direction of liberal democracy and capitalism. The advanced capitalist societies are at the vanguard of this movement. Through trade, exchange, innovation, and learning, all societies will tend to move in this direction.

Finally, out of all these modernizing changes, liberals assume that there is such a thing as progress. The human condition can and will get better. Liberals believe that individuals and groups do indeed learn. They respond to incentives to make their world better. They are sensitive to human rights and the moral correctness of the rule of law. As we have noted, liberals ground their theory of politics in the individual, and

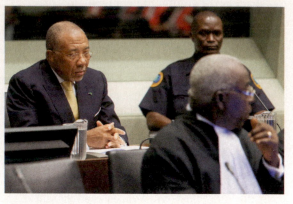

The Nuremberg Trials

The Hague Convention of 1907 established a list of war crimes for which individuals could be held accountable. After the Second World War, the highly publicized Nuremberg Trials, a list of military tribunals, prosecuted prominent members of the Nazi Party for major war crimes and crimes against humanity. In 2012 the ex-President of Liberia, Charles Taylor, was sentenced by a special UN-backed court to 50 years in prison for aiding and abetting the butchering of women and children during the civil war in neighboring Sierra Leone. Currently, the International Criminal Court prosecutes individuals accused of genocide, crimes against humanity, war crimes, and the crime of aggression. There are limits, however, to the reach of the ICC as it can only prosecute crimes committed on or after 1 July 2002 – the date of the court's establishment.

Source: Historical and Special Collections, Harvard Law School Library.

The Trial of Charles Taylor

Former Liberian President Charles Taylor, left, waits for the start of his appeal judgment at the Special Court for Sierra Leone (SCSL) in Leidschendam, near The Hague, Netherlands, Thursday September 26, 2013. Judges at a UN-backed tribunal are delivering their judgment in Taylor's appeal against his convictions and 50-year sentence for planning and aiding atrocities by rebels in Sierra Leone's bloody civil war. Taylor, 65, became the first former head of state convicted by an international war crimes court since World War II when the SCSL found him guilty on April 26, 2012, of 11 counts of war crimes and crimes against humanity including terrorism, murder, rape and using child soldiers.

Source: PA Images.

individuals possess rights and are worthy of respect. This puts liberals in a position to see progress within and between societies based on mutual recognition of rights and conduct based on the rule of law. Liberals look out at the international system and see that progress has, in fact, occurred; slavery has been abolished, genocide is now a crime against humanity, and despotic rule is seen as deeply illegitimate.

Liberal Propositions

Based on these assumptions, liberals advance a variety of concepts or propositions about how individuals and groups operate within and between states to shape international relations. These propositions involve commercial liberalism, democratic peace, liberal institutionalism, transnationalism, and cosmopolitanism.

The first proposition centers on the concept of commercial liberalism, which dates back to the writings of Adam Smith, an eighteenth-century Scottish social philosopher and pioneer of political economy. Liberals argue that market society and economic interdependence tend to have a *pacifying* impact on relations among states. As the economic relations between two states increase, the interests of these states in stable and continuous relations grow. This is because each country depends on the ongoing

Commercial liberalism: The idea that market society and economic interdependence tend to have a pacifying impact on relations among states. As the economic relations between two states increase, the interests of these states in stable and continuous relations grow.

trade and exchange with the other for its own economic well-being. War and destabilizing political conflict between these commercial partners jeopardize profits and employment at home. As a result, liberals argue that as economic relations between nation-states intensify, *vested interests* will emerge in these countries that advocate continued open and cooperative relations.

More generally, Adam Smith argued that the pursuit of wealth could contribute to moral perfection. A free market system could lead the consumer 'by an invisible hand to promote an end which was no part of his intention' (Smith 1937). In so doing, Smith and other liberals hold that a market society will eliminate some of the causes of war by causing states to abandon colonization and tariff barriers as policy tools. With democracy and capitalism, citizens become more rational and materialistic, and more resistant to belligerent nationalism. Liberals have developed these insights, arguing that the evolving character of economic interdependence between states will shape the foreign and security policies they adopt toward each other. Economic prosperity fueled by growing interdependence will make security competition and war less likely because the costs of conflict, particularly to domestic interest groups, will be unacceptably high.

The second and related liberal proposition is that democracies tend not to fight each other. This argument about the democratic peace, which as we noted in Chapter 1 is a leading example of a theory in the contemporary field of international relations, was first proposed by Immanuel Kant in an essay entitled 'Perpetual Peace' in 1795. The argument is that democracies, or what Kant called 'republics,' are unusually peaceful toward each other. Republics, or democracies, are understood as states that have elected governments, a free press, private property, and the rule of law. Kant's expectation was that as democracy spread around the world, so too would peace and stability. He foresaw a widening realm of peaceful relations among democracies, a sort of democratic federation or union of like-minded states that band together and cooperate to create a zone of peace. In this view, democracies are not necessarily more peaceful in their relations with non-democracies, but relations between democracies are special, and peace is to be expected.

Liberal scholars have proposed a variety of reasons why democracies do not fight each other. We will explore their reasoning in detail in Chapter 5, but here we highlight the main elements of their perspective. One reason is that democracies share common preferences; they have similar aspirations about how international relations should be organized. They all want open systems built around stable rules and institutions. In this way, democracies acknowledge each other as legitimate and worthy states whose interests and security must be honored and respected. It is hard for a democracy to declare war on another democracy when they have such strong bonds of shared values and interests. Another reason democracies do not fight each other is because in democracies, citizens bear the costs of war – the costly expenditures of blood and treasure – and they also choose their leaders. Leaders in democracies are held to account for their actions. Citizens are in a position to avoid the costs of war by voting for leaders who uphold the peace. Another reason for the democratic peace is that democracies tend to have transparent and accountable governments, and this makes it easier for these states to trust each other and cooperate (Russett 1993; Lipson 2003). In all these ways, liberals argue that democratic states have characteristics that allow them to transcend the insecurities of anarchy and build cooperative and integrated zones of peace.

A third liberal proposition is that states will build international relations around international law and institutions. We explore the contributions that such laws and institutions can make to peace in Chapter 6. For now we emphasize that, in general, liberals argue that international rules and institutions can play an important role in shaping the operation of relations among states. This view dates back to seventeenth-century philosophers such as John Locke and early modern theorists of international law. Political thinking emerged in this era that argued in favor of legal and constitutional rights of individuals within Western polities. The power of the state – and autocratic and monarchical rule – must yield to the rule of law and the sovereignty of individuals. Rights of individuals were seen to be anchored in the appreciation of the fact that all people were equal members of the human community. It was but a small step to recognize that the laws that informed and constrained the exercise of power within liberal societies were also of some significance in relations among liberal democracies. Individuals in other states were also rights-bearing members of humanity, and so leaders of liberal states must also respect the laws that protected these individuals within their own countries.

Liberals have also developed more pragmatic arguments about why and how rules and institutions matter in international relations. In some circumstances, states simply have different interests, so institutions will not help foster cooperation. But in other circumstances, states do not cooperate because they do not trust each other. States do not cooperate because they worry the other states will not hold up their side of the bargain. They are not sure the other state will be a reliable partner. Under these circumstances, when the interests of two states do not inherently conflict with each other, international institutions may serve the important function of reconciling those interests by increasing the flow of information, transparency, and trust. This is **functionalism**; institutions are tools that allow states to develop more efficient and durable forms of cooperation (Keohane 1984).

When states agree to abide by a set of rules and institutions, they are agreeing to limit their freedom of action. Liberals argue that states agree to bind themselves to institutional agreements when doing so creates incentives and obligations of other

Functionalism: The liberal idea that institutions are tools that allow states to develop more efficient and durable forms of cooperation.

states to do the same. These reciprocal agreements to operate according to rules and institutions create a predictable and functional environment in which all states can pursue their interests. Even powerful states may find a commitment to operate within mutually agreeable rules and institutions a way to protect their global interests and make their international leadership role acceptable to other states (Ikenberry 2001).

A fourth liberal proposition is that transnational relations provide important connections between states. Transnationalism refers to the tendency of groups within countries to build cooperative associations with groups in other countries. An extraordinary array of transnational groups operates across state borders. While realists argue that state-to-state interactions are most important, liberals stress that society-to-society interactions – that is, the interaction of individuals and groups across societies – can also shape patterns of cooperation and conflict within the global system. Transnational groups can come in many varieties, such as environmental groups, human rights organizations, religious sects, and scientific associations. In recent years, the world has also become aware of dangerous transnational groups, such as terrorist organizations, drug traffickers, and organized crime groups. Transnational groups can impact international relations in various ways. In some cases, the goal of these transnational organizations is to act as pressure groups seeking to alter state policies. Environmental groups such as Greenpeace and human rights organizations such as Amnesty International are of this sort. In other cases, transnational groups are associations of experts wielding scientific or other technical knowledge, and have an impact in informing the way in which states think about their interests. Some transnational business associations act as *private* governance institutions, facilitating cooperation between corporations on matters such as research and development, technical and regulatory standards, and so forth.

Finally, liberal theory stresses the importance of cosmopolitanism. Cosmopolitanism refers to the tendency of peoples in different countries to embrace each other as fellow global citizens. Cosmopolitanism can be contrasted with nationalism. If nationalism entails a shared identity of a particular national group expressed as an allegiance to others within the nation, cosmopolitanism involves the ability of people to identify with others in different lands and cultures. In emphasizing the cosmopolitan tendencies of mankind, liberals are suggesting that people are not trapped in their national identity. They can break out, seek people from other places, and build community between them.

Overall, liberal international theory offers a set of assumptions and propositions that stress the distinctive possibilities for cooperation among modern and advanced market democracies. The general claim is that these

Transnationalism: The tendency of groups within countries to build cooperative associations with groups in other countries.

Cosmopolitanism: The tendency of peoples in different countries to embrace each other as fellow global citizens. Cosmopolitanism can be contrasted with nationalism.

◀ Photo 3.5
Cosmopolitanism

This crowd is composed of people from different cultures and nations. It shows the principles of cosmopolitanism in action.

Source: Photoalto.

societies have incentives and capacities to build complex, stable, and mutually acceptable political relations. Liberal order is distinguished from other types of order, such as balance of power and imperial varieties, because of the way that state power is checked, restrained, and channeled. The problems of anarchy are reduced to such an extent that the distribution of power itself does not lead to balancing or coercive domination. Bargains, exchanges, reciprocity, specialization, and security cooperation are aspects of international relations that are captured by liberal theory.

But, not all people benefit equally from growing trade and cooperation, as liberal economic theory proposes. Rising inequality of wealth distribution during the industrial revolution gained support for the Marxist-Leninist theoretical framework, examined next.

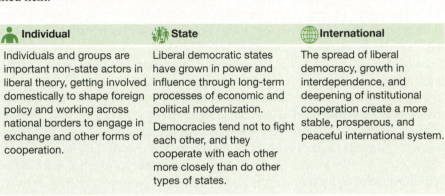

Levels of Analysis
The Liberal Tradition

🧍 **Individual**	👥 **State**	🌐 **International**
Individuals and groups are important non-state actors in liberal theory, getting involved domestically to shape foreign policy and working across national borders to engage in exchange and other forms of cooperation.	Liberal democratic states have grown in power and influence through long-term processes of economic and political modernization. Democracies tend not to fight each other, and they cooperate with each other more closely than do other types of states.	The spread of liberal democracy, growth in interdependence, and deepening of institutional cooperation create a more stable, prosperous, and peaceful international system.

The Marxist Tradition

When the European states entered the industrial revolution in the early nineteenth century, observers puzzled over how the rise of capitalism would impact the politics and economics of countries around the world. Traditional economies based on agriculture were rapidly transforming into industrial economies with modern corporations, wage workers, steam engines, and new manufacturing technologies. During the nineteenth century, countries in Europe went from rural societies of farmers and villagers to modern urban societies with bankers, businessmen, and a growing industrial working class. The countries of Europe grew in prosperity and their relations with the rest of the world changed, but not in the way hoped by liberal economists such as Adam Smith. That is, as we point out in Box 3.4, according to liberal economic theory, all would gain from trade. But, at least in the nineteenth century, too often the rich European countries became the wealth core of an emerging world economy, while peoples and nations in less advanced areas became the poorer periphery. Within the countries of the industrializing West, economic inequality also increased. Great wealth was created by the industrial revolution but working people and the poor benefited the least.

As scholars puzzled over the implications of the industrial revolution for domestic and international politics, a school of thought pioneered by the political economist Karl Marx emerged in the mid-nineteenth century that focused on class and class conflict. Marx sought to understand how the industrial revolution – and the rise of capitalism as an economic system – worked. He sought to identify capitalism's winners and losers and how capitalism and economic change shaped politics and political life.

Liberal Visions of Shared Benefits of Economic Growth

Aspiration: *Adam Smith, The Wealth of Nations*

Adam Smith argued in his seminal statement of market economics that nations will grow and prosper if their people are free to use their skills and capital to productive ends. Workers and businesses would be most efficient when they specialized at what they did best, creating a division of labor within and between nations. Governments were to protect property rights, enforce laws, and provide public infrastructure such as roads. As Smith argued, the individual's pursuit of his or her self-interest would indirectly and unintentionally promote the wealth and advancement of the general public.

> As every individual, therefore, endeavors as much as he can both to employ his capital in support of domestic industry, and so to direct that industry that its produce may be of the greatest value; every individual necessarily labors to render the annual revenue of the society as great as he can. He generally, indeed, neither intends to promote the public interest, nor knows how much he is promoting it. By preferring the support of domestic to that of foreign industry, he intends only his own security; and by directing that industry in such a manner as its produce may be of the greatest value, he intends only his own gain, and he is on this, as in many other cases, led by an invisible hand to promote an end which was no part of his intention. Nor is it always the worse for the society that it was no part of it. By pursuing his own interest he frequently promotes that of the society more effectively than when he really intends to promote it.
>
> (Adam Smith, *The Wealth of Nations*, Book IV, Chapter II, paragraph IX)

Reality: *Wealth Inequality between States during the Industrial Revolution, and Today*

The nineteenth-century industrial revolution that Smith foresaw entailed the growth of great wealth in countries like Great Britain and continued poverty and squalor elsewhere, such as colonial India. A similar dynamic takes place today and informs the debate over the advantages and drawbacks of globalization. Proponents of globalization point to the overall growth in the world economy that has occurred as borders have opened to the flow of goods, services, capital, and technology. Critics of globalization point to the growing disparities in income and wealth within and across states. Inequality, based on the workings of global capitalism, is the core concern of the Marxist tradition.

In sum, this Marxist tradition focuses on conflict and revolution thought to be associated with economic change and the rise of rich and poor classes within and across countries.

Marxism is not explicitly a theory about international relations. It is a theory about capitalism – its logic and unfolding dynamics in world history. Marxist theory is premised on the notion of historical materialism. This is the idea that history – and the actors that operate on the global stage across eras and regions – are shaped and motivated by their underlying material or economic basis. As the material basis of society changes, so too does history. In effect, the Marxist claim is that the most fundamental fact about people and societies is their material or economic circumstance. Societies are shaped and reshaped around the need to produce the material requirements of life. In the modern era, capitalism has provided the organizing logic shaping the productive forces within and between societies. This deeply rooted and ever-changing system of capitalism provides the structural setting in which peoples, classes, and states operate. Importantly, in the view of Marxist theory, it is the owners of the productive forces of capitalism who ultimately control politics and society as well. As we shall see, it is from this perspective that Marxist scholars have been able to say a great deal about the interests and motivations of actors within the global arena.

Marxist Assumptions

Mode of production: The basic organization of the economy – the way in which people relate to one another and to the material world.

Relations of production: The system by which the people in a productive system are related, or the relations between those people. According to Marxism, these relations are shaped by the mode of production. In a capitalist industrial mode, the relations of production will be characterized by class conflict.

Socioeconomic classes: Groupings of peoples based on their relationship to the economy.

Marxist theory about international relations begins with five assumptions. First, political interests and relationships are determined by a person's position within the transforming economic system. Economics – or the material setting in which people are situated – shapes politics. Or to put it in Marxist terms, the economic *base* shapes the political *superstructure*. The **mode of production**, organized in the modern era according to a capitalist logic, shapes the **relations of production**. The relations of production are the social and political relationships that emerge in society – for example, between workers and owners of businesses. The mode of production is the basic organization of the economy. It refers to the deep logic of economic life. In Marx's account, human societies were for centuries organized according to feudal relations of production, where serfs and peasants worked on the land that was owned by nobles or an aristocratic class. It was in the early modern era that capitalism arose as a mode of production, and with it came modern industrial society. Under capitalism, an industrial and commercial class emerged as owners of factories and corporations, and workers emerged as wage laborers. With the rise of capitalism as the mode of production, the relations of productions pitted the owners of capital and workers against each other. The world of politics evolved to reflect shifts in the underlying system of production. In other words, in this view, politics is what happens on the surface level of societies, and it is shaped by the deep underlying forces of capitalism and industrial development.

Second, the important actors in societies are not individuals or states, but **socioeconomic classes**, or groupings of peoples based on their relationship to the economy. With the rise of capitalism and the industrial revolution, the two most important classes are workers and capitalists. Workers are wage laborers and capitalists are the owners of the banks and businesses that make up the productive economy. While realists emphasize states as the key actors in the global system and liberals focus on individuals and groups, Marxist theory sees classes – within societies and between them – as the actors that directly or indirectly shape politics and international relations.

A third assumption is that the modern state is ultimately organized to serve the interests of the capitalist class – or what is sometimes called the ruling class. This is true even for constitutional democracies that elect their leaders. It is a fundamental claim of Marxist theory that modern states – despite their many differences around the world – have as their ultimate goal the protection and advancement of the capitalist class. Protecting and promoting the capitalist class is reflected in narrow instrumental ways when governments intervene to defend the property and profits of the capitalist class. But it is also manifest in a deeper and more structural way as the modern state upholds the rules, institutions, ideas, and privileges of the political order that support the capitalist system. Indeed, the capitalist class rules most effectively when its control over society is least visible.

A fourth Marxist assumption is that class conflict will increasingly define the relations among workers and capitalists. As capitalist industrialization unfolds, societies are expected to become increasingly divided between the two classes. The capitalist owners of wealth and industrial production will face off against workers. Class conflict is driven by their antagonistic economic interests. Workers are vulnerable to economic swings of boom and bust. They are exploited by the owners of capital who pay meager wages and keep the profits. For workers, unemployment and poverty always lurk around the corner. Capitalists, on the other hand, are enriched through economic growth. Moreover, these class relations are transnational. Workers share common interests across the industrial countries – a point captured in the old Marxist slogan, 'workers of the world unite!' Capitalists also tend to form transnational alliances, cooperating to protect their wealth, safeguard international trade and finance, and enforce the system of private property. Workers try to protect their interests by binding together in trade unions, such as the United Auto Workers, on the assumption that workers have more bargaining power if they act collectively rather than individually.

A final Marxist assumption is that revolution is the great source of political change. As class conflict grows more intense in the process of capitalist development, a breakpoint is eventually reached when the workers take control from the capitalist owners. The many overwhelm the few. Workers are expected to seize the ruling institutions of capitalist society – corporations, banks, and the state – and usher in a new political order. Society is to be transformed into a classless system. In Marx's ideal formulation, capitalism is to be turned into communism, a social system in which there is no private property or capitalist state, and workers collectively and harmoniously govern the economy and society. The Soviet Union, though characterized as a communist state, departed significantly from this Marxist ideal in that a small group of Communist Party officials, rather than the working class itself, took control of political power and the authority to allocate resources within society.

Marx foresaw a time when the conflicts and contradictions of modern capitalism would lead to revolution and a transformation in the mode of production – a transformation from capitalism to communism. But he also thought that capitalism was an extraordinarily dynamic and efficient system of production. Its powerful forces were transforming the world. Capitalist states would trade, invest, and expand outwards bringing the backward areas of the world into the arms of the capitalist system. In was in this sense that Marx was not an opponent of British or European colonialism. He saw it was part of the unfolding logic of capitalism, a process that would need to continue until capitalist societies were mature and ready for revolution.

In the twentieth century, Marxist theory of global capitalism evolved in various ways. The Russian revolutionary, Lenin, wrote perhaps the most influential Marxist-inspired treatise on the international politics of capitalism in his 1916 booklet, 'Imperialism: The Highest Stage of Capitalism'. Lenin argued that the capitalist class was becoming increasingly centralized in the major industrial countries, led by cartels of wealthy and powerful financial and industrial elites – what he called finance capitalism. To keep their workers peaceful, these elites in the advanced capitalist states were exporting their capital to poor underdeveloped countries to finance resources and cheap labor production. The poor and the backward regions of the world were being brought into the world capitalist system, and this was changing the relationship between capitalist states. This dynamic of finance capitalism allowed Lenin to explain

Class conflict: Conflict between the capitalist owners of wealth and industrial production and the workers they employ. Class conflict is driven by antagonistic economic interests and, according to Marxism, will increasingly define the relations between workers and capitalists.

Revolution: According to Marxism, in any instance of class conflict a breakpoint is eventually reached when the workers take control from the capitalist owners. Revolution is the dominant mode of political change in the Marxist school.

why revolution would not come – as Marx had predicted – in the most advanced countries but rather in the exploited less developed countries (Lenin 1917). With World War I as a backdrop, Lenin argued that the Western great powers, together with their finance capitalist elites, would be increasingly driven to compete with each other to divide up and exploit the undeveloped world. Thus it was imperialism and war – and not Marx's contradictions with the relations of production – that spelled the doom of advanced capitalism. Other Marxists during Lenin's time and later have continued to debate whether the global capitalist class would ultimately be divided into competing nation-states – reinforced by nationalism and geopolitics – or united in a global coalition to protect their shared interests.

In more recent decades, Marxist-inspired theory on international relations has explored the various ways in which global capitalism operates as a system of power. Some writings focus on the shifting winners and losers that emerge within global capitalism. Trade and open markets do not benefit all people in all places. The spread of capitalism worldwide has mobilized societies and raised many people up out of poverty. But the rich continue to get richer, while the poor – which is the vast majority of the people on earth – remain poor. Many non-Marxist scholars seek to explain these dynamics of inequality (see Stiglitz 2002), but Marxist theory is particularly committed as a theoretical tradition to identifying the divergent interests and outcomes that emerge from the expanding and transforming dynamics of capitalism. Other Marxist-inspired scholars have turned to the exploration of the ideologies and institutions that serve to preserve and protect the global capitalist system. Some scholars offer arguments about **hegemony** to explain the way in which leading capitalist states – most notably in the current era, the United States – dominate the resources and institutions of world politics (Cox 1987; Cox and Sinclair 1996; Gill 1992). Hegemony for Marxist scholars is a system of power where leading capitalist states exercise domination and control over weaker societies and peoples, often doing so indirectly through the influence of their ideologies and institutions.

Hegemony: The dominance of one state over other states. Many scholars believe that a hegemonic international system is most prone to peace.

Marxist Propositions

From these assumptions, Marxist theory offers a variety of insights about how capitalist states and international relations operate.

One proposition is that states – particularly those states in the advanced industrial countries – will act in ways that protect and advance the interests of capitalism and the capitalist class. This is not to argue that the governments of the leading capitalist countries will always promote the interests of specific businesses or banks. The proposition is that modern states will act to 'keep the world safe' for capitalism. This means that states will uphold property rights and the rules and institutions that support modern capitalism. In this regard, Marxist theory helps illuminate an entire history of state involvement in building, defending, and expanding the world capitalist system. This can be seen in the ways in which Western states over the last two centuries have pursed foreign policies that protect and advance the financial and commercial interests within their countries. The late nineteenth-century scramble for Africa, the partition of China, and the 'informal imperialism' pursued by Western capitalist states in Asia and Latin America were also episodes where states and capitalists worked together for economic and geopolitical advantage. While realists also expect to see states acting to advance the economic interests of their countries, they do so for national interest reasons. Marxists see states working on behalf of capitalism.

Marxists differ on precisely how business controls the state and argue that there are *structural* and *instrumental* capitalist influences on foreign policy. Structural influences of capitalism on foreign policy refer to the ways in which states automatically pursue policies that advance and protect the interests of capitalism. This is what Karl Marx himself argued when he said that 'the state is the handmaiden of capital.' Governments, after all, are dependent on a growing economy for taxes. They have an interest in making sure that the national economy is thriving. In this way, governments will protect the interests of capitalism. Governments will certainly not want to scare off businesses by imposing high taxes or expropriating their property. Governments will also seek to support rules and institutions within the global system that are supportive to trade and investment. In these ways, capitalism has a structural impact on what states do.

Marxists also point to instrumental influences of capitalism on foreign policy. In this case, it is the active lobbying of businesses that influences what states do. Capitalists are, in fact, well organized to influence government policy in most countries. Business associations have full-time representatives to lobby parliaments and presidents, and business elites are among the biggest donors to political campaigns. If 'money speaks' in politics, business groups use this advantage to influence governments. For example, in the United States, business groups with an interest in China have spoken loudly in favor of Sino-American trade and investment. More generally, the history of American foreign policy is full of episodes when business interests – oil companies or investment groups – pressure the government to intervene in the developing world on their behalf. Scholars continue to debate when and how these instrumental interests matter in international relations.

Another proposition is that **transnational business** will be a salient feature of world politics. As capitalism expands, businesses increasingly look outward into the international system for markets. In the nineteenth century and again in the decades after World War II, international trade grew rapidly. So, too, did international investment, where banks and corporations invest their money in foreign businesses. In recent decades, this *internationalization* of business has increased, and individual companies have established production operations in many different countries. These international businesses are called *multinational corporations* and include companies such as General Electric, Sony, Toyota, and Nestlé. Often, these companies become so internationalized that it is difficult to identify their home country; the world is their playing field.

Marxists argue that with the rise of transnational business, capitalists tend to win and workers tend to lose. That is, capitalists are able to cooperate to protect their wealth and maintain their privileged positions. International capitalists have options; they can establish operations in various countries and when conditions are not favorable to their business interests, they can shut down their operations and go elsewhere. National governments, therefore, have incentives to treat international business well, providing tax breaks and favorable deals so they will stay put. Workers, on the other hand, are not as mobile. They cannot move around as readily, and so their bargaining position is weaker. International capitalists are mobile. They fly around the world looking for business opportunities and they cooperate among themselves. Workers find it difficult to organize across countries. Marxists argue that international relations will bear the marks of this class conflict; national workers will press their governments for protection and international capitalists will lobby for an open world economy.

Taken together, Marxist theory sees the world in terms of class and economic interests. While realists see states struggling for power, Marxists see politics and

Transnational business: Businesses that operate across state lines. According to Marxism, as capitalism expands, businesses increasingly look outward into the international system for markets. This tendency enriches capitalists and impoverishes workers.

international relations as part of a deeper historical process of capitalist development. As the world capitalist system evolves, states and peoples organize and struggle accordingly. While liberals assert that economic interdependence is ultimately beneficial to all people and provides incentives for states to cooperate, Marxists believe that economic relations within and between countries are inherently unequal and exploitive. Economics does not breed peace – it generates conflict. Marxists do think that this conflict will someday be overcome through communist revolution. In the early decades of the twentieth century – before and after the Russian Revolution – some Marxists thought that the long-sought communist revolution had begun. But the Soviet Union ended up not establishing communism, but something very different – a despotic socialist state. Marxists believe that progress is possible, and class conflict can be overcome through revolution, but this dream for progressive change has yet to occur.

Marxism has enduring relevance as an analytic construct in international relations. In certain eras – such as the 'roaring 90s' – Marxism seems less relevant. Trade and investment expand and economic growth reaches around the world. Marxist ideas about class and class conflict give way to liberal ideas about mutual gain and the 'lifting of all ships.' But soon an economic crisis – such as the banking crisis and sharp economic downturn of 2008 – brings the insights of Marxism back into focus. The 2008 financial crisis highlights the tendency of capitalism to carry the seeds of its own destruction and to concentrate wealth – and by implication power – in the hands of fewer and fewer large actors, such as the large investment firms on Wall Street. Marxism also provides a useful counter-perspective to liberalism. Liberals tend to see globalization as a force for good, linking the world more closely together and generating economic gains for everyone. Marxism is more focused on the winners and losers in the global capitalist system. Globalization has drawn the world together, but it has also led to sharper divisions between haves and have nots. The United States and other advanced countries have seen their economies 'globalized' in recent decades. But globalization has led to concern in these countries over the hollowing out of their industrial sectors – the high-paying manufacturing jobs – leaving educated elites and those working low-wage service jobs to struggle within an increasingly unequal society.

Levels of Analysis *The Marxist Tradition*	👤 **Individual**	👥 **State**	🌐 **International**
	Individuals are divided into classes and their interests and political capacities are shaped by their economic circumstances.	Capitalist states are class societies, ruled by powerful economic elites. Capitalist states both exploit and dominate weaker societies and pursue war and foreign quest for economic gain.	The international system is shaped by the imperatives of capitalist growth and the powerful capitalist states that dominate it.

The Constructivist Tradition

In different ways, realists, liberals, and Marxists all make arguments about the impact of power and interests on international relations. Another theoretical perspective focuses on the role of ideas and the ways in which 'what people believe' shapes what individuals, groups, and states do. This constructivist perspective comes in several varieties, but it is unified by the view that ideas and beliefs matter in how actors define and pursue their interests. People do not simply act on self-evident interests or operate in a realist world of anarchy. International relations, according to constructivists, are 'socially constructed.' What people think and believe matters with regard to how they act in the world. While constructivism as a tradition in international relations is relatively new, the notion that ideas matter is an old notion reflected in a broader philosophical tradition known as idealism.

Constructivist Assumptions

Constructivist theory is built around four assumptions. First, the *interests* of individuals, groups, and states are not given or set in stone. Interests are shaped by the *identities* of actors. How people see themselves – for example, as a patriot, scientist, Christian, Muslim, Westerner, African, or citizen of the world – will shape how they think about their interests and what they want to achieve in politics. The realist, liberal, and Marxist theoretical traditions tend to see the interests of individuals as derived from specific social and political structures, such as anarchy, democracy, market society, or class position. In contrast, constructivists see much more diversity in the positions – and identities – of individuals.

Second, identities are molded by a variety of ideational factors – culture, religion, science, and normative beliefs. Constructivists do not fully discount the role of the material setting of individuals in shaping their identities. A steel worker or a bond trader operates within a setting that helps shape his or her thinking. But constructivists argue that identities emerge from interplay of these real world settings and the evolving ideas and beliefs inside the heads of people. Such differences in perspective on a given issue can be vitally important.

Third, elite individuals in both society and the state are the most important actors. The ideas and identities that these elites possess tend to shape the way the groups and states they lead take action within the international system. Thus, it is necessary to look closely at what leaders think and believe to explain what they do. Ideas shape the world.

Finally, communication plays an important role in shaping and changing identities. The interactions of elites and the networks they operate within are important in creating and reinforcing ideas and beliefs. Through communication and networking, elites tend to produce collective or shared world views that shape how interests are defined and pursued. The focus of constructivists is on critical historical moments when elites communicate and build consensus on who they are as groups and states, and how to think about problems. Interaction, process, networking, and communication all shape the way actors think and behave.

Constructivist Propositions

Four key concepts or propositions follow from this constructivist worldview. First, constructivists argue that 'the world is what you believe it is.' If people can be convinced and come to believe that the world is guided by universal moral standards, they will act that way. In a direct challenge to realism, one leading constructivist has argued: 'anarchy is what states make of it' (Wendt 1999). The world is anarchical, but this does not imply that inter-state relations will operate as realist theory predicts. Anarchy is shaped by how people think about it. As state elites learn more about each other, they

▶ Photo 3.6 NATO Soldiers on a Humanitarian Mission in Afghanistan, 2007

Since the end of the World Wars, and especially since the fall of the Soviet Union, new norms of humanitarian intervention have emerged to protect populations, especially minorities, within states. These norms give authority to the international community, including organizations such as NATO, to intervene in the domestic affairs of states to protect individuals from genocide or collective persecution. In the photo above, a soldier cuts webbing attached to a humanitarian aid-drop bundle in Parun, Afghanistan, June 27, 2007. The Nuristan Provincial Reconstruction Team worked side by side with the Afghan National Army to provide humanitarian aid and medical aid to Parun.

Source: ISAF, NATO.

Global civil society: The realm of private activity that lies outside the political system, where religious, ethnic, and civic groups flourish.. Civil society exists within countries but it also operates between countries, often manifest in transnational groups and associations. Global civil society is, in effect, the sum total of these transnational groups and activities.

can change their expectations and come to see each other as friends rather than foes. The United States does not worry about the United Kingdom's vast nuclear arsenal, but it frets that North Korea many have a small number of primitive nuclear bombs.

Indeed, anarchy can be manifest in several different ways. One type of anarchy is the harsh world that realists describe. This is a world in which states regard other states as enemies that deserve no respect, are not necessarily legitimate or sovereign, and can be conquered if circumstances allow. This is anarchy manifest as the law of the jungle. Another type of anarchy is where states view each other as rivals, but not enemies. States are not interested in conquering others simply because they can; instead, they seek to preserve the status quo, respect the rights of others to exist, and use force only for defensive purposes and in the name of stabilizing the system. The role of force is shaped by norms, absolute gains are often preferential to relative gains, and cooperation is possible. Yet another type of anarchy is one where states view other states as friends; states cooperate to maximize collective gains, the use of force is generally viewed as illegitimate, sovereignty is respected, and collective security replaces national security. According to the constructivist view, none of the types of anarchy is more natural or inevitable than the others, and through *learning* and *socialization*, which results from interaction between elites, the world can move toward more cooperative and collective security-oriented anarchy.

A second constructivist proposition is that states operate within a **global civil society**. In this sense, constructivism is compatible with liberalism's emphasis on cosmopolitanism. Civil society is the realm of private activity that lies outside the political system. It is the realm of private associations, where religious, ethnic, and civic groups flourish. Civil society exists within countries but it also operates between countries, often manifest in transnational groups and associations. Global civil society is, in effect, the sum total of these transnational groups and activities. Constructivists agree with liberal theorists that these transnational networks and exchanges are important mechanisms for spreading norms and ideas, and for building trust and consensus among countries. For constructivists, global civil society is what facilitates elite learning and socialization, providing the communication networks through which elites develop ideas and identities that shape state policy, and gives shape to the character of anarchy.

A third constructivist proposition is that normative change is a major way in which world politics evolved from era to era. Constructivists argue that the learning and socialization that takes place across the global system does tend to move the world in a progressive direction. Norms do change; often, although not always, for the better. The institution of slavery was outlawed by the end of the nineteenth century. The practice of apartheid was ended in South Africa in the 1980s. In the postwar era, as discussed in Chapter 11, new norms of humanitarian intervention emerged that give the international community the right and obligation to intervene in the domestic affairs of states to protect individuals from genocide or other forms of collective violence.

A final constructivist proposition is that state elites exist within and are influenced by strategic culture. As noted earlier, constructivists argue that states have *identities* that help shape how their leaders think about the nation's interests. Building on this view, constructivists go on to also argue that state leaders operate in a strategic culture that shapes foreign policy choices. Strategic culture refers to assumptions about the nature of the global system – for example, which states are friends and enemies – and strategies of action that are shared by government elites. Russia, Japan, Great Britain, France, China, and the United States all have different strategic cultures because of differences rooted in specific historical experiences and national security lessons crystallized in ideology and traditions of grand strategy (Johnston 1995). These differences in strategic culture give countries distinctive *personalities* as states, even as they operate in similar global situations. To understand how leading states will make choices, it is necessary to unpack the assumptions and ideational frameworks with which state leaders rank preferences and make grand strategic choices.

Recall our discussion in Chapter 2 of why the Cold War ended. Constructivists place great weight on the role of Gorbachev, and in particular on how he embraced a set of ideas to transform Soviet strategic culture. Gorbachev and his reformers believed war with the West was not inevitable, and there was greater room for cooperation with capitalism than traditional Soviet strategic culture had earlier believed. For constructivists, the world changed not because material power changed, but because ideas changed (Lebow and Risse-Kappen 1995).

In looking at the ways that ideas and identities shape the choices of states, some scholars have focused specifically on the role of gender as a shaping influence. We now turn to this emerging area of scholarship.

Normative change: The idea that as global learning and international socialization occur, ideas about what is or is not acceptable or 'normal' change. As normative change occurs, it can impact international relations.

Strategic culture: Strategic culture refers to assumptions about the nature of the global system – for example, which states are friends and enemies – and strategies of action that are shared by government elites.

👤 Individual	👥 State	🌐 International
Individuals are the most important actors in world politics. It is the ideas in their heads that shape what groups and societies do within the global system.	National political institutions and the reigning ideas and norms they embody shape the way states define their interests and act within the wider world.	The international system is composed of states and a global civil society. Anarchy does not necessarily breed conflict – it depends on what states make of it.

Levels of Analysis
The Constructivist Tradition

The Feminist Tradition

Alongside the theoretical approaches described above, feminist scholarship has emerged in recent decades to challenge traditional assumptions and visions of world politics, and it has developed its own distinctive theoretical tradition. Feminist thinking is wide ranging and offers provocative counter-points to old mainstream theoretical ideas about states, war, and power politics. The focus of feminist theory is on the role of gender – and the role of women – in society and world affairs. It seeks to illuminate biases and neglected ways of viewing international relations.

Feminist Assumptions

One of the groundbreaking feminist explorations of international relations is Cynthia Enloe's *Bananas, Beaches, Bases: Making Feminist Sense of International Politics* (Enloe 2000). The book provides a vivid historical account of the way women have been subordinated to men in various industries and institutions within the expanding global system such as tourism, agriculture, and the armed forces. In Enloe's portrait, women play a role in the world economy and geopolitical system primarily as subordinate and undervalued laborers – domestic workers, diplomatic wives, agricultural workers, and prostitutes outside military bases. Women are everywhere in international relations, but the lenses through which we view international relations tend to obscure and hide their presence. The great globalizing forces in world politics – multinational corporations, diplomatic relations, military alliances – are depicted as driven by the grand pursuits of men. In the background and with considerably less power, we find women playing undervalued and often demeaning supporting and subordinate roles. The important insight that Enloe advances – which is at the heart of the feminist critique – is that states and international relations have 'gendered' structures of domination and interaction. Feminism is similar to Marxism in that each emphasizes the structural inequality in political, economic, and social systems. Capitalism and the system of states is a system of domination, and women tend to be at the lower reaches and on the bottom. Traditional theories of international relations fail to acknowledge or analyze this hidden reality.

Building on this insight, beginning in the 1980s, scholars of international relations began thinking about the implications of gender for how we study world affairs. The focus was not just on the disadvantaged role of women in global affairs, but also the development of a feminist critique of traditional geopolitical and state power theories of world politics that have for the most part been constructed by men – that is, theories that look at the world from the perspective of state leaders, who also tend to be men. Scholar Robert Keohane poses the question that feminist theory asks: 'How have distinctively male values, and social structures in which male values are given priority, affected the concepts developed in international society?' (Keohane 1989). The goal of the feminist tradition in international relations is to expose the gender bias that pervades the traditional theories of states and power politics, and to offer alternative views of world affairs from the standpoint of the weak and powerless.

Two general lines of argument, or sets of propositions, have emerged most clearly and forcefully in the feminist tradition. One is a critique of male-oriented assumptions about world politics, challenging in particular the 'realist' orientation of prevailing theory. The other is the claim that gender bias has diminished the roles and capabilities of women in the actual conduct of international relations.

Feminist Propositions

In critiquing prevailing ideas and theories about international relations, feminist thinkers focus primarily on realist theory and its ideas about states, war, and power politics. Gender assumptions and biases are found at every level of this theoretical tradition. The language is male-oriented, sending the subtle or not-so-subtle message that world politics is a 'man's world'. After all, scholars talk of 'statesmen' and 'mankind'. The classic realist thinker, Hans Morgenthau, defines power as 'man's control over the minds and actions of other men' (Morgenthau 1967). The title of Kenneth Waltz's classic study is *Man, the State, and War*. The language of states and power – the 'high politics' of international relations that scholars focus on – suggests that the terrain of world politics is a man's terrain. The hidden assumption is that the rough and tumble 'public sphere' is a man's world, while the 'private sphere' of family and home is a woman's world.

Along these lines, in her influential feminist study, *Women and War*, Jean Bethke Elshtain argues that the great writings on war, by theorists from Thucydides to Machiavelli to modern realists, offer a vision of 'high politics' in which the public sphere is inhabited by men, wielding power and determining the fates of peoples and societies (Elshtain 1987). The scholarly study of international relations, Elshtain argues, has become a professionalized male-dominated world closed off from the wider values of society. 'Encumbered with lifeless jargon, systems and subsystems dominance, spirals of misperception, decision-making analysis, multipolar, intervening variables, dependence, interdependence, cost-effectiveness, IR specialists in the post-Second World War era began to speak exclusively to, or "at", one another or to their counterparts in government service' (Elshtain 1987). The discourse of international relations has become a closed intellectual system with deep assumptions about the masculinity of power and world politics. In making this feminist critique, Elshtain seeks to open up both the scholarly and political discussion of war and peace by calling for a more open 'civic' discussion of war and the exercise of power. By breaking down the gendered character of the study of international relations, the issues of war and peace can be seen and debated from more angles. More voices and sensibilities – including the voices and sensibilities of women – can be brought into the public debate over the great decisions of war and peace. The 'high politics' of international relations can become more open to a wider social and international conversation.

Feminist scholarship as a whole shares this aim of opening up and breaking down old gender-biased ways of thinking about international relations. If concepts such as state, power, anarchy, and war are masculine ideas, or at least ideas whose primacy in the study of international relations is reinforced by male gender biases, a feminine approach to international relations might emphasize cooperation, mutual gain, interdependence, and societal understanding. As Ann Tickner observes, 'Most feminists are committed to the emancipatory goal of achieving a more just society', which, for them, includes ending the subordinate position of women (Tickner 1997).

One implication is that if women are given more opportunities to hold power – to lead governments and make decisions about war and peace – they will do so with different priorities and sensibilities. Studies by anthropologists and biologists do give some evidence that males and females have different predispositions toward violence and aggression rooted in differences in their genetic and biological characteristics, such as the presence in males of the hormone testosterone. These biologically driven

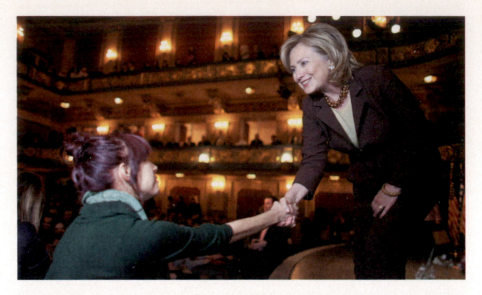

► **Photo 3.7 Secretary of State Hillary Clinton visits Sarajevo, October 2010**

US Secretary of State Hillary Rodham Clinton shakes hands with a student at a town hall meeting with university students and civil society representatives at the National Theater in Sarajevo, Bosnia and Herzegovina, on October 12, 2010.

Source: US State Department.

differences are seen by some experts to generate different social behaviors, including a greater tendency of males to engage in violence and aggressive actions. As we will see in Chapter 5, there are even some experimental studies that test male and female students, finding that males are more likely to be overconfident and attack the enemy in simulated war games (Johnson 2006). Some experts see culture as more important in shaping differences between the genders in social behavior – and there certainly is a lot of variation across history and countries of the world in the role of women in war and as wielders of power (Goldstein 2001).[1]

A second line of feminist argument is that women have been systematically under-represented in both the study and practice of international relations. The basic insight starts with the observation that although gender relations differ from country to country, they are nonetheless almost always unequal. In this respect, the historian Joan Scott argues that gender has been a way for societies to signify relationships of power. The claim is not that women are different – that they embody different values or sensibilities – but that they are simply under-represented in the scholarly world of international relations and the governmental corridors of power.

Despite advances in education and the modernization of societies, such as in Western Europe and the United States, there remains deep-rooted inequality of opportunity and representation for women. Within the field of political science, a recent study indicates that only 26 percent of the 13,000 professors are women, and an even smaller percentage of professors who study international relations are women (Malinak 2008). Women also tend to study and teach different subjects than men. Woman are more likely to study transnational actors and international organizations, specialize in developing regions, such as Latin America and sub-Saharan Africa, and focus on the role of ideas and identities in their work. Men are more likely to study American foreign policy and issues of war and peace, specialize in the great powers, and use realist theories of world politics.

In the world of foreign policy and diplomacy, the under-representation of woman is also striking. In the United States there has never been a female President, and only

---

1. For a summary of the evidence, see Goldstein (2001).

recently – since the 1990s – has there been a female US Secretary of State. When heads of state travel each September to the United Nations for its annual opening, the over-whelming majority of these leaders are men. While there have been female leaders in countries such as India (Indira Gandhi), Israel (Golda Meir), the Philippines (Corazon Aquino), and others, only British Prime Minister Margaret Thatcher and German Chancellor Angela Merkel have been leaders of one of the great powers. Worldwide, women fill only 17 percent of parliamentary seats and 14 percent of ministerial-level positions (Hunt 2007).

Feminists focusing on the problem of inequality and under-representation are not arguing that women would make better leaders or that the world would be more peaceful if woman ran the planet. Their argument is not that women are somehow morally superior to men. Rather, these feminist thinkers argue simply that it is a ques-tion of justice – and, indeed, that it is a lost opportunity not to draw upon the talents and capacities of fully half of the human race. Some writers do argue that women might be better diplomats and state leaders. Francis Fukuyama argues in a famous essay that women are in fact more sensitive to a wider set of social values and, if in charge, would be more inclined to seek peaceful solutions to the world's problems (Fukuyama 1998). But this view has been challenged by some leading feminist scholars. Ann Tickner argues that in fact this thesis that associates women with peace and moral superiority has the effect of keeping women out of power. 'The association of women with peace can play into unfortunate gender stereotypes that characterize men as active, women as passive; men as agents, women as victims; men as rational, women as emotional', Tickner notes. 'Not only are these stereotypes damaging to women, particularly to their credibility as actors in matters of international politics and national security, but they are also damaging to peace' (Tickner 1999). The goal of feminist theory is not to seek the advance of women into positions of power because they bring more lofty values and aspirations. It is because their under-representation in positions of power stems from the social injustice and inequities that speak ill of today's economic and political systems.

Considering the five theoretical frameworks, how do the roles of actors and actions in each tradition differ? We offer a brief comparison next.

Individual	**State**	**International**
Individuals are defined by their gender. This gender identity can be a powerful influence on how men and women think about world politics.	States tend to be led by men, who bring distinctively male impulses and sensibilities to the exercise of state power.	The conflict orientation of many men may reinforce the conflict-inducing character of international anarchy.

Levels of Analysis
The Feminist Tradition

Comparing Traditions

These five theoretical traditions provide useful ways to look at international relations. It is not necessary to decide if one is right and the others are wrong. They each provide a window on the world. Each claims to capture the dynamics of world politics. In the chapters ahead, we will make use of these traditions. In doing so, we can make some comparisons between them based on what they think are the important actors and forces at work in the global system.

Realism: War is a major source of change in world politics. In every historical era, war – particularly among major states – has dramatically changed the geopolitical landscape. In the wake of war, powerful rising states have emerged to dominate the system, while defeated states have gone into decline. War has forced states to mobilize their economies and societies, leading to innovations and changes in government capacities. War and security competition between states has fueled arms races and efforts to build new and more destructive weapons. World War I is a good example of how a major war transformed politics, economics, and world affairs. It was a war that led to the destructions of vast empires, brought the United States to the center of world politics, and fueled changes in European politics that played out over the next half century.

Liberalism: Liberals argue that change in world politics comes from ongoing trade, exchange, innovation, and learning that occurs within and between countries. Through these processes, societies advance and modernize. World politics changes as the countries themselves become more advanced – liberal, capitalist, and democratic – and as the relations between these countries become more interdependent and cooperative. The post-1945 rise of the European Community – later called the European Union – is a major example of what liberals see as advancement.

Marxism: Marxists argue that change in world politics is generated by political conflict that is rooted in the capitalist system. Economic inequality and the divergent economic interests between classes provides the setting for struggle between peoples, classes, and states. Marx originally argued that these conflicts would result in revolution within capitalist societies, ushering in communism. Later Marxist scholars have focused on a wider array of conflicts, including clashes between wealthy and poor countries.

Constructivism: Constructivists argue that change in world politics emerges from the evolution in norms and world views that guide the behavior of people and societies – including the behavior of state leaders. The decline in the acceptability of slavery during the nineteenth century and empire in the twentieth century are examples of major shifts in normative orientations.

Feminism: Like constructivists, feminist theorists argue that dominant ideologies and orientations in world politics are formed over long periods of time. Feminists point in particular to the way gender roles and expectations get established, leading to the marginalization of women in world affairs. For change to occur, societies need to become more aware of these often hidden or unremarked upon biases. Change comes when people's ideas about gender change. Women who do rise to prominence in world politics – as foreign ministers or heads of states – can become role models, thereby helping to change ideas and expectations.

In terms of the actors that dominate world politics, realists argue that state leaders speak for the national interests. Liberals argue that foreign policy reflects the diversity of people and groups within society, as well as the ties they develop across states. Marxists trace the broad patterns of world politics to economic classes, particularly business elites. Constructivism tends to look to government and societal elites who are the carriers of ideas that influence the actions of states. Feminism focuses on the gender of leaders and citizens and the male bias in the way people think about international relations.

The traditions differ regarding the behavior of these actors as well. Realists see states acting primarily to advance the power and interests of the state, and this brings states into conflict with each other. In other words, world politics, according to realists, is a struggle for power defined by conflict between states. Liberals see states as more inclined toward cooperation. Individuals and groups in society are always looking for ways to advance their interests by working with others, a dynamic most consistently seen in relations among liberal democracies. Marxists see economic inequality and class conflict as the fundamental dynamics within and between states. Constructivists focus on the ways in which elites within and across states communicate with each other, interacting in ways that share knowledge and build consensus on important questions of peace, prosperity, stability, and order. Feminist theories seek to expose the biases in how scholars think about international relations, showing how masculine values often get emphasized at the expense of feminine values – and these theories also emphasize how gender inequality exists in the 'man's world' of international affairs.

Realists see world politics shaped and reshaped by war. It is war that ultimately serves to destroy the old relations between states, paving the way for newly powerful states. Liberals, in contrast, see learning as a much more powerful force of change in world politics. States are not doomed to repeat their mistakes. Societies can learn and make advancements in their relationships with others. Marxists see revolution as the master mechanism of change. Economic classes are fundamentally antagonistic. When class relations become so prone to conflict and violence, revolutions can erupt that serve to overturn the old political order and usher in new social relations. Constructivists see the spread of ideas as the most important mechanism of change, a process that is pushed forward by political activist groups, including social groups and international non-governmental organizations. Feminists stress the pathways by which gender can influence both how leaders act in world affairs and how scholars understand and interpret that action.

Finally, the traditions differ in regard to the direction of history. Realists see history as cyclical. States are ultimately caught up in continuous cycles of war and change, rise and fall. Liberals see the direction of history as more linear. Peoples and societies can cooperate and make their lives better. Marxists see class conflict ultimately leading to revolution that ushers in more equal and just social relations. Constructivists tend to see a progressive logic to change in world politics, but are usually less certain than liberals that the world can and will be made better. In this sense, they do not have explicit visions of the advancement of mankind. But they do see elites across the world engaged in dialogue and communication. This dialogue and communication can lead to conflict, of course. But it can also give states opportunities to find common ground and remake world politics. Feminists believe that history is shaped by gender and that the prospects for peace, war, conflict, and cooperation among states will be influenced by gender relations within those states.

Individual	👥 State	🌐 International
Different theoretical perspectives place different weights on the importance of individuals; constructivism and feminism place the individual at the center of analysis; realism places the individual at the margins of its theory.	Realism, constructivism, and feminism downplay the significance of domestic institutions; liberalism and Marxism place them at the heart of their respective analyses, although the former stresses political institutions while Marxism-Leninism focuses on economic institutions.	Realism places its main emphasis on the international system; feminism and constructivism argue that the effects of the international system depend on how actors perceive that system; and liberalism and Marxism argue that the effects of the international system are contingent on the domestic institutions of states.

Levels of Analysis

Comparing Traditions

Revisiting the Enduring Question and Looking Ahead

This chapter has surveyed five competing theoretical traditions in the field of international relations. These traditions each provide assumptions and arguments about the way the world works. Do we need to pick between these five theoretical traditions? Is one of them right and the others wrong? The answer is no. The world is an amazingly large and diverse place. Over the centuries, it has exhibited an extraordinary array of human endeavor. No one theoretical tradition can explain everything that puzzles us about international relations. They are all potentially useful as tools of explanation. As we explore the enduring problems of international relations, we want to have a lot of tools in our toolbox to explain what is going on. The arguments of one tradition or another may be more convincing in specific circumstances or historical episodes, but we want to keep all of them ready to be used.

It is useful to think of these theoretical traditions as *lenses* through which we observe international relations. The traditions tell us where to look, even if they cannot always confidently predict what we will find in any given situation. Each theoretical tradition offers a different lens, and each lens highlights different actors and activities in the international system. When we put on the realist lens, we see states and the struggle for power. We see the problems of anarchy everywhere – security dilemmas, power balancing, and nationalism. When we put on the liberal lens, we see individuals and groups engaged in complex activities of cooperation and institution building. We see states organizing open systems of trade and the emergence of communities of democracies. When we put on the Marxist lens, we see class conflict and economic struggle between the rich and poor across the globe. We see an ever-changing system of world capitalism shaping and reshaping conflict and cooperation around the world. When we put on the constructivist lens, we see great movements of ideas and norms. We see elites communicating and learning through international networks, and state identities shaping the way countries make foreign policy and organize the global system. When we put on the feminist lens, we see both the importance of gender differences and the role of gender in the perpetuation of political, social, and economic inequalities within and across states.

Each of these lenses allows us to see different things and raises specific actors and dynamics to the foreground and moves other actors and dynamics to the background. As we explore the history and evolving character of international relations, we want to keep all of these lenses at the ready. In looking at international history, as well as foreign policy of states in the present period, we also want to have the analytical tools that students of foreign policy have developed. It is to the examination of that toolbox for the analysis of foreign policy that we now direct our attention.

Visit **www.palgrave.com/politics/Grieco** to access extra resources for this chapter, including:

- Chapter summaries to help you review the material
- Multiple choice quizzes to test your understanding
- Flashcards to test your knowledge of the key terms in this chapter
- Outside resources, including links to contemporary articles and videos, that add to what you have learned in this chapter

Study Questions

1. Which theoretical tradition of international relations is most appealing to you? Which is the least appealing? Why?
2. Is it important that we have theories of international relations? Why or why not?
3. Realist theory has been the most central or prominent theory in the past. Do you think it will be as important in the future? Why or why not? Which theory seems to have a more promising future?
4. How do we know if one or another theory of international relations is more helpful to us as we try to understand international relations?
5. Which theoretical tradition of international relations do you wish national leaders in major countries like the United States and China, for example, paid closer attention to as they formulate their foreign policies?

Further Reading

Bull, Hedley (1977) *The Anarchical Society: A Study of Order in World Politics*, 3rd edn (Basingstoke, UK: Macmillan). A founding statement of the English School of international relations, emphasizing both the existence of anarchy among states and an international community.

Buzan, Barry (1983) *People, States, and Fear: The National Security Problem in International Relations* (Chapel Hill: University of North Carolina Press). A pioneering exploration of the concept of national security in international relations and its implications for the security dilemma.

Doyle, Michael (1997) *Ways of War and Peace: Realism, Liberalism, and Socialism* (New York: Norton). A magisterial survey of the leading theoretical traditions in the study of international relations. It includes portraits of the philosophical thinkers whose ideas have informed these traditions.

Jervis, Robert (1976) *Perception and Misperception in International Politics* (Princeton: Princeton University Press). Explores the way psychology and perceptions influence relations among states.

Keohane, Robert O. and Joseph S. Nye (1977) *Power and Interdependence: World Politics in Transition* (Boston: Little, Brown). Offers a liberal internationalist perspective on world politics, emphasizing the fragmented and decentralized character of power within a complex and evolving modern international system.

Waltz, Kenneth (1954) *Man, the State, and War: A Theoretical Analysis* (New York: Columbia University Press). A landmark study of the ideas of classical political theories on questions of war and peace. Waltz famously divides these theories into 'images' or levels of the international system and sources of war – the individual, state, and international structural levels.

Wendt, Alexander (1999) *Social Theory of International Politics* (Cambridge: Cambridge University Press). Wendt offers foundational thinking for the constructivist approach to international relations.

4

The Analysis of Foreign Policy

Enduring question: What factors most influence the foreign policies of states

During the 1950s, China was allied with the Soviet Union and considered the United States its principle geopolitical adversary. China worked closely with the Soviet Union and fought opposite the United States during the Korean War of the 1950s and the Vietnam War of the 1960s. China did not even have diplomatic relations with the United States until the 1970s. Yet, by the end of the 1960s, Chinese foreign policy changed and China's leaders came to view the Soviet Union more as an adversary than as an ally. China and the Soviet Union fought a border war in 1969. By the 1980s, China not only established diplomatic relations, but moved closer to its former adversary, the United States, politically and economically.

Today, China enjoys cordial political relations, and limited economic relations, with Russia. It has close economic relations with the United States; in fact the two countries are highly dependent on each other commercially and financially. However, China's political relations with the United States are changing again, and have become significantly colder. Many believe the two countries are emerging as geopolitical competitors as they compete for influence in the South China Sea and in East Asia more generally.

These twists and turns in China's external relations point to the enduring question addressed in this chapter: which factors most influence the foreign policies of states? Also, which factors best account for significant changes in those foreign policies? We will address these questions by breaking them down into more manageable pieces in the sections to follow. First, we will consider the matter of what exactly is a foreign policy. Second, we will utilize the levels-of-analysis framework to investigate the sources of foreign policy or, more precisely, we will investigate the attributes of individuals, states, and the international system that influence the selection of foreign policies by governments.

Third, we will seek to identify the conditions under which states change their foreign policies.

The enduring question of what drives foreign policy is unresolved and consequential. Some analysts prefer 'inside-out' explanations; they focus on domestic sources of foreign policy, and debate the extent to which interest groups, public opinion, or the particular structure of government helps us to understand the behavior of states. 'Outside-in' analysts believe that international or external sources are the key determinants of foreign policy. External sources include how powerful or weak a country is relative to other countries, and the extent to which a country finds itself in a peaceful or threatening neighborhood. Scholarly debates over what accounts for foreign policy are unresolved in that no single factor is a clear analytical winner in explaining the foreign policies of different countries, across different issues, and across time. Understanding foreign policy is critical because the foreign policy choices that states make have profound implications for relations among states. Thus, it is important in an international relations text to devote sustained attention to the determinants of foreign policy.

© summersgraphicsinc–istockphoto.com.

Learning Objectives

By the end of this chapter, you will be able to:

→ Compare the study of international relations and the analysis of foreign policy, and appreciate how both are necessary to understand international affairs.

→ Identify the two core attributes, interests and strategies, of any country's foreign policy.

→ Analyze the range of policy instruments that a country may utilize in its foreign policy.

→ Apply the levels-of-analysis framework to explore the sources of a country's foreign policy.

→ Utilize the levels-of-analysis framework to identify the conditions under which a country may change its foreign policy.

Chapter Contents

- Foreign Policy Analysis: Connections to International Relations and Core Concepts
- The Sources of Foreign Policy
- How and Why States Change Their Foreign Policy
- Revisiting the Enduring Question and Looking Ahead
- Study Questions
- Further Reading

Foreign Policy Analysis: Connections to International Relations and Core Concepts

To explore the enduring question of which factors account for the foreign policies of states, we first examine how the analysis of foreign policy differs from and complements the study of international relations. We will then fine-tune language we introduced in Chapter 1 for the analysis of foreign policy, with particular attention paid to the two concepts of interest and strategy.

The Study of International Relations and the Analysis of Foreign Policy

In general, scholars of international relations are interested in interactions between two or more states, and particularly in why some of those interactions are cooperative while others are competitive and may even end in war. The theories we examined in Chapter 3 each fundamentally try to understand inter-state interactions, and especially the conditions that cause those interactions to be peaceful or in conflict. In contrast, foreign policy analysts want to understand why a *given country's government* has decided to take certain actions toward foreign governments or foreign non-state actors; why a government has decided that specific foreign policy interests are important to it; and why it has crafted a particular strategy to promote or defend those interests.

The negotiation of the Kyoto Protocol of 1997, which requires adherents (more than 191 states plus the European Union by the fall of 2012) to reduce greenhouse gases that contribute to global climate change, provides a good opportunity to see the differences between the relative emphases of scholars of international relations and scholars of foreign policy. A scholar of international relations would be interested in the international dynamics that brought the Kyoto Protocol into being. That scholar might ask whether the agreement on the Protocol was attained because more powerful countries bullied weaker countries into accepting it, because richer countries enticed poorer countries to do so, or because the global scientific community and globally active non-governmental organizations (NGOs) persuaded national leaders that global warming was a real threat and ought to be addressed through an international agreement.

A student of foreign policy might also be interested in how the Kyoto Protocol came about, but would focus on the decisions of specific countries on whether or not to adhere to it. So, for example, the student of foreign policy would want to understand why President Bill Clinton's administration helped negotiate the Kyoto Protocol in 1997 and signed the instrument in late 1998, but the Clinton team never submitted the Protocol to the US Senate for ratification, which the US Constitution requires in order for any treaty to come into force for the United States. Similarly, a foreign policy analyst might want to know why China and India, industrializing countries that produce significant amounts of greenhouse gases, were willing to sign and ratify an agreement that promised to constrain their future economic behavior. The study of foreign policy can focus on a particular country, such as the United States, India, or China, or can focus comparatively across the foreign policies of two or more countries.

Scholars of international relations and foreign policy specialists appreciate the importance of one another's work. Foreign policy analysts understand that a country's international context matters a great deal when its leaders identify interests and formulate strategies. In turn, students of international relations recognize that the international interactions of governments have firm roots in the foreign policies of the countries involved in those interactions. If you wish to understand international affairs and why countries sometimes work together, sometimes compete with each other, and sometimes even fight each other, then you must understand both sides of the coin in world affairs, international relations and foreign policy.

Foreign Policy Interests

We often say that a government is pursuing a particular foreign policy because it advances some interest (Jentleson 2010; George and Keohane 1980). An interest, as noted in Chapter 1, is a situation in the world that the leaders of a government want to exist, so much so that they are willing to pay costs to bring it about. National leaders often have to accept that there is a gap between their hopes to promote a given interest and their capacity to do so, and there are often trade-offs between interests; the pursuit of one requires giving up the pursuit of another.

For example, many US leaders believe that the extension of democracy and human rights to China is a US interest. However, those leaders often find it necessary to curtail their efforts to promote China's internal transformation due to the reality that they must gain the current Chinese government's cooperation in order to advance other US interests, including stabilization and growth of the international economy, finding a solution to global climate change, and management of numerous international security issues, including Iran's nuclear weapons program and North Korea's often provocative behavior toward South Korea. We explore in Making Connections Box 4.1 this clash between aspirations and realities involving the interest of US leaders in spreading human rights and democracy to present-day China while also working with its current government.

Foreign Policy Strategy

To advance or defend an interest, a government's leaders develop a foreign policy strategy. A foreign policy strategy, you will recall from Chapter 1, consists of the specification by leaders of objectives (the outcomes that help advance an interest), and policy instruments (the concrete measures the government takes to reach its objectives and thus advance its interest). For the purposes of discussion, we can distinguish between instruments that seek to reach policy objectives through the *persuasion* of a relevant foreign actor (that might be private or governmental in character), and those instruments that seek to reach policy objectives through the *coercion* of a foreign actor.

Instruments of Persuasion

Governments sometimes seek to achieve foreign policy objectives by trying to persuade foreign actors to act or desist from acting in one manner or another. One key instrument of such persuasion by governments is **diplomacy**. We will discuss diplomacy in more detail as a means toward peace in Chapter 6. However, diplomacy in general terms is the process by which representatives of two or more governments meet and discuss matters of common concern either bilaterally or in a multilateral forum. During these meetings, the representatives seek to persuade each other of the merits of their respective positions with a view toward finding a mutually agreeable solution to some problem or to develop a mechanism by which they can achieve individual gains through some form of joint action. These representatives may be ambassadors who are sent from their respective home countries to reside in the capital city of a host country, or they may be ministerial-rank officials, such as the British Foreign

Diplomacy: The process by which representatives of two or more governments meet and discuss matters of common concern.

US Foreign Policy toward China, 2009

US policy makers consistently argue that they place high value on the spread of democracy and human rights around the world. But, as this example shows, those concerns are often forced to take a back seat to other pressing issues such as climate change, the economic crisis then gripping the world, and security problems including the spread of nuclear weapons.

Aspiration: *Secretary of State Hillary Clinton on Human Rights and China, December 2009*

> The United States seeks positive relationships with China and Russia, and that means candid discussions of divergent views. In China, we call for protection of rights of minorities in Tibet and Xinxiang; for the rights to express oneself and worship freely; and for civil society and religious organizations to advocate their positions within a framework of the rule of law. And we believe strongly that those who advocate peacefully for reform within the constitution, such as Charter 2008 signatories, should not be prosecuted. With Russia, we deplore the murders of journalists and activists and support the courageous individuals who advocate at great peril for democracy. With China, Russia, and others, we are engaging on issues of mutual interest while also engaging societal actors in these same countries who are working to advance human rights and democracy. The assumption that we must either pursue human rights or our 'national interests' is wrong. The assumption that only coercion and isolation are effective tools for advancing democratic change is also wrong.

Source: Secretary of State Hillary Clinton, 'Remarks on the Human Rights Agenda for the 21st Century', address at Georgetown University, December 14, 2009.

Reality: *Secretary of State Hillary Clinton on Human Rights and China, February 2009*

In February 2009, Hillary Clinton was about to leave Seoul, South Korea, for Beijing, China, during an inaugural visit to Asia as Secretary of State. She told reporters that while she would raise with her Chinese hosts the controversial issues of human rights, as well as Chinese policy on Tibet and Taiwan, she thought it might be more productive to focus on issues on which real progress was possible, namely, climate change, the global economic crisis, and a range of security issues. According to the report in the *New York Times*, Clinton said 'There is a certain logic to that', and further, 'That doesn't mean that questions of Taiwan, Tibet, human rights, the whole range of challenges that we often engage on with the Chinese, are not part of the agenda', she said. 'But we pretty much know what they're going to say'. For that reason, according to Secretary Clinton, 'We have to continue to press them,' yet at the same time, she indicated 'But our pressing on those issues can't interfere with the global economic crisis, the global climate change crisis and the security crises. We have to have a dialogue that leads to an understanding and cooperation on each of those.'

Source: 'Clinton Softens Her Tone on China', *New York Times*, February 20, 2009.

Secretary or the Indian Minister of External Affairs, or they may be the heads of state or governments, such as the US President or the Canadian Prime Minister.

Diplomatic representatives from the five permanent members (P5) of the UN Security Council (China, France, Russia, the United Kingdom, and the United States) plus Germany have negotiated with representatives of the government of Iran in recent years on the latter's nuclear program. The P5 plus Germany have sought to persuade Iran that it should accept limitations on its nuclear activities since its past actions raise questions about its nuclear-weapons intentions. The Iranian representatives in turn have sought to persuade the P5 plus Germany that its nuclear activities are not directed toward the attainment of nuclear weapons, but instead are necessary for nuclear energy and medical research, and are in accord with Iran's rights and obligations as a signatory to the Nuclear Non-Proliferation Treaty (NPT). A diplomatic breakthrough occurred late in 2013, when Iran agreed to freeze temporarily much of its nuclear program and in exchange the P5 plus Germany agreed to grant Iran limited relief from international economic sanctions.

Diplomacy, then, is one instrument of persuasion in foreign policy. As the above example shows, economic incentives constitute another. Economic incentives are basically carrots: country A promises some economic gain to B, and delivers it if B does what A wants it to do. For example, West Germany extended very substantial economic aid to the Soviet Union to help facilitate Soviet acceptance in 1990 of the absorption of East Germany into West Germany (Newnham 2002). In the same vein, the European Union provided economic assistance to members such as Greece, Ireland, and Portugal to help those members meet their short-term funding requirements in the midst of the economic crisis that began in 2008, but on condition that they undertake internal reforms that will make them more competitive and self-supporting in the future.

Instruments of Coercion

Leaders sometimes find that diplomacy or incentives are not enough to cause another country to change its behavior. In those cases, leaders may turn to another class of foreign policy instruments, those that are designed to coerce a target government to act or stop from acting in some manner. One class of coercive policy instruments consists of economic sanctions (Hufbauer et al. 2007; Mastanduno 2011).

Economic sanctions are basically sticks: A threatens B with some form of economic loss if B does something A does not want it to do, or fails to do something A wants it to do. Such sanctions can include the imposition of tariffs or quotas on goods imported from a target country, the boycotting of purchases of particular goods from suppliers from the target country, or the seizure of financial assets owned by target-country residents that are held in the initiating country's banks or other financial institutions. In late 2011 and early 2012, the United States and member countries of the European Union began a boycott of purchases of oil from Iran, and a prohibition of financial transactions with Iran's central bank, in an effort to compel that country to negotiate an end to its efforts to build nuclear weapons. These actions were taken very seriously by the Iranian government: it raised the possibility that it might close the critically important Strait of Hormuz, through which passes approximately one-fifth of the world's oil exports (see Map 4.1). The United States responded that it would use military force to keep open the Strait of Hormuz – in other words, it would go to war with Iran. The deal the P5 plus Germany and Iran made in 2013 allowed the two

Economic incentive: An instrument of persuasion in foreign policy. Economic incentives are basically carrots: country A promises some economic gain to B, and delivers it if B does what A wants it to do.

Incentives: Rewards of some form offered by one state to another designed to influence the foreign policy of the recipient. Incentives are a form of persuasion.

Economic sanction: An instrument of coercion in foreign policy. Economic sanctions are basically sticks: A threatens B with some form of economic loss if B does something A does not want it to do, or fails to do something A wants it to do.

► **Map 4.1 Critical Waterway for Oil Exports: the Strait of Hormuz**

When in late 2011 and early 2012 the United States and its European allies sought to organize an oil embargo against Iran's oil exports, Iran threatened to retaliate by using naval forces to close the Strait of Hormuz, through which passes oil to world markets from such major producers as Kuwait and Saudi Arabia.

Covert operations: Activities that a government directs against the interests of another government or non-state actor in such a way that the foreign targets and others are kept from knowing that the initiating government is responsible for the activities.

Propaganda: The selective use of information, and at times misinformation, in order to advance a state's interests.

sides to scale back tensions. It also shows that yesterday's sticks (the initial imposition of economic sanctions) may be turned into today's carrots (the relaxation of those sanctions in exchange for some type of political concession).

Another class of coercive policy instruments involves covert operations and propaganda. Propaganda is the selective use of information, and at times misinformation, in order to advance a country's interests. Propaganda is frequently used as a tool to mobilize one's own population or to demoralize other populations in times of conflict or war. Nazi Germany, for example, relied on a Ministry of Public Enlightenment and Propaganda to produce documents and posters glorifying Germany's accomplishments and belittling its adversaries. During the Cold War, the United States used government-sponsored radio stations (Radio Liberty and Radio Free Europe) in an effort to influence the communist-controlled populations of the Soviet Union and Eastern Europe. Today, North Korea's autocratic government uses a steady stream of propaganda to keep its adversaries off balance, and to convince its deprived population that the more prosperous South Korea yearns to be 'purified' from capitalist influences and re-united with the communist North.

Covert operations are activities that a government directs against the interests of another government or non-state actor in such a way that the foreign targets and others are kept from knowing that the initiating government is responsible for the activities. In recent years Iran's government has provided covert support to anti-Israeli groups such as Hamas in Gaza and Hezbollah in southern Lebanon, and may have been providing logistical support to Shiite groups that had carried out lethal operations against US forces in Iraq. In May 2011, the United States killed Al Qaeda leader Osama bin Laden as the culmination of a covert operation in Pakistan, and did not inform the Pakistani government until after the actual raid against bin Laden's compound was completed, leading to a serious diplomatic rift between the two countries (Schmitt and Mazzetti 2011).

Similarly, the United States has used covert operations against Iran to try to cripple that country's nuclear program. In 2010 a highly destructive computer virus or 'worm'

◀ Map 4.2 Covert
Operation: the Killing
of Osama bin Laden

As a result of US covert
intelligence gathering,
including covert on-
site surveillance,
Osama bin Laden was
found to be living in a
large compound in the
Pakistani city of
Abbottabad. The com-
pound was attacked by
a US Navy SEAL team
early in the morning
on May 2, 2011, and
resulted in the killing
of bin Laden.

Source: US Department
of Defense image. (Use of
military imagery does not
imply or constitute
endorsement of Palgrave
Macmillan, its products,
or services by the US
Department of Defense.)

called Stuxnet was introduced into the computer systems that Iran was using to control important nuclear equipment, destroying much of it in the process. There are also signs that a country that does not want Iran to acquire nuclear weapons – it is probably Israel – has conducted covert operations in Iran that entail the assassination of Iranian nuclear scientists. Four Iranian scientists were killed in car bombings in the two years between January 2010 and January 2012, and Iran may have retaliated with covert bomb operations in February 2012 that sought to kill Israeli diplomats stationed in New Delhi, India, and Tbilisi, Georgia.

States may resort to coercive policy instruments involving differing degrees of military force. For example, a state sometimes may turn to **coercive diplomacy** – actions short of the immediate large-scale use of military force such as moving an aircraft carrier closer to the shores of another country to help convince it to rethink some behavior (Art and Cronin 2003). We noted in Chapter 1 that China and many of its neighbors have competing claims to the South China Sea and its potentially large undersea oil and gas reserves. On June 21, 2012 the parliament of Vietnam passed a bill that included an official reiteration of that country's claim of sovereignty over the two main island chains in that area, the Paracel Islands and the Spratly Islands. The Chinese escalated almost immediately to the non-violent use of military force. On June 28, China's government announced the undertaking of 'combat-ready patrols' in the areas claimed by Vietnam. On July 22, the Chinese government announced that Chinese military forces would establish a garrison at Yongxing Island (called Phu Lam Island by Vietnam), a 2.6-square-mile area of land where China maintains its main administrative outpost on the Paracel Islands (*The Economist* 2012). China used no actual military violence in response to the Vietnamese parliamentary action; however, it practiced coercive diplomacy by sending two non-violent military signals that it was preparing itself to use force to back its own territorial claims in the South China Sea.

Finally, the direct use of military force should also be considered a coercive foreign policy instrument. The German strategist Clausewitz famously stated that warfare is just the continuation of diplomacy by other means. After the 2001 terror attacks in New York and Washington, D C, the US government threatened the Taliban leaders in Afghanistan that they had to transfer Osama bin Laden and his aides to US custody, or

Coercive diplomacy:
Aggressive actions short of
the immediate large-scale
use of military force (such
as moving an aircraft
carrier closer to the shores
of another country)
designed to convince a
country to rethink some
behavior.

► **Photo 4.1 Chinese Administrative Facility, Paracel Islands, 2012**

In July 2012 China reinforced its claim over the South China Sea by establishing a military garrison at its administrative post in Yongxing Island (known in Vietnam as Phu Lam Island). Notice in this photo that China has already constructed an air facility that takes up a good proportion of the island.

Source: © Zha Chunming/Xinhua Press/Corbis.

the US would go to war with the Taliban. The Taliban continued to harbor bin Laden and his Al Qaeda fighters. During 2001 and 2002, the United States used a combination of covert operations, air strikes, and ground forces to help local Afghan factions topple the Taliban authorities, forcing Al Qaeda to retreat to the west of Pakistan. Since 2002, the United States has provided most of the military forces operating in Afghanistan and is trying to keep the Taliban and its Al Qaeda allies from retaking power in that country.

In short, states have many interests, and they can select from a range of strategies to promote or protect them. Where do these interests come from, and why do governments choose particular strategies to pursue them?

Levels of Analysis

The Practice of Foreign Policy

Individual	**International**
National leaders choose which interests to promote in foreign policy, and select strategies (goals and instruments) to advance those interests.	Given that they usually need the active cooperation of other states to achieve their interests, most states find it necessary to make some trade-offs with other states in the pursuit of their interests.
Individuals are often the target of foreign policy: these individuals may be leaders of foreign governments; key diplomatic, military, or scientific personnel; or non-state actors like terrorist leaders.	

The Sources of Foreign Policy

What are the sources of foreign policy, or more precisely, the sources of foreign policy interests and strategies? The levels-of-analysis framework can be helpful in addressing this question. As we noted in Chapter 1, levels of analysis are used in different ways by scholars. A well-known approach to using levels to illuminate foreign policy was developed by Graham Allison in the early 1970s (Allison and Zelikow 1999).

Allison and Zelikow use three models to understand the origins, conduct, and ending of the Cuban Missile Crisis. These models focus respectively on a nation-state as a single, cohesive actor, on the operating procedures of particular government departments, and on political bargaining among top decision makers. The cohesive nation-state model is situated at the international level of analysis; the government department model is situated at the state level of analysis; and the political bargaining model, which largely centers on individuals and their interactions, is situated at the individual level of analysis. Although Allison's models have become a standard way to use the levels of analysis to study foreign policy, his framework does not take into account dynamics that reside within a country's society, such as interest groups and public opinion, that might also influence foreign policy, and they do not examine factors that operate at the level of the personal history or psychology of decision makers. Therefore, in this chapter we take a somewhat different and more comprehensive approach, yet one that still relies on levels of analysis.

Sources of Foreign Policy at the Individual Level of Analysis

National leaders play a disproportionately large role in defining a country's foreign policy (Bueno de Mesquita et al. 2003; Chiozza and Goemans 2011). It is useful and important to understand the beliefs of national leaders about foreign policy, for those beliefs are likely to shape how leaders assess threats and opportunities in the international arena (Jervis 2006; Saunders 2009).

Where do national leaders get their beliefs about foreign policy? One possibility is that leaders have well-established personalities before they assume office. These personalities arise from a host of sources, including genetic make-up, childhood socialization, and early adulthood experiences. These personalities in turn may powerfully influence what leaders think about international affairs and foreign policy. For example, some analysts have suggested that Barack Obama's racial identity and early childhood experience living in Indonesia make him America's first 'global' president with particular sensitivity to multi-ethnic and multi-racial concerns at home and abroad (Sharma 2011). Below we discuss how the personality and experiences of Saddam Hussein may have prompted him to take great risks in deciding to lead Iraq to war in the 1980s and 1990s.

Leaders may also subscribe to particular beliefs as a result of their having experienced, witnessed, or perhaps learned about some attitude-shaping event in the international domain. Such events might not only influence the ideas of leaders, but perhaps those of many individuals in a particular generation, and even in subsequent generations. In the first Iraq war in 1990–91, President George H.W. Bush behaved in ways that suggested two major past events were influencing his beliefs: Munich and Vietnam. On the one hand, in his arguments for using military force to eject Iraq from Kuwait, he compared Saddam Hussein's aggression against its weaker neighbor to that of Adolph Hitler against Czechoslovakia. Yet, Bush ended the war abruptly – right after Iraqi forces were expelled from Kuwait but with Saddam still in power in Baghdad – in part because he believed, on the basis of the US experience in Vietnam, that the American public would not support a long and costly war (Record 2002).

The field of political psychology offers rich insights about foreign policy decision-making at the individual level of analysis. Some psychologists argue, for example, that leaders are 'cognitive misers' who, instead of making comprehensive analyses of costs and benefits, rely on simple mental short-cuts when making decisions (Fiske and Taylor 1984). Decision makers become cognitive misers to save time and effort when confronted with large amounts of information or when dealing with a series of issues under conditions of uncertainty. In the above example, President Bush may have been acting as a cognitive miser; his mental short-cut was to assume that the Iraq crisis was similar to other salient international crises and therefore required a certain type of response. Along similar lines, Russell Leng has argued that because India and Pakistan have engaged over time in a series of confrontations and wars with each other, Indian and Pakistani leaders have adopted the mental short-cut of assuming the worst possible motives of the other in subsequent conflicts of interest (Leng 2005). To break the cycle of conflict requires new leaders with different experiences, or existing leaders to avoid this short-cut and make different cognitive assumptions, including the willingness to view new situations from the perspective of their rivals.

Sources of Foreign Policy at the State Level of Analysis

Every country's foreign policy is likely to be influenced to some degree by the domestic political, social, and economic institutions and dynamics of that country. For the purposes of discussion, we can place these institutions and dynamics into two general categories: those that are situated largely within the national government of the country under review, and those that are situated largely within its national society. We take up each category in turn, highlighting which dynamics in one or another of the categories spills over and influences dynamics in the other.

Institutions and Politics within National Governments

It is useful initially to distinguish democratic from non-democratic (that is, authoritarian or autocratic) types of national governments. In general, the foreign policy processes in democratic governments are less centralized and more accessible to society than those processes in non-democratic governments. As Box 4.2 shows, Iraq's decision to go to war against an international coalition in 1990–91 was driven largely by the preferences and calculations of that country's autocratic leader, Saddam Hussein. By comparison, before initiating that war, the democratically elected leaders in Great Britain and the United States (Margaret Thatcher and George H.W. Bush respectively) felt it necessary to mobilize the support of their respective legislatures and general publics. They also took the trouble to mobilize an international coalition, in part to convince their domestic populations that there existed a widespread global consensus for military action.

Bureaucratic politics: A possible influence on a country's strategy characterized by national leaders and their subordinates engaging in foreign policy debates, building coalitions, and generally seeking to influence each other.

National leaders, both in democratic and autocratic regimes, do not make policy by themselves. Instead, they rely on officials in the executive branch of government (as opposed to the legislative or judicial branches), which consists of their immediate advisors, the heads of ministries or departments that are concerned with foreign affairs, and the professional staff of those ministries and departments. Leaders and their subordinates in a country's national government often engage in foreign policy debates, build coalitions, and generally seek to influence each other, and this **bureaucratic politics** can influence that country's interests and strategic choices.

This foreign policy process will look different across different countries. Compare, for example, the United States and China. In the United States, the parts of the executive branch that are chiefly concerned with foreign policy include the Departments of State and Defense, the Central Intelligence Agency, the Joint Chiefs of Staff on military matters and, on foreign economic matters, the Departments of Commerce and Treasury. To assist them in coordinating this large machinery of government, presidents since the late 1940s have had a National Security Advisor. At moments of major decision, the President, the National Security Advisor, and the heads of the departments most directly concerned meet as the National Security Council (NSC). The National Security Advisor and a staff of experts coordinate the activities of different

In 1990 Iraq occupied its small, oil-rich neighbor Kuwait. An international coalition, led by the United States and Great Britain, formed to oust Iraq from Kuwait, first by imposing economic sanctions, and second by setting a deadline for Saddam Hussein to withdraw from Kuwait or face a devastating military attack. The coalition was far superior militarily and made strong efforts to convince Iraq that it would attack if Iraq did not retreat. Yet, Saddam Hussein refused to back down, ended up in a lopsided war and suffered a significant military defeat. How might we explain this puzzling Iraqi foreign policy choice? We cannot know for sure, but there are a number of plausible arguments from different analytical perspectives (Gause 2001).

Saddam's Personality

Leaders always matter in decisions to go to war, particularly so in non-democratic countries where political power is heavily concentrated in the hands of one or a few individuals. Saddam Hussein was ambitious and paranoid, had a proclivity towards violence, and was willing to take risks. Saddam ordered Iraq to invade a more powerful Iran in 1980, hoping to exploit Iran's revolutionary instability and gain advantage over its traditional adversary. That risky war ended as a bloody stalemate eight years later. Saddam also appeared to believe that international actors were continually conspiring against him. He perceived neighbors such as Saudi Arabia and Kuwait conspiring to squeeze Iraq economically, and others such as Israel and America conspiring to undermine his power at home.

Misperception and 'Groupthink'

Saddam may have believed that the coalition, and in particular the United States, would not carry through on their threat to attack. Saddam seemed influenced by the US experience in Lebanon in 1983. When a car bomb struck the US embassy and killed over 200 Marines, the Reagan administration pulled its peacekeeping force out of Lebanon. On the eve of the 1991 war, Saddam in effect told US Ambassador April Glaspie that the United States did not have the stomach for war because it was unwilling to suffer large numbers of casualties.

What about other Iraqi leaders, in particular the small group of Ba'ath Party officials that advised Saddam Hussein? Some appear to have worried that Iraq was about to suffer a big defeat given the forces arrayed against it. But, they were generally reluctant to disagree with Saddam or share with him views or information contrary to his preferred course of action. Saddam was intolerant of dissent; when he took power in 1979, he summarily executed two dozen Ba'ath Party leaders who had opposed his rise to power. He surrounded himself with like-minded individuals who, even if inclined to disagree, knew better than to do so.

National Economic Distress

The war with Iran exhausted Iraq financially. Iraq demanded 'contributions' from other Gulf states to finance its war effort. When the war ended and the money stopped flowing, Iraq was in severe economic distress. It needed oil prices to remain high to earn hard currency for economic recovery. Saddam believed Kuwait was overproducing oil and driving down the global price. But by taking over Kuwait he could control Kuwaiti oil supply and keep the global price higher. From this perspective, once Saddam had Kuwait he could not afford to give it up, and therefore he was willing to try to 'ride out' a coalition attack rather than back down.

Geopolitical Opportunism

Iraq under Saddam Hussein fashioned itself as a regional power and the leader of the Arab world. Saddam attacked Iran because its new fundamentalist Shiite regime (Iraq's Ba'ath Party leaders were Sunni Muslims) had aspired to dominate the region. He threatened the Arab world's common enemy, Israel. By taking Kuwait, he hoped to signal the Arab countries (especially Saudi Arabia) that Iraq was the regional leader and they should accommodate its wishes. By standing up to the United States and international coalition, even if he lost a war, Saddam may have believed that Iraq's prestige would be enhanced on the 'Arab street'.

Students should recognize the operation of the levels of analysis in the differing perspectives described above. Arguments for Iraq's seemingly puzzling decision to go to war range across individual, state, and international levels. Some explanations view Iraq as a rational actor making cost–benefit calculations, while others see non-rational personal characteristics and group dynamics driving the decision.

parts of the government on security and foreign policy matters.

At each point in this policy process, advisors and subordinates may or may not fully share the beliefs of the President about what the country should do abroad. If they do share those beliefs, they may differ about how best to act to advance US interests, or they may agree about goals but disagree about what their particular department or agency ought to be tasked with doing to contribute to the American effort on a given issue. These differences in views occur in part because of the different life experiences officials may bring to their job, or because of differences in the interests of their respective organizations. An often-heard phrase in Washington is, 'Where you stand depends on where you sit.' In other words, if an official sits in the State Department he or she might give special emphasis to good diplomatic relations with other countries; if that same person were to sit in the Defense Department he or she might be more concerned about whether those countries can serve as a base for US forward military operations.

On looking forward to leaving office in 1952, President Harry Truman thought that General Dwight D. Eisenhower, if he were elected President, would incorrectly believe that executing the duties of that office was more or less the same as being a military commander. Truman said of Eisenhower, who had been a brilliant Supreme Commander of Allied Forces during World War II, that if he were to win the presidency, 'He'll sit here [the president's desk] and he'll say, "Do this! Do that!" And nothing will happen. Poor Ike – it won't be a bit like the Army. He'll find it very frustrating' (Neustadt, 1976).

The President is the key actor in the US foreign policy process. But the big executive bureaucracies play key roles as well and, as Photo 4.2 suggests, sometimes require the President to step in and resolve difficult inter-agency disputes. Unless the President is skilled in managing institutional and bureaucratic political maneuverings, he or she may inadvertently relinquish foreign policy leadership.

In China, political power over foreign policy is more concentrated. The key decision makers are found in the Politburo Standing Committee, China's top executive ruling body. Recently there have been important power transitions every decade or so, which happen behind closed doors and without voting or input from the mass public. China is a one-party state, but different factions within the Communist Party and especially within the elite Politburo compete for power generally and over China's foreign policy in particular. In recent decades 'reformers,' or top leaders who value

▲ **Photo 4.2 A Difficult Partnership**

Secretary Rumsfeld and National Security Advisor Condoleezza Rice often had sharp disagreements. Rice became Secretary of State in January 2005; Rumsfeld was fired by President Bush in November 2006.

Source: PA Images.

Name	Age	Confirmed and designated leadership post	Factional Background
Xi Jinping	59	Party Secretary General, Chairman of the Central Military Commission, PRC President	Princeling
Li Keqiang	57	Premier of the State Council	Tuanpai
Zhang Dejiang	66	Chairman of the National People's Congress (NPC)	Princeling
Yu Zhengsheng	67	Chairman of the Chinese People's Political Consultative Conference (CPPCC)	Princeling
Liu Yunshan	65	PRC Vice President, Executive Secretary of the Secretariat	Tuanpai (also close tie with Jiang)
Wang Qishan	64	Secretary of the Central Commission for Discipline Inspection (CCDI)	Princeling
Zhang Gaoli	66	Executive Vice Premier of the State Council	Jiang's protégé

◀ Table 4.1 China's New Top Leaders: The Politburo Standing Committee, 2012

Source: Cheng Li, Brookings Institution.

closer ties with Western countries and deeper Chinese integration into the world economy, have competed with 'conservatives' who place more emphasis on the state-run part of China's economy and who would prefer to see China act more assertively in East Asia and perhaps even globally. Some scholars make different factional distinctions, between 'generalists' who try to maintain initiative in the Chinese provinces and 'technocrats' seeking to maintain control in Beijing (Shih 2008).

An important political transition took place in China in 2012 (Li, 2012). The previous Communist Party Secretary General, Hu Jintao (in charge since 2002) handed power to a new leader, Xi Jinping. Xi is a 'princeling', or part of a faction of Chinese leaders who come from families of veteran revolutionaries (that is, the communist founding fathers) or other high-ranking officials, and are closely associated with a former Chinese leader Jiang Zemin. Another faction, known as *taunpai* includes leaders who build their careers by rising through the ranks of the Communist Party, usually starting from a young age. Professional China watchers note carefully the balance of power among these competing factions; in the 2012 transition princelings seemed to dominate, especially in the Politburo Standing Committee (see Table 4.1). Given the foreign policy preferences of princelings, this suggests, for example, that China will seek better relations with the United States and the West, and accelerate economic liberalization, all while seeking to avoid political liberalization and greater freedom for Chinese people domestically.

Dynamics between Executives and Legislatures

In democracies, executive-branch leaders must usually obtain cooperation, approval, or at least consent from the legislative branch for their foreign policies. This is true in parliamentary systems, such as that of Great Britain, in which the leader of the executive branch (the Prime Minister) and members of his or her cabinet are drawn directly from the elected legislative branch (the parliament). It is also true in presidential systems, in which the executive branch leader – for example, the Chancellor in Germany or the President in the United States – is elected independently of the legislature and appoints his or her own cabinet.

For example, the American political system presents important opportunities for the Congress to constrain the executive branch in foreign policy. The US Constitution stipulates that the President possesses the sole authority to negotiate any treaty with a foreign government, but the Constitution also mandates that any such treaty comes into force if and only if the US Senate ratifies the treaty by a two-thirds majority vote.

As we noted in Chapter 2, the significance of the Senate's treaty ratification power was evident in 1919–20 when the Senate refused to ratify the Versailles Treaty, frustrating President Woodrow Wilson's effort to engage the United States fully in the reconstruction of European security after World War I. President Jimmy Carter was thwarted in 1979 when the Senate refused to ratify the SALT II arms control treaty his administration negotiated with the Soviet Union, and in the late 1990s President Bill Clinton quietly gave up his efforts to get the Senate to ratify the Comprehensive Test Ban Treaty that his administration signed in 1996. As Box 4.3 shows, although different presidents approach Congress differently, it is impossible in the US system to ignore the role of Congress in foreign policy.

The need for executive leaders to engage politically and gain the support of the legislative branch is true, in varying degrees, across democracies. In 2013, British Prime Minister David Cameron preferred military action against Syria after there were claims that the Syrian regime used chemical weapons against rebel groups fighting for control of the Syrian capital, Damascus. However, the British parliament refused to go along and voted not to authorize Britain's use of force. British Members of Parliament, perhaps reflecting the unease of the British public, felt that the risks of getting involved in another Middle East war outweighed the sense of moral outrage directed at Syria's leader for using chemical weapons (*Guardian* 2013). Britain's response to Syria was being coordinated with that of the United States; after the British vote US President Barack Obama decided to step back and request formal approval from the US Congress before committing US military forces. Autocratic leaders, such as Syria's Bashar al-Assad, who was accused of using chemical weapons against the Syrian rebels, typically do not face similar types of domestic political constraints.

National Politics and Societal Actors

To this point, we have been focusing on political dynamics within governments as a source of foreign policy. Equally if not more important as a source of foreign policy are politics within a country as a whole (Snyder 1991). We explore below three particularly powerful classes of national political dynamics, and societal actors within countries, that influence foreign policy: public opinion and elections, the media, and interest groups.

Public Opinion and Elections

Public opinion and elections can play an important role in shaping foreign policy (Holsti 2004). The case of Syria, discussed above, is instructive. A survey conducted by the German Marshall Fund found that 72 percent of Europeans preferred that the European Union stay completely out of Syria's ongoing civil war. A majority of Americans – 62 percent – expressed a similar view of the role their government should play. In light of this clear public sentiment, it is not surprising that both European and American governments proved reluctant to intervene. That same survey revealed a more general difference between Europeans and Americans that both reinforces and

Romney–Obama Presidential Debate on Foreign Policy, October 22, 2012

Foreign policy is an important element of presidential elections. During the 2012 election the last of three debates between President Barack Obama and Governor Mitt Romney, held on October 22, was devoted solely to foreign policy. President Obama, right, and Republican Romney discuss a point during the third presidential debate at Lynn University, in Boca Raton, Florida.

Source: PA Images.

is reflected in the conduct of their respective approaches to foreign policy: 68 percent of Americans, but only 31 percent of Europeans, agreed with the statement that war is sometimes necessary to obtain justice (German Marshall Fund 2013: 6).

Scholars have demonstrated very clearly that US citizens vote on the basis not just of their views on domestic issues, but on foreign policy as well (Hurwitz and Peffley 1987). It is for this reason that presidential candidates spend significant time on foreign policy, and debate the subject. Moreover, there is good evidence that US presidents try to accommodate American public opinion on foreign policy issues. For example, a recent study demonstrates that presidents from Lyndon Johnson to Bill Clinton were aware of public opinion on foreign policy matters, and that when it came to that issue area, presidents 'follow[ed] the polls for both governing and electoral purposes' (Sobel 2001: 238–9).

An important line of research on the matter of public opinion and foreign policy concerns the conditions under which public opinion is likely to turn against a war once hostilities have commenced. A long-standing thesis on this subject is that a democratic public will inexorably turn against a policy action that includes the use of force in direct proportion to the number of casualties (Mueller 1973). The Vietnam War, which the US public initially supported but gradually turned against, appears to support this thesis. A more recent alternative view is that the public does not necessarily turn against a war as casualties mount. Instead, according to this line of analysis, how the public assesses a war that entails growing casualties depends upon how that war is going: if the public believes that the country is winning, then it will support military operations notwithstanding battlefield casualties. World War II is a clear example of how the US public continued to support a war effort in spite of very high US battlefield casualties. It is the persistence of casualties and a loss in confidence that victory is likely, as occurred in Vietnam, which causes public opinion to turn against continuation of the war (Gelpi *et al.* 2009).

The relationship between national leaders and public opinion in the context of war is complex and multi-dimensional. War and, more generally, external conflicts often boost the popularity of a leader. This phenomenon is often termed the **rally 'round the flag effect**. Fidel Castro of Cuba became a more popular leader at home after the ill-fated Bay of Pigs invasion of 1961 because he was perceived as having stood up for Cuba against external aggression sponsored by the more powerful United States. President George H. W. Bush enjoyed a spike in his approval ratings in 1991 after the United States and its allies expelled Saddam Hussein's forces from Kuwait, although

Rally 'round the flag effect: A commonly observed boost in the popularity of a leader due to external conflicts or war.

that boost in approval did not carry over to the 1992 presidential election, when Bush was defeated by Bill Clinton in large part because of a lackluster US domestic economy. We noted above that a US covert operation killed Osama bin Laden in early May 2011: in the immediate aftermath President Barack Obama's overall job approval jumped 11 percentage points, from 46 to 57 percent (Dao and Sussman 2011). Not surprisingly, scholars and commentators sometimes suspect that political leaders fabricate or embellish external threats precisely to instigate a rally 'round the flag effect, and to deflect attention from other political problems.

The News Media and Foreign Policy

The foreign affairs media are those individuals and organizations who report or comment on foreign developments in print, on television, over radio, and through the internet. For example, reporters play a key role in providing information about world events, often at great risk to themselves, and particularly when they operate in war zones (see Photo 4.4). However, the news media not only provides information; scholars have found that news media participants – reporters, commentators, and editors – can indirectly influence national leaders as they grapple with foreign policy problems. The mechanism by which this influence is exercised is termed framing. Framing is the process by which media participants select or present particular elements of a news story in such a way as to influence the opinions of recipients of the story (Entman 2004). The way the media frames a story can help shape public opinion on particular foreign policy matters; the choices media participants make about framing a particular issue can affect the degree of freedom political leaders have in positing interests and designing strategies.

A recent study systematically explored the degree to which media framing of a foreign policy matter can influence the recipients of such reporting (Berinsky and Kinder 2006). In an experiment carried out in two phases in the years 2000 and 2002, scholars recruited volunteers, divided them into three groups, and presented each group with slightly different sets of news stories about Serbian forces' brutal attacks in 1999 against civilian residents in the province of Kosovo, which ended with a NATO air strike campaign to stop the Serbian attacks. Volunteers in one group (the *control* group) were given news reports about the Serbia–Kosovo conflict that were, to the extent possible, devoid of a political slant. Individuals in the second group (what the research team termed the *humanitarian* group) were given reports that were largely the same as the straight news reports, but had been slightly adjusted to highlight the atrocities that the Serbs had been committing against the Kosovo residents. Members of the third group (what the team called the *risk to America* group) were given reports that highlighted the risks that American air force personnel could encounter in undertaking air attacks against Serbia. The research team found that, compared to the straight-news group and the risk-to-America group, those in the humanitarian group remembered more facts about the Kosovo case that related to Serbian atrocities and, looking back, they were more likely than individuals in the other two groups to say that the US decision to intervene against Serbia was the right thing to do. Even quite small differences across the groups in how the Serbia–Kosovo story was framed led to significant differences in what individuals in the different groups remembered about the issues at stake and how they assessed the wisdom of the air campaign against Serbia.

The media play a larger role in democratic countries than in autocratic countries, where the media typically face restrictions imposed by the central government, or are expected to report and frame stories in a manner favorable to the central leaders. Technological changes, however, are making it more challenging even for autocratic governments to control the media. In China, for example, 'online public opinion' has become a new social force that is beginning to influence foreign policy. The Chinese Ministry of Foreign Affairs has become more sensitive to public sentiments because it recognizes how much and what types of international information ordinary Chinese people can obtain over the internet (Junhao 2005; Xin-An 2005). Although Chinese leaders still closely monitor and restrict internet coverage of foreign affairs, the government's monopoly of media control is gradually breaking down.

Interest Groups

An interest group consists of individuals or organizations that share a common set of political concerns. They band together in an association, which may be more or less institutionalized, and work through that association to persuade leaders and the public to pursue, support, or accept policies that are in accord with the preferences of the association. Interest groups can be found in virtually every country and type of political system. They tend to be most prominent in democracies in which freedom of expression and the right to organize are protected by law. In advanced democratic nations, business, ethnic-religious, humanitarian, and environmentalist groups have long been active in seeking to influence foreign policy (Mearsheimer and Walt 2007).

Interest groups usually organize according to issue; particular groups wish to influence, for instance, their government's trade policies, environmental policies, or overall policies toward a particular country. In France and Japan, politically connected farmers work effectively to influence their country's position in regional and global trade negotiations. In the United States, Jewish and Arab lobby groups try to influence US policy toward Israel and the Middle East. In many cases the preferences of interest groups are sensitive to geographic location. In China, corporations that operate in coastal areas, where factories assemble goods for export, are more supportive of China's integration in the world economy, while state-run enterprises that reside in China's interior and produce (inefficiently) goods for the local market are more skeptical of global integration. In Russia, the largest private energy companies (such as

Interest group: Individuals or organizations that share a common set of political concerns and band together in an association to persuade leaders and the public to pursue, support, or accept policies that are in accord with the preferences of the association.

Presidents Woodrow Wilson, Harry Truman, and Barack Obama on Working with Congress on Foreign Policy

Over time, American Presidents have gained more and more decision-making power, relative to Congress, in the conduct of foreign policy. However Presidents must still enlist the cooperation of Congress in order to carry out foreign policy effectively. This is as true today as it was one hundred years ago. Presidents who choose to ignore or disdain Congress sometimes pay a heavy price, as the experience of Woodrow Wilson demonstrates. Presidents who commit to cooperation with Congress will often reap foreign policy benefits, as the early presidential experience of Harry Truman demonstrated. When Presidents and Congress find themselves in confrontation, it is difficult to get very much done in domestic or foreign policy, as Barack Obama found.

Then: *President Woodrow Wilson, 1919*

In July 1919, President Wilson submitted to the US Senate the Treaty of Versailles and the Covenant for the League of Nations. Several senators who favored ratification wanted to add reservations that would limit US obligations under the Covenant to protect other League members in the event they were attacked.

Asked if he would accept such Senate-imposed reservations on the Covenant, President Wilson said, 'Anyone who opposes me in that, I'll crush.' The Senate ultimately refused to support Wilson's ambitious initiative, leaving him incapable of carrying out the US commitment to the League.

Source: Thomas G. Paterson, J. Garry Clifford, Shane J. Maddock, Deborah Kisatsky, and Kenneth J. Hagan (2006) *American Foreign Relations, Volume I: to 1920* (Boston: Houghton Mifflin), p. 208.

Then: *President Harry Truman, 1946*

In a statement made before White House correspondents in November 1946, President Truman made it clear that he would continue his predecessor's efforts to work with the Congress, including members in the Republican Party, on matters relating to foreign policy.

Lukoil) are locked into West European energy markets; despite China's rise, and with the exception of arms exporters, no strong 'Asia lobby' is yet evident in Russian foreign economic policy (Rutland 2006). In light of China's ongoing demand for raw materials, it would not be surprising for such a lobby to emerge among powerful private actors in Russia's mineral-rich region of Siberia.

Since its independence in 1991, Ukraine's foreign policy has balanced between tilting toward Russia and edging closer to the European Union. Western and central Ukraine is home to Ukrainian-speaking Catholics who see their interests served by connecting with the West. In eastern and southern regions are a majority of Russian speakers and followers of the pro-Russian Orthodox Church, who more naturally lobby for their government to orient its foreign policy toward Moscow (Krushelnysky 2013). In 2013, Ukraine's President, Viktor Yanukovich, pivoted decisively towards Russia by accepting Russian leader Vladimir Putin's multi-billion dollar offer to bail out Ukraine's struggling economy. At the same time, Yanukovich turned away from Ukraine's planned economic partnership with the European Union. Pro-Western Ukrainians rose up in protest, taking to the streets, occupying local and regional gov-

Truman said at that time: 'I shall cooperate in every proper manner with members of the Congress, and my hope and prayer is that this spirit of cooperation will be reciprocated.' Truman faced a Congress generally reluctant to engage the United States deeply in European affairs after the war. Yet he managed to cultivate sufficient Congressional support for his signature foreign policy initiatives, the NATO alliance and the European Recovery Program (commonly known as the Marshall Plan).

Source: 'Statement by President Truman to White House Correspondents', November 11, 1946, in Henry Steele Commager (ed.) (1949) *Documents of American History*, fifth edition (New York: Appleton-Century-Crofts), p. 718.

Now: *President Barack Obama, 2013*

Obama faced widespread Republican opposition to his legislative agenda during his first term (2009–12) and into his second. He and his Congressional adversaries proved unwilling or incapable of finding sufficient common ground to move policies forward. The result was a shutdown of the government due to the failure of the two sides to reach a budget compromise, and a lack of significant legislative achievement with the exception of Obama's controversial health care reform initiative which he managed to force through Congress only because his party held a majority in both houses during his first two years in office. In foreign policy, Congressional opponents sought to stymie Obama whenever possible, for example in his handling of an attack on the US consulate in Benghazi, Libya in 2012, and by opposing his 2013 diplomatic opening to Iran and lobbying for a tightening rather than a relaxation of economic sanctions against Iran.

On the morning that the US government reopened after having been shut down, Obama expressed his frustration directly to his Congressional opponents:

> You don't like a particular policy or a particular President? Then argue for your position. Go out and win an election. Don't break what our predecessors spent over two centuries building. That's not being faithful to what this country is about.'

Source: Leigh Ann Caldwell, 'Obama may have won now, but next three years could be tough', CNN, October 18, 2013.

ernment buildings, and declaring their loyalty to a People's Council set up by the political opponents of Yanukovich. Early in 2014, Yanukovich was chased from office, and Russian President Vladimir Putin intervened and eventually annexed Crimea, which is part of Ukraine, setting off an international crisis between Russia and the West.

Interest groups use a variety of means to try to influence national leaders and the public. In democratic states, interest groups publish or fund the publication of policy papers, purchase advertisements in major newspapers and other media, organize letter-writing campaigns to political representatives, and undertake lobbying, or personally meeting and speaking with members of legislatures and officials in executive departments. Interest groups also contribute to political candidates and political parties, or organize political fundraisers. As the Ukraine example above shows, some interest groups organize protests and demonstrations in major cities around their country in order to attract media attention to their concerns.

While we know that interest groups have sought to shape the foreign policies of most countries, foreign policy studies are only beginning to produce systematic research on how much influence such groups actually have on foreign policy-making.

Lobbying: Meeting and speaking with members of legislatures and officials in executive departments in an attempt to influence policy. Interest groups often engage in lobbying.

One challenge is that while we can observe instances in which interest groups have tried to influence leaders and officials responsible for foreign policy, it is difficult to know if they have been successful even if the government does what the groups have called for. For example, looking at some US policy decisions relating to trade with China or arms sales to Israel, we may know that one or more interest groups pressed for the United States to act in a particular manner on those issues, and we may also know that government leaders took the stance on these issues that matched the position the interest group or groups had been advocating. However, what we do not know is whether the leaders took the stance they did because of the interest groups, or if they would have taken the stance even if the groups had not been active. Scholars try to set up research strategies that allow them to isolate the preferences of interest groups and the impact of interest group activity on foreign policy. A nice example of this type of comparative foreign policy research is described in Box 4.4.

Sources of Foreign Policy at the International Level of Analysis

At least three factors that are situated at the international level of analysis may shape how a country's leaders define that country's interests and strategies: the country's geography, its relative economic development, and its overall relative capabilities, or power.

Geography

A country's geographic characteristics, combined with its demographics, are likely to influence how its leaders think about interests and strategy. During the nineteenth century Great Britain, separated from the great powers of Europe by the English Channel, developed its naval power and expanded its influence overseas while seeking to maintain a balance of power among the European states on the continent. Similarly, from the 1780s to the 1930s, many people in the United States believed that the country could remain free of European entanglements because it was separated from the Old World by the Atlantic Ocean. Mexican and Canadian leaders have also believed that geography matters. One of Mexico's longest-ruling autocratic leaders of the late nineteenth and early twentieth century, Porfirio Diaz, is reported to have said, 'Alas, poor Mexico! So far from God and so close to the United States!' In the same vein, Canada's Prime Minister Pierre Trudeau told an American audience at the National Press Club in Washington that 'Living next to you is in some ways like sleeping with an elephant. No matter how friendly and even-tempered is the beast, if I can call it that, one is affected by every twitch and grunt' (Canadian Broadcasting Company 1969).

A country's immediate neighborhood helps to shape its foreign policy. Israel's simultaneously defensive and aggressive foreign policy is influenced by the fact that Israel lives in close proximity to countries it has long seen as adversaries. India borders its traditional rivals, China and Pakistan; much of its foreign policy is pre-occupied with managing those relations. Germany's size and prominence in the center of Europe has long been a source of anxiety, and at times opportunity, for its smaller neighbors such as Poland. The United States is concerned by North Korea's behavior, but the stakes are arguably larger for China, which borders North Korea and worries that a collapse of that country would lead to large refugee flows into China.

Relative Level of Economic Development

A country's relative economic wealth, and the sources of that wealth, can influence how the country defines its interests and strategies. Historically, countries with the largest and most dynamic economies have had opportunities to translate their wealth

The Influence of Bankers on Foreign Policy across Countries

Theory

Marxists believe banks have significant influence over the decisions of governments to go to war. As we discussed in Chapter 1, Lenin's theory of imperialism, for example, expected big banks, or finance capital, in Western countries to press their governments to adopt aggressive foreign policies in order to obtain access to new markets. Lenin believed governments would comply in order to serve the interests of powerful economic actors.

Practice

Recent research suggests this theoretical approach may be off the mark. Jonathan Kirshner shows that bankers do have significant influence on foreign policy, though not always on the critical decision to go to war. More importantly, the preferences of bankers differ from what Marxists expect (Kirshner 2007). In a study of bankers in different countries across different time periods, Kirshner finds that bankers consistently prefer peace to war. Financial actors, whether in France in the 1920s, Japan in the 1930s, America in the 1890s, or Britain in the 1980s, are interested in economic stability above everything else. A stable economic environment is the best for profit-making, and war is disruptive to economic stability. Kirshner shows, for example, that British bankers failed to support their natural ally, Conservative Prime Minister Margaret Thatcher, during the Falklands crisis of 1981–82 in which Thatcher took Great Britain to war against Argentina. During the 1930s, Japanese financial interests opposed the aggressive turn in foreign policy which led Japan to occupy China in 1931 and again in 1937. Japanese bankers preferred a more cautious foreign policy, but were overwhelmed by the Japanese military which took control of the state and moved foreign policy in a more belligerent direction.

into military power and exert considerable influence in global affairs. This was true of Great Britain and eventually Germany in the nineteenth century, and the United States during the twentieth century. The rise of China in the early twenty-first century is a direct function of its rapid economic growth. A country's relative level of wealth and prosperity also affects how it views specific foreign policy issues. For example, many European countries, in possession of mature, developed economies, place a high priority on environmental protection. In sharp contrast, leaders in countries with industries that are only now reaching world-class competitiveness, such as India, Brazil, and especially China, do not believe that their countries are yet able to afford stronger environmental or worker standards, and these leaders have set as an interest the prevention of the imposition of stricter standards.

Relative National Capabilities

A country's relative capabilities are likely to condition both its interests and its selection of goals and policy instruments. A country's relative capabilities determine its international influence, its positive ability to cause others to act in ways it prefers, and its negative ability to resist the efforts of other countries to induce it to do things it would rather not do. A country's relative capabilities are a function of many factors: its demography (including population size but also the balance between young and old, working-age and retired); territorial expanse and such natural resources (if exploited wisely) as arable land, oil, and economically important minerals; literacy as well as scientific and technological sophistication; and the degree to which governing institutions are effective and enable leaders to convert national economic resources into military power and political influence (Mearsheimer 2001 and Waltz 1979).

Leaders of especially powerful countries often believe that, in the absence of an effective international government, they have a special responsibility to contribute to the existing international order (Gilpin 1975; Ikenberry 2001). In these circumstances foreign policy may be significantly influenced by a country's relative position in the international system. When war breaks out in central Africa, it is of great concern to Africans. When Serbs and Bosnians fight, it is of great concern to neighboring Europeans. But these situations are also of special interest to far away powerful states who believe, for better or worse, that they share responsibility for managing regional crises and assuring global order.

We have to this point explored what a foreign policy looks like and from what sources it emerges. We now may turn to the chapter's final question: why do states sometimes *change* their foreign policy?

Levels of Analysis *Sources of Foreign Policy*	👤 **Individual**	👥 **State**	🌐 **International**
	A national leader's beliefs, which are likely to be shaped by his or her personality, formative political experiences, and motivated biases, play a large role in influencing that leader's approach to foreign policy.	Within a government, institutional and bureaucratic politics, as well as relations between different branches such as the executive and legislative in democratic systems, influence foreign policy.	Several international-level factors can influence both the foreign-policy interests and strategies of a country, including its geography, relative economic development, and relative overall power.
	Once a leader has made a foreign policy decision, cognitive dynamics may constrain his or her ability to change course in the face of new information.	Within a country, dynamics that largely take place within its society, including elections, public opinion, the news media, and interest groups, substantially shape its foreign policy.	

How and Why States Change Their Foreign Policy

We will organize our investigation of the sources of change in foreign policy with the aid of the levels-of-analysis framework, beginning with the individual, then focusing on domestic features of states, and ending with the international level of analysis.

Sources of Foreign Policy Change at the Individual Level of Analysis

At least two mechanisms that operate at the individual level of analysis have the capacity to bring about substantial changes in foreign policy. The first mechanism is that of learning by national leaders in such a way that they make significant shifts in foreign policy; the second is the sometimes dramatic impact of changes in leadership on foreign policy.

Leadership Learning and Changes in Foreign Policy

In accord with the expectations of constructivists that we discussed in Chapter 3, national leaders, as a result of their own foreign policy experiences or those of their predecessors, sometimes change their understanding of world politics or the particular circumstances of their country in the international system. Such learning can bring about significant changes in the way leaders define interests or what they consider to be the best strategies to promote them (Levy 1994).

For example, prior to the Great Depression, government leaders in the United States, Canada, Britain, Germany, and other industrialized countries mostly subscribed to *laissez-faire* economic ideas; governments should not interfere with market dynamics either at home or in the international sphere. As we saw in Chapter 2, at the outset of the Great Depression, those leaders had few international cooperative mechanisms available to them to deal with the collapse in national demand they were all experiencing, which in turn prompted them to turn to beggar-thy-neighbor prohibitive tariffs on imports or prohibitions on the inflow or outflow of capital. Since the Great Depression, government leaders in the United States, Canada, and Europe have largely believed that government should allow for the free operation of markets at home and overseas, *but* there is room for government intervention both through national monetary and fiscal policies and by way of international governmental coordination (as we will see in Chapter 8, through such entities as the International Monetary Fund and the Group of 20) to mitigate the kind of shocks that we have seen in the world economy during the crisis of 2008–13. The economic beliefs of leaders changed, and major changes in domestic and foreign economic policies were the result (Frieden 2006).

Similarly, an important line of recent research has shown that learning in the face of policy failure adds a key element to our understanding of why the United States switched from neutrality to internationalism at the close of World War II (Legro 2000). In particular, President Franklin Roosevelt reflected on President Wilson's failure to obtain America's entry into the League of Nations, and the United States' subsequent shift to a policy of political isolationism during the 1920s and 1930s, and learned that these failures enabled Nazi Germany, Fascist Italy, and Imperial Japan to pursue aggression. That aggression ultimately directly threatened America's security, Roosevelt thought, and that threat could have been averted or halted at lower cost had the United States been more active in world security matters and, in collaboration with other powerful states in a collective security organization, confronted the aggressors.

Roosevelt inferred that, to pursue its interest in security, the United States had to shift from a strategy of neutrality to one of internationalism, a strategy in which the US would be fully engaged with other states through institutionalized arrangements directed at maintaining world security and promoting global economic prosperity. The American strategy of neutrality during the 1930s clearly failed to keep the United States secure, and made Roosevelt's case for internationalism more credible in the US political system.

Over time, a given leader may change ideas about his or her country's interests or strategy. For example, Soviet leader Mikhail Gorbachev appears to have fundamentally changed his ideas about Soviet foreign policy from the time he took power in 1985 to the period during which he took steps that decisively ended the Cold War in 1988 (English 2005). At first, Gorbachev appears largely to have accepted the traditional Marxist ideas we discussed in Chapter 3: world politics is basically a continuation of domestic class struggles, the Soviet Union and the United States possessed fundamental conflicts of interest, and core Soviet interests in security could only be advanced by a strategy that included political dominance in Eastern Europe and, as

Isolationism: A strategy in which a state avoids or minimizes engaging with other states through any sort of international institutions or agreements and focuses solely on itself and its domestic politics.

Internationalism: A strategy in which a state is fully engaged with other states through institutionalized arrangements directed at maintaining world security and promoting global economic prosperity.

much as possible, military superiority over Western Europe. By 1988, however, Gorbachev radically shifted his foreign policy perspective to what was termed *new thinking* about Soviet foreign policy. Gone from Gorbachev's rhetoric and actions were global class struggle, permanent struggle with the United States, and the need for pro-Soviet regimes in Eastern Europe. He replaced these with an emphasis on shared interests with the West and acceptance of greater freedom of political choice in Eastern Europe.

Leaders' experiences with officials from other countries may change those leaders' beliefs about their own country's situation and strategic options. The experiences of leaders and policy officials in international institutions might also affect their perceptions and values. For example, Gorbachev moved to his *new thinking* stance on Soviet interests and the benefits of cooperation with Western countries as he interacted with decision makers from those countries, especially US Secretary of State George Shultz (Stein 1994). In the same vein, Chinese officials, as a result of participating in regular talks during the mid-1990s that included several East and Southeast countries, as well as the United States, appear to have moved from skepticism to support for the idea that regional dialogue is an effective mechanism by which China can reassure neighbors of its peaceful intentions (Johnston 2008).

The cases of Roosevelt, Gorbachev, and the recent leaders of China may leave us with the idea that policy makers typically learn what, from the viewpoint of a country's interests, are the *right* lessons from history, and then make the *right* policy adjustments. However, while learning may be a reasonably pervasive feature of foreign policy, the particular lessons leaders learn may not always yield successful outcomes. For example, while Belgian leaders inferred from World War I that neutrality had left them open to German invasion, the main diplomatic instrument they subsequently devised, a military alliance with France, did not prevent Germany from defeating and occupying Belgium in 1940. Many factors, not just correct learning, play a role in determining the success or failure of a country's national strategy.

Learning by leaders seems to occur in foreign policy-making, and such learning can materially influence how leaders view the interests of their countries and adjust their strategies to promote those interests. What is not guaranteed is that the lessons leaders learn necessarily increase or decrease their chances of success in foreign policy. An important scholarly task then is to identify and understand more fully the conditions under which leaders do or do not learn the right lessons in foreign affairs.

Leadership Turnover

Leaders play a key role in crafting foreign policy, so changes in leadership can bring about changes in foreign policy. Perhaps the most dramatic example of the impact of leadership change on foreign policy during the twentieth century occurred in the former Soviet Union in the 1980s. As we discussed in Chapter 2, Soviet leaders from Joseph Stalin to Leonid Brezhnev maintained iron-fisted control over Eastern Europe, using military force as necessary against Hungary in 1956 and Czechoslovakia in 1968. Mikhail Gorbachev between 1985 and 1988 reversed course on Soviet policy, most notably accepting the loss of Poland, Hungary, and other countries in what had been its empire in Eastern Europe, rather than relying on military force to keep them within the Soviet empire.

Postwar China offers a second example. From the 1950s until well into the 1970s, China was controlled by Mao Zedong, who was committed to making China communist, powerful, and independent through a strategy that combined a high level of state control over the national economy with an almost complete separation from global commerce. The coming to power of Deng Xiaoping in the late 1970s transformed China's economic and foreign policies from an emphasis on communist ideological purity toward to a more pragmatic strategy aimed at economic growth, a strategy that included economic engagement with capitalist countries.

Sources of Foreign Policy Change at the State Level of Analysis

Two mechanisms that originate and largely operate at the state level of analysis have the capacity to induce substantial change in a country's foreign policy: dramatic changes in a country's domestic political regime, and the political efforts of non-governmental organizations.

Domestic Regime Change and Shifts in Foreign Policy

Dramatic political changes within a country, such as a change in its political regime, may induce large changes in its foreign policy interests and strategies. A clear example of such an impact of regime change on foreign policy is Germany in the twentieth century.

At the outset of the 1900s, Germany had a political regime headed by the Kaiser and, as we saw in Chapter 2, his aggression, together with his unchecked control over Germany's foreign and military policies, led Germany to start but ultimately lose World War I. Germany's enemies in the war, Britain and France, with the acquiescence of the United States, imposed the very harsh Versailles peace treaty on Germany. By virtue of the Versailles Treaty, Germany lost much territory to its east, had Allied occupation forces in its western territories, was forbidden to have strong military forces, and was required to pay massive reparations to France, Britain, and other Allied countries.

In 1919, Germans succeeded temporarily in crafting a democratic constitution. This new Weimer Republic wanted to revise much of the Versailles Treaty. For example, Germany's new leaders wanted foreign forces out of Germany and a reduction in the reparations it owed to the countries it had fought during the war of 1914–18. However, Germany under the Weimar Republic pursued this goal in a cautious, non-confrontational manner, and sought revisions of the Versailles Treaty with the consent of the main European powers, particularly France and Britain, and in the framework of German integration into the League of Nations. In sharp contrast, when Adolph Hitler's Nazi regime came into power in 1933, it reversed Weimar's policies, overturned the Versailles settlement, and ultimately unleashed a war in Europe that almost perpetrated the destruction of all Jews in Europe. Then again, after World War II and the destruction of the Nazi regime, a new democratic Federal Republic in the western part of Germany turned to a policy of moderation and integration. West Germany aligned itself with the United States and Britain, became a loyal and important member of such Western institutions as NATO and the European Community (today's European Union), forged a durable peace with its eastern and western neighbors, especially France, and became a key supporter of the state of Israel.

The German case drives home a key point: what a state does abroad is likely to be influenced by how it is organized at home.

4.5   Differing Theoretical
      Approaches

Why Did the United States and the European Community
Impose Economic Sanctions against South Africa?

Background

South Africa long practiced a political system of institutionalized discrimination known as apartheid. A small minority of white South Africans ruled over a large majority of black South Africans. The apartheid regime controlled the economy and the political and legal system, and determined where black South Africans were allowed to work and live. Beginning in the early 1960s, a majority of members of the United Nations protested apartheid, imposed an arms embargo against South Africa, and sought to isolate the apartheid regime diplomatically. Several key countries, however, including Great Britain and the United States, maintained cordial political and close economic relations with South Africa until the 1980s. Then, in a significant policy shift, the United States and members of the European Community imposed economic sanctions against South Africa in 1986. What explains their initial reluctance to take action against apartheid, and their subsequent shift to opposing apartheid through the use of economic sanctions?

Realism: For realists, foreign policy is designed and executed to serve the core national interests of states. For the United States and its European allies, the central national security issue of the Cold War was the struggle against the Soviet Union and international communism. To Western leaders, South Africa's political regime was morally repugnant, but South Africa was an important ally in the global struggle against communism because it was an unambiguously anti-communist state in the key region of southern Africa. Western powers opted to maintain close ties with South Africa despite their distaste for apartheid. Security interests trumped democratic and human rights ideals.

The shift to sanctions in the 1980s is harder for the realist perspective to explain. One possibility is that once Mikhail Gorbachev came to power in the Soviet Union, the Cold War was moving towards its end, and thus support for the anti-communist regime in South Africa was less geopolitically vital. The problem with this explanation is that in 1986 it was difficult for Western leaders to foresee that the Cold War was actually ending and would do so within five years. A second and perhaps more persuasive realist argument is that the sanctions imposed were more symbolic than instrumental. They allowed Western leaders to take what had become a popular political stand against apartheid without doing significant damage to the South African economy. Realists might also point out that in the United States the sanctions were passed by Congress but opposed by President Ronald Reagan. Congress overrode the President's veto and the sanctions legislation became law. The US President, in other words, continued to pursue the national interest of close relations with South Africa; the foreign policy change was driven instead by the legislative branch, reflecting popular sentiment.

Constructivism: Constructivists focus on the importance of norms and ideas in international relations. For constructivists, the sanctions decision was the culmination of a gradual and global mass movement in favor of an anti-apartheid norm (Klotz 1995). The idea that apartheid was a politically and morally

Non-Governmental Organizations and Changes in Foreign Policy

Constructivists, as we discussed in Chapter 3, argue that non-governmental organizations (NGOs) have had significant success in influencing the foreign policies of states, as well as the policies of international institutions those states control (Keck and Sikkink 1998). NGOs have sought to exercise this influence by working individually and in networks to persuade the leaders of national governments that they should broaden their definition of interests beyond traditional security or economic concerns, and to include in that definition issues such as human rights and the environment.

Some NGOs, such as Oxfam, Doctors Without Borders, and Catholic Charities, pursue projects in poorer countries relating to health or economic development, and unacceptable regime type for a state in the international community took hold and spread over time. This anti-apartheid normative movement was led as much by international organizations (such as the Organization for African Unity) and non-state actors as by the governments of nation-states.

By the 1980s, this anti-apartheid norm became too powerful even for major states to ignore; countries such as Great Britain and the United States that refused to isolate South Africa began to appear themselves as outliers in the international community. The pressure for foreign policy change in the United States and Western Europe came from below, from domestic political forces, and transnationally, from international and non-governmental organizations. Western leaders continued to place geopolitical value on the South African connection, but eventually were swept along by the movement and could no longer resist it. Global normative change trumped prior conceptions of national interest.

Constructivists might argue further that even if sanctions had limited economic impact on South Africa, their psychological impact on the South African government was significant. So long as Great Britain and the United States supported the regime, South Africa's minority government could continue to feel they were part of an anti-communist coalition rather than a pariah within the international community. The sanctions signaled that even their most loyal international supporters no longer considered apartheid tolerable.

Marxism: Marxists could explain the willingness of liberal Western governments to tolerate apartheid as a function of the economic interests of private economic actors. South Africa's economy was the largest and most profitable in southern Africa. Western banks, manufacturing firms, and raw material producers long considered South Africa a lucrative host for trade and investment. Government policy in Western countries followed and supported the interests of dominant economic classes.

How then to account for the shift to sanctions? Marxists argue that by the 1980s, South Africa was increasing less attractive as an economic partner. The well-publicized campaign, led by college students, to convince universities and other large resource holders to divest their portfolios from companies doing business in South Africa forced companies to calculate increasing 'social costs' of their South African activities. At the same time, domestic unrest and uprisings among the black majority population in South Africa (the Soweto uprisings of 1976 were a key turning point) created an atmosphere of economic uncertainty. The apartheid regime responded with repression including the declaration of a state of emergency in 1985. Shortly thereafter, Chase Manhattan Bank decided it would not renew its loans to South Africa, and other big banks followed suit. For Marxists, the key variable was that private economic actors reluctantly turned against South Africa for business reasons before Western governments signed on to economic sanctions against the regime. Government actors, in other words, followed rather than led a shift in private economic interests.

advocate for better foreign aid policies by wealthy donor countries like the United States and key international organizations like the World Bank and the International Monetary Fund. Other NGOs, such as Human Rights Watch and Amnesty International, publicize abuses of human and political rights in countries around the globe through newsletters, reports, and direct contacts with members of the news media. They also press national governments, as well as the European Union and United Nations Human Rights Council, for stronger international protections of such rights. Many environmental NGOs, such as the World Wildlife Fund, the Worldwatch Institute, and the International Union for the Conservation of Nature, use similar strategies to draw public and governmental attention to problems in the environmental realm. Others NGOs use more dramatic strategies: for example, Greenpeace has employed

▶ **Photo 4.5**
Greenpeace Protests

Greenpeace is an NGO that is especially adept at using public actions to draw attention to policies with which it disagrees. In this instance Samcheok villagers participate in a demonstration to oppose the planned construction of a nuclear power plant in their community, 192 km from Seoul.

Source: © Jean Chung/ Greenpeace.

small boats and a helicopter to interfere with what it considers to be illegal and immoral operations of large whaling ships.

There is evidence that internationally active NGOs have sometimes changed the ideas of policy makers and shaped, to some degree, their definition of foreign policy interests or strategies. For example, according to an important study by Margaret Keck and Kathryn Sikkink, networks linking international and domestic activist groups centered on Amnesty International and Americas Watch, helped move the US government to take more seriously human rights abuses in Latin America, particularly in Argentina and Mexico during the 1970s, 1980s, and early 1990s. The study reports similar dynamics involving NGOs influencing important governments in the issue areas of protection of women and the natural environment (Keck and Sikkink 1998).

Moreover, NGO advocacy groups have influenced the policy instruments that national governments employ to protect interests even in the sensitive area of national security. For example, during the 1990s, hundreds of NGOs, coordinated by the International Campaign to Ban Landmines and led by Jody Williams, who would receive a Nobel Peace Prize for her work with the campaign, publicized the manner in which innocent civilians were being killed by anti-personnel landmines. The work of the NGOs helped prompt 122 governments to ban that class of weapons by virtue of a treaty signed in Ottawa, Canada, in 1997 (Price 1998). As we will see in Chapter 12, NGOs have sometimes been effective in influencing global policy regarding the natural environment. Finally, constructivists argue that NGOs played a decisive role in forcing leaders of Western countries to take a strong stand against South Africa's white minority government during the 1980s (Klotz 2005). As Box 4.5 shows, Marxists, constructivists, and realists rely on different types of explanations for that critical example of foreign policy change.

Sources of Foreign Policy Change at the International Level of Analysis

Finally, factors situated at the international level of analysis, in particular internationally-induced shocks and changes in the relative power of a country, can induce changes in its foreign policy.

External Shocks

National communities – leaders, officials, commentators, and politically attentive citizens – may sometimes be jarred out of their ideas about foreign policy by a major external shock. For example, the Japanese attack in December 1941 against the American naval fleet at Pearl Harbor discredited the isolationist position in American politics, and helped paved the way for the United States' more internationalist stance after World War II. In the same vein, the experience of Iran's revolutionary leaders after they attained power in 1979 – an invasion in 1980 by Saddam Hussein's Iraq, the receipt of no outside aid and, in fact, some American aid for Saddam Hussein – has probably scarred those leaders and made them deeply suspicious of the United States and committed to acquiring military power, including nuclear weapons.

Changes in Relative Power

You will recall from Chapter 2 that US leaders and much of the US political elite during and after World War II came to believe the United States had to do more to support a world order than had been true when the United States occupied a much less important place in the international system. In other words, as the US relative power position changed, so too did its conceptions of interest and appropriate strategy. These changes do not happen immediately; the United States was already very powerful by the 1930s but did not change its foreign policy significantly. Some analysts see China in a comparable position today – its relative power is rising, but it has not yet adjusted its foreign policy to do more to support international order. This 'lag effect' works in reverse as well. Great Britain and France maintained international responsibility typically associated with the strongest states in the system long after their power positions declined in relative terms.

Individual	State	International
Foreign policy can take a markedly different course either because new leaders come into office or because current leaders change their beliefs about the country's interests or strategy options.	A change in country's political regime, or intensive lobbying by non-state actors within the country, can bring about large changes in a country's foreign policy.	External policy shocks as well as changes in a country's relative power may contribute to significant changes in foreign policy.

Levels of Analysis

Sources of Foreign Policy Change

Revisiting the Enduring Question and Looking Ahead

In this chapter, we have examined the enduring question of what accounts for the foreign policies of states. We reviewed the main elements of foreign policy, namely, interest and strategy, with the latter concept entailing two ideas of goals and policy instruments. We employed the levels-of-analysis framework both to understand why governments, by virtue of the influence of their national leaders, domestic institutions and societal actors, and international conditions, choose certain interests to advance and devise particular strategies to pursue them.

We used that same levels-of-analysis framework to investigate an important question derived from our central one: why do states' governments make substantial changes to their foreign policies? In accounting for both foreign policy and foreign policy change, the chapter has showcased the ongoing and unresolved debate among students of international relations and foreign policy. That debate cuts across the levels of analysis and also across the theoretical traditions introduced in Chapter 3. Students who grasp the different types of arguments made by scholars at different levels, and from different theoretical perspectives, will be well equipped to engage the literature on foreign policy analysis, to understand and explain current foreign policy decisions, and eventually to conduct their own research as well.

With this chapter and the previous chapter, we have explored the key language, ideas, and overall approaches that scholars, many media observers, and even some government leaders and officials employ when they think, write, and speak about international relations and foreign policy. As you reflect on these chapters, you will recall that we often talked about military disputes, including war. Although war is a rare event in world politics, it does occur and it can be awesome in its human lethality and political, social, and economic consequences. In the nuclear age, war can be a recipe for national self-destruction. Why do states sometimes turn to war? Fortified with knowledge of international history, aware of international relations theory, and in possession of analytical tools to explore foreign policy, we are now in a position to turn to and confront that fundamental problem in international relations.

Visit **www.palgrave.com/politics/Grieco** to access extra resources for this chapter, including:

- Chapter summaries to help you review the material
- Multiple choice quizzes to test your understanding
- Flashcards to test your knowledge of the key terms in this chapter
- An interactive simulation that invites you to go through the decision-making process of a world leader at a crucial political juncture
- Pivotal decisions in which you weigh up the pros and cons of complicated decisions with grave consequences
- Outside resources, including links to contemporary articles and videos, that add to what you have learned in this chapter

Study Questions

1. Is the formulation of a coherent strategy by a complex government like China, the United States, or Great Britain really possible? Aren't foreign policies the sum of bureaucratic and institutional in-fighting within governments, rather than the result of a rational, systematic assessment by national leaders of what's best for the country?
2. Can you think of how the geographic location of the United States, or Japan, or France has influenced its foreign policy? Has that influence continued or waned over time?
3. Do you think that a country's domestic political institutions influence its understanding of its interests in the foreign domain? Do those institutions play a role in influencing which instruments the country is likely to turn to in advancing its interests?
4. In general, do you think leaders are good 'learners' when it comes to foreign policy?
5. What makes it more or less likely that a leader will learn appropriate lessons from his or her experiences in foreign policy?
6. Do you think NGOs have too much, just about the right amount, or too little influence on the foreign policies of countries in the international system?

Further Reading

Allison, Graham and Philip Zelikow (1999) *Essence of Decision: Explaining the Cuban Missile Crisis*, 2nd edition (New York: Longman). This classic work, first published by Allison in 1971, shaped a generation of scholarship on foreign policy by showing that the same set of foreign policy decisions – the Soviet decision to place nuclear weapons in Cuba and the US response – could be understood several different ways. Allison challenged the then conventional rational-actor approach by looking 'inside' the state at the institutional and bureaucratic politics of governments.

Kang, David (2009) *China Rising: Peace, Power, and Order in East Asia* (New York: Columbia University Press). In this foreign policy analysis Kang argues that the states of East Asia are more likely to accommodate China than to balance against it. He draws on constructivist thinking to make the case that historical and cultural norms in East Asian countries lead states to embrace, rather than resist, a hierarchy of authority with China at the top.

Kapstein, Ethan B. and Michael Mastanduno (eds) (1999) *Unipolar Politics: Realism and State Strategies after the Cold War* (New York: Columbia University Press). A collection of essays that examine how the changing structure of the international system – the shift from a bipolar to a unipolar world – affects the foreign policy calculations of countries including China, Russia, France, Germany, Poland and the United States.

Legro, Jeffrey W. (2007) *Rethinking the World: Great Power Strategies and International Order* (Ithaca: Cornell University Press). Legro makes the case that ideas drive foreign policy change. He develops the argument in a broad comparative framework that includes analysis of major foreign policy transitions in Russia, China, Japan, and the United States.

Narizny, Kevin (2007) *The Political Economy of Grand Strategy* (Ithaca: Cornell University Press). Narizny argues that foreign policy strategies are driven by the particular pattern of interest group coalitions found within a country. He uses this framework to explain the overall foreign policies, or grand strategies, of Great Britain and the United States during the nineteenth and twentieth centuries.

II

War and Peace: An Introduction to Security

5 War and its Causes

6 Pathways to Interstate Peace

7 Weapons of Mass Destruction

Visit **www.palgrave.com/politics/grieco** to watch the authors debating the issues discussed in this Part.
Video 1: Are China and Russia 'revisionist states'?
Video 2: Is war between great powers a thing of the past?

5

War and Its Causes

Enduring question: Why is war a persistent feature of international relations

President George Bush of the United States and Prime Minister Tony Blair of Great Britain led a coalition of states in a war against Iraq in March 2003 because they believed that Iraq under Saddam Hussein was trying to build nuclear weapons. Just before the US invasion, US Deputy Secretary of Defense Paul Wolfowitz dismissed as 'wildly off the mark' an estimate by General Eric Shinseki, the US Army Chief of Staff, that, after the allies had defeated Saddam's military, hundreds of thousands of US troops might then be needed to occupy and pacify Iraq (Milbank 2005). As it turns out, there were no Iraqi nuclear weapons. The United States, Britain, and their allies did, as expected, readily defeat Iraq's military, but an insurgency soon threatened allied forces and the new Iraqi government, and the United States and its allies only achieved a modicum of stability in Iraq with a force that included 160,000 US troops. More than 4,400 American and almost 200 British military personnel were killed during the Iraq war and the subsequent insurgency. After the allied withdrawal in December 2011, Iraq's political future was highly uncertain.

Why does a war like that against Iraq occur? Why, more generally, do wars remain a persistent feature of the world around us? We devote this chapter to an exploration of that enduring question in international relations. In the chapter's first section, we establish a foundation of factual knowledge about international military conflict by identifying the main types of conflicts that occur between countries, and investigate how international military conflicts have varied across time in their incidence and severity. We then, in the chapter's second main section, discuss the kinds of disagreements between countries which can make them turn to military threats or violence. In the chapter's subsequent three main sections we examine the underlying causes of war and other serious military conflicts between states, using the levels-of-analysis framework, with its emphasis on arguments pitched at the level of the individual, the internal characteristics of countries, and the inter-state system, to organize the discussion and the efforts by the main theoretical traditions in international relations to understand the causes of war.

We then, in the chapter's last main section, shift our focus from war *between* states and toward war *within* states, or internal wars. In that section, we highlight the reasons why students of international relations must understand internal wars; discuss different types of internal wars, as well as their incidence and severity; and identify and examine the range of causes that may bring about such wars within countries.

Source: © MoD/Crown copyright (2014).

Learning Objectives

By the end of this chapter, you will be able to:

→ Distinguish among and have a grasp of the different kinds of international military conflicts, including their frequency and lethality.

→ Understand the different kinds of conflicts of interest between countries that can be the immediate cause of war.

→ Compare and assess the different underlying causes of international military conflict at the individual level of analysis, with a focus on errors by national leaders arising from misperceptions, small-group dynamics, or a propensity toward over-confidence.

→ Recognize and analyze causes of conflicts at the state level of analysis, with a focus on domestic economic systems, political institutions, and governmental processes.

→ Evaluate the causes of military conflicts at the international level of analysis.

→ Identify the causes and effects of internal wars and understand their impact on the prospects for war and peace between states.

Chapter Contents

- Wars between Countries
- Immediate Causes of War
- Underlying Causes of War: the Individual Level of Analysis
- Underlying Causes of War: the State Level of Analysis
- Underlying Causes of War: the International Level of Analysis
- Internal Wars and their Causes
- Revisiting the Enduring Question and Looking Ahead
- Study Questions
- Further Reading

Wars between Countries

Before we explore the immediate and underlying causes of international military conflicts, we first lay down three foundations: we define and examine different kinds of military conflicts that take place between countries, present information on the incidence of those different types of military conflicts that have taken place between countries over the past two centuries, and consider how lethal those conflicts have been in terms of deaths of combatants and civilians.

Types of Military Conflicts between Countries

We begin with **interstate war**, which occurs when two or more national governments direct military forces against each other in organized, sustained, and highly deadly clashes.

There are many types of interstate war (Levy and Thompson 2011). For example, several that we examined in Chapter 2 – the Thirty Years War and the wars against Napoleonic France, Germany under William II and Hitler, and Imperial Japan – were **general wars** or **major wars** in the sense that they involved many or all of the most powerful states in their respective historical eras. Some, such as the Napoleonic wars and World War II were also **hegemonic wars**, that is, their outcomes determined which states would have predominant influence in the international system for years and even decades. World War I and especially World War II were instances of **total war**, where warring governments sought to mobilize as much of their human and economic resources as possible, and some or all of the main belligerents systematically sought to weaken or kill the civilian populations of their enemies as a part of their war strategies.

Since 1945, there has been no total war between or among the most powerful states, that is, the United States, the Soviet Union (now Russia), Britain, France, and China. With the exceptions of large-scale US–Chinese clashes during the Korean War of 1950–53, and minor skirmishes between Soviet and Chinese forces on their mutual border in 1969, the major powers since 1945 have avoided fighting each other directly. One important reason for the lapse in total war and in particular the absence of war between the major powers is the existence of nuclear weapons. During the Cold War, the Soviet Union and the United States (and two US allies, Britain and France) possessed large arsenals of nuclear weapons, and as we will see in Chapter 7, the fear of nuclear war contributed greatly to the prevention of World War III. Moreover, Japan and Germany, which under authoritarian and dictatorial governments were highly aggressive states during the first half of the twentieth century, became stable democracies in the wake of World War II, and, as we will see below, democracies are unlikely to fight among themselves. At the same time, these states were less likely to fight each other because they all found it necessary to work together to resist (but, in the face of nuclear weapons, not to fight) the Soviet Union during the Cold War.

This does not mean that the major states since 1945 have avoided all forms of military conflicts with one another or with other states. As we saw in Chapter 2, during the Cold War the United States and the Soviet Union fought proxy wars against each other. Moreover, we have witnessed what have been termed **limited wars** between one or more of the major states and less powerful countries, such as between China and India in 1962, or between less powerful states, including multiple wars between India and Pakistan and between Israel and Egypt and Syria.

Interstate war: When two or more national governments direct military forces against each other in organized, sustained, and oftentimes deadly clashes.

General war: A war that involves many or all of the most powerful states in a particular historical era. Synonymous with major war.

Major war: A war that involves many or all of the most powerful states in a particular historical era. Synonymous with general war.

Hegemonic war: A war the outcome of which determines which states will have predominant influence in the international system in the coming years or even decades.

Total war: War in which belligerent states mobilize all resources and target civilians as part of their war strategy.

Limited war: Smaller war in which major powers avoid fighting each other directly, contrasted with general or major war.

There is in the field of international relations no universally agreed upon threshold of violence that must take place between governments before that violence is classified as an interstate war. Many scholars, however, utilize a threshold proposed by the Correlates of War (COW) project, a path-finding data-collection program on different kinds of armed violence within and between countries. The COW data project stipulates that interstate wars are those organized clashes between the military forces of states that results in at least 1,000 combat fatalities during a 12-month period (Sarkees and Wayman 2010).

Interstate wars comprise the first of three COW-identified categories of international military conflicts. The second type is that of **militarized interstate disputes**, or MIDs. An MID is an international conflict in which states seek to win a dispute through military coercion. The concept of an MID covers a broad range of state actions: from the issuing by states of *threats* of military force against one another; to the making of *displays* of military power against one another, such as moving troops up to a common border; to the actual use of force by a state against an adversary, which in turn can run the gamut from using forces to seize territory, declaring war, or engaging in violent clashes with the adversary at levels below that of full-scale war (Ghosn, Palmer, and Bremer 2004). We presented a recent example of what will probably be classified by COW researchers as an MID in Chapter 4, namely, China's announcement in July 2012 that, in reaction to the Vietnamese parliament's claims to the South China Sea, it was undertaking 'combat-ready' naval patrols and dispatching troops to its administrative center in the Paracel Islands.

Extra-state wars represent the third COW category of international military conflicts. An extra-state war is a violent clash – resulting in at least 1,000 combat deaths – between the national government of a recognized state and an entity in a foreign territory that is not an internationally recognized state, or is a non-state actor located in a foreign state. The conquests that European states undertook against African tribal communities during the 1800s were extra-state wars, as were the wars for independence that colonies such as Algeria and Vietnam undertook against France after World War II. More recently, the United States has undertaken extra-state wars with remotely piloted armed drones against Al Qaeda or Al Qaeda-affiliated terrorist personnel and bases in Yemen, Somalia, and Pakistan.

Modern international conflicts can often have both interstate and extra-state dimensions. For example, after the Al Qaeda attacks against the United States in September 2001, US forces destroyed the bases that terrorist organization had established in Afghanistan. The United States also helped indigenous Afghan groups topple the Afghan government, which was then under the control of the Taliban, an Islamist fundamentalist group that had given Al Qaeda a safe haven in Afghanistan. Two wars thus occurred at the same time during 2001 and 2002: that against Al Qaeda was an extra-state war, while that against Taliban-controlled Afghanistan was an interstate war. The Taliban soon recovered from their defeats in 2001–02, and utilizing bases in Pakistan and Afghanistan launched an insurgency against the US-backed government in Kabul. By consequence, since 2002 the United States, Britain, and a number of allied countries have fought an extra-state war against a resurgent Taliban in Afghanistan and in neighboring Pakistan. Similarly, the Iraq war that began in March 2003 began as an interstate war, but an extra-state war soon developed in which the United States and its allies fought Iraqi opposition groups and outside fighters, including some affiliated with Al Qaeda.

Militarized interstate dispute: An instance in which a state threatens to use force against another state, mobilizes or moves military forces against the other in a threatening manner, or two states engage in military clashes at a level of severity below full-scale war.

Extra-state war: A violent clash – resulting in at least 1,000 combat deaths – between the national government of a recognized state and an entity that is not an internationally recognized state, or a non-state actor located in a foreign state.

Incidence of International Military Conflicts

Figure 5.1 employs COW data to explore the incidence of full-scale interstate wars from the end of the Napoleonic wars up through 2007. Each bar in the figure represents the average annual number of COW-level wars that began during the designated time period. The total number of wars that began during each time period is reported in parentheses below each bar. We can see by summing those figures that, between 1816 and 2007, there were 95 interstate wars using the COW coding rule, namely an interstate clash that produces at least 1,000 battlefield deaths in 12 months.

▶ **Figure 5.1**
Incidence of Interstate Wars, 1816–2007, and During and After the Cold War

In this chart, for each designated time period, the bar represents the average annual number of interstate wars launched during the period; the number in parentheses is the total number of interstate wars launched during the period. In this figure we can see that after steadily increasing for almost two centuries, the average annual incidence of interstate wars has declined since the end of the Cold War.

Source: Meredith Reid Sarkees and Frank Wayman (2010) *Resort to War: 1816–2007* (CQ Press). Data-set available from *Correlates of War*, Inter-State War Data (v4.0), at http://www.correlatesofwar.org/.

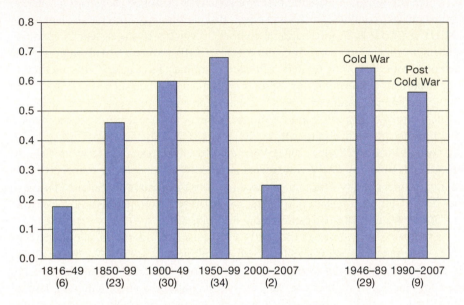

As can be observed in the figure, interstate wars increased in frequency over the course of most of modern history: from 0.2 new wars per year between 1816 and 1849 all the way up to almost 0.7 new wars per year between 1950 and 1999. However, the incidence of interstate wars has declined in recent years. In the last period we can analyze with COW data, the years between 2000 and 2007, only two COW-level interstate wars were launched (the war against Afghanistan beginning in 2001 and the war against Iraq beginning in 2003), which translates into an average annual incidence of about 0.25 wars per year.

Finally, particularly close attention should be paid to the two bars on the far right of Figure 5.1. The first bar represents the incidence of interstate wars during the Cold War era, that is, between 1946 and 1989, and the second represents the incidence of such wars in the immediate years of the post-Cold War period, that is, between 1990 and 2007. Notice that there is a modest decrease in the incidence of new international wars over the two periods, from a bit more than 0.6 wars per year to a bit less than that in the post-Cold War era. Hence, it is possible that after a constant, even relentless upward trend in the frequency of wars from the early nineteenth to the late twentieth century, with the end of the Cold War we are now seeing a reversal of that trend. We should be very careful in drawing an inference from less than two decades since the end of the Cold War, but, going back to our enduring question, if this trend were to hold it would raise questions about whether war is, in fact, necessarily a persistent

◀ **Figure 5.2**
Incidence of
Militarized Interstate
Disputes, 1816–2010,
and During and After
the Cold War

In this chart, for each
designated time
period, the bar repre-
sents the average
annual number of
MIDs launched during
the period; the number
in parentheses is the
total number of MIDs
launched during the
period. In contrast to
the pattern we
observed in connec-
tion to interstate wars,
the average annual
incidence of new MIDs
has not declined since
the end of the Cold
War, and perhaps has
slightly increased.

Source: Faten, Ghosn and
Scott Bennett (2003)
Codebook for the Dyadic
Militarized Interstate
Incident Data, Version
4.01. Available online:
http://correlatesofwar.org.

feature of international politics (Mueller 2009). For that reason it is a trend that is clearly worthy of continued attention in the years ahead.

We may now turn to the second type of military conflicts, MIDs, which, as noted above, are international conflicts in which states seek to win a dispute through military coercion. The COW data project has presented a data set that identifies 2,586 MIDs between 1816 and 2010. We noted above that the average annual incidence of inter-state wars has been on a downward trend in the post-Cold War era. The pattern of MIDs is more complicated: while their incidence has not gone down since the end of the Cold War, the average level of violence of MIDs has perhaps become somewhat attenuated in the most recent period.

The incidence of MIDs is reported in Figure 5.2. As with interstate wars, there was a long-term increase in the average number of MID initiations between 1816 and 1999, from about four MID initiations per year in the second half of the nineteenth century to ten MIDs per year in the first half of the twentieth century, and then to about 28 MIDs per year between 1950 and 1999. In the most recent period, from 2000 to 2010, the annual MID rate has stayed at almost the same level as it was during the previous fifty years. The particular years that constituted the Cold War era and the first two decades of the post-Cold War period are presented in the right-most two bars in the figure. They indicate that while 26 MIDs were launched per year on average between 1946 and 1990, an average of 28 MIDs were initiated per year in the post-Cold War years up to 2010. As with the data on interstate wars, we should be cautious in drawing inferences about MIDs in the post-Cold War era since we are still early in the period. However, at least in this early post-Cold War phase, MIDs have persisted as a prominent feature of international relations.

At the same time, it is possible that the severity of MIDs has decreased in the post-Cold War era. We can assess this possibility by reference to Figure 5.3. Consider the first pie chart in the figure. It reports the percentage of the 477 MIDs that occurred between 1900 and 1945 that took the form solely of threats issued by one state against another (5 percent of the total), the percentage that were more severe than threats,

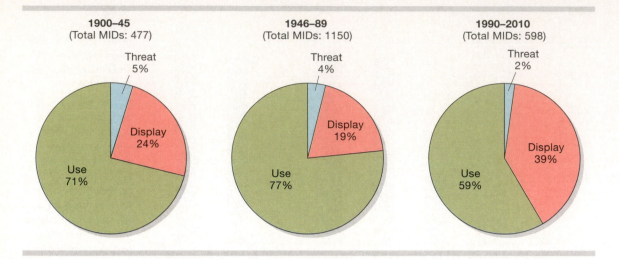

| 1900–45
(Total MIDs: 477) | 1946–89
(Total MIDs: 1150) | 1990–2010
(Total MIDs: 598) |

Threat 5%
Display 24%
Use 71%

Threat 4%
Display 19%
Use 77%

Threat 2%
Display 39%
Use 59%

▲ **Figure 5.3 Severity of Militarized Interstate Disputes, 1900–2010**

Compared to the first half of the twentieth century, uses of force more typically characterized MIDs during the Cold War. The use of force during MIDs has abated to some degree in the post-Cold War period compared to the Cold War era or to the years between 1900 and 1945.

Source: Faten, Ghosn and Scott Bennett (2003) *Codebook for the Dyadic Militarized Interstate Incident Data*, Version 4.01. Available online: http://correlatesofwar.org.

namely, displays of military force (24 percent), and finally, at the highest level of hostility, the percentage of MIDs that entailed the actual use of force between the contesting states, including violent clashes short of war (71 percent). Turning next to the second pie chart, we see that during the Cold War years of 1946–89, during which there were 1150 MIDs, the percentage of that total that were of the most severe type, the use of force, reached 77 percent. Notice, finally, the third pie chart: it indicates that during the first twenty years of the post-Cold War period, during which there were 598 MIDs, 59 percent of that total entailed the use of force, substantially below that of both the Cold War era and the first half of the twentieth century. It would seem then that while the annual incidence of MIDs has not declined with the end of the Cold War, a smaller percentage of the MIDs that have occurred are reaching the highest level of severity. This mixed pattern of trends regarding MIDs certainly invites research in the years ahead.

We next focus on extra-state wars, which, you will recall, involve a violent clash – resulting in at least 1,000 combat deaths – between the national government of a recognized state and an entity in a foreign territory that is not an internationally recognized state, or is a non-state actor located in a foreign state. Figure 5.4 reports the frequency with which countries initiated extra-state wars between 1816 and 2007. Countries launched a total of about 162 such wars, placing this category much closer to interstate wars than to MIDs. Extra-state wars display a historical trajectory quite different from the other two categories we have examined, reflecting what we discussed in Chapter 2 about the great burst of nineteenth-century imperialism, which peaked in the second half of that century, and then declined in the twentieth century as colonial peoples fought for and ultimately acquired independence.

Lethality of International Wars

The COW data project does not present battlefield fatalities for each MID, but we do have reasonable estimates for such deaths that were incurred during interstate and extra-state wars. At least 32 million combat deaths resulted from the 95 interstate wars that were fought between 1816 and 2007. Of that total, more than 8 million combat deaths occurred during World War I, and 16 million during World War II. Approxi-

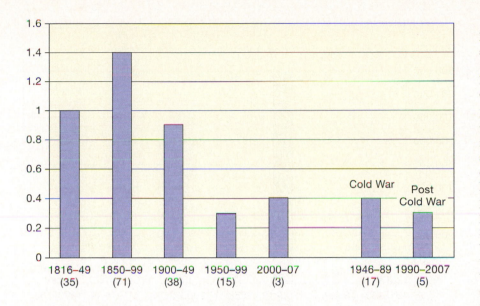

◀ **Figure 5.4 Incidence of Extra-state Wars, 1816–2007, and During and After the Cold War**

For each designated time period, the bar represents the average annual number of extra-state wars launched during the period; the number in parentheses is the total number of extra-state wars launched during the period. Extra-state wars declined in incidence during the first and especially the second half of the twentieth century, reflecting in part the end of colonialism during the first half of the twentieth century.

Source: Meredith Reid Sarkees and Frank Wayman (2010) *Resort to War: 1816–2007* (CQ Press). Data-set available from *Correlates of War*, Inter-State War Data (v4.0), at http://www.correlatesofwar.org/.

mately 2.1 million or more combatants were killed during that period in extra-state wars.

As we can see in Panel A of Figure 5.5, the lethality of interstate wars increased dramatically from the first to the second half of the nineteenth century, and then exploded in the first half of the twentieth century. More powerful weapons, such as heavy artillery, tanks, and machine guns; industrialization and thus the ability of states to produce vast quantities of those weapons; and a stronger capacity of governments to mobilize national populations and to put together ever larger militaries: all of these factors combined during this period to produce armed forces that could inflict truly massive casualties on one another. Thereafter, reflecting perhaps the fact that the major powers avoided direct war with one another as a result of nuclear weapons and democracies, wars on average dropped in lethality. We can also see that the two wars that have occurred in the post-Cold War era (Iraq and Afghanistan) were less lethal for combatant forces than were the wars that took place during the Cold War.

We may also observe in Panel B of Figure 5.5 that extra-state wars became more lethal during the twentieth as opposed to the nineteenth century. Wars of decolonization could be especially lethal: for example, some 270,000 combatants were killed during France's unsuccessful war between 1946 and 1954 to hold onto Vietnam, and 34,000 combatants were killed during France's failed bid between 1954 and 1962 to retain Algeria. There appears to have been a decrease in the lethality of extra-state wars with the end of the Cold War.

Interstate wars also cause vast numbers of non-combatants deaths (Downes 2008). Perhaps 50 million civilians were killed during the wars of the twentieth century. At least 30 million civilians were killed in World War II alone. Many civilians died during that war as a result of malnutrition or disease or as a result of air bombings that were conducted by the Germans as well as the British and the Americans. World War II also witnessed genocide in the form of the Holocaust – the highly organized campaign by the Nazi state to destroy the Jewish community throughout Europe. That campaign resulted in the Nazi murder of 6 million Jews. Approximately 3 million of the 6 million

► **Figure 5.5**
Battlefield Deaths in Interstate and Extra-state Wars, 1816–2007, and During and After the Cold War

For each designated time period, the bar represents the average number of battlefield deaths that occurred during the wars (inter-state in Panel A and extra-state in Panel B) during the period; the number in parentheses is the total number of such wars that began during the period.

Source: Meredith Reid Sarkees, and Frank Wayman (2010) *Resort to War: 1816–2007* (CQ Press). Data-set available from *Correlates of War, Inter-State War Data* (v4.0), at http://www.correlatesofwar.org/.

(a) Interstate Wars

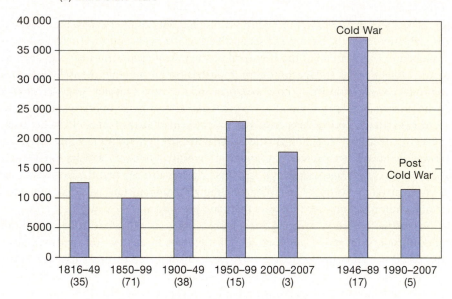

(b) Extra-state Wars

Jewish people killed by the Nazis were Polish citizens. The Nazi government killed at least an additional 1.9 million non-Jewish Polish citizens. The Nazis also conducted a massive murder campaign when they occupied the western part of the Soviet Union: the total number of Jewish and non-Jewish Soviet civilians killed by the Nazis is not known with precision, but estimates range from 13 million to 15 million people. The Nazis killed an additional 5 million Soviet prisoners of war through intentional mass starvation. The Nazis also killed prior to and during the war approximately 200,000 Roma (Gypsies), and tens of thousands of disabled people, political prisoners, homosexuals, and other individuals the Nazis thought did not fit in the world they were

◀ Photo 5.1 The Holocaust in Europe During World War II

This aerial photograph, taken in August 1944, shows the layout of Auschwitz, in Poland, the largest concentration and death camp the Nazis established during their effort to exterminate all Jews in Europe during World War II.

Source: PA Images.

seeking to create. Such mass killings and attempts at genocide are not a thing of the past: since World War II, perhaps two million or more civilians have been killed during interstate wars such as the Korean and Vietnam wars.

Immediate Causes of War

To this point we have sought in the main to *describe* international military conflicts: their types, incidence, and lethality. Now we shift our attention to developing a capacity to *explain* why such conflicts occur. We will proceed in two steps: in this section we will identify the immediate causes of war, and in the next section we will identify possible underlying causes of war. In particular, in this section we will look at how a strong disagreement between states about a specific issue – that is, a conflict of interest between those states – can prompt them to undertake MIDs or even full-fledged wars. As we will see below, conflicts of interest can revolve around economic resources, policy disagreements, political regimes, ethnic or religious identity, and territory.

Conflicts of interest involving scarce *economic resources* have served to foment militarized violence between states (Gleditsch et al. 2006). For example, disagreements between Israel and its Arab neighbors over water resources may have helped set the stage for one of the major Arab–Israeli wars in June 1967. When, in 1964, Israel began to draw water from the Jordan River, Egypt's President Nasser coordinated an Arab plan that would effectively divert water flows in Jordan, Syria, and Lebanon away from Israel. Israel responded with military strikes against the constructions sites for this project in Syria three times during 1965 and 1966 (Cooley 1984; Amery 1997).

Economic conflicts involving energy have also led to militarized conflicts. As we noted in Chapter 1, China and its neighbors have been locked into a struggle for control of the oil and natural gas resources that may lie beneath the South China Sea,

Conflict of Interest over Domestic Political Regimes: the French Revolutionary Period in the 1790s and the Build-up to the US Invasion of Iraq in 2003

Then: *Austrian Rationale for Fearing a Democratic Regime in France, 1791*

In the early 1790s, a top Austrian official, Baron Thugut, feared that the democratic character of revolutionary France would undermine the Habsburg dynasty. He said:

> Austria has certainly fought more wars in which threatening danger was much closer. But one cannot compare those with such an all-embracing struggle that we are now in ... Just as [earlier] wars weakened us, so they weakened the enemy, and at the end military victory or a more or less advantageous peace would bring them to a halt. But now this House [the Habsburgs] ... must fight a nation which has not only become utterly fanatical but which tries to drag along with it other peoples and which has prepared its current efforts for a long time in all of Europe through the voices of its prophets.

Source: Baron Thugut, in the summer of 1791, who became Foreign Minister of Austria in 1793, quoted in Karl A. Roider (1987) *Baron Thugut and Austria's Response to the French Revolution* (Princeton: Princeton University Press), p 129.

Now: *American Rationale for Overthrowing Iraq's Authoritarian Regime, 2003*

In 2003, the United States launched a war against Iraq in part because President George W. Bush and his advisors believed that Saddam Hussein's dictatorship in Iraq represented a threat both to the region and to the United States and the replacement of Hussein's regime with a democratic regime would yield a more peaceful Iraq and a more stable Middle East. President Bush at that time said:

> The success of a free Iraq will be watched and noted throughout the region. Millions will see that freedom, equality, and material progress are possible at the heart of the Middle East. Leaders in the region will face the clearest evidence that free institutions and open societies are the only path to long-term national success and dignity. And a transformed Middle East would benefit the entire world, by undermining the ideologies that export violence to other lands. Iraq as a dictatorship had great power to destabilize the Middle East; Iraq as a democracy will have great power to inspire the Middle East. The advance of democratic institutions in Iraq is setting an example that others, including the Palestinian people, would be wise to follow.

Source: Bush 2003.

In two very different historical eras, leaders and officials have been similarly motivated to go to war out of concern about the domestic political regimes of other countries.

and this conflict of interest has produced low-level MIDs. Saddam Hussein justified Iraq's August 1990 invasion of neighboring Kuwait in part with the claim that oil companies were using lateral drills to steal Iraqi oil. The United States then led an international coalition to expel Iraq from Kuwait. The United States decided to invade Iraq in 2003 in part because it worried that if Iraq had nuclear weapons, it would use them to dominate the Middle East and its economically crucial oil resources. This fear was expressed in July 2002 by Vice-President Dick Cheney:

◀ **Photo 5.2
Strategically
Important Territory:
The Golan Heights**

Israel captured the
Golan Heights during
the 1967 war, and con-
siders it to be a
strategic piece of terri-
tory since it is well
suited for military pur-
poses, including sur-
veillance and artillery
fire.

Source: PA Images.

Armed with an arsenal of these weapons of terror, and seated atop ten percent of the world's oil reserves, Saddam Hussein could then be expected to seek dom-ination of the entire Middle East, take control of a great portion of the world's energy supplies, directly threaten America's friends throughout the region, and subject the United States or any other nation to nuclear blackmail. (Cheney 2002)

Policy disagreements can also produce conflicts of interest between states that have the potential for military conflict. In early September 2007, Israeli warplanes destroyed what appears to have been a nuclear reactor that Syria had under construction. Israeli leaders had concluded that the Syrian government intended to employ the reactor to build nuclear weapons, which they deemed an unacceptable possible threat to Israel. In this instance, Israel's intolerance of Syria's possible policy of acquiring nuclear weapons produced a militarized interstate dispute. It did not produce an interstate war because Syria chose not to escalate by retaliating against Israel.

States can also find themselves in serious conflicts of interest as a result of disagree-ments about one or another's *political regime*. Box 5.1 highlights two very different instances, one at the outset of the modern era and one much more recent, in which disputes over political regimes have led to war.

Issues of *ethnic identity* can also lead states into serious conflicts of interest. By ethnic identity, we are referring to the linguistic, cultural, and religious beliefs and practices, common ancestral or kin ties, or other historical experiences that people believe they share in common and cause them to believe that they constitute a com-munity. In 1999, members of the NATO alliance attacked the Balkan country of Serbia. Why? Ethnic Albanians, who comprise the majority of residents in Kosovo, then a province in the south of Serbia, were pressing for greater self-governance, which they felt had been long denied to them while they remained part of the national commu-nity. In the late 1990s, an ultra-nationalist Serbian government under the leadership of Slobodan Milosevic abused and murdered Albanian civilians in Kosovo as a part

Perspective of the People's Republic of China (PRC), 1993

From People's Republic of China, 'White Paper on Taiwan, "The Taiwan Question and Reunification of China,"' August 31, 1993:

> There is only one China in the world, Taiwan is an inalienable part of China, and the seat of China's central government is in Beijing.... Peaceful unification is a set policy of the Chinese Government. However, any sovereign state is entitled to use any means it deems necessary, including military ones, to uphold its sovereignty and territorial integrity. The Chinese Government is under no obligation to undertake any commitment to any foreign power or people intending to split China as to what means it might use to handle its own domestic affairs.

Perspective of the Republic of China (ROC), 2002

Statement by Taiwan's President Chen Shui-bian, Opening Address to the 29th Annual Meeting of the World Federation of Taiwanese Associations (in Tokyo, Japan) via live video link:

> Taiwan is our country, and our country cannot be bullied, diminished, marginalized, or downgraded as a local entity. Taiwan does not belong to someone else, nor is it someone else's local government or province.... China's so-called 'one China principle' or 'one country, two systems' would change Taiwan's status quo. We cannot accept this, because whether Taiwan's future or status quo should be changed cannot be decided for us by any one country, any one government, any one political party, or any one person. Only the 23 million great people of Taiwan have the right to decide Taiwan's future, fate, and status.

Source: Kan 2007: 50–1, 72.

Ethnic cleansing: Sustained, organized violence perpetrated against a particular ethnic group with the goal of eradication of that group.

of an effort to suppress an armed Albanian secessionist movement, the Kosovo Liberation Army. The United States and its NATO allies became concerned that Milosevic might unleash a war aimed at '**ethnic cleansing**,' that is, the Serbs might murder and commit atrocities against local residents of Albanian background with the goal of inducing the survivors to flee and thus leave Kosovo open for Serbian control. By consequence, between March and June 1999, the United States and its NATO allies launched air strikes against Serbia to compel the Milosevic government to cease its anti-Albanian campaign and accept a NATO peacekeeping force in Kosovo. Kosovo has since declared its independence from Serbia and is today administered by the United Nations.

Finally, conflicts of interest regarding territory have a high potential for engendering military conflict (Senese and Vasquez 2005). Territorial disputes are fraught with the risk of war for three reasons. First, as discussed above, the territories in dispute may possess important economic resources. Second, countries may assign military importance to a borderland. For example, Israel seized the Golan Heights from Syria in 1967; it has been reluctant to return the area because Israel uses it to monitor Syrian military activities.

Moreover, in circumstances in which countries border one another and contain populations with similar ethnic characteristics, one side or the other might be tempted to go to war to 'unite the nation' under the rule of one sovereign state. Decolonization and the onset of the Cold War often divided similar cultural groups into separate states. After the new states were established, one often sought reunification with the other through military conquest. Examples of this type of culture-based international territorial conflict include the two Koreas, where unification has not occurred; the two Vietnams, where unification eventually took place in 1975; and Taiwan and the People's Republic of China (PRC), where the outcome is unknown but will greatly determine the future of peace in East Asia. Box 5.2 illustrates the radically differing perspectives of Taiwanese and PRC officials on the status of the island, notwithstanding the ethnic similarities of the two nations – or perhaps because of them.

Most states resolve conflicts of interest with other states through diplomacy. Thus, the presence of a conflict of interest cannot by itself explain the onset of war. When we see the onset of a MID or a war, there must be, in addition to an immediate conflict of interest, the operation of one or a number of other, underlying or fundamental causes of war. What are those underlying or fundamental causes? It is to that question that we now direct our attention.

👤 Individual	🌐 International
Individuals are the main victims in war, either as combatants or as civilians.	Interstate wars involve two or more states in intensely violent military conflict; MIDs also take place between states; and extra-state wars involve states and non-state actors.

Levels of Analysis
International Military Conflict

Underlying Causes of War: the Individual Level of Analysis

Individuals must be at the heart of the study of the causes of war, for leaders and other policy makers are the actors who ultimately make the decision for or against war. In this section we examine important examples of scholarship that emphasize the role of leaders (and their policy subordinates) in causing wars.

This scholarship is interesting in its own right, but it is also important in terms of our theoretical understanding of international relations. Realist international theory, which we examined in Chapter 3, assumes that states are rational and unitary actors. That is, realist theory works with the assumption that when we analyze international affairs we need not take into account the preferences, beliefs, and decision-making procedures of individual leaders and their policy officials. Instead, realist theory works with the assumption that we can gain strong insights into the behavior and interactions of states if we assume that states are unitary actors in the sense that they act as if they were integrated, coherent entities: government leaders may be assumed to react more to their international circumstances than to their personal characteristics. In addition, according to realist theory, we may gain good leverage on international affairs by assuming that states (including their leaders) are rational: they perceive international circumstances correctly and act after a full and careful search for and assessment of policy options. Those states that do not do so suffer costs and adjust, or make so many mistakes, and suffer so many costs, that they are ultimately selected out of the international system.

In this section we examine different lines of scholarship on the impact made by individual leaders and their policy officials on the probability of war. These lines of scholarship differ among themselves, but they are united by a resolute rejection of the realist view that we can understand international relations well by assuming that states are rational unitary actors. Instead, they put forward arguments that emphasize that to understand the sources of war we need to understand how state leaders may find it difficult if not impossible to act in accord with perfect rationality as assumed in realist theory. Then, in the next major section, we will see in the scholarship on domestic institutions how the assumption of states as unitary actors is also highly questioned in the field of international relations.

Misperception, Crisis Escalation, and War: the Role of Stress and 'Motivated Biases'

A national leader may go to war as a result of misperceptions: that is, he or she may perceive something about the world that is factually incorrect (Jervis 1988; Leng 2004). As we noted in the previous section, US leaders thought Saddam had a threatening nuclear program, but he did not; at least some US leaders thought a US occupation of Iraq would be easy to accomplish, and it was not. When are leaders more likely to succumb to misperceptions in a way that propels their countries toward war?

One possibility is stress. Scholars have suggested that when national leaders and their subordinates find themselves in a diplomatic crisis and perceive that the risk of war is present and growing, they are likely to experience severe physical and emotional stress. That stress could cause them to make mistakes in how they perceive their own policy options and those of their adversaries. These stress-induced misperceptions and mistakes, in turn, could increase the risk that the crisis might escalate to war.

Political scientist Ole Holsti (1972) has produced the classic work on the possible link between stress, impaired decision-making, and the decision for war. Holsti argues that, during the diplomatic crisis of July–August 1914 that led to the outbreak of World War I, discussed in Chapter 2, a dramatic upsurge in communications between Britain, France, Germany, and Russia in a short period of time appears to have contributed to rising stress among the leaders of those countries. That stress led the leaders to believe that time was working against them and their options in the crisis were decreasing in number, while the policy options of their adversaries were still wide open. Each leader began to say that it was up to the adversary to resolve the crisis before war engulfed Europe. As a result of this stress-induced tendency to perceive that others had more options, the main European leaders all inferred that it was not their responsibility, but that of others, to take decisive steps to stop the crisis that was moving toward war. Since none acted, the crisis spiraled out of control.

Stress may not be the only source of misperceptions. Cognitive psychologists have also identified a tendency for individuals to have 'motivated biases.' A motivated bias is any belief or attitude that a person holds because it advances or protects some interest, desire, or preference. Such motivated biases can impair the capacity of a decision maker to revise his or her beliefs in the face of new information. For example, one study has found that, during the Anglo-German crisis over Morocco in 1906, those German decision makers who had initially sought a confrontation with Britain were more reluctant to change course as the crisis began to take a turn against Germany than were German decision makers who had not made a commitment to the initial course of action leading to the crisis (Kaufman 1994). Motivated biases may account for the difference in views about how many US forces would be needed for Iraq in 2003, a matter we highlighted in the introduction to this chapter. Deputy Secretary Wolfowitz had been the main early proponent for the invasion, and so might not have wanted to anticipate how hard the invasion would be; General Shinseki appears to have played a less central role in deciding to attack Iraq, and therefore might have been more dispassionate in estimating what it would take to stabilize the country.

Social Psychology of Small Groups: Groupthink

The capacity of leaders and officials to process information and make sound judgments in the midst of a crisis might be impaired not just because of stress, but also as a result of psychological needs that those leaders and officials bring to their jobs. The groupthink thesis (Janis 1982) in particular suggests that a psychological need on the part of individuals to be accepted and liked by their work colleagues can lead national leaders and especially their advisors to make serious errors of analysis and judgment in the midst of a foreign policy crisis. For example, in April 1961, the new US president, John F. Kennedy, decided to press ahead with a Central Intelligence Agency (CIA) plan that had been developed in the last years of the Eisenhower administration to overthrow Cuba's pro-Soviet regime under Fidel Castro. The operation involved transporting about 1,500 anti-Castro rebels to beaches in Cuba called the Bay of Pigs, who were supposed to instigate a larger uprising by Cubans against their government. Cuban military forces quickly surrounded and attacked the anti-Castro force; Kennedy ceased support for the rebels, who were soon killed or captured; and Castro's victory fortified his grip over Cuba.

Several senior advisors to President Kennedy had doubts about the Bay of Pigs operation, but failed to express them. From the groupthink perspective, this silence was due to the fact that the doubters liked belonging to an elite group of advisors, and since most of those advisors *seemed* to support the operation, the doubters stayed quiet rather than jeopardize their positions in the group. Arthur Schlesinger, one of the doubters, recounted later that he did not want to appear soft while the other members of Kennedy's new team were expressing a strong 'we can do it' attitude.

The groupthink thesis may shed some light on why Kennedy's advisors failed to give the President their full assessment of the prospects for success of the Bay of Pigs operation. However, constructivist IR theory and feminist IR theory might suggest that the groupthink thesis raises at least as many questions as it answers. We take up this engagement of the groupthink thesis by those two perspectives in Box 5.3.

Moreover, one study (Kramer 1988) has suggested that the Bay of Pigs failure occurred not because of groupthink but because President Kennedy made the political calculation that if he canceled an operation that President Eisenhower had already approved, and this became known, Kennedy would suffer a serious loss of confidence both at home and abroad. On the other hand, more recently, and in seeming support of the groupthink thesis, a US Senate Intelligence Committee report invoked the groupthink thesis to explain how, in the lead-up to the Iraq war of 2003, the CIA overrated the status of Iraq's nuclear, biological, and chemical weapons programs. Commentaries on the Senate report emphasize that CIA analysts likely made errors in their assessments because they knew that national decision makers wanted to be told that Iraq had large-scale programs directed toward weapons of mass destruction (Phythian 2006).

Groupthink: The idea that a psychological need on the part of individuals to be accepted and liked by their work colleagues can lead national leaders and especially their advisors to make serious errors of analysis and judgment in the midst of a foreign policy crisis.

Constructivist and Feminist Interpretations of Groupthink and the Bay of Pigs

Background

As we discuss in the main text, President John F. Kennedy approved in April 1961 a CIA-backed invasion of Cuba by a force of Cuban exiles, an operation that ended in failure.

Groupthink explanation: Prior to the final go-ahead, advisors to President Kennedy who otherwise harbored doubts about the chances of success of the operation remained silent because they worried that if they expressed their doubts they would lose the respect and esteem of colleagues and the President. The result was that the advisors, by staying silent, helped propel Kennedy and the United States into a serious military debacle.

Constructivism: For a constructivist scholar, the groupthink argument raises but fails to ask a question about what transpired when groupthink dynamics were activated. In particular, the constructivist would ask, why did Kennedy's advisors believe that expressing doubts would lead to a loss of esteem with their colleagues and access to the President? A constructivist would suggest that the foundation for that fear was a network of shared understandings among the advisors and between them and the President. In particular, they all shared the view that Castro presented a serious threat to the United States, and that covert operations like the Bay of Pigs presented at least some prospect of success. The advisors knew that colleagues and the President had these ideas, and knowing that they feared that voicing doubts meant revolting against the group, which in turn would trigger exclusion. Hence, a constructivist would say that to understand how groupthink operated and contributed to the Bay of Pigs disaster, it is necessary to understand that the advisors and the President shared common understandings, namely, about the character of threats facing the United States and the prospects for success of a military response to those threats.

Feminism: A feminist IR scholar might criticize the constructionist viewpoint on the same grounds that constructivist criticizes the groupthink thesis; namely, that the constructivist argument is helpful but insufficient, for it raises but fails to answer a number of key questions. In particular, why did Kennedy's advisors believe that Castro was a threat to the United States, why did they believe that a covert military operation would have any prospect of success, and perhaps most importantly, why did they each feel so strongly that they could not risk losing the comradeship of their colleagues and access to the President as a result of expressing doubts about the whole enterprise? A feminist IR scholar would suggest that gender might be a part of the story, for not only was Kennedy a male, but so too was each and every one of his advisors on the Bay of Pigs. Perhaps, the feminist IR scholar would suggest, Kennedy and his advisors, by virtue of how they were socialized as males, and perhaps because of their male-based psychiatric make-up, were more inclined than was objectively true to see an independent and non-pliable Castro as a fundamental threat to them and the United States, and to believe that it was entirely appropriate and rational to think of using violence to deal with the problem of Castro. Most crucially, the feminist IR scholar might suggest, it could be the case that men have an especially high need for approval from other men, and an especially great desire for proximity to power. Thus, Kennedy's advisors might, by virtue of their gender, have been especially prone to think that violence was the answer to Castro, and may have been especially fearful that expressing doubts about that answer would lead to their expulsion from the group. Those male advisors were essentially biased by their gender both to make a recommendation to use violence and paralyzed in expressing doubts about that approach to the Castro challenge.

Pre-Conflict Aspirations of Leaders and the Realities of War

The United States Invades Iraq, March 2003

Aspiration: On March 16, 2003, three days before President George Bush announced that the United States would invade Iraq, Vice President Dick Cheney, predicted that 'I think things have gotten so bad inside Iraq, from the standpoint of the Iraqi people, my belief is we will, in fact, be greeted as liberators.' When asked if he thought Americans were ready for a 'long, costly and bloody battle,' the Vice President replied that 'Well, I don't think it's likely to unfold that way. . . . [the Iraqi people] want to get rid of Saddam Hussein, and they will welcome as liberators the United States when we come to do that.'

Reality: The United States readily defeated Iraqi regular military forces. However, an insurgency soon took hold and required several years to contain, and entailed the loss of more than 4,000 US military personnel, including 3,500 combat deaths. It was not until December 2009, more than six years after the war had begun, that the United States did not sustain a combat fatality during the course of a month. US forces were unable to withdraw from the country until 2011.

Sources: NBC (2003); GlobalSecurity.org (undated).

Personality Trait of Leaders: Over-Optimism

Leaders have often believed – falsely as it turns out – that if war were to occur their side would win a quick and easy victory, and thus be more willing to fight. One scholar has gone so far as to suggest that a crucial clue to understanding the causes of war is the 'optimism with which most wars were commenced by nations' leaders' (Blainey 1988:35).

Scholars have identified at least three reasons why leaders may be overly optimistic in estimating what they can achieve with military force. First, individuals in general may be prone to **positive illusions** – what we think we can accomplish is often greater than what we would expect to achieve if we had a truly accurate picture of our capabilities (Johnson 2004). Individuals may be prone toward positive illusions because they inspire confidence and confidence impels us to strive harder than we otherwise would. National leaders may be particularly prone toward positive illusions. Optimism and a 'can-do' attitude are among the characteristics that cause an individual to attract and instill confidence in others, and thus they are an attribute of successful leadership. The characteristics that make a person attractive and effective as a leader, in fact the very characteristics that helped that person ascend to power in the first place, might also make that person prone toward overestimating what can be achieved in a foreign crisis through different policy instruments, including the use of military force.

Second, it is possible that sudden increases in a country's military power may cause at least some of its leaders and policy makers to become more belligerent. For example, Pakistan's successful testing of a nuclear weapon in May 1998 may have contributed to its decision to use force against India later that year. A scholar of nuclear proliferation, Scott Sagan (Sagan *et al.* 2007: 139), notes that:

Positive illusions: The idea that what we think we can accomplish is often greater than what we would expect to achieve if we had a truly accurate picture of our capabilities.

When Pakistan acquired nuclear weapons there were many inside its military who said, 'This is our chance to do something about Kashmir,' so they misled then-Prime Minister Nawaz Sharif into approving an operation which sent Pakistani soldiers disguised as Mujahedeen guerillas to conduct low-level military actions in India-controlled Kashmir near the town of Kargil in the winter of 1998.

This infiltration in turn sparked a war between Pakistan and India, also in possession of nuclear weapons, between May and July 1999. Hence, the Pakistani military may have been emboldened by its acquisition of nuclear weapons, and this may have contributed to Pakistani aggression against India.

Feminist international theory, as we discussed in Chapter 3, suggests that men and women might differ systematically in the manner in which they view and approach international relations. One specific way in which this might occur is through gender's role in the generation of positive illusions (Johnson *et al.* 2006; McDermott *et al.* 2009; Rosen 2005). As you will recall from Chapter 3, Dominic Johnson and his co-authors conducted a study on the confidence of individuals prior to playing a computer-based conflict simulation game that included different ways of resolving disputes with other players, including the launching of 'wars.' Among the findings the study revealed were (a) prior to playing the game, males in the study were much more likely than females to predict that they would achieve above average scores; (b) individuals who were overconfident before the game started were substantially more likely to launch wars as a way of trying to win the game; and (c) males who were especially confident prior to the game were especially likely to launch wars. From these findings, the research team concluded that males may have a propensity toward overconfidence and this overconfidence may have led males to tend to launch wars to win the game. The research team could not identify what it might be about males that seemed to link them to overconfidence and then to the tendency to launch wars, and this question demands future research. However, the study does point to the possibility that there may be connections between gender, overconfidence, and decisions for war.

Recent studies have identified significant associations between the status of women within countries and the likelihood of those states becoming embroiled in military conflicts with other countries. For example, one study (Caprioli and Boyer 2001) finds that states with higher levels of gender equality tend to use less military violence in military crises than do those states with lower levels of gender equality. In addition, scholars have found that states where there is greater domestic security for women are also more likely to have cordial ties rather than violent relations with other countries (Hudson *et al.* 2008/2009).

In sum, and in strong contention with the realist view that individual characteristics can be put aside in the analysis of war, scholars have found that a range of individual-level factors – misperceptions, groupthink, and positive illusions – may contribute to the risk of war between states.

Levels of Analysis

The Individual as the Cause of War

Individual

Misperceptions may cause leaders to make errors resulting in war. These misperceptions may be due to stress or motivated biases.

Groupthink may cause the advisors to refrain from expressing doubts about the wisdom of using force, thus increasing the chances such force will be used.

Leaders may be especially prone to over-optimism in what they think they can accomplish through the use of military force, thus enhancing the chances they will choose that option.

Gender may play a role in generating positive illusions and groupthink.

Underlying Causes of War: the State Level of Analysis

Realist theory, we noted above, suggests that we can obtain good insights into international affairs by assuming that states act as unitary actors. That is, we may assume that state leaders act in the foreign domain more in reaction to circumstances in that domain, and not so much if at all in response to domestic institutions or conditions. Many scholars challenge this realist approach to international analysis. As we will see below, they suggest that domestic institutions and policy processes within countries shape the way leaders deal with international problems and, apart from and in addition to the impact of individual-level factors, might contribute to decisions by leaders to go to war. As we will see below, these scholars focus on a variety of domestic economic, political, and policy-making features of countries that may influence the risk of war.

Domestic Economic Systems and War

Some scholars, drawing often from the Marxist tradition that we described in Chapter 3, have suggested that the economic organization of a country, and in particular whether the country has a capitalist or socialist economy, may determine whether that country is more or less inclined to use military force to resolve foreign conflicts of interest. As we saw in Chapter 3, in a capitalist economic system (or market-based economy) consumers, enterprises, and workers interact in relatively unregulated markets. This interaction determines which goods and services a country produces and consumes, how much workers are paid, and how much money is used for consumption as opposed to saving and investment. In contrast, in a socialist economic system the government plays a central role in the organization and coordination both of the supply of the factors of production, such as the number of workers in a particular industry, and the quantity of goods and services that are produced in that industry.

As noted in Chapter 1, Russian Bolshevik leader Vladimir Lenin suggested that the main cause of World War I was the fact that the European states had capitalist economies. He argued that these capitalist countries necessarily underpaid their workers and, consequently facing insufficient demand at home, they competed for colonies abroad and thus ultimately came to war against one another. More recent work in international relations (Rosecrance 1999; Gartzke 2007) suggests that, in fact, capitalist countries are particularly likely to remain at peace with one another. Such countries avoid conflict with each other because they want relatively open trade and a stable international monetary system, and territorial issues among them have ceased to matter because they mutually recognize that they can obtain economic prosperity much more readily through trade and financial integration than through conquest of each other or other countries.

Domestic Political Institutions and Governmental Processes

The most important challenge to the realist view about the immateriality of domestic factors in world politics is situated firmly in the liberal tradition: it is the democratic peace thesis, that is, democracies almost never fight each other. As we discussed in Chapter 3, scholars have suggested that two sets of causes account for the democratic peace: the first relates to institutional constraints (Russett 1993); the second to normative constraints (Owen 1994). We now examine in more detail how these two causal processes may produce the democratic peace.

Institutional Politics and War: The US Oil Embargo against Japan, 1941

Theory: *The Unitary-Actor Assumption in Realist International Theory*

Realist international theory assumes that states are unitary actors. That is, having established a national strategy, top state leaders can then execute it in the manner that reflects their preferences and ideas by effective orchestration and control of the actions of various parts of the national government. According to this assumption, state leaders have a high capacity to monitor and control subordinate officials.

Practice: *The US Oil Embargo Against Japan, 1941*

In response to Japan's invasion of French Indochina (today's Vietnam, Cambodia, and Laos), President Franklin Delano Roosevelt on July 24, 1941 ordered a freeze on Japanese financial assets in the United States. When Roosevelt announced the freeze, he promised that Japan could apply to the US government for licenses to import oil, that such licenses would be issued, and that funds held by Japanese importers in the United States would be released so the Japanese could pay for licensed oil sales. Assistant Secretary of State Dean Acheson (who later, under President Harry Truman, served as Secretary of State), the official responsible for releasing Japanese funds, refused to do so in the first weeks of August, while Roosevelt was out of the country. When Roosevelt returned at the end of August and learned of Acheson's refusal to release the funds, the President apparently decided he could not reverse Acheson's actions. Thus, a financial sanction that Roosevelt wanted to exclude oil came to include oil, as Acheson had wanted. The oil embargo contributed to the Japanese decision to attack Pearl Harbor in an ill-conceived effort to achieve a quick victory against the United States.

Acheson later claimed that even though Roosevelt had said he wanted the oil shipments to go through, Acheson knew that what Roosevelt really wanted and what the US national interest really required was a total embargo of oil shipments to Japan. Acheson suggested that '[If] President Roosevelt lacked decisiveness in the degree his successor [President Truman] possessed it, he had a sense of direction in which he constantly advanced. It seemed to those in government [that is, Acheson] that our most useful function was to increase in so far as we could the rate of that advance.'

Source: Sagan 1994: 70.

Institutional constraints:
The constitutional or customary checks within a country that impede, slow, or limit the capacity of a leader unilaterally to undertake some action.

Institutional constraints are the constitutional or customary checks within a country that impede, slow, or limit the capacity of a leader unilaterally to undertake some action. Citizens of democratic states, knowing they and their children will pay most of the costs of war, use their political influence – and especially their right to elect leaders – to constrain leaders from going to war except in the direst of circumstances. By contrast, authoritarian leaders can use coercion to shift the costs of war onto the general public, and may positively embrace war as a way of seeking power and glory for themselves, and to divert the attention of citizens from domestic problems (Chiozza and Goemans 2011). Thus, authoritarian leaders may have a greater motive and ability to start wars than is true of democratic leaders.

Normative constraints are the beliefs, values, and attitudes that inform and shape the behavior of a leader. The normative constraints on democratic leaders might give democracies time and political space to solve their problems with each other. The kind of person who is likely to rise to power in a democratic state must demonstrate that she or he values compromise over total victory, peaceful change over violence, and the rule of law over the use of force to solve disputes. Exactly the opposite characteristics are likely to propel a person to the top leadership position in an authoritarian state. Authoritarian leaders often gain and maintain power through the use of violence. Both kinds of leaders are likely to bring their very different orientations to political life to foreign policy interactions. If that is so, then leaders of democratic states will likely find it much easier to amicably resolve any conflicts of interests with leaders of other democratic states than they would with leaders of autocratic countries. Moreover, leaders of autocratic states would have grave difficulties in reaching peaceful accords with each other if they faced serious conflicts of interests.

Democratic institutions and norms may be doing more than maintaining the democratic peace. They may also be serving as brakes on the possible risk that military conflict abroad might undermine those democratic institutions. In January 1961, Dwight D. Eisenhower, in his farewell address as President, warned that a **military-industrial complex**, a growing US military bureaucracy together with a network of large American defense-related firms, was acquiring too much influence over US national security policy. Eisenhower (1961) also warned that 'In the councils of government, we must guard against the acquisition of unwarranted influence, whether sought or unsought, by the military industrial complex. The potential for the disastrous rise of misplaced power exists and will persist … We must never let the weight of this combination endanger our liberties or democratic processes.' Sociologist Harold Lasswell (1941) had issued a similar warning when he suggested that there might be emerging at that time what he termed the '**garrison state**,' that is, highly militarized countries in which governments controlled economic, social, and political life in order to maximize military power. Yet, the US system of political checks and balances, together with a widespread skepticism about government, have interacted to ensure that the United States has retained its republican character and has not become a garrison state working at the behest of a military-industrial complex (Friedberg 2000).

The democratic peace thesis is persuasive. However, we should keep in mind three points of caution. First, democracies rarely go to war with each other, but they often become involved in militarized conflicts with non-democratic states. Second, while there is strong empirical support for the democratic peace, there is as yet no consensus on why we observe it. Finally, even in democracies, policy subordinates will misinterpret – possibly even purposely – the directives of leaders and essentially begin to pursue something approaching their own foreign policies. During a political-diplomatic crisis such policy incoherence can contribute to the risk of war, as can be observed in the example in Box 5.5.

In sum, the economic and political systems of countries play a large role in inclining those countries toward peace or war with each other in the context of a serious conflict of interest.

Normative constraints: The beliefs, values, and attitudes that inform and shape the behavior of a leader.

Military-industrial complex: The combination of a large military bureaucracy and a powerful network of defense industry firms, united to obtain a disproportionate and overly powerful influence over national security policy (generally applied to the United States).

Garrison state: A highly militarized state in which the government controls economic, social, and political life in order to maximize military power.

State

Democratic states may be less likely to fight each other than other kinds of pairings of countries (mutually non-democratic or mixed) because they possess a wider and more potent range of institutional and normative constraints on the use of force.

In all states, intra-governmental policy dynamics, including overly aggressive officials, can increase the risk of war.

Underlying Causes of War: the International Level of Analysis

International anarchy may act as a permissive cause of war, that is, it may enable factors situated at other levels of analysis to induce states to be inclined toward war. It may also serve as an active cause of war, that is, it might positively propel states to do things that increase the risk of war between them.

Anarchy as a Permissive Condition for War

If international anarchy, that is, the absence of an international government to which states can appeal for redress of grievances or protection, always inclined states to fight when they found themselves in diplomatic crises, then every time we see states having such a crisis then we should also see those states go to war. Most diplomatic crises do not end in war. Hence, anarchy by itself cannot cause states to go to war with each other.

International anarchy might instead give free rein to individual-level and state-level factors that push states toward war (Waltz 1959). The United Nations is available to offer a helpful framework for diplomatic resolutions of disputes, and in doing so it has probably helped states resolve disagreements before they escalated to war. However, the UN cannot itself provide protection to a state if it is attacked, or penalize a state that turns to violence. Because then there is no reliable international government, the risk of war weighs on state leaders in the midst of a crisis. If those leaders experience stress or groupthink or overconfidence and begin to make errors, no outside agency exists that can, with a high level of reliability, stop them from going over the brink to war.

Anarchy as a Propellant of International Conflict

Private information problem: The tendency of states to overstate their resolve and capabilities during a diplomatic or military crisis because there is no international authority to force states to reveal their true preferences, intentions, and capabilities. This tendency can make a diplomatic solution more difficult to obtain and war more likely.

International anarchy may not just allow other factors to propel states toward conflict, it may itself positively and independently induce states to initiate military crises and even war (Fearon 1995). Anarchy may, in the first place, generate what international relations scholars call the problem of **private information**. Because there is no international authority to force states to reveal their true preferences, intentions, and capabilities, they have the capacity and thus the incentive to overstate their resolve and capabilities during a diplomatic or military crisis. This tendency toward bluff could make a diplomatic resolution more difficult to attain and war more likely to occur by virtue of each side pressing too hard with threats and counter-threats. For example, after he was soundly defeated in the first Iraq War of 1991, Saddam Hussein sought to maintain power at home and security abroad by *seeming* to have a nuclear weapons program and taking actions that seemed to be directed to hiding Iraq's nuclear weapons activities from Western intelligence agencies and the International Atomic Energy Agency (IAEA). Actually, Hussein had ceased serious efforts to develop a nuclear military capability sometime during the 1990s, but US, British, and other intelligence services were convinced that he was going for the bomb. Toward the end of the crisis of 2002–03 that culminated in the second Iraq war, Hussein's government sought to signal that Iraq really had no nuclear weapons program, but by then it was too late. US and British leaders were convinced that Hussein was lying, and the only way to do away with Iraq's nuclear threat was to invade and destroy his regime.

Second, anarchy may produce what is often called the **commitment problem**. Given the absence of an international government, states must fear that any diplomatic agreement they reach with an adversary to stave off a war might be violated at some point in the future when that adversary is in a position to be more deadly and demanding. In those circumstances, one or both sides may decide that it may be better to fight today rather than be cheated upon and attacked at a moment of weakness in the future. For example, as noted above, it is quite likely that US and allied leaders in 2002 and early 2003 simply ceased to believe that Saddam would keep his word if he signed an agreement to make no future demands on Kuwait and to refrain from reconstituting his nuclear program. Without that trust, or a capacity to ensure compliance, it seemed a safer path for the US and allied leaders to invade and remove Saddam from power once and for all.

Scholars of international relations use a helpful analytical device from game theory to explore this type of situation, namely the **Prisoner's Dilemma**. Imagine that the police catch two criminals as they are breaking into a liquor store. The police search and find evidence in the getaway car that indicates they have just apprehended not two break-in thieves but possibly two professional contract killers who work in tandem and have killed several people. The police place the two criminals in two separate holding cells at the station. They cannot communicate with each other. The local district attorney arrives. She goes into each holding cell. She tells each prisoner that if he stays quiet, he will, at the very least, go to prison for five years for the break-in. She also tells each prisoner that if he agrees to testify at trial that both he and his partner are contract killers, and the other does not, then the one who testifies will go free while the other will get 50 years in prison. She also adds this: if both prisoners admit to being contract killers, they will each receive a sentence of 20 years in prison.

The situation the prisoners are facing is depicted in the payoff matrix in Figure 5.6. A's payoffs are listed in the left side of each cell; B's payoffs are listed in the right side of each cell. Each year of jail is a bad experience, so for each year a negative 1 is assigned: a jail sentence of 20 years therefore translates into a payoff of –20.

Prisoner A may think along the following lines: if I stay quiet (which we call a strategy on the part of A to cooperate with B), and B does the same thing (an outcome of cooperate–cooperate), we both receive five years in jail for the break-in, or a payoff of –5. That is bad but better than a lot of the other options I am facing. Still, I am not going to stay quiet, for two reasons. First, I might be able to walk out of here a free man, if I agree to testify about the contract killings and my partner stays quiet (which we will call a strategy by A to 'defect' from B). Second, if I stay quiet, and he agrees to testify (a strategy of defect by B), he goes free and I go to jail for 50 years! So, I'll admit to the murders, and if my partner does the same I'll receive the 20-year sentence, but there's the chance he'll stay quiet and then I'll walk free, and in any event if I talk I'll

Commitment problem: A state's fear that any diplomatic agreement it reaches with an adversary to stave off a war might be violated at some point in the future when that adversary is in a position to be more deadly and demanding. The commitment problem arises due to the anarchic nature of the international system.

Prisoner's Dilemma: A helpful analytical device from game theory used to model certain instances of state behavior.

The Prisoner's Dilemma game illustrates how two actors can fail to achieve mutually beneficial cooperation and end in mutually costly non-cooperation. They face a particular combination of pay-offs – they do well by cooperating with each other, but even better by cheating, and they do the worst if they are cheated upon. Because they lack some overarching mechanism to ensure that they faithfully comply with an agreement, they end up doing a lot worse than if they cooperated with each other.

		Prisoner B	
		Cooperate	Defect
Prisoner A	Cooperate	−5, −5	−50, 0
	Defect	0, −50	−20, −20

avoid 50 years in prison. B thinks exactly along the same lines. The likely result: A and B both admit to being contract killers, and both go to jail for 20 years. Each loses a chance to serve no more than five years in prison, but each has avoided the worst possible outcome, namely, a 50-year sentence.

Let us now return to Iraq, the United States, and the lead-up to their war in 2003. For the sake of conversation, the United States may be viewed as state A in Figure 5.5, and Iraq may be viewed as state B. Let us imagine that, prior to the outbreak of hostilities, the two sides might have considered making the following deal: Iraq would forego any future nuclear weapons program or aggressive designs on Kuwait or other neighbors, and the United States would agree not to invade the country and to lift economic sanctions that had been in place since the early 1990s. The two sides in this instance would grudgingly have to live with each other, but they would avoid a costly war. This arrangement would correspond to the cooperate–cooperate outcome in the northwest corner of the payoff matrix in Figure 5.6. However, the United States would worry that if it lifted sanctions and forswore attacking Iraq, the latter might be tempted to develop nuclear weapons secretly, and after it had those weapons it might become extremely dangerous toward Kuwait and other countries in the Middle East. In that case, the United States would find itself in the cooperate–defect cell in the north-east corner of the matrix. Iraq on the other hand would worry that if it adhered to the agreement, the United States would find some other pretext at a later date to undermine it: the result would be for Iraq to find itself in the highly unfavorable southwest corner of the matrix. Hence, for both sides, a war – the defect–defect cell in the southeast corner of the matrix – is clearly costly but at least it gives each the hope that it can avoid its worst outcome, that is, making a deal but then later being cheated upon by the other. The mutual fear of the United States and Iraq of defection is being driven by the absence of an effective international government to enforce agreements, that is, international anarchy.

International anarchy may establish a context in which states overstate their claims and resolve, and fear that a deal to avert war today might lead to a situation in the future that is actually worse than commencing a war. In these two ways, international anarchy might propel states with a conflict of interest toward war.

Levels of Analysis

The International System as the Cause of War

🌐 **International**

Anarchy may be a permissive condition for war: the absence of an international government may increase the risks of war.

States may be actively propelled toward war by virtue of international anarchy because the latter encourages states in a crisis to retain private information and undertake strategic lying during a crisis.

International anarchy generates Prisoner's Dilemma-like impediments to resolving conflicts of interests by states with diplomatic agreements.

Internal Wars and their Causes

In general, an **internal war** is an instance in which politically organized groups within a country, including most often the national government, become engaged in sustained military operations against one another. Students of international relations have good reasons to be interested in internal wars, and especially civil wars, as we shall see in the next section.

Internal Wars and International Peace and Security

Internal wars may have important repercussions for international peace and security. In particular, an internal war may spread to other countries, it may cause the state experiencing the internal war to be more aggressive towards other states, or it may cause other states to become hostile toward the state experiencing domestic violence.

An internal war in one country can instigate international violence through at least three different pathways. First, an internal war in one country can bring about **contagion**, that is, it can spread to neighboring countries (Buhaug and Gleditsch 2008; Braithwaite 2010). Rebels in one country often find shelter in a neighboring country, and they sometimes begin to fight the government of that country. The Taliban, who originally held power in Afghanistan, moved in large numbers to Pakistan after the US invasion of 2001, and in recent years have been conducting an insurgency against the US and the US-supported government in Kabul while also fighting an insurgency aimed at Pakistan's central government. Alternatively, refugee flows from a war-torn country into a neighboring country can lead to instability and the outbreak of violence in the latter country, as occurred in the mid-1990s when refugees from Rwanda's civil war fled to neighboring Zaire and overwhelmed its infrastructure, which in turn contributed to the onset of a civil war in that country.

Second, a state that has experienced an internal war and political change arising from that war may for a time become more aggressive toward other states. It may do so both out of a fear that other states are hostile to it, and to divert domestic attention from the problems the new government is having in establishing the legitimacy of its rule as well as domestic order and stability (Maoz 1989; Walt 1996; Colgan 2013).

The third pathway by which internal war within a country might lead to international military conflict is that a state experiencing violence at home might attract invasions or other military confrontations from abroad. This could take place in at least two ways. On the one hand, a foreign state may believe that the country experiencing internal war may be vulnerable and easy to defeat militarily. Saddam Hussein appears to have made this calculation when he decided to invade Iran in September 1980, just as Iran was enmeshed in revolutionary change. As it turned out, the war dragged on for eight years and ended in a stalemate that favored Iran.

Another form of international military intervention against a state involved in internal war might arise from outrage by other states about the manner in which domestic violence is taking place within the country. Internal wars often produce social chaos, mass hunger, and a collapse of medical care, and combatants, as we will see below, often deliberately kill massive numbers of civilians. Combatants sometimes commit war crimes during these conflicts – mass killings of civilians, using rape as a military strategy, or employing children as soldiers – as has happened in numerous internal wars in recent years in the Balkans (for example, in Bosnia-Herzegovina and Kosovo) and in sub-Saharan Africa (such as in Sierra Leone and the Central African

Internal war: Any war within a state, contrasted with war between two or more states.

Contagion: The spread to neighboring countries of an internal war in one country, often caused by rebels seeking shelter in a neighboring country and beginning conflict there.

► Photo 5.3 Child Soldier in Civil War in Liberia, 2003

In the mid-2000s, up to 300,000 children were being forced to fight in 30 armed conflicts around the world. The problem is especially acute in sub-Saharan Africa. This file photograph dated July 28, 2003 shows a nine-year-old Liberian child soldier fighting for Charles Taylor's government forces during the civil war in Monrovia, Liberia. In 2006, Taylor was arrested and transferred to the Hague, the Netherlands, to stand trial for instigating a civil war in the neighboring country of Sierra Leone, and for violating numerous terms of the Geneva Convention in that country, including the use of child soldiers.

Source: © NIC BOTHMA/epa/Corbis.

Republic), and in Asia (for example, in Sri Lanka). In some of those instances, one or more outside states have reacted to the atrocities by intervening militarily to try to bring the internal strife to an end. Such humanitarian interventions raise the possibility that there is developing a 'responsibility to protect' by outside powers when non-combatants are targeted by governments and rebels in civil wars. We will discuss humanitarian interventions in greater detail in Chapter 11.

Given their repercussions for international relations, we need to understand internal wars. It is to that task that we now direct attention.

Internal Wars: Types and Trends

There are many types of internal wars. The most prevalent form is **civil war**. A civil war is a sustained clash between forces that are controlled by the national government and forces that are controlled by an organized opposition group within the country. Those opposition groups typically have one of two goals. First, they may seek to overthrow the current regime and seize control of the central government, especially its military and national police. Several 'Arab Spring' revolutions that swept through North Africa and the Middle East in 2011–12 are in this class of civil wars. The Libyan civil war that began in February 2011 was complex in its origins and conduct, but was essentially a military struggle on the part of several loosely allied domestic opposition forces, supported by a coalition of outside powers including the United States, that fought to overthrow Colonel Muammar Gaddafi and his dictatorship centered in the capital city of Tripoli. It ended with the defeat of forces loyal to Gaddafi, the fall of the dictatorship, the formation of a transitional government that was recognized by the United Nations in September 2011, and the capture and killing of Gaddafi the following month.

Sometimes the opposition group or coalition does not wish to seize control of the national government, but instead to bring about the secession of a part a country to form a new state. An example of such a **secessionist civil war** concerns Sudan. Forces in the southern part of Sudan fought two prolonged civil wars (1955–72 and 1983–2005) against the central government in Khartoum, and in 2012 finally achieved independence and became the sovereign state of the Republic of South Sudan. Different

Civil war: A sustained clash between forces that are controlled by the national government and forces that are controlled by an organized opposition group within the country.

Secessionist civil war: A civil war in which the rebel group seeks to bring about the breaking away of a part of the territory of a country to form a new, separate state.

◀ Figure 5.7
Incidence of Internal Wars, 1816–2007, and During and After the Cold War

For each designated time period, the bar represents the average annual number of internal wars that began during the period; the number in parentheses is the total number of such wars that began during the period.

Source: Meredith Reid Sarkees, and Frank Wayman (2010) *Resort to War: 1816–2007* (CQ Press). Data-set available from *Correlates of War*, Intra-State War Data (v4.0), at http://www. correlatesofwar.org/.

opposition groups in Darfur, in the western part of Sudan, have also fought a civil war aimed at secession since 2003, but have not succeeded in breaking away from the central government. We will return to the Darfur civil war below, in our discussion of the causes of internal wars.

Civil wars constitute about 92 percent of the 334 internal wars that occurred between 1816 and 2007, according to the COW research team. Two other types of internal wars do not involve the central government fighting an opposition group. The first type consists of **inter-communal wars**: they constitute about 5 percent of COW-identified internal wars, and take place when members of different religious communities in a country become embroiled in large-scale organized violence. For example, several militias that fought one another during the civil war in Lebanon between 1975 and 1990 were organized along sectarian lines – among others there were several different Shia Muslim, Sunni Muslim, and Maronite Christian fighting forces. Finally, in a few instances – about 3 percent of the total – internal conflicts have consisted of violence between military forces of governmental entities below the national level and non-governmental entities. For example, in 1967, fighting broke out in China between Red Guard radicals and regional military forces during the Cultural Revolution that communist leader MaoTse-Tung sought to instigate against what he thought were increasingly conservative party comrades.

In Figure 5.7 we offer COW-generated data on the incidence of internal wars that occurred between 1816 and 2007. Internal wars began at a remarkably steady rate of about 1.3 internal wars per year during the bulk of the nineteenth century and the first half of the twentieth. Then, during the period of decolonization and its aftermath, we see a sharp upward spike, to about 2.8 new internal wars per year, during the years between 1950 and 1999. Finally, the incidence of new internal wars actually increased during the 2000–2007 period and, if we compare the 1946–89 era to the post-Cold War years between 1990 and 2007, we observe an increase in the annual incidence of new internal wars, a phenomenon that demands further research.

We present in Figure 5.8 tentative estimates of trends in the lethality of internal wars: these are rough estimates because good data on battlefield deaths during internal

Inter-communal wars: A war in which members of different religious communities in a country become embroiled in large-scale organized violence.

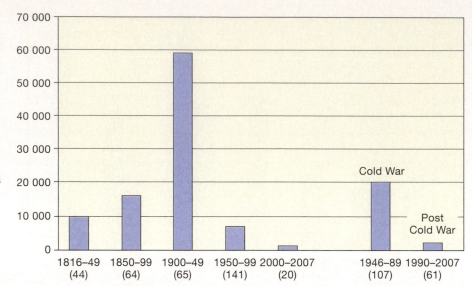

► Figure 5.8
Lethality of Internal Wars, 1816–2007, and During and After the Cold War

For each designated time period, the bar represents the average number of battlefield deaths that occurred during the period; the number in parentheses is the total number of internal wars that began during the period.

Source: Meredith Reid Sarkees, and Frank Wayman (2010) *Resort to War: 1816–2007* (CQ Press). Data-set available from *Correlates of War*, Intra-State War Data (v4.0), at http://www.correlatesofwar.org/.

wars is much less systematic than what is available on interstate or extra-state wars. Keeping that note of caution in mind, we are able to observe that at least 6 million combatants were killed in internal wars between 1816 and 2007, the vast majority of whom were killed in the civil wars of the twentieth century. In more recent times, the lethality of internal wars appears to have gone down, both in terms of total killed and killed per war.

Internal wars may be at least as lethal for non-combatants as the various types of international wars. Civilian deaths during internal wars are often due to intentional wartime killings by one or more sides involved in the war (Kalyvas and Kocher 2009). For example, a recent study identified 115 civil wars during the years between 1945 and 2000, and it found that during 27 of those wars at least one of the warring sides carried out a strategy of mass civilian killings (Valentino *et al.* 2004).

There have been numerous instances in which civil wars spark civilian killings on an enormous scale. In Cambodia, the Khmer Rouge rebel force overturned the central government in Phnom Penh in 1975, and then began what it called a 'purification' campaign that, by 1979, resulted in the murder of somewhere between 1.5 and 2 million men, women, and children, or something approaching 20 percent of Cambodia's population in 1975. Just nineteen years later, in the sub-Saharan country of Rwanda, a civil war began during which government-supported armed groups composed mainly of individuals from one tribal group, the Hutu, killed in a matter of months approximately 800,000 unarmed civilians belonging to individuals of another tribal group, the Tutsi, or other Hutu civilians who were thought to be protecting Tutsi or who were thought in one way or another to oppose the massacre. In that case, as in Cambodia, approximately 20 percent of Rwanda's pre-war civilian population was murdered.

Finally, with the aid of Figure 5.9 we turn to the issue of the **internationalization of civil wars**, by which we mean that, during the course of the internal war, one or more foreign states intervened and provided support to one or another of the warring sides, including sometimes the introduction of combat forces, but did not take over the bulk of the fighting. We can make at least three observations about external interventions in internal wars from the data in the figure. First, for reasons that scholars

Internationalization of civil war: The process by which, during a civil war, one or more foreign states intervenes and supports one or another of the warring sides, possibly by introducing combat forces, but does not take over the bulk of the fighting

▼ Photos 5.4 and 5.5 Genocide in Cambodia and Rwanda

Genocide after the Cambodian Civil War, 1975–79

Photos of the victims of the Khmer Rouge are displayed at the Tuol Sleng Genocide Museum, which is in Phnom Penh, the capital of Cambodia. The site is a former high school that was used by the Khmer Rouge as a torture and killing center.

Source: PA Images.

Genocide in Rwanda, 1994

The Rwanda killings of 1994 tell us that genocide remains a fundamental problem even in contemporary times.

Source: © lifegallery – istockphoto.com.

have not yet identified, international interventions do not take place in connection to all civil wars. Second, such interventions are not a new phenomenon: they occurred during the nineteenth and twentieth centuries, and have continued in the twenty-first century. Third, the frequency with which foreign states intervened in internal wars was roughly twice as high during the second half of the twentieth century, and in particular during the Cold War, than in earlier periods, or since the end of the Cold War. Part of the explanation is that the Cold War was conducted through a series of proxy wars consisting of interventions by one or both superpowers in civil wars and other internal military conflicts in the Third World.

◀ **Figure 5.9 International Interventions in Internal Wars, 1816–2007, and during and after the Cold War**

Percentage of Internal Wars in which International Intervention Occurred

Source: Meredith Reid Sarkees, and Frank Wayman (2010) *Resort to War: 1816–2007* (CQ Press). Data-set available from *Correlates of War*, Intra-State War Data (v4.0), at http://www.correlatesofwar.org/.

Causes of Internal Wars

Just as the levels-of-analysis framework helps us learn about the causes of inter-state war, it is also helpful in exploring what observers have suggested might be the causes of internal wars, and in particular civil wars.

The Individual and Internal War

Many of the factors discussed above that prompt individual national leaders to go to war probably operate on the leaders of factions in internal wars. Beyond that, scholars have suggested that at least two additional individual-level mechanisms may increase the likelihood of internal wars, namely, **greed** and **grievance** (Collier *et al.* 2009). By greed we mean a person's intense desire to possess goods or money, and by grievance we mean a person's belief that he or she is being victimized by or excluded from important institutions in a country. Individuals may believe they are being victimized or excluded for many reasons, including their religion, race, ethnic background, gender, or social class.

Greed may be a part of what motivates individuals in internal (and international) wars of all sorts, but it may play a particularly large role in countries that possess natural resources that can be readily acquired, transported, and sold for cash. Such resources, sometimes termed **lootable wealth**, may include diamonds, gold, minerals, timber, narcotics, and oil. Countries where lootable wealth has played a role in prompting or prolonging civil wars are concentrated in sub-Saharan Africa, including Angola, Congo, Liberia, and Sierra Leone (Weinstein 2005).

In addition to greed, grievance might be a powerful individual-level factor in prompting internal wars. Scholars in recent years have found that ethnicity-based grievances have played a key role in motivating individuals to take up arms in civil wars (Cederman *et al.* 2010). Ethnic identity-based grievances were very much a part of the tensions that led to the civil war between the Hutu and the Tutsi in Rwanda, for example. More generally, perhaps 60 ethnicity-based conflicts occurred between 1946 and 2005 and reached the COW standard for a civil war, namely, 1,000 battlefield deaths within 12 months, which suggests that ethnic conflicts made up a substantial portion of all civil wars during the second half of the twentieth century.

Competition over natural resources can interact with ethnic differences and contribute to individual and ultimately group-level grievances and the onset of an internal war. One example of this dynamic can be observed in the secessionist civil war in the Darfur region of Sudan. That civil war, which began in 2003 and was ongoing in 2014, has pitted the central government in Khartoum and local Arab militias called the **Janjaweed** against two indigenous rebel groups, the Sudanese Liberation Movement/Army (SLM/A), and the Justice and Equality Movement (JEM). The war has been brutal: perhaps 450,000 civilians have been killed and 2.75 million persons displaced from their homes. The United Nations since late 2007 has undertaken a peacekeeping mission in the region, replacing an earlier effort by the African Union, but periodic violence has continued. The United States and other countries have accused the central government in Khartoum of perpetrating genocide in Darfur, and the International Criminal Court (ICC) has issued an international arrest warrant for Sudan's president, Omar Hassan Ahmad Al Bashir, for directing war crimes and crimes against humanity in Darfur.

The continuing civil war in Darfur has many roots, and among them has been the overlay of ethnicity and competition over scarce resources. In particular, at the heart

Greed: A person's intense desire to possess goods or money. On the individual level of analysis, a primary mechanism that increases the likelihood of internal war.

Grievance: A person's belief that he or she is being victimized by or excluded from important institutions in a country. On the individual level of analysis, a primary mechanism that increases the likelihood of internal war.

Lootable wealth: Natural resources that can be readily acquired, transported, and sold for cash. In some countries, greed and lootable wealth combine to make internal conflict more likely.

Janjaweed: Local Arab militias in Sudan allied with the central government in Khartoum against the Sudanese Liberation Movement/Army and the Justice and Equality Movement in the Sudanese civil war.

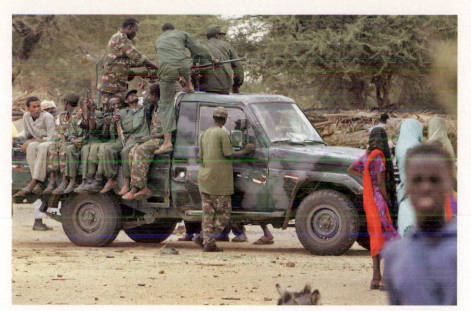

◀ Photo 5.6
**Janjaweed Militia
Fighters, October
2004**

The Janjaweed is an
armed militia com-
posed mainly of
Sudanese Arabs that
has perpetrated many
of the atrocities against
African civilians that
have occurred during
the Darfur civil war.

Source: PA Images.

of the Darfur war is a dispute between African farmers who wish to settle and cultivate
land and Arab semi-nomadic livestock herders who want periodic access to that land.
The latter group has been supported by the Khartoum government. Herder–farmer
tensions had long been present in Darfur. However, a drought that began roughly in
the mid-1980s and was still in effect in the mid-2000s sharpened the competition
between farmers and herders over scarce land and water resources, making the settlement of this underlying resource dispute more difficult and turning it into a driver
of what has become an inter-ethnic war in that region (Straus 2005).

The State and Internal War

Two characteristics of countries at the state level of analysis may play a role in the outbreak of internal wars, namely, the degree of inclusiveness of different elements of
society in the control of the state, and the capacity of the state.

Governments in ethnically divided societies that favor one ethnic group, and systematically discriminate against other groups, are much more likely to induce the
latter to take up some form of resistance, perhaps leading to a secessionist war. The
degree of inclusion or exclusion on the basis of ethnicity by a national government
is an important state-level contributor to civil peace or civil war. The presence of
democratic political institutions does not appear to reduce the likelihood of civil
wars, so while inclusiveness is important it appears that there may be several political arrangements whereby that goal can be achieved (Fearon and Laitin 2003;
Collier *et al.* 2009).

Second, the capacity of the government to resist an armed insurgency has a
strong influence on the likelihood that a country will experience some form of
internal war (Fearon and Laitin 2003). A number of statistical studies have shown
that wealthy countries are markedly less likely to experience internal wars. Such
countries may be characterized by less severe or widespread grievances on the part
of individuals within those countries. In addition, a country's wealth creates the
basis for the strength of its government. If the society is wealthy, then the govern-

ment will have a relatively larger pool of tax revenues and a more sophisticated and educated work force. This strong government in turn will be able to reduce the risk that the country will experience a civil war. For example, it will have sophisticated military and police intelligence resources, so it can identify and suppress domestic dissident groups that might have the potential to turn to arms. It is also likely to have built a network of roads, and these roads give government military leaders an advantage in moving troops to trouble spots, overcoming possible terrain advantages that rebels might otherwise enjoy, such as mountainous regions, and suppress early signs of rebellion. A strong government is also better able than a weaker government to conscript fighters to defeat insurgencies before the latter reach a high level of effectiveness.

In sum, characteristics of governments – whether they are inclusive or exclusive, and, perhaps most important, whether they have strong and effective societal-control capabilities – play an important role in the incidence of internal wars.

The International System and Internal War

At least three conditions at the international level affect internal wars: interstate wars, colonialism and its aftermath, and the Cold War.

Wars between states can increase the chances of a civil war in one or the other combatant state. Political scientist Theda Skocpol (1974) has shown how the multiple wars that the French kings fought in the eighteenth century, and Russian monarchies fought during the nineteenth and early twentieth centuries, alienated important domestic groups, weakened the regimes, and pushed them toward revolution and civil war. China's defeat by Japan in 1895 caused the Ch'ing dynasty to undertake a number of political and administrative reforms, but those reforms themselves led to a weakening of central governmental authority and paved the way for a period of successive revolutions in China between 1911 and 1949.

Since World War II, ex-colonies have been at a high risk of internal war. Colonialism may be a risk factor for internal war for three reasons. First, European great powers drew colonial borders not on the basis of the ethnicity of the peoples in the colonies, but the relative power and degree of competition among the great powers themselves. In sub-Saharan Africa, for example, the countries that therefore emerged from colonialism had highly diverse ethnic populations, with members of the same ethnic group often located in two or more neighboring states. This mismatch between borders and ethnicity in post-colonial Africa may have made domestic stability more difficult to attain and maintain (Englebert *et al.* 2002).

In addition, colonial powers in sub-Saharan Africa focused mainly on extracting natural resources, and did little to create institutions, such as courts systems, that would promote long-term economic growth (Acemoglu and Robinson 2012). The countries that emerged from colonialism in that region were hence weak economically, and thus less able to co-opt or defeat anti-regime opposition groups. Third, the colonial powers maintained order through the deployment of their own military and police forces. Once those forces were withdrawn, the newly independent countries had weak armies at their disposal: the door was left open to civil war (Fearon and Laitin 2003: 81).

The Cold War also had a very large impact on internal wars. We saw in Figure 5.7 that the average annual incidence of such wars during the years from 1950 to 1999 was double that during most of the nineteenth century and the first half of the twentieth century. It is likely that the underlying causes of that spike in internal wars after World War II are to be found in the factors we discussed above, especially the destabilizing legacies of decolonization in many countries that won independence after 1945. However, as we discussed in Chapter 2, the Cold War meant that both rebels and national governments would have the material resources and training to fight each other.

The end of the Cold War did not bring about an end of internal wars: this can be observed in Figure 5.7. This suggests that the US–Soviet competition enabled, but was not the sole cause of such wars. More recently, the post-Cold War years of 1990–2007 witnessed an increase in the incidence of new civil wars compared to previous decades. That upsurge can be attributed to two specific consequences of the end of the Cold War: the break-up of the Soviet Union (six internal wars) and Yugoslavia (four internal wars). If we take those wars out of the analysis, the post-Cold War incidence of internal wars, at 2.9 new wars per year, converges with the 1950–99 experience of about 2.8 wars per year and is not very different from the Cold War experience of 2.4 new wars per year. At the same time, it may be recalled that the lethality of internal wars has declined in the wake of the Cold War. It is possible, given a recent analysis of the changing character of civil wars after the end of the Cold War, that the end of that conflict has meant internal war combatants – both governments and the opposition – in recent years are fighting with relatively fewer heavy armaments, since they have lost their Soviet and US suppliers, and as a result they are less able to inflict heavy casualties on each other (Kalyvas and Balcells 2010).

In sum, international factors, particularly interstate wars, colonialism and its legacy, and the Cold War and its termination, have all played a role in the onset and character of internal wars in the contemporary era.

Individual	👪 **State**	🌐 **International**
Individuals may participate in an internal war because of greed, especially in the presence of lootable wealth.	A state's capacity for inclusiveness of individuals from different backgrounds into important political and societal institutions is likely to influence its susceptibility to internal war.	A state's participation in costly international wars may increase its susceptibility to internal wars.
Grievances, such as exclusion from a country's institutions, may motivate individuals to participate in an internal war.	A country's wealth may affect the likelihood of sparking, and its capacity to wage grievance-based internal wars.	Colonialism and its legacies, including the creation of states with multiple and sometimes competing ethnic groups, and poor foundations for governance, have contributed to the onset of internal wars.

Levels of Analysis
The Causes of Internal War

Revisiting the Enduring Question and Looking Ahead

Military conflicts, including full-scale wars, have been and remain a central feature of international politics. Why do they happen, given that they are often horrifically costly in terms of the deaths of both combatants and civilians? This is the enduring question that we pursued in this chapter. We have shown that wars and other types of military conflicts between states, and within them, are rare but have taken place persistently through history. We also showed that war occurs in the most immediate sense because states have conflicts of interest with one another. Yet, that explanation is not satisfactory by itself, because states often have conflicts of interest and their disagreements over those interests do not end in war.

Why, then, do some disagreements between states, and the conflicts of interests on which those disagreements rest, escalate to MIDs or even full-fledged wars? Given that arguments that stress the immediate causes of wars are not sufficient, we then shifted our focus to different possible underlying causes of wars and other violent conflicts between states. These causes are situated and operate at the individual, state, and international level of analysis, and many of them are emphasized by realist, liberal, constructivist, and feminist theories of world politics. Those theories and the causes they identify provide us with a quite substantial menu of possible fundamental causes of war.

We also discussed wars within countries. We examined why internal wars matter on their own terms, for example, in respect to their lethality for civilians, and by virtue of their capacity to affect international relations. We also explored different types of internal wars, and sought to understand the multiple causes for such wars, causes that again are situated at the individual, state, and international levels of analysis.

War is a persistent and dangerous part of the international domain. Yet, consider the case of France and Germany during the past 150 years. These two countries fought each other in three major wars between 1870 and 1945. During most of that period, when they were not actually fighting each other, they were bitter diplomatic adversaries. Yet, after 1945 these two countries reconciled and became close partners in the European Union. Just as there are many pathways to war, there must be factors in world politics that provide states with pathways to peace. We turn to this possibility in the next chapter.

Visit **www.palgrave.com/politics/Grieco** to access extra resources for this chapter, including:
- Chapter summaries to help you review the material
- Multiple choice quizzes to test your understanding
- Flashcards to test your knowledge of the key terms in this chapter
- An interactive simulation that invites you to go through the decision-making process of a world leader at a crucial political juncture
- Pivotal decisions in which you weigh up the pros and cons of complicated decisions with grave consequences
- Outside resources, including links to contemporary articles and videos, that add to what you have learned in this chapter

Study Questions

1. Is war an inevitable feature of international relations?
2. What one thing would you change about the internal features of a specific country that you believe would decisively lower the risk of war in the modern era?
3. How does a constant, like international anarchy, possibly influence the onset of interstate wars, which vary across time?
4. Is there a link between gender and war?
5. Given what we know about internal war, what can be done to reduce its incidence and severity?

Further Reading

Blainey, Geoffrey (1988) *The Causes of War*, 3rd edn (New York: Free Press). Blainey identifies the main theoretical arguments about the causes of war, and provides a superb critique of them.

Gurr, Ted Robert (2011) *Why Men Rebel: Fortieth Anniversary Edition* (Boulder: Paradigm Publishers). This book pioneered the systematic study of internal war, and remains a helpful intellectual gateway to this important subject.

Jervis, Robert (1997) *Perception and Misperception in International Politics* (Princeton: Princeton University Press). This book remains the best overview of different forms of misperceptions and their impact on the risk of war. It also presents a superb discussion of the levels-of-analysis framework for the study of international relations.

Pinker, Steven (2011) *The Better Angels of Our Nature: Why Violence Has Declined* (London: Allen Lane). Pinker puts forward the provocative thesis that human beings in general are becoming less violent toward one another, of which one manifestation is a decline in war.

Waltz, Kenneth (1959) *Man, State, and War: A Theoretical Analysis* (New York: Columbia University Press). This is the seminal work on viewing the causes of war from the perspective of factors situated at the individual, state, and inter-state levels of analysis, or what Waltz himself termed 'images.'

6

Pathways to Interstate Peace

Enduring question: What factors make it more likely that states will resolve their differences and avoid war **?**

War has been a constant feature of world politics over the centuries – but so too has been the search for peace. As soldiers have marched across distant battlefields and generals have plotted their military campaigns, diplomats and scholars have pondered the best ways to prevent war and establish stable international order. As we saw in Chapter 5, wars have come in many shapes and sizes. So too have the visions and strategies of peacemaking.

What scholars and policy makers believe will work to promote peace depends on their assumptions about what causes war. For example, if you believe that dictators are likely to be prone to war, you might favor the creation of democratic communities as a solution to the war problem. If you believe the real problem is the existence of nation-states in anarchy, you might be inclined to favor the much discussed yet never realized alternative of world government, or even the elimination of sovereign states. If men cause war, then a practical solution might be to have more female leaders in power. The point is not that any of these particular claims is necessarily correct; it is that the solution to a problem such as war must go hand in hand with analysis, or one's argument about the causes of war.

This chapter traces the various ways that peoples and governments throughout history have attempted to construct a stable and peaceful international system. We begin by looking at the background conditions that allow for a stable peace: a balance of power on the one hand or hegemony on the other. After this, we go on to examine the different strategies or instruments of peacemaking, which range widely. The strategy that perhaps comes to mind most immediately is diplomacy. But often diplomacy is not enough. Nation-states also form alliances or collective security arrangements to deter potentially aggressive states. Moreover, states over time have developed a series of international laws and institutions to avert war and promote peace, and we will devote substantial attention to the role of international law and institutions as a mechanism for peace. We will also move beyond states and state leaders and focus on three transnational forces that may promote peace, namely, economic interdependence, the possible emergence of a community of democratic nations, and the efforts of nongovernmental actors who together may be thought to constitute elements of a transnational civil society.

Source: © Dean Calma/IAEA

Learning Objectives

By the end of this chapter, you will be able to:

→ Recognize how two very different distributions of international power may contribute to peace among states: the balance of power and hegemony.

→ Analyze the two most important policies that governments have used to promote peace: diplomacy and power balancing.

→ Identify and evaluate the ways international law and institutions may promote peace.

→ Examine the capacity of transnational interactions, such as economic interdependence, the spread of democracy, and peace movements and civil society, to prompt states to resolve their disputes in peaceful ways.

→ Discuss the importance that leaders and especially ordinary people have assigned to peace.

Chapter Contents

- The International Distribution of Power as a Condition for Peace
- State Strategies for Achieving Interstate Peace
- International Law and Institutions as Mechanisms for Peace
- Transnational Mechanisms for Peace
- Revisiting the Enduring Question and Looking Ahead
- Study Questions
- Further Reading

The International Distribution of Power as a Condition for Peace

The distribution of power among states may be a factor that influences the prospects for peace. Two possibilities regarding peace and the distribution of power have been investigated by scholars: one is that peace is more likely in periods when there is a more or less equal distribution of capabilities among a number of states, while the other, in a completely different line of analysis, is that peace is most likely when there is a single overwhelmingly powerful state in the international system.

Balance of Power

Balance of power: Any situation in which a rough equality of power exists between the major states in the international system at a given moment in time. Balance of power is thought by many scholars to be an important condition for peace.

In a situation of a **balance of power**, a rough equality of power exists between the major states in the international system at a given moment in time. If several great powers are roughly equal in their material capabilities, the balance of power has taken the form of a multipolar system. In those circumstances, peace and stability may be attained because coalitions of states form alliances or partnerships to ensure that no single state – or coalition of states – gains power dominance. When two states overshadow all others – as the United States and the Soviet Union did during the Cold War – the balance of power is established through bipolar balancing. Each of the two superpowers gathers allies and seeks to muster sufficient collective capabilities to counterbalance the other side.

In both bipolar and multipolar settings, peace is maintained when there is a rough equilibrium of power. After the European wars of the eighteenth and nineteenth centuries, the balance of power was the dominant condition for re-establishing peace. During the Cold War, the balance of power was again a crucial mechanism for preserving stability. The United States and the Soviet Union were each convinced by the power of the other side that war was not worth the risks. Nuclear weapons and the threat of retaliation against a 'first strike' figured prominently in this calculation. Each

▶ **Map 6.1 The Roman Empire in 116 CE**

The Roman Empire experienced great prosperity and stability prior to its fall. The Pax Romana was one of the earliest examples of what scholars call hegemonic stability.

side went to considerable efforts to establish the credibility of its own power position to ensure that the other side would indeed make sober calculations of restraint.

Hegemony

Hegemony, or the dominance of one state over other states, is a second condition that can allow for stable peace. In this situation, the ability of a powerful state to organize and enforce order creates peace among states. Over the centuries, there have been a number of occasions when a powerful state has been able to organize and rule over large parts of the world. Examples of these occasions include the Pax Romana, Pax Sinica, Pax Britannica, and Pax Americana. The historian Edward Gibbon coined the term *Pax Romana* to refer to the Roman Empire of the first and second centuries CE, when Rome maintained political control over vast reaches of Europe and Northern Africa (Gibbon 1996). During this period, Rome's extended imperial order existed in relative peace and tranquility, undisturbed by internal civil war or foreign invasions. China – beginning with the Han Dynasty in 200 BCE to 200 CE – dominated East Asia and established a stable peace that lasted for centuries. This era of peace, known as the Pax Sinica, involved the establishment of hierarchical relations of status – the so-called tribute system – between China and its Japanese, Korean, and Vietnamese neighbors (Kang 2010; Fairbanks 1992).

Later, scholars characterized the British leadership and dominance of the international system in the nineteenth century and American leadership and dominance of the latter half of the twentieth century as similar eras of international peace. Peace was established not through a balance of power – at least in large parts of the world that Britain and the United States dominated – but by the hegemonic presence of the major power. Hegemonic peace here was not derived through direct imperial control but through leadership. States within the British and American hegemonic orders became willing partners, as these leading states used their economic, political, and military capabilities to establish and maintain order – and ensure the peace. For example, after World War II, Western European countries and Japan joined the United States to jointly manage the capitalist world economy. Cooperation between these countries was not simply a result of American power. It was also manifest in their common interests and values and the way they shared leadership responsibilities.

◀ **Map 6.2 The Han Empire in 100 BCE**

The Han Empire dominated East Asia from 200 BCE to 200 CE and used its commanding position to impose peace and stability on the region.

Hegemony: The dominance of one state over other states. Many scholars believe that a hegemonic international system is most prone to peace.

🌐 **International**

A balance or equilibrium of power among states can be a source of stable and peaceful order.

The dominance of a single state can also be a source of stable and peaceful order.

Levels of Analysis

The Distribution of Power as a Source of Peace

State Strategies for Achieving International Peace

Policy makers within states rely on diplomacy as a key foreign policy instrument and power balancing as a major foreign strategy to promote peace.

Diplomacy

One of the oldest and most time-honored peacemaking instruments that states employ for a variety of reasons is diplomacy. Diplomacy, as noted in Chapter 3, primarily consists of actions that governments undertake as their representatives negotiate with representatives of other governments to resolve disputes and establish collaborative bilateral or multilateral arrangements through which their countries can mutually achieve individual gains. The British scholar-diplomat, Harold Nicolson, defined diplomacy as 'the process and machinery by which … negotiation is carried out' (Nicolson 1963). The historian Jeremy Black describes diplomacy as the activities that states undertake to manage their relations abroad, particularly as they make representations, acquire information, and conduct negotiations (Black 2010). Diplomacy, then, is what states do when they engage in dialogue and negotiation. Diplomacy can be used by states for many purposes – but perhaps its most important use is the search for peace.

The tradition of diplomacy dates back to the rise of the system of states in early modern Europe, beginning in the sixteenth century with the development of permanent representatives among the city-states in northern Italy (Black 2010). The small Italian states posted diplomats in neighboring city-states and used them to collect and disperse information and conduct negotiations relating to war and peace. This practice spread throughout the European continent as states became sovereign political entities and began to conduct foreign policies. By the nineteenth century, this formal system spread worldwide, with governments dispatching official representatives – **ambassadors** – to the other capitals of the world. Embassies and diplomatic staffs were established and rules, protocols, and traditions of diplomacy gradually emerged, providing mechanisms for states to communicate their intentions and exchange information (Mattingly 1988).

At the heart of this modern system of diplomacy were the evolving norms of state sovereignty in which states recognized and respected each other as independent and self-governing political entities. States existed in a world of states – and diplomacy was the institutional network of offices and officials that provided the means for the management of these interstate relationships (Bull 1977).

The breakthrough in this system of sovereign statehood, as noted in Chapter 2, came with the Treaty of Westphalia of 1648, the peace settlement that followed the bloody Thirty Years War in which Protestants and Catholics fought to impose their religious views on each other. The victorious states in the war – particularly France and Sweden – disavowed and sought to undermine the religious universalism and hierarchical control of the Holy Roman Empire. As Kalevi Holsti argues, Westphalia 'represented a new diplomatic arrangement – an order created by states, for states – and replaced most of the legal vestiges of hierarchy, at the pinnacle of which were the Pope and the Holy Roman Empire' (Holsti 1991). Power was dispersed into the hands of sovereign states, and the international order was organized around sovereign states that acknowledged one another as legal equals. Territorial rulers were given the right to choose their religion for themselves and their terri-

Ambassadors: Official representatives of a state's government representing that state diplomatically in another state.

The Growth of Modern International Diplomacy

Over the last hundred years, the number of nation-states in the global system has grown dramatically and their diplomatic interactions have intensified. One way of seeing this intensification of diplomacy is the expansion in nongovernmental organizations and international bodies. Nation-states are doing more diplomatic business with each other and more non-governmental groups are linking these states together.

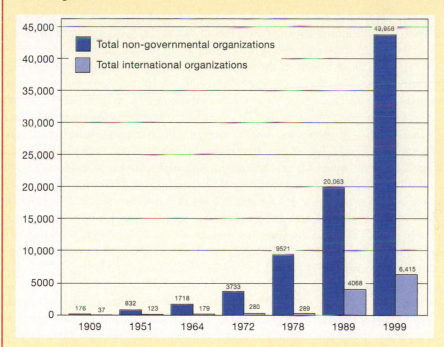

▲ **Figure 6.1 International Organizations by Year and Type, 1909–99**

Source: Data from Union of International Associations, 'Statistics: International Organizations by Year and Type, 1909–1999'.)

tories. The treaty countered Europe-wide religious-imperial domination by strengthening the legal and political autonomy of territorial rulers to achieve a stable peace. A state system managed through diplomacy and statecraft was the pathway to peace.

Over time, rules and norms have evolved to govern the ways ambassadors and other state officials represent their governments abroad. In the seventeenth century, when European states began the practice of posting permanent diplomatic representatives in foreign capitals, delegations were small, typically consisting of only an ambassador and a small staff. After the Napoleonic Wars of the early nineteenth century, European diplomats meeting in Vienna agreed to formalize the roles and rankings of diplomatic representatives within international law. Previously, all ranks of government representatives had been called 'ministers.' With the Vienna agreement, ambassadors were designated as ministers of the highest rank, with 'plenipotentiary authority' to represent their heads of state. This was the term for high diplomats who represented the crown or state in foreign capitals. During the nineteenth century, the more common term became ambassador. By the twentieth century, the world's leading states had established large embassies in major world capitals with hundreds of ministers and staff. These embassies have continued to grow, with ministers and officers charged with making contact with foreign governments in areas such as business, military, energy, environment, labor, human rights, law enforcement, and cultural affairs. In recent decades, diplomacy has also been increasingly carried out in a wide range of settings – summit meetings, international conferences, and other multilateral gatherings.

In capitals around the world, this far-flung diplomatic system of ambassadors and embassies is visibly on display. Often the embassies of foreign governments are grouped together along an 'embassy row,' as they are in Washington, DC. Under international law, these embassies are the 'territorial sovereignty' of the foreign government and, as such, are above the law of the local host country. The privileges and immunities granted to the ambassador and the embassy staff exempts them from the full force of local laws. This principle of **diplomatic immunity** – accepted by governments on a reciprocal basis – developed to allow the foreign state to maintain government relations and the chain of authority over its overseas embassies, necessary if the ambassador is to truly speak for the sovereign. Although this practice of diplomatic immunity is deeply rooted in international law and historical tradition, average citizens of countries often find out about it in less lofty ways. For example, residents of New York City, which hosts the United Nations and thousands of foreign embassy officials, periodically read newspaper reports about how these officials never pay their parking tickets. Disgruntled New Yorkers have discovered one of the practical implications of diplomatic immunity.

Although diplomacy between states has been institutionalized into a worldwide system of embassies, ambassadors, norms, and traditions, it has also grown beyond this system. Traditionally, the Foreign Office – or, in the United States, the State Department – has carried out diplomacy. But this practice has changed over time. In recent times, presidents and prime ministers have often resorted to 'personal envoys' to conduct diplomacy. In 1971, President Nixon turned to his White House foreign policy advisor, Henry Kissinger, to undertake a secret trip to China to explore the possibilities of closer ties. Nixon did not just bypass the State Department in this groundbreaking diplomatic overture; he did not even inform the department about it. Leaders sometimes turn to members of Congress or even private citizens to undertake diplomatic trips. In 2009, President Obama sent former President Bill Clinton to North Korea to obtain the release of captured American journalists. Sometimes diplomacy is even further removed from traditional channels. In efforts to improve relations with other countries, governments have encouraged private groups – orchestras or sports teams, for example – to help break the ice. In 2008, the New York Philharmonic Orchestra visited and performed in North Korea as a gesture of goodwill and friendship between American and North Korean peoples. In previous centuries, diplomacy was a more scripted craft, with diplomats conducting formal state-to-state dialogues. In today's world of growing economic interdependence and open democratic societies, diplomacy has become more multifaceted.

The most dramatic – and high stakes – moments for diplomacy occur when states appear to be on the brink of war. Diplomacy then becomes a tool to try to diffuse the conflict and prevent war. The border between North Korea and South Korea is the

Diplomatic immunity: The privileges and immunities granted by a host country to foreign ambassadors and embassy staff, exempting them from the full force of local laws.

◀ **Photo 6.1 The Embassies of Greece and Georgia on Embassy Row in Washington, DC**

Embassy Row in Washington, DC is a wonderful example of the institutionalized system of diplomacy between states.

Source: David Hunt, www.davidrehunt.com.

most militarized in the world, and the United States, South Korea, and Japan – joined by China – have periodically pursued negotiations with North Korea to avert a military clash. When North Korea took steps in the 1990s to build nuclear weapons, the United States launched intensive negotiations to end these efforts, offering energy and food aid in exchange for North Korean promises to step back from the nuclear brink. In the early twenty-first century, North Korea relaunched its nuclear programs and tested nuclear weapons devices. In response, the United States, China, North Korea, Japan, Russia, and South Korea initiated the **Six-Party Talks** to explore a settlement of the nuclear standoff. These talks – now suspended – attempted to draw North Korea into an agreement under which it would agree to end its nuclear program in exchange for normalization of relations with the outside world. Frustration has been a consistent theme in these negotiations, but the states of Northeast Asia see few options besides patient diplomacy.

Six-Party Talks: Diplomatic talks between North Korea, South Korea, the United States, China, Russia, and Japan intended to convince North Korea to suspend its nuclear program in exchange for normalized relations with the rest of the world.

The Clinton administration also engaged in diplomacy in 1998 in an effort to avert war between India and Pakistan over Kashmir, when Pakistani and Kashmiri insurgents moved across the border into India and armed conflict followed. Long-standing disputes over territory and the status of Kashmir increased the risk that these clashes would escalate into a major war. Indeed, the United States received evidence that Pakistan had moved nuclear weapons into forward positions, in anticipation of a general war. The Pakistani government appealed for American assistance to end the crisis, and the Clinton administration agreed, but only after Pakistani troops withdrew from across the Indian border. The diplomatic intervention of the United States helped diffuse the situation. Clinton officials facilitated a settlement of the dispute by identifying steps that each side could take to reduce tensions, and applied pressure on Pakistan, which relied on the United States for foreign aid and military assistance. Diplomacy made a difference.

Diplomacy, however, does not always work. For example, it failed during the run-up to the first Gulf War in 1990. In 1990, Iraq – led by President Saddam Hussein – charged Kuwait with **economic warfare** by overproducing oil and stealing oil from

Economic warfare: Aggressive actions by a state intended to damage another state economically.

Iraqi fields near the border. In August 1990, roughly 100,000 Iraqi troops invaded Kuwait and within a day seized control of the country. The United Nations Security Council voted to impose sanctions on Iraq, and the United States, Great Britain, and France began a military build-up in the region, deploying troops to Saudi Arabia and imposing a naval blockade against Iraq. An international military coalition had been assembled, and the George H. W. Bush administration was committed to a war to push Iraq out of Kuwait. But the United States made one last attempt to convince the Iraqis to leave without a fight. In early 1991 US Secretary of State James Baker began talks with Iraqi Foreign Minister Tariq Aziz about the withdrawal of Iraqi forces from Kuwait. In his memoirs, Baker recalled the thinking behind the American proposal for direct talks with Aziz:

> A face-to-face meeting might create its own psychological and political imperatives that could lead Saddam to withdraw. It certainly would give him an opening he could use to avoid war if he were seeking one. And if we could not convince Iraq to withdraw in direct talks, then no one would be able to question that we had done all we could. This would also help us with the Soviets and others who were reluctant to see force used. (Baker 1995)

In the end, the Iraqis were unwilling to use this opening to withdraw from Kuwait and avert war. Operation Desert Storm began a week later, and by the end of February 1991, the Iraqis had been expelled from Kuwait and the war was over.

In reflecting on the relationship between diplomacy and war, we might say that in one sense, the two activities are alternatives. Diplomacy is the tool a state uses to alter the actions of other states short of war. Prussian theorist of war Carl von Clausewitz famously argued that war is the pursuit of diplomacy by other means. But war and diplomacy are also complements. Diplomacy can be an important tool for state leaders who find themselves on the road to war. In the first Gulf War, as noted earlier, the Bush administration found that offering diplomatic contact with Iraq was a way to build support – both internationally and at home – for military action. The message that the United States was seeking peace and wanted a settlement made other states more willing to acquiesce. Moreover, war itself is rarely total. Wars are aimed at specific objectives, and even if the use of force is successful, diplomacy is typically a necessary tool in the aftermath of war to ratify the result of the war and rebuild peace.

Power Balancing

Power balancing: Efforts by states to protect themselves in a dangerous world by arraying power against power, consisting of both **internal balancing** and **external balancing**.

External balancing: The process by which states enter into security alliances with other states to balance the power of a particularly strong state or coalition of states.

Internal balancing: The process by which states muster their own power to balance rival states by mobilizing their economy and increasing their defense capabilities.

Diplomacy is a policy instrument whereby states seek advantages and settle disputes short of war. States also pursue a more general strategy, that is, a goal and associated policy instrument that can promote peace, namely, **power balancing**, which consists of efforts by states to protect themselves in a dangerous world by arraying power against power. States can attempt to counteract powerful or threatening states through internal and external balancing. **Internal balancing** is the process by which states muster their own power by mobilizing their economy and increasing their defense capabilities. In **external balancing**, states enter into security alliances with other states. In amassing counterbalancing force, states seek to dissuade other states from resorting to war. If a state knows that its power will be met with resistance – if it knows that its capabilities on the battlefield are no greater than those of its enemies – it will hesitate to start a war. In an international system in which power is balanced, states have incen-

◀ **Map 6.3 The Wars of German Unification, 1866–1871**

During the late nineteenth century, Bismarck unified the German states through a series of wars. This unification led Britain to pursue a strategy of balancing against Germany, eventually leading to the world wars of the twentieth century.

Map legend:
- Prussia before 1866
- Conquered by Prussia in Austro–Prussian War, 1866
- Austrian territories excluded from German Confederation, 1867
- Joined with Prussia to form German Confederation, 1867
- South German states joining with Prussia to form German Empire, 1871
- Won by Prussia in Franco–Prussian War, 1871
- German Confederation boundary, 1815–66
- Bismarck's German Empire, 1871

tives to act with restraint and caution. According to this logic, a world in which power is balanced is a world that will tend toward peace.

Much of international politics in the modern era has involved states using balancing strategies to advance their interests. In the late eighteenth and nineteenth centuries, Great Britain pursued a strategy of power balancing to prevent the European continent from being dominated by a hostile hegemonic state. This strategy involved staying 'off shore' and watching over developments on the continent. If and when a continental great power became too powerful or sought to dominate Europe as a whole, Great Britain would endeavor to organize a balancing coalition to undercut the challenger. In the late eighteenth century, Napoleonic France made a bid for European dominance, and Great Britain assumed leadership of the coalition of states that fought and eventually defeated Napoleon. In the late nineteenth century, Britain again cast a wary eye on the rise of Germany, led by 'Iron Chancellor' Otto von Bismarck. The British Foreign Office codified this balancing strategy in strategic documents, and it was reflected in Lord Palmerston's famous dictum that Britain had 'no permanent friends, no permanent enemies, only permanent interests.' This balancing strategy had as its objective the use of British power to maintain the balance between the great powers on the European continent, undercutting efforts by any state to make war and try to dominate the region.

During the Cold War, the United States employed power balancing as a tool for managing its relations with the Soviet Union. The internal strategy involved mobilization of the American economy, reflected in investments in research and development, education and training, and massive expenditure to boost military capacities. External balancing took the form of building alliances, providing foreign and military assistance, and championing economic and political cooperation within the non-communist world. This so-called bipolar power balancing lasted for decades and, in retrospect, it appeared to play an important role in preserving peace between the two superpowers, although proxy wars were fought in other countries.

States today still often pursue a strategy of balancing, either directly or indirectly. The rise of China has led countries in Asia to explore ways to counter or guard against the possibilities of China's domination of the region. India, another large and growing Asian country, has looked warily at the rise of China – and has taken steps to strengthen its military capacities and political relations in the region as counter-measures. Southeast Asian countries, such as Singapore, Australia, and the Philippines, seek to engage China and benefit from good political and economic relations. But indications suggest that at least some of these countries also want the United States to remain in the region as a balance against Chinese power. The United States has responded to this situation by reassuring East Asian states of its security commitments and leadership in the region. The announcement by Secretary of State Hillary Clinton in the summer of 2010 that the United States would play an active role in brokering territorial disputes in Southeast Asia – disputes that pit China against the smaller states – reflects this use of power balancing as a tool of diplomacy. China, in return, has adopted a strategy of diplomacy, reassuring its neighbors and offering to participate in various regional economic and security institutions to mitigate the worries that other states have about a rising China, thereby undercutting the urge these states might have to seek to balance power against China.

Bandwagoning: When smaller, weaker states ally with a larger, powerful state for protection. Contrasts with **balance of power**.

We can contrast balancing with **bandwagoning**. If balancing involves aggregating capabilities to resist the threats of an increasingly powerful rival state, bandwagoning occurs when smaller states flock to a state for protection. Rather than resist the power of a leading state, weaker neighbors affiliate with the more powerful state. Their strategy is to tie themselves to the leading state, thereby gaining protection and other benefits from it. States often pursue this strategy in conjunction with power balancing. So, for example, as the United States balanced against the Soviet Union during the Cold War, smaller states bandwagoned with the United States.

Levels of Analysis

State Strategies in Pursuit of Peace

 State

States employ diplomacy and undertake balancing to advance their interests, and in doing so may bring about peace.

International Law and Institutions as Mechanisms for Peace

States have tried to establish stable peace by building systems of international law and institutions. We begin our exploration of this potential pathway to peace with a discussion of the meaning, origins, and efficacy of international law and institutions. We then focus on their impact on peace in three important instances: the League of Nations, the United Nations, and the European Union.

Essential Features of International Law and Institutions

International law consists of the body of rules, norms, and standards that states have crafted over time that give those states and other actors rights and obligations in their interactions with one another. International law specifies the rules and principles governing the relations among states, although in recent decades the scope of international law has been expanded to include relations between states and individuals and with international organizations. Less formal or binding than domestic law, law in international relations is embodied in a wide array of written treaties and customary practices (Cali 2010). International institutions are international laws plus organizational arrangements that are designed to facilitate the implementation by states of international law. In the next section we will examine in detail three examples of international institutions. The origins of international law date back to the seventeenth century. The Treaty of Westphalia was itself an effort to establish agreed-upon rules and norms for the conduct of relations among European sovereign states. As noted earlier, the emergence of a tradition of diplomacy and statecraft – conducted within a system of states – was premised on the existence and legitimacy of a fundamental set of laws and principles guiding the international conduct of states. In the early seventeenth century, Dutch jurist and legal scholar Hugo Grotius, who is widely considered to be one of the founders of international law, wrote *The Law of War and Peace* (1625), a monumental work in which he sought to demonstrate the existence of a universal law among nations.

International law seeks to govern relations among states by setting out principles and standards of conduct that states are expected to obey. It seeks to establish a rule-based framework within which states expect each other to operate. In the contemporary world, international law is grounded in a multitude of rules and principles that cover all sorts of state action, including rules about war, human rights, and various aspects of international trade and finance. Champions of international law say that it offers a vision of world politics in which the laws of nations are expected to strengthen peaceful relations and provide a stable environment for states to cooperate and prosper.

International law differs from domestic laws within nations. Domestic law is applied to all people within a country's borders. Formal mechanisms of representative government are in place to generate law. Law is, in turn, interpreted through an independent judiciary and enforced by police and the courts. Constitutions exist – at least in established liberal democracies – to set limits and restraints on what power holders can do. In short, domestic law is formal and enforceable. In a fully functioning constitutional democracy, law has the last word. In international relations, law is more limited as a governing mechanism. International law applies primarily to states as sov-

International law: The body of rules, norms, and standards that states have crafted over time that give those states and other actors rights and obligations in their interactions with one another.

ereign 'personalities' and not individuals. There are exceptions to this generalization. In the decades since the end of the Cold War, governments have acknowledged that individuals can be guilty of war crimes and crimes against humanity. The International Criminal Court (ICC), established in 2002, is a permanent international tribunal that tries individuals for war crimes and genocide. The ICC is an example of small but important steps that states have taken in recent decades, building on the United Nations Charter and other international human rights agreements, to strengthen international law in the area of war and mass violence. But international law remains largely a tool of sovereign states, as there is no international body that stands above nation-states to enforce its terms.

However, international law does not totally lack enforcement. Groups of states can impose sanctions on states that are seen to violate international law. States that join the ICC and other international courts do – by their membership and ratification of these treaties – accept the authority of these courts. They acknowledge that these judicial bodies do have some authority to make decisions. Even though the ICC and other courts cannot force states to abide by their rulings, the authority of these bodies does put pressure on governments to comply. International court decisions can also make it easier for other governments to organize sanctions against the offending government or leaders. But enforcement is not binding. It is up to states to impose costs on other states and, in this sense, states – not the law – have the last word.

Where does international law come from? If domestic systems of law are established at a specific historical moment – such as a constitutional convention in which a state's basic laws are drafted – international law has emerged more piecemeal over the centuries. International law has several sources. Many of the most basic principles and norms of international law have emerged through customary practice. **International customary law** is the accumulation of principles and norms that states have put forward over the centuries and which have come to be widely seen as legitimate and authoritative. International customary law enshrines basic ideas about the organization and standing of states in the international system, reflecting principles such as sovereignty, recognition, freedom of the seas, international responsibility, and self-defense. In this regard, for example, international law has emerged that distinguishes between the lawful and unlawful use of force. States can take action against what international law defines as illegal acts by other states, such as seizure of ships or territorial invasion. Once a war breaks out, international customary law provides rules and principles about such matters as the conduct of war and neutrality.

Another source of international law has been treaties, written agreements that states establish with one another and which spell out commitments and expectations in specific areas of conduct. Because governments recognize **treaties** as having high legal standing they have some of the authority of law. Treaties might initially be negotiated among just a few states, with the rules and norms embodied in the treaties eventually spreading to the wider system of states. Treaties often provide more specific rules and norms than customary law. For example, formal treaties between states spell out legal understandings about such matters as territory and diplomatic immunity; the protection of nationals abroad; freedom of navigation and commerce; and extradition and asylum. A number of treaties exist that specify how states are allowed to operate in territories and waters that are not part of the territory of sovereign states. For example, the 1959 Antarctic Treaty bars any further exclusive appropriation of territory in that region. Treaties governing how states can use outer space include the

International customary law: The accumulation of principles and norms that states have put forward over the centuries and which have come to be widely seen as legitimate and authoritative, enshrining basic ideas about international organization and the standing of states and reflecting basic principles such as sovereignty, recognition, freedom of the seas, international responsibility, and self-defense.

Treaty: A formal agreement between two or more states designed to settle a dispute or set down guidelines for future action.

Realist Theory on International Law, Institutions, and Government Actions

Theory

Realist theory suggests that international law, norms, and institutions are of little or no significance to states. Power rather than the rule of law or international institutions matters in how states act. Anarchy and competition for wealth and power create the conditions in which states operate. In world politics, power rules.

Practice

Governments in the modern era have spent an extraordinary amount of time and energy to create international institutions and enshrine their actions in international law. At critical moments, even when national security is at stake, governments care about being seen as acting according to international laws and norms. For example during the Cuban Missile Crisis in 1962, the Kennedy administration sought the approval of the Organization of American States as a way of ensuring that the embargo and possible use of force was widely seen as consistent with regional and global law and norms.

1967 Treaty on Principles Governing the Activities of States in the Exploration and Use of Outer Space.

In recent years, one of the most important efforts at strengthening international law has occurred in regard to the world's oceans. The so-called Law of the Sea Treaty establishes a framework of rights and responsibilities for states in their claims over coastal territories and the uses and management of the ocean environment and natural resources. This treaty – which has now been ratified by 161 states, with the United States as a prominent exception – replaced the older 'freedom of the seas' principle that dates from the seventeenth century. The old understanding established three nautical miles – the length of a 'cannon shot' – as the distance off the coast that a nation could claim territorial rights. This legal principle was overturned in the twentieth century by many states claiming extended zones off their coasts, doing so in pursuit of mineral resources or seeking to protect fish stocks. By the 1960s, very few states still adhered to the 3-mile standard, with many claiming a 12-mile zone of control – and some claiming as much as 200 nautical miles. Negotiations on a new Law of the Sea Treaty lasted over ten years, culminating in a new and wide-ranging agreement in 1982 that became active law in 1994 when sixty countries had ratified it. This new treaty set limits of national claims to offshore territories, established navigation and transit rules, and created regimes to govern rights relating to the continental shelf, deep seabed mining, scientific research, protection of marine environment, and the settlement of disputes.

The Law of the Sea Treaty is now an operational body of international law. States have used it to settle disputes over maritime rights, exclusive economic and fishing zones, and natural resource claims. Today, for example, China has advanced controversial claims to island and other territorial rights in the South China Sea, triggering anger and worry from smaller states in the region. The dispute was brought to a head when one Chinese military spokesman claimed that China has 'indisputable sovereignty' over the entire South China Sea, but would nonetheless allow others to freely navigate the 1.3 million-square-mile waterway. Japan, Taiwan, Vietnam, Indonesia,

Malaysia, and the Philippines have advanced competing claims to these waters and island territories. In July 2010, US Secretary of State Hillary Clinton countered the Chinese by urging a multilateral approach to the resolution of competing claims. While this conflict is still unfolding, the Law of the Sea Treaty has been an important body of authoritative rules and understandings to guide settlement of the dispute (Rothwell and Stephens 2010).

Why might states adhere to international law? One reason is that much of international law reinforces the sovereignty and authority of states. Indeed, the cornerstone of international customary law is the independence of the state. Customary law establishes principles and norms that uphold freedom of armament, access to raw materials and markets, and the admission of migrants. Moreover, states are free to decide on their own if they will participate in international congresses and sign treaties and other agreements. Many international agreements and conventions do not take force until a majority of the world's states ratify them, so there are limits on how much constraint international law imposes upon states. So international law can be attractive to states that only want to guard their own sovereignty.

Beyond this, the accumulated body of international law provides a loosely rule-based environment in which states can pursue their national interests. In effect, international law works on the idea of reciprocity. If states want other states to behave according to established rules and norms – enshrined in international law – they need to offer their own compliance in return. Any one state would like to see other states operate in a predictable way, adhering to international law, while remaining, itself, free of the constraints of international law, however minimal those constraints might be. But to get other states to bind themselves to the rules and norms of international law, this state must reciprocate. Each state gives up a tiny bit of freedom for the benefits of a more predictable and rule-based international order (Ikenberry 2001).

Great powers might adhere to international law because it gives **legitimacy**, or a sense of rightness and acceptance, to power. International law provides rules and principles that give the international system a sense of justice. If a majority of states in the system agree to and uphold principles of international law such as universal access to markets and freedom of the sea, the great powers do not need to use force to coerce other states to behave properly. Moreover, some aspects of international law give the great powers special rights and advantages. The United Nations Security Council, for example, gives the major states permanent membership and the veto. To the extent that these rights and advantages are codified in international law, the power advantages of the major states are made more legitimate. British international relations scholar E.H. Carr argued that international law was really a disguise for the exercise of power by the strong (Carr 1939). But for international law to truly be legitimate in the eyes of all states, the great powers themselves must obey the rules and norms – and doing so requires at least some restraint on their part. Thus, while international law places some limits on what strong states can do with their power, it also creates a more predictable and hospitable environment where they can pursue interests.

Three Experiences with International Law and Institutions: the League of Nations, the United Nations, and the European Union

During the past century, state leaders have made multiple efforts to build international institutions – again, the combination of laws and associated organizations – that would help keep the peace. The most ambitious of these efforts have been the effort after World War I to establish a global collective security system, that is, the League of Nations; then the creation after World War II of the United Nations; and finally, in Europe, a succession of institutions aimed at regional integration and peace, currently called the European Union.

Collective Security and the League of Nations

A peacemaking instrument that combines elements of international law and alliances/balancing is **collective security**. In this arrangement, member states agree to come to the aid of any member that is attacked by an aggressor from either within or outside the collective security arrangement. The basic idea is 'all for one and one for all' or 'safety in numbers.' Weaker states find collective security attractive because it offers the opportunity to lock stronger states into a commitment to protect them.

The classic example of collective security – and its problems – is the **League of Nations**, the international organization designed and proposed by US President Woodrow Wilson after World War I. In Wilson's vision of this universal membership organization, member states committed themselves to act in concert to protect territorial borders and enforce the peace. If a member of the League was attacked by another state, the other states in the League were to come to its defense. The idea of collective security was based on several assumptions. First, the League was to be a global organization in which membership would be near universal. All states would need to agree to uphold the commitments and obligations of membership. Second, states would not be able to veto or block actions of the organization. If they could, the collective security organization would likely find itself on the sidelines precisely when it was needed. Third, states would need to be sufficiently interdependent such that the threat of sanctions would be persuasive. Finally, all the states in the international system would need to be convinced that the members of the organization would indeed come to the aid of any member that was attacked. If these conditions held, as Wilson and other champions of the League of Nations argued, would-be aggressors bent on war would think twice.

The League of Nations was meant to embody this collective security idea and provide an institutional form to manage disputes around the world. The League's principal mission was the avoidance of war largely through arbitration and a reduction of armaments, and then, if necessary, the threat of collective sanctions. States would agree to act – imposing sanctions or employing force – when confronted with territorial aggression by an outlaw state. International relations scholar Inis Claude described the logic of collective security in this way:

> The twentieth-century hope that international organizations might serve to prevent war, or, failing that, to defend states subjected to armed attack in defiance of organized efforts to maintain the peace, has been epitomized in the concept of collective security . . . Collective security can be described as resting upon the proposition that war can be prevented by the deterrent effect of overwhelming power upon states which are too rational to invite certain defeat. (Claude 1956)

In the League of Nations, states were to come together as equals. The League had an Executive Council but, adhering closely to the principle of the equality of states, the council's powers were simply to initiate investigations and make recommendations

Collective security: Security provided by the members of an international cooperative institution in which, if any state threatened or actually used military force illegally against a member state, the other members pledged to form an overwhelming coalition to defeat the aggressor.

League of Nations: An international body established by the Treaty of Versailles at the end of World War I and designed to provide states with an ongoing international legal and institutional framework to solve their disputes and avoid war.

to the body of the whole. The League of Nations embodied a universal set of laws and principles intended to provide the foundation for a new era of peace and stability, reflecting Wilson's belief in the virtues of a world ordered by international law. As Wilson put it, 'the same law that applies to individuals applies to nations' (Wilson 1917). International law and the system of collective security anchored in the League of Nations would provide a socializing role, gradually bringing states into a 'community of power.' The League of Nations held its first council meeting in January 1920, a week after the Treaty of Versailles came into force.

The League of Nations was weakened at the outset by the failure of the United States to join it. President Wilson campaigned across the United States for ratification of the Treaty of Versailles, which included membership in the League of Nations. But in a stinging defeat for Wilson and League of Nations supporters, the vote in the US Senate fell short. Part of the opposition came from conservative and isolationist senators who did not want the United States to be involved in foreign affairs. Other senators were willing to vote for the Treaty but only with formal reservations that affirmed the Senate's constitutional right to decide when and if the United States would commit military forces abroad. President Wilson agreed that League of Nations membership did not entail giving up America's sovereign authority over decisions about war and peace, but he resisted the Senate's efforts to formalize these qualifications in the treaty. For reasons that diplomatic historians still debate, Wilson was unwilling to compromise with these 'reservationist' senators who would have insured ratification of the treaty (Knock 1995). Ironically, the United States helped inspire the idea of the League of Nations – and the vision of world peace based on collective security – but was not part of its organizational founding.

Soon after the League of Nations was established, its ability to foster a peace system based on collective security was called into question. As we observed in Chapter Two, by the 1930s, the world was entering into a global economic depression, and protectionism and nationalism were on the rise. In Asia, Japan responded by invading its neighbors and building an empire. This development put the League of Nations to the test. In 1931, Japan, a League of Nations member, invaded and occupied Manchuria, a part of China. League members initially debated imposing economic sanctions on Japan. But the world economy was weak and many countries depended on trade with Japan, so there was little support for sanctions. Unable to penalize Japan, the League resorted to diplomatic persuasion. The League sent a delegation to study the problem, reporting back a year later. In 1933, after two years of deliberations, the League passed a resolution condemning the invasion and calling for Japan to withdraw from Manchuria. But the resolution did not commit members of the League to any specific actions, because member states could not agree on actions. Japan refused to leave Manchuria and instead withdrew from the League of Nations.

A second blow to the League of Nation's system of collective security came in 1935 with its inaction in response to Italy's invasion of Abyssinia (now Ethiopia). Both Italy and Abyssinia were members of the League of Nations. By the early 1930s, Mussolini's fascist regime ruled Italy and – as part of an aggressive foreign policy – it threatened Abyssinia with military invasion from its bordering imperial territory of Italian Somaliland. The Abyssinian Emperor, Haile Selassie, went to the League of Nations to appeal for help. The League initially proposed to give some of Abyssinia to Italy, but rather than work with the League, Mussolini simply invaded Abyssinia. As in the case of Japan's invasion of Manchuria, the League was unable to rally states to stop the aggres-

Collective Security versus Britain's Abandonment of Czechoslovakia

Aspiration: *Article X, League of Nations Covenant, 1919*

In the Covenant of the League of Nations, members pledged to preserve the territorial sovereignty of fellow members of the League.

> The Members of the League undertake to respect and preserve as against external aggression the territorial integrity and existing political independence of all Members of the League. In case of any such aggression or in case of any threat or danger of such aggression the Council shall advise upon the means by which this obligation shall be fulfilled.

Reality: *British Prime Minister Neville Chamberlain, September 1938*

In practice, leaders of the world were more cautious and reluctant to go to the aid of other League members who faced military aggression.

> How horrible, fantastic, incredible it is that we should be digging trenches and trying on gas masks here because of a quarrel in a far-away country between people of whom we know nothing ... However much we may sympathize with a small nation confronted by a big and powerful neighbor, we cannot in all circumstances undertake to involve the whole British Empire in war simply on her account.

Source: Prime Minister Neville Chamberlain, in address to the British people during the crisis over Czechoslovakia, September 27, 1938.

sion. Indeed, in the case of Abyssinia, two of the leading members of the League, Britain and France, secretly agreed to hand over Abyssinia to Italy. They chose not to stand up against Italian aggression, fearing that doing so would push Italy closer toward an alliance with Hitler's Germany. The fact that the United States was not a member of the League simply compounded these failings. By the mid-to-late 1930s, the promise of world peace based on collective security had disappeared, as the example in Box 6.3 further shows, and would fail entirely with the eruption of World War II.

The United Nations: A Modified Collective Security System?

After the World War II, the United States and other countries again had an opportunity to build an international order – and again they sought to strengthen the role of rules and institutions as a basis for lasting peace. Between 1944 and 1950, the United States and other countries proposed a wide variety of postwar political, economic, and security institutions, including the United Nations, the Bretton Woods economic institutions, and the North Atlantic Treaty Organization (NATO). Like Wilson, President Franklin Roosevelt, his successor, President Harry Truman, and other American leaders in the 1940s wanted to build a system of order that would provide for a new era of peace. A global institution – the United Nations – was to be the cornerstone of this new attempt to create an open system built around collective security and the peaceful settlement of disputes.

But with his vision, President Franklin Roosevelt also wanted to avoid the problems Wilson and the League of Nations had encountered. So the United Nations (UN) was established as a 'modified' collective security system with several significant differences from the League of Nations. First, the UN gives the great powers a large role in managing international peace and security. The UN is composed of six principal organs (with numerous specialized funds and agencies in its wider system), but of most relevance to the issues of war and peace are: the General Assembly in which all member states participate on an equal basis; and the Security Council, with five permanent members (the United States, France, Great Britain, the Soviet Union, and China) along with an additional group of rotating temporary members. Second, these permanent members are given a veto over resolutions mandating UN action. This provision makes the great powers more likely to join the organization because actions without unanimous support would be vetoed. The League of Nations became discredited because it was not able to deliver on its basic promise to marshal the actions of all states in the face of territorial aggression. The UN would avoid this fate by allowing the major states to veto action where their interests were at stake. This veto power meant that the UN would not act in all instances, but only when the major states agreed that action was needed and when action was possible. Success or failure would hinge on the ability of the permanent members of the Security Council to cooperate.

While the UN avoided the fate of the League of Nations, it too gave way to the realities of power politics. The Cold War between the Soviet Union and the United States doomed Roosevelt's vision of the great powers collectively upholding peace and stability. Instead, the United States took on more direct responsibilities for organizing and leading the non-communist world and began building alliance partnerships – with Europe and East Asia – as an alternative pathway to international security. NATO became the central mechanism for establishing security in Europe. In East Asia, the United States built bilateral security alliances with Japan and other states. These alliances did not provide collective security for all states in the international system. They only provided security – what might be called cooperative security – for those countries which were part of the alliances. The vision of a global system of collective security managed by the great powers narrowed to became a Western-oriented security community organized around cooperative security.

The UN did act – at least indirectly – in matters of war and peace as it assumed new responsibilities in the decades following World War II. First, the UN became the 'voice of the South' as it represented the states of the developing world. The UN was designed primarily to address the problems of war and peace, as had been experienced in the two world wars. Great power wars in which a powerful state invaded another country were the pre-eminent threat to world peace, and the UN was the embodiment of the world community's desire to prevent such wars in the future. But in the post-World War II era, the struggles for security and prosperity in the developing world emerged as a new problem for the global system. The new problems focused on establishing political independence and stable order and grappling with the challenges of economic development. The UN gave these developing countries a forum for debate on development and governance. The UN was a 'great power club' but it was also a thriving venue for small and poor countries to advance their ideas. Second, the UN became increasingly focused not on **peacemaking**, but on **peacekeeping**. Peacemaking involves actually trying to end wars. In peacekeeping operations, UN-sponsored troops, drawn from various UN member states, are deployed in countries in the aftermath of war or civil violence to keep the warring groups apart and enforce the peace settlement. The UN could not prevent war. The Cold War and the stalemate between

Peacekeeping: UN operations in which UN-sponsored troops are deployed in countries in the aftermath of war or civil violence to keep the warring groups apart and enforce the peace settlement.

Peacemaking: UN action before war breaks out designed to prevent two states from going to war with each other by brokering peaceful settlements. Contrasts with **peacekeeping**, which occurs in the aftermath of war.

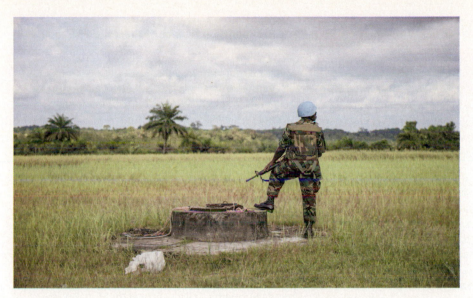

◀ Photo 6.2 UN Peacekeeping Operations

A Ghanaian peace-keeper with the UN Mission in Liberia (UNMIL) is pictured on guard duty.

The United Nations Security Council has the authority to deploy peacekeepers. In doing so, it draws upon military and civilian personnel from various UN member states.

Source: UN Photo/Staton Winter.

the Western powers and the Soviet Union meant that the UN Security Council would not be able to act, as its permanent members could not reach unanimous decisions. But the UN did play a role in deploying peacekeeping operations to keep war from reccurring. The UN Charter gives the Security Council responsibility to take action to maintain peace and security. As a result, countries often come to the Security Council for help in implementing peace agreements. When the Security Council authorizes the deployment of peacekeepers, it draws upon military and civilian personnel from various countries to work together as a combined UN operation. Since 1948, the UN has sponsored 63 peacekeeping operations; 16 of these are ongoing.

In her exhaustive study of peacekeeping operations, Virginia Page Fortna shows that these UN-sponsored interventions are a very effective policy tool, dramatically reducing the risk that war will break out. Fortna cites evidence to show that where civil war ceasefire agreements are backed up with peacekeepers, the peace tends to last much longer. Peacekeeping operations have several potential impacts. They can help raise the costs that combatants face if they were to return to the battlefield, they can increase the confidence that each side has in the terms of the ceasefire agreement, and they help prevent accidental incidents that might spark a return to violence. The warring parties need to find some way to the peace table, but if they do get there – and agree to a ceasefire – UN peacekeepers can help keep the peace going (Fortna 2008).

The role and significance of the United Nations in world politics is a source of ongoing debate among international relations scholars. In Box 6.4, we compare liberal and realist views of the manner and extent to which the UN matters as a mechanism of peace.

The Rule of Law and Institutions: The Case of the European Union

Europe has developed the most elaborate form of stable peace through international law and institutions. After World War II, Western European countries began a decades-long process of building a cooperative regional order. The violence and destruction of World War II led postwar European leaders to search for new ways to create peace. Rather than return to a balance of power, these leaders chose a path of

Background

The United Nations is a large global institution that supports a wide array of activities. How important is this international organization in the promotion of peace and justice in world affairs? The theoretical traditions offer different answers.

Liberalism: Few liberal theorists argue that the United Nations has had a transformative impact on global peace and security, but they do emphasize its various contributions. The UN General Assembly provides a forum for debate, giving a louder voice to weaker states that might not otherwise be heard. The UN Security Council provides a venue for the great powers to consult – and possibility act – on questions of war and peace. In these ways, the UN offers space for diplomacy – and it is up to states to use it as they can to overcome differences and rivalries that can lead to war. Overall, liberals argue that the UN plays a valuable role as it enshrines a set of ideals and aspirations for the conduct of world affairs that in small ways or at critical moments can help states move away from armed violence and toward a stable peace.

Realism: Realists are more skeptical of what the UN can do in world politics. States act in their own interests whether they are making decisions at the United Nations or in their own capitals. The UN Security Council reflects this reality. It gives the great powers that created the UN – the United States, Russia, China, France, and Great Britain – a veto over UN resolutions. In effect, power politics can always trump UN action. The fact that the permanent members of the UN Security Council do not seem willing to give permanent SC membership to other powerful states – such as India, Germany, and Japan – only underscores the dynamics of power that lurk in the background of the global body.

regional integration and institution building, beginning with the European Coal and Steel Community and later the European Economic Community. Beginning with a core group of countries, led by France and West Germany, the European project both expanded to include most of the states of Europe and deepened relations by reducing trade barriers. In the 1990s, European states inaugurated the European Union with formal institutions such as the European Parliament, Court of Justice, and a Commission and created a common currency, the euro; these arrangements bind the countries together as a political community.

The European Union is a new type of political community, a group of liberal democracies tied together by shared institutions and a commitment to governance through the rule of law. Like the League of Nations and the United Nations, it is an experiment in overcoming the age-old problems of conflict and war. Like these other experiments, the European Union has had its successes and failures. It has succeeded in building a framework for economic and political cooperation and at least limited joint governance. It has expanded its members across the European continent, integrating many of the countries from the former Soviet Union. However, it has struggled in recent years with its common currency and monetary order. The economic misfortunes of many member states – such as Greece and Spain – have put tremendous strains on the European Union. Like all efforts to build a system of peace and prosperity, it is an ongoing experiment.

The various mechanisms that states have used to promote peace are not mutually exclusive. Interstate peace may be built on a combination of them. The peaceful order that emerged in Europe in 1815, after the Napoleonic wars, was built around both the balance of power and an elaborate set of rules among the great powers. At the same

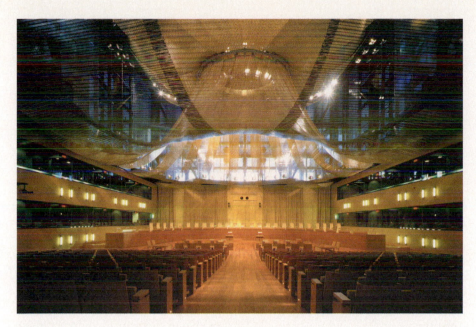

◀ **Photo 6.3 The European Court of Justice in Luxembourg**

The European Court of Justice is one of the many formal institutions established by the European Union. The Court of Justice serves many legal purposes, including settling disputes between EU countries and EU institutions.

Source: Court of Justice of the European Union.

time, the European great powers continued to dominate smaller states through empire and other forms of control. Likewise, the American-led order that emerged among the democracies after World War II combined all three structures – balance of power, hegemony, and international law and institutions. During the Cold War, the United States stepped forward to organize a Western or 'free world' order, doing so as it pursued a balance of power strategy against the Soviet Union. This order had characteristics of hegemony as well. The United States took the lead in organizing and running the order, providing security, and managing the open world economy as it built partnerships with other states in Europe and Asia. This American-led order was also characterized by multilateral rules and institutions that both reflected American power and also established limits and restraints on how power could be exercised within this order. The result was a distinctive political order – stretching across the Atlantic and Pacific oceans – that has provided stable peace (at a global level) for many decades, even after the end of the Cold War.

State	International
States have established international rules and institutions to facilitate cooperation and reinforce stability and peace.	International law may inform and constrain the behavior of states in ways that avert war and promote peace.
Western democracies have made repeated efforts to build global and regional systems of collective security and rule-based relations.	The European Union is the most successful example of how international institutions can promote peace.

Levels of Analysis

International Law and Institutions as Mechanisms for Peace

Transnational Mechanisms for Peace

To this point we have discussed mechanisms for peace that mostly rely on states and national leaders. However, there are at least three pathways by which private individuals and non-governmental actors can play a central role in promoting peace and averting/ending war, sometimes by pressuring national leaders. These three pathways relate to economic interdependence, a possible international community of democratic nations, and peace movements and global civil society.

Economic Interdependence

States have also sought to build peaceful international relations through the promotion of open trade and economic interdependence. The relationship between economics and peace is a complex one, and scholars continue to debate the specific ways in which the economic relationships that states pursue alter their conduct in matters of war and peace – if they do at all. Many liberal thinkers are convinced that extensive economic interdependence between countries creates domestic interests and constituencies that favor stable and peaceful relations. When countries are tied together in mutually beneficial trade and exchange, disrupting those relations is costly – and states should be sensitive to this consideration in their security relations. Others are more skeptical. Today, the rise of China – and its growing economic ties with Western states – provides a new test for the way in which economic interdependence influences the way states make decisions about security and cooperation.

Leaders of liberal democratic states such as Britain in the nineteenth century and the United States in the twentieth century and today have acted on this conviction. Both countries have had powerful economic incentives to do so – after all, they were the most advanced and productive economies of their day. But British and American leaders also promoted the building of an open world economy because of the more general effects this would have on international relations. As US Secretary of State Cordell Hull argued in the 1930s, 'if goods cross borders, soldiers won't'. Hull's logic was simple: trade fosters economic growth; growing and prosperous countries have fewer reasons to wage war. Moreover, the joint gains from trade and the mutually beneficial economic ties that would grow between countries would also create interests – and stakeholders – in these countries that favor peaceful and stable relations. Free trade creates expanding 'vested interests' that favor peace.

British economists and politicians made the first serious efforts to champion free trade as a way to promote world peace in the early nineteenth century. The British free trade movement came on the heels of the ideas advanced by economist Adam Smith whose *Wealth of Nations* (1776) had argued in favor of the many virtues and benefits of free markets and international trade. Britain was just beginning to lead the world in a new stage of rapid industrialization. Business leaders and workers were a growing force in British politics – and they increasingly identified their interests with open markets. In a dramatic political battle, the British Parliament debated – and eventually repealed – the Corn Laws, which were key protectionist blocks to the free flow of goods across borders. In their speeches to Parliament, John Bright and Richard Cobden, two of the leading political figures who opposed the Corn Laws, made eloquent pleas for free trade, linking expanding markets and trade with the movement toward a more peaceful world.

Over the next decades, Britain and other countries lowered tariffs and established the first great age of an open world economy. By the end of the nineteenth century, goods and capital flowed throughout Europe and around the world. Steamships, telegraph wires, and railroads provided the new infrastructure for a global economy. But all this changed abruptly with the coming of World War I. Despite the extensive trade and financial ties between the European states, peace did not last. In *The Grand Illusion* (1909), British politician Norman Angell, reflecting the liberal conviction that economic interdependence would deter war, argued that economic integration had grown so extensive between the European states that war between them was utterly futile. Angell's thesis was not that war was impossible – after all, political leaders could do what they wanted to do – but that it was economically irrational. Nonetheless, a bloody world war did come, dramatically revealing the limits of the economic sources of peace.

In the years leading to World War II, the United States saw its geopolitical operating space shrink as the other great powers began to construct closed and competing regional blocs. Japan was establishing an imperial regional order in East Asia, the Soviet Union dominated its region, and Germany was seeking to dominate Western Europe. After the war's end, the United States hoped to build a peaceful world around trade and an open world economy and committed itself to rebuilding such an economy. US officials believed that a nondiscriminatory commercial system would be the cornerstone of a stable peace. Open markets would provide the essential foundation for a wider multilateral system organized around the rule of law. This conviction about how to organize the global system brought together economic, ideological, and geopolitical strands of thinking among American policy makers.

Both the Roosevelt and Truman administrations championed a postwar effort to reopen the world economy. Free traders in the State Department, led by Secretary Cordell Hull, were at the forefront of this effort. Hull and his colleagues embraced economic interdependence, led by the United States, as the only way to ensure prosperity and stable peace. In a speech in November 1938 Hull said:

> I know that without expansion of international trade, based upon fair dealing and equal treatment for all, there can be no stability and security either within or among nations … I know that the withdrawal by a nation from orderly trade relations with the rest of the world inevitably leads to regimentation of all phases of national life, to the suppression of human rights, and all too frequently to preparations for war and a provocative attitude toward other nations. (Hull 1938)

Hull's emphasis was less on free trade than it was on nondiscrimination and equal commercial opportunity. Open markets, according to this widely shared American view, would simultaneously advance two objectives. They would ensure that the United States would have access to markets and raw materials around the world, a goal that Washington officials had pursued since the Open Door policies of the turn of the century. Beyond this, open markets would contribute to economic growth and interdependence, in turn creating shared interests among countries in a peaceful international order.

President Truman believed strongly that World War II had its roots in economics. It sprang from the rivalries and insecurities generated by protectionism, closed markets, and imperial blocs. If the world was to return to a period of stable peace, the barriers to free trade and nondiscrimination would need to be swept away. Assistant Secretary of State Dean Acheson argued in April 1945 that there was 'wide recognition that peace is possible only if countries work together and prosper together. That is why the economic aspects are no less important than the political aspects of peace' (Acheson 1945).

The promotion of peace through the expansion of markets was a critical strategy that the United States and its European partners brought to bear on postwar Europe. In the first decade after 1945, American and European officials worried that Europe would become an economic and political failure. The memory of World War I and the economic depression that followed was still fresh in the minds of postwar leaders – and the lesson was clear: economic contraction, rising unemployment, and social hardship provided the ugly conditions of political radicalism and instability. The challenge was to rebuild Europe in a way that would allow Germany to integrate into the continent without reigniting old hostilities and insecurities. Economic integration became a key component of reconstruction policy. Robert Schuman, French Finance Minister and later Foreign Minister after the war, was a leading architect of this vision of European economic integration. One part of this strategy was to tie together the old rivals – Germany and France – in new forms of economic cooperation. The European Coal and Steel Community was established to bind together these two industrial sectors in Europe's heartland. The 'industries of war' would no longer be national but European. The United States further pushed its postwar partners to create a Europe-wide common market. An integrated Europe that was growing together as a single whole would be less nationalist, militarist, and geopolitically divided.

The American strategy for the wider postwar international order was also grounded in the opening and expansion of world markets. The United States took the lead in the 1940s in negotiating with Britain and other market democracies to establish trade and monetary rules. The system of agreements reached at the 1944 conference in Bretton Woods, New Hampshire, provided mechanisms for governments to manage economic openness, which we shall explore further in Chapter 8. In the decades that followed, the advanced democracies continued to liberalize trade, lowering tariffs and non-tariff barriers. Trade and investment grew steadily though the postwar decades. American and European multilateral corporations expanded their operations worldwide. After the end of the Cold War, the world economy expanded to include most of the developing and former communist world.

The globalization of the world economy does not in itself ensure a stable peace. But it does create incentives for countries to settle their differences short of war. The interconnectedness of countries increases the number of stakeholders committed to a stable, open system. Yet interdependence also creates new problems with which states must struggle collectively. Globalization brings with it such problems as transnational crime, drugs, and terrorism, and it makes countries more vulnerable to economic crises and upheavals in other parts of the world. But it also creates incentives for governments to develop rules and institutions – and international capacities – to manage their joint vulnerabilities.

Liberal thinkers and liberal states believe free trade leads to peace, but the results of scholarly studies offer a mixed picture. There is empirical evidence for both the liberal view that economic interdependence can promote peace and the realist view that it does not. Economic interdependence does not – in itself – stop states from going to war. World War I remains the classic case that shows that statesmen do not always listen to businessmen and bankers. There is no evidence that governments make straightforward decisions about war and peace based on simple calculations of economic gain or loss. War has many causes and so it is unrealistic to think that the presence of mutually beneficial economic ties, by itself, will stand as an absolute brake on war.

Nonetheless, there is evidence of some relationship. One scholar has discovered that since 1850 the level of international trade has been inversely related to the occurrence of major power war (Mansfield 1994). Another study of the period 1950–86 found a significant correspondence between increased interdependence and democracy, on the one hand, and a reduction in the incidence of military conflict on the other (Oneal and Russett 1997). On the realist side, scholars have found that during the early decades of the twentieth century, the costs of disrupting interdependence did not restrain countries from going to war (Blanchard and Ripsman 1996/97). One scholar looking at the full array of recent studies of interdependence and conflict found that ten supported the liberal position, four supported the realist position, and six found mixed results (McMillan 1997).

What seems to be most telling in recent research on economic interdependence and war is that specific circumstances – what scholars call 'intervening variables' – tend to matter (Mastanduno 1999). Economic interdependence does have impacts on domestic groups and political coalitions. Economic interest groups that benefit from trade will push for stable relations with other states, but whether they are influential will hinge on many factors, including the character of the governing elite's political coalition. Some scholars also point to how state leaders think about their future economic prospects, while others look at the more general security environment surrounding economic relations. In the end, these contingent factors seem to matter in determining the nature of the relationship between interdependence and conflict.

A Possible International Community of Democratic Nations

As we saw in Chapter 5, liberal democracies tend not go to war against each other – and, in fact, they are unusually capable of working together to build cooperative relations. This simple insight lies behind one of the most celebrated and debated strategies of peacemaking, the democratic peace thesis, which focuses on democracy and the building of community among democracies. The characteristics of liberal democracies – the rule of law, free speech, private property, and leaders that are accountable to citizens – makes them predisposed not to go to war with other liberal democracies. It is not that liberal democracies are pacific states; they frequently attract and make trouble. But when democracies confront each other, they often find ways to settle their differences short of war. As democracy spreads around the world, so too does the **zone of peace** in world politics, that is, the number of countries and the geographic space they possess within which states do not want to use military force or believe it will be used against them. President Bill Clinton expressed this view as the United States sought to build international order after the Cold War: 'Ultimately, the best strategy to ensure our security and to build a durable peace is to support the advance of democracy elsewhere. Democracies don't attack each other' (Clinton 1994).

As we noted in Chapter 3, the German philosopher Immanuel Kant first advanced this argument in his 1795 essay, *Perpetual Peace*. Writing at a historical moment when democracies were just beginning to appear in the Western world, Kant suggested that what he called 'republics' – that is, countries with legal equality of citizens and repre-

Zone of peace: The number of democratic countries and the geographic space they possess within which states do not want to use military force or believe it will be used against them, in keeping with the Democratic Peace Theory.

sentative government – would be driven to affiliate with each other and build peaceful forms of community.

Kant's thesis was not only that republican states lack reasons to attack each other in war, but that they actually have incentives to draw closer together. Their market economies lead them to seek opportunities for trade and exchange, and their common political orientations make collaboration particularly easy. Kant argued further that building a democratic union would provide security in a world where democracies still faced threats from non-democratic states. Strength exists in numbers. A grouping of democratic states is more likely to withstand the assaults of other states than democracies operating individually on their own. Kant was less specific about what the democratic union might look like. It was to be something more than formal peace treaties between democratic states; it was to be a union or community of states. But Kant certainly did not see a democratic union as a prelude to world government – a formal international government structure that might jeopardize civic freedoms and limit republican rule.

Democracies in the contemporary era have tended both to cooperate and to behave peacefully toward each other. Leaders in democracies have embraced the ideas of a democratic peace. Woodrow Wilson's vision of a universal system of law and collective security was premised on his view that a worldwide democratic revolution was underway. In his case for war against Germany in 1917, Wilson made it clear that it was the authoritarian and militarist nature of Germany that produced aggression and war. 'No autocratic nation could be trusted to keep faith within it [a concert of peace] or observe its covenants,' Wilson argued. 'Only free peoples can hold their purpose and their honor steady.' Wilson believed that the post-1919 international order would need to incorporate non-democracies. But he was convinced that over time these autocratic and authoritarian states would join the world democratic community.

American leaders after World War II were even more determined to anchor the postwar international order in an alliance of democracies. While Roosevelt hoped that the United Nations might provide the master mechanism for world peace, the other US leaders placed greater reliance on political, economic, and security cooperation with Europe and the wider free world community of democracies. As the Cold War loomed, American leaders made far-reaching commitments to build and manage the international order. The shared democratic traditions of its Western partners made it easier for the United States to honor these commitments. In arguing for economic aid to Europe in 1948, for example, Secretary of State George Marshall told a congressional committee that American assistance was necessary to prevent 'economic distress so intense, social discontents so violent, political confusion so widespread, and hopes for the future so shattered that the historic base of Western civilization, of which we are by belief and inheritance an integral part, will take on new forms in the image of the tyranny that we fought to destroy in Germany' (Marshall 1948). Europeans also invoked this notion of Western civilization in arguing for postwar cooperation. British Foreign Secretary Ernest Bevin argued for a European security alliance with the United States – what became NATO – as part of a 'spiritual union' that would link the Atlantic world. 'While, no doubt, there must be treaties or, at least, understandings, the union must primarily be a fusion derived from the basic freedom and ethical principles for which we all stand. It must be on terms of equality and it must contain all the elements of freedom for which we all stand' (Bevin 1948; Jackson 2003). The failure of peacemaking after World War I and the search by the United States for a stable group of like-minded countries with whom to build institutionalized relations made officials on both sides of the Atlantic receptive to these appeals to Western democratic solidarity (Jackson 2006; Hampton 1995; Hampton 1996).

After the end of the Cold War, the United States and the other leading democracies again affirmed their commitments to one another. Speaking at the United Nations in September 1991, President George H. W. Bush noted that the two great breakthroughs in the modern world had been the rise of individual enterprise and international trade. 'As democracy flourishes,' Bush said, 'so does the opportunity for the third historical breakthrough – international cooperation.' The Clinton administration also enshrined democratic community as the great reality of world politics after the Cold War – and its strategy of global peacemaking involved the 'enlargement' of this globalizing, democratic, market-oriented world system. The trade system was strengthened with the establishment of the World Trade Organization in 1995, which provided rules and dispute settlement mechanisms for the expanding world economy. In the late 1990s, the Clinton administration also supported the creation of the Community of Democracies, which was a forum for the leaders of the world's democracies to gather periodically to discuss ways to support and strengthen democratic institutions in transitional and developing countries.

After the September 11, 2001, terrorist attacks the George W. Bush administration raised the stakes in the importance of democracy for global peace. Nongovernmental groups of terrorists who might gain access to deadly weapons of mass destruction presented new threats to American and world security. As we discuss more fully in Chapter 11, failed and despotic states – even in remote parts of the world – are a danger to the world because they could be breeding grounds for terrorists. The only way to be secure in this new age was with a democratic transformation of all countries. As President Bush stated: 'We are led, by events and common sense, to one conclusion: the survival of liberty in our land increasingly depends on the success of liberty in other lands. The best hope for peace in our world is the expansion of freedom in all the world' (Bush 2005).

The rise of China today will test these liberal ideas. As China becomes more powerful, will it peacefully integrate into the existing international order or seek to overturn it? Liberals and realists offer strikingly different visions of the future. Liberal thinkers argue that a 'peaceful rise' of China is possible if its domestic system evolves toward liberal democracy. In this view, China would follow a pathway similar to that of Japan after World War II. As a liberal capitalist state China will grow wealthier and gradually integrate into the world economic and political system. It will become a stakeholder in the existing order. Realist thinkers are more skeptical that democracy is a sufficient brake on conflict. For realists, the changing power position of China and the United States will matter more. China, regardless of its internal system, will

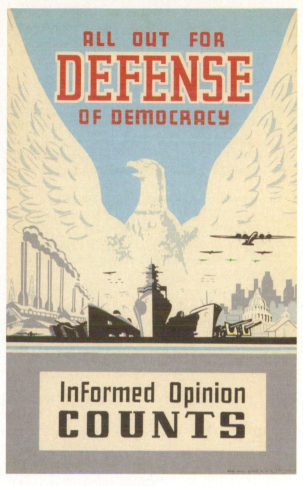

▲ Photo 6.4
American Poster from World War I

In this poster from World War I, the American eagle forms the background of a depiction of the American military effort. Such imagery portrays the strength of America as a democracy. In the postwar years, American officials became convinced that world order had to be rooted in democratic states.

Source: © Corbis.

6.5 Differing Perspectives — Liberals and Realists on Interdependence and the Rise of China

Former President Bill Clinton, a Liberal Voice:

- China should be brought into the World Trade Organization.
- The United States has a fundamental interest in promoting building prosperity and partnership with Asia. The key to getting the China relationship right is to increase China's interdependence with the outside world. A more interdependent China will be a more cooperative China.
- 'The world will be a better place over the next 50 years if we are partners, if we are working together.'

Political scientist John Mearsheimer, a Realist Voice:

- China will attempt to be a 'regional hegemon,' the undisputed power in its part of the world, and will not tolerate meddling by an outside state like the United States.
- The rise of China – and its likely desire to dominate East Asia – will pose a fundamental threat to the United States in the near future.
- 'The best way to survive in this system is to be the biggest and baddest dude on the block. . . Nobody fools around with Godzilla.'

(Quoted in Nathan Swire, 'Mearsheimer explores threat of China', *The Dartmouth*, November 14, 2008.)

seek to use its power to expand its influence and control over its region and perhaps the wider world. The United States, in turn, will resist China's quest for domination. Conflict – perhaps even war – will be the inevitable result.

The United States and other advanced democracies believe strongly that a world of democracies is more likely to be peaceful than the alternative – a world of autocratic and authoritarian states. Many observers also believe that democracy – at least when it is deeply rooted within stable societies – facilitates other international developments that foster peace: international interdependence and the rule of law. Democracies are predisposed to trade with other states and collaborate to establish rules and institutions that allow them to collectively manage their relations.

Peace Movements and Global Civil Society

States make war – and so, not surprisingly, do states also take charge to make peace. But nongovernmental organizations, that is, citizens' groups and political movements, have also played a role in pushing governments to the peace table, particularly over the last two centuries with the rise of liberal democracy and the increasingly destructive experiences of war. While these nongovernmental groups do not directly end wars or make peace agreements, they serve to draw attention to the costs of wars and to lobby governments to address issues of human suffering and social justice.

Before the twentieth century, citizen groups were not a major presence when states went to war. In both Europe and the United States, pacifist groups formed to seek alternatives to war and made small acts of resistance. For example, in Britain, the National Peace Council, established in 1908, brought together citizens from voluntary groups around the country to seek disarmament and the peaceful resolution of disputes. With World War I, however, large-scale groups of citizens organized to oppose government policy. During and after the war, peace activists in Britain and the United States also put forward ideas about world peace, offering proposals for a world organization that would promote peace – ideas that Woodrow Wilson drew from in his proposal for a League of Nations. The massive outpouring of people into the streets of cities across Europe to greet Wilson on the eve of the Paris peace talks lifted and reinforced Wilson's peacemaking agenda.

▲ Photo 6.5 A Vietnam War Protest in Washington

A crowd of demonstrators gather at the Washington Monument for the Moratorium Day peace rally, November 15, 1969, to protest the Vietnam War. The attendance is estimated at 200,000 people.

Source: PA Images.

The devastation of the two nuclear bombs dropped on Japan at the end of World War II provided the political and symbolic catalyst for a new generation of peace activism, which gained additional participants in the early decades of the Cold War. The dangers of nuclear war provided the focal point for these peace campaigns. Political activists, philosophers, theologians, and public intellectuals were active participants in the worldwide Cold War peace movement. Even nuclear scientists who had helped in inventing atomic weapons became involved in the search for arms control and disarmament. In 1957, for example, a group of scientists from both sides of the Cold War divide met in Pugwash – a remote location in Canada – to promote understanding and reconciliation between Western and Communist countries. The Pugwash Conferences, so named for that first meeting, continue today to bring together scholars and public figures to seek to reduce the dangers of armed conflict and find cooperative solutions to global problems.

Peace movements have had many different specific aims. In the United States, the Vietnam War triggered the most organized and vocal peace movement in the country's history. Hundreds of thousands of protesters marched on Washington on various occasions to demand that the United States withdraw from the war and bring the troops home. Opposition to the Vietnam War sparked protest demonstrations at the 1968 Democratic National Convention in Chicago, culminating in violence and hundreds of arrests. The antiwar movement touched many facets of life – music, art, education, and lifestyle. Rock groups such as the Grateful Dead and the Beatles incorporated messages of peace in their music, spreading those sentiments within American and international youth culture. The anti-Vietnam War movement ended when American troops finally left Vietnam in the spring of 1972.

In the 1980s, the American and European peace movements came to life again in protests over the escalation of hostilities between the United States and the Soviet Union. Huge crowds in the major capitals of Europe protested the decision by the Reagan administration to introduce new mid-range nuclear missiles on the European continent. Campaigns for nuclear disarmament that had been active during the earlier decades of the Cold War resumed. Church groups – including Catholic bishops, and doctors – through an organization called Physicians for Social Responsibility – issued statements about the catastrophic loss of life that nuclear war would bring to the planet.

More recently, the 2003 American war in Iraq also triggered an outpouring of anti-war protests in the United States, Western Europe, Japan, Turkey, and around the world. Protests began in 2002, even before the war was launched, and continued thereafter. Hundreds of thousands of people flooded into public squares to demonstrate against the war in cities such as Washington, DC, Paris, Berlin, and London. In Rome, on February 15, 2003, three million people came out to demonstrate against the war, which might be the largest anti-war rally in history. On the same day, anti-war protests were held in nearly 600 cities worldwide.

It is difficult to measure the influence of the peace movement on the actions of governments. Peace demonstrations likely played some role in helping to pressure the US government to end its involvement in Vietnam. In the 1980s, the Western peace movement provided the backdrop of the diplomacy between the United States and the Soviet Union, which ultimately brought the Cold War to an end. The anti-war demonstrations against the American war in Iraq – and the widespread opposition to the war particularly in Western Europe – made it easier for elected leaders to criticize US policy and oppose the war in places such as the United Nations.

Levels of Analysis *The Transnational Pursuit of Peace*	👤 **Individual**	👪 **State**	🌐 **International**
	Citizens and societal groups promote peace by building coalitions across national borders and putting pressure on governments.	Philosophers and political leaders have championed the building of 'zones of peace' among democratic states.	Liberal thinkers argue that the growth of economic interdependence between states can create pressures and incentives for states to pursue peace.

Revisiting the Enduring Question and Looking Ahead

As the weapons of war have become more destructive over time, the search for stable peace among states has also gained ground. Over the centuries, states have traveled many different pathways to peace. Until the sources of war completely disappear, the search for peace will remain a persistent feature of world politics.

Two international distributions of power may influence the prospects for peace, a balance of power and hegemony. Diplomacy and power balancing represent actions by states to advance their interests but may also help promote peace. International law and institutions, and in particular the European Union, may offer important new opportunities for peace. The extension of democracy to more countries, the intensification of trade and investment across the world, and the rise of peace movements and international civil society have also helped maintain international peace, particularly among democratic states.

Nuclear weapons have also perhaps had a pacifying effect on world politics. Indeed, nuclear weapons are so important that it is sometimes suggested that they brought about a revolution in the very character of world affairs. It is to that possibility that we now turn our attention.

 Visit **www.palgrave.com/politics/Grieco** to access extra resources for this chapter

Study Questions

1. Among the forces for peace today are democracy, economic interdependence, diplomacy, and international law. Which of these do you consider the most powerful force for peace today? Could it be some other force? On what grounds are you basing your answer?

2. As noted in this chapter, a single big power, a hegemonic state, might be a force for peace. If you live in a small country that neighbors that hegemonic state, what questions might you pose to the leaders and citizens of the hegemonic state about their intentions as they bring peace into being?

3. A Roman writer of the fourth century A.D. advised: 'If you want peace, prepare for war.' To what extent do you find his advice persuasive?

4. In today's international system, how much overlap do you perceive among the two main power structures which reinforce stable peace – balance of power and hegemony?

5. With the advent of the Internet and new forms of social media, do you expect the role of citizens as a source for peace to increase or decrease in the years ahead? Explain your reasoning.

Further Reading

Claude, Inis (1956) *Swords into Plowshares: The Problems and Progress of International Organizations* (New York: Random House). A classic study of the efforts by states in the modern era to build international peace organizations, with a focus on the League of Nations and the United Nations. Claude provides one of the best statements of the logic of collective security.

Falk, Richard A., Friedrich V. Kratochwil, and Saul Mendlovitz (eds) (1985) *International Law: A Contemporary Perspective* (Boulder: Westview Press). Essays in this volume discuss the various ways that international law is useful in the pursuit of peace and justice in world affairs.

Hamilton, Keith and Richard Langhorne (2010) *The Practice of Diplomacy: Its Evolution, Theory, and Administration*, 2nd edn (New York: Routledge). A survey of the rise of diplomacy among states as a tool for managing relations and establishing the conditions for peace and problem solving. The book also looks at the current experience of diplomacy in the areas of climate change, human rights, and the activities of NGOs.

Ikenberry, G. John, Michael Mastanduno, and William C. Wohlforth (eds) (2011) *International Relations Theory and the Consequences of Unipolarity* (New York: Cambridge University Press). This book features various scholars exploring the consequence of a unipolar or hegemonic organization of world politics, particularly on international peace and stability.

Kaufman, Stuart, Richard Little, and William C. Wohlforth (2007) *Balance of Power in World History* (New York: Palgrave Macmillan). A sweeping study of the role of balance of power and empire across world history.

Wooley, Wesley T. (1988) *Alternatives to Anarchy: American Supranationalism Since World War II* (Bloomington: Indiana University Press). A vivid portrait of the ideas of postwar globalists and peace activists and their political efforts to usher in radical shifts in the governance of the global system to overcome the dangers of war and geopolitical conflict.

7

Weapons of Mass Destruction

Enduring question: How have weapons of mass destruction, and in particular nuclear weapons, changed the practice of international relations

Although it may seem counter-intuitive, the best way for two countries to avoid a nuclear war is for each one to try *not* to defend its own people in the face of a possible nuclear attack. This curious conclusion has been reached by many scholars and strategists who have thought long and hard about the connection between nuclear weapons and world politics. Nuclear weapons are so destructive that a nuclear war is unwinnable. The best way to avoid a nuclear war is to prevent countries from having nuclear weapons. But once countries have them, the best strategy may be to make sure no country sees a possible way to use nuclear weapons without facing massive destruction itself.

This chapter explores the impact nuclear weapons and other weapons of mass destruction have had on international relations. It is common to think that governments develop weapons so they can be used in war. But nuclear weapons are different, so different in fact that their existence has changed the way most governments actually think about war itself. They are weapons not to be used in war, but to be used instead to deter war. It is striking that prior to the nuclear age, the great powers of the international system fought major wars with other each to settle their differences. In the nuclear era, however, the type of great power wars the world witnessed between 1914 and 1945 has not taken place. Do nuclear weapons constitute an extraordinary "pathway to peace" for nation-states? Have they changed fundamentally the relationship between diplomacy and warfare? This latter question has been an enduring and consequential one in international relations since the dawn of the nuclear age.

We will look first at what nuclear weapons are and how they work. Then we examine that peculiar logic of nuclear strategy that says the best way to avoid war is not to be prepared actually to fight it. That logic applied to the

United States and Soviet Union who had massive nuclear arsenals facing each other during the Cold War. Does it also apply to countries like India and Pakistan, who face each other today with smaller nuclear arsenals? Does it apply to a world in which many countries including North Korea, Iran, and Syria are either developing or seeking nuclear capabilities? We will also examine other weapons of mass destruction – weapons designed to kill very large numbers of civilians or armed forces – such as biological and chemical weapons, and explore the ongoing efforts by the international community to control the spread of all types of destructive weapons. Finally, we will look at the special problem of terrorism and weapons of mass destruction, and recognize the possible new threat of cyber-warfare.

Source: © Giovanni Verlini/IAEA

Learning Objectives

By the end of this chapter, you will be able to:

→ Recognize the unprecedented destructive capacity of nuclear weapons and their influence on modern international relations.

→ Analyze the peculiar logic of nuclear deterrence and its impact on governmental policy.

→ Understand the spread of nuclear weapons and evaluate efforts to halt it.

→ Analyze the dangers posed by chemical and biological weapons for modern society.

→ Demonstrate the connections between non-state actors, terrorism, and weapons of mass destruction.

Chapter Contents

- Nuclear Weapons
- The Nuclear Revolution
- Nuclear Proliferation and Efforts to Halt it
- Chemical and Biological Weapons
- Weapons of Mass Destruction and Terrorism
- Revisiting the Enduring Question and Looking Ahead
- Study Questions
- Further Reading

Nuclear Weapons

We use the word 'blockbuster' today to describe a big event, such as a hit movie. The term was popularized during World War II, when the largest conventional bombs the combatants used were called blockbusters because they were powerful enough to destroy an entire city block. The original blockbusters that US and British forces dropped on their enemies contained *two tons* (4,000 pounds) of high explosive. Blockbusters were designed to blow the roofs off buildings so that smaller bombs could be dropped to destroy building interiors.

On July 16, 1945, the United States detonated a very different type of bomb at a remote testing site near Alamogordo, New Mexico. That device – by today's standards, a very simple and crude nuclear bomb – released the energy equivalent of *nineteen thousand tons* of TNT. The explosion in the New Mexican desert, which American nuclear scientists labeled the Trinity test, ushered in a new era for military technology and international politics (Rhodes 1986).

Manhattan Project: The secret project that brought together expert scientists to build a super weapon, culminating in the creation of the first atomic bomb. The Manhattan Project was begun by the United States around the time it entered World War II.

Fission: An atom-splitting chain reaction that is central to the working of a nuclear weapon.

The Trinity test was the culmination of a secret project that began just as America entered World War II. Code-named the **Manhattan Project**, it brought together some of the best scientific minds of the United States and Europe to develop a super-weapon that would take advantage of recent discoveries in atomic physics. Albert Einstein, whose work on relativity served as the foundation of nuclear physics, helped to prompt the Manhattan Project by sending a letter to President Franklin Roosevelt in 1939 to alert him that German scientists were trying to exploit these key findings for military purposes (E-World 1997). Manhattan Project scientists worked to design a weapon that could harness and then release the tremendous energy created by **fission**, or an atom-splitting chain reaction, before the Germans did.

On August 6, 1945, a US Air Force B-29 plane dropped a nuclear weapon called Little Boy on the Japanese city of Hiroshima. Three days later, a second bomb known as Fat Man was detonated over Nagasaki. The destructive effects were startling. The Hiroshima bomb killed between 70,000 and 80,000 people and injured 70,000 others. The Nagasaki bomb exploded over a relatively isolated part of the city, resulting in about 40,000 killed and 40,000 injured. Japan surrendered shortly after the nuclear attacks on Hiroshima and Nagasaki, effectively ending World War II. As we show in Box 7.1, historians continue to debate the morality of the nuclear attack and whether it was truly necessary to cause the Japanese surrender.

Thermonuclear bomb: A type of nuclear weapon, even more powerful than a conventional nuclear weapon, that relies on the power of a contained fission explosion to trigger the fusing of hydrogen particles, a process that yields even greater amounts of destructive energy than a **fission** reaction alone. Also known as a **fusion** bomb.

America's nuclear monopoly did not last very long. In 1949, the Soviet Union shocked the world by successfully testing its own version of a fission atomic bomb. By 1952, the United States had developed an even more powerful and sophisticated device – a **thermonuclear**, or fusion bomb, also known as the hydrogen or 'H' bomb. Fusion bombs rely on the power of a contained fission explosion to trigger the fusing of hydrogen particles, a process that yields even greater amounts of destructive energy than a fission reaction alone. The United States tested its first fusion bomb in November 1952, and the explosion released 10.4 megatons, or millions of tons of TNT equivalent. That blast, more than 500 times more powerful than the Trinity test, vaporized an entire South Pacific island and replaced it with a crater 6,000 feet across and 164 feet deep.

That first thermonuclear device was too cumbersome to be used as a weapon. It was the size of a small building and weighed about 70 tons. As countries mastered nuclear technology, however, they abandoned the 'bigger is better' theme and sought

Background

During August 1945, the United States dropped two atomic bombs on Japan, the Soviet Union declared war on Japan, and Japanese leaders surrendered to the United States and its allies. For decades, scholars, scientists, and journalists have debated whether the use of atomic weapons was necessary to end the war and morally justifiable. Newly declassified materials and other primary source documents have gradually become available to stir the debate (Burr 2007).

Supporters of President Truman's historic decision believe that the use of nuclear weapons was the most viable and least costly way to force a Japanese surrender. The Japanese fought with almost fanatical resistance and signaled a determination to fight to the last man rather than surrender. Supporters argue that an invasion of Japan would have resulted in casualties far exceeding those caused by the attacks on Hiroshima and Nagasaki. The shocking effect of the dramatic new weapon convinced Japan's unyielding leaders to surrender, and ended the war quickly enough that the Soviet Union could not make any plausible claim to occupy Japan jointly with the United States.

Critics argue that the United States had viable alternatives to nuclear attack on two cities filled with Japanese civilians. They believe that by August 1945 Japan was already close to surrender due to the destruction by conventional bombing of over 50 of its cities, the blockade of its territory by the US Navy, and the fact that the Soviet Union had now joined the war against it. The threat of a final invasion under these circumstances should have been credible and sufficient to prompt capitulation. Moreover, if US leaders believed the shock effect of the nuclear device was really needed to prompt Japanese surrender, they could have detonated a weapon over Tokyo Harbor or a similarly visible location in order to achieve the desired political response while minimizing civilian casualties. Critics of Truman's decision suspect that US leaders were more interested in containing Soviet ambitions in the Pacific, or perhaps seeking to justify the massive costs associated with developing the atomic weapon, than in finding the least costly way to end the war.

Henry Stimson, US Secretary of War in 1945

I felt that to extract a genuine surrender from the Emperor and his military advisers, they must be administered a tremendous shock which would carry convincing proof of our power to destroy the empire. Such an effective shock would save many times the number of lives, both American and Japanese, than it would cost...The decision to use the atomic bomb was a decision that brought death to over one hundred thousand Japanese. No explanation can change that fact and I do not wish to gloss over it. But this deliberate, premeditated destruction was our least abhorrent choice. The destruction of Hiroshima and Nagasaki put an end to the Japanese war. It stopped the fire raids, and the strangling blockade; it ended the ghastly specter of a clash of great land armies. (Stimson 1947: 101)

Admiral William D. Leahy, Chief of Staff to President Truman

It is my opinion that the use of this barbarous weapon at Hiroshima and Nagasaki was of no material assistance in our war against Japan. The Japanese were already defeated and ready to surrender because of the effective sea blockade and the successful bombing with conventional weapons...The lethal possibilities of atomic warfare in the future are frightening. My own feeling was that in being the first to use it, we had adopted an ethical standard common to the barbarians of the Dark Ages. (Leahy 1950: 441)

to make nuclear devices smaller, more efficient, and able to penetrate enemy defenses and deliver weapons more accurately to chosen targets.

Today's most sophisticated nuclear arsenal belongs to the United States, and contains an array of compact and miniaturized nuclear weapons that can be delivered from land, sea, and air. Weapons may be dropped from 'stealth bombers', or planes

► **Photo 7.1 'Ivy Mike' thermonuclear explosion in the Marshall Islands**

The mushroom cloud rises from the Ivy Mike test on Enewetak Atoll in the Marshall Islands, South Pacific Ocean. Operation Ivy was the code name given to America's plan to develop a hydrogen bomb. 'Mike' was shorthand for 'megaton' explosion.

Source: Science Photo Library.

Intercontinental ballistic missile (ICBM): Missile that in under an hour can travel thousands of miles through outer space and release multiple nuclear warheads, each carrying a payload of several hundred kilotons and independently guided to explode within several hundred feet of a separate target.

Submarine-launched ballistic missile (SLBM): Missile that can produce much the same effect as an **intercontinental ballistic missile (ICBM)** from a platform deep beneath the ocean's surface.

Cruise missile: Missile, capable of being launched from land, air, or sea, that can travel below radar detection and guide itself around obstacles to deliver the warhead it carries.

Blast effect: The immediate explosive effect of a nuclear weapon. Can be powerful enough to level all buildings in a several-mile radius and to produce destructive winds of between 100 and 200 miles per hour.

that can fly up to 6,000 miles without refueling and are invisible to enemy radar despite their large size. In less than one hour, **intercontinental ballistic missiles** (ICBMs) can travel thousands of miles through outer space and release multiple nuclear warheads, each having a yield of several hundred kilotons and independently guided to explode within several hundred feet of a separate target. **Submarine-launched ballistic missiles** (SLBMs) can accomplish the same mission, with a similar degree of accuracy, from a platform deep beneath the surface of the world's oceans. **Cruise missiles**, measuring about 20 feet long, can travel 'below the radar' at low altitudes, and possess a terrain-matching guidance system that enables them to fly across valleys and around mountains to deliver their nuclear warheads. Cruise missiles may be launched from the ground, aircraft, or ships (Schwartz 1998).

Regardless of how they are delivered, the distinctive feature of nuclear weapons is their unprecedented destructive capacity. Never before in history have humans created a weapon that could destroy property and people so easily and quickly, with little discrimination between combatants and civilians.

Nuclear explosions create blast, heat, and radiation effects. An authoritative study by the Office of Technology Assessment (OTA) for the US Congress in 1979 found that the **blast effect** of a one megaton explosion would be sufficient to level all buildings not specially reinforced within a four-mile radius (Office of Technology Assessment 1979). People in the vicinity of 'ground zero' would be crushed by debris or experience fatal collisions with nearby objects due to winds of up to 180 miles per hour. The heat or **thermal effect** of a one-megaton blast would cause third-degree burns on exposed skin up to five miles away from the explosion. Because a nuclear explosion causes dirt and air particles to become radioactive, the radiation or **fallout effect** would spread much further, with the potential to expose people hundreds of miles from the blast site to fatal cancers over time.

The OTA study estimated the likely effects of a variety of hypothetical nuclear exchanges between the United States and the Soviet Union during the Cold War. An attack of one nuclear weapon on a US or Soviet city (the OTA modeled Detroit and Leningrad as the hypothetical targets) would result in up to two million deaths imme-

Estimated nuclear casualties for attacks on 10 large Indian and Pakistani cities

City name	Total population within 5 kilometers of ground zero	Number of persons killed	Number of persons severely injured	Number of persons slightly injured
India				
Bangalore	3,077,937	314,978	175,136	411,336
Bombay	3,143,284	477,713	228,648	476,633
Calcutta	3,520,344	357,202	198,218	466,336
Madras	3,252,628	364,291	196,226	448,948
New Delhi	1,638,744	176,518	94,231	217,853
Total India	14,632,937	1,690,702	892,459	2,021,106
Pakistan				
Faisalabad	2,376,478	336,239	174,351	373,967
Islamabad	798,583	154,067	66,744	129,935
Karachi	1,962,458	239,643	126,810	283,290
Lahore	2,682,092	258,139	149,649	354,095
Rawalpindi	1,589,828	183,791	96,846	220,585
Total Pakistan	9,409,439	1,171,879	614,400	1,361,872
India and Pakistan				
Total	24,042,376	2,862,581	1,506,859	3,382,978

◀ **Table 7.1 Ten Bombs on Ten South Asian Cities**

A nuclear war between states that possess even modest stockpiles would result in several million persons killed or wounded.

Source: NRDC, Natural Resources Defense Council, 2002, http://www.nrdc.org/nuclear/southasia.asp. Reproduced with permission.

diately. A limited nuclear exchange in which each side fired ten missiles at oil refineries would result in the loss of about two-thirds of each country's oil capacity and the deaths of one to five million people. An all-out exchange utilizing large fractions of the nuclear arsenals of the two sides would result in between 20 and 160 million deaths and 'incapacitating psychological trauma and the breakdown of social order.' During the 1980s scientists speculated that a large-scale nuclear war might even result in a **nuclear winter**, as the smoke and soot resulting from explosions blocked out the sunlight from the earth's surface for extended periods of time.

The National Resources Defense Council recently produced an estimate of the effects of a 'small' nuclear war between India and Pakistan. They simulated India and Pakistan each exploding five nuclear bombs over five major cities of their neighbor. Each bomb in the Indian and Pakistani arsenals is about the size of the Hiroshima weapon. In this scenario, almost 3 million Indians and Pakistanis would be killed instantly, and another 1.5 million would suffer severe injuries (National Resources Defense Council 2002). Table 7.1 presents the cities targeted and the specific casualties estimated for each one.

Thankfully nuclear weapons have not been used since the attacks on Hiroshima and Nagasaki. But the **nuclear club** of nation-states believed to have possession of nuclear weapons has grown gradually to include nine members (see Table 7.2). The United States possesses the world's most diverse and technologically sophisticated nuclear arsenal, totaling over 7,000 nuclear warheads, of which about 2,100 are 'active' or operational. Although its former Cold War capacity has been diminished, Russia remains a major nuclear power with a stockpile of about 8,500 warheads, of which about 1,800 are operational. It inherited the nuclear arsenal of the former Soviet

Thermal effect: The secondary effect of a nuclear explosion, in which the heat waves from the explosion can cause third-degree burns up to five miles from the detonation site.

Fallout effect: The tertiary effect of a nuclear explosion. Because nuclear weapons cause dirt and air particles to become radioactive, an explosion can expose people hundreds of miles from the blast site to fatal cancers over time. This exposure to radiation is the fallout effect, and affects a much wider range than the blast or thermal effects.

Nuclear winter: A situation, feared by many scientists in the 1980s, in which the smoke and soot resulting from numerous nuclear explosions blocked out the sunlight from the earth's surface for extended periods of time.

Nuclear club: The group of states believed to possess nuclear weapons.

► Table 7.2 World
Nuclear forces,
January 2013

Today there are nine
nuclear weapons states,
and even with the end
of the Cold War, the
nuclear arsenals of the
former superpowers
are still very large.

Source: *SIPRI Yearbook
2013: Armaments,
Disarmament and
International Security,*
Stockholm International
Peace Research Institute,
2013, www.sipriyearbook.
org.

Country	Year of first nuclear test	Deplyed warheads[a]	Other warheads[b]	Total inventory
United States	1945	2,150[c]	5,550	7,700[d]
Russia	1949	1,800	6,700[e]	8 500[f]
United Kingdom	1952	160	65	225
France	1960	290	10	300
China	1964	–	250	250
India	1974	–	90–100	90–100
Pakistan	1998	–	100–120	100–120
Israel	–	–	80	80
North Korea	2006	–	–	6–8?
Total		4,400	12,865	17,270

a 'Deployed' means warheads placed on missiles or located on bases with operational forces.
b These are warheads in reserve, awaiting dismantlement or that require some preparation (e.g. assembly or loading on launchers) before they become fully operationally available.
c In addition to strategic warheads, this figure includes nearly 200 non-strategic (tactical) nuclear weapons deployed in Europe.
d This figure includes the US Department of Defense nuclear stockpile of c. 4,650 warheads and another c. 3,000 retired warheads that are awaiting dismantlement.
e This figure includes c. 700 warheads for nuclear-powered ballistic missile submarines (SSBNs) in overhaul and bombers, 2,000 non-strategic nuclear weapons for use by short-range naval, air force and air defence forces, and c. 4,000 retired warheads awaiting dismantlement.
f This includes a military stockpile of c. 4,500 nuclear warheads and another c. 4,000 retired warheads awaiting dismantlement.

Union; former Soviet republics such as Belarus, Ukraine, and Kazakhstan transferred nuclear weapons left on their territory after the collapse of the Soviet Union to Russia during the 1990s. Great Britain, France, and China were the third, fourth and fifth nation-states to test a nuclear weapon, in 1952, 1960, and 1964 respectively. Each country currently possesses an arsenal of several hundred warheads.

It is difficult to make precise estimates of the holdings of other members of the nuclear club. Israel is widely thought to possess at least 80 warheads, even though it has not conducted a public test and refuses to acknowledge the existence of its arsenal. Nuclear experts believe India possesses between 90 and 100 warheads. Experts at the Federation of American Scientists estimate Pakistan to have between 100 and 120. North Korea tested a nuclear weapon in 2006 and is believed to have sufficient nuclear material to construct up to 8 warheads. South Africa was a member of the nuclear club, having produced 6 warheads during the 1980s, but it dismantled its program and weapons in 1991 after its apartheid, or racially segregated, regime was overthrown in a popular revolution.

You now have a good grasp of what nuclear weapons are, how they work, and who has them. In the next section, we explore the implications of these weapons for international relations.

Levels of Analysis
Nuclear Weapons

🧍 Individual	👥 State
The best scientific minds were drafted by governments to develop new weapons with the potential to transform warfare and international relations.	A relatively small number of states in the international system set themselves apart by having a special weapon not possessed by other states.

The Nuclear Revolution

The traditional purpose of military innovation has been to create new and more effective weapons that can be used to defeat an enemy in wartime. The machine gun, battle tank, aerial bomber, and submarine are some of the most important weapons in the modern era. Nuclear weapons are qualitatively different and cannot be thought of as simply the next generation of war-fighting instruments. Bernard Brodie, one of the first military theorists of the atomic age, put it succinctly in 1946: 'Thus far the chief purpose of our military establishment has been to win wars. From now on its chief purpose must be to avert them. It can have almost no other useful purpose' (Brodie 1946: 76). Brodie captured the paradoxical essence of the nuclear revolution – nuclear weapons are so powerful that they cannot actually be used. As noted in Chapter 6, the nineteenth-century German strategist Carl von Clausewitz famously stated that warfare is 'the continuation of politics by other means.' Warfare, in other words, is a rational instrument of statecraft to be used by policy makers to achieve political goals. Warfare and diplomacy are two sides of the same coin; where diplomacy fails, military action might succeed. Even the all-out world wars of the twentieth century fit Clausewitz's model; military power was used to achieve a politically meaningful objective, even if at great cost. But nuclear weapons seem to nullify Clausewitz's rule. It is hard to imagine a politically meaningful purpose being served by an all-out nuclear war, or even by a 'limited' one. As Nina Tannenwald (2008) points out, much of the international community has internalized this understanding; a 'nuclear taboo' developed gradually after 1945, prompting most states to embrace the non-use of nuclear weapons as a political and moral imperative. Tannenwald's work is an important constructivist contribution to the debate over nuclear weapons, showing how norms and ideas develop and spread across the international system.

If nuclear weapons are not useful as weapons of war, then what purpose might they serve? The most basic answer is **deterrence** (Freedman 2004; Jervis 1989a). Instead of being used to fight wars, these weapons may be used to deter war or other types of behavior government leaders might find unacceptable. The nuclear strategy of the United States, for example, is designed to deter a nuclear attack on America, and to deter a nuclear or even a non-nuclear attack against America's closest allies. Many analysts believe that the purpose of the Israeli nuclear force has long been to deter any kind of attacks from an array of hostile neighbors, including Syria, Iran, and, prior to the 2003 war between Iraq and the United States, Saddam Hussein's Iraq. Iran, in turn, may be acquiring nuclear weapons to deter what it perceives as potentially aggressive Israel and United States. Recall the importance of viewing the world from multiple perspectives: any state's nuclear program might be viewed as prudent and defensive by its leaders, yet as aggressive and alarming by its neighbors.

Deterrence: Using the threat of retaliation to protect oneself from an attack. Nuclear states use the threat of nuclear retaliation to deter other states from attacking them.

Assured Destruction and the Peculiar Logic of MAD

To understand nuclear deterrence theory, consider the simplified situation of just two states, each with sizable nuclear forces. The United States and Soviet Union during the Cold War inspired this model. What was required for the United States to effectively deter the Soviet Union from attacking America with nuclear weapons? First, the United States needed the ability to retaliate and deliver nuclear weapons against the territory and population of the Soviet Union even after the Soviet Union had struck the United States first. Second, the threat of US retaliation had to be credible; Soviet leaders had to believe the United States would retaliate. If Soviet leaders felt their US counterparts would be reluctant to use nuclear weapons, perhaps for moral reasons, then the Soviets would be less likely to be deterred. Third, the costs of retaliation had to be judged by the Soviet leadership as unacceptably high. In other words, even after being struck first, the United States had to have sufficient forces remaining, and the will and capacity to deliver them, in order to inflict unacceptable damage on the Soviet population and territory.

Unacceptable damage is difficult to define precisely. For some countries, the prospect of a single nuclear attack against one city might be sufficient to deter them. Others, depending on the stakes involved in a particular conflict, might be willing to contemplate far greater losses in order to achieve a particular political objective. During the Cold War, American military planners tended to apply 'worst-case' analysis and presumed that the Soviet threshold for unacceptable damage was fairly high. In the early 1960s, the United States government developed a nuclear arsenal with the premise that, to deter a possible Soviet first strike, the level of damage the United States had to inflict in a second strike was approximately 25 percent of the Soviet population and about 50 percent of the country's industry.

Once the United States possessed the ability and will to inflict unacceptable damage on the Soviet Union – even after the Soviets hit first with their best nuclear attack – it had what nuclear strategists call a **second-strike capability**. This is also called an **assured destruction** capability. Once the Soviet Union also acquired a comparable second-strike capability in relation to the United States, the two countries were in a situation of **Mutual Assured Destruction**, or MAD.

In the terminology of nuclear deterrence theory, a **first-strike capability** is the negation of another country's second-strike capability. In other words, if the United States possessed a first-strike capability (as it did during the early 1950s, when the Soviet Union had a small number of nuclear weapons and vulnerable delivery systems) it could strike the Soviet Union first in a nuclear attack, and the Soviets would not have sufficient residual nuclear forces to strike the United States in response and inflict unacceptable damage.

Assuming two countries have sizable and dispersed nuclear forces, it is difficult to achieve a first-strike capability. But we can conceive of ways it might be accomplished. For example, one country's nuclear forces could become so accurate that they could locate and destroy most or all of the nuclear weapons of their adversary in a coordinated first strike. Second, a country might figure out how to defend its own territory and population from nuclear attack, perhaps by developing a space-based defensive system that would shoot down the other side's nuclear warheads before they could detonate on their targets. Since the early 1970s, the United States government has spent billions of dollars to research the possibility of a missile defense system that might thwart a nuclear attack against the United States. For example, Walt discusses a proposed space-based defense system with a 'railgun' that would electronically launch 'smart' projectiles to destroy incoming missiles (Walt 2000). Critics of missile defense argue that it is impossible to stop a determined nuclear attack because if even one of several warheads gets through, they will render unacceptable levels of damage on the target. Critics also worry that if any state believes it might be able to defend itself against a nuclear attack, it may be more tempted to use nuclear weapons itself in a conflict with an adversary.

Unacceptable damage: The level of damage that a state is absolutely unwilling to sustain.

Second-strike capability: The ability and will to inflict unacceptable damage on an adversary – even after the adversary hits first with its best nuclear attack. Also known as assured destruction.

Assured destruction: The ability and will to inflict unacceptable damage on an adversary – even after the adversary hits first with its best nuclear attack. Also known as second-strike capability.

Mutual Assured Destruction (MAD): [1] A situation in which two adversaries each possess **assured destruction** capability, meaning that a nuclear conflict would likely inflict **unacceptable damage** on both countries. [2] A theory favored by many Cold War policymakers. This theory argues that a state should want **second-strike capability** but not **first-strike capability**.

First-strike capability: The negation of another country's second-strike capability. A state has first-strike capability if, and only if, it has sufficient nuclear capability to entirely eliminate an adversary's capacity to respond to a preliminary strike.

◀ **Map 7.1 Israel, Iran and the Middle East**

Although it struck a separate peace with Egypt in 1979, Israel continues to view some of its neighbors, in particular Iran, as implacably hostile. Iran and other regional actors such as Hamas (which governs the Gaza Strip) and ISIS (the self-proclaimed Islamic State that, as of 2014, controlled parts of Syria and Iraq), in turn, question Israel's right to exist and view it as a regional aggressor that continues to occupy Arab lands, and to repress Palestinian peoples. These actors also resent that powerful Western states seem willing to tolerate Israel's nuclear arsenal while seeking to prevent Iran and others from acquiring nuclear weapons.

Most nuclear deterrence theorists believe that second-strike capabilities are desirable and first-strike capabilities are undesirable. They believe, in fact, that MAD is the best of all possible nuclear worlds. The reasoning is simple yet powerful. If two adversaries each have secure second-strike capabilities, neither has any incentive to start a nuclear war. No matter how good your initial nuclear attack might be, your adversary will still be able to destroy your territory and society in retaliation. MAD represents stability because no one can win a nuclear war, even if you catch your adversary by surprise.

In contrast, first-strike capabilities create instability. If the United States or any other country achieves a first-strike capability, they might be tempted in a crisis or a war to use nuclear weapons, on the assumption that they might be able to limit damage to their own society and perhaps 'win' a nuclear war. The situation is most unstable if two adversaries each believe they have a first-strike capability. In that case, there are great incentives to 'go first,' because the state that launches its nuclear forces first has the potential to come out of any conflict in a relatively advantageous position. Mutual first-strike capability gives each side the incentive to be 'trigger happy.' This is especially troubling in times of crisis, when government leaders are under considerable stress.

The policy implications are counter-intuitive if one follows the logic of MAD. The most important advice for policy makers is to protect their weapons instead of their people. As long as governments can retaliate effectively and credibly, their adversaries will have no incentive to attack them with nuclear weapons. Policy makers should also avoid deployments that might enhance their own first-strike capability, because the appearance of a first-strike capability will only heighten the anxiety of adversaries and give them incentives to develop their own in response. For this reason, proponents of MAD oppose missile defense systems; any efforts to develop an effective defense

The Logic of MAD versus the Cold War Nuclear Strategies of the United States and Soviet Union

Theory: *The inescapable logic of MAD, as described by Robert Jervis, Professor of Political Science, Columbia University*

> A rational strategy for the employment of nuclear weapons is a contradiction in terms. The enormous destructive power of these weapons creates insoluble problems. For this reason, much of the history of nuclear strategy has been a series of attempts to find a way out of this predicament and return to the simpler, more comforting pre-nuclear world in which safety did not depend on an adversary's restraint. Short of developing an effective defense, however, these efforts cannot succeed. Instead, they can only produce doctrines which are incoherent and filled with contradictions, which though they are super-ficially alluring, upon close examination do not make sense. (Jervis 1984: 19)

Jervis's point is the core of nuclear deterrence theory, which holds that it is both futile and dangerous for states to try to escape the logic of MAD. It is futile because there is no practical way to limit damage from a nuclear attack, and dangerous because the attempt to limit damage only increases the incentive to use nuclear weapons. Nevertheless, in practice countries do try to escape the logic of MAD, as the discussion below of Soviet and American nuclear strategy during the Cold War demonstrates.

Practice: *American Nuclear Strategy during the 1980s*

American strategy for the past several years – the 'countervailing strategy' – has been based on the assumption that what is crucial is the ability of American and allied forces to deny the Soviets military advantage from any aggression they might contemplate. The US. must be prepared to meet and block any level of Soviet force. The strategy is then one of counterforce – blocking and seeking to destroy Soviet military power.

> The nuclear policy of the Reagan administration – which is essentially the same as that of the Carter administration and which has its roots in the developments initiated by even earlier administrations – is particularly ill-formed ...the strategy rests on a profound underestimation of the impact of nuclear weapons on military strategy and attempts to understand the current situation with intellectual tools appropriate only in the pre-nuclear era. (Jervis, 1985: 85)

Practice: *Soviet Nuclear Strategy during the 1980s, described by Richard Pipes, Professor of Russian Studies, Harvard University*

> The classic dictum of Clausewitz, that war is politics pursued by other means, is widely believed in the United States to have lost its validity after Hiroshima and Nagasaki. Soviet doctrine, by contrast, emphatically asserts that while an all-out nuclear war would indeed prove extremely destructive to both parties, its outcome would not be mutual suicide; the country better prepared for it and in possession of a superior strategy could win and emerge a viable society... Clausewitz, buried in the United States, seems to be alive and prospering in the Soviet Union...The strategic doctrine adopted by the USSR over the past two decades calls for a policy diametrically opposite to that adopted in the United States by the predominant community of civilian strategists: not deterrence but victory, not sufficiency in weapons but superiority, not retaliation but offensive action. (Dyson 1985: 96)

might tempt a country into thinking it could combine offensive and defensive measures to limit damage to its territory in a hypothetical nuclear war. The most striking policy implication of MAD logic is that governments should not try to defend their populations from nuclear attack. In the logic of MAD, keeping the American and Soviet populations as 'mutual hostages' during the Cold War, and by implication, keeping the Chinese and American populations as mutual hostages today, represents the best way to ensure that no government is tempted to use its nuclear arsenal.

Should Governments Prepare to Fight Nuclear War?

Not everyone is convinced by the logic of MAD. Beginning in the 1980s, a small group of scholars and practitioners in the US defense community, some of whom were close advisors to US President Ronald Reagan, argued that MAD is impractical and have urged the United States to enhance its nuclear war-fighting capabilities (Gray 1979). MAD proponents dubbed adherents to this view as **Nuclear Utilization Theorists**, or NUTS (Keeny and Panofsky 1981–82). It is important to understand their perspective to gain a fuller appreciation of the logic and consequences of nuclear deterrence.

Proponents of nuclear war fighting argued that MAD left the United States with an immoral and impractical response to the threat of a Soviet nuclear attack. MAD was immoral because the responsibility of the federal government was to protect the US population from attack, but the logic of MAD suggested that the government abdicate that responsibility and leave the population exposed. MAD was not credible because, in the event of a limited Soviet nuclear attack, it left the United States with a retaliatory choice of 'all or nothing.' If the Soviet Union launched even one or two nuclear weapons at US targets, would US leaders unleash the full US arsenal in response, knowing full well that the Soviets could then do the same? The Soviets were less likely to be deterred by non-credible threats to destroy the planet than by the realization that the United States was prepared to fight and try to win a nuclear war even though it had no intention of starting one.

The policy implications of nuclear war-fighting logic meant that the United States needed to get as close as possible to a first-strike capability. It needed to emphasize weapons that could target and destroy Soviet nuclear forces and develop strategies to eliminate the Soviet leadership and disrupt communications in the event of war so that the Soviets could not retaliate. And it needed to do its best to protect the US population by developing space-based missile defense technologies and enhancing **civil defense** (for example, underground bomb shelters) to protect against any Soviet warheads that reached US territory.

The debate between proponents of MAD and NUTS mirrored an important dichotomy within both the US and Soviet governments during the Cold War. The *civilian leaders* of each country embraced, in their public statements, the logic of MAD. American and Soviet leaders argued consistently that there could be no winners in nuclear war; the only outcome was mutual annihilation. At the same time, however, the American and Soviet *military establishments* were busily preparing to fight a nuclear war in the event one occurred. Each side developed accurate land-based missiles that could be used in a first strike against the land-based forces of the other side. They targeted each other's command and control systems, and spent billions of dollars and rubles conducting research on missile defense systems. Civilian leaders aspired to avoid war, but the job of professional militaries was to prepare for war, and develop strategies for winning in the event war took place.

Nuclear Utilization Theory (NUTS): Contrary to **MAD** proponents, many Cold War policy makers followed this strategy, which argues that the United States should do everything it can to be prepared to fight a nuclear war.

Civil defense: Defenses, such as fallout shelters, designed to protect civilians in case of a nuclear strike from an adversary.

Government Advice on Preparing for Nuclear War versus Government Response to Hurricane Katrina

Aspiration:

In 1977, the US Defense Civil Preparedness Agency published a pamphlet entitled 'Protection in the Nuclear Age' (US Department of Defense 1977). This pamphlet was written for ordinary citizens with the purpose of reassuring them that in the event of a nuclear war, the US government at all levels would be there to help and protect them. The pamphlet was circulated among public libraries and opened with the following:

> If an enemy should threaten to attack the United States, you would not be alone. The entire Nation would be mobilizing to repulse the attack, destroy the enemy, and hold down our own loss of life. Much assistance would be available to you – from local, State, and Federal governments, from the US armed forces units in your area, and from your neighbors and fellow Americans. (p. iii)

Chapter One explains in simple terms the 'hazards of nuclear attack' including blast, heat, and radiation effects. Subsequent chapters provide detailed instructions and diagrams for constructing a fallout shelter in the basement of one's home, including advice on how much dirt would need to be packed around the home foundation in order to absorb radiation produced by exploded nuclear warheads. It advised citizens that they should, upon hearing a warning signal from their local government:

> go immediately to a public fallout shelter or to your home fallout shelter. Turn on a radio, tune it to any local station that is broadcasting, and listen for official information. Follow whatever instructions are given. (p. 12)

Chapter Seven explains that in a nuclear crisis 'relocation' might be necessary:

> Your Federal Government and many State and local governments are currently planning for the orderly relocation of people in time of an international crisis. These plans call for 1) allocating people from high-risk areas to go to appropriate low-risk host areas for reception and care, and for 2) developing and improvising fallout protection in host areas. (p. 49).

The authors anticipate that nuclear war could prompt tense moments and anti-social temptations. They instruct:

> If you get caught in a traffic jam, turn off your engine, remain in your car, listen for official instructions, and be patient. Do not get out of the line to find an alternate route. All routes will be crowded. Be sure you have adequate gasoline when you start out. DO NOT BUY ANY MORE GAS THAN YOU WILL NEED. (p. 54, caps in original)

The pamphlet shows a picture of one motorist offering a can of gasoline to another whose car is stalled. Upon arrival at a public fallout shelter, it advises people to 'elect a leader and form working groups' for tasks such as cooking, maintaining order, caring for the injured, and 'organizing recreation and religious activities' (p. 55).

Reality:

The desire of any government to try to prepare its citizens for disaster is understandable. Our point is not to criticize that effort but to highlight the almost certain futility of it. An actual nuclear attack would pose individual, social, and organizational challenges that are virtually unimaginable. Instead of following plans and instructions, it is more likely that people would panic, chaos would reign, and government agencies, to the extent they still exist, would be incapable of developing strategies and directing citizens to respond in a calm and orderly fashion.

In order to appreciate the gap between aspiration and reality, consider the public response to Hurricane Katrina, which battered New Orleans in 2005. Katrina was one of the deadliest natural disasters in US history, with nearly 2,000 people losing their lives in the hurricane and subsequent flooding. Although there was ample warning, government response at the local, state and national level is widely regarded to have been a dismal failure. According to a congressional report following the crisis, entitled 'A Failure of Initiative,' government officials neither executed emergency plans nor shared information that would have saved lives (Hsu 2006).

The report cited 90 failures at all levels of government including that the White House failed to act on the collapse of the New Orleans levee system which led to catastrophic flooding; that the US military and the Federal Emergency Management Agency (FEMA) set up rival and conflicting chains of command on site; that the Secretary of Homeland Security, Michael Chertoff, and the Governor of Louisiana, Kathleen Blanco, could neither cooperate effectively nor agree on who should have primary responsibility for response to the crisis; and that inadequate training, lack of qualified emergency personnel, and poor communication among first responders hampered rescue and relief efforts. The report asserted that 'blinding lack of situational awareness and disjointed decision making needlessly compounded and prolonged Katrina's horror.'

The evacuation plan initiated by New Orleans Mayor Ray Nagin did not account for the fact that 100,000 city residents had no cars and relied on public transportation. Shelter sites were overwhelmed; the Louisiana Superdome was intended to host less than 1,000 evacuees, but more than 30,000 showed up.

The congressional report found that the single biggest government failure was in not fully anticipating the consequences of the storm.

Reflecting on these nuclear debates in 1989, political scientist Robert Jervis observed that 'MAD is a fact, not a policy' (Jervis 1989). He sought to remind us that nuclear weapons are so profoundly destructive that it is an illusion for any country, facing an adversary with sizable nuclear forces, to escape the logic of MAD. It takes so very few nuclear weapons to inflict a level of damage on a territory or population that most reasonable governments would consider unacceptable. A space-based defense system might be flooded with warheads or fooled by decoys. An effective civil defense would require people to behave calmly and rationally while cities were being destroyed and hundreds of thousands, if not millions, of their fellow citizens were being killed or irradiated. Box 7.3 shows the difficulties US governing authorities faced, even though they had considerable warning time, in trying to respond to a local crisis – Hurricane Katrina that struck New Orleans in 2005. Just imagine the difficulty of responding to a nuclear attack with little or no warning that devastated dozens of US cities at the same time.

Living with MAD: Arms Control Efforts

Recognition that there would be no winners in nuclear war helped to inspire governments to undertake nuclear arms control efforts that have spanned more than five decades. The Cuban Missile Crisis of 1962, which brought the world as close as it has ever been to nuclear war, was a key catalyst. In 1963, the Soviet Union, United States, and Great Britain signed the Partial Test Ban Treaty, which prohibited tests of nuclear devices in the atmosphere, outer space, and under water, but allowed them deep underground. Over 100 countries subsequently signed and ratified the treaty. The signatories of the Test Ban Treaty acknowledged both the danger of nuclear weapons and their potential to contaminate the natural environment.

By 1969, the two superpowers were prepared to take the next step and begin placing limits on nuclear capabilities. The first Strategic Arms Limitation Treaty (SALT I) was signed in 1972. It essentially froze US and Soviet land-based and submarine-based ballistic missiles at their current levels. The Anti-Ballistic Missile (ABM) Treaty, also signed in 1972, prohibited the development, testing, and deployment of comprehensive missile defense systems. SALT I was followed by SALT II, a more complicated treaty that sought to limit the arms race in particular types of nuclear warheads and delivery systems. SALT II allowed the United States and Soviet Union to each field no more than 2,400 ICBMs, SLBMs, and strategic bombers.

Nuclear freeze: A plan that would stop an arms race in its place by simply preventing two adversaries from developing or deploying any new warheads or delivery systems.

Many proponents of arms control in the United States complained that the SALT process did not actually limit or stop the nuclear arms race; by setting ceilings on the number of weapons each side could have, it simply provided incentives to American and Soviet planners to develop more sophisticated and potent nuclear weapons. As we saw in Chapter 6, a mass movement during the early 1980s including peace activists, politicians, scientists, and religious leaders emerged in support of a **nuclear freeze**. The idea of the freeze was to avoid complicated negotiations and simply stop the arms race where it was by preventing the superpowers from developing or deploying any new warheads or delivery systems.

Although the nuclear freeze was never implemented, it influenced politics in the United States. The administration of President Ronald Reagan responded with its own idea for a new agreement with the Soviets – the Strategic Arms Reduction Treaty or START. Reagan presented START as an improvement over SALT because it called for actual reductions in superpower arsenals, rather than setting high limits to which each side could legally race. Soviet leaders were initially skeptical of START because they did not want to reduce their arsenal while the United States was simultaneously exploring the possibility of a sophisticated, space-based missile defense system, popularly known as the Reagan Star Wars plan. But the Soviet position softened as the end of the Cold War drew near and it became clear that an effective space defense against thousands of missiles and decoys would be almost impossible to accomplish. In 1991 START I was signed, calling for the United States and Soviet Union to each reduce their strategic nuclear arsenals to no more than 6,000 warheads on a maximum of 1,600 land-based and sea-based missiles and nuclear-capable aircraft. START I did produce a radical reduction in forces. By the deadline for implementation in 2001, the two sides destroyed over half of their strategic nuclear weapons.

A START II treaty was signed by US President George W. Bush and Russian President Boris Yeltsin in 1993. The treaty required each side to reduce their deployed

Year	Event
1959	Antarctic Treaty
1963	Treaty banning nuclear weapon tests in the atmosphere, in outer space and under water (LTBT)
1967	Treaty for the prohibition of nuclear weapons in Latin America
1968	Non-Proliferation Treaty (NPT)
1972	First round of Strategic Arms Limitation Talks (SALT I) ends
	Treaty between the United States of America and the Union of Soviet Socialist Republics on the limitation of underground nuclear weapons tests (TTBT)
	Interim agreement on Strategic Offensive Arms (SALT I Treaty)
1974	Treaty between the US and the USSR on the limitation of underground nuclear weapon tests (TTBT)
1976	Treaty between the US and the USSR on underground nuclear explosions for peaceful purposes (PNET)
1979	Treaty between the United States of America and the Union of Soviet Socialist Republics on the limitation of Strategic Offensive Arms, together with agreed statements and common understandings regarding the treaty (SALT II Treaty)
1985	South Pacific Nuclear-Free Zone Treaty (Treaty of Rarotonga)
1987	Treaty between the US and USSR on the elimination of their intermediate-range and shorter-range missiles (INF Treaty)
1991	Treaty between the United States of America and the Union of Soviet Socialist Republics on the reduction and limitation of Strategic Offensive Arms (START I Treaty)
	Presidential nuclear initiatives
1993	Treaty between the United States of America and the Russian Federation on further reduction and limitation of Strategic Offensive Arms (START II Treaty)
1995	Treaty on the South-East Asia Nuclear Weapon-Free Zone (Bangkok Treaty)
1996	African Nuclear Weapon-Free Zone Treaty (Pelindaba Treaty)
	Comprehensive Test Ban Treaty (CTBT)
2002	The Moscow Treaty on Strategic Offensive Reductions (SORT)

◀ **Figure 7.1**
Timeline of Nuclear Arms Control Agreements and Treaties

Negotiations to control, limit, or reduce nuclear weapons have been a part of world affairs for half a century.

nuclear warheads to 3,500 and banned the use of MIRVs (Multiple Independently Targetable Re-entry Vehicles, or missiles that could deliver multiple warheads to different targets at the same time) on land-based missiles to discourage each side from having a potent means to attack the land-based missiles of the other. However, START II was never implemented due to Russia's objections to US plans to develop a limited missile defense system. US diplomats emphasized that this missile defense initiative was not directed at Russia, but at rogue states such as Iran and North Korea, or terrorist groups, whose leaders might not be deterred by the threat of retaliation. Nevertheless, when in December 2001 the United States notified Russia (as per the terms of treaty) that it was withdrawing from the ABM Treaty, Russia announced that it no longer considered itself bound by the provisions of START II.

Arms control efforts continued, however, and a so-called New START Treaty was signed by the United States and Russia and ratified by the US Senate at the end of 2010. The Treaty limits each side to 1,550 deployed strategic warheads (warheads placed on missiles and planes and ready to be used), and 700 deployed land-based missiles, sea-based missiles, and strategic bombers. It also allows each side to have up to 100 *non-deployed* missile launchers and bombers. The Treaty stipulates that each side must be in compliance with the limits by 2017, and these limits will stay in effect until the Treaty expires in 2020. Each side also gets to conduct on-site inspections to ensure the compliance of its partner.

The Obama administration hailed the treaty as a major improvement over the existing START agreement and a major step forward in arms control. Critics pointed out that the counting rules of the New START Treaty actually allow for each side to deploy many more nuclear weapons than it first might appear. This is due to the fact that every bomber equipped with nuclear weapons counts as one warhead under the terms of the treaty. In other words, heavy aircraft could carry many nuclear warheads even though it counts as only one. Arms control proponents were also disappointed that the treaty did not place significant limitations on missile defense systems.

Does MAD Still Exist Today?

Arms control efforts have come a long way since the Cold War. As late as 1986, the United States had over 23,000 nuclear warheads and the Soviet Union had over 40,000. As Table 7.2 shows, currently the Soviet Union has about 1,800 operational nuclear warheads, and the United States has about 2,100. These deep reductions have been welcomed by those concerned with the threat of nuclear weapons. However, the reductions have taken place in a context very different from the Cold War. America and Russia are no longer equivalent superpowers; the United States is far more capable in relative terms. This gap in capabilities has raised the concern that MAD's stabilizing effect among major nuclear powers, including China, may be disappearing.

Numerical comparisons may be deceiving. Russia may have more warheads, but the United States is a decidedly superior nuclear power in terms of the quality and readiness of its forces. The US submarine force, long the world's dominant one, now has new, more accurate missiles with higher-yield warheads that are capable of striking not only Russian (and Chinese) cities but also land-based missile sites. The relatively new cruise missiles mounted on B-52 aircraft are hard to detect by Russian (and Chinese) radar. The newly developed B-2 'stealth' bomber' can fly low enough to evade radar and drop its bombs over enemy territory. The United States continues to improve its land-based missile force and work on the development of space-based missile defense.

Russia, on the other hand, has witnessed the remarkable decline of the Soviet Union's once formidable nuclear posture. Russia still has thousands of weapons but operational readiness has deteriorated badly. Its submarine force has decayed, and what is left spends more time sitting in port than patrolling (or hiding) under the oceans. Submariners are no longer effectively trained for nuclear missions. The same is true of Russian strategic bombers; as of 2006, they were concentrated at two bases with their warheads stored elsewhere. Russia's early warning system has deteriorated and cannot 'see' any missiles launched from a large slice of the Pacific Ocean. Russia's land-based missile force has become old and unreliable.

China, as we noted earlier, has a small force of about 250 operational nuclear warheads. Its systems are relatively antiquated. It has perhaps two dozen warheads capable of reaching the United States, and they are carried by old, single-warhead ICBMs utilizing liquid fuel that cannot be stored in the missile itself. China, however, has been steadily modernizing its nuclear forces over the past ten years, including the development of a new class of submarine (the 'Jin class) capable of launching nuclear weapons at sea. In 2010 Chinese officials justified nuclear modernization, terming it a defensive effort to maintain a limited but effective second-strike capability in the face of technologically superior possible adversaries (Buckley 2010).

The relative states of US, Russian, and Chinese nuclear forces has led some analysts to question whether the United States may be moving closer to achieving a first-strike capability. In 2005, two political scientists speculated that the United States might be on the verge of nuclear primacy (Lieber and Press 2006). They ran computer simulations that found a US surprise attack had a very good chance of destroying Russian bomber bases, submarines, and ICBMs. Russian radar and early warning systems would give their leaders very little warning. China's more rudimentary nuclear forces would be even more vulnerable. And, even if unable to withstand a comprehensive attack, the missile defenses the United States hopes to deploy in the near future might be able to stop a small residual response after a US first strike.

None of this is meant to suggest that the United States is eager to start a nuclear war or that US or foreign leaders actually believe the United States has a first-strike capability. Keep in mind that any large-scale surprise attack would require a significant mobilization of US forces in advance, which might be detectable by other countries even if they lack the technological sophistication to detect a cruise missile flying over their territory. There is also, of course, the political and moral taboo against nuclear use which would weigh on any leader even remotely tempted to employ the ultimate weapon.

The logic of nuclear deterrence and its associated arms control efforts were developed in a world of two major nuclear powers. But what are the implications as more and more states possess nuclear weapons? We turn next to that important question.

Individual	State	International
The logic of MAD suggests that individual leaders, even in times of great psychological stress, have no incentives to start a nuclear war.	Nuclear weapons forced two states that were geopolitical enemies to cooperate in arms control efforts.	The nuclear revolution changed international relations by making the most destructive weapon of war unusable on the battlefield.

Levels of Analysis
Nuclear Deterrence Theory

Nuclear Proliferation and Efforts to Halt it

For the first 40 years of the nuclear era, the possibility of all-out nuclear war between the superpowers preoccupied international relations scholars and practitioners. Today, the more important concern is the spread of nuclear weapons and the possibility that, as more actors obtain them, nuclear war becomes more likely either by accident or design. In this section, we explore how difficult it is to obtain nuclear capability and why some states choose to make that effort. We also examine different perspectives on the dangers of nuclear proliferation. Finally, we look at efforts to halt the spread of nuclear weapons and abolish them altogether.

► **Figure 7.2 A Schematic Diagram of an Implosion Bomb**

Schematic diagram of an implosion bomb similar to one designed by Iraq

Source: 'Nuclear Weapons,' Wisconsin Project on Nuclear Arms Control, accessed at http://www.wisconsinproject.org/bomb-facts/nuclearessay.htm.

Reflector: 100 to 250 kg of natural uranium

Tamper: 50 to 200 kg of iron

High explosive: 250 to 200 kg

Detonators: 32

Initiator: Polonium, Berylium

Firing set: energy source, timer, switches

Core: 15 to 18 kg of high-enriched uranium

Obtaining Nuclear Capability: Difficult But Not Impossible

The basic design features of a nuclear weapon are readily available to anyone with a computer or access to a good public library. Fortunately, understanding the basic idea of how to build a nuclear weapon is very different from obtaining the materials and configuring the device with the necessary precision so that it actually works. It is very difficult, but not impossible for a state or non-state actor to develop a viable nuclear weapon.

The highest hurdle is to obtain fissionable material. The only materials that can achieve a self-sustaining, atom-splitting chain reaction in the core of a nuclear bomb are **plutonium** and **uranium**. Neither is easy to produce in *weapons-grade* form. Plutonium is rarely found in nature, but created as a by-product when energy is generated by a nuclear power plant. Plutonium needs to be extracted and then *reprocessed* or refined in a technically demanding procedure in order to become weapons grade. Uranium does occur in nature, but the predominant isotope (U-238) is unsuitable for nuclear weapons use. It needs to be *highly enriched* in a sophisticated technical facility to concentrate the minority isotope (U-235) that can sustain a chain reaction. Facilities to enrich uranium or reprocess plutonium are large and the processes are complicated. Nuclear inspectors are trained to find clues that reveal whether a country is engaged in the production of weapons-grade material.

Reprocessed plutonium or highly enriched uranium form the core of a nuclear weapon. But for the chain reaction to become self-sustaining, the core material must be placed under incredible pressure. Typically, this is done by surrounding the nuclear core with an outer ring of conventional high explosives, which have to be detonated at precisely the same time so the pressure on the nuclear material is intense and uniform. Thus, in addition to the necessary ingredient of uranium or plutonium, the nuclear shopping list would include air pressure measuring equipment, detonating heads, explosive charges, fuses, lead shields, neutron deflectors, and a team of scientists who could put it all together without destroying themselves and their facility in the process.

Countries that already possess nuclear weapons do not sell them to others on the open market. They also guard their nuclear arsenals carefully so weapons are not lost

Plutonium: Along with **uranium**, one of the two materials that can be used to create a nuclear weapon. Rarely found in nature, plutonium is found as a byproduct when energy is generated by a nuclear power plant, and must then be extracted and reprocessed to become weapons grade.

Uranium: Along with **plutonium**, one of two materials that can be used to create a nuclear weapon. Unlike plutonium, uranium can be found in nature, but is not suitable in that form (U-238) for nuclear weapon use. It needs to be *highly enriched* in a sophisticated technical facility to produce the concentrated uranium (U-235) that can sustain a chain reaction.

◄ **Photo 7.2 Iran's Nuclear Power Plant at Bushehr**

In this photo taken on August 23, 2010, and released by the International Iran Photo Agency, Iranian technicians work at the Bushehr nuclear power plant, outside the southern city of Bushehr, Iran.

Source: PA Images.

or stolen. If it is not possible to buy one or easily steal one, how do countries develop nuclear weapons? Since fissile material is the key ingredient, a typical starting point is to develop a civilian nuclear power capability to generate energy. The expertise, equipment, and materials gained from this peaceful application of nuclear technology could subsequently be diverted to a weapons program. India, for example, developed a civilian nuclear capability during the 1960s with the help of companies from more advanced countries such as Canada, and then shocked the world in 1974 by testing a nuclear weapon it had obviously been developing as a by-product of its peaceful activity.

Israel, Iran, Iraq, North Korea, and Pakistan attempted similar strategies with varying success. Israel developed a large nuclear complex near the city of Dimona, with French assistance, beginning in the late 1950s. Israel's diversion from nuclear power research to weapons production is assumed from the pattern of activity at that complex and satellite pictures of weapons bunkers and launch sites. Pakistan began during the 1970s with a nuclear power plant near Karachi that led to a diversion of material over several decades, with considerable help from China, before testing its weapon in 1998. China transferred to Pakistan nuclear weapon designs, technical expertise, and some of the sophisticated ancillary equipment.

International inspections revealed that North Korea had a plutonium reprocessing facility and subsequently had developed a uranium enrichment program. China assisted North Korea during the Cold War and, during the early 1990s, Pakistan swapped its nuclear technology for North Korean missile technology. North Korea announced in 2005 that it had a functional nuclear weapon and conducted a partially successful test in 2006.

Iran raised concerns when international inspectors discovered a uranium enrichment plant south of the capital, Tehran, in 2002. In 2004, Iranian leaders agreed in the Paris Accords to suspend nuclear enrichment activity, but they resumed those activities in defiance of the UN in 2005, claiming that their nuclear facilities were intended solely to produce electricity. Western countries responded with international sanctions, but Iran continued its efforts; President Ahmadinejad announced in 2010 that Iranian scientists had improved their ability to enrich uranium for the purpose of medical research. The diplomatic stand-off between Iran and Western governments suspicious of its nuclear ambitions continued into 2013, and as discussed in Chapter 4, in that year Iran and the P5 countries plus Germany struck a deal in which Iran halted its nuclear activities temporarily in exchange for relief from international economic sanctions.

Iraq's nuclear ambitions were frustrated in 1981, when Israel destroyed an Iraqi nuclear reactor that Israel claimed was being used to produce weapons-grade fuel. It became apparent after the first Gulf War (1990–91) that Saddam Hussein had revitalized the Iraqi nuclear program, only to have it destroyed by international inspection teams as part of the surrender terms after the war. The US attack against Iraq in 2003 was premised, in part, on the belief that Saddam Hussein still possessed and was hiding a nuclear weapons program. No evidence was found to support this suspicion, leading many countries, including close allies of the United States such as Germany and France, to question US motives and protest its decision to attack Iraq.

Globalization has increased opportunities for nuclear aspirants to obtain the necessary materials, equipment, and expertise. In 2003, the world discovered that Abdul Qadeer Khan, the 'father' of Pakistan's nuclear program, had been orchestrating a global black market in nuclear technology for years. Khan's network stretched across Europe, Russia, the Middle East, and Southeast Asia. He apparently assisted North Korea, Iran, and Libya in furthering their nuclear programs. Like any good salesman, Khan even published brochures and catalogues advertising the materials and services his 'team' could offer to clients. His ring was broken up in 2004, but he remained defiant in justifying his activities as appropriate to enhance the security needs of developing countries.

Why do States Want Nuclear Weapons?

Given the insecurity of an anarchical international system and the potency of the 'ultimate' weapon, we might expect every country to be in hot pursuit of a nuclear capability. Surprisingly, most are content to be non-nuclear weapon states. Only a relatively small number of states are determined to join the nuclear club, and it is important to understand why. We should resist the temptation to conclude that, beyond the 'responsible' states that already possess them, only 'irrational' states or leaders seek nuclear weapons.

We can identify at least three general reasons why states might be willing to bear the substantial financial costs and risk the disapproval of the international community by pursuing nuclear weapons. Conflicts with neighboring states or geopolitical rivals constitute the most important rationale for proliferation efforts. India and Pakistan are long-standing rivals. Once India tested the bomb, Pakistan's leaders felt that nuclear capability was essential to deter and prevent intimidation by India. Resource-poor Pakistan was determined to match India even if the effort took decades. Israel's not-so-secret nuclear weapons program clearly inspired some of its regional rivals – Iran, Syria, Libya, and Iraq – to pursue their own projects. Not surprisingly, Iran's leaders find it hypocritical that powerful Western countries tolerate Israel's nuclear program – presumably because Israel faces hostile neighbors – but refuse to tolerate Iran's, even though Iran, too, faces a hostile neighbor, Israel.

A second motivation concerns status or prestige. Nuclear weapons, like a space program, confer great power status or, in a regional context, major power status on their holders. The great powers of an earlier era, Great Britain and France, developed and maintained their own nuclear forces after World War II to signal that they still merited great power status despite their decline in relative influence and membership within the NATO alliance. Iraq's nuclear program was clearly tied to Saddam Hussein's ambition to make Iraq a dominant regional power, the self-appointed leader of Arab states mobilizing against the common enemy of Israel. China and India each had plausible geopolitical reasons (including fear of each other) to develop nuclear weapons, but also sought respect as large, emerging great powers in the international system.

Third, nuclear weapons are great equalizers, and are especially attractive to states or regimes that perceive themselves as facing threats to their very existence. Israel, at least initially, perceived itself as weak and vulnerable in a neighborhood of hostile Arab states that did not accept its right to exist. South Africa developed nuclear weapons during the decades it was treated as a pariah state; the apartheid regime was widely challenged by neighboring black states and the international community as a whole. North Korea, particularly after the fall of communism globally, views itself as a fragile state in a precarious position in part because the United States has expressed its desire for the regime to collapse.

We should also ask why states with the clear potential to develop nuclear weapons refrain from the attempt or abandon it. **Extended deterrence** – the threat by one country to use its nuclear forces to protect other countries – is one key reason. Many of America's allies in NATO and others, including Japan and South Korea, are technologically capable of joining the nuclear club, but instead have relied on the protection provided by the US 'nuclear umbrella.' The United States has committed to protecting them, with nuclear weapons if necessary, from attacks by neighboring states who themselves may possess nuclear weapons. One important reason for America's continued military presence in East Asia after the Cold War is to discourage nuclear proliferation. If the United States abandoned its commitment, Japan and South Korea, surrounded by nuclear-capable states (China, North Korea, Russia, and India) might feel compelled to develop their own nuclear equalizers.

Some states recently abandoned well-developed nuclear programs in order to earn approval and material benefits from other states in the international system. South Africa produced six nuclear weapons by the end of the 1980s, yet dismantled them with the collapse of the apartheid regime. Giving up the weapons was part of a larger strategy for South Africa to integrate into an international community that had long considered it an outcast. Libya suddenly announced in 2003 that it would terminate its nuclear weapons program. It had been subject to international economic sanctions since the late 1980s for support of terrorism and development of weapons of mass destruction. Libya had not yet developed warheads but had acquired the technology and materials needed to enrich uranium. Its renunciation of nuclear weapons helped to end its isolation and expose the smuggling ring of A.Q. Khan.

Since 1994, when it struck a deal with the United States, North Korea has hinted that it would renounce its weapons program in exchange for international recognition, security guarantees, and the right amount of economic aid. As of 2013, negotiations had not succeeded. Finally, three countries – Ukraine, Kazakhstan, and Belarus – inherited a number of nuclear weapons (respectively 5,000, 1,400, and 81) stationed on their territory when they became independent states after the Soviet Union collapsed. All three new states eventually transferred their nuclear holdings back to

Extended deterrence: The threat by one country to use its nuclear forces to protect other countries.

Russia in the mid-1990s; in exchange, they received economic aid and diplomatic support from many other states.

Giving up nuclear weapons brings international approval, but might it make weaker states more vulnerable to attack? This question was raised in 2011, with the decision by NATO countries to intervene in Libya's civil war in support of rebel forces seeking to overthrow Libya's government. Libya had given up its nuclear program in 2003 in exchange for Western diplomatic and economic concessions; in 2011, Western countries saw the Libyan civil war as an opportunity to oust Libya's dictatorial government. North Korea observed these events, and the North Korean official news agency released a statement in March 2011 suggesting that Libya had been deceived by the West when it gave up its nuclear program. A North Korean Foreign Ministry official called the West's earlier bargain with Libya 'an invasion tactic to disarm the country' (McDonald 2011). These comments appeared to be intended to signal the international community that North Korea would refuse to abandon its own nuclear quest.

The reasons why states seek to acquire, or not acquire, nuclear weapons capabilities are debated by scholars from different theoretical perspectives. Box 7.4 showcases constructivist, liberal, and realist views on why technologically capable states might forego nuclear weapons.

How Dangerous is Nuclear Proliferation?

The answer to this question might seem obvious, but it is not to all political scientists. Kenneth Waltz and Scott Sagan published a book in 1995 (updated in 2002) that debated whether the gradual spread of nuclear weapons would have a stabilizing or destabilizing effect on international politics. Waltz argued that more may be better, while Sagan worried that more will be worse (Sagan and Waltz 2002).

Waltz's counter-intuitive argument rests on a belief in the strong deterrent effect of nuclear weapons. Because they are so destructive, nuclear weapons make states act cautiously. Once a state has nuclear forces – even a small amount – its rivals become wary of attacking because the possibility of nuclear retaliation is such a costly outcome. Would the Bush administration have invaded Iraq in 2003 if Saddam Hussein had even a small handful of nuclear weapons, or would it have decided that the risk of even one retaliatory strike against the United States was too great to bear? Waltz believes the United States would have reconsidered. He also believes that India and Pakistan, bitter neighboring rivals who have clashed in the past, will be less likely to fight any kind of war with each other now that both are nuclear powers.

In Waltz's view, nuclear weapons make their holders responsible as well as cautious. He detects a Western bias in the belief that a nuclear-armed United States will act more responsibly than a nuclear-armed Iran or North Korea. States learn by doing, and the very act of developing and deploying nuclear weapons instills a sense of responsibility in the holder who learns to protect the force and avoid accidental use. Waltz reminds us that during the 1950s and 1960s China was considered a revolutionary state determined to upset the international status quo. China acquired nuclear weapons and has possessed them for over four decades without using or losing them. Today China would hardly be considered an irresponsible state or dangerous nuclear power.

Sagan and other critics accept the logic of deterrence but believe that Waltz underestimates the dangerous characteristics and circumstances of states that have recently

Nuclear weapons are regarded by many as the 'ultimate' weapon. When a state possesses them, it can deter potential adversaries, even more powerful ones, from attacking it. A relatively small number of states have pursued nuclear capability with determination. But many others have decided to pass up the opportunity to develop the ultimate weapon. Constructivists, liberals and realists can offer different insights, highlighting different explanatory factors, into why states forego nuclear weapons.

Constructivism: Constructivists emphasize the development and spread of international norms in shaping state behavior. The 'nuclear taboo' and 'chemical weapons taboo' are clear examples of norms that have developed over time and been embraced by most member states in the international community. Constructivists might note that even states that developed or inherited nuclear weapons, for example South Africa and Ukraine, were willing to give them up to conform to international normative expectations.

Liberalism: Liberals share with constructivists a belief in the power of international norms, but emphasize even more strongly the importance of international institutions. For liberals, the nuclear non-proliferation regime provides an institutional framework to enable states to forego weapons, for example by rewarding states willing to give up nuclear weapons with access to civilian nuclear technology. In other words, the institutional agreement, backed by United Nations monitoring and verification, is that if a state gives up nuclear weapons programs it can gain the technology to develop and run nuclear power plants.

Realism: Realists emphasize calculations of power and interest. Technologically capable states might bypass their own nuclear forces if they are confident that the 'nuclear umbrella' of a stronger ally will protect them by deterring potential aggressors from attacking them. Many realists expect Japan, for example, to continue to forego nuclear weapons as long as the United States remains credibly committed to protecting Japan. Constructivists see it differently, and would argue that Japan's nuclear reluctance is more a function of a political culture shaped by Japan's difficult history as both an international aggressor and a victim of nuclear attack itself.

acquired or are likely to acquire nuclear weapons. One problem is that not all states have stable, civilian-run governments. Some have weak civilian governments or military rulers, while others, like Pakistan, flip back and forth between civilian and military rule. Recall our earlier discussion of US and Soviet nuclear strategy; civilian leaders were more inclined to stress deterrence, while military leaders placed greater emphasis on being ready and able to fight nuclear wars if necessary. The lack of robust civilian control of the military in a new nuclear state could mean a greater likelihood of using these weapons, especially under the pressure of a crisis.

Second, deterrence works best when the states involved have large forces with secure second-strike capabilities. But what if rival states had small forces that might be vulnerable to attack? If India and Pakistan each had several thousand weapons deployed on land, in the air, and under the oceans, neither side's military might feel a nuclear first strike would be a viable strategic option. But what if each side had only several dozen weapons, believed to be stored at a few military sites? In that scenario, a government might be tempted, in a crisis situation, to try to eliminate its rival's nuclear forces. The danger is heightened by the fact that nuclear weapons tend to spread unevenly to rival states. India had the bomb long before Pakistan. Israel is in a similar position with respect to Iran, and tensions between the two countries have led many analysts and government officials to wonder whether Israel will seek to destroy Iranian nuclear capability pre-emptively in order to deny its adversary the nuclear equalizer.

Sagan also worries that, as more states obtain them, the possibility of nuclear accidents increases. We cannot assume that new nuclear states who develop their weapons programs covertly will simultaneously figure out how to safeguard those weapons from unauthorized use or premature detonation. UN inspectors poring over Iraq's nuclear program in the early 1990s speculated that an Iraqi bomb would have been so unstable it might have detonated if it fell off a desk. Even if we could be confident that new members of the nuclear club would develop safeguards over time, the learning period might still be precarious. Nuclear weapons, Sagan tells us, are controlled by 'imperfect human beings in imperfect organizations.' The potential for error accumulates as more imperfect humans in imperfect organizations gain access to the ultimate weapon.

The possession of nuclear weapons may make your neighbor think twice before attacking you. But a world of many nuclear states might encourage more risk taking in overall terms. More aggressive states might believe they can take advantage of the fact that other states, fearing nuclear escalation, will be cautious and back down rather than risk war over something relatively small. This is the seductive logic of 'chicken,' the dangerous game in which two drivers speed directly at each other to determine who will be more frightened and swerve first. The game often ends sensibly, with one or both drivers swerving. But sometimes each miscalculates, assuming the other will swerve, and they find themselves in an avoidable but tragically fatal head-on collision.

Efforts to Halt Proliferation: The Grand Bargain

The potential dangers of proliferation were recognized early in the nuclear era. In 1968, the Nuclear Non-Proliferation Treaty (NPT) was signed by 98 countries. As of 2012, there were 189 signatories, making the NPT almost universally accepted in the international system (as discussed below, some key states have not signed the treaty or have signed, but are not in compliance with its terms). The NPT is sometimes called a grand bargain because it offers benefits and demands obligations from both nuclear and non-nuclear states.

Non-nuclear signatories agree to renounce nuclear weapons and refrain from developing, obtaining or deploying them. In exchange, they are entitled to receive civilian nuclear technology, such as nuclear power plants and the know-how to produce nuclear energy for peaceful purposes, from nuclear weapon possessing states, as well as other advanced industrial states. Non-nuclear states also agree to allow their peaceful nuclear operations to be monitored and inspected to ensure that diversion to weapons programs is not taking place. An international organization under the UN known as the International Atomic Energy Agency (IAEA) is charged with carrying out this monitoring function.

The major benefit for nuclear weapon possessing states is the stability derived from maintaining a selective nuclear club. The treaty legitimizes a division between nuclear haves and have-nots. In exchange, the nuclear weapons states must commit to transferring civilian nuclear technology to non-nuclear signatories in compliance with the terms of the NPT. As part of the NPT, nuclear weapon possessing states also pledged to take effective measures to reduce their own nuclear arsenals and work toward disarmament. This disarmament provision is a key component of the NPT because it provides some political cover for non-nuclear states to sign on without having to accept that a world of similarly sovereign states will be divided by international law into those states who are allowed to have the ultimate weapon and those who are not. In 2010, the Obama administration completed a Nuclear Posture Review, which sought to make the bargain more attractive for non-proliferators by stating publicly and explicitly that the United States would not introduce nuclear weapons into any conflict with a non-nuclear state or a nuclear-capable state in compliance with the NPT (US Department of Defense 2010).

The effectiveness of the NPT has been mixed. On one hand, it has established and institutionalized an international norm that nuclear proliferation, like nuclear use, is unacceptable. It has created legitimacy for nuclear weapon possessing states, working through the IAEA, to intrude upon the sovereignty of non-nuclear states and inspect their facilities and activities. By creating the expectation of civilian technology transfer, the treaty gives states a plausible economic rationale to renounce an option for protecting their security. The NPT also provides reassurances to some states that if they deny themselves nuclear weapons they won't be at a disadvantage relative to their neighbors. Latin American rivals Brazil and Argentina, for example, decided during the 1990s to give up their respective nuclear weapons efforts and join the NPT. They also signed the Treaty of Tlatelolco, which bans nuclear weapons from Latin America.

On the other hand, the clear problem with the NPT is that those countries most determined to proliferate will either not sign the treaty, or, if they do sign, at some point exercise the option to renounce it. Israel, India, and Pakistan, now members of the nuclear club, never signed. North Korea did sign the NPT, but subsequently created an international crisis in 2003 by withdrawing from the treaty, announcing that it was on the verge of testing a nuclear weapon. Iran was found in non-compliance with the NPT in 2003 for its failure to declare its uranium enrichment program.

The NPT is not well-designed to prevent 'hard' cases from proliferating. The treaty lacks adequate enforcement measures; for example, it does not call for collective sanctions against violators. Furthermore, even states that make compliance and inspection agreements with the IAEA can find room to maneuver if they are covertly pursuing nuclear weapons. It became clear after the Gulf War of 1990–91 that during earlier decades, Iraq had been allowing inspectors to view some nuclear facilities, but was developing weapons at other sites not subject to inspection. North Korea sounded a similar alarm in 1993 when it asserted its sovereignty and refused to allow international inspectors to view its plutonium reprocessing facilities.

If the NPT, despite its significant benefits, cannot achieve it, is there any way for interested states to stop the small number of determined proliferators? Several strategies are available, though none guarantees success. Collective economic sanctions and diplomatic isolation sometimes work if applied consistently over an extended time period. Libya, which had not been a signatory to the NPT, joined the effort in 2004 when it announced that it would abandon its nuclear weapons efforts. Sustained diplomatic pressure from a select group of powerful countries may sometimes prove effective as well. Since 2003, the United States, Russia, Japan, China, and South Korea have engaged North Korea in the Six Party Talks, designed to find ways to persuade North Korea to abandon its weapons program. Negotiators have mixed threats of punishment (harsher economic sanctions and further international isolation) with the promise of rewards (economic assistance, diplomatic recognition) in the effort to convince North Korea that going nuclear is just not worth the cost. As of 2014, these efforts had not met with success.

As the NPT suggests, it is important to recognize that 'carrots' as well as 'sticks' are valuable instruments in preventing proliferation. After the Soviet Union collapsed, the United States passed the Soviet Nuclear Threat Reduction Act (also known as the Nunn–Lugar program, after its sponsors, Senators Sam Nunn of Georgia and Richard Lugar of Indiana), which authorizes the United States to spend billions of dollars helping its former Soviet-bloc enemies to destroy nuclear, chemical, and biological weapons and establish verifiable safeguards to prevent their proliferation. Nunn–Lugar has involved retraining thousands of Soviet-era nuclear scientists and helping them find civilian sector jobs, so they might resist the temptation to peddle their nuclear weapons skills on the black market.

Export control efforts are also an important strategy to halt proliferation. The Nuclear Suppliers' Group (NSG) was created in 1985 to establish guidelines restricting the export of nuclear-related equipment and technologies to non-nuclear states pursuing or contemplating a weapons program. As the A.Q. Khan ring demonstrated, the NSG is hardly leak-proof, but it does provide a way for the principal nuclear supplier states to exchange information and coordinate efforts to restrict technology transfer. A similar arrangement, the Missile Technology Control Regime, was established in 1987 to stem the proliferation of missiles that could deliver weapons of mass destruction.

Pre-emptive military action is a controversial non-proliferation strategy open to the selected states with the means to employ it. We noted earlier that Israel destroyed an Iraqi nuclear reactor in 1981. It employed a similar strategy against Syria in 2007, bombing what it claimed was a nuclear reactor under construction. The strike followed a visit to Syria by a North Korean ship suspected of delivering reactor components.

A similarly controversial strategy is missile defense. As a response to proliferation, the United States continues to pursue a missile defense system designed to prevent limited attacks by nuclear states using short- or medium-range ballistic missiles. Both the Bush and Obama administrations worked on missile defense with selected allies such as Turkey, Romania, and Poland to protect against a possible future attack from

Iran. Although these defense plans are ostensibly aimed at Iran, they have created anxiety in Russia whose leaders worry that NATO-based missile defense could one day, if successful, compromise Russia's nuclear deterrent. For similar reasons, China objects to US plans to develop missile defense in collaboration with Japan. Although the stated purpose of US–Japan collaboration is to deflect a possible North Korean attack, China fears any effective system would be detrimental to its own deterrent.

One of the most significant constraints on non-proliferation efforts for policy makers is the fact that non-proliferation may compete with other foreign policy priorities. This problem is evident in US policy toward recent entrants to the nuclear club. For some time, the United States proved willing to tolerate Israel's nuclear development because Israel is a close ally of the United States. The fact that Israel has proliferated silently, without an obvious public test of a nuclear weapon, has made it easier for the United States to maintain what many view as a hypocritical stance. US non-proliferation efforts have been inconsistent with respect to Pakistan. At times, US policy makers have imposed sanctions but, at other times, they have quietly reduced the pressure in exchange for Pakistan's cooperation on issues of importance to the United States. Pakistan helped the United States provide support to insurgents resisting the Soviet occupation of Afghanistan during the 1980s, and assisted the United States in the war on terrorism after 2001. With the rise of China in East Asia, the United States has been strengthening existing alliance relationships and cultivating new ones, particularly with China's long-standing rival, India. Despite the fact that India had defied the NPT and developed nuclear weapons, in 2005 the United States recognized it as a 'responsible state' possessing nuclear technology, paving the way for full nuclear cooperation between the two countries.

Given their danger to human beings and the international system, can nuclear weapons ever be abolished? Most scholars would argue, perhaps reluctantly, that the nuclear genie cannot be put back into the bottle. Nuclear weapon states may be willing to control or reduce their arsenals, even substantially, but unwilling to give them up completely. Aspiring nuclear states would be reluctant to forego the influence and prestige that comes with nuclear weapons, and the ability to deter neighbors they do not trust. Even if we could find a way to achieve the improbable feat of getting all states to agree to eliminate nuclear weapons, the production and deployment knowledge would remain, with the potential to be exploited by states or groups seeking to take advantage of the restraint of others.

Despite these practical difficulties, the idea of 'getting to zero,' or total nuclear disarmament, remains alive and well and, in fact, has been with us throughout the nuclear era. The idea has obvious appeal to pacifists and anti-war activists. But, as Box 7.5 shows, it also attracts less likely proponents, such as the conservative US President Ronald Reagan and the veteran realist statesman and writer, Henry Kissinger. Kissinger, along with former Senator Sam Nunn, former Secretary of State George Shultz, and former Defense Secretary William Perry, formed a non-governmental organization called the Nuclear Security Project to mobilize global action to reduce nuclear threats and build support for eventually eliminating nuclear weapons.

Nuclear weapons are the most significant but not the only weapons of mass destruction. We next turn to chemical and biological weapons and efforts to control them.

Proposals from US Political Elites for a Nuclear-Free World

Then: *1946, The Baruch Plan*

Bernard Baruch was an American financier and close advisor to Presidents Woodrow Wilson and Franklin Roosevelt. President Truman appointed Baruch as US representative to the newly created United Nations Atomic Energy Commission. At its first meeting in June 1946, Baruch proposed that the United States would turn over its nuclear weapons and the designs to produce them to the United Nations, on the condition that all other countries pledge not to produce atomic weapons and subject themselves to an effective system of inspection. Americans perceived this as a generous offer since, at the time, the United States enjoyed a nuclear monopoly. Stalin's Soviet Union rejected the Baruch Plan because it felt the United Nations would be dominated by the United States and its allies and could not be trusted to implement the plan fairly. Lacking Soviet agreement, the Baruch Plan was not viable and both superpowers proceeded to develop their nuclear arsenals.

Then: *1986, Ronald Reagan and the Reykjavik Summit, October 20, 1986*

> It is my fervent goal and hope...that we will some day no longer have to rely on nuclear weapons to deter aggression and ensure world peace. To that end the United States is now engaged in a serious and sustained effort to negotiate major reductions in levels of offensive nuclear weapons with the ultimate goal of eliminating these weapons from the face of the earth.

As President, Ronald Reagan intensified the Cold War with the Soviet Union, but also surprised many people by arguing forcefully for the elimination of nuclear weapons. Reagan shocked his own advisors in 1986 by proposing, at a summit meeting with then Soviet leader Mikhail Gorbachev, that the two superpowers work together to reduce and then eliminate completely their nuclear arsenals. Gorbachev was receptive, but ultimately resisted when it became clear that Reagan was unwilling to give up American efforts to develop his Strategic Defense Initiative or 'Star Wars' plan to defend the United States from any nuclear attack.

Now: *2007, The 'Gang of Four' Calls for a Nuclear-Free World*: On January 4, 2007,

George Shultz, William Perry, Henry Kissinger, and Sam Nunn published an essay called 'A World Free of Nuclear Weapons' [Shultz, *et al.*, 2007]. Each played an important role in US national security policy during the Cold War; Shultz and Kissinger as former Secretaries of State, Perry as former Secretary of Defense, and Nunn as a prominent Senator from Georgia. They wrote:

> Nuclear weapons today present tremendous dangers, but also an historic opportunity. US leadership will be required to take the world to the next stage – to a solid consensus for reversing reliance on nuclear weapons globally as a vital contribution to preventing their proliferation into potentially dangerous hands, and ultimately ending them as a threat to the world.

They argued that reliance on nuclear weapons only increases the chances of accidents, misjudgments, and catastrophic terrorism. They called for substantially reducing the size of nuclear forces in all states that possess them, providing the highest possible standards of security for all stocks of weapons and weapons-grade plutonium and uranium, and halting the production of fissile material for weapons globally. They concluded that 'we endorse setting the goal of a world free of nuclear weapons and working energetically on the actions required to achieve that goal.'

State	🌐 **International**
Many countries have relied on nuclear deterrence as well as physical defense to prevent attacks against their territory and people.	The NPT is an important example of global governance – an effort by many states to find cooperative solutions to the dangers posed by nuclear weapons.
	The NPT also reflects the inequality of nations in that it reinforces that some states have nuclear weapons and others do not.

Chemical and Biological Weapons

Nuclear weapons are by far the most destructive weapons ever created. But other types of weapons also qualify as weapons of mass destruction or weapons with the ability to do significant harm to massive numbers of people. Many analysts place chemical and biological weapons within this category.

How They Work and Efforts to Control Them

Chemical weapons use manufactured chemicals to kill people. Common examples include chlorine gas and mustard gas, both of which were used by combatants in World War I. These chemicals do their damage by blistering lung tissue. More sophisticated chemical weapons include sarin gas, a nerve agent that causes suffocation through uncontrollable muscle contraction. One milligram of sarin in the lungs is sufficient to kill someone, as compared to ten milligrams of mustard gas. In 1995, a Japanese group of extremists named Aum Shinrikyo released sarin in the Tokyo subway system, killing twelve, injuring thousands, and causing mass terror. An even more lethal form of sarin is called VX. In a 1996 film, *The Rock*, a renegade US Marine threatens to launch a missile containing VX nerve gas into San Francisco (Sean Connery and Nicholas Cage help to save the day).

Biological weapons kill people by spreading bacteria or viruses. Examples of potential bioweapons include smallpox, a highly contagious virus that has been eradicated worldwide but could be recreated in new strains for destructive purposes. Botulism is a highly lethal bacterium that kills by causing muscle paralysis.

Anthrax is a durable bacterium, and if anthrax spores find their way into a person's lungs they can create a fatal toxin. Americans have learned first-hand just how dangerous anthrax can be: just after the September 2001 Al Qaeda attacks against the Twin Towers and the Pentagon, someone mailed letters containing anthrax to the offices of two US senators in Washington, DC, as well as to several news media offices in New York City, and caused five deaths.

Chemical or biological agents may be delivered in various ways. Low-flying crop duster planes could spray a lethal agent from the air, just as a truck equipped with a fire hose could spray a fine mist on the ground. Chemical or biological agents could be placed in a bomb to explode in a populated area, or perhaps used to contaminate a water supply. Aum Shinrikyo used several small explosive canisters in their Tokyo subway attack.

Chemical weapons have a long history, both on the battlefield and at the negotiating table. The Hague Conventions of 1899 and 1907 banned the use of poisonous weapons in warfare. These prohibitions were ignored during World War I, as both France and

Chemical weapons: A category of WMD that uses manufactured chemicals to kill people.

Biological weapons: A category of WMD that kills people by spreading bacteria or viruses.

▶ **Photo 7.4 The Trial of 'Chemical Ali'**

Ali Hassan al-Majid, known as 'Chemical Ali', was condemned to death by hanging by an Iraqi court in January 2010, after being found guilty of orchestrating the Halabja massacre.

Source: PA Images.

Germany made extensive use of chlorine and mustard gas. Other agreements – the Washington Arms Conference Treaty of 1922 and the Geneva Protocol of 1929 – subsequently prohibited chemical weapons use, again with limited effect. Japan's army used chemicals against Asian populations it sought to subjugate before and during World War II. On the European front, both Allied and Axis powers developed and deployed chemical agents, though neither side relied heavily on chemical warfare.

The most extensive use of chemicals in the postwar era took place during the Iran–Iraq War of 1980–88. Iraq deployed mustard gas and other agents against advancing Iranian forces and Kurdish groups within its own population. In one such attack in March 1988, 5,000 civilians, mostly women and children, perished in the Kurdish town of Halabja. Ali Hassan al-Majid, known as 'Chemical Ali', was condemned to death in 2010 by an Iraqi court that found him guilty of masterminding the massacre. Many feared that Iraq might use chemical weapons against coalition forces or Israel during the 1990–91 Gulf War. Those attacks never materialized, possibly because the United States threatened nuclear retaliation in the event of a chemical attack.

A second tragic use of chemical weapons occurred more recently, in the context of Syria's civil war. In August 2013, rockets containing sarin killed hundreds and possibly thousands of Syrian civilians, and several dozen Syrian opposition fighters, in the Ghouta suburbs of the Syrian capital, Damascus. The Syrian government of Bashar al-Assad and the rebel forces seeking to overthrow it blamed each other for the chemical attack. (Assad's government claimed the rebels launched the attack and even killed some of their own forces to frame the Syrian government and prompt international outrage against it.) After a UN investigation, the European Union, United States, and neighboring Arab countries concluded that the attack had been carried out by forces loyal to the Syrian government.

The Syrian chemical attack prompted debates within the EU and United States over military intervention. US President Barack Obama had asserted one year before the attack that the use of chemical weapons by the Syrian government would cross a 'red line' and trigger US military intervention in the civil war. As discussed in Chapter 4, however, public pressure in the United States and Great Britain led those two countries to avoid military intervention. They pursued a diplomatic alternative with Russia's assistance, and in September 2013 Russia and the United States announced an agreement designed to result in the elimination of Syria's remaining chemical stockpile by the middle of 2014. The deal drew both praise and criticism – praise because it avoided outside military intervention and convinced Syria to agree to give up its chemical weapons; criticism because the deal left the dictator al-Assad in power, gave him international legitimacy as a negotiating partner, and left his forces to continue killing tens of thousands of Syrian civilians using conventional weapons in the ongoing and brutal Syrian civil war.

The Iraq and Syria experiences helped to strengthen the international consensus on the desirability of banning chemical warfare and eliminating chemical weapons. A major international treaty, the Chemical Weapons Convention (CWC), was established in 1993 and came into force in 1997. As of 2012, 188 countries had signed the treaty. The CWC forbids outright the production and possession of chemical weapons. Signatories must destroy their existing stockpiles and must allow a UN entity, the Organization for the Prohibition of Chemical Weapons (OPCW), access to their territories to inspect plants designed for the production of chemicals for civilian uses such as fertilizers. As a result of the Russia-US agreement described above, Syria joined the CWC in 2013 and allowed the OPCW access to its territory to locate and eventually dismantle its chemical weapons.

The CWC is a major arms control accomplishment in that it completely forbids an entire category of lethal weapons. Its implementation is not straightforward because the destruction of existing stockpiles is costly and requires complicated safety precautions to be carried out effectively. Between 1997 and 2008, roughly one-third of global stockpiles had been destroyed. All 65 chemical weapon-producing facilities in signatory states stopped production, and inspections took place in some 80 countries. One remaining challenge is whether the United States and Russia manage to destroy their large existing stockpiles by the treaty deadline. A second challenge is to persuade states in the Middle East with probable or definite chemical programs (such as Egypt) to sign the treaty, and to convince Israel, which has signed it, to ratify it.

Biological weapons have an even longer history of use in warfare. In ancient times, city-states at war would use biological agents to poison the food and water supplies of their enemies. In the modern era, both Nazi Germany and Imperial Japan conducted extensive experiments on human subjects using lethal biological agents. Biological weapons did not play a major role during World War II, although Japan did use germs against China. In 1940, the Japanese Air Force dropped ceramic bombs on China that contained fleas carrying botulism. The Soviet Union and United States developed bioweapons programs during the war and carried out extensive research and production during the Cold War. The United States had bioweapons ready for battlefield delivery in aerosol spray cans, cluster bombs, or missile warheads.

As in the case of chemical weapons, an international consensus formed during the Cold War that biological weapons should be outlawed. The Biological and Toxic Weapons Convention (BWC) of 1972 reflected this sentiment, and banned the development, production, and stockpiling of microbes except in the small amounts needed for peaceful research. As of 2011, 165 countries had signed and ratified the treaty. In 1992, the head of the former Soviet Union's biological weapons effort, Ken Alibek, defected to the United States and revealed that the Soviet Union, despite signing the BWC, secretly continued research and production of biological weapons until its collapse in 1989. The BWC is weaker than the CWC because it has no provisions for monitoring or verifying compliance and implementation.

Comparing Nuclear, Biological and Chemical Weapons

Although nuclear, chemical, and biological weapons are commonly lumped together under the heading of weapons of mass destruction, we should recognize significant differences across these categories. Most importantly, nuclear weapons are qualitatively different in terms of their destructive power because a few weapons can do so much damage to lives and property. Biological weapons have great potential to be lethal, but their success depends on the widespread yet precise distribution over an exposed population. They must be spread carefully and survival depends on environmental conditions. Similarly, chemical weapons can be lethal but only under specific conditions. The attacker must disperse a large amount of chemical agent in order to kill a great number of people and must recognize that dispersal of the agent may be hard to control. Shifting winds, for example, may carry chemical agents beyond the range of intended target populations or may blow chemical agents back upon the attackers themselves. During the World War I Battle of Loos, in France in September 1915, British soldiers released chlorine gas intended for the Germans, but some of the gas was carried back by the wind onto Britain's own soldiers who were deployed in trenches.

There are also significant differences across these weapons categories with regard to the possibility of defense. We argued earlier that it is almost impossible to defend effectively against a nuclear attack. Defense against biological and chemical agents is not easy, but it is possible. Troops can be equipped with gas masks and protective clothing when operating in a military environment under the threat of chemical attack. Even civilians may be offered some protection in anticipation of attack; the Israeli government distributed gas masks to its citizens during the 1990–91 Gulf War in case Saddam Hussein launched missiles with chemical warheads at Israel in retaliation for the US-led attack against his forces in Kuwait. In the face of biological warfare, preventive vaccination has some potential to be effective, yet only if one is

◀ **Photo 7.6 Israeli Citizens Prepare for Possible Chemical Attack from Iraq During 1990–91 Gulf War**

Israelis don gas masks to stare at the sky outside a café in Tel Aviv, February 23, 1991, after air raid sirens wailed throughout Israel just minutes before the deadline for Iraq to begin withdrawing from Kuwait.

Source: PA Images.

certain of the type or strain of the agent in question. US troops were vaccinated against possible anthrax attacks during the Gulf War.

Nuclear weapons are also more difficult to develop than biological or chemical weapons. Reprocessed plutonium and enriched uranium require a complex technical infrastructure to produce. In contrast, the basic building blocks of chemical weapons are more readily available. Chlorine, for example, is a common chemical used to kill bacteria in water systems. Anthrax may be found in nature and grown in laboratories from existing spores. This is not to suggest that developing a biological or chemical weapon is a simple task, only that it is a more achievable task than developing a nuclear weapon.

International legal norms governing these classes of weapons also differ. Biological and chemical weapons are completely outlawed. The consensus codified by international law is that no state, great power or otherwise, should be allowed to use them, deploy them, or even stockpile them. International law with regard to nuclear weapons divides the world into have and have-not states. A handful of states have the legal right to possess and deploy the weapons while the great majority of states do not. A state that 'crosses the line' in defiance of legal norms might later try to become accepted as a legitimate member of the club, as India has recently attempted with the support of the United States. Arms control advocates hope the more universal prohibitions that apply to chemical and biological weapons will one day apply to nuclear weapons.

Weapons of mass destruction in the hands of numerous nation-states are a cause of great concern in international politics. The same holds true for non-state actors, and below we discuss the connection between terrorism and weapons of mass destruction.

Individual	🌐 **International**
Individuals or small groups can obtain and disseminate biological or chemical weapons, causing the type of death and destruction that we usually associate with the armed forces of sovereign states.	The CWC is a landmark arms control agreement in that it completely forbids an entire category of WMD.

Levels of Analysis
Chemical and Biological Weapons

Weapons of Mass Destruction and Terrorism

The attacks of September 11, 2001 in the United States, the 2002 bombings in Bali, Indonesia, the 2004 train bombings in Madrid, and the July 2005 bombings in London greatly heightened the fear of terrorism around the world. After these attacks, it was natural to ask the horrifying question of what might happen if terrorists managed to gain control of weapons of mass destruction, in particular of a nuclear weapon. This final section explores the likelihood and consequences, and briefly addresses the new threat of cyber-warfare.

From the perspective of deterrence theory, the consequences of a terrorist group acquiring a nuclear weapon are profound and disturbing. The international system has endured nuclear weapons on the presumption that the use of those weapons may be effectively deterred by the threat of nuclear retaliation. The problem is that terrorist groups may be harder than nation-states to deter. Deterrence against nation-states rests on the threat of inflicting unacceptable damage on something of value to the nation-state in question, such as its territory, population, national identity, or sovereign integrity. Terrorists are usually stateless; they have no fixed territory to defend, and no population that might credibly be held hostage by the threat of nuclear retaliation. It is often said that terrorist groups have 'no return address,' or no specific home to direct the threat or actuality of retaliation.

One could, of course, threaten to retaliate against states that harbor terrorists. The United States followed this logic by invading Afghanistan because the Taliban regime provided sanctuary for Al Qaeda prior to the September 11 attacks. Threatening the host state might cause the host government to think twice about harboring terrorists on their territory. Yet that same threat might be less effective in deterring the terrorist group operating within the borders of the host state. The host territory itself might not be of sufficient value to the terrorist group; it could simply move its operation to a different host or to multiple hosts. Retaliation against populations which are sympathetic to the terrorist groups in question might be another alternative, but the pitfalls here are obvious; the threat would be made against innocent civilians and the threat itself might serve to mobilize political sympathy for the terrorist group. In short, the usual reassuring rules of deterrence do not operate as easily in the case of a terrorist threat.

A terrorist group in possession of nuclear weapons may be difficult to deter, but how likely are terrorist groups to acquire nuclear weapons? The difficulties nation-states face in developing a nuclear capability apply even more forcefully to stateless groups. As we have seen, nuclear weapons development requires a far-reaching technical infrastructure and support system; it is not something that can be accomplished in one's basement or backyard. Terrorists typically do not have the resources – appropriate and ideally hidden facilities, sophisticated equipment, scarce raw materials, scientific talent, and ample time (measured in decades) – to put it all together. Press reports occasionally speculate that terrorists would not need a missile or other sophisticated delivery system and instead could rely on a small 'suitcase' bomb. But to develop a *small* nuclear weapon that works effectively is an even more demanding task technologically; the first nuclear weapons developed by determined nation-states were large and cumbersome.

The difficulty of developing a nuclear weapon does not imply that the problem of nuclear terrorism is trivial. If terrorists cannot do it alone, there is always the possibility of stealing an existing weapon, or having one transferred voluntarily from a nuclear weapons possessing nation-state. The United States invaded Iraq in 2003 in part because it feared Iraq might possess nuclear weapons (it did not turn up evidence to confirm that fear), and out of fear that Iraq might one day share its nuclear capability with a terrorist group. Leaving aside the political particulars (Al Qaeda and Saddam Hussein were not allied), deterrence theory suggests that the nation-state sharing nuclear weapons with a terrorist group would at least have to take into account the possibility of being the target of retaliation – the return address – in the event the nuclear hand-off was traced back to it.

The most likely route to a terrorist nuclear capability involves the so-called '**dirty bomb**', or radiological dispersal device. This would be a device that, without the profound power of a nuclear explosion (and its attendant heat and blast effects), disperses some type of radioactive material. The damage from a successful dirty bomb would be far less than from a nuclear weapon, and the effects (radiation poisoning) would likely be long term instead of immediate. The most important effect would be psychological; the detonation of a radiation dispersal device would surely terrorize any population it victimized.

In a recent book, Graham Allison (2004) describes nuclear terrorism as 'the ultimate preventable catastrophe.' He urges nation-states to cooperate in a global alliance to guard against the theft of weapons or weapons-grade material, ban the new production of highly enriched uranium or reprocessed plutonium, and ensure that no other states join the nuclear club.

Dirty Bomb: A device that, without the profound power of a nuclear explosion (and its attendant heat and blast effects), disperses some type of radioactive material.

The Emergence of Cyber-Warfare

Finally, we should recognize the destructive potential of a relatively new technological threat, that of **cyber-warfare**. Cyber-warfare is a form of information warfare; it is the use of the internet and related technologies by governments to damage or disrupt the activities or systems of an adversary or a private entity of value to an adversary. A related term, cyber-terrorism, refers to the use of cyber-warfare techniques by groups or individuals operating independently of national governments. A number of states, including Israel, the United States, Iran, and China have indicated that they have active cyber-warfare programs. Intelligence analysts believe that Iran's cyber-warfare was behind a string of attacks in 2012 that disabled the websites of numerous US banks and disrupted the operations of the Saudi Arabian oil company Aramco. US and Israeli operatives developed a computer virus named Stuxnet that was targeted against Iran's nuclear enrichment facility at Natanz. Stuxnet damaged Iran's facility, and escaped to the internet when an Iranian nuclear technician inadvertently transferred the virus from Iran's nuclear facility to the internet through his personal computer.

Cyber-warfare: The use of the internet and related technologies by governments to damage or disrupt the activities or systems of an adversary or a private entity of value to an adversary.

Is cyber-warfare an anti-proliferation device, or a potential new weapon of mass destruction? It is too early to tell, but some scientists see eerie parallels to the dawn of the nuclear age (Kemp 2012). As we saw at the beginning of this chapter, nuclear weapons were developed in an environment of interstate competition and used by one government without a full appreciation of their implications. Although the destructive potential may differ, governments developing cyber-warfare may be heading down a similar path, creating weapons that could possibly destroy stock markets and banking systems, flood dams, and poison water supplies. The extent to which cyber-warfare 'arms races' take place and whether the international community will seek to control or ban their use remain to be seen.

State	International
Some states see cyber-warfare as a new form of statecraft, one with uncertain implications.	Deterrence is one solution to the destructive potential of nuclear weapons, but the logic of deterrence applies differently to states and non-state actors.

Revisiting the Enduring Question and Looking Ahead

This chapter examined the extent to which nuclear weapons and other weapons of mass destruction have transformed international relations. Nuclear weapons may have an important stabilizing effect – they discourage great powers from fighting the kind of all-out wars that characterized the pre-nuclear history of the international system. The spread of nuclear weapons to a number of additional states and potentially to non-state actors, however, raises a host of concerns about the potential for international conflicts to escalate in truly destructive ways. The existence of nuclear weapons makes war less likely, yet potentially more catastrophic should it occur. Although they have less destructive capacity, the same argument applies to biological and chemical weapons.

In these last three chapters we have explored the enduring problem of war, the strategies statesmen and citizens have employed in pursuit of peace, and the special challenges posed by nuclear and other weapons of mass destruction. The questions of what causes war and what are the conditions for peace are among the most fundamental in world politics. But international relations, both in the sense of what is happening in the international domain and as a field of study, are not just defined by the military dimensions of war and peace. International relations are also vitally concerned with international commerce and finance, the exchange of goods and services between countries, and the investing of money across borders. Those economic relations, the political conditions that hinder or facilitate those relations, the impact of economics on politics and military affairs, and the special question of whether international economic ties help or hurt the prospects of poorer countries, constitute the study of international political economy (IPE).

IPE is vital to our understanding of international affairs, and we now turn to it. We explore how international politics and economics interact, and why economic relations often inspire international cooperation and sometimes lead states to conflict. We examine why some states develop their economies more rapidly than others, and what that implies for the stability of the international system.

Visit **www.palgrave.com/politics/Grieco** to access extra resources for this chapter, including:

* Chapter summaries to help you review the material
* Multiple choice quizzes to test your understanding
* Flashcards to test your knowledge of the key terms in this chapter
* An interactive simulation that invites you to go through the decision-making process of a world leader at a crucial political juncture
* Pivotal decisions in which you weigh up the pros and cons of complicated decisions with grave consequences
* Outside resources, including links to contemporary articles and videos, that add to what you have learned in this chapter

Study Questions

1. Imagine that, during the twenty years after 1945, neither the United States nor the Soviet Union possessed nuclear weapons. Do you think those two countries would have gone from a cold war to major hot war during that period?

2. How many nuclear weapons do you think the United States needs to deter any potential nuclear weapons state from using its arsenal against America? 200 warheads? 500 warheads? More? Fewer? Explain your answer.

3. Imagine this world: your home country does not have nuclear weapons, and is a signatory to the NPT. All the rest of the countries that now possess nuclear weapons have them. In this imaginary world, would you favor or oppose the acquisition of nuclear weapons by your country, even if it had to break its obligations under the NPT? Why or why not?

4. Are nuclear weapons morally justifiable?

5. To what extent are biological and chemical weapons substitutes for nuclear weapons?

6. Do you think the threat of terrorism will increase international efforts to contain nuclear proliferation and the spread of biological and chemical weapons? Why or why not?

Further Reading

Alibek, Ken (2008) *Biohazard: The Chilling True Story of the Largest Covert Biological Weapons Program in the World* (New York: Random House). A physician and microbiologist, Alibek ran the Soviet Union's massive bioweapons program during the Cold War. He emigrated to the United States in 1992 and provided a full account of this ongoing program to the US government. This book tells his story and that of the secret program.

Allison, Graham (2004) *Nuclear Terrorism: The Ultimate Preventable Catastrophe* (New York: Times Books). Allison assesses the dangers of nuclear terrorism – who might attempt it and how they might obtain the weapon. He views the threat as preventable assuming a broad coalition is willing to work together to control weapons-relevant materials at the source.

Cohen, Avner (1988) *Israel and the Bomb* (New York: Columbia University Press). Cohen provides a detailed account of when, how, and why Israel developed its nuclear capability. He draws on interviews and declassified documents to piece together this important political history.

Hersey, John (1946) *Hiroshima* (New York: Alfred Knopf). A war correspondent during the 1940s, Hersey tells the horrifying story of the impact of the world's first nuclear explosion on ordinary people. He also traces the path of a handful of Japanese who survived the attack.

Jervis, Robert (1989) *The Meaning of the Nuclear Revolution: Statecraft and the Prospect of Armageddon* (Ithaca: Cornell University Press). This is perhaps the clearest academic statement of the logic and inevitability of MAD once states have nuclear weapons. Jervis explores the political, psychological, and moral dimensions of statecraft in the nuclear age.

Kaplan, Fred (1991) *The Wizards of Armageddon* (Stanford: Stanford University Press). This is a readable account of the lives and times of the civilian architects of the nuclear age. Kaplan explores the role and impact of key scientists and policy makers who developed the field of nuclear strategy after World War II.

Tannenwald, Nina (2008) *The Nuclear Taboo: The United States and the Non-Use of Nuclear Weapons since 1945* (Cambridge: Cambridge University Press). Tannenwald makes the constructivist case that a nuclear taboo, or the shared social inhibition against nuclear use, is more important than the standard arguments about deterrence in accounting for why no state has used nuclear weapons since 1945.

III

Wealth and Power: An Introduction to International Political Economy

8 International Economics: Basic Theory and Core Institutions

9 Power, Politics, and the World Economy

10 Dilemmas of Development

Visit **www.palgrave.com/politics/grieco** to watch the authors debating the issues discussed in this Part.

Video 1: What does globalization mean and what are its effects?

Video 2: Do International Organizations promote peace, prosperity and justice?

8

International Economics: Basic Theory and Core Institutions

Enduring question: How do politics shape the global economy

In 2012, trade between the United Kingdom and Vietnam reached about $4.4 billion, having increased by about one-third in just one year. Two important products Vietnam supplies to UK residents, tea and coffee, cannot readily be produced in the British Isles, but one of the major products that Vietnam sells to the UK is shoes. Why does the UK possibly need or want to buy shoes from Vietnam, rather than making them at home? At the same time, a major British export to Vietnam is prescription medications. Why doesn't Vietnam develop and rely upon its own pharmaceutical industry? To address these and a host of other important questions relating to the international economy, we turn in this section to the sub-field of International Relations that is called International Political Economy (IPE).

We begin our exploration of IPE in this chapter with a brief overview of basic ideas from the discipline of economics that help us understand why countries undertake international trade and international financial transactions. We also provide you with an introduction to one of the most important agents in the international economy, the multinational enterprise (MNE). We then turn our attention to an overview of the main international institutions that states have created since World War II to help them both expand the international economy and cope with some of the problems that have been engendered by that expansion.

Our goal in this chapter is to provide you with a firm base of understanding of the economic and political dynamics as a result of which countries have created an international economy. We then, in Chapter 9, examine how states sometimes utilize their international economic linkages to advance their political interests, including an enhancement of their overall power, or sometimes seek to limit their exposure to the international economy for fear that such exposure hinders the attainment of their national interests abroad and even curtails their internal economic and political autonomy. To understand how international economic linkages create political opportunities and also political risks for countries, which is at the core of our discussion of IPE in Chapter 9, it is vital first to understand why those countries, in the first place, engage with that international economy, why they have the particular kinds of interactions that they have – for example, why Vietnam exports shoes and imports pharamaceutical products, while the United Kingdom does the opposite – and what are the basic international institutions that states have created so that they can work together on international economic matters.

Source: © Auris – istockphoto.com

Learning Objectives

By the end of this chapter, you will be able to:

→ Understand the basic concepts of international trade theory, and appreciate why governments sometimes embrace trade and sometimes seek to insulate their economies from it.

→ Recognize how exchange rates between national currencies are determined, why governments change them, and how they matter to international trade and investment.

→ Understand the characteristics of multinational enterprises and assess their importance in the world economy.

→ Appreciate the relationship between world politics and the international institutions that govern the world economy.

Chapter Contents

- Basic Elements of International Trade
- Basic Elements of International Money
- Multinational Enterprises and International Political Economy
- The Institutions of the World Economy
- Revisiting the Enduring Question and Looking Ahead
- Study Questions
- Further Reading

Basic Elements of International Trade Theory and Policy

During much of international history, governments either avoided trade by pursuing **autarky**, the separation of the country from the world economy, or they pursued mercantilism, which we discussed in Chapter 2, and which you will recall consists of efforts by governments to supervise and manipulate international economic contacts with the aim of maximizing exports, minimizing imports, and acquiring gold in exchange for exports in order to pay for a stronger military. Yet, between the mid-1700s and the mid-1800s Adam Smith and then David Ricardo put forward a critique of mercantilism and provided the intellectual underpinning for a gradual turn first by the United Kingdom and then other countries toward freer trade, that is, the relaxation by governments of controls on private commerce both within and between countries.

Subsequent generations of economists have elaborated on the central ideas of Smith and Ricardo. Taken as a whole, economists argue, as we will see below, that trade encourages and allows countries to use their national resources more efficiently, and it allows them to consume more goods than would be possible if residents could only buy things that are produced at home. Trade, in short, makes good sense economically for the country taken as a whole. But as we shall see, trade does not always seem beneficial to every individual or all groups of individuals within a country, and those individuals and groups have a rational incentive to enter the political realm so as to push back and reverse or at least seek protection from freer trade. Politics thus is at the heart of trade: it can facilitate it, but it can also serve as a brake on it.

Building Blocks for Analysis: Consumption and Production

We begin with the individual person. Economists assume that an individual attains **utility**, or well-being, as a result of consuming goods and services. Economists further assume that, in the same way an individual improves his or her well-being through consumption of goods and services, so too an entire country enjoys greater well-being if it can somehow consume more goods and services. Economists have put forward, we will see in a moment, a theory that suggests that, compared to the country's consumption of goods and services in autarky, it can improve its consumption of goods and services by engaging in trade. This outcome, according to economists, explains why countries undertake trade.

In order for goods and services to be consumed, they must in the first instance be produced. To understand what a country can produce, economists employ a model they call the **production possibilities frontier (PPF)**. A production possibilities frontier is a graphical representation of the different combinations of goods that a country may produce during some period of time, for example, a year, with the resources it has in its possession. When we refer to productive resources, we usually mean the land, labor (working people and managers), capital (factories and equipment), and technology located in the country.

To see what a hypothetical PPF looks like, let us imagine that the United States produces only two goods, computers and shoes, and that, given its endowment of productive resources, it has the PPF depicted in Figure 8.1.

Notice that the US production possibilities frontier in Figure 8.1 drops downward as we move from left to right. This downward slope represents the existence of what economists call an **opportunity cost** in the production of either computers or shoes,

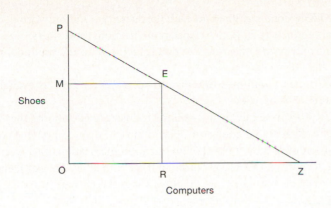

◀ Figure 8.1
Hypothetical US
Production
Possibilities Frontier

This production possi-
bilities frontier illus-
trates what the United
States hypothetically
could produce if it put
all its productive
efforts into making
shoes, computers, or
different combinations
of shoes and com-
puters.

that is, an increase in the production of one of the goods requires the forgoing of some amount of the other good. To see why this is the case, imagine that the United States is devoting *all* its productive resources to shoe manufacturing. In the figure this is represented by point P, at which the United States is producing and consuming OP pairs of shoes and zero computers. If the United States decides it wants a different combination of the two goods depicted in the figure – for example, it would like to be at point E, at which it is producing and consuming OM pairs of shoes and OR computers – it needs to reduce its production of shoes by MP pairs of shoes and move the productive resources thus released into computer manufacturing. Hence, in order for computer manufacturing to go up, shoe output must go down, and thus we have the downward slope in the PPF in the figure. Note that if we had said that the PPF in Figure 8.1 was that for the United Kingdom, Canada, India, or Sweden, those PPFs would also be downward sloping: economists argue that opportunity costs in the production of goods hold for all countries.

Although all countries have downward-sloping PPFs, suggesting that they all must decrease the production of one good in order to produce more of another good, the extent to which they have to reduce one good to produce more of another is likely to be different, sometimes radically so. As we will see in a moment, these *differences* in opportunity costs between countries make possible the establishment of mutually beneficial trade between countries.

Comparative Advantage

Recall that the benchmark for evaluation of whether trade is worthwhile is greater consumption by each country. If we can show that two countries, for example, Vietnam and the United Kingdom, each achieve greater consumption as a result of trade, we can understand not only why those two particular countries trade with each other, but in general how trade can be beneficial to trading partners, which in turn explains why those partners engage in trade. The United Kingdom in the discussion below stands in for a range of advanced industrial countries that includes, for example, Japan, Germany, Sweden, and the United States; Vietnam is standing in for many developing countries, a group that includes among others Bangladesh, India, and China.

We present our analysis of why countries trade with one another with the aid of four assumptions. These assumptions are by no means an accurate depiction of real-world countries, but they do help us focus on how countries can gain from trade. The four assumptions are:

- The United Kingdom and Vietnam each produces two and only two goods, pharmaceutical products (that is, prescription medications) and shoes.
- Labor is the only productive resource that is required for the production of either product.
- Each country has 1 million workers, and so each country has available to it 1 million labor-years of work.
- Because UK workers are living in a wealthy industrialized country, they have been trained to be efficient in manufacturing, and thus we may assume that any one UK worker can produce more bottles of prescription medications each year than any one worker can in Vietnam (500 bottles in the UK to 50 in Vietnam), and any one UK worker can also produce more pairs of shoes than a Vietnamese worker (200 to 175 pairs).

Absolute advantage: A situation in which one state has a productive advantage over another in two (or more) goods, but trade can still be mutually beneficial due to the principle of **comparative advantage**.

The last assumption means that the United Kingdom has an **absolute advantage** over Vietnam in both prescription medications and shoes. In these circumstances, we might reasonably ask, how could the UK possibly gain from trade with Vietnam?

The reason why the United Kingdom and Vietnam can both gain through trade in spite of the UK's absolute advantage in pharmaceutical products and shoes is that there are *differences* in the opportunity costs between the two countries in the production of those medications and shoes. As we can see in Table 8.1, a UK worker in one year can produce either 500 bottles of prescription medications or 200 pairs of shoes, so the UK opportunity cost to produce one additional pair of shoes is 2.5 bottles of medications (500 bottles of medication given up/200 extra pairs of shoes made = 2.5 bottles given up for each additional pair of shoes). By the same logic, the UK opportunity cost for one additional bottle of prescription medications is 0.4 pairs of shoes (200 pairs of shoes given up/500 bottles of medications fabricated = 0.4 pairs of shoes foregone for each additional bottle of medications). We can also see in the figure that any one worker in Vietnam can produce either 50 bottles of prescription medications or 175 pairs of shoes. The opportunity cost of making one additional pair of shoes in Vietnam is about 0.3 bottles of medications (50 bottles foregone/175 shoes made = about 0.3 bottles of medications foregone for each extra pair of shoes produced). The opportunity cost of producing one additional bottle of prescription medications in Vietnam is 3.5 pairs of shoes (175 pairs of shoes foregone/50 additional bottles of medications produced = 3.5 pairs of shoes given up for each additional bottle of medication).

Comparative advantage: One country has a comparative advantage over another in the production of a good if, in order to make one more unit of that good, it has to forego less of another good.

This example illustrates the concept of **comparative advantage**. One country has a comparative advantage over another in the production of a good if, in order to make one more unit of that good, it has to forego less of another good. You will recall that the way we constructed this example, the UK has an absolute advantage over Vietnam both in prescription medications and shoes. However, Vietnam has a comparative advantage in shoes. This is because it is *relatively* cheaper to produce an additional pair of shoes in *terms of foregone bottles of prescription medications* in Vietnam (0.3 bottles) than in the United Kingdom (2.5 bottles). Another way of making the same point is to observe that the cost of producing an extra pair of shoes in Vietnam in terms of bottles of medications foregone is about one-eighth the amount that is required in the United Kingdom. At the same time, the UK has a comparative advantage over Vietnam in prescription medications. This is because it is *relatively* cheaper

	Worker Output per Year		Opportunity Cost	
	Bottles of Rx	Pairs of Shoes	1 Bottle Rx	1 Pair Shoes
UK	500	200	0.4 pairs shoes	2.5 bottles Rx
Vietnam	50	175	3.5 pairs shoes	0.3 bottle Rx

◀ **Table 8.1**
Hypothetical Output and Opportunity Costs, Bottles of Medications and Pairs of Shoes, UK and Vietnam

This figure shows how countries can differ in opportunity costs in production, and thus differ in the goods for which they have a comparative advantage.

to produce an additional bottle of prescription medications *in terms of foregone shoes* in the UK (0.4 pairs) than in Vietnam (3.5 pairs). Put another way, in the United Kingdom the cost of producing one additional bottle of prescription medications in terms of shoes foregone is about one-ninth the amount that must be foregone in Vietnam.

The Gains from Trade

Even if it is true that, in light of differences in opportunity costs in the two countries, the UK enjoys a comparative advantage in prescription medications, and Vietnam enjoys a comparative advantage in shoes, how exactly do both of those countries do better by trading with each other? We are now in a position to answer that question. Figure 8.2 illustrates how such a mutually beneficial trading situation can arise.

◀ **Figure 8.2**
Specialization and Trade: the United Kingdom and Vietnam

The theory of international trade suggests that differences in opportunity costs in the United Kingdom and Vietnam, specialization by them on the basis of comparative advantage, and mutually voluntary exchange between them, can combine to allow both countries to improve their consumption and thus their national well-being.

Let us begin with both countries in autarky. Each country's production possibilities frontier – depicted for the UK on the left side of Figure 8.2, and for Vietnam on the right side of the figure – dictates its consumption opportunities, since by definition each country in autarky can consume only what it itself produces. Let us assume that in autarky each country allocates 600,000 labor-years to producing pharmaceuticals and 400,000 labor-years to making shoes. In these circumstances, the UK in autarky is at point 1 in the left panel of Figure 8.2: it produces and consumes 300 million bottles of prescription medications and 80 million pairs of shoes. Vietnam in autarky is at point A in the figure's right panel: it produces and consumes 30 million bottles of prescription medications and 70 million pairs of shoes.

What happens if trade becomes possible? The UK first specializes on the basis of its comparative advantage: it entirely stops making shoes and increases its production of medications from 300 million to 500 million bottles. This is represented by the movement from point 1 to point 2 in the left side of Figure 8.2. Vietnam also specializes: it stops making pharmaceuticals altogether and increases its shoe production

Terms of trade: The rate at which goods will be exchanged between two states.

from 70 million pairs to 175 million pairs; this is noted by the movement from point A to point B in the right side of the figure.

Each country can now offer to exchange some of the good it makes for the good it no longer produces. In order to make an exchange, the two countries must agree on the **terms of trade**, that is, the rate at which UK bottles of prescription medications will be exchanged for Vietnamese shoes. Imagine that Vietnam and the UK each send a representative to negotiate on behalf of their respective country on this matter of the terms of the trade. Let us also imagine that the Vietnamese representative in the first instance offers less than 0.4 pairs of shoes for each bottle of prescription medications it receives (for example, the representative suggests a terms of trade of 3 bottles per pair of shoes, which translates into 0.33 pairs of shoes per bottle). In those circumstances, the UK representative declines to agree to trade, for at anything less than 0.4 pairs of shoes per bottle the UK can acquire shoes more cheaply by shifting UK labor back into shoes and then obtaining 0.4 pairs for each bottle of medications it forgoes. On the other hand, if the UK representative were to propose a terms of trade that required Vietnam to give up more than 3.5 pairs of Vietnamese shoes per UK bottle of medications – for example, let's imagine the UK representative suggests that the UK should receive 4 pairs of Vietnamese shoes for each bottle of UK pharmaceuticals – then the Vietnamese representative declines to trade, for it would be cheaper for Vietnam to shift labor out of its production of shoes and into the manufacturing of prescription medications and thereby obtain bottles of domestically made medications at an opportunity cost of 3.5 pairs of shoes.

The opportunity costs in the two countries require that the terms of trade must fall somewhere between 0.4 pairs of Vietnamese shoes for one bottle of UK prescription medications and 3.5 pairs of Vietnamese shoes for one bottle of UK medications. Let us assume that the United Kingdom and Vietnam mutually agree to set the terms of trade at 1 pair of shoes for each bottle of medications, and on that basis they agree further to a trade whereby Vietnam provides 100 million pairs of shoes in exchange for which it receives 100 million bottles of UK medications. Returning to Figure 8.2, Vietnam produces at point B, but with the exchange we just described above it now consumes at point C; the United Kingdom UK produces at point 2 but consumes at point 3.

In Table 8.2 we present the changes in consumption by the UK and Vietnam that their new trading relationship makes possible. Before trade, Vietnam consumes 70 million pairs of shoes and 30 million bottles of prescription medications; with trade, Vietnam consumes 75 million pairs of shoes and 100 million bottles of medications. Vietnam, by virtue of specialization and exchange, increases not only its consumption of prescription medications by 70 million bottles, but it also increases its consumption of shoes by 5 million pairs. For its part, in autarky the UK consumes 300 million bottles of medications and 80 million pairs of shoes; with specialization and trade, the UK consumes 400 million bottles of medications and 100 million pairs of shoes. With specialization and trade the UK not only consumes 20 million additional pairs of shoes, it is also able to consume an additional 100 million bottles of prescription medicines.

For economists, in sum, countries benefit in terms of total consumption if they pursue specialization on the basis of their comparative advantage and they undertake trade, and this explains why they pursue this dual strategy of specialization and trade.

Consumption	United Kingdom		Vietnam	
	Bottles Rx	Pairs Shoes	Bottles Rx	Pairs Shoes
After Trade	400	100	100	75
Before Trade	300	80	30	70
Gain from Trade	100	20	70	5

Note: all figures are in millions.

◄ Table 8.2
UK–Vietnam Trade: Gains in Consumption

In this hypothetical scenario, both the UK and Vietnam enjoy increases in their consumption of prescription medications and shoes, which for international trade theory explains why they undertake trade with one another.

Why do Countries Protect Themselves from Trade?

While trade theory's depiction of the benefits of trade is elegant and persuasive, almost every government at one time or another places restrictions on goods coming into its territory, that is, it pursues one or another form of **protectionism**. Why does this occur? Governments turn to protection either because of their understanding of what constitutes the interests of the country as a whole, or because of pressures they may receive from some groups in society that are harmed by trade.

Let us consider how governments might decide that, from the viewpoint of the country as a whole, protectionism is a necessary policy. In the example above, Vietnam improves its total consumption if it specializes in shoes and buys prescription medications from the United Kingdom. From the viewpoint of liberal international theory, which we reviewed in Chapter 3, this opportunity for absolute gains in consumption is sufficient to motivate Vietnam's government to open its country to trade on the basis of comparative advantage.

Yet, Vietnam's government might face incentives and constraints highlighted in realist theory. For example, the Vietnamese government might worry that if it allows UK prescription medications into its market, Vietnam will have no prospect of ever having a local pharmaceutical industry. Given that the UK has had a head start in that industry, free trade would simply lock in its advantage and doom the formation of an indigenous Vietnamese industry in that important field. The Vietnamese government might calculate that such free trade will prevent Vietnam from developing a strong research capacity in chemistry and the chemicals industry, which might have implications for Vietnamese national security. The Vietnamese government might also calculate that trade on the basis of current comparative advantage industry would make Vietnam dangerously dependent on the UK for medicines. Given how important pharmaceuticals are to modern life, Vietnamese leaders might fear that if they become dependent on Britain in that area they will be open to British pressure or even blackmail if those two countries found themselves in a dispute and Britain threatened to apply economic sanctions if Vietnam did not comply with its diplomatic demands .

To address these concerns, Vietnam might adopt **infant-industry protection**, that is, a policy by a government of restricting imports of a good so that potential or actual domestic producers of that good have a large enough domestic market that they can grow and become efficient and thus eventually not need trade protection. The goal in this instance would be a decision by the Vietnamese government to restrict UK medications and thereby to create a temporarily sheltered market for its own pharmaceutical industry. Having that sheltered market would give the Vietnamese industry a chance to develop and ultimately stand on its own in its home market and perhaps

Protectionism: Any of a number of policies in which a country puts restrictions on incoming goods in an effort to protect the domestic economy.

Infant-industry protection: A policy in which imports of a certain type of good are restricted (in theory temporarily) to allow for the development of the capacity to produce that good domestically.

even to be able to engage in international competition. Of course, while the protection was in place, Vietnamese consumers would need to pay more for 'home-grown' prescription medications, and the country would not be using its economic resources most efficiently. In this case, Vietnam's government would believe that the country's long-term economic and political interests would need to override the economic interest of its consumers.

An example where infant-industry protection has worked in modern history is the United States, which was highly protectionist until well into the early twentieth century and was protectionist precisely to allow US industry to develop. Countries that in the second half of the twentieth century provide further evidence that infant-industry protection can sometimes be effective include Japan and South Korea. We will return to this issue in Chapter 10; for the moment, we present differing views on this contemporary debate in Box 8.1.

Governments might also turn to protectionism in order to address the legitimate concerns of societal groups that are made economically vulnerable as a result of foreign competition. Liberal theory – for example, as articulated in democratic peace theory – accents the point that individuals and domestic interest groups drive foreign policy. While there are many grounds to believe that individuals and groups press democratic governments in peaceful directions, there are also good reasons to believe that, in international economic matters, different interest groups often pressure governments in different directions, some pressing for openness while other press for closure, with trade policy usually in consequence possessing both free-trade and protectionist elements.

In the above discussion of trade, we can imagine that UK pharmaceutical producers would press for freer trade with Vietnam. However, UK workers in British shoe factories might reasonably see imports of Vietnamese shoes as a threat to their jobs, livelihoods, and way of life. For those workers, it is largely impractical to believe they can give up making shoes and return to school for retraining to learn how to produce prescription medicines, so they might pressure politicians to restrict Vietnamese imports of shoes. If these UK shoe makers and their friends and families are clustered in politically sensitive parts of the United Kingdom, politicians in those districts might indeed press for protectionism, and to some degree they might prevail over the preferences of pharmaceutical manufacturers, or at least slow the rate at which UK–Vietnamese trade is liberalized. Although it might make economic sense for the United Kingdom as a whole to import most of its shoes, a regional political logic in which domestic interest groups have political influence might dictate that the UK avoids completely free trade in that industry. For a striking example of how economically inefficient yet politically powerful producers have used government restrictions to further their parochial interests, see Box 8.2 on rice farming in Japan.

Tariff: A tax collected by the government on goods coming into the country.

Non-tariff barrier (NTB): Policies, such as anti-dumping duties, import quotas, or controlled government procurement, by which a state can control imports and import prices without imposing tariffs.

Protectionism itself can take many forms. Until quite recently, governments routinely employed **tariffs**, which is a tax collected by the government on goods coming into the country. Governments around the world quite often deploy one or another **'non-tariff' barrier (NTB)** to trade, which in general is a government policy that restricts the supply of imported goods and gives market advantage to home producers. As tariffs have come down since World War II, something we will discuss below, non-tariff barriers have become more important both as a government policy instrument and as a subject of international trade negotiation.

In her presidential address to the American Economic Association, Anne O. Krueger, a former World Bank Chief Economist and Deputy Managing Director of the IMF, argued that infant-industry policies are typically unsuccessful; in contrast, a UN international panel headed by former Mexican president Ernesto Zedillo argues that there remains a place for them.

The Argument against Infant-Industry Policies in Developing Countries: Economist Anne O. Krueger

A second misapplication of good theory arose because of the nonoperational nature of the theory itself, and the failure to identify circumstances under which policy implementation might be incentive compatible and potentially increase welfare. A key culprit in this was the interpretation of the infant industry argument…[it was] generally recognized as a 'legitimate' case for a departure from free trade…The problem with the argument, as a basis for policy, is that it fails to provide any guidance as to how to distinguish between an infant that would grow up and a would-be producer seeking protection because it is privately profitable.

Source: Anne O. Krueger, 'Trade Policy and Economic Development: How We Learn', *American Economic Review* 87 (March 1997): 11–12.

The Argument for Infant-Industry Policies in Developing Countries: UN International Panel Headed by Former President of Mexico Ernesto Zedillo

However misguided the old model of blanket protection intended to nurture import substitute industries, it would be a mistake to go to the other extreme and deny developing countries the opportunity of actively nurturing the development of an industrial sector. A requirement for international approval of such protection could be a help to the governments of developing countries in resisting excessive demands from their domestic lobbies (and from multinationals considering local investment).

Source: United Nations, 'Report of the High-level Panel on Financing for Development', June 21, 2001, p. 41, available at: http://www.un.org/en/events/pastevents/financing_for_development_report.shtml.

There are many types of NTBs. One class involves the **anti-dumping** practices of importing countries. **Dumping** is the sale of goods by producers in a foreign market at prices that are lower than what those producers charge in their home market. Producers might engage in dumping to gain market share in the targeted foreign markets, or to drive out local producers in those markets, and having done so then to increase prices and obtain very high profits. In most countries, governments have procedures as a result of which local producers can claim that foreign producers are engaged in dumping. If the governments find merit to such claims, they can impose **anti-dumping duties**, that is, tariffs that offset the price cuts offered by foreign suppliers below what they charge in their own markets.

Anti-dumping is allowed under international trade law. However, suppose, returning to our UK–Vietnam example, that the British government puts into place anti-dumping procedures whereby it is extremely easy and inexpensive for UK shoe makers to press their claims against Vietnamese shoe exporters, while at the same time Vietnamese shoe exporters must hire lawyers and undertake lengthy and expensive efforts to demonstrate that they are not dumping. Those exporters might decide that, even if they are not dumping, it makes sense to avoid the legal expenses and business uncertainty that would flow from an anti-dumping dispute and instead simply to raise their prices for shoes sold in the UK, or to turn away from the British market

Anti-dumping: A type of policy designed to prevent **dumping** by other states. Permitted by international law, **anti-dumping** policies constitute one sort of **non-tariff barrier (NTB)**.

Dumping: The sale of goods by producers in a foreign market at prices that are lower than what those producers charge in their home market. Producers might engage in dumping to gain market share in the targeted foreign markets, drive out local producers in those markets, and, having done so, then increase prices and obtain very high profits.

Anti-dumping duties: Tariffs that offset the price cuts offered by foreign suppliers below what they charge in their own markets (**dumping**).

The Economic Logic of Specialization and Trade versus the Political Power of Domestic Interest Groups

Theory

The economic logic of comparative advantage holds that countries should specialize in what they produce most efficiently based on their factor endowments of land, labor, and capital, and trade with other countries to obtain goods and services that they produce less efficiently.

Practice

Countries often provide trade protection to their less efficient but politically sensitive producers. A good example is rice farming in Japan. Rice is produced cheaply and efficiently in Southeast Asian countries and other parts of the world. In Japan, rice is produced inefficiently and at high cost by a multitude of farmers tending very small plots, typically less than three hectares and often less than one hectare (one hectare equals approximately 2.5 acres). Japanese rice farmers are also part-time farmers, deriving less than half their income from this activity.

Nevertheless, Japanese rice has long enjoyed special protection from trade competition. Many in Japan consider rice a sacred cultural commodity because it is the key staple in the Japanese diet. Rice farmers have long been a key constituency of the Liberal Democratic Party, which ruled Japan from 1955 to 1993 and again from the mid-1990s to 2009. Liberal Democratic politicians insisted on protecting Japanese rice producers and until the 1990s would not allow, in the words of one politician, 'a single grain of rice' to enter Japan from abroad. In return, rice farmers and their communities served as a loyal voting bloc to help Liberal Democrats maintain power.

In the 1990s, and under intense pressure from its trading partners, Japan reluctantly agreed to allow some foreign-produced rice into the country. The government also provided subsidies to make sure that most of the high-cost Japanese rice farmers could stay in business. One result is that Japan in recent years has found itself with more rice than it could consume, and it holds the surplus in storage. As of 2010, the Japanese tariff on imported rice remained at a very steep rate – 788 percent!

Protectionist pressures remain very strong in some sectors even in countries that rely heavily on international economic integration.

Government procurement: The purchase by government agencies of goods and services from private suppliers. Because national governments spend so much money every year, government choices in how to purchase such goods and services can have a major impact on international trade. Thus, government procurement may constitute a **non-tariff barrier (NTB)**.

and instead to focus on other foreign markets. Anti-dumping procedures that are tilted in favor of domestic producers in this instance would serve to give protection to UK shoe producers, and constitute a non-tariff barrier to trade.

A second type of NTB involves government procurement, that is, the purchase by government agencies of goods and services from private suppliers. Given that government expenditures can run into the hundreds of billions of dollars per year, how the government awards purchasing contracts can either promote or hamper international trade. For example, the American 2009 stimulus package, totaling almost $900 billion, included 'Buy America' provisions that required US infrastructure spending programs (for example, roads, tunnels, and public transportation) to give preference to US over foreign suppliers.

Import quotas represent a third type of NTB. Import quotas are government-imposed numerical limits on how much of a particular good or service may be imported during some period of time, usually one year. Returning to our illustration of trade theory, to mollify the concerns of British manufacturers and unions in the shoe industry, the UK government could impose annual quotas on Vietnamese shoe imports. If British consumers want to buy 5 million pairs of shoes from Vietnam each year, but the UK government allows only 2 million pairs to be imported, customers will bid up the price of those shoes, forcing customers to look for alternatives – including UK domestically produced shoes.

The use of import quotas is restricted under international trade law. Because of this, governments sometimes employ **Voluntary Export Restraints (VERs)**. Imagine that the British government announces that if Vietnam does not reduce its shoe exports to the UK, then the British government will impose quotas not just on shoes, but on other Vietnamese products, such as clothing. The Vietnamese government might then persuade or compel Vietnamese shoe manufacturers to agree 'voluntarily' to restrict their sales in Britain.

In sum, international trade theory helps us understand why states engage in trade. At the same time, the study of politics helps us understand how governments may turn to protectionism. Politics can also bend the logic of international monetary affairs, to which we turn next.

👤 **Individual**	👥 **State**	🌐 **International**
Individuals, alone and as members of households, are at the heart of international trade theory, for it is their preference for consumption that animates specialization and trade.	Nations as a whole can improve their consumption opportunities from trade, and this explains why countries trade. Workers and producers in import-competing industries can lose out from trade and thus pressure their governments for protectionism.	States may turn away from freer trade and pursue infant-industry and other forms of protection in order to promote national autonomy or strengthen national defense.

Levels of Analysis

International Trade Theory

Basic Elements of International Money

In the previous section, Vietnam and the United Kingdom literally exchanged pairs of shoes for bottles of prescription medications. Yet, in the real world, UK pharmaceutical exporters want to be paid in British pounds sterling, and Vietnamese shoe exporters want to be paid in their national currency, the dong. Moreover, if foreign investors want to invest in Britain, they need pounds sterling to do that, just as non-Vietnamese investors who wish to invest in Vietnam need dong. Consider these investment transactions, and notice how each requires the investor to acquire the currency of the country in which the investment is taking place:

- *Foreign Direct Investment*: Residents in one country – most typically multinational enterprises, about which we say more below – may establish wholly-owned foreign subsidiaries, or buy enough shares of a foreign firm to control the operations of that firm. For example, Siemens, a large manufacturer of electronics and electrical equipment, is headquartered in Germany, but in 2013 roughly two-thirds of its 362,000 employees worked in Siemens-owned factories and research centers around the world.

- *Portfolio Investment*: Residents in one country – individuals, mutual funds acting on behalf of individuals, or firms acting on their own – may purchase foreign securities such as bonds, or purchase equities of foreign firms in amounts that do not confer managerial control. Large US and UK financial services firms – such as Vanguard and Fidelity in the former, and Aberdeen Asset Management and Barclays in the latter – offer to investors a wide range of funds that invest partly and even wholly in foreign firms.
- *Bank Deposits and Lending*: Banks headquartered in one country might extend loans to a foreign individual or enterprise. For example, if Deutsche Bank lends euros to a Vietnamese shoe manufacturer, that represents a German loan to a Vietnamese enterprise.

A person, household, or firm that wishes to acquire the currency of a foreign country typically does so through a purchase of the relevant currency on what is termed the foreign exchange market, that is, the marketplace (important locations are in London, New York, Frankfurt, and Tokyo) in which individuals, firms, and even governments sell and buy foreign currencies. Through a process of offering and bidding foreign currencies, market participants establish foreign currency exchange rates, that is, the amount of one currency that must be offered to purchase one unit of a foreign currency. Table 8.3 presents examples of such rates in February 2014.

National Exchange-Rate Systems

If a government allows supply and demand in foreign exchange markets to determine the exchange rate for its currency, then the government is pursuing a flexible (or floating) exchange-rate system. Examples of countries that utilize largely flexible exchange-rate systems include the United States, United Kingdom, Canada, and Switzerland. The alternative, used often in past decades but less so in recent years, is for a government to establish a fixed (or pegged) exchange-rate system. In that instance, a government announces that its currency will trade at a specific rate or within a band of values against a particular foreign currency or a group of currencies. The government is then obliged, as we will see below, to intervene in the foreign exchange market or to take policy measures to maintain the pegged rate, that is, monetary policy (efforts usually by the country's central bank to raise or lower interest rates) or fiscal policy (government decisions on spending and taxes). China today is an example of a country that has a largely fixed exchange-rate system.

Flexible Exchange-Rate Systems

Both Canada and Switzerland allow their currencies to float against each other. We can see how the exchange rate between their two currencies, the Canadian dollar (often called the CAD by participants in foreign exchange markets) and the Swiss franc (often called the CHF) is determined, and can change, in Figure 8.3.

In Figure 8.3, we use demand curves and supply curves to explain how, as a result of market forces, the exchange rate is established between the Canadian dollar and the Swiss franc. A demand curve specifies the quantity of a good that consumers wish to purchase at different prices; a supply curve specifies how much producers are

Foreign exchange market: The marketplace in which individuals, firms, and even governments sell and buy foreign currencies.

Exchange rate: The amount of one currency that must be offered to purchase one unit of a foreign currency.

Flexible (or floating) exchange-rate system: A system in which a government allows supply and demand in foreign exchange markets to determine the exchange rate of its national currency.

Fixed (or pegged) exchange-rate system: A system in which a currency trades at a government-specified rate against a particular currency or a group of currencies, and the government intervenes in the foreign exchange market or takes monetary or fiscal policy measures to keep those rates in place.

Demand curve: A demand curve specifies the quantity of a good that consumers wish to purchase at different prices. Along with **supply curves**, demand curves can show the likely price of goods, including currencies, in international markets.

Supply curve: A curve specifying how much of a good producers are willing to offer at different prices. Along with **demand curves**, supply curves can show the likely price of goods, including currencies, in international markets.

Currencies	GBP £	EUR €	USD $	JPY ¥
Australia 1.00 AUD	0.56140	0.67900	0.94140	95.70000
Canada 1.00 CAD	0.54720	0.66170	0.91740	93.28000
European Union 1.00 EUR	0.82660	N/A	1.38620	140.93000
Hong Kong 1.00 HKD	0.07691	0.09303	0.12897	13.11260
Japan 1.00 JPY	0.00587	0.00709	0.00984	N/A
Switzerland 1.00 CHF	0.67850	0.82090	1.13800	115.71000
United Kingdom 1.00 GBP	N/A	1.20950	1.67680	170.48000
United States 1.00 USD	0.59630	0.72130	N/A	101.67000

◀ Table 8.3
Selected Currency Rates

This chart depicts the rates of exchange among major economies as of April 2014. Columns two through five indicate how much of the currency listed at the top of the column needs to be offered to purchase one unit of the currency listed in the first column. You will observe that, for example, to purchase one euro, a person would have to pay £0.83 or US $1.39. Some version of this chart may be found daily in the business section of most national newspapers and online.

willing to offer at different prices. In Figure 8.3, D_0 and D_1 represent two hypothetical demand curves that Canadian residents have for Swiss francs over some period of time, for example, a year, while S represents the amount of Swiss francs that Swiss residents are willing to offer during that same period at different rates of exchange against the Canadian dollar.

Notice that both Canadian demand curves are downward sloping. Assume that a Swiss watch sells for 100 francs in Switzerland. At an exchange rate of CAD1.20/ 1 Swiss franc, the watch costs CAD120 in Canada; if it only costs one Canadian dollar to buy a Swiss franc, the watch costs CAD100. As the price of a Swiss franc declines, Swiss watches become less expensive in Canada; more Canadian residents want to purchase them; and therefore Canadian demand for Swiss francs will be greater. Notice also that the supply curve for Swiss francs, S, is upward sloping. As the Swiss franc becomes more valuable in terms of the Canadian dollars it can purchase, Cana-

◀ Figure 8.3
Determination of Exchange Rates: Canadian Dollar and Swiss Franc

This figure shows how the interplay between demand and supply determines exchange rates.

dian goods fall in price in terms of Swiss francs; Swiss residents will offer more of their currency so they can buy those cheaper Canadian goods.

In Figure 8.3 we assume that, at first, Canadian demand for and Swiss supply of Swiss francs equals one another at CAD1.20 per Swiss franc. How might this exchange rate change? Imagine that Canadian residents wish to purchase more Swiss products or financial assets, and therefore they demand, *at any given exchange rate*, more Swiss francs. This across-the-board increase in Canadian demand for Swiss francs is represented by a shift in the Canadian demand curve from D_0 to D_1. The new exchange rate where demand equals supply is CAD1.25 per Swiss franc.

In a flexible exchange-rate system, currency values are determined on the market, without government manipulation. Yet, even governments that normally prefer a flexible exchange-rate system occasionally intervene in currency markets. For example, in 2011, many individuals and companies began to sell euros (the common currency of several European countries, about which we will say more in a moment) for Swiss francs. The Swiss National Bank, the official central bank for that country, became alarmed that the resulting appreciation of the Swiss franc was making Swiss exports uncompetitive. It entered the foreign exchange market, offered Swiss francs for euros, and thereby capped the former's rise against the latter.

Fixed Exchange-Rate Systems

A government will sometimes pursue a fixed exchange-rate policy, that is, it will try to maintain its currency at a fixed value relative to one or more other currencies. For example, in the 1990s, the Mexican government sought to keep the peso fixed against the dollar. As noted above, China today pegs its currency against the dollar, although in recent years it has permitted some increase in the value of that currency relative to the dollar.

To see how a fixed exchange rate operates, imagine that the Canadian government wishes to fix the CAD-CHF rate at CAD1.20 to one Swiss franc. That rate would be the *official exchange rate* between the Canadian dollar and the Swiss franc, and, as noted above, the Canadian government would commit to maintain it through **currency market interventions** (purchases or sales of currency by the Canadian government), or by making changes in Canadian fiscal and monetary policy. What would happen if the Canadian government wanted the exchange rate to stay at CAD1.20 to the Swiss franc even if Canadian demand for Swiss goods and financial assets increased from D_0 to D_1? Returning to Figure 8.3, imagine if Canadian residents wished to import Swiss goods and buy Swiss financial assets at an annual rate totaling CHF 800 billion (see the dashed lines in the figure), while the Swiss supply of francs to buy Canadian goods and financial assets was CHF 400 billion. In those circumstances, Canada would soon experience a deficit in its current account.

Let us explain what we mean by a nation's current account. To do that, we need to introduce to you the idea of a country's overall **balance of payments**, and to the manner in which a country can experience a balance of payments deficit or a balance of payments surplus. The balance of payments for a country is a summary of the international transactions of its residents, including individuals, households, private enterprises, and the government, with residents in the rest of the world during some fixed period of time, usually a quarter (three months) or a year. One key part of the balance of payments is the **current account**. The current account consists of the country's balance of trade in goods and services (the value of exports minus the value of imports), plus its income receipts such as the receipt of earnings from past investments abroad or the

◀ **Map 8.1 Members of the European Union Using the Euro, 2014**

A wide range of EU countries have elected to utilize a common currency, the euro.

Map legend:
1 Albania
2 Bosnia and Herzegovina
3 Croatia
4 Macedonia
5 Slovenia
6 Montenegro
7 Serbia
8 Kosovo

Eurozone
Non-euro EU states

payment of such earnings to foreigners, and other transfers such as remittances that workers send out of the country or local residents receive from abroad.

Imagine Canada has a fixed exchange-rate system and begins to run a current-account deficit with Switzerland. Without intervention by the Canadian government the Canadian dollar would drop in value, reaching perhaps CAD1.25 per Swiss franc rather than the official peg of CAD1.20. To prevent that, the Canadian government would need to use some of its holdings of Swiss francs to buy Canadian dollars and thereby bid up their price so that the market rate would stay at the official rate of CAD1.20 to the Swiss franc. As we will see below, a very wealthy country like Canada can do that for quite some time; a poorer country is likely to find itself more severely constrained in its capacity to maintain a peg in the face of a persistent current-account deficit.

There are two other policy options available to governments when it comes to their national currencies. First, governments may agree to establish a **currency union**, the giving up by countries of their respective national currencies in favor of a common currency. The most prominent currency union today is the **euro zone**. As of 2014, eighteen of twenty-eight member-states of the European Union had converted their

Currency union: A group of countries in which each has given up its respective national currency in favor of a common currency.

Euro zone: The world's most prominent **currency union**, consisting of eighteen countries in Europe all using the euro as a national currency.

Dollarization in Central and South America

Aspiration: *Governments must defend the value of their currency*

For most governments, the national currency is an important symbol of sovereignty and power. They must also defend the value of their currency so that their own citizens, as well as investors abroad, have confidence in it as a store of value.

Reality: *Not every government manages to create and defend a viable national currency*

Some governments decide, informally or formally, to allow their citizens to use a foreign currency either alongside or as a substitute for the local currency. This process is called 'dollarization' because, especially since the end of World War II, the US dollar has been the currency of choice as a substitute for local currencies in trouble. For example, in the late 1990s, the Asian financial crisis spread to Brazil and threatened the stability of neighboring Ecuador. In March 1999, after a steep drop in the Ecuadorian sucre, the government froze its entire banking system to prevent money from flowing out of the country. Shortly thereafter, Ecuador's government adopted the US dollar as its official currency. Other examples include Panama, which has been dollarized officially for over 100 years, since 1904. Lebanon uses the US dollar as an official currency alongside the Lebanese pound. El Salvador dollarized its currency in 2001. Cuba, though still a communist country, began to rely more heavily on the US dollar following the collapse of its economic benefactor, the Soviet Union, in 1990. Today, Cuban citizens use the Cuban peso, which is not convertible into foreign currencies. They also may use a second currency, the 'convertible peso,' which trades officially at 1 to 1 with the US dollar, but unofficially trades at about 25 to 1 with the dollar. The US dollar itself is used extensively in Cuba.

Why adopt someone else's currency as your own? An important reason is price stability. Many weaker governments may be unable to resist the temptation to print money in response to demands by citizens and workers for higher incomes, or to buy support, particularly at election time. Of course, printing money without restraint leads to inflation and, in many cases, even bigger problems. Relying on an outside currency ties the hands of the government; it can no longer print money and monetary circulation more closely reflects the actual level of economic activity in the local economy. The decision to dollarize, of course, has potentially detrimental effects on national pride, especially in Latin and Central America, where nationalist sentiment runs high in the face of 'Yankee imperialism.'

Adopting the currency of another country is perhaps the strongest form of fixed-currency system a country can undertake in the contemporary era.

---

national currencies to the euro (see Map 8.1). A common currency may help draw economies closer together. However, the euro crisis that began in 2009 underscores the point that currency unions are prone to crises: investors and governments may become unsure whether some of the countries can stay in the union, or that they might be forced to withdraw and return to using their national currencies.

A second monetary policy option is when a country substitutes a foreign currency for its own in its home market. This practice is called dollarization because, as discussed in Box 8.3, the foreign currency most likely substituted has been the US dollar.

Dollarization: A monetary policy in which a country substitutes a foreign currency for its own in its home market. Historically the US dollar has been the most commonly substituted foreign currency.

Fixed Exchange-Rate Systems: Benefits and Problems

Governments that peg their exchange rates often find it necessary to intervene in the foreign exchange markets or to adjust their monetary and fiscal policies to maintain their desired official rates of exchange. But why would a government want to have a fixed rate in the first place? To answer that question, let's look at the benefits and risks of fixed exchange-rate systems.

One reason governments may fix their exchange rates is to fight **price inflation** (usually simply the term 'inflation is employed) where too much money is chasing too few goods, pushing up prices of goods and services. If a government has had a poor track record in controlling inflation, it may stoke **inflationary expectations**, the belief on the part of individuals, firms, unions, and other economic agents that price increases are always just around the corner. In those circumstances, domestic and foreign holders of that country's currency are constantly on the lookout for any signs of inflation, and if they see them they sell their holdings of the currency, causing its value to drop on currency markets, and by so doing increasing the price of imports and therefore actually bringing on more price inflation.

Governments in the first place often try to counteract inflation and inflationary expectations through a policy of **austerity**; that is, by raising interest rates, or by reducing government spending and increasing taxes, governments seek to discourage consumption and investment at home, and by dampening domestic demand also reduce inflationary pressures in the economy. However, another way a government can signal that it is resolved on fighting inflation is to fix the exchange rate of its currency against the currency of a slow-inflation country, and announce it will maintain the fixed rate, even if this means using fiscal and monetary policies that will slow a nation's economy and thereby keep inflation in check. A second reason a government might seek to peg its currency below what would be the free-market rate is to spur exports by its domestic producers. For example, the US government has claimed for many years that the Chinese government has pegged its currency, the renminbi (which is also known as the yuan, and whose trading symbol on foreign exchange markets is CNY), at an official rate below the free-market rate, precisely in order to promote Chinese exports.

Fixed-rate exchange systems provide governments with a mechanism by which they can dampen inflationary expectations or attain a competitive edge in global trade. However, there are risks in fixing exchange rates for either purpose. Consider the case of China and the possible undervaluing of the renminbi against the US dollar. China, by virtue of an undervalued currency, sells more goods to the United States than it purchases from that country; China in turn experiences large current-account surpluses; and, over time, it accumulates a large holding of US dollars – in recent years, something like $3 trillion.

There are three risks with this strategy. First, persistent large current-account surpluses accentuate the risk of Chinese domestic price inflation. As Chinese firms earn US dollars and other foreign currencies, they submit them to the Chinese central bank (that is how China's government has amassed $3 trillion); in return they receive renminbi. The firms deposit these renminbi in Chinese banks, which in turn lends them to Chinese residents to start new businesses, buy homes, or buy other goods and services. More and more renminbi are thus moving through the Chinese economy, and if the growth in the domestic supply of goods in China does not grow at the same rate as the growth in the currency, price inflation is likely to go up in China.

Price inflation: A situation in which too much money is chasing too few goods, pushing up prices of goods and services.

Inflationary expectations: The belief on the part of individuals, firms, unions, and other economic agents that price increases are always just around the corner.

Austerity: A policy by which governments raise interest rates or reduce government spending in an effort to discourage consumption and investment at home and, in so doing, reduce inflation and inflationary pressures.

▶ Figure 8.4 US Dollar/Chinese Renminbi Exchange Rate, 2000–12

The Chinese government has allowed the renminbi, or CNY, to appreciate against the US dollar in recent years. While the exchange rate was fixed between 2000 and 2005 at 8.3 CNY per dollar, the CNY gradually began to appreciate from 2006 onward (fewer CNY were needed to buy one US dollar), and by 2012 only 6.3 CNY were needed to purchase one dollar. This movement may have been due to US pressure on China to allow its currency to float upward.

Source: Data from IMF, World Data Bank, *World Development Indicators*, available at http://databank.worldbank.org/data/databases.aspx.

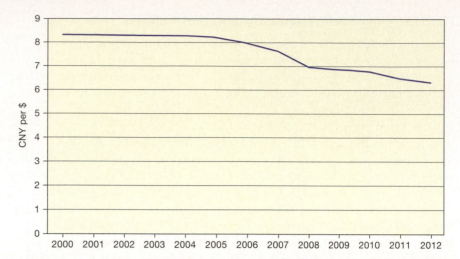

Second, Chinese monetary officials use the US dollars they accumulate to purchase US Treasury bonds. They need to believe their US counterparts will maintain the value of those bonds, and more generally the international purchasing power of the dollar. Think of it this way: if you are holding $3 trillion in bonds, and the dollar's value falls 10%, your bonds are worth $300 billion less. In light of recent US fiscal policy problems, including a credit downgrading in August 2011 of US debt by the rating agency Standard & Poor's, Chinese monetary authorities must sometimes wonder if their faith in the United States is entirely well placed. By early 2012 Chinese authorities were diversifying their official reserve portfolio by holding fewer US dollars and more Swiss francs, Japanese yen, and EU euros.

Finally, utilizing a fixed exchange-rate system to attain a competitive edge will work so long as a country's trading partners do not take some form of retaliation to offset the edge gained through a government-maintained undervalued currency. To date, China's exchange-rate system has not prompted strong retaliation from major trading partners like the United States, Japan, or the European Union. However, there have been persistent criticisms of China's currency peg in the US Congress, where several members have repeatedly introduced a law that would impose very high tariffs on Chinese goods entering the United States for the explicit reason of penalizing China's pegged-rate system.

China also came under intense pressure regarding its currency peg at the April 2011 meeting of the Group of 20 Finance Ministers. The risk then of retaliation by trading partners, together with possible Chinese fears about domestic price inflation, may help explain why, as noted above, the Chinese government in recent years has begun to allow the renminbi to appreciate slowly against the dollar, as can be observed in Figure 8.4.

Fixed exchange-rate systems create challenges for countries with current-account surpluses. They can be much, much harder on countries that begin to experience serious current-account deficits, for example, Mexico in the mid-1990s and Argentina in the early 2000s. As we saw in the hypothetical case of Canada and Switzerland, a country that wants to maintain a peg when its current account deficit is growing must intervene in the currency markets and buy its own currency with its holdings of foreign currency. That strategy is limited by two powerful constraints: its holdings of foreign currency, and its ability to borrow foreign currency to purchase its own currency.

In time domestic and foreign investors may come to question whether the central bank of a deficit country might run out of currency reserves or might no longer have the ability to borrow them from foreigners. Fearing that the government must finally allow the currency to devalue, holders of the currency – both local and foreign – begin to sell assets they hold in the country, and buy foreign currency and assets. The result is that local stock markets and real-estate markets fall, and the supply of the local currency on foreign exchange markets grows even faster, making it even harder for the country to maintain the peg. The government then faces a hard choice: either extreme austerity even as the national economy is already contracting, or going off the peg, which will in the short term prompt even more currency sales and a sharper domestic economic contraction.

👤 **Individual**	👥 **State**	🌐 **International**
As in trade, individuals are prime movers in international monetary affairs, for their demand for foreign goods and assets requires their attainment of foreign currency.	Governments need to make several key decisions about what kind of foreign-exchange system they wish to implement.	Governments interact with one another on international monetary issues, and sometimes claim that one or another is manipulating exchange rates to advance their interests at the expense of others.

Levels of Analysis
International Monetary Theory

Multinational Enterprises and International Political Economy

We will explore multinational enterprises (MNEs) and their important role in world affairs in three steps: first, we will provide a definition of such firms and examine their key characteristics; second, we will examine their economic importance in the modern global economy; and third, we will examine several ways in which they are important political actors in the modern world.

Definition and Characteristics of Multinational Enterprises

Multinational enterprises (MNEs) are firms that have their headquarters in one country and ongoing business operations in one or (more typically) several other countries. For example, as can be seen in Map 8.2, at the outset of 2014 the Ford Motor Company owned and operated manufacturing facilities in 21 countries outside its home country of the United States.

Multinational enterprises often own substantial assets (property, equipment, financial assets, and intellectual property), generate a great deal of their total sales, and have large numbers of their employees in countries outside the country in which they are headquartered. For example, the Nestlé Corporation in 2011 had the vast majority of its assets outside its home country of Switzerland ($116 billion out of a total of about $121 billion); so too most of its sales were in foreign markets ($92 billion out of a total of $94 billion); and most of its employees were located in foreign countries (318,000 out of 328,000).

Why do firms not just stay at home and simply export from their home countries to foreign markets? Why do they instead sometimes become multinational enter-

Multinational enterprise (MNE): A firm that has its headquarters in one country and ongoing business operations in one or (more typically) several other countries.

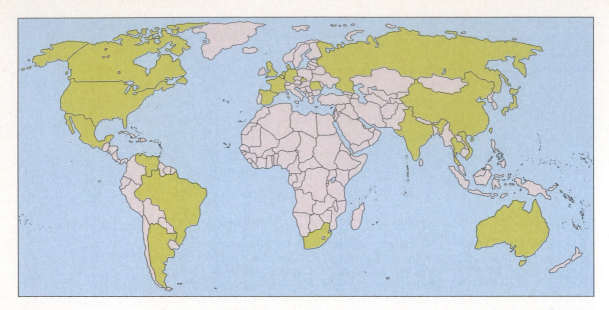

▲ Map 8.2 A Multinational Enterprise: Ford Motor Company's Worldwide Operations

At the outset of 2014 the Ford Motor Company had manufacturing facilities in 21 countries outside its home country of the United States (colored segments).

National treatment: A clause in the EEC (non EU), negotiated by the United States, that allows for American firms to be treated as though they are European firms.

prises? As a purely business matter, some firms by virtue of the industry in which they are active must go abroad: international petroleum firms such as Exxon Mobil and BP long ago become global in orientation in order to explore and exploit oil deposits in the Middle East, Latin America, Africa, and, in the years ahead, possibly in East and Southeast Asia. MNEs in manufacturing industries may decide that placing manufacturing or research and development facilities in foreign markets allows them to understand better what the customers in those countries want. For example, Nestlé's global presence allows it to observe changes in consumer tastes more quickly than would be true if it relied on exports alone. Taking on international operations also allows firms to take advantage of skills that might be particularly widespread in those countries. For example, US auto firms that produce in Germany can take advantage of that country's highly effective apprenticeship system for the training of young people in machine-tool operations. Japanese auto firms such as Honda and Nissan can benefit from an entry point into European markets, an English-speaking base, and a flexible workforce through their investment in the UK. In some instances moving abroad allows an MNE to employ labor that costs less than is the case in their home markets: many MNEs from the United States, Japan, and Europe have moved to Mexico, China, and countries in Southeast Asia for precisely this reason.

Sometimes firms elect to become multinational in orientation as a result of changes in their political environment. For example, many US firms established or enhanced their European manufacturing operations during the late 1950s and early 1960s because of the establishment in 1957 by Germany, France, Italy, and the three Benelux countries (Belgium, Netherlands, and Luxembourg) of the European Economic Community (EEC). The EEC established a common external tariff (CET) to imports of a variety of goods. However, the United States persuaded the European governments to include in the EEC founding treaty a '**national treatment**' clause that was worded in such as way as to treat European subsidiaries of US firms as if they were national firms of one or another of the EEC members. By virtue of this national treatment provision in the EEC treaty, the subsidiary of General Motors (GM) incorporated in

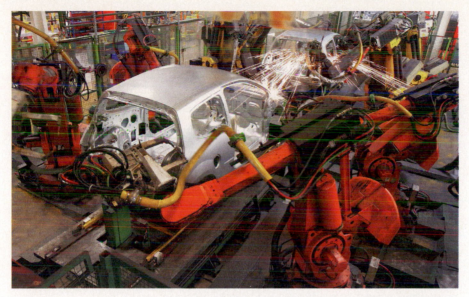

Germany, for example, would be treated by the German government and the EEC exactly as each would treat Volkswagen (VW) or BMW. That meant that GM automobiles manufactured in Germany could enter Italy with exactly the same favorable EEC tariff treatment (compared to tariffs imposed on autos coming in from outside the EEC) as automobiles made by VW or BMW or Mercedes. The only way to attain national treatment was for a US firm to have sufficient manufacturing operations in one or more EEC countries that its goods would be viewed as local in origin and thus subject to the relatively more favorable CET tariff rates.

A firm might also decide to develop international operations in order to overcome non-tariff barriers. For example, Japanese firms like Honda and Toyota responded to an automobile Voluntary Export Restraint (VER) agreement that the United States imposed on Japan in the late 1970s by establishing large manufacturing and assembly plants in the United States. The VER was designed and implemented in such a way as to only limit cars imported directly from Japan, not cars made in the United States by Japanese-owned automobile manufacturers.

Importance of MNEs to the World Economy

We can observe the importance of MNEs to the world economy in Figure 8.5, which shows how MNEs have been responsible for substantial proportions of global capital formation, global output of goods and services, and global trade.

Fixed capital is the value of assets a company utilizes in an ongoing way in the production of a good or service: we can think of fixed capital as what remains at a production site after everyone goes home at night: buildings, computers, and machinery used for production. **Gross fixed capital formation** represents the total increase in fixed capital that occurs in a country or in the world during a given period of time, usually a year. Foreign direct investment (FDI) that flows into a country is usually associated with the formation of new fixed capital, since it often entails the building of a new factory, or the introduction of new equipment for an existing factory. As we can observe in Figure 8.5, FDI inflows accounted for roughly 4 percent of capital formation throughout the world in 1990. It then almost tripled by the years prior to

Fixed capital: The value of assets a company utilizes in an ongoing way in the production of a good or service.

Gross fixed capital formation: The total increase in fixed capital that occurs in a country or in the world during a given period of time, usually a year.

▶ **Figure 8.5 Global Economic Significance of MNEs, 1990–2011**

The global operations of multinational enterprises have for some time accounted for a substantial proportion of world trade, and since 1990 they account for a growing proportion of global capital formation and world output.

Source: For the year 2008, see UNCTAD, World Investment Report 2011, p. 24, available at http://www.unctad-docs.org/files/UNCTAD-WIR2011-Chapter-I-en.pdf, for remaining years see UNCTAD, World Investment Report 2012, p. 24, available at http://www.unctad-docs.org/files/UNCTAD-WIR2012-Chapter-I-en.pdf (accessed October 2014).

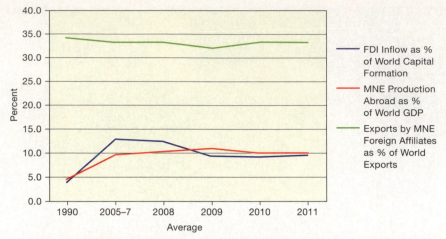

Notes: the data for 2010 and 2011 are UNCTAD estimates.

Intra-firm trade: The cross-country movement of different components that are put together at one or more final assembly plants in one or more countries.

the great recession that began at the end of 2008 and the beginning of 2009, and still represented almost 10 percent of world capital formation up to 2011.

MNEs also play a large and growing role in the production of the world's gross domestic product (GDP), the total monetary value of all goods and services produced by all countries of the world in a year. A branch of the United Nations, the UN Conference on Trade and Development (UNCTAD), reports data on the total value of exports of goods and services by the foreign affiliates that are owned or controlled by multinational enterprises. As we can see in Figure 8.5, the total output by foreign affiliates of MNEs has gone from about 5 percent of world GDP in 1990 to about 10 percent in recent years. More concretely, in 2011 the value of goods and services produced around the world totaled about $70 trillion; of that total, about $7.2 trillion was produced by foreign affiliates of MNEs. The foreign production efforts of MNEs, then, are quite salient when it comes to the production of goods and services around the world.

Finally, consider MNE exports relative to global exports, or the sum of all exports by all countries of the world. Here we can observe in the figure a relationship that appears to have taken hold by 1990, for throughout the period covered in the figure we can see that exports by MNE foreign affiliates have accounted for about one-third of total world exports. Again, for the purposes of perspective, consider that global exports totaled a bit more than $22 trillion in 2011, and of that total, about $7.4 trillion consisted of exports by the foreign affiliates of multinational enterprises.

Many of the exports by MNE foreign affiliates represent **intra-firm trade**, or the cross-country movement of different components that are put together at one or more final assembly plants in one or more countries. For example, Ford Motor Company produces automobile engines at a Ford-owned plant in Chihuahua, Mexico. If that plant then ships those engines to Ford USA, this transfer takes place as an intra-firm sale and it appears as an export from Mexico to the United States. Intra-firm trade accounts for many of the exports by MNE foreign affiliates, and it has been for several decades an important feature of the world trading system.

Political Issues Surrounding MNEs

Multinational enterprises have attracted close attention and oftentimes strong criticisms on a host of issues from scholars, civil society activists, national governments, and international institutions. A great deal of attention is focused on whether multinational enterprises help or hinder poorer countries in achieving economic development, and we will devote substantial attention to that issue in Chapter 10. The important issues surrounding multinational enterprises that we will examine at present can be divided into three clusters: the effects of multinational enterprises on the autonomy of home and host countries, and in particular how their operations affect or constrain environmental policies and the status of workers; the domestic political consequences of MNE operations, and especially their effects on civil rights and the prospects for democracy around the world; and the impact that MNEs might have on the prospects for international peace.

MNEs and National Autonomy: the Environment and Workers' Rights

An important issue surrounding multinational enterprises is whether their ability to move in and out of countries relatively easily means that governments – of both developed and developing investment-receiving countries – experience a loss in their capacity to make independent choices in the kinds of economic and environmental policies they can pursue. Take, for example, a government that wishes to impose more stringent environmental rules or more robust health and safety rules in workplaces. These will necessarily generate costs for employers. The concern is that multinational enterprises already operating in the country, seeing their production costs go up, might be inclined to shift production to other countries where rules and standards may not be so high and expensive. In consequence, the Canadian government, for example, might fear that if it brings into effect stronger environmental standards or health and safety rules for workers, Canadian firms might shift investments from Canada to countries with lower standards, such as Mexico or China, and it might therefore be reluctant to put those stronger measures in place. Alternatively, Mexico and China, wanting to attract MNE investments and aware that they are competing with other developing countries such as Vietnam, might be reluctant to raise environmental or worker standards for fear of scaring away multinational investments. In consequence of MNEs, then, governments around the world might find that they are engaged in a 'race to the bottom,' that is, they put into place progressively lower policy rules and standards regarding the environment and workers' rights out of a fear of losing, and perhaps out of greed for attracting, foreign investments from multinational enterprises.

Recent scholarship presents a mixed picture about MNEs and national policies on the environment and workers' rights: MNEs may be a positive force when it comes to workers' rights, but less than positive when it comes to the environment.

First, there is support for the thesis that MNEs seek out 'pollution havens', that is, countries that have low standards or lax enforcement of their environmental rules and regulations. Early work on the pollution-haven thesis (Eskeland and Harrison 2003) found no association between the location by MNEs of their production plants and the environmental laws and regulations of host countries. However, that scholarship tended to focus particularly on firms in 'heavy' industries such as mining, chemicals, and steel making. Plants in those industries are large and expensive to build, and so firms in them are likely to be resistant to moving in response to anything but the most extreme policy changes. More recent work (Kellenberg 2009) examines a wider range of firms, including those in 'footloose industries,' that is, firms whose plant costs are lower and plant mobility is therefore higher, such as in electronic components, computer assembly, and

Race to the bottom: A situation in which two or more countries put into place progressively lower policy rules and standards regarding the environment and worker rights out of a fear of losing, and perhaps out of greed for attracting, foreign investments from multinational enterprises.

Pollution haven: Countries that have low standards or lax enforcement of their environmental rules and regulations, which may attract foreign companies.

appliances. In that work it appears that MNEs in the years from 1999 to 2003 did increase their production in countries that were perceived to be lax in environmental policy enforcement; this finding held in respect to decisions by MNEs to shift production among developed countries, and especially to developing countries.

On the other hand, multinational enterprises appear to bring about improvements in governmental labor policies, suggesting that in that policy domain there may be a 'race to the top' by countries that are more closely tied to MNEs (Mosley and Uno 2007). Three mechanisms might be producing this positive association between FDI and workers' rights and conditions of employment. First, MNEs have a stake in law-governed business environments, for they themselves gain greatly from legal protection of their patents, trademarks, and investment in plant and equipment. Hence, in their own interests MNES may as a general rule press host-country governments to adhere to the rule of domestic and international law, including those regarding workers' rights. Second, MNEs may bring into a new country in which they become active relatively better policies that have become engrained in the way they do business, perhaps because these firms are aware that their operations are being scrutinized by non-governmental organizations and activist groups. Finally, MNEs may be more interested in having high-quality rather than low-cost labor, and thus will tend to prefer to invest in countries where workers are accorded education, training, and generally favorable treatment. Interestingly enough, trade integration may have the opposite effect to FDI: trade is statistically associated with a reduction in workers' rights in the area of collective organization and bargaining (typically associated with trade unions). Hence, the manner in which developing countries are integrated with the world economy, via FDI or trade, may influence the policy pathway they follow when it comes to workers' rights.

Domestic Political Consequences of MNEs: Human Rights and Democracy

An important question about MNEs is whether their operations help improve the human rights situation in authoritarian countries and whether their presence improves the prospects for movement by those countries from authoritarian rule to democratic government.

Critics of multinational enterprises have suggested that multinationals in extractive industries such as oil or minerals, for example, provide authoritarian governments with tax revenues that they can use to purchase police and military capabilities to repress domestic dissent and retain authoritarian control over their countries. A more optimistic view is that foreign direct investment, like international trade, promotes economic development and in particular a business community and middle class, and these two groups are ultimately powerful forces for democratization (Maxfield 1998; Maxfield 2000). A growing middle class wants its rights to be protected, and a responsive government is the best mechanism to ensure that. Hence, integration through trade and finance promotes growth; this in turn promotes the emergence of a middle class; and this middle class eventually, in order to attain an effective political voice, will ultimately move their respective countries towards democracy (Eichengreen and Leblang 2008).

It is possible to think of instances of authoritarian countries that became economically more open to the world and thereafter also became robust democracies: South Korea and Taiwan are two strong examples. More generally, statistical studies have identified a positive association between increases in trade and financial flows of *all types* and democratization (Eichengreen and Leblang 2008). However, it is not clear that FDI by multinational enterprises is in itself a force for improved human rights or democratization. For example, political scientist Nita Rudra (2005) determined that while greater trade by and *portfolio* capital flows to developing countries from the early 1970s to the late 1990s were positively associated with improvements in human rights and democracy, FDI flows were not a reliable predictor of change in either political dimension. Moreover, in the case of China, it is possible that MNE operations have unintentionally delayed the prospects for democratization in that country by impairing the development of a large and politically unified Chinese business community (Gallagher 2002).

MNEs and International Peace

As we noted in Chapter 6, scholars in the liberal tradition have long argued that countries that share stronger economic ties via trade and foreign direct investment may be less likely to go to war with one another. There has been a lively debate in particular about whether *trade* between countries leads to a reduced risk of war between them. Relatively less attention has been paid to the role that foreign direct investment may play in attenuating the risk of military conflicts. This is surprising, for two reasons: first, there is a well-developed set of arguments as to why FDI might have at least as much, if not more of a pacifying effect on relationships between countries than trade; and second, in contrast to the mixed findings that we see in quantitative studies on the matter of trade and conflict, studies that use statistical techniques have been notably consistent in finding that FDI has the capacity to reduce the risk of military conflicts between countries.

Let's consider the theoretical argument that states might become less oriented to fighting each other as they become the homes and hosts of foreign direct investment. Writing from the liberal perspective, Richard Rosecrance (1999) has suggested that many states have learned that foreign investment affords them growth, welfare, and technological sophistication – in other words, they can attain all the attributes of success in the modern world. On the other hand, with that success comes a risk, a risk that the country might do something that frightens away foreign firms and with them access to foreign technology and markets. One way to frighten foreign firms, Rosecrance points out, is for a country to become involved in military disputes. It will not just be firms from the countries involved in the dispute that will shun investing in one another's countries; instead, firms from countries other than those immediately involved will wish to avoid the disputants, given that they have become risky places in which to do business. Thus, benefiting greatly from foreign direct investment, and fearing what would happen if they were cut off from such flows, national governments, Rosecrance argues, have strong reasons to resolve their disputes with others peacefully. In fact, scholars have been consistent in finding that FDI may promote peace, at least since 1945, including through the amelioration of territorial disputes, which we found in Chapter 5 to be among the most war-prone of types of conflicts of interests between nations (Gartzke and Li 2003; Bussmann 2010; Lee and Mitchell 2012).

State	International	
MNEs can have significant effects on a wide range of domestic circumstances of countries, including their environmental policies, treatment of workers, human rights and prospects for democracy.	Cross-border direct investments, typically by MNEs, may reduce the incentives of governments to use military force to solve diplomatic problems, including conflict-laden territorial disputes.	*Levels of Analysis* *Multinational Enterprises*

The Institutions of the World Economy

Regional blocs: Groups of smaller countries dominated by great powers, put in place by those great powers to help their domestic economies in the face of the Great Depression.

As we saw in Chapter 2, major economic powers like Britain, France, Germany, and the United States almost succeeded in resuscitating the global economy during the 1920s, but in the face of the global contraction in world output that we call the Great Depression of the 1930s they each turned to extreme protectionism both in trade and in money. The result was a dramatic downward spiral in the volume of world trade, as can be observed in Figure 8.6. Almost all countries imposed high national tariffs and extensive controls on capital, and the leading powers organized regional blocs they could dominate and use to gain preferential trade advantages. Britain and France each created an imperial preference system with their respective colonies: each colonial power and its colonies charged much lower tariffs against one another's imports than they charged for goods coming from countries outside the bloc. Germany organized and dominated economic relations with smaller countries in central Europe. Japan adopted a militarist and coercive strategy of conquering its Asian neighbors to ensure its access to vital raw materials. The United States and Soviet Union each turned their large domestic economies inward; the United States in an attempt to recover from the Depression, and the Soviets in an effort to mobilize internal resources to catch up with the West industrially.

After the war, the United States and its allies made another effort to rekindle the international economy. The goal was not the immediate creation of totally free international markets in goods or money. Instead, and in accord with constructivist theory, leaders and officials in the two most powerful states that were active in the negotiations, the United States and Britain, shared a consensus that they and other governments in the negotiations should create relatively freer markets in trade and finance across borders over time, and there should be mutual acceptance of limited government intervention and sometimes even controls over the level and tempo of that liberalization so that national governments could employ fiscal and monetary policies when needed to promote national employment (Ruggie 1982). To attain this goal of gradual economic liberalization, the major states, especially the United States and Britain, created a number of international economic institutions. We will examine these international institutions in three categories: trade, money, and governance.

International Trade: From ITO to GATT to WTO

Bretton Woods system: The international system created in 1944 to encourage progressive trade liberalization and stable monetary relations between all the countries of the world. Although initial membership was fairly low due to Cold War tensions, membership in the resulting organizations steadily increased to include the vast majority of the world's countries. The ITO, GATT, WTO, IMF, and World Bank were all created as a result of the Bretton Woods system.

During three weeks, July 1–22, 1944, diplomats from 44 countries allied against Nazi Germany met at the small resort town of Bretton Woods, New Hampshire, in the US to develop a plan for the reconstruction of the world economy after depression and war. The resulting Bretton Woods system was originally designed to include all countries of the world, but with the onset of the Cold War, the Soviet Union and its satellites remained outside the system. The Bretton Woods system nonetheless was the central focus for the development by countries of rules and norms governing international trade and monetary relations. Although parts of the original design have changed, the overall themes of progressive trade liberalization and stable monetary relations remain in place today and apply to almost all countries across the globe.

International Trade Organization (ITO): An ambitious scheme for global trade management proposed in 1947. The ITO eventually failed because the United States refused to support it, and was largely replaced by the less ambitious GATT.

By 1947, international negotiations had produced an ambitious scheme for global trade management, the International Trade Organization (ITO). The ITO reflected compromises among different national interests. The United States had the world's most dynamic and powerful economy and wanted international rules to maximize

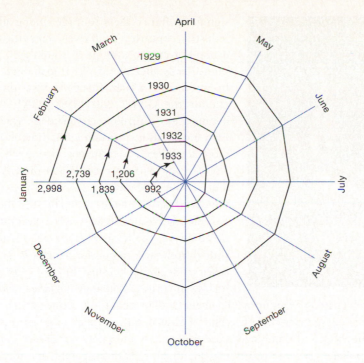

April
May
March
June
February
1929
1930
1931
1932
1933
2,739   1,206
2,998   1,839   992
January
July
December
August
November
September
October

◀ **Figure 8.6 The Kindleberger Spiral of Declining World Trade**

If you begin looking at the spiral in January 1929, you will see how, month by month, and year by year, the value of world trade became smaller and smaller. This was the result of slower global growth as a consequence of the Depression and government policies of protectionism in response to that slower growth. As the 'economic pie' became smaller, each government tried to preserve its share of it by imposing protection and devaluing its currency. The overall effect was that the pie became even smaller.

Source: Kindleberger, Charles (1973) *The World in Depression, 1929–1939*, (Berkeley: University of California Press), with permission.

free trade. France and Great Britain, weakened by war, lobbied to retain their imperial preference systems. Less developed countries felt unprepared for open international competition and demanded infant-industry protection for their new manufacturing sectors and a host of other preferential arrangements. The ITO could only succeed with the support of the United States, but the Truman administration felt the final compromise departed significantly from US preferences, and declined to submit the agreement to Congress for ratification. Without American participation, this first attempt to develop global trade rules was aborted.

A more modest trade initiative emerged in its place. Under the auspices of what was supposed to be an interim agreement pending global acceptance of the ITO, the 1947 General Agreement on Tariffs and Trade (GATT) represented an initial attempt by the United States and other Western countries to lower their respective tariff rates on a wide variety of goods and to establish a first set of rules to resolve trade disputes among nations. For example, within the 1947 GATT agreement the participants agreed to extend any tariff reductions to which two or more members agreed to all other members of the agreement. In the United States, this practice means conferring *most favored nation status* on various trading partners; those partners get the lowest or 'most favored' tariff rates that the United States offers to any country.

With the ITO not coming into effect, the GATT became the nexus for a global trade order. GATT was given a home in Geneva, Switzerland, and its members entered into a succession of negotiating rounds to reduce trade barriers, establishing rules and procedures whereby members could seek to resolve trade disputes. The GATT was upgraded in 1995 to an institution that enjoys a more formal legal status, the World Trade Organization (WTO), which we will discuss more fully in a moment.

Diplomats have given each GATT (and now its successor organization, the WTO) negotiating round a name, such as the Geneva Round in 1947 and the Kennedy Round in 1962. By 1969, so much progress was made that tariff barriers were no longer a

General Agreement on Tariffs and Trade (GATT): When the ambitious **ITO** fell through, **GATT** represented an initial, less ambitious attempt by the United States and other Western countries to lower their respective tariff rates on a wide variety of goods and to establish a first set of rules to resolve trade disputes among nations (finalized in 1947).

▲ **Photo 8.2 The Bretton Woods Conference**

The great economist John Maynard Keynes attended the Bretton Woods summit in 1944; here he is speaking at the summit.

Source: Intrenational Monetary Fund.

significant impediment to trade among advanced industrial countries. Tariff levels across the Atlantic dropped from an average of roughly 50 percent immediately after World War II to about 5 percent twenty-five years later. This period was the golden era for the GATT. After 1970, GATT rounds became more difficult to complete for two reasons. First, negotiations became more difficult because more countries joined the negotiating table as the world economy recovered. When the GATT was founded it had 23 member states; by the early 1960s the GATT had 62 members; and by 2013 there were 152 member states in the WTO. Second, as we noted above, the focus of trade negotiations has shifted from tariff to non-tariff barriers. Tariffs are easier to negotiate because they are quantitatively precise and transparent: they can take the form, 'I'll reduce my tariff on shoes from 50 percent to 40 percent if you reduce yours on computers from 35 percent to 25 percent.' Non-tariff barriers such as government procurement rules, anti-dumping procedures, health and safety standards, and border control policies are more varied, less quantifiable, less transparent, and more subtle as means of trade protection. In addition, such barriers are often deeply embedded in the domestic political and economic values of the countries around the table. Convincing France to reduce its tariffs on machinery by 10 percent is a lot easier than convincing French negotiators to relax domestic content restrictions on Hollywood-produced films when they believe that a thriving French film industry is essential to the national culture.

The Tokyo Round, so named to symbolize the importance of bringing Japan more fully under the rules of the liberal trading order, sought to discipline non-tariff barriers. Negotiations were protracted (the round began in 1973 and concluded in 1979) and results were modest. It took seven additional years for GATT members to even agree to begin a next round, called the Uruguay Round to symbolize the importance of bringing developing countries more fully under the auspices of GATT rules. The Uruguay Round took until 1994 to complete. It is no surprise that commentators came to refer to the GATT as the 'General Agreement to Talk and Talk.'

The Uruguay Round was very ambitious. It sought a grand bargain between developed and developing countries for developed countries to reduce protectionist barriers in agriculture and textiles, two politically sensitive areas that had long been handled outside the GATT rules for free trade. For their part, developing countries agreed to consider liberalizing trade in new areas not previously covered by the GATT, including trade in services such as banking and insurance, and to develop new rules to protect intellectual property rights. For example, it would be illegal for developing country entrepreneurs to copy Western-made pharmaceutical products, movies, or music DVDs. In the end a deal was struck, although neither group was fully satisfied. Developing countries, led by India and Brazil, felt that the more powerful governments of the United States and European Union wrested concessions from weaker developing country negotiators without making sufficient concessions to open their own markets for food and clothing promptly and meaningfully.

Trade-Dispute Settlement in the GATT and WTO

Then: *Dispute Settlement under GATT*

The GATT had a procedure for settling trade disputes, but it was relatively ineffective. There were no fixed timetables, so dispute negotiations could drag on inconclusively for years. Equally important, rulings could only be adopted by consensus, which meant that any single country – including the loser in the dispute! – could object and block a ruling from taking effect. There was no effective way to enforce rulings that were accepted, and there was inadequate protection for third parties, or countries affected by the dispute but not directly part of it.

It is not surprising that powerful countries tended to take matters into their own hands, seeking to resolve disputes outside of the GATT process. The United States was the most well-known practitioner of 'aggressive unilateralism,' or the attempt to coerce other states into changing trade practices that the US considered unfair. American trade legislation, generally referred to as Section 301 (originally part of the Trade Act of 1974) gave the President broad powers to single out unfair traders, force them into negotiations, and retaliate against them with protectionist measures if they refused to agree to US demands. Other members of the international trading community found it outrageous that the United States felt it had the right to act simultaneously as prosecutor, jury, and judge in trade disputes. The United States typically responded that it had no choice given the importance of opening markets abroad and the lack of an effective dispute settlement mechanism in the GATT.

Now: *Dispute Settlement under WTO*

The WTO sets out specific (though somewhat flexible) timetables for dispute settlement, emphasizing that prompt settlement is crucial for the WTO to function effectively. Countries are encouraged to settle disputes on their own, but if they cannot, a case may be brought to the WTO. Within fifteen months, the WTO is expected to form an impartial panel of three to five experts from different countries to examine the evidence, have that panel deliberate and issue a final report, allow the countries in question to appeal, and have the Dispute Settlement Body adopt the report. The 'losing' country is expected to change its practices to bring them in line with international expectations. If it cannot, for whatever reason, it must negotiate with the injured party to determine some type of mutually acceptable compensation. In the absence of acceptable compensation, the complaining side may ask the Dispute Settlement Body for permission to impose limited retaliatory sanctions against the offending member.

The adoption of rulings is now far easier than it was under the GATT. Instead of requiring a consensus to adopt a ruling, the WTO requires a consensus to *overturn* a ruling. In other words, a country seeking to block a ruling must persuade all other WTO members, including its adversary in the case, to agree that the ruling should be invalidated.

The robust dispute-settlement provisions and procedures under the auspices of the WTO constitute one of the most important developments in multilateral trade diplomacy to have occurred during the 1990s and the first decade of the 2000s.

An important institutional innovation did emerge from the Uruguay Round – the agreement to create the World Trade Organization (WTO), which on January 1, 1995, took effect as the successor to the GATT. The WTO has more explicit rules and guidelines than the GATT, and involves the great majority of the world's countries as members. Most importantly, the WTO contains a more highly developed mechanism for resolving trade disputes among countries than was available under the GATT. This move toward stronger dispute settlement procedures underscores the liberal international view of the importance of international institutions to states in mitigating problems of compliance with agreements and the achievement thereby of mutually positive gains. Box 8.4 compares *dispute settlement mechanisms* in the GATT and now in the WTO.

The first multilateral trade negotiation under the auspices of the WTO has been the Doha Development Round. It was launched in 1999, but took until the end of 2013 for member countries to reach an initial preliminary agreement. Throughout the negotiations industrialized countries, in particular the United States and European Union, have been reluctant to make concessions in agriculture, while developing countries, which believe they conceded too much in the prior round, have become better organized and slow to offer many additional concessions.

In recent years, and perhaps because global trade agreements are increasingly difficult to complete, many countries have turned to regional trade agreements and bilateral free trade agreements (FTAs) as alternatives. In the early 1990s, the United States concluded the North American Free Trade Agreement (NAFTA) with Canada and Mexico. The United States has bilateral FTAs with at least twelve other countries, including Australia, Chile, Israel, Honduras, Morocco, and Singapore. In 2012, agreements with Columbia, Panama and South Korea received Congressional approval. The European Union is perhaps the world's most advanced free trade agreement; the EU aspires to create a single integrated market for trade among its members. In South America, Mercosur (the 'common market of the south' or Mercado Común del Sur) was formed in 1991 by Argentina, Brazil, Paraguay, and Uruguay; Chile and Bolivia were added later in the decade.

Most governments still recognize that a WTO-based global trade order is desirable, even when they do not follow WTO rules. The WTO creates opportunities for states to resolve trade disputes and it has created a set of expectations among members that makes it difficult politically to impose new trade barriers. Yet, the advance of free trade also faces significant challenges. Key areas of world trade such as agriculture are still highly protected and others, such as trade in services, investment, and intellectual property, have only basic agreements in place and large gaps in coverage. New concerns have emerged at the intersection of trade and social policy. For example, environmentalists worry that free trade and investment agreements enhance the risk of something we noted in connection to MNEs, namely, a 'race to the bottom' in which developing countries relax environmental regulations to gain competitive advantage in the marketplace.

The most important challenges are political. In the United States, few politicians today would cite NAFTA approvingly without risking a popular backlash. The concern is that cheaper labor and lax standards in developing countries are leading to the loss of jobs at home. For their part, in developing countries the worry is expressed that the more advanced world is forcing them to accept free trade in areas where they are not ready for full competition, such as finance and information technology. Despite its status as an improvement over GATT, the WTO has managed to attract passionate protests almost anywhere in the world that it holds a meeting.

International Finance: Why is the IMF so Controversial?

The main goal of the Bretton Woods negotiators was to create a new international monetary order. They recognized the close relationship between international trade and international monetary policy, and in particular had fresh memories of how competitive currency devaluations helped destroy world trade during the Great Depression.

To prevent competitive currency devaluations in the future, American and British negotiators settled on a plan to create a system of exchange rates that were presumed to be fixed and could be changed only by mutual consent. Each government pledged to maintain a fixed rate for its currency relative to the US dollar. For example, the British government agreed to defend the rate of 1 pound sterling = $2.40, and the Japanese agreed to $1 = 360 yen (as an exercise you might wish to check business news websites to learn what the current exchange rates are between the dollar and pound sterling and the yen). Governments pledged that if the market value of their currencies moved too far from this official value, they would intervene in currency markets, as we discussed above in connection to fixed exchange-rate systems, and buy or sell their own currencies in amounts sufficient to bring market prices back into line with official rates.

The negotiators at Bretton Woods created an international institution to facilitate and reinforce this postwar exchange-rate system, the **International Monetary Fund (IMF)**. The IMF, based in Washington, DC, began operations in 1946 and remains one of the world's most important international economic institutions. Bretton Woods planners created a sister organization for the IMF, the International Bank for Reconstruction and Development, more commonly known as the **World Bank**, which is also headquartered in Washington. The original purpose of the World Bank was to provide loans to countries to help them with economic recovery from the war. Today, the World Bank finances and manages projects – for example, the construction of a dam, the development of a communications grid, the building of highways – to foster the economic growth of developing countries.

International Monetary Fund (IMF): An international institution created in 1946 to facilitate and reinforce the exchange-rate system created in the aftermath of World War II. The IMF remains one of the world's most important international economic institutions.

World Bank: The International Bank for Reconstruction and Development. Initially created to provide loans to countries to help them with economic recovery from World War II, today the World Bank finances and manages projects to foster the economic growth of developing countries.

▲ Photo 8.4 IMF Headquarters in Washington, US

The IMF plays a central role in today's international monetary system and in the management of global economic crises.

Source: International Monetary Fund.

The original role of the IMF was to assist governments – especially those running balance-of-payments deficits – in meeting their fixed exchange-rate obligations under the Bretton Woods agreement. A country running deficits needed to use foreign reserves, or the currencies of other countries, to buy its own currency on international markets. But what if the government did not hold adequate amounts of foreign reserves in its central bank? The IMF held a fund of foreign reserves (mainly US dollars) that it could lend to countries in balance-of-payments distress. In return, IMF officials typically asked these borrowing governments to take certain steps in their domestic economies, such as reducing government spending to control inflation, as a condition for receiving the loan. This practice has become known as IMF **conditionality**.

But what if, despite repeated tries, the market price of a currency kept falling and the government could not buy enough of its own currency to defend its fixed rate? The more drastic next step would be **devaluation**, a downward change in the *official* price of the currency to more accurately reflect its market value. Devaluation would however also confer export advantages to the country in question, thus creating a temptation for them to do so under the guise of being unable to maintain an official exchange rate. Here the Bretton Woods agreement was critically important: by virtue of it countries could only devalue in the event of a 'fundamental disequilibrium' and only with the approval of the IMF. The IMF was there to ensure that countries only devalued as a last resort, and not in an effort to attain trade advantages against other countries.

What determines which states are especially powerful within the IMF? The IMF requires contributions from member states in order to have the funds on hand to lend out to countries with balance-of-payments problems. Member countries receive voting power in proportion to the contributions they make to the fund. In the early years of the IMF, when most other countries were still recovering from the war, the United States contributed about half the reserves. As a result, the United States at first had overwhelming power in IMF decision-making and could use the IMF as an instrument to influence the domestic economic policies of other governments. Today, the United States still has the relatively largest share of IMF votes, but the shares of other countries have moved up as well. Table 8.4 shows the voting shares of the seven largest contributors to the IMF in 2014.

The dollar played a special role in the Bretton Woods system, especially from the late 1940s to the late 1960s. Governments held dollars in their central banks for use

Country	Voting Weight (Percent of Total)
United States	16.75
Japan	6.23
Germany	5.81
France	4.29
United Kingdom	4.29
China	3.81
Italy	3.16
Saudi Arabia	2.80
Russian Federation	2.39
India	2.34
Total	**51.87**

◀ Table 8.4 Largest Voting Shares in the IMF by Individual Country, 2014

A relatively small number of states in the international system provide the bulk of the lending resources at the disposal of the IMF, and therefore have a dispropor-tionate voice in voting at the Fund.

Source: IMF Members' Quotas and Voting Power (March 7, 2014), available at http://www.imf.org/external/np/sec/memdir/members.aspx.

in emergencies, to buy goods and services on world markets, and to buy back their own currencies when their exchange rates fell. Private individuals and companies also used the dollar in their international transactions. The US government, to reinforce everybody's confidence in the dollar, pledged to other governments that it would give them gold for dollars at a fixed rate, or $35 for one ounce of gold. With this pledge, the US government was essentially claiming that its paper currency was 'as good as gold;' others should treat it as the world's money.

Playing the role of banker to the world gave special privileges to the United States. As long as other countries were willing to hold its money as an 'IOU,' the United States could make international purchases without having to balance its payments right away. But if the United States abused this privilege and spent too many dollars abroad, other governments and private actors might begin to question whether the dollar was really as good as gold. This happened during the 1960s, when the United States spent more dollars abroad to provide foreign aid, paid the costs of stationing its troops in Europe and Asia, fought the Vietnam War, and bought more goods from its recovering Western trading partners. Some US allies, led by France, felt the United States was acting irresponsibly and should raise taxes or spend less on programs at home to help pay for the things it was doing abroad. They demanded gold in exchange for the dollars that were piling up in their national accounts. The United States claimed it was running national deficits because it was bearing the burden of Western defense. It argued that its Western allies were now sufficiently recovered to open their markets more fully to American goods and to pay more of the price of defending the West against the Soviet Union.

This conflict was finally resolved in August 1971 when the Nixon administration simply announced it would no longer meet its stated obligation of trading gold to other governments for US dollars. This decision, taken unilaterally by the United States, was so shocking to the world financial community that it became known as the 'Nixon shock.' The United States had created the fixed exchange-rate component of the Bretton Woods system, but twenty-five years later, when that component no longer served US interests, US officials ended it. If the United States was no longer committed to defending the value of its dollar relative to gold, then other governments would not defend their currency values relative to the dollar.

The world's leading economic powers transitioned during the 1970s, by default, to a flexible exchange-rate system. The IMF members revised the Fund's Articles of

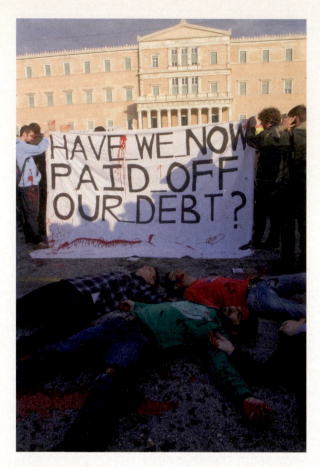

▲ **Photo 8.5 Greek Citizens Protest Austerity Imposed by IMF and EU**

In this February 2012 protest in Athens, Greece, young people pretend to be dead in front of the Greek parliament. Thousands of demonstrators clashed with police as the Greek parliament prepared to vote on an EU/IMF austerity deal designed to help the country through its economic crisis.

Source: PA Images.

Agreement in 1976 to allow member states to follow whatever exchange rate practices they chose, as long as they maintained reasonable price stability, took actions necessary to avoid or mitigate undue short-term fluctuations in exchange rates, and avoided the manipulation of exchange rates 'to gain an unfair competitive advantage over other members' (IMF 2011).

Exchange rates continue to be politically controversial, notwithstanding this general IMF guidance that countries be good international economic citizens. Economic partners of the United States have often complained that the US dollar is too strong, attracting money away from their countries, or too weak, thereby giving the United States unfair trade advantages. American officials in turn complained during the 1980s that Japan was manipulating its currency to obtain unfair trade advantages, and it makes a similar complaint about China today.

Members of the European Union, to insulate themselves from the effects of the powerful US dollar, went back to a fixed exchange-rate system among themselves during the 1980s and, as we discussed above, in the 1990s many of them (with some notable exceptions including the United Kingdom) abandoned their national currencies altogether for a common currency, the euro. The euro has been a mixed blessing for some of the more fragile economies of Europe, like that of Greece, which no longer have the option of allowing their currency to float downward to help ease the impact of balance-of-payments deficits. In the face of the 2008 financial crisis, the Greek government, at the urging of the IMF as well as the EU, cut government services and payments to workers, sparking a series of ongoing street riots.

The IMF and its Critics Today

The IMF remains at the center of international political economy, continuing to serve as a fund for member countries in economic distress. Yet, as in the Greek example above, its lending practices frequently spark 'IMF riots' in recipient countries. If the IMF is there to help countries in need, why are its efforts so controversial?

IMF conditionality – that is, the conditions the IMF places on a government in exchange for its loans – is the main reason. The IMF generally prescribes what, to a country in distress, can appear to be harsh and bitter medicine. That medicine comes in the form of austerity or economic belt-tightening. A typical package of structural adjustments recommended by the IMF might include sharp reductions in government spending which affect the jobs and salaries of public sector workers, the benefits of the unemployed, and the pensions of retirees. If the government had been subsidizing basic necessities like food and electricity, complying with the IMF might require sharp price increases. The package might also call for interest rate hikes to slow inflation.

Membership

The G-20 is made up of nineteen countries and the European Union:

- Argentina
- Australia
- Brazil
- Canada
- China
- France
- Germany
- India
- Indonesia
- Italy
- Japan
- Mexico
- Republic of Korea
- Russia
- Saudi Arabia
- South Africa
- Turkey
- United Kingdom
- United States of America
- The European Union, which is represented by the rotating Council presidency and the European Central Bank, is the 20th member of the G-20.
- The Managing Director of the International Monetary Fund (IMF) and the President of the World Bank, plus the chairs of the International Monetary and Financial Committee and Development Committee of the IMF and World Bank, also participate in G-20 meetings on an ex-officio basis.

◀ **Table 8.5 The Group of 20**

The G-20 brings together important industrial and emerging-market countries from all regions of the world. Together, member countries represent around 90 percent of global gross national product, 80 percent of world trade (including EU intra-trade) as well as two-thirds of the world's population. The G-20's economic weight and broad membership gives it a high degree of legitimacy and influence over the management of the global economy and financial system.

But higher interest rates mean slower growth for the economy as a whole, and possibly even an economic recession. The IMF also urges governments to reduce the size of the state sector and liberalize trade and financial markets.

Governments, of course, could choose not to do business with the IMF. But another reason the IMF is so controversial is that it is so powerful. A country that is in financial distress may seek infusions of cash from international banks. But before lending, bankers often look to make sure that the country's policies have received the IMF 'seal of approval.' In other words, accepting the harsh medicine of the IMF is more likely to lead private money to flow into the economy, while defying the IMF might leave the country more or less on its own.

The controversial policies often prescribed by the IMF – smaller state sectors, privatized markets, and liberalized trade and financial sectors – are policies preferred by the US government. During the 1980s, this collection of policies became known as the Washington Consensus – a consensus supported by the US Treasury Department and the Washington-based IMF and World Bank – and was put forth as the necessary path to prosperity for all countries to follow. The great financial crisis of 2008, however, has cast considerable doubt on the desirability of the Washington Consensus. Governments and citizens around the world perceived these policies, and the idea of unregulated liberal capitalism, as the cause of the crisis rather than the necessary recipe for economic growth and prosperity.

Washington Consensus: A group of controversial US-backed policies (smaller state sectors, privatized markets, and liberalized trade and financial sectors) set forth by the IMF as the necessary path to prosperity from the 1980s until the Great Recession of 2008, when the Consensus began to be widely questioned.

Global Governance: From the G-7 and G-8 to the G-20

The new controversies sparked by the IMF and Washington Consensus have highlighted a long-standing debate on the question: who should govern the world economy? As in other areas of international relations, the answer frequently raises a clash between aspirations and reality. Developing countries argue they should have a greater say in international economic governance because the world economy affects their development prospects so profoundly. In reality, more powerful countries tend to make the rules and manage the system. During the Bretton Woods era, the United

The G-20 has a much larger and more diverse set of member countries than the G-7 and G-8. Given the larger membership, which as noted in the text includes all of the members of the original G-7 advanced industrialized countries, together now with not only Russia but also such countries as South Korea, China, India, and South Africa, it is possible that any policy decisions the G-20 makes will be more likely to be consequential for the world economy, for a larger number of important countries would help make the decisions and thus have a stake in their faithful implementation. On the other hand, it is also possible that large-group dynamics will make it more difficult for the G-20 to reach important decisions than was true for the G-7.

What, then, are the prospects that, compared to the G-7 experience, the G-20 countries will be able to agree on bold initiatives in trade or monetary affairs? Major theories of international relations are skeptical about the ability of the G-20 countries to pursue an ambitious international economic agenda, although they have different grounds for the skepticism.

Realism: A realist would not be optimistic about the G-20. The realist would argue that the G-7 countries during the 1970s and 1980s shared many common interests, including a common need to remain strong in the face of challenges from the old Soviet Union, and that this commonality of interests, including in the security domain, helped underpin the efforts by the G-7 countries to work together. In contrast, the G-20 countries include states that have relatively few foreign policy interests in common, and many of them are geopolitical rivals to one degree or another (India and China, the United States and Russia, China and the United States). The group actually includes at least one pair of countries that has had recent militarized international disputes (China and Japan). Given the heterogeneity in foreign policy interests of G-20 countries, the agreements they reach are likely to be very modest in scope.

Liberalism: A liberal with a domestic-institutions focus would have serious doubts about the capacity of the G-20 to embark on large initiatives. The issue for the liberal/domestic institutions theorist, as with

the realist, is that the G-20 is characterized by too high a level of heterogeneity of interests. However, the liberal would argue that the problem is not just that there may be differing geopolitical interests among the G-20 countries that will impair their ability to reach agreements on trade and monetary matters, there is also the more fundamental problem that the G-20 includes countries with extremely different political systems, from highly authoritarian (China and Russia) to highly democratic (United Kingdom, Canada, and Germany). Liberals with an international institutional perspective would argue that the G-7 worked reasonably well because there were numerous informal cross-country linkages among ministries of finance and central banks and that these linkages helped the G-7 embark on serious joint actions. The G-20 association lacks strong informal bonds such as the G-7 enjoyed and continues to enjoy, and it lacks the kind of formal organizational features – for example, a permanent secretariat and procedures for ensuring compliance with group decisions – that make bold action possible with such a large coterie of states.

Constructivism: A constructivist might also have doubts about the capacity for bold action by the G-7. That theorist would note that leaders and policy officials from the G-7 countries shared and continue to hold many ideas and beliefs in common. In particular, they all hold more or less similar beliefs about the proper role of government in the national and global economy, namely, that government should let market forces largely determine economic outcomes but governments should intervene in limited ways when necessary to prevent sustained economic recessions. In contrast, the G-20 countries includes countries with radically different elite views about the role of government in the economy, from those that rely more on markets with limited government management (United Kingdom) to those that believe the government should be very directly active in the national economy (China and Russia). Countries with elites holding such different views about the proper role of government in economic affairs are unlikely to be able to find common ground on how to address international economic challenges.

States was powerful enough to not only make the rules, but also break them when they no longer served US interests. Since those days, international economic power has gradually diffused, first to other advanced industrial states and now even more broadly to newly emerging economies powers like China and Brazil.

After the collapse of Bretton Woods, the informal grouping that governed international economic relations was known as the Group of 7 (G-7): the United States, United Kingdom, France, Germany, Japan, Italy and Canada. For many years the G-7 held annual summit meetings at which heads of governments, finance ministers, and the governors of central banks of these seven major industrialized countries sought to resolve international economic problems by coordinating their exchange rates and their domestic monetary and fiscal policies. The G-7 enjoyed notable achievements; the Plaza Agreement of 1985, for example, helped to ward off protectionism through coordinated efforts to increase the value of some currencies, such as the Japanese yen and German mark, and decrease the value of others, especially the US dollar.

After the end of the Cold War the G-7 countries began to invite Russia to participate in parts of their meetings, and thus was launched the Group of 8 (G-8). The G-7 summits now take place among ministers of finance and central bank governors; the G-8 meetings bring together the heads of states of the old G-7 plus Russia. Alongside economic coordination, G-8 summits typically address pressing political issues, such as the war on terrorism or the proliferation of weapons of mass destruction. The inclusion of Russia was part of a broader effort by Western countries after the Cold War to integrate their former adversary into supporting the rules and sharing the governance of the international system.

Today, the G-8 is no longer the main locus of international economic governance. It has been supplemented and in time it might be replaced by a broader group, the Group of 20, or G-20, which includes the G-8 members along with newly rising economic powers like China and India, oil producers like Saudi Arabia, and middle powers such as Australia, Turkey, and Argentina. Table 8.5 displays the full membership of the G-20.

The G-20 was formed after the Asian financial crisis of 1997–98, and achieved political prominence in the context of the deeper and broader global financial crisis that began in 2008. The rise of the G-20 reflects the diffusion of international economic power; the United States and its close allies are no longer powerful enough to shape the world economy by themselves. G-20 members represent 90 percent of global GDP, 80 percent of trade, and two-thirds of the world's population. The G-8, in contrast, represents only 15 percent of world population, 65 percent of GDP, and 65 percent of world trade. The G-20's membership is more representative but it is also more diverse. Whether this informal association of countries can provide effective leadership to the world economy remains to be seen; some of the main factors that are emphasized by different theories of IR in estimating how ambitious the G-20 policy agenda might become are highlighted in Box 8.5.

Group of 7 (G-7): The group of seven countries (United States, United Kingdom, France, Germany, Japan, Italy and Canada) that governed international economic relations after the collapse of the Bretton Woods system by coordinating their exchange rates and their domestic monetary and fiscal policies.

Group of 8 (G-8): The Group of 7 (G-7) plus Russia. In the aftermath of the Cold War, Russia was added as a significant, symbolic, political move. Russia was suspended from the G8 in 2014 for its annexation of Crimea in March 2014.

Group of 20 (G-20): A broader group of states, including the G-8 members along with newly rising economic powers like China and India, oil producers like Saudi Arabia, and middle powers such as Australia, Turkey, and Argentina, which has replaced the G-8 in international economic decision-making.

Individual	State	International
Individuals who worry about the effects of economic globalization and the power of MNEs and institutions like the IMF have participated in mass protest movements.	Civil society activist groups that are critical of modern economic globalization, including the operations of MNEs, have influenced national economic policies.	Major states, and especially the United States, but also Britain, both destroyed the international economy during the 1930s and created a new basis for international economic integration during the 1940s.

Today, a wider range of states, including such countries as China, Japan, and India, play key roles in important international economic institutions as the IMF and the Group of 20. |

Levels of Analysis

Institutions of the World Economy

Revisiting the Enduring Question and Looking Ahead

This chapter has introduced you to the dynamics of international trade and money, and it has provided you with an introduction to some of the key international institutions, both private and public, that constitute and drive the world economy. With this knowledge you are well on your way toward engaging the enduring problem we presented at the outset of the chapter, what is the relationship between politics and economics at the international level?

An understanding of international economic dynamics, such as the economic sources and effects of trade, or why we have exchange rates and how are they derived from market forces as well as government decisions and actions, is vital for making sense of both historical and contemporary international relations. We began by using concepts from the field of economics, most importantly comparative advantage, to show why countries trade. We also explained how both domestic and international political considerations sometimes lead states to disrupt the flow of trade. We examined the link between trade and money, again focusing on the political choices governments make to control (or not control) the price of their national currency, and the consequences that follow. We also paid substantial attention to a vitally important agent in the modern world economy, the multinational enterprise. Developing one further connection between international politics and economics, we examined key political international institutions that govern the world economy of today, the WTO, the IMF, and the G-20.

Chapter 9 moves more explicitly to the level of foreign policy analysis and continues our exploration of international political economy. We look in more detail at states and markets, and the tools and strategies that governments use in the world economy to provide economic benefits for their people at home as well as power and influence for their countries as they interact with one another on the international stage.

 Visit **www.palgrave.com/politics/Grieco** to access extra resources for this chapter

Study Questions

1. Trade theory assumes that countries gain from trade because, overall, they consume more goods and services through specialization and exchange. What are we assuming when we say 'the country is better off overall because it enjoys greater consumption overall?' Does that mean that every individual or family is better off? Is it possible that everyone might not be better off?

2. Is free trade in every country's best interest? Why or why not?

3. The United Kingdom, Sweden, Canada, Australia, Switzerland, and the United States have sought to maintain a reasonably flexible exchange-rate system. What are the main benefits of having a flexible as opposed to a fixed exchange-rate system? Do you think it might be better to shift to a fixed exchange rate? Why or why not?

4. What are the main benefits that MNEs provide to the world economy? What are the main problems that they may pose for individuals and countries?

5. Does the IMF have too much power in international economic relations? If it does, how might you reform it?

6. As an instrument of international economic governance, is the G-20 an improvement over the G-7/G-8?

Further Reading

Brooks, Stephen (2005) *Producing Security: Multinational Corporations, Globalization, and the Changing Calculus of Conflict* (Princeton: Princeton University Press). Brooks develops in detail the thesis that, in the modern world, foreign direct investment by multinational enterprises ties countries together in ways that makes military conflict between them irrational and unlikely.

Gilpin, Robert (2000) *The Challenge of Global Capitalism* (Princeton: Princeton University Press). This is a wide-ranging survey of the world economy at the turn of the twenty-first century, with attention to trade, finance, and foreign investment. Gilpin emphasizes the importance of a stable political foundation for international economic relations.

Lipset, Seymour Martin (1959) 'Some Social Requisites of Democracy: Economic Development and Political Legitimacy', *American Political Science Review* 53 (1): 69–105. Lipset put forward an early and highly influential statement of the argument that a country that undergoes economic development is more likely also to follow a path of democracy. This essay is therefore essential for students who want to engage with the thesis that multinational enterprises, and, more generally, international economic integration through trade and finance, are forces for democratization in the modern world.

Ruggie, John (1982) 'International Regimes, Transactions, and Change: Embedded Liberalism in the Postwar Economic Order', *International Organization* 36 (2): 379–415. In this essay Ruggie puts forward the thesis that the post-World War II international economic order reflected a consensus among the leaders and officials of the major industrial economies, and especially the United States and Britain, that international trade and financial liberalization should take place in the context of government controls and intervention both in domestic and foreign economic matters so as to promote growth and, more important, employment. This is an important essay not only because it helps us understand the intellectual and political foundation of the modern world economy, it is also an early statement of constructivist international theory.

Yarbrough, Beth, and Robert Yarbrough (2006) *The World Economy: Open-Economy Macroeconomics and Finance*, 7th Edn (Mason, OH: Thomson/South-Western). This intermediate-level text provides a rigorous but accessible introduction to modern economic theory of international trade and finance.

9

Power, Politics, and The World Economy

Enduring Question: How do governments use international economic relations to further national political objectives

Did you know that even the most powerful states in the world – those with the largest military establishments and most destructive weapons – are deeply dependent on their economies to support such vast amounts of military power? Did you know that bankers and businessmen around the world are able to engage in trade and exchange because states have created rules and institutions to support the free flow of goods and money? The world of international relations and power politics on the one hand, and the world of business and economics on the other, seem to be quite separate. Students tend to study these subjects in different classes and university departments. But, in fact, they are quite interconnected. Countries that are wealthy and fast-growing will tend to be more powerful on the world stage. Poor and slow-growing countries will find it harder to be active and influential on the world stage.

Chapter 8 introduced you to basic economic concepts: trade, monetary, and investment relations, and the core institutions of the world economy. This chapter takes you more deeply into international political economy by exploring how states, the key political actors, and markets, the key economic mechanism, interact. The world of states and the world of markets co-exist within the global system; they shape and influence each other. While diplomats and political leaders pursue foreign policy and national security, ordinary citizens are forming corporations, hiring workers, producing goods and services, and selling them in home markets and around the world. Citizens and corporations also invest heavily in sophisticated stock, bond, and currency markets across the global landscape. Businessmen and traders depend on governments to support and uphold national and international economic rules and institutions. Governments depend on business; in the long run, states are only as powerful as their economies are wealthy and prosperous. International politics shape and are shaped by the changing character of the world economy.

We will look first at the rise, decline, and re-emergence of an open world economy over the last two centuries. Then we examine the three great traditions of thinking about politics and economics – economic liberalism, economic nationalism, and Marxism. Each offers a different view about how states and markets shape and constrain each other. After this, we look at the ways in which states – as they compete with each other for power and influence -- seek to both foster economic growth and protect themselves from economic dependency. We look at the way in which great powers seek to use markets – fostering the expansion of economic openness and integration – as tools for promoting their national interests and fostering global peace and security. We end the chapter by looking at the role of leadership in maintaining an open system of trade and economic exchange, and current debates about the future of today's globalized and complex world economy.

© Photodisc

Learning Objectives

By the end of this chapter, you will be able to:

→ Recognize and distinguish different schools of thought on how international politics and economics interact.

→ Understand the relationship between states and markets in the world economy.

→ Appreciate the economic choices of states in a geopolitically competitive world.

→ Identify ways that powerful states use economic tools to pursue foreign policy goals.

→ Explore the links between hegemony, open markets, and security.

→ Analyze the role of globalization, and challenges to it, in the current world economy.

Chapter Contents

- Two Great Eras of Economic Globalization
- States and Markets: Three Great Traditions of Thought
- States and Markets in a World of Anarchy
- Great Powers and the World Economy
- The Contemporary World Economy: Globalization and its Challenges
- Revisiting the Enduring Question and Looking Ahead
- Study Questions
- Further Reading

Two Great Eras of Economic Globalization

Globalization: The ongoing process of international economic and technological integration, made possible by advances in transportation and communication.

Economic relationships among sovereign nation-states may be relatively open and market-driven, or relatively closed with governments imposing many types of restrictions on cross-border economic activity. In a striking development over the past two hundred years, the world has witnessed two great eras of globalization and open markets characterized by the freer flow of economic transactions across state borders. As noted in Chapter 2, globalization is the ongoing process of international economic and technological integration, made possible by advances in transportation and communication. Globalization involves the broader and deeper movement of goods, capital, technology, ideas, and people within and across borders.

In the late nineteenth century, Great Britain led the establishment of an open world economy in which goods, capital, ideas, and people moved relatively freely across Europe and beyond. By the beginning of the twentieth century, this system had generated unprecedented levels of economic interdependence within Europe, across the Atlantic, and between the more developed industrial core of the world economy in Europe and North America and the relatively less developed periphery of Asia, Africa, and Latin America. Multinational enterprises, many of which were based in one country but with far-flung operations around the world, emerged as key actors in this interdependent world economy.

▶ **Map 9.1 The Dutch East India Company**

The Dutch East India Company, founded in 1602, is considered by many to be the first multinational enterprise. During the seventeenth and eighteenth centuries, the company acted on behalf of European countries, especially Britain, in expanding markets to Asia. The company established trade routes to the East and opened up many new markets to European consumers and investors. However, it would not be until the late nineteenth century that an open world economy was fostered by the British Empire.

Source: Jean-Paul Rodrigue.

Amsterdam	Dutch East Indies	Arabia	Ceylon	India	China	Japan
From	*From*	*From*	*From*	*From*	*From*	*From*
Silver	Pepper	Coffee	Cinnamon	Cloth	Porcelain	Precious metals
To	Nutmeg	Silk	Pepper	Yarn	Tea	Lacquer
Pepper	Mace	*To*	Cardamom	Silk	Sugar	*To*
Nutmeg	Cloves	Spices	Ivory	Indigo	Silk	Silk
Cinnamon	*To*		Arecanuts	Pepper	Precious metals	Porcelain
Cloves	Cloth		Sappanwood	*To*	*To*	Spices
Mace	Silver		Gems	Silver	Spices	Luxury goods
Cardamom	Ivory		*To*		Luxury goods	
Coffee			Cloth		Cloth	
Sugar						
Tea						
Sappanwood						

Map legend:
- Regional Trade Network
- Inbound Route to Batavia
- Inbound Route to Galle
- Return Route

Map labels: Japan, China, Arabia, India, Ceylon, Galle, Dutch East Indies, Batavia, Spice Islands, Amsterdam, Cape Town

The Rise of a Liberal World Economy

The chart below measures exports as a percentage of Gross Domestic Product across countries and time. It gives us a visual means to understand the evolution of the world economy in a more liberal direction since 1870.

Notice first the pattern for the entire world. Exports increased significantly between 1870 and 1913, during the first great wave of globalization. But between 1913 and 1950 – the era of two world wars and the Great Depression – world trade not only stagnated, but actually declined. Since World War II, and particularly beginning in the 1990s, the world has experienced a second great wave of globalization as countries have become more dependent on trade as a percentage of their overall economic activity.

Note also that the United States, Germany, France, and the United Kingdom each follow more or less the same pattern over time. But the United States is relatively less dependent on trade in overall terms. US exports have grown significantly over time, but by 2007 still represented only about 12 percent of US GDP, while for Germany, the proportion in 2007 was about 45 percent, and for France and the United Kingdom, about 25 percent.

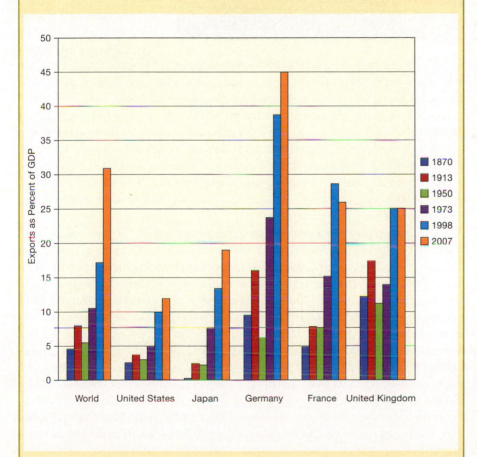

◀ Figure 9.1
Merchandise Exports as Per Cent of GDP in 1990 Prices, 5 Countries and World, 1870–2007

Sources: For 1870 to 1998, see Angus Maddison, *The World Economy: A Millennial Perspective* (Paris, Organisation for Economic Co-operation and Development, 2001), Table F-5, p. 363. Both exports and gross domestic product are based on 1990 constant international dollars; for 2007 data, see International Monetary Fund, *World Economic Outlook* database for real GDP, April 2008, and for trade see World Trade Organization, 'International Trade and Tariff Data', available at http://wto.org/english/res_e/statis_e/statis_e.htm .

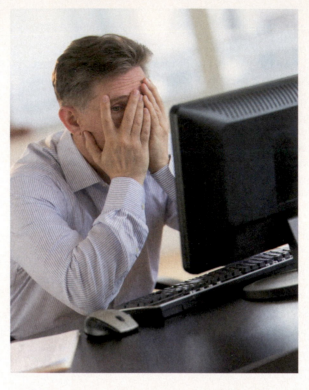

► Photo 9.1
Witnessing the Effects of the 2008 Financial Crisis

The 2008 global financial crisis and economic meltdown has raised new questions and debates over the hazards and benefits of open and relatively unregulated financial markets. Such a system offers opportunity for great prosperity but can also result in economic disaster in part because money now moves across borders electronically and instantaneously at the click of a mouse. The body language of the trader pictured suggests his inability to control today's rapid financial movements.

Source: © tetmc – istockphoto.com.

As we saw in Chapter 8, this open system collapsed in the wake of World War I and the economic depression of the 1930s. The United States led the way toward a second era of globalization after World War II. Trade tariffs were reduced. Currencies became convertible, which meant the paper money of one country could be exchanged at a market price for the paper currencies of other countries. Commerce and investment spread, first within the trans-Atlantic world of Western Europe and the United States and gradually into other regions. In the 1980s, East Asian countries integrated more fully into this expanding world economy. After the Cold War, many countries from the former communist world, most importantly China, also pursued market reforms and joined the open world economy.

By the turn of the twenty-first century, the world economy was truly a globalized system, encompassing all regions. The current 'center of gravity' of the world economy is shifting away from the Western economies toward Asia and the developing world. China is growing rapidly, and it could eventually overtake the United States as the world's largest economy. As we discuss in Chapter 10, India, Brazil, Indonesia, South Africa, South Korea, and other non-Western developing countries are also gaining a greater share of world economic activity.

Globalization has brought wealth and prosperity to millions of people around the world. But it also created new problems and pressures. The rapid flow of money into different economies has led to destabilizing currency crises, such as in Latin America in the 1980s, East Asia in the 1990s, and the entire world economy in the great financial crisis that began in 2008. The 2008 financial crisis and global economic recession has been particularly consequential because it is a crisis that began in the United States, the leader of the world economy and champion of open markets for the past 60 years. With the 2008 financial crisis and global economic slowdown, new debates have arisen over the virtues and dangers of open and relatively unregulated financial markets. Questions have been asked, for example, about whether banks should be allowed to engage in complex packaging of assets and loans that make it difficult to assess their risk and reliability (Johnson and Kwak 2010; Lewis 2010). The crisis has also raised questions in capitals around the world about the ability of the United States to continue to be the global economic leader, providing stability and support in times of economic turmoil.

Convertible currency: A currency that can be exchanged at market price for the currency of another country.

Google has become a part of many people's daily lives, providing users access to the world of information online. When people search the internet, they prefer to have access to the full range of information available so that they may individually pick and choose what to view.

The Chinese Government View

Officials within the Chinese government have a different agenda. The government allows the Chinese people increasing degrees of economic freedom, yet more closely restricts political freedom and freedom of speech. It fears that the Chinese people, with access to the full range of information available around the world, might come to question or even organize opposition to the Communist party's monopoly over political authority. Google's interest in maximizing the free flow of public information and the Chinese government's interest in regulating the flow of information are at odds with each other.

Google's View

In 2006, Google set up business in China. It agreed to create 'filters' that would censor some search results. For example, if a Chinese user typed 'Tiananmen Square' or 'Dalai Lama' into Google, many of the sites that would otherwise be displayed were blocked. Google was unhappy with these restrictions but accepted them. A Google official said in 2006: 'Our decision was based on a judgment that Google.cn will make a meaningful – though imperfect – contribution to the overall expansion of access to information in China.' There were good

business reasons to do so. China has more web users than any other country in the world – as many as 400 million users – and Google has made millions of dollars a year as a result (300 million dollars in 2009 alone, according to CNNMoney). In January 2010, however, the situation changed. Google announced that Chinese hackers had tapped into the Google Gmail accounts of Chinese human rights activists and conducted a 'highly sophisticated and targeted attack on our corporate infrastructure.' Google suspected that these hackers might have been acting with the support and encouragement of the Chinese government.

In response, Google promised to stop censoring results in China unless the Chinese government changed its ways. It redirected Chinese Google users to Google's Hong Kong link which provides uncensored searches. A standoff occurred and the Chinese government threatened not to renew Google's license to operate in China.

The Compromise

The two sides essentially both blinked. Google agreed not to automatically redirect Chinese users to the Hong Kong site. Users now need to actively click to transfer to the uncensored Hong Kong site. But Google did agree to the previous policy of filters on access. The Chinese government got the restrictions it wanted and Google can claim that uncensored access to its search results is only a click away. Given the obvious conflict of interests, it is likely that this struggle will continue.

Moreover, today's economic globalization has created anxiety over culture and identity; some Japanese, Americans, and Europeans worry about excessive immigration, some Europeans resist the fast food culture common in the United States, and some traditional groups and societies in the Middle East, Asia, and Africa are alarmed by the rapid spread of more permissive Western ideas about sex and life style. As Box 9.2 shows, certain governments, including that of China, worry about maintaining domestic political control while their people engage in more economic transactions around the world. China's trading partners, in turn, worry about whether seemingly unlimited supplies of Chinese labor will gobble up the world's natural resources and manufacturing jobs. Over these two great eras of globalization, states unleashed the dynamic forces of trade and investment in an effort to increase prosperity and power. The resulting expansion of global economic activity has generated power and wealth for some, and new challenges for all. To provide the framework for globalization, we will examine the major philosophies concerning the relationship between states and markets in the next section.

States and Markets: Three Great Traditions of Thought

Over the centuries, political thinkers have offered a wide array of perspectives about the relationship between states and markets and their effects on international relations. Understanding these different 'philosophies' will help to guide you through the arguments and debates of international political economy. Three major schools of thought on the relationship between politics and economics stand out: economic liberalism, economic nationalism (or statism), and the capitalist class theory of Karl Marx (Gilpin 1975). These philosophies of international political economy are linked respectively to the broader perspectives of liberalism, realism, and Marxism that we discussed in Chapter 3.

Economic Liberalism

The classical liberal view of international political economy dates back to Adam Smith, a Scottish pioneer of political economics, and the early decades of capitalist growth in Britain in the late eighteenth century. Liberal economic thinkers believe strongly in free markets, the harmony of interests between countries, and the positive effects

▶ **Photo 9.2 Adam Smith**

Adam Smith's *The Wealth of Nations*, published in 1776, marks the foundation of classical economic theory. Smith advocated for an open economy with minimal government intrusion. His imagery of the invisible hand guiding the market is still widely utilized today.

Source: © GeorgiosArt – istockphoto.com.

an open world economy will have on politics and foreign policy. Because open economic relations bring so many positive benefits to all, Smith and other classical liberals argued that the role of the state in the national economy should be quite limited. The government should try to minimize its intrusions. The basic functions of the state were to provide property rights, enforce the rule of law, and provide for the national defense. According to Smith, the government was to be a 'night watchman,' standing guard over the economy to ensure that production and trade took place freely. In a similar way, we might think of the state in economic liberalism as a referee; it maintains and enforces the rules of the game without disrupting the flow of the game itself. The main players are private citizens as workers, producers, traders, and investors.

Smith speaks for an entire tradition of thinkers in emphasizing the natural and autonomous logic of markets. According to this view, people are inclined by nature to 'truck, barter, and trade.' That is, people are naturally predisposed to buy, sell, and make deals. There is a deep human desire to build productive and commercial relations within and between nations. The appropriate role of the state is to provide a hospitable environment for these private deals and transactions to occur. Properly organized, commercial society will flourish.

Smith argued that a thriving world of commerce would generate wider benefits for society. He believed that the **invisible hand** of the marketplace – the uncoordinated behavior of individuals and firms acting in their own selfish interest – would lead to the best economic outcome for society as a whole. For liberals, economics is not a game in which some win while others lose; Smith and others believed in **absolute gains**, where economic interaction creates only winners, even if some benefit relatively more than others. Smith also believed that market society would bring the out the best in people. It provides a 'civilizing spirit' as people go about their pursuits. Smith's view was that people think rationally and understand their mutual interdependence and that this is true within and among nations. Trade among nations will leave all countries better off. It leads to the efficient allocation of resources and stimulates growth. And, as we discussed in Chapters 3 and 6, economic relations form an integral part of the liberal theory of international relations. Trade and economic interdependence create 'vested interests' in favor of stable and peaceful relations. Governments themselves, as Adam Smith suggests, should be encouraged to let these natural commercial impulses spread around the world. In doing so, the dangerous dynamics of power politics and security competition can be tamed. Open economic relations lead to prosperity for all and, as a bonus, promote peace as well.

Smith's logic was pushed a step further by another British political economist, David Ricardo, who developed the now famous law of comparative advantage that we discussed in detail in Chapter 8. Recall that the law of comparative advantage is the classic statement on why trade between two countries is advantageous to both, and why it makes sense for all countries to specialize and trade.

In the long run, liberals see states and societies adapting themselves to the imperatives of economic integration and wealth generation. This conviction has led the United States and other capitalist states around the world to pursue policies that promote open trade and exchange. In the view of liberals, economic growth is facilitated by specialization and the division of labor, leading businessmen and traders to seek out ever-expanding geographical realms for the exchange of goods and services. As the technologies of communication and transportation improve, the scale and scope of markets will tend to expand outward. States will face pressure to reduce barriers and support the growth of markets. In this process, states will adapt, yielding to incentives for global political integration and cooperation (Neff 1990).

Invisible hand: A term coined by Adam Smith to describe the uncoordinated behavior of individuals and firms acting in their own selfish interest in the marketplace.

Absolute gains: An important element of economic liberalism, absolute gains is the idea that economic interactions create only winners, even if some gain more than others. Contrasts with **relative gains**.

Economic Nationalism

We might think of economic liberalism as believing that states should make way for markets. A second great tradition puts states first, and emphasizes the key role of the state in shaping market relations to national advantage. In American economic history, this world view is associated with Alexander Hamilton and other early industrial 'state builders' who focused on the political dynamics of state competition. Hamilton was an American founding father who championed a strong federal government that actively promoted economic development as a way to help a young and vulnerable United States increase its chances of survival in a world of powerful European nation-states. In the nineteenth century, the cause of economic nationalism was taken up by German thinkers, in particular Friedrich List, who worried that Germany would never compete economically with Great Britain unless the German state protected and nurtured Germany's infant industries (Earle 1971).

Economic nationalists, unlike liberals, do not trust in the magic of Adam Smith's invisible hand. They emphasize the importance of states as facilitators of economic growth. Economic development and the benefits of international trade do not in their view happen automatically; governments must build banks, nurture industries, and plan institutions to facilitate economic advancement at home and assure that the nation-state gets the best deal from engaging economically abroad. The state must act strategically to promote the social and political infrastructure that allows market society to emerge and prosper. In this tradition, the state is not merely a referee, but an important player with unique resources.

The Hamiltonian view emphasizes that countries are in competition with each other. States must seek to promote – and if necessary protect – the national economy from the economic exploitation and domination of other countries. Whereas liberals emphasize absolute gains, economic nationalists worry about relative gains, or the idea that even if both sides gain from economic relations, one side might gain disproportionately more and use its gains to dominate the other side. Economic nationalists believe that prosperity and even national security might be compromised if international markets are left to themselves. This view has inspired many countries – particularly less developed countries – to intervene in the economy to protect and promote industries. In Asia, for example, beginning in the 1960s, the governments of Japan, South Korea, and Taiwan protected their domestic industries in sectors such as consumer electronics and automobiles, allowing them to grow strong and become successful export-oriented businesses (Kohli 2009). Recall our discussion of 'infant-industry' protection in Chapter 8; economic nationalists worry that more advanced economies can be at a competitive advantage, threatening to outperform and displace infant industries in developing economies. So the state becomes vital as a shield, creating protected space and support as the industrial economy grows stronger.

Within the world economy, states become important as strategic players seeking to develop congenial political relationships that support national advancement. In this view, states are not obstacles to the functioning of national economic systems or the global economy; rather, they are architects and champions of commercial societies that seek to advance in a competitive and potentially threatening international environment. In light of its focus on the need to protect national interests and autonomy in a dangerous world, we may consider this Hamiltonian perspective as the economic component of realist international relations theory.

Relative gains: [1] The gains a state makes **relative** to other states. As opposed to **absolute gains**, which are simply the total materials gains made by a state, relative gains focus on the gains one state makes compared to a rival. Realists emphasize the importance of relative gains. [2] An important element of economic nationalism, relative gains is the idea that some gain more than others in economic interactions, and those who gain less lose out, even if they have positive absolute gains.

Marxism

A third tradition of thinking about states and markets is inspired by the ideas of Karl Marx. Recall from Chapter 3 that in this view, the rise of market economies brings new divisions between the owners of businesses, or the capitalist class which possesses the productive assets of society, and the workers. Marxism argues that economic relations tend to shape political relations, and the main economic actors are classes, rather than individuals or the state.

For Marxists, the state within a capitalist society is neither a neutral referee nor a facilitator of economic development for the nation-state as a whole. Instead, the state has a special mission – to protect and advance the interests of the capitalist class. The state, in Marx's terms, is the 'executive committee of the bourgeoisie,' and its role is to shape the economic game to the advantage of the capitalist class, at the expense of the working class.

Despite the fact that capitalists held all the economic and political advantages, Marx was confident the underdog would ultimately win. The underlying conflict of interests between capitalists and workers would lead to a series of political struggles and the ultimate triumph of the working class, ushering in a new post-capitalist society in which all people were the owners and beneficiaries of economic activity.

While liberals argue that there is a deep harmony of interests between different groups and classes in society – and between societies – Marxists see a zero-sum struggle in which one side's gain is the other's loss. Capitalists seek to protect their advantages and workers seek to gain a greater share of wealth and power. Until the economic system is overturned in a political revolution, the capitalist class will retain their power advantages within society. Workers will work and capitalists will prosper until workers so outnumber capitalists that an effective leader can mobilize them into a meaningful political movement.

Within the wider international system, Marxist thinkers see the state operating in the service of national capitalist interests. As we discussed in Chapter 1, to the Russian revolutionary and Soviet leader Vladimir Lenin this meant that states would be driven by capitalist competition into geopolitical struggle and even war. Indeed, this was the Soviet leader's explanation for World War I. It was a conflict between states seeking to advance their national capitalist interests, particularly the giant banking and manufacturing conglomerates that held sway over these antagonistic states.

In the later decades of the twentieth century, Marxist thinkers acknowledged the remarkable spread of trade and investment, noting the rise of global business firms. National capitalists had become international capitalists, and their states tended to follow, providing international support – including global rules and institutions – for their expanding commercial and financial interests. In this way, Marxists see international economic relations as a continuing drama in which capitalists in rich countries – backed by their states – dominate those in weaker and less developed countries. Today's international economic institutions, in particular the International Monetary Fund and the World Bank, are, they believe, instruments of the rich countries, protecting their interests even as they offer aid and assistance to less developed states. The struggle between workers and the capitalist class within societies is matched by the struggle between the advanced capitalist states and the struggling societies in the poor and less developed parts of the world. Marxist analyses flourish in eras of capitalist crisis, so it is not surprising that many books and articles from this perspective have appeared in the wake of the 2008 financial crisis (Ticktin 2011; Harmon 2009).

Despite their differences, however, most economic liberals, nationalists, and Marxists would acknowledge that states exist within a competitive state system, and this helps shape the way they act within the world economy. We now examine state behavior in the international economic arena, focusing on how governments use markets to strengthen their economies, protect their political autonomy, and compete militarily with other states.

👤 **Individual**	👥 **State**
Individual thinkers such as Adam Smith, Alexander Hamilton, and Karl Marx articulated influential ideologies of state–market relations.	Both economic nationalists and Marxists argue that the state – represented by centralized governmental officials – plays a critical role in shaping markets and capitalist economic development.
	Liberals argue that the state has a more limited role.

States and Markets in a World of Anarchy

States are both politically sovereign and economically interdependent. The world of commerce and trade must co-exist with sovereign-territorial states that compete and cooperate with each other. These two systems – the capitalist world economy and the international state system – emerged together on the world historical stage in the seventeenth century. It has been an uneasy relationship ever since.

Each system has its own ways of operating. Capitalism tends to be transnational; nation-states are inherently territorial. Each has, at various moments, been threatened and destabilized by the other. Market booms and busts and rapid economic change have undermined the political standing of ruling regimes and fueled political conflict within and between states. The Great Depression of the 1930s is probably the most dramatic instance when growth and trade in the world economy plummeted – unemployment climbed to unprecedented levels – and governments were thrown into chaos. The economic crisis led to the collapse of some democracies in Europe and provided the conditions that brought to office such fascist leaders as Germany's Hitler and Italy's Mussolini. The financial crisis that began in 2008 thankfully has not brought war, but has led to political turbulence and conflict, most prominently in the European Union and in particular in Greece. Likewise, inter-state competition – and at the extreme, war – has disrupted international flows of trade and investment and set limits on the integration of world markets. As we showed in Box 9.1, the era of world wars in the first half of the twentieth century brought with it a retreat from global economic integration and growth. But the two systems have also worked together: states have taken steps to establish property rights and construct international rules and institutions that support trade and investment between countries; and capitalism has grown into a global system of production and exchange that provides states with taxes and other resources to compete with each other.

If these are the circumstances in which states find themselves, what are the implications for the goals of states in the world economy? Generally, the competitive structure of inter-state relations creates incentives for states to get involved in their national economies to promote economic growth and advancement, protect national autonomy, and be responsive to the relative power consequences of international economic relationships. But states also realize the potential benefits of an open system of trade and investment; they find themselves making trade-offs between concerns for security and independence, on the one hand, and opportunities to promote economic growth through trade and exchange, on the other. States, in other words, seek both power and wealth, the ability to protect themselves in a world of competing states and to prosper in the world economy. Generally, the two goals go hand in hand: the more prosperous states economically tend to be the most powerful ones politically. As the Soviet Union eventually found out, it is difficult for a state to be a dominant military power in the long run if it lacks a prosperous economy.

The Two-Sided Government: Managing Domestic and International Relations

The world economy is embedded within the broader system of states. Each individual state, however, must manage its national economy, and to do so requires that it operate simultaneously within domestic and global markets. Regardless of whether one is primarily a liberal, nationalist, or Marxist, it is useful to think of governments as facing both directions, inward to their own societies and economies, and outward to the world system.

From a historical perspective, the relationships of governments to the outside world and to their domestic societies have developed hand in hand. The rise of the modern state in Europe prior to the twentieth century involved the simultaneous process of fighting off foreign rivals while also strengthening the government's relationship with its own society and economy. The more intense the inter-state competition, the more governments needed to mobilize and extract resources from their societies. States won wars if they had a strong military, and this depended on the ability of governments to tax and spend. This, in turn, provided incentives to encourage a productive economy and a legitimate role for the state within the society. The more the state needed to make demands on the society and economy, the more incentives it had to make its rule agreeable to domestic individuals and groups, including businessmen, banks, and workers. This dynamic of war making and state building is perhaps best seen over the two centuries of armed conflict between Britain and France, from the 1660s to the end of the Napoleonic War in 1815. These struggles led each government to seek new ways to bolster and extract taxes and resources from their economies – and from the economies of conquered territories (Liberman 1996). Each developed more elaborate national financial systems to tax and borrow and thereby strengthen the ability of state leaders to pursue war and peace (Kennedy 1987).

As states interact with their own societies, the institutions and traditions of government and society impose some limits and constraints on what state leaders can do. States differ in their relations with society; this will shape and channel how states can operate at home and within the world system. These differences can be understood as variations in the capacities of states. Some states are more centralized and insulated from society than other states, and as a result they are better able to act in an independent and strategic manner. Other states are more decentralized and less autonomous, and as a result their policies will tend to more directly reflect the class

► **Photo 9.3 Beijing 2008 Olympic Games**

In 2008, China hosted the Summer Olympics in Beijing. In preparation for the events, China built a new Olympic complex which became a symbol of modern China. The stadium cost a reported $423 million USD to build, demonstrating Chinese economic prowess. The photo captures part of the opening ceremonies in the stadium.

Source: PA Images.

or group interests within society. Among the advanced Western countries, France is often seen as a particularly centralized state in which the government has considerable capacity to shape and direct the economy. The United States is often seen as a decentralized state, with power divided between branches of government and between the national government and state and local governments. Some states are able to formulate policies and strategies that are independent of society and implement them effectively. Other states are less capable – unable to act coherently and lacking the policy tools with which to pursue independent goals (Krasner 1978; Mastanduno et al. 1989).

Some observers see China and the United States as examples of these two types. China is governed by a single party – the Communist Party – and it commands all the levers of government. It has the authority to intervene in the society and economy to pursue its goals. This ability to 'get things done' was on display during the 2008 Olympics, when the Chinese government acted quickly to build huge athletic facilities and public transportation. When the Olympic Games were being held, the Chinese government was also able to shut down factories to reduce pollution emissions.

The more purposeful Chinese government is often contrasted today with America's more divided government. The leaders of the US government pursue objectives in a multi-party system where frequent elections and political bickering between the two major political parties make it more difficult to pursue goals in the way China appears to be able to do. The 'fiscal cliff' negotiations of late 2012, in which Democrats and Republicans took the US economy to the brink of deep recession in trying to resolve their disagreements over taxing and spending policy, are a good recent example of how frustrating the more decentralized US political system can be. However, when faced with a national challenge, the United States can set goals and mobilize resources with great effectiveness. During the Cold War, the United States competed with the Soviet Union to show its abilities to 'do great things.' The space program – and the mission to put a man on the moon – was a showcase of the American effort to engage in a great feat of science, technology, and human imagination. On the other hand, many observers today question whether China's more rigid political system will enable the kind of creativity and innovation needed for its economy to become a true global leader.

◀ **Photo 9.4 Twenty-First-Century Greece**
The global recession led to widespread riots in Greece in 2010. Clouds of tear gas mingled with smoke in Athens as police and stone-throwing protesters clashed during the demonstration. During the 2000s, the Greek government borrowed heavily and lived beyond its means. Public-sector wages almost doubled, while widespread tax evasion within the country meant that the government consistently spent more than it took in.

Source: PA Images.

A variety of factors will shape the capacities of states; the most basic is the sovereign integrity of the state and military and administrative control of its territory. Most developed states around the world have stable governments and territorial borders. The government taxes and regulates the economy. The national borders are protected. But, as we discuss fully in Chapter 11, other states are less fully in control of their borders and territory. In countries such as Sudan or Afghanistan, the central government is weak and its authority does not reach outward to all the regions of the country. Tribal leaders and war lords compete with the state for rule over outlying parties and territorial borders are left unguarded. In these weak or failed states, the basic capacities of government are not yet established.

In some cases, governments of what we think of as more developed countries may exhibit limited capacity. In the 1990s, after the Cold War ended, the government of Russia lost control over its society – the rule of law broke down, businesses and households evaded taxes, and organized crime plundered major parts of the economy (Taylor 2001). During the 2000s, it became apparent that the government of Greece was bankrupt because it had spent lavishly but had a limited ability to collect taxes from its population. Greece's financial problems affected all members of the European Union and created particular resentment in Germany since the more financially disciplined German people felt they should not have to provide the money to bail out the less disciplined Greeks. Germany offered in 2012 to send experts to Greece to assist in the craft of tax collection – an offer many Greeks saw as an insult and an intrusion on their sovereignty (*The Guardian* 2012).

Promoting National Economic Growth

Economic growth is a vital component of state power. In a competitive system, governments are likely to care a great deal about the wealth and prosperity of their respective societies. In the short run, it might be possible for ambitious governments to extract resources from their society forcefully and build up their military capabilities, taking capital and other assets away from more productive uses. Stalin used this technique in the 1930s to modernize the Soviet Union and ensure its place as a great power.

But in the long run, as Soviet leaders ultimately learned when they could no longer sustain the Cold War, the power of the state will depend on the wealth of the society it commands. As a result, we should expect states to encourage economic growth and the accumulation of wealth. There may be other reasons why state leaders would want to promote economic growth and wealth creation at home, such as responding to interest group pressures or creating a prosperous electorate that will re-elect the leaders in office. But the competitive international system itself provides a powerful incentive for states to care about the health and welfare of the national economy.

If a government wants its country to gain economic strength, to what extent should it participate in the world economy? As we saw in Chapter 8, liberal economic theory answers yes on the grounds that trade openness promotes specialization and maximizes economic gains. South Korea and Taiwan, for example, have over the last forty years been able to grow particularly fast and foster the development of more advanced and high-technology industries by gradually opening up to foreign investment and joint ventures with leading international businesses. Along the way, they have acquired knowledge and experience that has allowed them to develop their own world-class businesses in many areas.

But states interested in promoting long-term economic growth and advancement have also found reasons to protect domestic industries at their initial stage of development and shelter critical industries and technologies from foreign competition. South Korea and Taiwan were careful not to open up their economies too quickly or fully to outside investment. They regulated foreign investment, allowing time and space for their domestic businesses to grow and develop. But they were not completely protectionist. They opened up their economies to outside investment gradually to create competition and gain knowledge and experience. As we shall see in Chapter 10, developing countries have experimented with both open, liberal strategies and more insulated nationalist strategies in their efforts to promote growth and develop strong national economies (Haggard 1990).

Protecting Autonomy

Governments operating in a competitive state system will generally have a second important goal – to protect their country's autonomy. They will not want their economy to be too dependent on others and put the country's security at risk. An open system of world markets may stimulate the growth of the national economy, but too much exposure can create dangerous vulnerabilities and dependencies. States will try to prevent themselves from becoming too dependent on other states, particularly if the other states could eventually become adversaries. But states might also try to make other states dependent on them by providing favorable terms of trade, drawing other states into a dependent relationship that allows the one state more advantages and power. The American government's active encouragement of Japanese imports after World War II, for example, was aimed at stimulating economic revival in East Asia – warding off communist-led political instability – and drawing Japan into America's emerging Cold War alliance system as a reliable junior partner. In these circumstances, states must make difficult choices and trade-offs between interdependence and autonomy.

The problem of dependence on other countries for resources and trade has become an important issue as the world economy has become more interdependent. For example, Ukraine is heavily dependent on neighboring Russia for its energy supplies,

◄ Map 9.2 European Gas Pipelines

The majority of Europe's gas pipelines emanate from Russia, a major global supplier of natural gas. Russia has used its energy dominance as a political tool, most notably in attempts to constrain Ukrainian economic and foreign policy.

Source: *Petroleum Economist.*

particularly oil and gas. In recent years, the government of Ukraine has attempted to strengthen its ties to NATO and the West, a move resisted by Russia, which prefers that Ukraine have a more 'Russia-friendly' than 'West-friendly' orientation. Russia has used its economic leverage over Ukraine by making Ukraine's access to Russian energy supplies dependent on the maintenance of close political ties between the two countries. When Ukraine strays too far from Russia, Russia threatens to restrict, or actually restricts, the flow of natural gas. Ukraine's energy dependence on Russia potentially constrains the freedom and ability of the government of Ukraine to reorient its foreign policy (Olearchyk and Buckley 2010).

As China's economy has become more powerful, it has exploited the economic dependence of its Asian neighbors for political gain. In September 2010, the Japanese coast guard arrested and detained the captain of a Chinese fishing vessel after it rammed a Japanese coast guard ship in waters off of a disputed island in the East China Sea (see Map 9.3). After Japan refused to immediately release the captain, China announced an 'informal embargo' on export of rare earth materials to Japan. China mines and sells over 95 percent of the world's market in rare and expensive minerals used in advanced technologies, such as solar collectors, computers, and mobile phones. China used the dependence of Japanese companies on these resources from China to intensify the pressure on Tokyo to back down. The Chinese sailor was eventually released and the crisis was defused. Not surprisingly, Japan and other countries took note of China's use of its near monopoly on rare earth resources; these governments responded by taking steps to reduce their dependence on China (Bradsher 2010).

► **Map 9.3 East China Sea**

The map illustrates the source of ongoing conflict at sea between China and Japan. Each side claims an Exclusive Economic Zone (EEZ) in the East China Sea and the two zones overlap. Each side claims the right to control and patrol the area of overlap. The Senkaku Islands (the Chinese call them the Diaoyudao), a roughly 4-square-mile area of uninhabited islets, fall within the area of overlap. Japan claimed the territory in 1895; China made a counterclaim in 1970. Why fight over uninhabited islets? One reason is economic – the disputed area of the East China Sea holds great potential for oil and gas exploration, fishing, and the mining of sea-bed metals.

Sensitivity: A state is sensitive to another state's actions if those actions can temporarily hamper a state until it finds a replacement for the good or service from another location.

Vulnerability: A state is vulnerable to another state's actions if it is unable to compensate effectively for losses caused by the other state's actions.

A state that opens itself up to dependence on another state must make a series of calculations. First, the threat that energy supplies or other critical resources might be cut off is not as straightforward as it seems. It is useful to make a distinction between **sensitivity** and **vulnerability** to resource cut-offs (Keohane and Nye 1977). If Ukraine is able to shift the source of its energy imports from Russia to Saudi Arabia (which is eager to sell the same resources to Ukraine), the security implications of dependence on Russia are not that serious. In that case, Ukraine is merely 'sensitive' to disruptions. Alternatively, Ukraine might be able to undertake domestic efforts to substitute the discontinued flow of energy with the building of nuclear energy facilities that serve the same purpose. Again, the implications of disruption are not that severe; Ukraine will pay some cost for the loss of Russian supplies but it will be inconvenienced more than significantly harmed.

But what if Ukraine was not able to make up for the disruption of energy flows from Russia and could not find a domestic substitute? In this situation, Ukraine's dependence on Russia is more severe. Ukraine is not just sensitive to a Russian cut-off, it is vulnerable to it. This vulnerability has more serious implications in that Ukraine is putting its security at risk by allowing itself to become dependent on one energy source. In cases of extreme dependence, we should expect the dependent state to try to broaden and diversify its imports and trade relationships to limit the power of the single exporting state. The importing state may also try to find domestic substitutes for the resources.

Dependence and vulnerability may apply as much to financial relations as trade relations. As Figure 9.2 shows, the United States has found itself increasingly dependent on China as a source of capital. By 2010, China was holding almost $1 trillion of bonds issued by the US Treasury. By borrowing this way, the US government has been able to engage in massive spending, including major wars in Iraq and Afghanistan, without imposing the immediate costs on American taxpayers. For its part, China has had its own reasons to be such a generous lender. As we discussed in Chapter 8, it has bought American Treasury bonds to take pressure off its own currency, reinforcing an exchange rate that favors Chinese exports.

This situation in which China has been America's *de facto* banker has led some in Washington to worry if the United States has become indebted to China politically as well as financially. Has the United States developed a dependency on China's financing of budget deficits that gives Beijing leverage over American foreign policy? If China sold its holding of American treasury notes, the value of the dollar might plummet

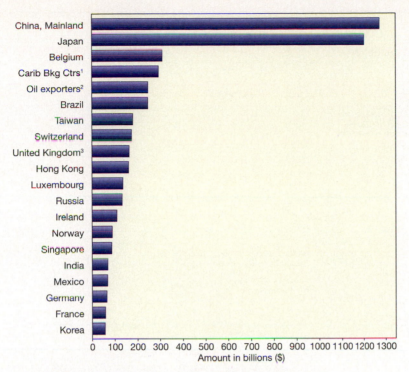

◀ **Figure 9.2 Top 20 Foreign Holders of US Treasury Securities, end January 2014**

Source: Data from the Department of the Treasury and Federal Reserve.

1   Caribbean Banking Centers include Bahamas, Bermuda, Cayman Islands,
    former Netherlands Antilles and Panama. Beginning with new series for June 2006,
    also includes British Virgin Islands.
2   Oil exporters include Ecuador, Venezuela, Indonesia, Bahrain, Iran, Iraq, Kuwait, Oman,
    Qatar, Saudi Arabia, the United Arab Emirates, Algeria, Gabon, Libya, and Nigeria.
3   United Kingdom includes Channel Islands and Isle of Man.

and the United States government would be forced to raise interest rates, choking off economic growth and creating a political crisis. Many experts do note that China would also suffer if it actually did sell off its debt holdings. Their value would also plummet and the very act could destabilize the world economy on which China depends so heavily. In this sense China and the United States may be symmetrically interdependent – depending so much on each other that neither can afford to disrupt the economic relationship for relative political gain (Drezner 2009).

China and the United States may be mutually constrained because both are large economic powers. But interdependence between larger and smaller economies is usually more one-sided. As we saw in Russia's relations with Ukraine, a large state seeking to expand its political power and enhance its own autonomy might actually want to promote the dependence of its smaller neighbors (Hirschman 1980). In the classic study of this strategy, the famous political economist Albert Hirschman looked at Germany's inter-war trade relations with the small countries in Southeast Europe during the 1930s. In order to enhance its own autonomy, Germany drew these states into trade relations that made them dependent on Germany over the longer term by securing access to raw materials and increasing its leverage in the region. Germany offered very favorable terms to these small states to reorient and deepen these trade relations. As these small states became more dependent on trade with Germany, their 'exit' options were made more costly. But because these same trade relations played a smaller role in the much larger German economy, the potential costs of disruption were asymmetrical and the

► Map 9.4 China and East Asia

China is the world's second largest economy and it has developed rapidly by relying on trade both with the developed world of the United States and Europe and with its smaller neighbors in East Asia. Not surprisingly, economic relations with China figure prominently in the calculations of surrounding countries including Thailand, Vietnam, Malaysia, and even Australia. In 2007, China overtook the United States and Japan to become Australia's largest trading partner.

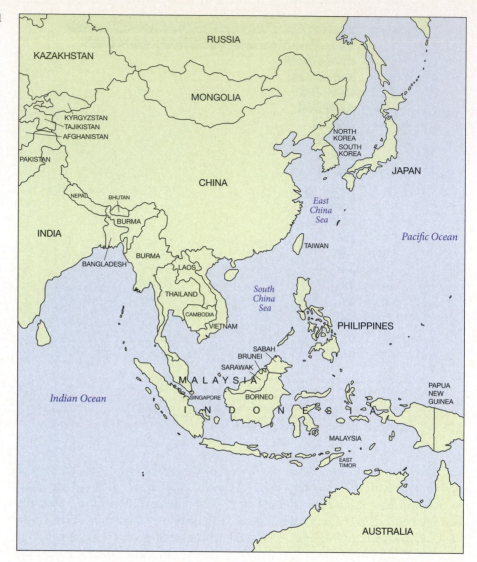

dependent trade relationship also created political dependence. Germany used its own internal market as a tool of state power, enhancing its political autonomy by using trade and economic dependence to develop asymmetrical power relations.

Today we should consider the extent to which China is pursuing a 'Hirschman-like' strategy with regard to its smaller neighbors in East Asia. The Chinese economy has grown so rapidly that it has become a magnet for the imports and exports of the Philippines, Thailand, and South Korea, among others. These countries have become increasingly dependent on China economically while continuing to maintain long-standing political and security ties to the United States. The natural concern of American policy makers is that over time, 'the flag will follow trade,' and these American allies will see fit to reorient their foreign policies to a greater extent in the direction preferred by China.

In summary, an open system of trade, money, and finance creates efficiency gains that leave all states better off than if they simply remained national economies. But, a

The Trade Dispute over China's 'Rare Earth' Mineral Exports

Theory

Countries will seek to minimize extreme levels of dependence on their trading partners for items vital to their economies. This is especially true when the trading partner in question is a potential geopolitical competitor.

Practice

Governments find it difficult to forego the economic benefits of specialization, even when it leaves their economies vulnerable to calculations made by their trading partners.

In 2012, the United States, the European Union, and Japan filed complaints at the World Trade Organization against China over China's restrictions on the export of 17 'rare earth' minerals. The rare earth minerals, with exotic names such as Dysprosium, Neodynium, Yttrium, and Europium, are essential to the production of many technology-intensive products such as iPads, hybrid car batteries, mobile phones, and photovoltaic films. The more developed countries making the complaint are heavily dependent on China for the supply of rare earths. In 1995, China produced 40 percent of the world's supply of rare earth metals; by 2012, it produced an astonishing 95 percent. The problem emerged because China decided to impose restrictions on its exports of rare earths, allowing in 2012 only about one-half the exports of rare earths that it had allowed in 2005. China's reasons seemed sensible; it cited environmental concerns and a desire to sustain its supply of these minerals over the longer term. But China's trading partners cried foul, contending that Chinese firms were happy to sell their product to other countries, but that the Chinese government was using unfair trading practices to hoard the vital materials for its own domestic use.

China has the largest proven reserve of rare earths (about 55 million metric tons as of 2011). But other countries have sizable reserves as well: Russia has 19 million metric tons, and the United States has 13 million. So why then does China provide 95 percent of the world's supply? Rare earths are expensive to mine, and China has large amounts of inexpensive labor. Rare earth production is also environmentally costly, in some cases producing radioactive waste that most countries would prefer not to have on their territories. China has been more willing to absorb these environmental costs. Its trading partners have been happy to avoid these costs and simply buy the minerals from China.

By restricting the supply of rare earths, China will force their prices to go higher. At some point, the higher prices will attract new suppliers into the market from other countries. As of 2012, in response to the Chinese restrictions and higher prices, companies in Colorado, Wyoming, Australia, Canada and South Africa announced plans to open or re-open mines to produce rare earths.

state contemplating expanding its exposure to the world economy must calculate the trade-off between the absolute economic gains from trade and the possible loss of political autonomy that might accompany greater economic dependence. A state that cares about its security in a world of anarchy will be attentive to this trade-off: it will want to achieve all the economic gains it can, because this is part of what creates the national basis of its power position, but it also may be willing to forego some of those economic gains if they create dependence and vulnerability. As Box 9.3 shows, in an era of globalization governments find it increasingly difficult to forego the economic benefits of specialization and trade, even though it may mean extreme dependence on others countries as sources of supply.

Pursuing Relative and Absolute Gains

Finally, states operating within a competitive international environment will care about both absolute gains and their *relative standing* with other states (Baldwin 1993). Liberal economic theory tells us why states should care about absolute gain. Countries will trade freely based on specialization and comparative advantage. In doing so, these countries experience more economic gains than they would if they did not engage in free trade. Each country is economically better off. But in some circumstances, it is the *relative* economic gains that governments worry more about. This will be particularly true if the other country is a rival or a potential enemy in war. Generally speaking, the more secure a state feels, the more content it will be to think in terms of absolute gains.

As we showed above, the United States and China today, for example, appear relatively content to trade and exchange with each other without regard to considerations of relative gains. Both are gaining in absolute terms. The United States has found China to be a source of cheap imports, reducing costs for US consumers. Trade is a large part of Chinese economic growth, and economic growth is vital to economic and political stability within China. But it is possible that in future a moment might arrive when the United States and China start to worry more about relative gains. The United States, for example, might come to eye China increasingly as a rival and potential enemy. If China comes to look more like a threat than a trading partner, the United States will worry about China profiting more than it is. Relative gains will become more significant.

We can look more closely at the logic of relative gains, introduced earlier in the chapter. In making choices about economic relations, states can think about the payoffs in one of two ways. One way is to simply make choices that give the state the most economic gains in absolute terms. This is the logic of the neo-classical theory of trade. If policy X leads to 20 units of economic gain for my state, and policy Y leads to 10 units of gain for my state, the choice is obvious: in maximizing my state's absolute economic gains, I will choose policy X. But, in an insecure and dangerous world, conditions may exist that prompt a state to calculate its interests in terms of relative gains. If policy X gives my state 20 units and the other state receives 40 units of economic gains, we both gain but the other state gains more. If policy Y gives me only 10 units of gain, but it gives the other state 5 units of gain, my state's absolute gains are less but its relative gains are greater in comparison to the other state. If my state's goal is to look after its relative power position, the incentive to pursue relative gains over absolute gains may exist.

The ultimate reason a state would worry about the distribution of gains within an economic relationship is the risk of war. The possibility that a state's trading partner might someday be a grave and dangerous adversary will create incentives for that state to calculate in terms of relative gains. But, if the costs of war are huge and the possibilities of war are tiny, then that state will likely calculate that the absolute gains from trade are worth pursuing.

Consider two examples. In trade between the United States and Canada, neither side pays much attention to relative gains. The two neighbors are long-standing allies and the militarily weaker country, Canada, does not fear invasion or conquest from its superpower neighbor. Alternatively, consider that during the Cold War, the United States and Soviet Union were potential military adversaries, each of which thought seriously about the relative gains implications of economic exchange. The Soviets sought to buy or steal Western technology as a way to 'catch up,' or close the relative gap in economic and military capabilities between the two sides. The United States and its NATO allies organized a system of export restrictions, preventing their companies from trading certain technologies to the Soviet Union in order to maintain the West's relative advantage (Mastanduno 1992). NATO governments believed that free trade with the Soviet Union would benefit both sides, but would benefit their potential adversary relatively more.

State Building, War, and Markets

By now it should be clear that most governments have a conflicted view about world markets. They are both attracted to economic openness and in some ways threatened by it. An open world economy can stimulate trade and investment that fuel economic growth, raise living standards, and create a wealth base from which the state can extract resources to pursue its geopolitical goals. But it can also undermine domestic industry, destabilize employment, and leave the society dependent on an external world it cannot control. Governments must continually choose between these dangers and opportunities. For most governments, as the world economy has become more integrated, the balance between interdependence and autonomy has clearly shifted in favor of interdependence. Many governments today claim a commitment to open markets and free trade. Yet, as Box 9.4 shows, the reality does not always match the rhetoric.

The dilemma governments face between economic interdependence and political autonomy goes all the way back to early modern European history when capitalism and state formation were both beginning to take shape (Tilly 1985). Political leaders at that early moment were attempting to build themselves up and engage in 'state making,' which also involved protracted wars with neighboring world-be state builders. It is true that the state, or government, makes war; it is also true that war made the state, in the sense that the need to fight wars created incentives for political leaders to assert great control over their territories and populations in order to mobilize the resources needed to fight wars effectively. Wealth and power were inextricably linked at the dawn of the state system and they still are today.

In the years between 1400 and 1700, rulers mostly contracted with mercenary troops to fight their wars and relied heavily on private capitalists within their region for loans and the collection of taxes. After 1700 and into the present era, states created mass armies and navies, with soldiers drawn increasingly from their own populations. The military establishments became a formal part of the state, and the administrative organs of the state became directly responsible for the fiscal management of the national territory.

Over time it became easier for governments to extract resources from their populations. In traditional, non-monetized societies, leaders had to rely mainly on coercion – their representatives had to go out and extract tribute from private actors within its territorial reach. As societies became more commercial and monetized, the ease with which the government could monitor and extract funds increased. In more commercial societies, taxation could shift from tribute, rents, and tolls at strategic ports to trade tariffs and, ultimately, income taxes. States with societies at higher levels of com-

Free Trade in Principle, Not Practice

Aspiration: *George W. Bush, speaking in a Republican Primary Debate, January 7, 2000*

> I would be a free trading President, a President that will work tirelessly to open up markets for agriculture products all over the world. I believe our American farmers can compete as long as the playing field is level. That's why I am such a strong advocate of free trade and that's why I reject protectionism and isolation because I think it hurts our American farmers.

Presidential candidate Bush was simply reiterating a long-standing aspiration in American foreign economic policy: free trade benefits all, as long as the playing field is 'level.' In other words, the United States supports open markets and expects other states to do so as well.

Reality

The reality is quite different, particularly in the area of agriculture. From the early years of the General Agreement on Tariffs and Trade, the United States insisted on special treatment for its agricultural products. US officials have long provided protection for American dairy, sugar, and peanuts in two ways. First, the government provides price supports for domestic producers to ensure that they receive high prices for their crops even if the supply is greater than the demand. In 1986, for example, the US domestic price for sugar was about four times the world price. Consumers, left on their own, would substitute cheaper sugar from Central America for the more expensive US production. But, the US government does not allow free trade in sugar; instead, it negotiates a set of quotas with foreign producers to limit the amount of sugar coming into the US market. In this case, the rhetoric of free trade does not match the reality of a controlled market that benefits less efficient US producers.

Among developed countries, the United States is not alone in practicing agricultural protectionism. The European Union protects its farmers in similar ways and, for decades, Japanese policy makers vowed not to allow a single grain of foreign rice in the Japanese market. As we shall see in Chapter 10, agricultural protectionism is a key issue of contention in relations between developed and developing countries, because many countries in Africa, Latin America, and Asia are producers and exporters of agricultural products. Their economic growth depends, in part, on access to the consumer markets of the United States and Europe.

mercialization and capital intensiveness could extract resources more efficiently; those at lower levels of commercialization were at a competitive disadvantage and required a larger and more coercive state apparatus.

The trick for successful governments has always been twofold: to encourage a rising economy and find efficient ways to extract resources from that economy without stifling growth. Put differently, governments want the economy to lay golden eggs, so they can take a few of those eggs for their own purposes. But they need to play the game right: to encourage egg production and pursue egg extraction, without threatening the goose's ability to lay the eggs.

Today, most (but not all) people accept as legitimate that their government has the right to collect taxes and use the proceeds for the collective good of the country as they see it. Companies withhold part of the pay of their employees and send it to the government, and citizens participate in the annual ritual of preparing their individual tax returns for the government. The government uses these resources to build roads and bridges, provide services to those in need, and to redistribute income from the more wealthy to the less wealthy. It also uses some part of those resources to conduct foreign policy, including at times the resort to war. Crises such as the Cold War or the attacks of September 11, 2001 tend to expand the size and powers of government, as political leaders react to what they and their populations perceive as a more threatening international environment. Even today, the state makes war and war makes the state.

After laying the foundation for how states balance territorial concerns with economic growth, we now turn to the examination of great national powers, or superpowers, who use open markets to pursue security policy and international order.

State	🌐 **International**
States differ in their capacities to intervene in the domestic economy to stimulate and direct economic development.	The anarchic environment in which states operate creates incentives for governments to get involved in the national economy, promoting economic growth and protecting the country's sovereignty and vital industries.

Levels of Analysis
State versus Market in a World of Anarchy

Great Powers and the World Economy

All states must manage the trade-off between economic interdependence and political autonomy. But the most powerful states, with the most dynamic economies, have additional opportunities. They can use their disproportionate political and economic power to shape the world economy in which they participate.

More so than 'ordinary' countries, great powers may use markets and the expansion of economic openness and integration as a tool of security policy and international order building. Britain after the Napoleonic wars of the nineteenth century and the United States after World War II are the most dramatic examples of major states that have had the power and opportunity to build and manage the world economy. The economic goals pursued by these leading states have been closely tied to general political and security goals and ambitions in the creation of an international political order.

There are a variety of ways the expansion of world market relations and increased economic interdependence might serve the political and strategic interests of a leading state. Here we highlight three key political goals states may pursue through economic means: increasing national wealth, influencing the economic and political orientation of other states, and shaping the overall political direction of the international system.

First, a powerful state may take special advantage of the fact that an open world economy increases the nation's access to markets, technology, and resources, fostering greater domestic economic growth and increasing national wealth. This basic logic informed the American proposals for rebuilding the world economy after 1945. The United States emerged from the war as the most advanced and productive economy in the world. Its leading industries were well positioned for global competition. An open world economy, organized around non-discriminatory multilateral rules, was an obvious national interest. American policy makers concerned with national economic advancement were drawn to a postwar agenda of trade barrier reduction and the promotion of global multilateral economic openness (Gilpin 1987).

The construction of an open world economic order in the aftermath of World War II remains one of the more remarkable accomplishments of the twentieth century. As discussed in chapter 8, agreements reached by the United States and Britain during the war and ratified at Bretton Woods in 1944 marked a decisive move toward openness. This was a surprising feat given the ravages and dislocations of war and competing postwar interests. It came only because the United States had formidable political and economic power and was willing to use it to push the postwar world economy in its preferred direction of openness and non-discrimination. For example, America offered postwar recovery assistance to European countries, but only on the condition that they open their economies to multilateral trade and make their currencies convertible on international currency markets.

A second political-strategic interest that might prompt a leading state to pursue market openness and integration is the opportunity to influence the political and economic orientation of other states and regions. Specifically, a world economy divided into closed and rival regional blocs may be contrary to the economic and security interests of the leading state. During World War II, American postwar planners were in agreement that the United States could not remain a viable great power and be isolated within the Western hemisphere. The American economy would need to integrate itself into a wider pan-regional world economy. The war itself was in part a struggle over precisely this matter. German and Japanese military aggression was aimed at the creation of exclusive regional blocs in Europe and Asia. The American economy would thrive best in a world without blocs; its status as a leading great power depended on economic openness. And, in the context of the Cold War, American security depended on having reliable anti-Communist allies. US leaders used American economic power to drive Western Europe and Japan into economic interdependence and military alliance with the United States.

In the decade after World War II, the United States took the lead in helping Japan find new commercial relations and raw material sources in Southeast Asia to substitute for the loss of Chinese and Korean markets. The United States also fostered integration within Europe. The solution to the German problem after World War II was to economically integrate the allied zones of occupied Germany within the wider Western European economy. The celebrated European Coal and Steel Community, which created joint French and German ownership of basic war industries, embodied this strategic goal. Economic integration can create mutual dependencies that make autonomous and destabilizing security competition more difficult. The same logic reappeared more recently during the process of German unification when Germany agreed to tie itself even more fully to Europe through monetary union.

Finally, a leading state may use economic openness and integration to *shape the overall political orientation* of the international system. American officials who embrace liberal beliefs about politics and economics had long anticipated that expanding world trade and investment would indirectly promote and reward movement by states toward liberal democracy. A world of democratic states would reduce security threats and allow the United States to more fully realize its international goals. Trade and investment strengthen the private sectors of countries, empowering civil society as a counterweight to strong states. Economic openness would create vested interests within countries in favor of pluralistic political order and stable and continuous relations between states. This is the view most forcefully made by the American Secretary of State Cordell Hull during World War II. Free and open trade would not just stimulate economic growth but strengthen democratic regimes around the world and make war less likely. In Secretary Hull's words, 'when trade crosses borders, soldiers don't.'

Over the decades, it has been a staple of American foreign policy thinking that the spread of trade and investment into the non-democratic world would stimulate and reinforce the economic and political forces pushing for political change. An expanding market society acts as a counterweight to autocratic states and encourages the rise of a middle class that favors democratic institutions. This concept is at the center of American thinking about the rise of China, and US foreign policy that advocates integration of China into the world economy. In the wake of the deal between the two countries in 2001 over Chinese entry into the World Trade Organization, a reporter captured this logic:

> For a president who talks constantly these days about harnessing the forces of economic globalization, the agreement to integrate China into the global trading system marked the culmination of Mr. Clinton's single biggest imprint on American foreign policy: the use of American economic power for strategic ends. That is what this agreement is all about, locking in China's commitment to economic reforms and with it, he is betting, a further opening of Chinese society. (Sanger 1999)

During the Cold War, the Chinese government was skeptical of international institutions, viewing them as a tool used by Western states to constrain Chinese foreign policy and force China to comply with Western norms and values. Since the mid-1990s, however, China's leaders have embraced international institutions, for example, joining the WTO, CTBT, and leading the Six Party Talks on North Korea. What explains this shift in policy?

Constructivism: Western states have engaged China, encouraging it to be a responsible player as a way to gain status as a great power. As China has participated in these institutions, it has become socialized into embracing their role and utility. This socialization process occurs when Chinese officials actually participate in these institutions, slowly acquiring their norms and orientations.

Realism: China's embrace is tactical and instrumental. It needs to reassure its neighbors that its rise is non-threatening. Embracing international institutions is one way to do that. As China becomes more powerful, we should expect it to be more selective in its willingness to abide by the rules and norms of international institutions.

Liberalism: China's interest is functional. Its key goal is economic development, and its key strategy is global integration. Joining the WTO is a direct way to integrate into the global trading system. Cooperation in security institutions reinforces the image of China as a responsible rising power providing a stable environment for long-term investment in its economy.

To promote economic interdependence is to allow the grand forces of economic change to move countries around the world in the direction of the United States. Trade and investment is a solvent of authoritarian politics. To the extent that an expanding world economy stimulates the rise of democracy around the world, American security and political interests are advanced. Other countries, of course, have their own reasons for pursuing interdependence and engaging with international institutions. In Box 9.5, we review liberal, constructivist, and realist arguments on why China has become more willing to embrace international institutions.

Leadership and the Liberal World Economy

The experience of the United States after World War II led political scientists and economists to theorize more generally about the role of leadership in promoting a liberal or open world economy. The link between openness and leadership was first stressed by Charles Kindleberger in his study of the great depression in the 1930s. In exploring various causes of the collapse of the world economy after 1929, Kindleberger looked at a variety of potential causes, such as specific government policies and long-term shifts in economics and technology, but he ultimately focused on leadership. In his view, Britain was unable and the United States unwilling to provide measures to ensure openness and stability in the world economy during this inter-war moment of crisis. By the late 1920s, Britain was no longer the leading world power and the United States, while newly powerful, had not fully recognized its increasing leadership importance and responsibilities. According to Kindleberger, the leading state can exercise leadership during a crisis by keeping its domestic market open to trade in goods from other countries, providing international financing and liquidity, and pursuing expansionary macro-economic policy measures (Kindleberger 1973). In 1929, the United

States failed to recognize its special leadership role and pursued narrow, short-term interests. It followed, along with other major countries, protectionist interests and competitive devaluation of currencies. Rather than attempt to counteract the collapse of world markets, the United States made the situation worse by enacting the infamous Smoot-Hawley tariff, one of the most protectionist bills in American history.

In Kindleberger's view, leadership is more than the wielding of power. The leading state must have some recognition of its special responsibilities for management of the world economy. In the 1930s, the United States did not yet understand its role. The leading state must be able to use its domestic market to stabilize the larger international economy, and it must be able to resist domestic pressures. Leadership requires reforming the leading state's understanding of interests and capacities. Policy makers must grasp the state's larger role and conceive interests in a far-sighted and dynamic way. The state may forgo some short-term gains by resisting protection and restrictive policies, but better serve the country's long-term interests.

This focus on leadership of the world economy directs us to questions about the future. The United States has played a leadership role for many decades, using its economic, military, technological, and political capabilities to open up and manage the postwar world economy. On balance, the United States used its dominant position to encourage open trade, rules, and institutions that would facilitate economic stability. But, while the United States is still the largest economy in the world and possesses unrivaled military and technological capabilities, other countries are growing bigger and richer. China has become a key player in the world economy, and is likely to become more important. So are countries such as India and Brazil. As the United States loses its commanding position, how will this impact the world economy? Will other countries, such as China, join the United States to provide more collective leadership? Alternatively, will China seek to pursue a less liberal-oriented organization of the world economy? Will it engage in more mercantilist and state-to-state trading relationships that undercut the openness of the world economy?

The United States provided leadership of the world economy during and after the Cold War, relying on economic partnerships with Japan and European countries, particularly Germany. These countries shared a great deal. They were all liberal democracies and they were alliance partners. But, increasingly, it is now China that the United States must work with over the management of the world economy. China is neither a liberal democracy nor an alliance partner. It is, however, seen by many observers as a potential geopolitical rival. How will this new and dynamic situation play itself out? Can China and the United States work together to provide leadership, or will these countries find themselves in competition with each other, reluctant to cooperate to keep the world economy open and stable? This is a key question for the future of the liberal world economy.

State	🌐 **International**	*Levels of Analysis*
Great powers have special incentives and opportunities to use trade and market relations to influence the orientation of other states and, over time, alter the basic organization of the world economy so as to advance their national interests and the order and stability of world politics.	The distribution of power within the global system creates limits and opportunities for major states to lead and manage the world economy.	*Great Powers in the World Economy*

The Contemporary World Economy: Globalization and its Challenges

The world economy today is truly a global system of markets and exchange. Trade has been steadily expanding across the regions of the world. People buy, sell, and invest across vast reaches of the Earth. American consumers buy goods made in China, Malaysia, and Vietnam. Chinese companies invest in mining operations in Africa. Global multinational enterprises operate in dozens of countries. Indian firms provide accounting and legal services for offices in New York. Buildings in Beijing are designed in London, and built with supplies from all corners of the world. Markets in stocks and bonds link traders and investors in Europe, Asia, and North America. In this integrated global financial system, money speeds across borders in increasing volumes and velocity. In the background, the American dollar provides a 'key currency' for the world economy, facilitating the exchange of currencies and the stability of trade and investment. We live in an era of economic globalization.

Will globalization move forward or retreat? The world economy has become increasingly integrated, but it has also encountered many challenges. To some, globalization is a wonderful development which has united the world and brought people together in new and positive ways. To others, globalization is a process controlled by wealthy states and corporations that has created global winners and losers and generated threats to stability and security. There are several aspects to worries about the future of globalization.

First, the recent global financial crisis has raised new doubts about the virtues of unfettered economic openness. The global financial crisis began in the fall of 2008 with several large American banks suddenly becoming insolvent. Their balance sheets were built on sophisticated and highly leveraged credits and loans, backed by inflated and unsustainable real estate values. In a spiraling crisis, several leading banks defaulted on their obligations, other banks quickly stopped lending, and the global financial system almost came to a standstill. The American government launched a massive and controversial 'bailout' of the banks, but the abrupt stoppage in bank lending triggered a slowdown in the world economy. The most severe recession since the Great Depression enveloped the world. The major industrial countries responded to the crisis with new ideas about the regulation of banks and international financial transactions. But, questions remain about the virtues of an open and globalized system of finance.

Second, the American dollar has also been under pressure. As we noted earlier, the United States has exercised leadership over the world economy, partially through the international use of the dollar as a key currency. The dollar has been seen as a stable currency that countries can use to 'store value' and facilitate transactions. It has been the global currency. But, with the rise of Asian economies and the relative decline of America's pre-eminent role, there are new questions about the future of the dollar. Will countries such as China seek to establish an alternative global currency? What happens if there is a general breakdown in the key currency arrangements and a more fragmented monetary system emerges?

Third, there is growing competition for energy supplies worldwide. China has become the second largest economy in the world and continues to grow rapidly; it has made systematic efforts to secure deals with supplier countries to stable flows of oil and gas. A scramble for energy has returned to the global stage. Will this competition for energy turn into a geopolitical struggle that will tear the multilateral trading system apart? Will the rise of state-to-state deals between countries like China and energy suppliers undermine the principles of open market access and free trade? China, along with other rapidly industrializing market countries such as Brazil and India, uses a tremendous amount of energy. Scarcity and the insecurity of access to energy resources reinforce tendencies of these high-growth states to pursue exclusive state-to-state deals.

Fourth, as we described in Chapter 8, the World Trade Organization is the global body dedicated to the promotion of open trade. In past decades, the WTO, or the GATT which preceded it, presided over successive rounds of trade liberalization. Tariffs and non-tariff barriers were eliminated and the flows of trades increased. But the most recent effort to liberalize trade – the Doha round – has stalled and there is no prospect of completion any time soon. Tough issues are on the WTO agenda. Agriculture, for example, is one area that has not been fully liberalized. Developing countries have much to gain from global reductions on barriers, but Europe, Japan, and the United States face powerful domestic interests that resist further openness of agricultural trade. What happens when a 50-year period of global trade barrier reductions comes to an end? The recent global economic recession has also produced new voices in countries around the world questioning the virtues of free trade.

These developments do not necessarily herald the end or a sharp decline in economic globalization. But the optimistic vision of the 1990s, that with the end of the Cold War globalization would spread fully and inevitably throughout the international system, seems less convincing today. After the Cold War, writers such as Thomas Friedman were enthusiastic champions of globalization (Friedman 1999). Good things would come from the expansion and integration of market societies. Democracy would be encouraged and reinforced. Growth would lift all boats on the global economic sea. Economic globalization would encourage peaceful settlements of disputes. Economically isolated countries would join the modern world. Internationalism would grow and nationalism would wane. In retrospect, these optimistic projections seem a bit premature. Globalization has lifted some societies upward and trade has been integral in facilitating economic growth. But, worries persist about the stability of such an open, far-spreading system.

In the midst of the Great Recession of 2008–09, new forms of global economic governance began to emerge. Countries such as China, India, Brazil, Mexico, and South Africa became more important participants in the world economy, and sought and attained greater voice in managing global economic rules and decisions. In the fall of 2008, the then US President Bush hosted a meeting of the G-20, an expanded grouping of states that includes developing countries such as India and China and oil producers such as Saudi Arabia. In the years ahead, the G-20 and other state groups will likely grow in importance as world leaders seek to manage the crises and instabilities of a globalized world economy.

The emergence of the G-20 at the height of the Great Recession of 2008–2009, and the increasing importance of fast-growing developing countries such as China, Brazil, and India to global recovery and expansion are signals of great change; a 'changing of the guard' among states that lead and direct the world economy.

Levels of Analysis	**State**	**International**
Globalization and its Challenges	As China grows more wealthy and powerful, it joins the United States as a leading world economic power, and this raises questions about how the two countries will cooperate or compete in managing stability and openness of the world economy.	The globalization of the world economy – in which most of the countries of the world are increasingly interconnected – raises fundamental questions about world politics – political stability, economic fairness, and the future of global leadership.

Revisiting the Enduring Question and Looking Ahead

International politics and economics go hand in hand, and this chapter has continued our exploration of how a world of states and a world of markets interact. We have focused at the level of individual governments and explored the challenges and opportunities they face in simultaneously managing domestic politics – relations with their own citizens – and foreign policy – relations with other governments, peoples, and organizations around the world. We have examined the many ways that states rely on their domestic economy for taxes and resources to support their international ambitions. We have seen the complex calculations that states must make to foster open trade but also protect domestic industries from foreign competition. We have analyzed how great powers often seek to use policies of trade and economic integration to promote friendly and stable relations with other great powers. And we have seen the complex ways that a globalized world economy shape and constrain modern international relations.

In the next chapter, we look in more detail at the challenges faced by developing countries in the world economy. We know that powerful states and corporations have the resources to make the world economy serve their interests. What about poorer or weaker states – what strategies are available to them, and why do some weaker states develop more fully and quickly than others? We will explore the characteristics and problems of development generally, and will pay particular attention to some development states that are rising rapidly both politically and economically, including India, China, and Brazil.

Visit **www.palgrave.com/politics/Grieco** to access extra resources for this chapter, including:

- Chapter summaries to help you review the material
- Multiple choice quizzes to test your understanding
- Flashcards to test your knowledge of the key terms in this chapter
- An interactive simulation that invites you to go through the decision-making process of a world leader at a crucial political juncture
- Pivotal decisions in which you weigh up the pros and cons of complicated decisions with grave consequences
- Outside resources, including links to contemporary articles and videos, that add to what you have learned in this chapter

---

Study Questions

1. What major assumptions distinguish the three major schools of thought in international political economy: liberalism, Marxism, and economic nationalism? Which worldview do you find most compelling, and why?

2. Governments are territorial; they control pieces of land and the populations upon them. Economic actors are mobile; traders and investors cross borders and potentially operate anywhere in the world. In what ways can this tension between the logic of states and the logic of markets be resolved?

3. Do international economic relations promote peace? Why or why not?

4. Is it possible in the international system to be a great military power without being a great economic power? Is it possible to be a great economic power without being a great military power?

5. If economists are correct that free trade benefits all who trade, why do governments sometimes pursue free trade, and sometimes pursue protectionism?

Further Reading

Kennedy, Paul (1987) *The Rise and Fall of Great Powers: Economic Change and Military Conflict from 1500 to 2000* (New York: Random House). A masterful history of the cycles of rise and decline of the great powers in five centuries of the modern era, tracing the implications of the advancing and receding economic fortunes of states on their geopolitical ambitions and accomplishments.

Keohane, Robert (1984) *After Hegemony: Cooperation and Discord in the World Political Economy* (Princeton: Princeton University Press). A major statement of why states in the postwar era have incentives to build multilateral institutions that facilitate exchange and cooperation.

Kindleberger, Charles (2013) *The World in Depression, 1929–1939*, 40th anniversary edition (Berkeley: University of California Press). Kindleberger seeks to explain the Great Depression and the collapse of the world economy in the 1930s, emphasizing the failure of British and American leadership.

Polanyi, Karl (2001) *The Great Transformation: The Political and Economic Origins of Our Time*, 2nd edn (Boston: Beacon Press). In this classic work of economic history, originally published in 1944, Polanyi offers an account of the rise of market societies in the Western world beginning with the industrial revolution. He argues that the idea of the 'self-regulating market' is a myth. Markets emerged through deliberate government actions as state building and geopolitics gave birth to a modern world economy.

Rosecrance, Richard (1987) *The Rise of the Trading State: Commerce and Conquest in the Modern World* (New York: Basic Books). Rosecrance argues that the nature of capitalism and the world economy has changed, allowing states to trade and grow rich without engaging in old-style imperialism and territorial conquest.

Rodrik, Dani (2012) *The Globalization Paradox: Democracy and the Future of the World Economy* (New York: Norton). Rodrik challenges the widespread view that ongoing increases in globalization – manifest in open and increasing levels of trade and capital integration – is overwhelmingly good for peoples and societies.

Smith, Adam (2013) *The Wealth of Nations* (New York: Simon and Brown, originally published in 1776). The classic statement of the origins and working of markets and commercial society, making the case for the virtues of free trade and enlightened self-interest.

10

Dilemmas of Development

Enduring question: How does participation in the world economy help or hinder the economic development of poorer countries

South Korea today is wealthy: it has a bustling, modern economy, and its citizens are among the best educated and healthiest in the world. But did you know that, in 1980, the total output of goods and services that Argentina produced per person was perhaps twice that of South Korea? Starting from behind Argentina, and many other countries, South Korea surged ahead. By 2010, South Korea and Argentina had completely reversed their relative economic standing: while South Korea that year produced goods and services worth about $27,000 per person, Argentina's production of goods and services was a little over $14,000. Although surpassed by South Korea, Argentina did experience a growing economy. The East African country, Kenya, in contrast, made little to no progress during this period on the economic front: in 1980, its economy produced goods and services totaling about $1,375 per person; in 2010, its economic output was about $1,481.

Why do developing countries differ so much in attaining higher standards of living for their people? This question is clearly important: whether countries do or do not develop economically determines in large measure whether their populations enjoy a full life or suffer an early death, and whether they have growing hope or persistent despair. It is also important from a practical viewpoint: as we will see in later chapters, countries that fail at development are often prone to internal war and the terrible consequences of that both for the people living in those countries as well as for neighbors and the larger international community.

A great deal of the answer to the question of why some countries develop economically while others do not concerns what happens within them. However, every national economy is also embedded, to a greater or lesser degree, in the global economy. Then the question becomes: does participation in the world economy help or hinder the economic development of poorer countries? This external side of the development question is the focus of this chapter. We will see below that there are many answers to this question, and debates about the international economy and development form a core element of the field of international political economy.

We will in the first section describe exactly what we mean when we use terms such as economic development and developing country, and show that different groups of countries have had radically different degrees of success in attaining economic development. In the second section, we pay close attention to the challenges that developing countries face that arise from their historical as well as their contemporary linkages with the global economy. We then investigate whether commercial and financial linkages between developing countries and the world might present important opportunities for these countries to move ahead economically. Finally, we will look at a group of large and increasingly important developing countries, the so-called BRICS states of Brazil, Russia, India, China, and South Africa.

Learning Objectives

By the end of this chapter, you will be able to:

→ Recognize the defining characteristics of a developing country and appreciate the recent economic growth experiences of different groups of developing countries.

→ Consider the challenges developing countries face in achieving economic goals that result from past and current linkages to the global economy.

→ Analyze opportunities and problems that globalization of trade present to developing countries.

→ Evaluate opportunities and problems that globalization of finance present to developing countries.

→ Compare the economic development strategies of countries that may emerge or re-emerge as great powers, such as China, India, Brazil, Russia, and South Africa.

Chapter Contents

- What and Where Are the Developing Countries?
- International Relations and Challenges to Developing Countries
- Is International Trade a Path to Development?
- Is International Finance a Path to Development?
- Development Strategies and Emerging Great Powers – the BRICS
- Revisiting the Enduring Question and Looking Ahead
- Study Questions
- Further Reading

What and Where Are the Developing Countries?

A **developing country** is a country whose residents have not, on average, attained the living standards typically enjoyed by residents of wealthy countries, such as the United States, Canada, Japan, and the nations of Western Europe. At present, the developing countries are mainly located in Latin America, Northern and sub-Saharan Africa, the Middle East (with the exception of Israel), and East, South, and Southeast Asia. China is an interesting case. It was until recently an economic laggard, but it is now bursting with growth and possesses the world's second largest national economy. However, its population is so large that its *average* living standard is not yet on a par with countries we typically consider developed. In more technical terms, developing countries have lower levels of average gross domestic product (GDP) per capita than wealthy nations. As you will recall from Chapter 8, a country's annual total GDP is the final monetary value of the goods and services that are produced in that country in a given year. A country's GDP per capita is therefore a country's total GDP divided by its total population. One important analysis (Collier 2007) suggests that countries around the world with residents totaling between them around four billion people have seen improvement in their standard of living, but about one billion people live in countries that have made little or no economic progress. These individuals live, for the most part, in sub-Saharan Africa, but also in such countries as Afghanistan in Central Asia, Laos and Cambodia in Southeast Asia, and Haiti and Bolivia in the western hemisphere. These very poor countries face high barriers to growth, including corrupt governments, poor transportation links to the outside world, and high dependence on exports of natural resources.

What is Economic Development?

GDP per capita is often employed by economists, governments, and international institutions such as the World Bank and the IMF as a rough measure of the quality of life that individuals can attain through their consumption of goods and services, including basic items like food, education, and medical care. However, GDP per person is an imperfect measure of the economic well-being for each person in a country in a given year. Because it reports only the average level of income that individuals have attained in a country, GDP per capita may mask large inequalities in the distribution of income within a country, and, therefore, life opportunities. Moreover, as the UN Development Program (UNDP) an agency of the UN, emphasizes, **human development** is a process of enlarging people's choices and giving them a means to lead lives that they value. The UNDP thus has created the Human Development Index (HDI), which consists of average life expectancy, literacy and educational attainment, and per capita income. The UNDP presents a report each year on changes in HDI around the world, and while the index has yet to attain widespread acceptance or use it deserves examination by students of international development.

GDP per capita and the HDI index are highly correlated with one another, so the former seems to capture much of what is measured by the latter, but there are exceptions which are what make the HDI index so useful. For example in 2011, Qatar, a small oil-rich country in the Gulf, had the world's largest per capita GDP at $107,700, more than double that of the United States. But the Human Development Index ranked Qatar thirty-seventh when life expectancy and literacy and other educational features were taken into account.

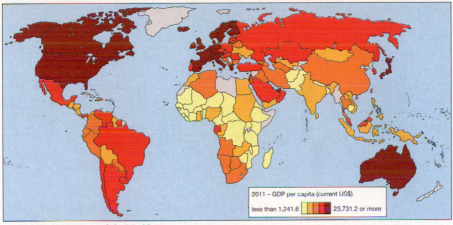

A   GDP Per Capita around the World, 2011

2011 – GDP per capita (current US$)

less than 1,241.6   23,731.2 or more

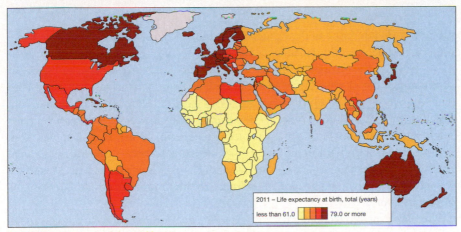

B   Life Expectancy around the World, 2011

2011 – Life expectancy at birth, total (years)

less than 61.0   79.0 or more

◀ **Map 10.1 A World of Different Life Opportunities**

This pair of maps shows that countries with higher levels of income tend also to have higher life expectancies. This suggests that, in general, countries that have achieved a higher level of economic development in terms of per capita income enable residents to live longer.

Source: World Bank, World Databank, World Development Indicators, available at http://databank.worldbank.org/ddp/home.do?Step=12&id=4&CNO=2.

More generally, when comparing the above pair of maps (Map 10.1), we can see there is a close relationship across countries between GDP per capita and average life expectancy at birth. Some of the differences around the world on both dimensions are shocking. In 2011, for example, Norway's GDP per capita was almost $100,000, and Norwegian babies born that year had an average life expectancy of 81 years; that very same year, GDP per capita in the Democratic Republic of Congo was only about $244, and babies born in that country had an average life expectancy of only 48 years.

Given the connection between GDP per capita and a basic measure of human well-being such as life expectancy, most developing countries seek progressively higher levels of GDP per capita. By consequence, economic development is usually taken to mean the attainment by a poorer country of an increase in its rate of growth of GDP per capita.

Growth Experiences of Different Groups of Developing Countries

Despite most developing countries aiming to increase their rate of growth of GDP per capita, different regions of the world have had very different experiences. Indeed, as we can see in Figure 10.1, from the 1980s up through the first decade of the 2000s, developing countries in East Asia and the Pacific enjoyed a consistent record of rapid

Economic development: The attainment by a poorer country of an increase in its rate of growth of GDP per capita.

► **Figure 10.1 Annual Rates of Growth in Per Capita GDP, by Region and Decade, 1980–2010**

This figure shows how different groups of developing countries have attained different rates of growth in per capita income from the 1980s through the first decade of the 2000s or, in the case of the newly free countries that emerged from the Cold War, from the 1990s up to 2010.

Source: World Bank, World Databank, World Development Indicators, available at http://databank.worldbank.org/ddp/home.do?Step=12&id=4&CNO=2.

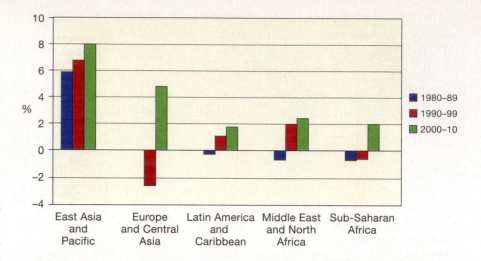

economic growth; those in the former Soviet bloc in Europe and Central Asia had a difficult first decade of independence but are now attaining strong growth; those in Latin America, the Caribbean, the Middle East, and North Africa have had slow but accelerating rates of growth during the period; and countries in sub-Saharan Africa had negative per capita growth during the 1980s and the 1990s, but in the most recent decade have begun to attain modest rates of economic growth. Africa's recent success might be due to short-term circumstances (Collier 2007: 9–10) such as increases in prices for the natural resources they export, which is recorded as growing national income, rather than movement to long-term, sustained growth trajectories. Cautious, watchful optimism might be the best approach to thinking about development in this part of the world.

We have explored what we mean by economic development and developing countries, and emphasized how different groups of developing countries have fared in terms of growth in recent decades. But how might international relations have affected economic development in these countries in the past and at present, and shaped their prospects for development in the future? That is the central question we want to address, and having now set the stage we next analyze the effects of history and current global trends on economic development.

Levels of Analysis	👤 **Individual**	🌐 **International**
Characteristics of Developing Countries	Per capita GDP is an important overall measure of a country's prosperity, but individual citizens also are greatly affected by 'quality of life' measures such as literacy and life expectancy.	Just as there is great inequality among states in international security affairs, there is great inequality among states in the world economy.

International Relations and Challenges to Developing Countries

Why are countries like Germany, Japan, and now South Korea relatively wealthy and prosperous, while countries like Mexico, Uganda, and India are relatively poor and are still in the process of achieving development? Economists have not settled on a single theory of development, but they have learned there are many factors that account for variation in the economic fates of poorer nations, including geography; reliable, extensive access to foreign markets; and the availability of growth-producing national endowments of land, labor, capital, and natural resources. Good governance is also very important for growth. A country with good governance at home typically possesses transparent and consistent political and legal systems, combats official corruption, and protects property. These factors encourage individuals to save, make investments, and pursue technological innovations that promote economic growth.

Scholars of international relations have sought to learn whether international connections – trade, investment, and foreign aid – help or hinder poorer countries as they seek to develop. In this section, we look at what scholars have learned about two *challenges* that past and present external conditions may present to poorer nations. Then, we will see what kinds of helpful *opportunities* international participation may provide developing countries as they try to attain faster growth.

Failure to Develop: A Legacy of Colonialism?

Many scholars in the 1960s and 1970s suggested that the lack of growth plaguing many developing countries was due to their colonial heritage. They suggested that former **colonies** or countries that were highly dominated by European countries or the United States in Latin America, Asia, and Africa might be formally independent, but their economies were still oriented to serving the dominant states at the cost of achieving their own economic well-being. These scholars, often informed by some of the Marxist ideas we discussed in Chapter 3, constituted the *dependencia* school of underdevelopment (Frank 1966; Dos Santos 1970; Cardoso and Faletto 1979). In response to our enduring question of whether international economic linkages help or hinder development, the dependencia school has offered the fullest and most consistent answer in the negative.

Dependencia scholars have argued that developing countries' elites were controlled by the governments and large corporations in the advanced countries, mainly the United States and the industrial countries of Western Europe. The local elites in particular directed their national economies toward the needs of the rich nations, serving as a source of raw materials and a market for goods from the rich countries that would be sold to the elite. The result was that a small segment of the population in developing countries prospered, but the country as a whole failed to develop indigenous manufacturing and a vibrant working and middle class.

Dependencia theory commanded progressively less attention from students of development and international relations by around the late 1980s. Perhaps the central reason the approach became less salient and persuasive is that several developing countries, including South Korea, Taiwan, Chile, Mexico, and Brazil, began to achieve economic growth, in some cases dramatically so, even though they were former colonies or were otherwise tightly linked to rich countries through trade and invest-

Good governance: A country with good governance at home typically possesses transparent and consistent political and legal systems, combats official corruption, and protects property. These factors encourage individuals to save, make investments, and pursue technological innovations that promote economic growth.

Colonies: Areas conquered by a colonizing power over which the colonizer has political and economic control. Colonizers exploit colonized lands and peoples through trade or settlement for economic and political gain.

Dependencia: A school of thought that argues that international economic linkages hinder development in developing countries. Proponents of *dependencia* argue that the connections between developing countries and wealthy countries are designed for the benefit of the wealthy countries (often former colonial powers) and the only people in the developing country who benefit are in the small elite that promotes the international linkages.

ment. As we will see below, the most prominent dependencia writer, Fernando Henrique Cardoso, actually came to favor global economic integration as a pathway to development.

Still, there are good reasons to believe that the impact of colonialism on development has been mixed at best. In some instances, colonial powers created economic infrastructure – roads, railways, ports, and telecommunications systems – that laid the foundation for future growth. In many other instances, colonial powers did little to promote long-term growth. They dictated that their colonies trade exclusively or preferentially with the mother country, instead of having broad access to the markets and products of many other countries. Colonial powers also used coercion to extract economic value. Portugal, for example, used forced or conscript labor in its African colonies of Angola and Mozambique, often compelling women and children to work without pay building and paving roads (Anderson 1962). Farmers in Mozambique who traditionally grew subsistence crops for their local communities were forced to cultivate and pick cotton, a cash crop for which Portuguese companies held monopoly rights and reaped the profits.

The development prospects of some former colonies were stunted by the repressive and exploitative practices of their colonial masters. Yet, some former colonies – think for example of the United States, Canada, and South Korea – grew and prospered over time. Moreover, some countries that have faced development challenges are not former colonies (for example, Iran), while others, such as Latin American states that achieved independence in the 1820s and 1830s, broke free of colonial ties long ago. As we noted earlier, what happens within countries over time is, alongside external relations, an important factor in accounting for the development of that country or its lack thereof.

Finally, there is evidence that a colonial legacy *of a certain type* unambiguously imparted harmful dynamics to numerous developing countries (Acemoglu et al. 2012). So whilst in places like North America and Australia, where many of the indigenous inhabitants were killed by disease, large numbers of Europeans settled and created laws and political institutions that protected private property and set the stage for long-term economic growth, in Latin America, the Caribbean, and sub-Saharan Africa, where smaller numbers of colonialists settled, the Westerners who did arrive employed highly exploitative legal arrangements to maximize their own short-term profits. The result was a legacy of laws, courts, and regulatory bodies that afforded an inhospitable environment for long-term growth. Hence, in response to our enduring question, there is good reason to say that colonialism kept many countries from achieving long-term growth even after they became independent.

Difficulties in Development

In the years immediately after World War II, many developing countries exported agricultural products and raw materials to advanced countries and, in return, imported manufactured goods they needed, such as automobiles, aircraft, or pharmaceuticals. This arrangement would seem to be in everyone's best interest, if we think back to the trade theory presented in Chapter 8. However, as Box 10.1 shows, and reflecting realist concerns that we discussed in Chapters 3 and 8, leaders and top policy makers of new countries, from Secretary of the Treasury Alexander Hamilton in the United States in the 1790s to Prime Minister Jawaharlal Nehru of India in the early 1960s, have balked at dependency on other countries for manufactured goods, especially if these goods have an impact on national security.

State Leaders Describe the Importance of National Economic Self-Sufficiency

Then: *Treasury Secretary Alexander Hamilton on Promoting American Industry, 1791*

At the outset of its history, the United States had an overwhelmingly agricultural economy, and important American leaders such as Thomas Jefferson believed that America would safeguard its republican institutions most effectively if it remained rooted in agriculture. However, in a major report to Congress in December 1791, Secretary of the Treasury Alexander Hamilton argued that the new nation should possess an agriculture base but also encourage manufacturing. Summarizing his argument he suggested:

> From these circumstances collectively two important inferences are to be drawn: One, that there is always a higher probability of a favorable balance of trade, in regard to countries in which manufactures, founded on the basis of a thriving agriculture, flourish, than in regard to those which are confined wholly, or almost wholly, to agriculture; the other (which is also a consequence of the first) that countries of the former description are likely to possess more pecuniary wealth or money than those of the latter ... Not only the wealth, but the independence and security of a country appear to be materially connected with the prosperity of manufactures. Every nation, with a view to those great objects, ought to endeavor to possess within itself all the essentials of national supply.

Source: Alexander Hamilton, *Report on Manufactures*, Communication to the House of Representatives, December 5, 1791, reprinted as Document 162 by the US Senate in 1913.

Now: *Prime Minister Jawaharlal Nehru on Building MIGs in India, 1962*

In June 1962, Prime Minister Nehru announced to the Indian Parliament that India would purchase several Soviet MIG-21 fighter jets rather than seek to buy relatively more advanced fighters from the United States or Britain. Nehru acknowledged that the MIG-21s India would buy and later build were less advanced technologically than the F-104s that Pakistan had recently purchased from the United States. However, Nehru told the members of parliament that he had selected the MIG-21 option because the Soviets had agreed they would license and assist in Indian domestic manufacture of that model of jet fighters. For Nehru, even though the MIG-21 was not the most advanced fighter aircraft available, the licensing agreement with the Soviets, which would eventually see the production of several such aircraft built in India, was critically important:

> It was more practical to have the capacity to manufacture a second-rate thing in one's own country than to buy a first-rate thing from outside

While separated in time by almost two centuries, both America's Alexander Hamilton and India's Jawaharlal Nehru argued that national self-sufficiency in manufacturing is an important and valid economic policy goal for a new country.

Source: Ian C. C. Graham, 'The Indo-Soviet MIG Deal and Its International Repercussions', *Asian Survey* 4 (May, 1964), p. 826.

Reliance on agriculture and raw materials may be a path to development, to the extent that countries use the economic gains created by those activities to generate investments in new areas of manufacturing and services. However, from the 1950s to the present, economists and political scientists have raised concerns about the vulnerability of developing countries that rely too heavily on agriculture and raw materials.

For example, wealthy industrial countries – including the United States, Japan, the member countries of the European Union, and other European countries such as Switzerland – extensively protect their farmers from foreign agricultural competition. Developing countries specializing in agriculture therefore cannot count on full access to those markets. In addition, technological innovations – for example, the use of robotics and computers in the manufacturing of automobiles – improve **worker productivity**, that is, they enable increases in the amount of output any worker can produce in a fixed period of time. These technological innovations have been more pervasive in manufacturing than in agriculture or raw materials. These productivity gains promote higher GDP per capita, increasing the economic gap between producers of manufactures and producers of raw materials. Some raw materials, such as oil, are in high demand and can bring significant profits to their producers. But developing countries blessed with energy reserves must be wary of the 'resource curse'. That is, over-reliance on the proceeds from oil sales in some countries of the Middle East and Latin America has been associated with autocratic rule, large gaps in the distribution of income and wealth, and a failure to move beyond oil to a more diversified set of economic activities.

In summary, then, a colonial past and a lack of national manufacturing in the present may inhibit economic growth in the global economy for developing countries. But to what extent can international trade and the resulting globalization serve as a tool for economic development?

Worker productivity: The amount of output any worker can produce in a fixed period of time.

Levels of Analysis
International Challenges to Developing Countries

State	International
National laws and institutions, inherited from a colonial past, can sometimes promote yet often inhibit economic growth.	Reliance on agriculture and raw material production can spark economic growth, but may also trap countries in an international division of labor in which it becomes difficult to develop more diversified economies.

Is International Trade a Path to Development?

Since World War II, poorer countries have pursued different strategies to overcome the challenges we have previously described and to create opportunities for development. From roughly the 1950s into the 1970s, many developing countries, including such major countries as China, India, Mexico, Brazil, and Turkey, sought to restrict or at least control their trading linkages with developed countries. By the late 1970s and into the 1990s, when it became clear that those market-controlling strategies had failed to deliver sustained growth, these and other developing countries increasingly turned to more outward-looking strategies.

Developing Countries and Market-Controlling Trade Strategies

Developing countries have pursued three basic market-controlling strategies to improve their economic position: infant-industry oriented policies to promote national industries, international commodity cartels, and international commodity agreements.

Import-Substituting Industrialization

In the two decades after World War II, many developing countries, notably Brazil, India, Mexico, and Turkey, acted in line with the infant-industry logic we discussed in Chapter 8 and pursued import-substituting industrialization (ISI). The intellectual inspiration behind ISI came from an Argentine economist, Raúl Prebisch, who directed the UN's first Economic Commission for Latin America. The roots of ISI also take us once more to the Great Depression of the 1930s, when industrial-country markets for raw materials and agricultural products collapsed, and thereby forced developing countries that relied on those markets to search for alternative ways to generate economic growth. Anti-colonial sentiment also contributed to ISI's appeal. Prebisch and others were critical of the international division of labor that seemed to lock developing states into selling primary goods and buying finished goods from their former colonial masters.

The strategy of ISI was premised on answering our enduring question partially in the negative: under then-existing conditions most developing countries could not benefit greatly from international economic integration if that integration unfolded strictly under the terms of the logic of traditional trade theory. A different approach was needed. In particular, in adopting ISI, governmental leaders wanted their consumers to substitute imports of manufactured goods, such as automobiles, with comparable domestically produced goods. Governments pursued ISI with high tariffs on imports of goods targeted for substitution, and subsidies (such as cash grants and low-cost loans) to pre-selected local manufacturers. These national champions were firms the government believed could do the best job of producing the substituted industrial goods. Ultimately, the expectation was that these national champions could compete at home without protection, and even become leaders in foreign markets.

ISI registered some success in the initial postwar decades. India, for example, experienced rapid economic growth pursuing ISI, with industrial output doubling during the 1950s and growing by 9 percent annually between 1960 and 1965 (Krueger 1975). India decreased its imports of manufactured goods and created domestic capacity, particularly in the types of machinery and equipment needed to produce final goods. Similarly, Brazil, Mexico, and Argentina enjoyed rapid growth during the 1950s and 1960s and established indigenous capacity in automobiles, steel, and machinery production.

The weaknesses of ISI became apparent by the 1970s. National champions and other domestic firms were safely behind high tariff walls. They did not face international competition, and had little incentive to charge low prices at home or make internationally competitive products. The results were current-account deficits and domestic price inflation. Inflation and resulting periodic economic slowdowns sometimes led to political upheaval and military coups, such as in Brazil, Chile and Argentina during the 1960s. By the 1970s, larger developing countries abandoned the 'go it alone' spirit of ISI and tried to attract foreign direct investment from advanced economies, while smaller developing states engaged the world economy through export strategies, both of which we discuss below.

Import-substituting industrialization [ISI]: A national development strategy that seeks to avoid international economic linkages in favor of focusing on domestic production. High tariffs and other similar measures encourage the local economy to forego imported goods in favor of goods produced locally by national champions.

National champion: In a state pursuing a strategy of ISI, firms the government believe could do the best job of producing the substituted industrial goods.

International Commodity Cartels

Rather than seeking to diversify away from raw material production, some developing countries instead have banded together and tried to gain greater economic benefits from selling their natural resources. These countries have formed state-sponsored **international commodity cartels**, which are groupings of developing-country governments that try to control the supply of a raw material or agricultural product on world markets in order to drive up prices and maximize revenues received by participating countries for the raw material or agricultural product. In recent decades, there have been a number of such international commodity cartels; examples include bauxite, rubber, diamonds, and, most notably, oil. For a variety of reasons, such as the entry of new suppliers or the availability of substitutes, these cartels do not, in general, appear to have been very successful in maximizing cartel-member revenues.

A partial exception is the Organization of Oil Exporting Countries (OPEC), which was founded in 1960, has twelve members (including Saudi Arabia, Iran, Iraq, Kuwait, Nigeria, and Venezuela), and is headquartered in Vienna, Austria. Representatives of OPEC nations meet periodically to set an oil production level for the membership as a whole, and allocate production quotas for individual members.

OPEC has had some success in limiting oil supplies on global markets; less supply typically does lead to higher prices. Yet, OPEC's success has been constrained by the fact that cartel members often cheat and produce more than their quotas. Moreover, such oil-producing countries as Russia, Canada, and Mexico are not members of the cartel, and when prices go up these producers have an incentive to increase production.

Still, OPEC countries, and especially Saudi Arabia, will be important to the future of the oil industry. As can be observed in Figure 10.2, in 2012 OPEC countries produced about 41 percent of the world's oil, and that year OPEC countries possessed about 72 percent of the world's proven reserves of oil.

International Commodity Agreements

Cartels such as OPEC consist of agreements among suppliers of a good or commodity that seek to limit production in order to maximize prices and revenues. An alternative

International commodity cartels: Groupings of developing-country governments that try to control the supply of a raw material or agricultural product on world markets in order to drive up prices and maximize revenues.

▶ **Figure 10.2 Global Oil Production and Proven Reserves, 2012**

These two figures underscore the importance of OPEC, and particularly OPEC member Saudi Arabia, in recent world production of oil and especially in terms of proven reserves of oil.

Sources: US Energy Information Administration, International Energy Statistics, available at http://www.eia.gov/cfapps/ipdbproject/IEDIndex3.cfm.

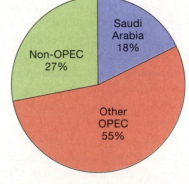

A   Oil Production, Percent of Total, 2012

Note: Total oil production in 2012 = 89.3 million barrels/day.

B   Proven Oil Reserves, Percent of Total, 2012

Note: Total reserves in 2012 = 1526 billion barrels.

approach used by some developing countries has been to press consumer countries (mainly advanced nations) to establish an **international commodity agreement**, or ICA, on the supply and prices for a particular commodity. In these cases, the developing countries have not sought agreements that lead to maximum prices for their commodity exports, but a reduction in price fluctuations for their exports. The objective for developing countries is to attain reasonably good prices and some sense of certainty about what their countries will be earning from their exports. Five ICAs were established from the 1950s to the 1970s for sugar, coffee, tin, cocoa, and rubber.

◀ **Photo 10.1 4th OPEC International Seminar, 2009**

Representatives of the member states of OPEC meet periodically to discuss whether they should increase or decrease amounts, or quotas, of oil each may sell on world markets. Here, OPEC representatives meet in Vienna, Austria in 2009 at the 4th OPEC International Seminar. Among other issues, the seminar, which had the theme 'Mapping the Future Energy Scene,' looked at the impact of falling prices caused by the global financial and economic crisis on the sustainability and long-term stability of the oil market.

Source: OPEC Secretariat, PR & Information Department.

However, these agreements often did not include all suppliers of the commodity in question (as in the case of cocoa). New suppliers could also enter an industry (the countries that now make up the European Union in regard to sugar) and existing members could exit an agreement (Thailand, Sri Lanka, and Malaysia in connection with the rubber agreement). As a result of these factors, all five ICAs were abandoned between the early 1980s and late 1990s (Gilbert 2004).

Developing Countries and Market-Accepting Trade Strategies

Countries that pursued ISI strategies often experienced high government debts and very low rates of national growth. As an alternative, a few developing countries with smaller domestic markets in the late 1950s and into the 1960s sought renewed growth through a strategy of **export-led growth (ELG)**. This strategy basically answers our enduring question in the affirmative: it is premised on the view that the international economy presents important opportunities for development. The strategy typically includes two basic components. First, national producers of goods for the local market are no longer offered preferential access to government credit or foreign exchange. Second, firms producing for export markets are now granted preferential access to credit and foreign currency.

ELG was not the preserve of small countries only; it was actually adopted by Japan after World War II, along with domestic protectionism, and was the basis of the 'economic miracle' that catapulted Japan from being a country demolished by war to the

International commodity agreement: An agreement, generally sought by developing countries exporting a particular commodity, on the supply and price of that commodity. The goal is not to maximize prices but rather to establish an acceptable, consistent price that the developing country can rely on.

Export-led growth (ELG): A strategy that argues that international economic linkages are good for developing countries because the international economy presents important opportunities for development. The strategy entails switching preference for government credit and foreign currency from firms producing for local markets to firms producing for export markets.

Asian Tigers: Originally Taiwan, South Korea, Singapore, and Hong Kong, countries that achieved rapid growth rates using a strategy of **export-led growth**, causing many Asian countries to follow in their path. Now many rapidly growing Asian countries are considered 'tigers'.

world's second largest national economy by the early 1980s. By the 1960s, the four Asian Tigers that had been early in choosing or switching to ELG – Taiwan, South Korea, Singapore, and Hong Kong – were achieving fast rates of growth in GDP per capita, and served as models for other East Asian countries that turned to ELG in the 1970s, such as Thailand, Malaysia, and mainland China.

Soon, even countries with large internal markets moved from ISI toward an export-oriented strategy of development. Turkey, Brazil, and Mexico made this shift during the 1980s, and India did so in the early 1990s. Many academics and policy makers shifted from skepticism to optimism about the possibilities of such integration. Indeed, as Box 10.2 shows, the most distinguished dependencia writer, Fernando Henrique Cardoso of Brazil, shifted his perspective on the benefits of economic integration, and took on a markedly strong pro-market and pro-integration orientation when he became Finance Minister and then President of Brazil. Cardoso shifted from a Marxist perspective (underdevelopment was a function of the capitalist world economy) and economic nationalist perspective (the solution was greater national self-sufficiency) to a more liberal perspective (development comes from embracing, not resisting, the liberal world economy).

Beijing Consensus: The idea that, for some poor countries, development can be best attained in a world of economic turbulence through systematic government controls on the pace of trade integration, capital inflows and outflows, the movement of labor within the country, and the external value of the national currency.

By the 1990s, many developing countries were not just turning to exports as the path to growth. They were also implementing packages of other policies reflecting what, as we noted in Chapter 8, came to be known as the Washington Consensus. Now, in the wake of the global economic crisis and the continuing rise of China, a potential new model of development has come into view, sometimes called the Beijing Consensus. This term is meant to suggest that, for some poorer countries, the necessary answer to our enduring question is once more at least partially in the negative: development can be best attained in a world of economic turbulence through systematic government controls on the pace of trade integration, capital inflows and outflows, the movement of labor within the country, and the external value of the national currency. Moreover, while the United States and other wealthy countries have argued that democratic political institutions are most likely to provide the best long-term environment for growth in poorer countries, the Beijing Consensus thesis holds that authoritarianism may actually enable growth to occur most rapidly in a developing nation. Only time will tell if the Beijing Consensus will gain traction and give state capitalism and authoritarianism new legitimacy in the years ahead.

Recall that Chapter 9 focused on the relationship between states and markets, and on the trade-offs governments face between economic efficiency and political autonomy. Now we see another dimension of the state–market relationship. Countries seeking economic development at times have relied more heavily on government intervention (the era of ISI) and at times on market forces (the era of the Washington Consensus). If the Beijing Consensus spreads, the pendulum may swing back to a renewed emphasis on the importance of the state in economic development.

Seeking a Better Deal in International Trade Negotiations

Many developing countries have accepted and benefited from economic integration and globalization, but this does not mean they have simply removed barriers to trade and allowed global market forces to dictate their trading patterns. Since the end of World War II developing countries have sought, with limited success, to shape the rules of the global economy more in their favor. In the 1960s, as we saw in Chapter 2, developing countries used their power in numbers in the UN to form the Group of

Fernando Henrique Cardoso on the Benefits of International Economic Integration

Cardoso Writing as Academic Critic, 1971/1979

Of course, imperialist penetration is a result of external social forces (multinational enterprises, foreign technology, international financial systems, embassies, foreign states and armies, etc.). What we affirm simply means that the system of domination reappears as an 'internal' force, through the social practices of local groups and classes which try to enforce foreign interests, not precisely because they are foreign, but because they may coincide with values and interests that these groups pretend are their own

It has been assumed that the peripheral countries would have to repeat the evolution of the economies of the central countries in order to achieve development. But it is clear that from its beginning the capitalist process implied an unequal relation between the central and the peripheral economies. Many 'underdeveloped' economies – as is the case of the Latin American – were incorporated into the capitalist system as colonies and later as national states, and they have stayed in the capitalist system throughout their history. They remain, however, peripheral economies with particular historical paths when compared with central capitalist economies." .

From Cardoso, *Dependency and Development in Latin America*, with Enzo Faletto, published in Spanish in 1971 and in English, by the University of California Press, in 1979.

Cardoso as Presidential Candidate and then President of Brazil, 1994, 2002

The international system is a field of opportunities, of resources, that must be sought naturally. We are a great country, with a clear vocation for an active and responsible participation in world affairs.

The process of liberalization of the economy and opening toward the outside world will continue, not an objective in and of itself, but as a strategic element in the modernization of our economy.

From 'Let's Work, Brazil,' the main campaign statement of the then Finance Minister Cardoso as he ran successfully for the first of two terms as President of Brazil.

Question: Mr. Cardoso, you are a sociologist and have studied, analyzed and written about the Brazilian society. As President and sociologist what is your advice to foreign investors when they come to invest in Brazil?

Response: My advice is probably superfluous, because the strength of the Brazilian economy speaks for itself. But I will say this: those who bet on Brazil's future stand to gain a lot, because the country has all it takes to continue in the path of social and economic development. For too long has Brazil suffered in stagnation and backwardness. This chapter is now closed. With democracy, economic stability and greater social justice, there is nothing that can stop Brazil in its progress. Our economic environment is business-friendly. Our people [are] hard-working, creative and eager to learn more. The country is not affected by any sort of ethnic rivalries or civil strife. We have world-class universities and world-class scientists. Investors who come to Brazil will be partners in our development and they will get the very significant returns of operating in a market of over 160 million people, or even more if you consider the integration with our neighbors in Mercosul.

From interview by World Investment News (WINNE) with President Cardoso, July 2002.

Sources: For statements from *Dependency and Underdevelopment*, and 'Let's Work Brazil', see Ken Brown, 'Word for Word: Fernando Henrique Cardoso: Having Left Campus for the Arena, Winner in Brazil Shifts to Right', *New York Times*, November 20, 1994.

77 and lobby collectively for development-friendly reforms in trade and finance. Their appeals, for the most part, were ignored by the stronger developed countries. As we also saw in Chapter 2, perhaps the most promising negotiating attempt took place in the 1970s, as many countries in the developing world sought to ally with OPEC and use its prominence to demand a New International Economic Order (NIEO). The NIEO demanded preferential trade arrangements, larger aid grants to less developed countries, and controls on multinational firms operating within their borders. OPEC countries eventually made their own deals with the United States and Europe, and the NIEO quietly faded away.

In recent years, influential developing nations, such as Brazil and India, have sought to forge a coalition of developing countries to press for better deals in the World Trade Organization (WTO). For example, these two countries, together with China and South Africa, brought together a coalition of developing countries that has blocked completion of the Doha round of WTO multilateral trade negotiations, which had been launched in 2001 in Doha, Qatar. If multilateral trade liberalization via the WTO is to have a future, it will require greater accommodation of the demands of these influential developing countries.

Fair trade negotiations may offer potential growth, but what role does international finance play in economic development? The next section will explore types of international financial flows and their impact on economic development.

Levels of Analysis

Trade as an Opportunity for Developing Countries

👥 **State**	🌐 **International**
Developing countries adopt different individual and collective strategies in their efforts to get a better deal from their interaction with the world economy.	Most collective negotiating efforts by developing countries to change the rules of international trade have not been successful, reflecting the lack of developing-country power in international politics and economics.
	Today the situation is changing, as developing countries, led by China, Brazil, and India, become more influential.

Is International Finance a Path to Development?

Developing countries often rely on foreign capital, but there is sharp controversy as to whether such capital is really helpful to them. To explore this matter, we need to define what we mean by international financial flows, examine the different types of such flows, and explore the opportunities and problems they pose for developing countries.

International Financial Flows: Meaning, Types, and Magnitudes

By an **international financial flow**, we mean the movement of capital – sometimes in the form of actual cash, but usually as a result of electronic transfers – from private or governmental individuals or organizations inside one country to private or governmental individuals or organizations inside another country. There are two basic forms of financial flows to developing countries: private and official. **Private finan-**

International financial flows: The movement of capital – sometimes in the form of actual cash, but usually as a result of electronic transfers – from private or governmental individuals or organizations inside one country to private or governmental individuals or organizations inside another country. These flows consist of both **private** and **official financial flows**.

Official financial flows: International financial flows that originate with governmental entities.

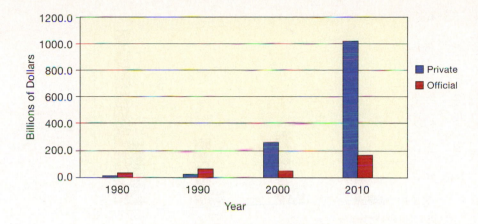

◀ Figure 10.3 Total Private and Official Financial Flows to Developing Countries, 1980–2010

This figure underscores how private financial flows to developing countries have grown compared to financial flows from official sources.

Source: World Bank, World Databank, World Development Indicators, available at http://databank.worldbank.org/ddp/home.do?Step=12&id=4&CNO=2.

Private financial flows: International financial flows that originate with non-governmental entities, such as individuals, private charities, or private firms such as banks or multinational corporations.

Foreign direct investment (FDI): when an enterprise (usually an MNE) in one country moves capital to another country with the intention of establishing an on-going business presence.

cial flows are flows that originate with non-governmental entities, such as individuals, private charities, or, private firms such as banks or multinational corporations. **Official financial flows** are flows that originate with governmental entities. These entities may be individual governments or inter-governmental organizations formed by governments, such as the World Bank, the International Monetary Fund, the European Union, the Asian Development Bank, and the Inter-American Development Bank.

As Figure 10.3 indicates, total financial flows to developing countries have increased steadily since the 1980s, reaching a total of $1.2 trillion in 2010. Moreover, while at the outset of the 1980s official sources of financial flows to developing countries were roughly twice those from private sources, by the end of the first decade of the 2000s the vast majority of financial flows to developing countries came from private sources. For example, private sources provided about 83 percent of the $1.2 trillion in total financial resources that went to developing countries in 2010.

There are four basic kinds of private capital flows to developing countries. First, **foreign direct investment** (FDI) occurs when an enterprise in one country moves capital to another country with the intention of establishing an ongoing business presence. The investing firm is usually a multinational enterprise (MNE). So, for example, when IBM establishes a wholly owned subsidiary in Mexico, this constitutes a US FDI

◀ Figure 10.4 Composition of Private Financial Flows to Developing Countries, 2000–10

This figure underscores two key points: first, private flows of capital to developing countries have grown substantially; and second, foreign direct investment is the largest type of private financial flow to developing countries.

Source: World Bank, World Databank, Development Indicators, available at http://databank.worldbank.org/ddp/home.do?Step=12&id=4&CNO=2.

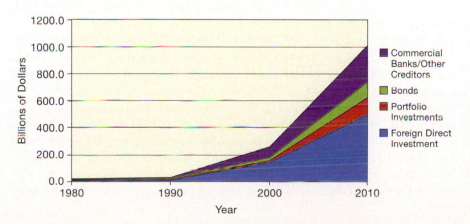

► Figure 10.5
Official Financial Flows to Developing Countries, by Type, 1980–2010

Bilateral ODA has been and remains the most important source of official financial flows to developing countries, although loans from official creditors like the World Bank are important.

Source: World Bank, World Databank, Development Indicators, available at http://databank.worldbank.org/ddp/home.do?Step=12&id=4&CNO=2.

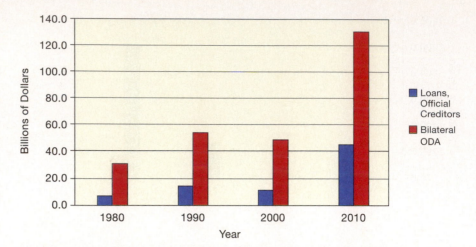

in Mexico. Another major type of private capital flow consists of **international bank loans**, whereby a bank in one country extends a loan to residents (which might be private individuals, firms, or a government) in another country. For example, if Deutsche Bank makes a loan to a private Mexican cement firm, that represents a bank-loan capital flow from Germany to Mexico. A third type of private financial flow to developing countries consists of **international portfolio investments**. If, for example, a Canadian-based mutual fund buys shares in the hypothetical Mexican cement firm noted above, *but not enough to have any management say in what that cement firm does*, then this is an instance in which there has been Canadian portfolio investment in Mexico. Finally, there are **international bonds**. For example, if a Mexican cement firm issues bonds in euros that are purchased by French pension funds, then this represents a bond-based capital flow from France to Mexico.

Figure 10.4 illustrates changes in the relative importance of these four kinds of private capital flows to developing countries. As it indicates, foreign direct investment has become by far the biggest single type of private financial flow into developing countries, followed by bank loans and similar credits, portfolio investment, and bonds. For example, FDI flows to developing countries in 2010 totaled about $509 billion, representing half of the total of roughly $1 trillion in private capital flows to developing countries that year, and totaled just about twice that of the next largest category of private capital flows to developing countries, bank loans.

There are two basic kinds of official financial flows to developing countries. First, there is bilateral **official development assistance (ODA)**, the provision by a donor government to a developing country of grants or loans with highly favorable repayment terms (for example, 50 years to repay, at 1 percent interest). Second, multilateral institutions such as the IMF and the World Bank, as well as regional financial institutions such as the Asian Development Bank, and the European Bank for Reconstruction and Development (EBRD), make loans to developing countries with near-market interest rates and repayment periods, to help those countries meet short-term cash needs or pursue big projects like dams and ports. These are termed financial flows from *official creditors*. With this background in mind, we can see in Figure 10.5 that, as of 2010, annual total official flows to developing countries have been in the range of about $176 billion, with about 75 percent of that consisting of ODA.

International bank loans: A kind of international private capital flow in which banks in one country supply loans to individuals in another country.

International portfolio investments: A type of international private capital flow in which an investor in one country buys shares (but not enough to have any management say) in a firm located in another country.

International bonds: A kind of international private capital flow in which individuals or firms in one country buy bonds originating in another country.

Official development assistance (ODA): The provision by a donor government to a developing country of grants or loans with highly favorable repayment terms (for example, 50 years to repay, at 1 percent interest).

Official flows are especially important for sub-Saharan Africa. As Figure 10.6 indicates, financial flows of all types to developing countries in sub-Saharan Africa totaled about $92 billion in 2010. Of that total, about $50 billion, or 54 percent, consisted of ODA and loans from multilateral institutions. Sub-Saharan Africa, then, while making substantial economic progress, still requires official economic assistance to meet its financial needs and attract resources from private investors and creditors.

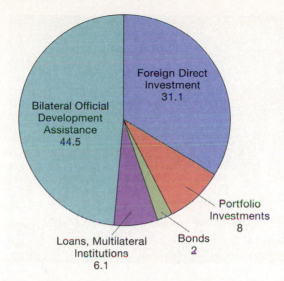

◀ **Figure 10.6 Private and Official Financial Flows to Countries in Sub-Saharan Africa, 2010**

(Billions of US Dollars)

While private sources make up the bulk of external financial resources to developing countries overall, official sources continue to represent the lion's share of resources committed to countries in sub-Saharan Africa.

Source: World Bank, World Databank, Development Indicators, available at http://databank.worldbank.org/ddp/home.do?Step=12&id=4&CNO=2.

Financial Flows: Opportunities and Challenges for Developing Countries

Official and private financial flows from abroad have allowed developing countries to gain access to foreign industry, technology, and managerial expertise. Multinational companies, for example, bring more advanced technology and their connections to the global economy when they set up shop in a developing country. As we discuss below, China has utilized foreign investment to attain its remarkable growth over the past three decades. Yet, although the potential benefits are significant, foreign capital can also create challenges for developing countries.

Bank Loans, Portfolio Investments, and Risk of Financial Crises

Many developing countries have learned that private capital flows from abroad, especially international bank loans and portfolio investments, can be quite volatile. Foreign investors seem to follow a pattern of becoming enthralled with, and then frightened by, prospects in particular developing countries, developing regions, or even developing countries as a whole. For example, a cycle of strong financial inflows followed by extremely rapid exits of capital contributed to a painful economic crisis during 1994–95 in Mexico. An even more dramatic financial crisis hit the developing world during 1997–98. At that time, a collapse in the stock market and currency in Thailand soon led foreign investors to pull their money out of the Philippines, Indonesia, and Malaysia, and even from seemingly strong countries like Taiwan and South Korea (Haggard 2000). Investors, afraid of having exposure to any developing or emerging market, soon pulled funds out of Russia and Brazil. The Russian government effectively defaulted on the country's debts, and Brazil radically increased the interest rates it paid to its creditors, to make the country attractive once more to foreign investors.

Multinational Enterprises: Opportunities and Concerns

As noted in Chapter 8, mainstream economic theory suggests that MNEs that undertake foreign direct investment in a host country, either developed or developing, contribute to the latter's stock of capital, technology, and managerial expertise, and thereby augment the growth of the industries in which the foreign investments occur and the

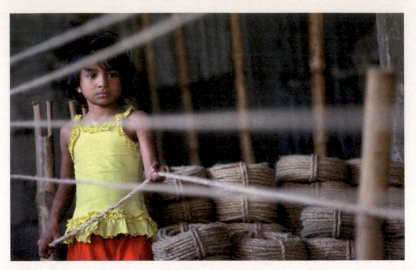

▲ Photo 10.2 Child Labor in Developing Countries

A concern about the operations of multinational enterprises in developing countries is that some foreign firms might rely on local contractors that employ child labor.

Source: PA Images.

economic growth of the country as a whole. Hence, for mainstream economic theory, just as the answer to our enduring question is positive in respect to trade, so too it is at least as much in the positive in connection to linkages with multinational enterprises. On the other hand, critics of globalization have suggested that multinational enterprises that move to developing countries exploit workers, especially women and children, and avoid the stronger legal and governmental regulatory standards that protect workers and the natural environment in the advanced industrial countries (Graham 2000; Evans 2000; Neumayer and De Soysa 2006).

One way multinational firms have responded to these charges has been to establish codes of conduct (Locke *et al.* 2009). For many years, for example, Pakistani suppliers of soccer balls for such firms as Nike, Adidas, and Puma used child labor. When this practice was made public in a June 1996 story in *Life* magazine, non-governmental organizations (NGOs) vigorously protested against the developing-country operations of Nike and other multinational sports firms. As a result, the firms entered into negotiations with the United Nations Children's Fund (UNICEF), the International Labor Organization (ILO), and several NGOs. In early 1997, the international firms and their Pakistani suppliers agreed to a code of conduct, the Atlanta Agreement, named for the city in which it was signed, that committed the international firms, as well as their Pakistani contractors, to stop using child labor. The trade association that represented the multinational sports firms later reported (Gorgemans 2008) that at least 6,000 children were taken out of soccer-ball workshops in the Pakistani city of Sialkot, where most of the largest suppliers were located.

The debate about FDI, multinational enterprises, and economic development has abated in recent years, in part because it appears that there is no single correct answer to the question of whether MNEs promote economic development. In Asia, for example, foreign investment in manufacturing sectors has had a strongly positive impact on economic development (Wang 2009). More generally, FDI is especially likely to foster growth in other both developed and developing host countries, but its effects to date have been more positive in the former than in the latter (Li and Liu 2005). One key reason for this difference appears to be the capacity of the different types of host countries to absorb the technology associated with MNE investments. Among developed countries MNE investments seems to spur technological innovation, and while this sometimes happens in developing countries the positive impact brought about by the technology transfer associated with MNE investments tends not to be as large or certain.

Official Aid Flows: Help or Hindrance to Developing Countries?

For many years there have been serious controversies on whether official aid helps or hurts developing countries. Indeed, it is in respect to foreign aid that we observe the most divergent answers to the enduring question about whether international linkages are a good or bad idea for developing countries. For example, critics suggest that the practice of tied aid reduces the beneficial impact of bilateral aid. In tied aid, donor governments often require that the funds they give to a recipient country must be used to purchase goods and services provided by firms from the donor country. The tying of aid bridles international competition among firms who supply goods and services for the project being funded, which in turn reduces the efficiency of the aid for the developing country. According to the World Bank (1998), the loss in efficiency may reduce the effective value of the aid by about 25 percent.

In recent years, there has also been a serious debate about whether foreign aid really promotes growth in developing countries. In theory, as illustrated in Box 10.3, foreign aid is supposed to act as a stepping stone to economic progress for developing countries. In Africa, no such positive association seems to be evident from the 1970s to the end of the 1990s.

Economist William Easterly (2002, 2006, 2007) has argued that the foreign aid strategies of wealthy donor countries (and the multilateral institutions they control, the World Bank and the IMF) have done little systematic good in the developing world. In addition to the data summarized in Box 10.3, Easterly emphasizes that if we look back over the past five decades, the rich industrial countries have provided $2.3 trillion in aid to developing countries. At the end of that period, three billion people were still living on $2 or less per day, 840 million were suffering from hunger, and 10 million children were dying each year from preventable diseases.

Easterly offers a number of reasons why aid has not promoted growth in the developing world and, in particular, sub-Saharan Africa. First, economists and aid bureaucrats simply do not understand the dynamics of economic growth sufficiently well to design large-scale aid programs that consistently promote growth throughout the developing world. Moreover, providing aid to often highly corrupt developing-country governments greatly reduces the effectiveness of aid. We have, for example, the case of Zaire under the notoriously corrupt government headed by Mobutu Sese Seko: between the late 1970s and 1990, the IMF provided the Mobutu government no fewer than eleven loans, none of which materially helped Zaire as a whole make progress in attaining economic development.

Easterly does not say that international aid should be altogether ended. Instead, he argues that donor governments should give up on the idea that there is a single 'grand strategy' to institute development in all poor countries. Donor governments should instead design more tailored aid programs that ensure feedback is generated on whether the aid is working, require accountability for national and international officials if the projects they put into place fail to produce results, find ways to bypass corrupt developing-country governments, and provide more targeted assistance to individual entrepreneurs or social activists in recipient countries.

In contrast, economist Jeffrey Sachs (2005a) has suggested that a new grand design for foreign aid by the rich countries could make a major contribution to ending poverty in the developing world. Sachs acknowledges that if a developing country has a deeply corrupt (what he terms a 'predatory') government, economic development is unlikely to occur. However, even a well governed developing country is unlikely to achieve economic growth, Sachs argues, without outside assistance if that country is caught in a poverty trap, that is, when it is so poor that most of its national resources must be used to satisfy the immediate day-to-day needs of the population, with insuffi-

Tied aid: A practice in which donor governments require that the funds they give to a recipient country must be used to purchase goods and services provided by firms from the donor country.

Poverty trap: When a country is so poor that most of its national resources must be used to satisfy the immediate day-to-day needs of the population, with insufficient resources left for savings or investment.

Foreign Aid and Economic Development in Africa

Theory: *Foreign Aid as a Spur to Development*

Foreign assistance from official sources is supposed to catalyze economic development in poorer countries through a number of pathways. Most important, such financial assistance is supposed to make up for shortfalls in domestic capital formation. Moreover, if foreign official donors provide funds for important infrastructure projects, such as shipping port facilities, roads, or airports, private investors from abroad will be more likely to invest in the country, since it will have stronger foundations for economic activity. Finally, foreign official assistance usually comes with foreign expertise and advice on how to implement economic development projects, providing greater chances of efficient utilization of the resources.

Practice: *Apparent Negative Relationship between Aid and Growth in Africa, 1970s–1990s*

The economist William Easterly constructed the figure below. It reports both the receipt of foreign aid (as a percent of GDP) received by African countries, and the growth in per capita GDP of those countries, from the early 1970s to the late 1990s. While aid increased as a percentage of GDP in the region during this time period, growth in GDP per capita went down.

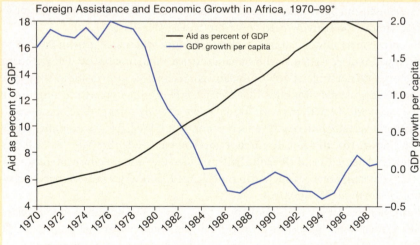

Foreign Assistance and Economic Growth in Africa, 1970–99*

* The data for each year represents the average per capita GDP growth rate and the average rate of aid (as a percenatge of GDP) over the previous 10 years.

▲ Figure 10.7

Source: William Easterly, 'The Cartel of Good Intentions', *Foreign Policy* 131 (July–August 2002), p. 45.

While foreign official assistance is supposed to serve as a motor of economic development of poorer countries, this positive impact of aid did not occur in Africa over a period of three decades.

cient resources left for savings or investment. According to Sachs, many of the especially poor countries in sub-Saharan Africa are in precisely that situation: forced to use all available resources essentially to keep the population alive today, they lack the resources needed to undertake investment in new productive facilities, such as better irrigation systems for farmers or better railways and roads for commerce, to propel the country toward higher incomes tomorrow.

The solution is to find an alternative source of investment resources. Sachs suggests that a massive injection of outside aid, in particular ODA, could serve that function for countries in sub-Saharan Africa that commit themselves to good governance. Well designed aid programs, Sachs suggests, that involved close coordination among the donors, as well as main international aid institutions like the World Bank, could effectively end poverty in that region if donor countries doubled their ODA flows.

The major donor countries and international development agencies have in fact made greater efforts to coordinate their objectives when it comes to development assistance. In September 2000, most of the world's leaders agreed at the United Nations in New York to what they termed the Millennium Declaration. In that declaration, the world's nations pledged their individual and joint efforts to achieve by 2015 a number of specific goals for the developing countries. The **Millennium Development Goals (MDGs)** include cutting extreme poverty by one-half, achieving universal primary education and gender equality at all levels of education, reducing the mortality rate of children under five and new mothers by two-thirds, and cutting the incidence of AIDs/HIV, malaria, tuberculosis, and other diseases.

In 2005, through a research effort he conducted for the UN Development Program, Sachs (2005b) put forward a concrete and ambitious strategy for donor and recipient governments to achieve the MDGs, including the recommendation that official development assistance from the rich countries be doubled from a national average of about 0.24 percent to 0.54 percent of GDP. That would be less than the target of 0.7 percent that rich countries had pledged to achieve as far back as 1970 and as recently as 2002. The problem, as explored in Box 10.4, is (with a few exceptions) the continuing failure of key donor countries to increase ODA as a percent of their respective national incomes.

The Millennium Project will not have achieved success by 2015. We can anticipate a major debate among economists and policy makers as to whether the shortcomings were due to the grand scale of the Millennium Project, or because the United States and other major donors failed to provide the resources needed to make the strategy a success.

The Issue of IMF Lending to Developing Countries

Many developing countries have found they lacked sufficient foreign exchange resources to cover debt obligations and even critical imports, such as oil, food, and medicine. As we discussed in Chapter 8, in those instances such countries often turn to the IMF for short-term loans. In order to receive short-terms credits from the IMF, a country must, in almost all circumstances, reach an agreement with the Fund regarding the terms and timing for repayment and, more important, a **stabilization program**. A stabilization program is essentially a contract between the IMF and the recipient country stipulating what the country will do to ensure that its short-term foreign exchange shortfall does not become permanent. Its main functions are to press the government to take actions to bring about an improvement in the country's balance of payments, and may include increasing interest rates, cutting government

Millennium Development Goals (MDGs): A series of goals agreed upon by world leaders at the UN in September 2000. They include cutting extreme poverty by one-half, achieving universal primary education and gender equality at all levels of education, reducing the mortality rate of children under five and new mothers by two-thirds, and cutting the incidence of AIDs/HIV, malaria, tuberculosis, and other diseases.

Stabilization program: Essentially a contract between the **IMF** and a country receiving an emergency short-term loan stipulating what the country will do to ensure that its short-term foreign exchange shortfall does not become permanent.

Developed Countries' Pledges and Performance on Official Development Assistance

Aspiration: *Donor Promises about ODA, 1970 and 2002*

Original International Pledge on Official Development Assistance, 1970

In recognition of the special importance of the role which can be fulfilled only by official development assistance, a major part of financial resource transfers to the developing countries should be provided in the form of official development assistance. *Each economically advanced country will progressively increase its official development assistance to the developing countries and will exert its best efforts to reach a minimum net amount of 0.7 per cent of its gross national product at market prices by the middle of the Decade.*

Source: United Nations General Assembly, Resolution 2626, October 24, 1970, available at http://www.un.org/documents/ga/res/25/ares25.htm, emphasis added.

Most Recent Affirmation of the Pledge, 2002

we urge developed countries that have not done so to make concrete efforts towards the target of 0.7 per cent of gross national product (GNP) as ODA to developing countries.

Source: 'Monterrey Consensus of the International Conference on Financing for Development,' in United Nations, *Report of the International Conference on Financing for Development*, available at http://www.unmillenniumproject.org/documents/07_aconf198-11.pdf, p. 9.

Moral hazard: When an individual or some other actor believes they can take very great risks because, if things go badly, someone else will pay for the consequences of the risky behavior. Some accuse the **IMF** of encouraging moral hazard.

spending, liberalizing the country's economy, and strengthening its regulatory frameworks in finance and other sectors.

The IMF's policies have produced two main lines of criticism. First, IMF lending may stunt the growth opportunities of developing countries that agree to take on IMF loans and their attendant harsh conditions. Second, it is possible that the IMF actually contributes to the risk that countries will behave in ways that bring about financial panics. The IMF, by acting as a lender of last resort, may produce moral hazard (Meltzer 2000) on the part of both developing-country governments and private lenders. Moral hazard occurs when an individual or some other actor believes they can take very great risks because, if things go badly, someone else will pay for the consequences of the risky behavior. It is possible that developing-country governments and foreign lenders believe that if they engage in what turns out to be overly risky economic behavior (over-spending by the governments and over-lending to those governments by outside banks and other financial actors), the IMF will bail them out. Those governments and lenders might, by consequence, be more likely to make choices that lead to financial crises and the need for IMF bailouts.

In sum, when we seek to answer the enduring question about international linkages and development, official aid and IMF lending produce extremely divergent views.

As we noted above, developing countries have had very different growth experiences. The next section highlights different paths to economic development that have been taken by a small number of emerging states that are particularly important both for the growth they have achieved and their potential for affecting in turn the growth of the world economy.

Reality

▼ **Figure 10.8**

Official Development Assistance as Percent of Gross National Income, Major Donors, Five-Year Average, 2008–12

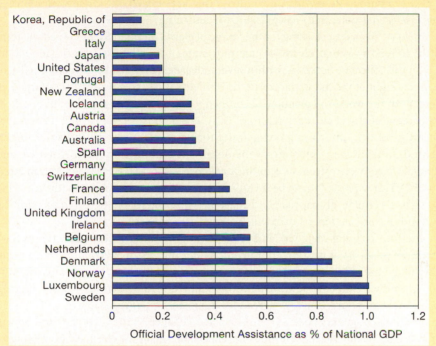

Official Development Assistance as % of National GDP

Source: United Nations, United Nations Statistics Division, Millennium Development Goals Indicators, 'Net ODA as percentage of OECD/DAC donors GNI,' available at http://mdgs.un.org/unsd/mdg/SeriesDetail.aspx?srid=568 (accessed October 2014).

In 1970, the major donor countries pledged to provide official development assistance (ODA) equal to 0.7 percent of their respective national incomes; they endorsed the 0.7 percent target again in 2002. However, only five donors have met (and in each case exceeded) that target. The United States is at the low end of the country-donor list in terms of ODA as percent of national income: its ODA between 2006 and 2010 averaged only about 0.2 percent of US annual income.

 State

Developing countries that accept international investment might grow more rapidly than they otherwise would, but in so doing they take on risks as domestic and international investment conditions change.

International

There is disagreement over the extent to which foreign aid and direct and portfolio investment have beneficial impacts on development.

Levels of Analysis

International Finance as an Opportunity for Developing Countries

Development Strategies and Emerging Great Powers – the BRICS

The discussion so far highlights that there are different pathways to the achievement of development. Some countries have clearly done better than others. This final section considers a group of developing countries that are singled out for special attention because each is potentially an emerging (or returning) great power.

In 2001, an analyst working for the financial giant Goldman Sachs coined the term BRIC to refer to a small cluster of emerging states – Brazil, Russia, India, and China – with the collective potential, within several decades, to overtake the combined economic weight of the industrial world. In 2001 this BRIC group already contained 40 percent of the world's population, accounted for 15 percent of global GDP, and held 40 percent of global currency reserves. BRIC countries also shared high future economic potential: China was growing faster than any other country, India was not far behind, Brazil was re-emerging as the dominant economy of South America, and Russia was recovering from its economic collapse at the end of the Cold War. In 2010, South Africa requested that it be included in the group, and it was formally invited to do so in December of that year, and so we now use the terms **BRICS** in recognition of South Africa's membership in this informal arrangement.

The four original members and later the five-member BRICS association have made some efforts at crafting joint positions on international economic issues, and have taken initial steps to create a new international institution. For example, in June 2009, what were then the four BRIC countries held their first summit in the Russian city of Yekaterinburg. The four agreed on the need for a more stable and diversified international monetary system (translation: less reliance on the US dollar) and reform of international financial institutions to reflect changes in the world economy (translation: more influence for BRIC countries, and less for the United States and Europe, in the World Bank and IMF). Moreover, during 2013 the now five-member BRICS were in intense negotiations and seemed to be making some headway in reaching an agreement for the creation of a new development bank. The BRICS would invest in the development bank something in the neighborhood of $50 billion, which would make the bank a significant new force in development finance.

It remains to be seen if the BRICS grouping will become a lasting, influen-

BRICS: Brazil, Russia, India, China.and South Africa. These five rapidly developing countries have the collective potential, within several decades, to overtake the combined economic weight of the industrial world.

▶ **Photo 10.3 National Leaders at the Fifth BRICS meeting**

At their fifth annual summit, held in Durban, South Africa, in March 2013, BRICS national leaders announced they would seek to establish a new development bank.

Source: PA Images.

Background

Brazil, Russia, India, China, and South Africa are working to create a new informal political-economic grouping in the world economy, the BRICS. Their goal is to craft and press common positions on international economic matters, and as such to wield more influence as members of a group of important economies than they might as individual countries, and they are seeking to create a new development bank. What are the prospects for the BRICS as a political-economic grouping? Scholars working in the realist, liberal, and constructivist traditions might share doubts about the future of the BRICS, but they would differ in the kinds of questions they would ask about the grouping in reaching their views as to its likely future health and vitality.

Realism: A realist would ask whether the BRICS countries are subject to threats in common – political, military, and economic – and if they do, then this would augur well for the grouping. A realist would also ask if the BRICS countries have serious conflicts of interest between or among group members, for if they do this would yield pessimism about the prospects for robust cooperation and development of the grouping. Here a realist might take note that India and China have been locked in a long-standing disagreement about the exact demarcation of their common border, a disagreement that caused a war between them in 1962. This split at the heart of the BRICS, a realist would suggest, might impose limits

on the future of the grouping. All the BRICS countries might oppose US pre-eminence in international relations, but while US–China and US–Russia relations have deteriorated in recent years, US–India relations have improved, and this too might again constrain BRICS political and institutional cooperation.

Liberalism: A liberal would argue that, if they were all democracies, the prospects for the BRICS countries to expand and deepen their cooperation would be reasonably good. As it is, the BRICS grouping is composed of countries with highly diverse domestic political regimes: Brazil, India, and South Africa are democracies, and China and Russia have authoritarian regimes. A liberal is likely to look at the differences among the BRICS in terms of domestic regimes and conclude that that variation is likely to hamper development of the group.

Constructivism: A constructivist would suggest that the prospects for the BRICS grouping depends upon the degree to which the political leaders, business elites, and other active members of the societies of the different BRICS countries share common ideas about such matters the proper role of government in the national economy, the value of working with other countries in international arrangements, and, in line with realist views, whether they were confronting common threats and opportunities in the international domain.

tial political force in world economic matters. Scholars working from the realist, liberal, and constructivist perspectives would probably all be cautious in their assessments of the prospects for the BRICS as a political grouping. We highlight in Box 10.5 how those theoretical perspectives would differ on the kinds of issues they would emphasize in trying to estimate the likely durability and salience of the BRICS as a group in the future.

Still, as individual countries, China, India, Brazil, Russia, and South Africa will be major actors in the world economy in the years ahead. Below, we briefly describe their development strategies and impending challenges.

China

China is by far the largest and most successful of the BRICS. During its first 30 years under communist rule (1945–75), China possessed a Soviet-type economy with most resource allocation decisions made by central planning authorities rather than market forces. A new Communist leadership took over in the mid-1970s and, in 1978, initiated economic reforms that have resulted in China's gradual transition to a market-based economy. These measures included allowing farmers to lease land from the state, the steady privatization of state-owned enterprises (SOEs), and an export-led growth strategy that established special economic zones for Chinese and foreign companies to produce goods for final markets in the West.

China's economic strategy has been remarkably successful. It export revenues jumped from about $10 billion in 1978 to about $500 billion in 2003, and to $1.2 trillion by 2009. Between 1985 and 2010, the economy grew at an astounding rate of almost 10 percent per year. By 2005, China's total GDP grew to $2 trillion using current exchange rate and $5 trillion in purchasing power parity (PPP) terms (PPP is a measure economists use to compare the value of a similar basket of goods across countries with different living standards and exchange rates). Economists at the Organization for Economic Cooperation and Development, an intergovernmental organization whose members are the advanced industrialized countries, reported in 2012 that China's economy was approaching that of the United States in PPP terms, and they predicted that China will have a markedly larger economy in terms of PPP than the United States by 2030 (see Figure 10.9).

We could therefore be witnessing a transition in global economic hegemony similar to the one that took place between Great Britain and the United States during the first half of the twentieth century. We might see financial power shift from New York to Shanghai and Beijing. China might become decisive in determining world trade rules and take on the leadership of the IMF and World Bank. Chinese leaders have already extended their diplomacy across Asia, Latin America, and Africa, using their formidable financial and commercial resources to extract political benefits and necessary raw materials on favorable terms. With an additional 20 years of sustained growth, China would be in a position to challenge American political dominance around the world, even if Chinese military capabilities still lagged behind.

But will China continue to grow at its rapid pace? We should not assume that its future will simply look like its recent past. China faces a series of difficult economic and political challenges that could derail its rise to the top. The Chinese economy, for example, has a problem of striking a balance between too much and too little growth; if it grows too fast, it will create inflation and a possible financial crisis, but if it does not grow fast enough, it will not be able to absorb the millions of workers looking to move from the countryside to the cities each year. Significant unemployment tends to breed social unrest. And China's leaders cannot fully control the pace of growth because the economy is so dependent on world export markets. When the world economy slows down, so does China's economy.

For China's communist leaders, economic performance and regime legitimacy are inextricably linked. So far, China has managed to sustain what the Soviet Union could not – a thriving, quasi-capitalist economy governed by an authoritarian one-party state. The legitimacy of the communist regime is no longer based on revolutionary fervor or the inherent political appeal of communist ideology. Instead, it is based on economic performance, or the ability of the regime to ensure that the economy delivers goods, services, and jobs to its growing population. Significantly slower growth would inevitably lead parts of the population to question the political monopoly of the Communist Party. The greater the questioning, the more tempted the regime would be to exercise repression, which would lead the population to ques-

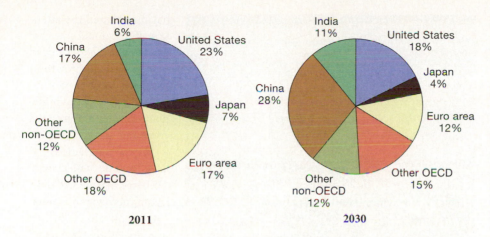

2011

2030

◀ **Figure 10.9** Shares of World GDP 2011 and Projection for 2030

In the foreseeable future China might have the world's largest economy. By the end of the next decade it might be the site of 28% of global economic activity, while in 2011 it was the location of about 17% of world economic output. By comparison, the United States, which in 2011 generated about one-fourth of world output, might be the source of 18% of such activity in 2030.

Sources: Johansson, Å., *et al.* (2012) 'Looking to 2060: Long-Term Global Growth Prospects: A Going for Growth Report,' *OECD Economic Policy Papers*, No. 3, OECD Publishing, p.23.doi: 10.1787/5k8zxpjsggf0-en. See also, Johansson, Å. et al. (2013) 'Long-Term Growth Scenarios,' *OECD Economics Department Working Papers*, No. 1000, OECD Publishing. http://dx.doi.org/10.1787/5k4ddxpr2fmr-en

tion regime legitimacy even further. For China's communist elite, the maintenance of rapid economic growth is a political and economic necessity. It is not surprising that China's leaders responded to the global slowdown sparked by the 2008 financial crisis with a massive domestic stimulus program in order to sustain high growth rates.

The communist regime must also deal with the social and economic inequalities that result from successful economic growth. Growing gaps have appeared between rich and poor, urban and rural populations, and residents on the economically vibrant coastline and those in less well-off inland parts of the country. Large gaps in income and life opportunities generate resentment among those at the bottom, who, during the communist era, could at least count on the 'iron rice bowl', a guarantee from the state of job security and access to basic necessities. But there is even discontent among the rising middle class who, as they become well off, have increasing expectations for a higher quality of life and demand a greater say in the political decisions affecting their lives.

In sum, China's prospects for *future* rapid growth are far less predictable than any linear projection of past trends would indicate. China may continue rapid growth for some time, and may even catch and overtake the United States. But it is also plausible that China will grow more slowly and, at the extreme, face a series of economic, social, and political dislocations.

India

India has long been an exceptionally large, but exceptionally poor, developing country. Why has it gained so much attention in the past decade, to the point of being included in the BRICS? One reason is economic; the other is geopolitical.

During much of the Cold War, the Indian economy was shackled by government intervention and regulation. Modest liberalizing reforms undertaken in the 1980s helped the country attain an annual growth rate of about 5 percent. A currency crisis in 1991 led to more far-reaching reforms: tariff cuts, business tax reductions, and the deregulation of industry. India grew at 6 percent annually between 1992 and 2002, a period that included a major economic disruption in its region, the Asian financial crisis of 1997–98. Between 2002 and 2008, India grew even more rapidly; at 8.8 percent annually, it achieved growth rates similar to China. With one billion people – about half under the age of 25 – and a rapidly growing economy, India caught and

Iron Rice Bowl: A guarantee from the government of Communist China of job security and access to basic necessities for Chinese citizens.

▶ **Photo 10.4 Slums and Skyscrapers: Two Faces of India**

The contrasting faces of Mumbai. The financial capital of India is home to glitzy malls and skyscrapers but, at its feet, squalor seethes in Dharavi, the second largest slum in Asia.

Source: © nstanev – istockphoto.com.

has maintained the attention of the global community. It has experienced especially rapid growth in the service sector, particularly computing and information technology. Its computer services leaders – Wipro and Infosys – have become well known. The same may be said of its leading auto manufacturer, Tata Motors; in 2009, Tata introduced what it claimed to be the world's least expensive car, measuring 10 feet by 5 feet and selling at a base price of $2,200.

India has gained geopolitical attention as well. It has taken on a self-appointed role as leader of developing states seeking a better deal in the world economy in negotiations with the more established industrial states. India helped to derail the Doha Round because it felt the United States and Europe did not make sufficient concessions, particularly in agriculture. As we will discuss in Chapter 12, India is a key player in global climate change negotiations because it is the world's third largest emitter of greenhouse gases. Here, too, it has proved reluctant to cooperate on the grounds that countries already economically developed, at a high cost to the global environment, are now urging developing countries to restrict their own growth in the interest of environmental protection. Finally, India has gained more positive geopolitical attention from the United States because it is a potentially valuable partner in the possible containment of China. In the administration of George W. Bush, the United States signaled its desire for cooperation by pressing forward a US–India nuclear deal. This deal meant the United States and the 45-member Nuclear Suppliers Group recognized India as a nuclear weapons state, despite its defiance of the international non-proliferation regime. The nuclear deal enhanced India's status and helped distinguish it as a great power rather than just one side of the India–Pakistan regional conflict.

Its recent success and prominence as a BRICS country should not blind us to the formidable development challenges that India continues to face. As of 2005 a remarkable 40 percent of the Indian population – over 450 million people – lived below the poverty line. Some 60 million children suffer from malnutrition, and literacy rates are only at about 65 percent (compared to 90 percent in China). Despite its ability to produce world-class information technology services and globally competitive cinema, India's basic infrastructure is remarkably underdeveloped. Hundreds of millions of people live without electrical power and, in many parts of the country, sanitary conditions are horrible, exacerbating disease, malnutrition, and infant mortality.

India's economic progress requires a continuation of economic reforms, along with sustained attention to its deficient infrastructure. Its democratic government is aware of the problems, but is not always in a position to address them effectively. Recall from early in this chapter the importance of good governance as a facilitator of economic development. Corruption plagues the Indian parliament; as of 2010, some 25 percent of sitting members were facing criminal charges. The ruling coalition government has at times contained more than one dozen parties, making it difficult to sustain itself in power, much less take decisive action to address pressing social and economic problems.

Brazil

Brazil was hit hard by the Great Depression of the 1930s. As Western markets for its coffee and other raw materials collapsed, Brazil's policy makers learned that the country should not excessively rely on the global economy. As a result, they adopted an ISI strategy. The government regulated trade and used tariff barriers and other incentives to encourage local Brazilian firms, sometimes in collaboration with foreign multinationals, to produce goods for the large Brazilian market. ISI produced some growth over the years but, by the 1980s, Brazil was afflicted with high inflation, large external debts, and inefficient industry. By the early 1990s, Brazil joined many other developing countries in shifting development strategy in a more liberal direction, as we discussed above, emphasizing freer trade and privatization of many state-owned firms.

Since many developing countries have embraced the world economy since the 1990s, why single out Brazil for special attention? The simple reason is that, like India and China, Brazil is no ordinary emerging economy; it has the potential to be a great power, economically and geopolitically. Brazil's land mass is similar in size to the United States. Its population is about 200 million, or two-thirds that of the United States. Its GDP of roughly $2.2 trillion in 2013 placed it among the top ten countries in the world. Unlike many developing countries, Brazil already possesses a sophisticated and diversified economy that has been growing at about 5 percent annually. It is a major agricultural producer and exporter of coffee, soybeans, cotton, tropical fruits, and biofuels such as ethanol. It is emerging as a global player in oil and gas. Within the past decade, the state-owned firm Petrobras has made huge new oil discoveries in Brazilian territorial waters, and industry experts estimate that Brazil's reserves have now tripled to about 40 billion barrels, among the top ten globally and equivalent to the reserve positions of long-time OPEC members Nigeria and Venezuela. With over 2,500 miles of coastline, further discoveries are likely. It is ironic that Brazil spent decades developing its manufacturing sector, and now finds raw materials and food to be just as much an engine of its current and future growth.

Brazil's central government has become stronger and more stable. Brazil returned to democracy in 1985 after two decades of military rule. Its extensive multiparty system ensures that governing coalitions have numerous participants. Yet, only two of the parties, the leftist Worker's Party and the center-left Social Democratic Party, have been able to produce viable presidential candidates, and they have alternated in power over the past 20 years. When in power, each party has managed to form governments capable of getting things done, even with seemingly unwieldy coalitions.

▶ **Photo 10.5 Brazil's Agricultural Miracle**

In many parts of Brazil's cerrado, or savannah, large tracts of eucalyptus and pine trees were cut down in order to make way for commercial farming of such crops as soy and cotton.

Source: © josemoraes – istockphoto.com.

Brazilian politics has become more stable and predictable in absolute terms, compared to other countries in the region, such as Venezuela, where populist leaders have sought to manipulate democratic rules in order to remain in power indefinitely.

The Brazilian state has become more competent in some of the good governance tasks those in the developed world often take for granted – the collection of taxes and implementation of government programs. Between 2003 and 2013 President Luiz Inacio Lula of the Worker's Party targeted resources to the large numbers of Brazilian poor, emphasizing health care, education, and housing. At the same time, he maintained the pragmatic and growth-oriented economic policies that enhanced Brazil's ability to compete internationally.

Brazil continues to face major challenges. Its average annual growth rate has been slower than China's (5 percent versus 10 percent), while the government's share of its economy is larger (20 percent versus 14 percent). Large gaps in income and wealth across the population remain. Brazil's emerging dependence on raw material and agricultural exports make it vulnerable to global economic slowdowns. Its Amazon region has become something of a 'wild west,' with loggers, miners, and farmers grabbing what they can at the expense of the local and global (Brazil is a leading emitter of greenhouse gases) environment. There is still much work to be done, but Brazil looks more able than ever to join the ranks of the major powers in the decades ahead.

Russia

Under Communist rule as the core of the Soviet Union (1917–90), Russia undertook a 70-year experiment in central planning of the economy. The state controlled virtually every aspect of economic interaction; it set prices for goods and services and determined what would be produced, how it would be produced, and in what quantities. The system produced some successes in aggregate economic terms. Stalin's *revolution from above* during the 1930s marshaled economic resources to achieve, at the expense of the peasantry, rapid industrialization and militarization. After World War II, the Soviet-style economic system was put forward as an alternative to liberal capitalism.

During the 1950s, it compared relatively well, when the Soviet Union recovered from war and achieved high levels of growth by devoting more land, labor, and capital to the production process. By the 1960s, however, it became apparent that the Soviet system was 'all thumbs and no fingers.' In other words, it was good at mass-producing basic commodities, but much less effective at producing a wide range of goods and services of appeal to ordinary consumers. The Soviet economy was a bit like the army; it could produce enough 'standard-issue' shoes or shirts for everyone, but could not compete with the variety and quality of goods produced in market economies around the world.

The Soviet Union was a global leader in the production of oil, natural gas, nickel, and other primary commodities, and the boom in commodity prices during the 1970s made the Soviet economy look stronger than it actually was. When commodity prices fell during the early 1980s, the Soviet economic weakness was exposed, and, as we discussed in Chapter 2, Mikhail Gorbachev took power with a bold plan to reform the Soviet economy while maintaining centralized political control. His experiment ultimately failed, as the Soviet economy was thrown into chaos; the subsequent demands for political liberalization led to the demise of the Soviet empire, the Soviet Union itself, and the Cold War. During the 1990s, Western governments hoped that Russia could be reformed into a liberal democracy and market economy. But economic reform meant that a small segment of powerful elites and their associates became very rich, while most ordinary people faced economic insecurity; the safety net of communism was ripped away but a fully functioning market economy was not really put into place. By 2000, Vladimir Putin took advantage of this situation by centralizing power in Moscow and promising the Russian people a return to the tradition of stability and order provided by a strong central government.

In the interim period of the 1990s, the Russian economy faced severe hardship: GDP contracted at the beginning of the decade by 10 to 15 percent annually. Investment slipped and unemployment and poverty levels rose significantly. Russia was hit hard by an international financial crisis during 1997–98: the ruble collapsed in value and the government defaulted on billions of dollars of its international and domestic debts.

Why, then, has Russia been singled out as a BRICS country? The simple reason is that Russia's economy staged a strong recovery after 1998. Between 2000 and 2008, annual growth averaged almost 7 percent. The government eliminated or repaid its debt and, by 2009, had piled up more than $400 billion in foreign currency reserves, more than any other country other than China and Japan. The benefits spread broadly as jobs were created, poverty levels dropped significantly, and personal incomes and consumer spending rose. The crisis of 1998 forced the government to rein in spending, and the cheaper ruble stimulated Russia's exports.

The key to Russia's success has been energy. Oil and gas prices shot up after 2003, with oil approaching and even breaking through the $100 per barrel mark. It is the world's second largest oil producer and exporter (after Saudi Arabia), and the world's largest natural gas producer and exporter.

Under Putin, Russia's economic revival has been accompanied by a more assertive foreign policy, particularly in the area of the former Soviet Union. Russia has used the threatened or actual cut-off of energy supplies to influence politics in Ukraine, Belarus, and Georgia. In 2008, Russia invaded Georgia to bolster the independence of the Russia-friendly regions of Abkhazia and South Ossetia. The fact that the rest of the world seemed incapable of deterring or stopping Russia from attacking its smaller neighbor (on the eve of the attack, US President Bush and Russian Prime Minister Putin were seen together attending the opening ceremonies of the Beijing Olympics) made Russia look all the more formidable.

It was Russia's revival, coupled with China's economic success, which led some observers to celebrate the authoritarian capitalist model that we discussed earlier in the chapter as an alternative to the liberal capitalist model of the West. In Russia's version of authoritarian capitalism, Putin's government stifled democracy and freedom of the press and expanded the power of the central government in the name of stability, law, and order. By 2008, the government had taken over all major television networks and controlled all major newspapers except one Moscow weekly. In exchange, the Russian people received a share of the economic benefits generated by oil and gas sales. The fact that Putin's approval rating as President approached 80 percent in 2007 seemed to suggest that the authoritarian model was not only effective, but popular. When Putin was replaced as President in 2008 by Dmitry Medvedev, he stayed on as Prime Minister and then as President in 2012.

Russia's authoritarian capitalist model and economic revival face major challenges and hide significant social and economic problems (McFaul and Stoner-Weiss 2008). Russia's population has been shrinking for at least 20 years, in part due to serious health afflictions. Heart disease, the leading cause of death, occurs at three times the rate of that in the United States. Alcoholism is rampant among young and middle-aged men. Russia has the highest HIV infection rate of any country outside Africa. 'Law and order' is a supposed benefit of rule under Putin but, over the past ten years, the murder rate has increased and Russia experienced the two worst terrorist attacks in its history, at a Moscow theatre in 2002 and in an elementary school in Beslan in 2004. Russia ranks very high in international rankings for corruption and has one of the least friendly business environments in the industrial world. The protection of property rights is weak, Russian authorities regularly harass foreign businessmen, and the government has used its political clout to redistribute Russia's vast energy and other resources into the hands of a small elite.

Russia's development model may be over-reliant on oil and gas. Energy profits, in fact, have facilitated authoritarianism by giving Russia's central leaders the resources to reward friends, crack down on enemies, and placate the general population. But such circumstances may not last because Russia, like a number of Middle Eastern oil countries, is susceptible to the resource curse; it has gotten richer, but it has not developed. The danger for Russia, in light of its other problems, is that the next energy downturn will lead to economic and social crisis. Finally, Russia's confrontation with Ukraine in 2014 may prompt Russia's isolation from the world economy.

South Africa

As a result of a multi-decade struggle led by Nelson Mandela and the African National Congress, South Africa achieved during the early 1990s a stunning transformation from a deeply racist and authoritarian regime – one that was based on apartheid, or separation of the races and subjugation of blacks by whites – to one that is democratic and multiracial. South Africa's post-apartheid economic performance has been reasonably strong (World Bank 2013a). The country's GDP has grown at a rate of about 3.2 percent per year, although GDP/capita has only grown by about 1.6 percent per year. Poverty has declined in South Africa very substantially, from about 50 percent of the population in 2000 to about 35 percent in 2010. While South Africa scores very high on some specific measures of economic advancement, such as child literacy, it faces serious challenges in such areas as infant mortality and life expectancy.

Going forward, South Africa faces both opportunities and challenges. It is a country that has substantial mineral resources including the world's largest reserves of manganese and platinum group metals and among the world's largest of gold and diamonds. It has a skilled workforce characterized by a high degree of gender equity. According to the World Economic Forum, South Africa has the 17th (out of 136 countries) narrowest gender gap in the world, measured in terms of participation in the economy, education, political opportunities, and health (World Economic Forum, 2013). Its democratic institutions give every sign of being robust. It has very solid government finances, and is able readily to tap international financial markets.

At the same time, the country faces serious residual problems from the apartheid period: South Africa is characterized by a high degree of income inequality, and according to the World Bank it has one of the most unequal distributions of land ownership in the world. National health problems and inequalities, including a high incidence of HIV/AIDS infections, constitute a serious barrier to economic development. South Africa is clearly an important state in Africa, enjoys global influence and respect by virtue of its transition to multiracial democracy, and could be poised to enjoy sustained economic development. However, the degree to which it prospers economically and retains global diplomatic importance will depend upon its capacity to resolve a number of deep-seated social and political problems. Just as many developing countries must address the legacy and lingering effects of colonialism, South Africa must confront the legacy of apartheid.

State	International	Levels of Analysis
BRICS countries have pursued different development strategies, reinforcing the idea that there is no single pathway to national economic prosperity.	The rise of the BRICS, especially China, demonstrates the connection between economic power and geopolitical influence in the international system.	*The BRICS*
The challenge of good governance plagues each BRICS country to a greater or lesser degree.		

Revisiting the Enduring Question and Looking Ahead

Economic development is one of the great challenges of our time. In this chapter, we have asked whether economic globalization helps or hinders poorer countries as they seek to attain such development. Globalization seems to be helping many once poor countries, such as South Korea and China, achieve a stunning level of economic development. Most developing countries are likely in the future to pursue at least limited integration with the global economy, through trade, foreign investment by multinational enterprises, and the receipt of financial assistance either from donor countries like the United States or by international institutions like the World Bank. Yet, in doing so, developing countries are likely to be concerned as to whether they are attaining the maximum possible gains from integration, and this concern is likely to translate into bargaining with the wealthier and more powerful countries in the global economy, including and perhaps especially the United States.

Developing countries are likely to become increasingly important for international economics. The BRICS may become a significant force in world politics. Individual BRICS countries, and especially China but also Brazil to a considerable degree and possibly India in the foreseeable future, are central actors in world trade, finance, and economic diplomacy. South Korea has joined and is an important part of the community of advanced industrial countries.

Still, it remains an open question whether all developing countries, especially the very poorest, can escape from poverty traps and propel themselves onto a trajectory of sustained growth. Moreover, there is still no strong consensus among academics or policy makers on whether trade, investment, and foreign aid can help in promoting or fortifying change in the poorest countries. Good governance and domestic civil peace are needed to bring about sustained growth and poverty reduction in those countries. The questions of whether, and under what conditions, external engagement promotes internal economic improvement in poorer countries will remain at the center of global politics in the decades ahead.

In many developing countries, economic progress is being challenged or undermined by serious civil conflicts, often driven or accompanied by ethnic political divisions. In addition, high levels of lawlessness in many developing countries contribute to the emergence of powerful drug lords, whose violence and corruption undermines possibilities for improved governance in these countries. The circumstances sometimes become so dire that they threaten the stability and security for the people living in them, neighbors, and even outside states to such a degree that the international community has forcibly intervened to avert humanitarian disasters and create a minimum of order. In the next chapter, we turn to these countries, their tragedies, and the outside interventions that sometimes occur in reaction to those tragedies.

Visit **www.palgrave.com/politics/Grieco** to access extra resources for this chapter, including:

- Chapter summaries to help you review the material
- Multiple choice quizzes to test your understanding
- Flashcards to test your knowledge of the key terms in this chapter
- An interactive simulation that invites you to go through the decision-making process of a world leader at a crucial political juncture
- Pivotal decisions in which you weigh up the pros and cons of complicated decisions with grave consequences
- Outside resources, including links to contemporary articles and videos, that add to what you have learned in this chapter

Study Questions

1. Recall the three key perspectives – liberalism, Marxism, and economic nationalism – discussed in Chapter 9. What do you consider the most important insight from each regarding the dilemmas of development?
2. What are the most important causes of failed efforts by many countries to achieve economic development? Are they more likely to be domestic or international? Are they more likely to be political, economic, or geographic?
3. Evaluate the costs and benefits of international trade, foreign direct investment, and official development aid as engines of development.
4. Imagine you are the foreign minister of Brazil. What strategies would you adopt toward other BRICS countries, the United States, and your immediate neighbors in order to enhance your country's development prospects?
5. How might developing countries be affected if the price of oil tripled over the next decade?
6. Is the term BRICS a useful analytical construct? Why or why not?

Further Reading

Acemoglu, Daron and James Robinson (2012) *Why Nations Fail: The Origins of Power, Prosperity, and Poverty* (New York: Crown Business). This widely read book provides a good argument about, and a vast amount of empirical materials on the manner in which, geography and domestic political institutions, as well as the legacies of colonialism, have affected the prospects for growth of development of countries around the world.

Easterly, William (2006) *The White Man's Burden: Why the West's Efforts to Aid the Rest Have Done so Much Ill and So Little Good* (New York: Penguin Press). This is perhaps the most thoughtful and persuasive book on the possible pitfalls and even counter-productive effects of foreign aid from developed to developing countries. It should be read in conjunction with Sach's *End of Poverty*, noted below.

Rodrik, Dani (2007) *One Economics, Many Recipes: Globalization, Institutions, and Economic Growth* (Princeton: Princton University Press). Rodrik puts forward a balanced analysis of the role of international economic integration in the process of economic development. He argues that countries that have benefited from economic integration did so by first building strong domestic institutions and industries, or at least the foundations for both. He then offers an interesting alternative perspective to the Washington Consensus view that developing countries should, without qualification or preparation, pursue free trade and capital market liberalization.

Ross, Michael (2012) *The Oil Curse: How Petroleum Wealth Shapes the Development of Nations* (Princeton: Princeton University Press). Ross shows how, paradoxically, the possession of oil can place serious obstacles before developing countries as they seek to attain good governance and economic development.

Sachs, Jeffrey (2005a) *The End of Poverty: Economic Possibilities for Our Time* (New York: Penguin Press). Sachs in this book puts forward a compelling case for the possible efficacy and moral necessity of foreign aid from developed to developing countries. It should be read in conjunction with Easterly's *White Man's Burden*, noted above.

IV

Contemporary Challenges and the Future of International Relations

11   Non-State Actors and Challenges to Sovereignty

12   The Environment and International Relations

13   Facing the Future: Six Visions of an Emerging International Order

Visit www.palgrave.com/politics/grieco to watch the authors debating the issues discussed in this Part.

Video 1: What are the main global challenges facing the international community?

Video 2: What might the future hold for international relations?

11

Non-state Actors and Challenges to Sovereignty

Enduring question: Can the state continue to overcome challenges to its authority

Many people think that states have always dominated world politics – and always will. But in fact states have long been challenged in various ways. The ancient and early modern world was dominated by empires, and the nation-state only gained dominance in Europe in 1648. In earlier chapters, we explored moments when single states have tried to take over all or part of the system, such as Napoleonic France and Nazi Germany. In the 1970s, multinational corporations grew to be major players in the world economy, challenging the sovereign authority of national governments. In the 1990s, the international financial system – and large global banks – encroached on the ability of national governments to manage the world economy. The rise of nuclear weapons also led some people to argue that since states could no longer protect their populations, the state would wither away.

In recent decades, the nation-state has appeared to be challenged both from above – by supranational bodies such as the European Union – and from below – by localism, tribalism, and sub-national ethnic groups. The growing prominence of failed states in many parts of today's world raises questions about the viability of nation-states, at least in some troubled underdeveloped areas. The growth of transnational groups – both political activist groups and dangerous terrorist organizations – also shows the ways in which modern technologies and globalization can challenge and possibly undermine the state's ability to protect its borders and pursue its goals.

In other words, the sovereign state has been continually challenged, both internally and externally, and these challenges have taken different forms in different eras and settings. In this chapter, we look at some of the contemporary challenges to the nation-state, while recalling the enduring nature of the problem.

The combination of violent non-state actors and weak or failed states raises several far-reaching questions. Are these non-state actors gaining a sufficient foothold in the global system to challenge the primacy of the state as the dominant actor in the system and one that monopolizes the effective use of force? To what extent are the forces of globalization, technological change, and political fragmentation eroding the power and authority of states as the central actors in world politics? What are the implications of weak and failed states for the international system?

We first look back at the Westphalian system of sovereign states. Then we examine several non-state challenges, including how pirates on the high seas exploit the weakness and vulnerabilities of states, and how war lords take advantage of the difficulties that some countries – such as Afghanistan, Sudan, and Colombia – have had in building a strong state. We also revisit the problem of terrorism and the growing threat that violent non-state groups pose for peace and security. Finally, we look at the international responses to terrorism, non-state violence, and failed states. When countries fall apart, governments do not function, and private actors are free to pursue crime and violence within and across a state's ungoverned borders, what can the rest of the world do?

Source: © MOD/Crown copyright (2014).

Learning Objectives

By the end of this chapter, you will be able to:

→ Recall the historic rise and spread of the nation-state system and how the world became organized around sovereign states.

→ Analyze how technology and globalization facilitate the ability of non-state actors to challenge the modern sovereign state and transform the international system.

→ Assess the powerful impact that violence by non-state actors has on the global system of states.

→ Understand the causes and consequences of weak and failed states.

→ Consider the reaction of the international community to terrorism, non-state violence, and failed states, and the global consequences of these non-state threats and actions.

Chapter Contents

- States, Sovereignty, and the Westphalian System
- Challenges to Sovereign States
- International Responses to Non-State Actors
- Whither the State?
- Revisiting the Enduring Question and Looking Ahead
- Study Questions
- Further Reading

States, Sovereignty, and the Westphalian System

Failed states: States that lack the basic institutions and capacities of government – taxing, policing, upholding the rule of law, protecting property, providing public roads and services, and maintaining control over territory.

Our starting point is the observation that international relations does not involve states alone. There are a multitude of other agents or actors in world affairs, non-state actors who are not beholden to national governments but pursue their agendas privately and transnationally across international borders. Most non-state actors are peaceful in their interests and actions. Human rights groups, such as Amnesty International, and environmental groups, such as the World Wide Fund for Nature, are well-known examples. But there are also non-state actors that behave more like criminal gangs – groups such as pirates, war lords, and terrorists. These non-state actors typically prey on their victims in parts of the world where states are weak or use these weak states as bases of operation to attack more advanced countries. Indeed, in some parts of the world states are so weak that they are often called failed states. Failed states are states that lack the basic institutions and capacities of government – taxing, policing, upholding the rule of law, protecting property, providing public roads and services, and maintaining control over territory.

In order to appreciate the significance of these non-state actors, we need to recall the historic rise and spread of the nation-state system. The rise of the nation-state is one of the great dramas of the modern world. In earlier chapters, we explored the history and implications of the growth and expansion of territorial states. You will recall from Chapter 2 that scholars often date the birth of the state system to the Peace of Westphalia in 1648. This is when the monarchs and other state leaders of Europe agreed that states – national territorial states – were sovereign, independent, and the dominant actors in the international system. Over the centuries that followed, beginning in Europe, the nation-state grew more capable as a political entity and spread to all corners of the world. States developed capabilities as national governments to organize the economy and society. They developed laws and political institutions, systems of taxation and regulation, judicial bodies and agencies of law enforcement, and expansive military organizations. Along the way, the modern territorial state became the dominant political entity in the world. The world became organized around sovereign states.

Two features are most important in characterizing the Westphalian state system, and they operate at different levels of analysis. First, domestically, states are territorial sovereign entities. As the German sociologist Max Weber famously observed, states in a Westphalian system have 'a monopoly on the legitimate use of physical force within a given territory' (Weber 1970). This is the classic understanding of the modern sovereign nation-state. The state, embodied in the national government, has the exclusive right and ability to exercise violence (physical force) within its own territorial boundaries. Groups in society have no rights to act as private armies or police. The state controls violence and force within the society. Second, at the international level, national governments recognize and respect the supreme authority of states as sovereign political entities. Outside actors have no legitimate rights to act inside the territory of a sovereign state. Together, these features capture the essence of the Westphalian system. As the political theorist Chris Brown observes, '[t]he actors in the Westphalian System are sovereign states – territorial polities whose rulers acknowledge no equal at home, no superior abroad' (Brown 2002).

It is important to distinguish the ideal norms of the Westphalian system and the actual capacities of states to live up to these norms. Throughout the modern era, many

◀ Photo 11.1 The Assassination of Paolo Borsellino, 1992

On July 19, 1992, Italian anti-Mafia Judge Paolo Borsellino was killed by a car bomb set by the Italian Mafia. The Mafia has persistently challenged the central state of Italy for decades, frequently engaging in the killing of government officials and lay persons alike. The charred remains of the car bomb are pictured here.

Source: PA Images.

states claimed status as sovereign entities but were not able to fully enforce their monopoly on the use of violence within their societies. War lords – private authority figures who control their own local armies or militias – and criminal gangs have plagued nation-states across the centuries in both the West and the rest of the world. Certain national governments and their law-enforcement capabilities have often proved incapable of preventing sub-state groups from wielding violence. Organized criminal gangs are notorious in the United States and other countries. Among the most infamous of these groups is the American Mafia, an Italian-American criminal society that emerged in the late nineteenth century in New York City and spread to other major cities on the East Coast and elsewhere. In Italy, the Mafia has challenged the central state for more than a century (see Photo 11.1). In Mexico, drug gangs have grown into multinational businesses, with private armies that smuggle contraband across the United States border, intimidating and killing politicians and law-enforcement officials. In Japan, the Yakuza are an infamous organized crime syndicate, operating in many sectors of the economy. In China, war lords and violent gangs operated along territorial borders and in waters off the coast for centuries.

Governments have running battles with these gangs as they terrorize towns and cities, and use the threat of violence to extract payments from frightened businesses. States may claim the legitimate monopoly of violence, but they often struggle to make good on this claim.

Recall as well that sovereign states, in a legal sense, are equal as members of the Westphalian system. In practice, however, they differ vastly in their capabilities. In this sense, the norms of equality within the Westphalian system coexist with a system of power inequality and political hierarchy. Some powerful states have more ability to get their way than weak states. Similarly, the norm of sovereign non-intervention exists as an ideal but is often violated. States can claim a supreme authority within their national borders but outside actors, such as strong states or non-state transnational actors, may be able to intervene inside states. States may be unable to enforce

War lords: Private authority figures who control their own local armies or militias.

border controls, and find their sovereign territorial boundaries transgressed by foreign actors. At the extreme, such transgressions would be the military intervention of a foreign power. A weak state can find itself unable to resist or defend against a more powerful invading state. But sovereign control by a state can fail in many less spectacular ways. Criminal groups, such as drug lords and gangs, can operate across borders without the national government being able to enforce laws or territorial boundaries.

Challenges to the sovereign authority of states by criminal groups are not new. Pirates, organized crime, and drug cartels have operated for centuries in various parts of the world. States have always been under challenge by non-state groups. There are challenges to the state today, but there have been challenges in the past as well. As a result, states must constantly find new ways to build and reinforce state control. Below we examine non-state challenges in more detail, and then consider the international responses to these challenges.

Levels of Analysis *The Westphalian* *System*	👥 **State**	🌐 **International**
	States claim sovereign authority internally and externally, but are not always able to enforce that claim.	The sovereign state system is a defining feature of world politics and has continually adapted to challenges from non-state actors.

Challenges to Sovereign States

The traditional Westphalian idea of the international system – and the modern sovereign state itself – has been challenged in recent decades by a cluster of inter-related developments: non-state actors empowered by technological change, failed states, and the changing norms and expectations of the international community.

First, advancements in technologies have made it easier for private groups, such as criminal gangs and terrorist groups, to operate and inflict harm across national borders and at longer distances. The internet makes it easier to communicate and transfer funds across the world. These groups can build extended transnational organizational networks. Technologies of violence – nuclear, chemical, and biological – also provide capabilities that allow non-state actors to wield destructive force that, previously, only states could possess. Modern technologies, such as monitoring and surveillance, also give states new tools with which to seek out transnational criminal and terrorist groups. In remains an open question whether these modern technologies give the advantage to non-state groups or the states which seek to detect and prevent their violent activities.

Second, the capacity of states to retain sovereign control over their national territories varies considerably. In the developing world, there are many nation-states that are sovereign more in name than reality. Afghanistan, Sudan, and Somalia are just some examples of states so weak that the central government has no effective control over major regions within the formal territorial borders. These un-ruled territories provide attractive havens for non-state criminal and terrorist groups to operate, offering training sites and launching pads for transnational operations. More established states with capable law-enforcement institutions and courts that uphold the rule of law provide less welcoming conditions for these private wielders of violence, though, as we have noted, even these advanced countries still struggle with organized crime and other violent groups.

Third, countries around the world have become increasingly concerned with the activities of non-state actors, particularly the violent ambitions of terrorist groups with increasing global reach. The Westphalian system is under threat, and established sovereign states are searching for ways to respond. One response is to target criminal and terrorist groups with intelli-

gence, special operations, covert actions, and counter-insurgent war. For example, in recent years, the United States has expanded its use of unmanned drones in places such as Pakistan, Afghanistan, and Yemen to strike terrorist havens (Harnden 2011). Another strategy of response is to seek to strengthen the weak and failing states that provide havens for outlaw groups. The dramatic events of September 11 gave birth to ambitious strategic plans from the George W. Bush administration; this agenda of state strengthening and political development gained new urgency.

At the same time, the norms of state sovereignty are evolving, reflected most clearly in the rise of the norm of the **Responsibility to Protect**. This is an international norm that says that if a particular state is inflicting harm or violence on its own citizens or if it is unable to protect its own citizens from harm or violence, the international community has the right – indeed the obligation – to act. As we will discuss later in the chapter, the emergence of this new responsibility norm reflects an evolution of thinking within the international community about state sovereignty. Failed states, terrorism, and violations of human rights are driving the international community to rethink the old Westphalian state system and the rules and norms of intervention.

Responsibility to Protect: An international norm that says that if a particular state is inflicting harm or violence on its own citizens or if it is unable to protect its own citizens from harm or violence, the international community has the right – indeed the obligation – to act.

The international system will be transformed by these challenges, struggles, and changing norms. States will either find ways to adapt and strengthen the capacity of their sovereign authority or the world will enter a new epoch of transnational violence and disorder. Technologies and the forces of globalization have brought the world together in new ways but, in the hands of violent and criminal non-state actors, they also threaten to tear the world apart. We can look at three 'faces' of this non-state world: pirates, war lords, and terrorists with global reach.

Piracy

Pirates have been among the most colorful and persistent challengers to the authority of states, threatening freedom on the world's oceans over the centuries. **Pirates** are non-state gangs who commit robbery or criminal violence on the high seas. The 1982 United Nations Convention on the Law of the Seas defines piracy as acts of 'violence, detention, or depredation' committed for private ends against the crew or passengers on board ships on international waterways. States care about piracy because the criminal activity itself can be costly, in human and economic terms, and these non-state groups amount to a direct challenge to states and their monopoly of control over the use of force in and between states. Pirates operate outside the law, and also outside the Westphalian system of states. The upsurge of piracy in the contemporary world, most prominently seen off the coast of East Africa, presents disturbing evidence that at least some states have lost control over the seas.

Early Piracy

Piracy dates back to some of the earliest recorded history in the West. In the Middle Ages, pirates appeared in the waters around Western Europe, the North Seas, and the Atlantic coast after the fall of the Roman Empire, which could no longer protect its declining territories. Shipping groups seeking to provide their own defense sometimes formed guilds, but some of these groups turned to piracy given the riches that were available. Famously, the Vikings engaged in piracy along the European coasts, from Scandinavia and the Baltic Seas to the Iberian coast and the Mediterranean Sea, traveling up the rivers running into Eastern Europe and the Black Sea. The absence of centralized states in Europe or a powerful state willing to enforce freedom and safe passage at sea ushered in an era of rampant piracy throughout medieval Europe. During the same period, Muslim pirates plundered the coastal cities of southern France, northern Italy, and the North African shores.

Pirates also preyed on other regions of the world. The Caribbean was famous for piracy in the centuries following Christopher Columbus' voyage to the New World in

Pirates: Non-state gangs who commit robbery or criminal violence on the high seas.

1492. The classic era of piracy in the Caribbean played out from 1560 until the mid-1720s as outlaw gangs attacked Spanish treasure ships transporting Aztec gold back to Spain. Spain was the dominant force in the Caribbean during these years, but England, France, and the Netherlands (rivals of Spain) also sought to gain a foothold in this region, awash in gold, silver, and other valuables. During the height of Caribbean piracy, all the conditions that allowed outlaws to flourish were in evidence: a region awash in treasure, expanding shipping traffic, and vast stretches of islands and waters that were outside the reach of Spanish naval power.

Pirates also flourished in Asia during these centuries. In the thirteenth century, the Japanese-based Wokou began 300 years of attacks across East Asia. Other pirate groups operated in the South China Sea with bases in Taiwan. As in other regions, piracy emerged when the protection of maritime states and their naval forces receded. In East Asia, it was the retreat of the Mongol Yuan fleet that opened the region to piracy, allowing these gangs to prey on the riches that came with the growth of the maritime silk and spice routes. The most powerful pirate groups in the region were Chinese, and they grew and flourished throughout the early nineteenth century.

The problem of piracy was one of the first diplomatic challenges of the newly independent United States. Prior to independence, American colonial ships were protected from Barbary raiders off the coast of North Africa by English forces. But when these protections lapsed, American ships were seized by privateers – private individuals who operate vessels with a government commission to capture enemy shipping – from Morocco and Algeria. The problem came to a head in 1785 when Algerian privateers seized two American ships, sold their cargo, enslaved their crews, and held them for ransom. The American ambassador to France, Thomas Jefferson, attempted to negotiate with the Algerian ambassador in Paris. The Barbary state demanded huge payments of tribute, which the American Congress refused to approve, leaving the crews to languish as slaves to Algerian Moors for over a decade. Out of these struggles, the American Navy was born in March 1794. American naval forces did battle with the privateers and their sponsoring states along the North African coast in the Barbary Wars.

Privateers: Privately owned ships hired by European governments, primarily in the seventeenth century, to attack and harass Spanish ships in the Caribbean. In addition to taking half of the spoils, European governments benefited from not having to build larger navies to deal with Spanish dominance.

Modern Piracy

With the rise of modern naval power in the late nineteenth and early twentieth centuries, piracy receded around the world. But it was not fully extinguished, and has reappeared in recent years. Many of the coastal waters around the globe, such as the coasts of North and South America, Western Europe, and Northeast Asia, are relatively safe. In these waters, established naval powers safeguard sea lanes and deter pirate gangs. In other regions, however, piracy is a fact of maritime life. In particular, piracy remains a significant problem in the waters extending from the Red Sea and the Indian Ocean, off the east African coast, and in the Strait of Malacca and Singapore; these waterways are used by as many as 50,000 commercial ships a year. One study indicates that worldwide losses from piracy amount to as much as $13 to 16 billion annually (Hahn 2012).

The most famous instances of modern piracy occur off the coast of Somalia. Major shipping routes take a large flow of cargo ships through narrow water passages, making it easy for pirates to overtake and board them with small motor boats. This is also a region dominated by developing countries with small navies. Somalia itself is a failed state, with ongoing clashes between various factional war lords and criminal gangs. The pirates are typically protected by these factional groups on shore, and the absence of centralized government authority makes effective law enforcement impossible. At the same time, the major naval powers in the region – which include India and the United States – are unable or unwilling to project consistent naval protection into the area, except in instances where commercial interests are particularly significant or are seen as growing completely out of control. As a result, piracy proliferates. The Somalia pirates are clever enough not to harm crews or vessels. They capture and hold the ships, and demand ransom. With few options, the commercial shipping companies tend to pay the pirates what they demand, and business continues. The US navy has intervened in some instances to rescue hostages taken by pirates (Gettleman 2012).

Modern piracy – much like piracy during its golden years – is a form of crime on the high seas that does not directly threaten established states. It shows the limits of state capacity to enforce order and provide security on open waters. Piracy comes to life when a leading power, such as the Roman Empire or the British Royal Navy or the United States, is not positioned to offer protection. When great powers are struggling among themselves or if their presence recedes from regions with active commercial maritime traffic, the 'rule of the sea' declines or disappears. Most importantly, piracy is aided by the weakness of states in the region. It is the failure of Somalia to establish the rule of law and a capable central government that allows piracy to prosper. The pirates can be attacked by navies dispatched to the area, but the problem will only be solved when weak or failed states in the area are able to achieve sufficient capabilities to resist the activities of pirates in their harbors and shores. Pirates conduct dangerous business on water, but require havens on land. The problem of piracy is felt off shore but the solutions, in part, are to be found on shore. The governments of the countries need to be strengthened so that they can establish stable order and defend their territorial waters against groups.

Weak/Failed States

We have already observed that a modern sovereign state has several key characteristics: it has a functioning central government, it is capable of controlling its borders,

Pirates in the Seventeenth and Twenty-first Centuries

Then: *Seventeenth-Century Pirates*

The Golden Age of pirates, 1650–1720, included famous figures such as Blackbeard (Edward Teach), Henry Morgan, William 'Captain' Kidd, and Bartholomew Roberts. Many of these pirates operated in the Caribbean Sea, seeking treasure aboard Spanish ships transporting gold and silver back to Europe. Pirate ships were heavily loaded with canons and sailors, making it easy for them to attack and over-whelm merchant ships. Pirating became so widespread and successful in the eigh-teenth century that European governments were forced to patrol the waters with heavily armed naval warships. Many famous pirates were killed or captured after these government-sponsored patrols began, and pirating in the New World declined.

Now: *Twenty-First-Century Pirates*

Beginning in the early 1990s, pirates operating off the coast of Somalia began to attack shipping vessels, kidnapping crews for ransom. The collapse of the Somali government and ensuing civil war provided the setting. The decline of the fishing industry off the coast of East Africa has intensified desperate economic circum-stances; some pirates were originally fisherman whose livelihoods were undercut by illegal fishing by foreign crews off Somali waters. Today, Somali pirates armed primarily with machine guns board cargo ships and hold the crew for ransom. War lords along the coast have organized the pirate networks and split the profits from their operations. Hundreds of attacks occur each year. Recently, warships from various countries, including the United States, Britain, China, and Japan, have patrolled the waters to deter attacks. These patrols do provide deterrence, but pirates still operate in these waters.

and it effectively claims a monopoly on the legitimate use of force over its territory. Most observers would agree that a stable, capable state has a defined territory, a dis-tinct population, an effective government, and the capacity to enter into formal rela-tions with other states.

Obviously, many states in the developing world are only a shadow of this ideal. Some states might be best seen as **weak states**. They have functioning central govern-ments, but they have only weak control over their territory and borders. They are unable to fully tax the population, establish police and military services, and provide other public services. Failed states are states where the government itself no longer functions; the state has essentially collapsed. As I. William Zartman, an academic who studies international organizations and conflict resolution, suggests in his widely accepted definition, a failed state is a state where 'the basic functions of the state are no longer performed' (Zartman 1995). Some observers see failed states primarily man-ifest in the inability of the state to enforce order. This absence of an established capable state will be seen most dramatically when insurgents attack the government and the country is torn by civil war.

As one expert on weak and failed states notes: 'In most failed states, government troops battle armed revolts led by one or more rivals. Occasionally, the official author-ities in a failed state face two or more insurgencies, varieties of civil unrest, different degrees of communal discontent, and a plethora of dissent directed at the state and at

Weak states: States with functioning central govern-ments but only weak control over their territory and borders.

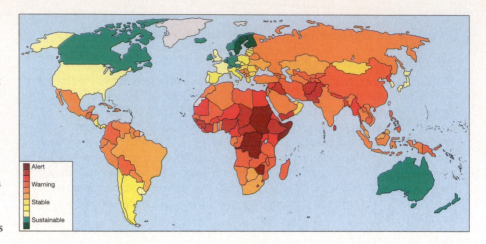

▶ **Map 11.1 The Failed State Index 2013**

Each year the Fund for Peace releases its index of failed states around the world. This is a graphical representation of that index for 2013, along with the scores used to derive the index and rankings for the twenty most vulnerable countries. Notice how those states that are categorized as in critical or dangerous condition tend to cluster together in geographic regions. The international community has tried to respond to the trouble created by the worst of these states, but international organizations are fighting an uphill battle.

Source: Fund for Peace, www.fundforpeace.org.

groups within the state' (Rotberg 2003). In today's world, countries such as Pakistan, Iraq, Afghanistan, and even Mexico and Peru are countries with violent internal rivals – or war lords – challenging the central government.

As in the case of pirates, rival groups and war lords have long been part of the history of the Westphalian state system. The first states that emerged in early modern Europe in the seventeenth century did not simply emerge whole and sovereign. They had to be created. Central government rulers had to build institutions and establish their supreme authority within an internationally recognized territorial boundary. The first states in Europe were composite states, built through the combining of several political entities. As Daniel Nexon, professor of government at Georgetown University, notes:

> Whether confederate or imperial, ruled by hereditary or elected princes, or operating as autonomous republics, most early modern European states were composed of numerous subordinate political communities linked to central authorities through distinctive contracts specifying rights and obligations. These subordinate political communities often had their own social organizations, identities, languages, and institutions. (Nexon 2009)

In Europe during this era, and around the world, the rulers of the central state had to struggle to establish their authority and maintain control over outlying areas.

In some cases, central governments fail to establish rule and order within a sovereign state because outlying provinces and regions want independence. In Europe today, there are active independence movements in northern Spain, Great Britain, and elsewhere. Along the Chinese border, provinces such as Tibet are attempting to gain autonomy or independence. Russia has also struggled with secession movements in provinces such as Chechnya along its southern border. In other cases, it is not an independence movement that threatens state sovereignty and control but criminal gangs and war lords that operate as mini-states within an outlying region. For example, Afghanistan is a country that has many war lords controlling territory in remote areas away from the capital in Kabul. The border area between Pakistan and Afghanistan is a 'no man's land' that has been a sanctuary for terrorists because it lies beyond the control of the central government of either country. These challenges to the centralized state are often associated with crime and violence since they operate beyond the reach of the police and the law.

◀ **Photo 11.5 The Kashirskoye Shosse Apartment Bombing, Moscow, Russia 1999**

For the past several decades, Russia has struggled to control secession movements in several of its provinces, most notably Chechnya. Chechen rebels are known to carry out attacks against populations in major Russia cities, specifically through the use of bombs. Here you see the bombing, and resulting demolition, of an apartment building in Moscow that left 118 people dead. Rescuers and firefighters work at the site of the massive explosion, which shattered a nine-story apartment building at Kashirskoye Shosse in Moscow, one in a series of 1999 apartment house bombings that triggered the second war in Chechnya, in this early Thursday, September 9, 1999 photo.

Source: PA Images.

The most dangerous cases of weak or failed states are those where regional or provincial leaders, or war lords, engage in violence that spills out into the wider region and international system at large. Often, these war lords engage in international criminal activity by selling drugs, buying weapons, smuggling diamonds, and pursuing other sorts of transnational violence. We can look more closely at three countries in different parts of the world, Afghanistan, Sudan, and Columbia, to better understand the processes by which such threats to the international system occur.

Afghanistan

Afghanistan sits at the crossroads of South Asia, bordered by Iran in the south and west, and Pakistan in the east. It is a landlocked and mountainous country situated over the centuries amidst great empires and trade and migration routes. Afghanistan is one of the poorest countries in the world, and its largest export is poppies, which are used in making heroin. Indeed, Afghanistan is the largest provider of poppies in the world, and the international heroin trade depends on its exports (Naim 2005). Afghanistan is also a country with a weak central government and a patchwork of tribal and ethnic groups that control provincial areas and compete with the national government in Kabul for the allegiance of the Afghan people.

Since the late 1970s, Afghanistan has been plagued by civil war. When its pro-Soviet government was threatened by internal tribal uprisings, the Soviet Union intervened with military force. This was followed by a long struggle between Soviet military forces, tied to a Soviet-backed regime in Kabul, and tribal groups resisting foreign domination. As many as two million Afghans died in the war with the Soviets. Rebel groups were led by the Afghan Mujahideen, US-supported resistance fighters that struggled against the Soviet invasion of their homeland. American involvement in Afghanistan was primarily motivated by its Cold War competition with the Soviet Union, so after the withdrawal of Soviet troops in 1989, the United States lost interest in Afghanistan. During the 1990s, in the void left by the departure of Soviet and United States troops, a civil war ensued among different tribal and provincial groups vying for control over the

Building the Afghanistan State

Aspiration: The United States intervened militarily in Afghanistan soon after the September 11, 2001 terrorist attacks, overthrowing the Taliban government. In the aftermath of this intervention, American and NATO forces have spent the last ten years trying to defeat an insurgency by Taliban forces and other tribal groups. The most ambitious goal that the United States and others have articulated for Afghanistan is to turn it into a functioning democratic state. The goal is to build a strong, legitimate, and accountable central government with all of the elements of modern government. Consider the following statement by President George W. Bush:

> With the steady leadership of President Karzai, the people of Afghanistan are building a modern and peaceful government. Next month, 500 delegates will convene a national assembly in Kabul to approve a new Afghan constitution. The proposed draft would establish a bicameral parliament, set national elections next year, and recognize Afghanistan's Muslim identity, while protecting the rights of all citizens. Afghanistan faces continuing economic and security challenges – it will face those challenges as a free and stable democracy.

(Remarks by President George W. Bush at the 20th Anniversary of the National Endowment for Democracy, November 6, 2003)

Reality: After ten years of military struggle, the Afghan government remained weak. Its powers and authority did not reach much further than the city limits of the capital. The possibility of building a Western-style democratic state was remote. Although voting took place for a national assembly and the leader of the country, the authority of the central government remains limited. Power-sharing schemes that leave tribal areas under separate rule became a more realistic option. Stability, rather than the lofty ideals of nation building and democracy, became the watchword for Afghan politics. Consider the statement by President Barack Obama:

> The goal that we seek is achievable, and can be expressed simply: No safe haven from which Al Qaeda or its affiliates can launch attacks against our homeland or our allies. We won't try to make Afghanistan a perfect place. We will not police its streets or patrol its mountains indefinitely. That is the responsibility of the Afghan government, which must step up its ability to protect its people, and move from an economy shaped by war to one that can sustain a lasting peace. What we can do, and will do, is build a partnership with the Afghan people that endures –one that ensures that we will be able to continue targeting terrorists and supporting a sovereign Afghan government.

(Remarks by the President on the Way Forward in Afghanistan, June 22, 2011)

country. Out of this struggle the Taliban, a radical Islamic group, developed into a politico-religious organization and seized power in the capital of Kabul, eventually capturing as much as 95 percent of the country by 2000. The Taliban instituted a radical political and religious order, restricting rights and freedoms, particularly of women and girls. Most importantly, under the Taliban, the Al Qaeda terrorist organization was able to set up training camps in the countryside, establishing a safe haven, from which it could launch the 2001 terrorist attacks on the United States.

America's new enemy now had its 'home address', and it was in Afghanistan. Nonetheless, the Taliban refused to hand over Al Qaeda's leader, Osama bin Laden, and other prominent terrorist leaders. In late 2001, the United States launched an attack on Taliban and Al Qaeda targets in Afghanistan, working with anti-Taliban groups across the country. These assaults on the Taliban culminated with the capture of Kabul by the Northern Alliance, a militia still recognized by the United Nations as the legitimate Afghan government. Along the way, many regional war lords switched their allegiance from the Taliban to the Northern Alliance. For a while, the new government made inroads in rebuilding and establishing rule across the country. But the Taliban slowly began to return to prominence, gathering forces in various outlying regions. The result was a new phase of insurgent civil war. The beleaguered central government struggled to maintain order in the face of rebel acts within regional strongholds. Beginning in 2007, the United States expanded its military operations in the country; to this day, a violent insurgency continues to pull the country apart. Entire parts of the country remain outside the control – and law enforcement – of the government in Kabul. Despite the capture and death of Osama bin Laden, the threat remains that this lawless country will again become a haven for terrorists.

Sudan

Sudan is the largest country in Africa with an ancient history, but one that has long suffered from civil war and has been labeled a failed state. It is also a country with rich oil deposits. Like Afghanistan, it is a country that over the centuries has been encroached upon by neighbors, such as Egypt. In the late nineteenth century, Sudan was under British control even as other European powers, such as France and Belgium, also pursued claims on parts of its territory. Eventually, Britain granted the country independence in 1956, but Sudan remained divided between the North, which maintained close ties with Egypt and was predominantly Arab and Muslim, and the South, which was mostly populated by Christians and members of other religious sects. The fact that Britain divided the country between the North and the South for purposes of administrative rule also reinforced these divisions. In the decades to follow, civil war was rife between the two factions. Military governments were formed in the North and rebel armies organized resistance in the South. The southern 'liberation army' formed in the 1980s and was a Marxist-inspired organization with support from the Soviet Union and Ethiopia. It gradually shed this identity and reached out for Western support by portraying the struggle as one between a Christian South and an Arab Islamic North seeking to dominate the nation.

After two decades of brutal war, peace talks in 2003 did lead to a truce and the granting of autonomy for the South for a period of years to be followed by a referendum on independence. The agreement also mandated joint leadership of the government and the sharing of oil revenues. A United Nations mission to Sudan was established to help implement the agreement. But by 2005, the Southern rebel army withdrew from the accord that ended the civil war, protesting its slow implementation. In the meantime, a bloody civil war was also occurring in the western region of Sudan, known as Darfur. Sudanese rebels were seeking autonomy from the central government, which they saw as neglecting the region. Government and rebel groups were both accused of violent atrocities, but the Arab militias operating on behalf of the national government were singled out by outside observers for engaging in acts of genocide. In 2004, American Secretary of State Colin Powell described the conflict in

Darfur as genocide, suggesting that it was the worst humanitarian crisis of the new century. Eventually, the Sudanese government and rebel groups signed an agreement, bringing an end to the conflict and establishing a temporary government in the region that would include rebel participation. Ultimately, the agreement did not stop the violence, and civil war continues to pit religious and ethnic tribal groups, both regionally and nationally, against each other (Natsios and Abramowitz 2011).

The civil war in Sudan is a tragedy for its own people, but is also a struggle that threatens the outside world. The fragmented and war-torn country has a government that cannot impose its authority or the rule of law throughout the north, south, and west regions. As in Afghanistan, the failure of the state created ungoverned regions that are prime locations for radical and terrorist groups. The United States has listed Sudan as a state sponsor of terrorism since 1993. In the late 1990s, the United States bombed a pharmaceutical factory in Khartoum because of its alleged production of chemical weapons and links to Al Qaeda. Beyond this, Sudan's rich oil reserves have attracted the attention of major outside powers and intensified the stakes in the civil war. China has extensive economic relations with Sudan, obtaining as much as 10 percent of its oil from Sudan, and China is a major arms supplier of the Sudanese government.

Colombia

Colombia is a country in South America with a constitutional government and a large economy. It gained independence from Spain in 1819 and established the Republic of Colombia in 1886. After several decades of political stability in the early twentieth century, the country found itself in new episodes of political violence and civil war beginning in the 1940s, when armed militias of the Liberal and Conservative parties descended into a vicious circle of violence and retaliation that persisted for decades. By the 1960s, violence between the political parties declined; leading political figures established a united front of shared power and pursued an agenda of economic and social reform.

Despite efforts at building a modern government, political violence and instability were never far in the background. Beginning in the 1970s, various guerrilla groups, some dominated by Marxist ideology, emerged to fight the government. Amidst this turmoil, in the late 1970s, violent drug cartels took hold of territory, increasing their power and control of outlying regions in the following decades. The most famous of these drug cartels were the Medellin Cartel, led by Pablo Escobar, and the Cali Cartel who, along with various associated groups, exerted increasing political and economic influence in Colombia over the decades. These cartels helped finance an array of illegal armed groups, both right-wing paramilitary groups and left-wing insurgents. These cartels and groups have undermined the rule of the central government. Guerilla groups emerged first, operating in the countryside under the influence of Marxist revolutionary ideas. Paramilitary groups have also been a prominent part of the Colombian political landscape, often employed by landowners seeking protection against guerilla groups when the central government could not do so. In the 1980s, these paramilitary groups who, in the past, had worked with agricultural landowners producing legal crops, began to come under the sway of drug lords, using their lands for the growing of coca. Soon, the drug cartels began supporting paramilitary squads (Kline 2003).

Drug groups used their money and firearms to build private security protection arrangements for towns and people, further weakening the state. The central government tried to re-establish its authority and the reach of law enforcement, but was largely helpless as the cartels and private security war lords continued to dominate large parts of the country. Harvey F. Kline, a specialist on Latin America, summarized the downward spiral of Columbia's central governmental power:

> Hence the weak state that existed in Colombia made it possible for drugs to become rooted in the countryside. This, in turn, made the Colombian state even weaker, as drug dealers established private governments in parts of the country. As their illicit wealth increased, they armed themselves and collaborated with both paramilitary groups and guerrilla groups, which made the state weaker yet. (Kline 2003)

Along the way, Colombia became the leading drug-producing country in the world. In recent years, the country continues to be plagued by drug cartels, insurgent movements, and paramilitary groups. Smaller drug trading groups have emerged, employing sophisticated financial and communication technologies to escape the law and operate across international borders. In the last decade, Colombian drug traffickers have found sophisticated ways to 'clean' their money, entrusting their dollars to intermediaries who use the funds to make legal purchases in the United States on behalf of Colombian customers. The customers pay the brokers in local currency that is passed on to the drug dealers (Naím 2005).

What Afghanistan, Sudan, and Colombia have in common is that the central state has failed to establish its authority and sovereign control over the national territory. These nations do not possess what sovereign states must possess – namely, a monopoly over the legitimate use of violence within the territorial borders of the country. Non-state groups such as ethnic militias, separatist forces, guerilla groups, and warlord armies usurp authority and violence capacities that are normally reserved for the state. The state is weak or failing, allowing private groups to take control of regions or provinces. This breakdown of political order becomes a vicious cycle; the groups take hold because the state is weak, which weakens the state further, which allows the groups to grow stronger, further weakening the state. Crime and violence remain outside the reach of law enforcement. Pierre Hassner, a renowned French lecturer in international relations, has described this breakdown of state authority as a 'return to the Middle Ages,' in which the modern state is undermined by a proliferation of competing sub-state power blocs (Hassner 1993). Through this process, these weak and fragmenting states become theaters for transnational crime and violence. As a result, other countries with established functioning states, and the international system itself, become threatened. If lawlessness emerges in one state or region of the world, it provides a platform for criminal groups to threaten other countries and regions.

Terrorism

The terrorist attacks of September 11, 2001, were a frightening introduction to the threats of violence in the twenty-first century. In one sense, the attacks were quite simple in their design. A group of twenty hijackers boarded four commercial airlines, took over the controls, and smashed them into buildings. The only weapons they brought with them were box cutting knives. What made the attacks shocking is that the hijacked airplanes became weapons used to inflict great violence on New York City and the Pentagon. Prior to 9/11, the security of the American homeland had really only been attacked in the modern era when Japanese bombers destroyed Pearl

Harbor at the beginning of World War II. But September 11, 2001 seemed to shatter the view of America as relatively invulnerable. Violence could come from any direction and hit any place on earth. No people are secure. Small groups of armed gangs, made up of people who hate and are prepared to die, can lash out at established societies and leave their cities burning.

As we discussed in Chapter 2, terrorists employ violence against civilians to achieve a political purpose. Used as a tool of war and political struggle, terrorism may be employed by a group seeking to intimidate, coerce, or manipulate the sentiments of another people by inflicting violence on innocent civilians. This violence may simply be an expression of hatred and anger, but it can also be a calculated step aimed at altering the behavior of an enemy. The immediate victims may be innocent civilians, but the ultimate target is the foreign policy of a state.

In this sense, terrorism, like piracy, is very old. In the nineteenth and early twentieth centuries, terrorism primarily took the form of violence committed by nationalist movements resisting occupation and seeking independence from imperial or colonial domination. In late nineteenth-century Russia, opponents, or **anarchists**, of the Tsarist state used bombs to kill state officials with the hope of inciting popular revolt. Anarchist figures were responsible for the assassination of Russian Czar Alexander II in 1881 and American President William McKinley in 1901. Also in the late nineteenth century, Armenian nationalist groups seeking independence from the Ottoman Empire used violence against public officials. During the same period, Irish nationalists carried out attacks in England, foreshadowing the later activities of the Irish Republican Army, a group that, for decades, carried out assassinations and political violence in their protests against British presence in Northern Ireland. In the early twentieth century, Zionist groups fought the British in their efforts to establish a Jewish state in Palestine. At the same time, the Muslim Brotherhood, which recently won control of the Egyptian government, and then lost it in a military coup, was formed in Egypt as a nationalist group resisting British control. As we discussed in Chapter 5, a terrorist act by a Serbian nationalist was the proximate cause of World War I.

After World War II, there was another surge in nationalist and anti-colonial movements, in which groups used violence against established authorities. Empires were in retreat around the world, with European states weakened by the toll of war, and movements for self-rule were on the rise. The Viet Minh fought against the French in Indochina, a Malayan resistance movement struggled against the British, and a liberation movement opposed French colonial control of Algeria. Other anti-colonial groups fought the British in Cyprus, while Basque guerillas in northern Spain waged open war against the military rule of General Francisco Franco. These Basque separatists, demanding independence, killed government officials, often by planting car bombs. Starting in 1959, Fatah, a Palestinian nationalist group, began attacks on the young state of Israel (established in 1948). In one of the defining moments of international terrorism, the Fatah splinter group, Black September, seized eleven Israeli athletes at the 1972 Summer Olympics in Munich. In a gun battle with police, all of the athletes and five of the terrorists were killed. Since the 1980s, Hezbollah, the Islamist revolutionary group founded in Lebanon, and Hamas, an Islamic Palestinian group, have carried out rocket attacks, kidnappings, and suicide bombings against Israeli military and civilian settlements.

By far the most notorious international terrorist group is Al Qaeda. Founded in 1988 by Osama bin Laden, this Sunni Islamist extremist movement has carried out

◄ **Photo 11.6 Mural Idolizing the IRA in Belfast, North Ireland**

The Irish Republican Army was arguably one of the most formidable insurgency groups in the world. For decades, the organization evaded the British government, while carrying out assassinations, bombings, and other political violence. The IRA used this violence as a means of protest against British control over North Ireland. Here, a man walks past a Republican mural in the Nationalist Derrybeg housing estate, Newry, on September 26, 2005.

Source: PA Images.

acts of violence with the aim of ending foreign influence in Muslim countries and establishing a new Islamic caliphate (transnational Islamic state). In October 2000, Al Qaeda carried out a bombing of the US Navy destroyer USS Cole in the port of Aden in Yemen. But it was the September 11, 2001 attack using hijacked commercial airliners that brought the threat of international terrorism into a new era.

The terrorist acts of September 11 share the basic characteristics of terrorism as it has appeared over the centuries. It is an act of violence by non-state actors directed at civilians and seeking to send a message. An Al Qaeda spokesman commented on the violence unleashed in the United States in September 2001. 'It rang the bells of restoring Arab and Islamic glory' (Richardson 2007). The violence is directed at the enemy, but it is not aimed at defeating an enemy in war. It is an act of violence that seeks to make a political point and alter how others see a political struggle. By reacting to an attack, people will force their government to change its policies. The symbolic aspect of the September 11 attacks was clear. It was an attack on icons of American power. The World Trade Center's Twin Towers served as a symbol of American global capitalism and the Pentagon as a symbol of American global military power. Another hijacked plane that crashed into the Pennsylvania countryside was headed for the Capitol Building or the White House.

So why do terrorists do what they do? What leads people to kill innocent civilians? There are many reasons why angry militants engage in terrorism (Richardson 2006). As in its early nineteenth-century manifestations, one motivation for terrorism still appears to be the quest for an independent homeland. The Basques in Spain, the Tamils in Sri Lanka, the Chechens in southern Russia, separatists in Northern Ireland, and many other groups have , over the last century, resorted to terrorist violence as they seek independence. Other groups have had more far-reaching political objectives. Revolutionaries in nineteenth-century Europe sought to overturn capitalism and usher in a new social order. Since the days of Mohammad, some Islamist groups have sought to transform the states in the Middle East into a trans-state caliphate. Most recently, the Al Qaeda terrorist group has sought to force the United States and its military forces out of the Middle East (in particular, Saudi Arabia as the home to Muslim holy sites) and oppose the autocratic Arab states in the region which they see as an obstacle to the realization of their trans-Arab aspirations for a caliphate.

The international sovereign state system is being challenged by the effects of piracy, weak nations, war lords, and transnational terrorist groups. We have discussed the conditions which make it possible for these groups to organize, but what tools can transform their power and reach on a global basis?

Technology and the Privatization of War

What pirates, war lords, and terrorists have in common is that they are non-state actors who employ violence to achieve their ends. They are not just citizens committing a crime. They are groups using violence capabilities ordinarily reserved for states to pursue economic or political gains by directly challenging the Westphalian state system. They have always existed at the edges of the state system. What has made these groups increasingly dangerous in the contemporary world is their potential global reach and the growing lethality of their violence. Communication technologies have allowed these groups to become transnational and organize at a great distance. They can operate far afield, sending messages, money, and agents around the world. At the same time, they are also able to gain access to ever more lethal violence capacities. These developments make non-state actors increasingly dangerous. They threaten not just particular cities or states, but global civilization and potentially the Westphalian system itself.

Privatization of war: The idea that states no longer have a monopoly on the effective use of violence. As technology advances, private parties have greater and greater capacities to wage war and engage in violence.

These new developments might be called the **privatization of war**. In the past, only states (primarily powerful states) were able to gain access to violence capabilities that could threaten other societies. It is still a remote possibility, but we can look to the future and foresee the day when small groups or transnational gangs of individuals might be able to acquire weapons of mass destruction (WMD). These technologies and knowledge will almost inevitably diffuse outward. Determined groups of extremists will increasingly be in a position to obtain WMD. The journalist Robert Wright has called this the 'growing lethality of hatred' (Wright 2006). The actual number of individuals in the world willing to inflict harm on others may not be growing. What is growing is the capability of these individuals. In the past, groups that were willing to use violence to express their hatred were limited in the damage they could inflict. In the future, this limitation may well drop away.

It is now possible to imagine a small group of determined individuals camped out in a weak or war-torn Middle Eastern country or elsewhere planning a massively destructive event. It would not take a lot of people, but it would take money, knowledge, and logistical capabilities. The group might find common cause with a few scientists or engineers who work for a government military agency with chemical, biological, or nuclear materials. Secretly, the government experts could find a way to transfer the materials to the non-state group. This could be possible because the state itself is weak or failing, has splintered into competing factions, or has lost the capacity to enforce safety and security for its WMD stockpiles. Organized crime groups or war lords from another state could act as an intermediary between government experts and terrorists. Once in the hands of a terrorist group, it is only a matter of logistics and determination to get the weapon to its target. The target might be a harbor city in Europe or the United States, perhaps New York City. Like the hijackers of September 11, these terrorists may be willing to die for their cause. An exploded nuclear device would kill hundreds of thousands of people, perhaps even a million or more,

State Sovereignty

Theory

State sovereignty is one of the most basic ideas about how the international system is organized. It emerged in Europe in the seventeenth century as a set of norms about the primacy and legal pre-eminence of the nation-state. The nation-state is sovereign. There is both an external and internal dimension to sovereignty. Externally, no other foreign government has the legal right to rule or intervene within the internal politics of the nation-state. The national government has the supreme authority and last word on what goes on within the nation-state's borders. Internally, the state – or central government – has an exclusive right to rule within the country, unhindered by private police or armies.

> *Sovereignty*: A government which exercises de facto administrative control over a country and is not subordinate to any other government in that country is a sovereign state.   [*The Arantzazu Mendi*, [1939] AC 256, Strouds Judicial Dictionary]

Practice

Many countries have weak governments that simply cannot live up to the ideals of state sovereignty. Externally, the state cannot protect its borders against the illegal movement of private criminal groups or terrorists. Foreign groups or the agents of foreign governments operate within the country without resistance from the central government. Internally, militias and private armies control territory and operate as sort of 'private governments' within regions of the country. The central government is too weak to enforce order within the country or protect its borders.

Yemen – a small country on the southern coast of the Arabian Peninsula – is a prominent example. The countryside is ruled by tribal war lords while government institutions are weak and failing. The President of Yemen has ruled for over three decades and maintains power through coopting and balancing off the warlord leaders in the provinces. As one Yemeni analyst notes: 'The government is a façade: the real power lies in the hands of the president, the house of the president and his network of patronage' (quoted in the *Financial Times*, January 3, 2010). There are more weapons in the hands of tribal groups than are controlled by the central security ministry. The terrorist group –Al Qaeda – has established affiliations with local radical Islamic groups and operates in safe havens within the country. The position of the president is weakening and the country is on the edge of civil war.

depending on its explosive capacities. A chemical or biological weapon would kill people more slowly, contaminating and poisoning people on a large scale across a metropolitan area. This is what terrorism could look like with global reach. It is a future spectacle in which the forces of technology and anger threaten the world in new and ominous ways.

In the wake of September 11, 2001, the United States government sounded the alarm about this new threat. In its famous National Security Strategy Report, issued a year after the terrorist attacks, the Bush administration proclaimed the danger:

The gravest danger our Nation faces lies at the crossroads of radicalism and technology. Our enemies have openly declared that they are seeking weapons of mass destruction, and evidence indicates that they are doing so with determination. The United States will not allow these efforts to succeed . . . America is now threatened less by conquering states than we are by failing ones. We are menaced less by fleets and armies than by catastrophic technologies in the hands of the embittered few. We must defeat these threats to our Nation, allies, and friends. (White House 2002)

The Bush administration's vision of danger in the twenty-first century was the nexus between technology and political extremism. In this vision, the most worrisome peril to the United States and other countries of the world was terrorist groups that gained access to WMD from hostile or rogue states and used this violence capability to kill massive numbers of civilians. The immediate threat was from Al Qaeda, but the threat was much more profound and troubling than one terrorist organization. It was the deeper shift in the global system – a shift away from states able to monopolize violence – toward a future in which small gangs of dangerous people could destroy everyone's way of life.

This is a scary view of the future. It is a future where a small group of violent extremists – perhaps a group of radicals that the world does not even know exists – finds a way to acquire a nuclear device or a chemical weapon and detonate it in a major city, killing millions of people. Alternatively, the group might gain the knowledge to develop a deadly biological agent spread into the air over a major metropolitan area, again killing millions. The danger is that these non-state actors can operate 'under the radar screen.' They are small groups that hide in the shadows of world politics. Small groups with advanced technologies of violence operating transnationally across the globe are a new and worrisome face of the future.

These developments constitute a transformation in the ways and means of collective violence in international politics that is driven by technology and the political structure of the Westphalian system itself. This transformation causes problems for the old norms of sovereignty and the use of force. It raises troubling new questions about the relationship between domestic politics and international relations; regions of the world previously ignored must now be closely scrutinized. It also creates new functional challenges that will, inevitably, influence patterns of security cooperation. A global consensus does not exist on how to deal with this new type of diffuse non-state threat, which plays havoc with old notions of deterrence, alliance, self-defense, and Article 51 of the United Nations Charter (which defines the rights of states for collective self-defense).

Non-state actors engaging in crime and violence have co-existed with states and the states system throughout history. But technological advances and globalization have made them more dangerous and consequential for the global system. These non-state actors are triggering new efforts by states and international organizations, such as the United Nations, to work together to find ways to diminish their activity and impact. Ultimately, this has meant trying to eliminate the political conditions that allow these transnational groups to engage in violence and crime.

Individual	State	International
Small groups of terrorists are able to operate beyond the reach of states or the state system.	Weak or failed states are breeding grounds for challenges by non-state actors.	Technology and globalization have increased the vulnerability of states and have created new opportunities for terrorists, war lords and pirates to operate.

Levels of Analysis
Challenges to
Sovereign States

International Responses to Non-State Actors

In the years since September 11, 2001, the international community has debated how to respond to the danger of terrorism with global reach. Generally, there have been three types of response: attacking terrorist targets, building capacities for deterring terrorism, and long-term efforts to strengthen weak and failing states. As time has passed since the dramatic events of 2001, the focus has tended to be on the long-term necessity of strengthening weak states and promoting stable, sovereign states able to enforce the rule of law.

The first type of response, attacking terrorist targets, involves direct military action. The United States invaded Afghanistan in late 2001 to overturn the Taliban regime, which had been harboring Al Qaeda terrorists. In the meantime, the Bush administration articulated a doctrine of pre-emptive action that justified future efforts to go after terrorists before they could strike. In 2003, the United States invaded Iraq and overturned the regime of Saddam Hussein. In the run-up to this war, the Bush administration argued that the Iraqi government was actively acquiring WMD, including materials to build a nuclear bomb. From their perspective, the invasion was justified both as combating a direct and gathering threat and as part of the larger 'war on terror' where despotic and hostile regimes, such as Saddam's Iraq, could threaten the world by passing WMD to terrorist groups. It was the nexus of despotism, technology, and terrorism that the Bush administration focused on to justify war. More than a decade after the September 11, 2001 attacks, the United States has only recently left Iraq and is ending its war in Afghanistan, and the justification continues to be the threat posed by terrorist groups that operate within and out of these states.

A second type of response to the new terrorist threats has been a series of international conventions and agreements that are aimed at giving states the authority to track down groups seeking to transport WMD around the world. In the decades before 2001, the United Nations had already developed conventions and protocols that provided universal legal instruments related to the prevention and suppression of terrorism. In 2005, the General Assembly adopted a series of conventions aimed at reducing the power and capabilities of these terrorist organizations and individuals, such as the International Convention on the Suppression of Acts of Nuclear Terrorism and the Convention on the Physical Protection of Nuclear Material (Ward 2003). Altogether, the United Nations has passed sixteen international conventions and protocols aimed at establishing a legal framework for international cooperation in countering terrorism. In addition, the UN Security Council has passed resolutions, both before and after the 2001 attacks, calling upon member states to ratify these anti-terrorism agreements and urging states to implement domestic measures to fulfill their obligations.

In addition, outside of the UN framework, states have cooperated to expand monitoring and tighten up safety at nuclear sites. The United States and Russia, for example, have been cooperating for some years on securing Cold War-era nuclear facilities and weapons in the former Soviet Union. The United States has also worked with other states to develop a counter-terrorism regime worldwide. Major countries with intelligence agencies have also increased their cooperation in tracking terrorist suspects and organizations through the sharing of intelligence information. As one expert on the financial networks behind terrorist groups reports: 'Beneath the loud shout of unilateralism present from the creation of the Bush administration's invasion of Iraq, a veritable orchestra of institutions have continued to play sotto voce to build capacities against global terrorism' (Winer 2003). Individual countries have also taken steps to increase security at harbors and border crossings. Even the borders between friendly countries, such as the United States and Canada, have been tightened, subjecting travelers to more demanding inspections and documentation checks. In all these ways, countries are seeking to gain more information on what terrorist groups are doing, and prepare against their operations and attacks.

In recent years, a third type of response has focused on the longer-term problem of promoting political stability and the rule of law in weak and failing states. In the view of the George W. Bush administration, terrorist groups were threats, in part, because states in troubled parts of the world were weak and failing, providing safe havens for these groups. Other autocratic states, such as Iraq under Saddam Hussein, were directly threatening to the world if they acquired WMD or passed weapons or materials on to terrorist groups. These new security worries grew the agenda for regime transformation. Threats by terrorists and hostile autocratic states could only be confronted by altering the character of these states. Secretary of State Condoleezza Rice captured the essence of the Bush administration's new view in a January 2006 speech at Georgetown University:

> Since its creation more than 350 years ago, the modern state system has rested on the concept of sovereignty. It was always assumed that every state could control and direct the threats emerging from its territory. It was also assumed that weak and poorly governed states were merely a burden to their people, or at most, an international humanitarian concern but never a true security threat. Today, however, these old assumptions no longer hold . . . The fundamental character of regimes now matters more than the international distribution of power. (Rice 2006)

The United States could not render itself safe in the existing system. States around the world would now need to be confronted, strengthened, and democratized.

All of this government activity and foreign policy prescription comes from a particular perspective about the root causes of terrorism. The motivation and development of terrorism dictates how the United States, Europe, and other countries should act to prevent it. Implicit in this perspective is a two-fold claim: terrorism with global reach is an almost revolutionary new development that threatens the very existence of societies and civilizations; and this revolutionary threat can only be undercut or diminished by extraordinarily ambitious and long-term efforts to strengthen states and promote liberty and freedom worldwide.

Other views make different claims about the causes and solutions to the threat of terrorism. Some see terrorism as a danger, but one that can be managed without the

George W. Bush Administration

The growing threat of 'terrorism with global reach' is caused by extremists who have resorted to violence because 'they hate who we are.' Al Qaeda and other Islamic extremists are the most prominent and dangerous terrorists operating today. As the Bush administration argued after September 11, the terrorists are threatened by our freedom and liberty. They will not stop until we find them and kill them. We must go directly to their hideouts and build functioning states that are based on representative government and the rule of law. We need to go get them before they come to our shores and get us.

Other Voices

Robert Pape, scholar from the University of Chicago: Terrorists are provoked primarily by the occupation of their lands by foreigners, or at least by their beliefs about such occupation. In this view, the September 11 terrorists were motivated primarily because of American military presence in Saudi Arabia – the land most holy to Islam – and American support for the conservative Arab regimes in the region and the state of Israel. To reduce the religious and political motivation of terrorism, the United States needs to reduce its presence in the Middle East.

Robert Wright, journalist: Wright was the author of a series of essays in Slate online magazine after September 11, where he argued that American force in the region was catalyzing Islamic terrorism rather than undercutting it. The focus needs to be on reducing the grievances and ideological motivations that propel radicals to engage in violence.

need for massive commitments to rebuild weak and troubled states. To the extent that Al Qaeda is motivated by American political and military support for conservative Arab states in the Middle East, the solution might actually be to reduce American presence in the region. Others argue that Al Qaeda terrorism is triggered by unresolved political problems in the Middle East, including the failure to establish peace between Israel and Palestine. It is perceived injustices and historical grievances that provide the impulses for violence. Some see the threat of terrorism not originating in weak and troubled regions of the world, but within Europe and the United States. It is a domestic social problem of integrating Muslim immigrants and strengthening peace and cooperation within civil society.

Global Response to Failed States

How the international community, and particularly the United Nations, should respond to the problem of weak and failed states has become a defining issue for world politics in the twenty-first century. Officially speaking, all internationally recognized states are sovereign entities. The United Nations Charter observes in Article 2(7) that the United Nations shall not intervene in 'matters, which are essentially within the domestic jurisdiction of any state.' Chapter VII of the Charter does indicate that exceptions to this general principle of non-interference exist when a country poses a threat to international peace and security. In earlier decades, most of the major powers did not consider weak or failed states to be major threats to international peace and security, so the UN was not seen to have responsibilities in this area. More recently, the UN Security Council has been willing to define dangers to international peace and security more broadly. Beginning in the 1990s, the Security Council invoked Chapter VII to authorize various interventions: Somalia in 1992–93, facing a major humanitarian disaster; Haiti in 1994, when a military coup deposed the democratically elected

► Photo 11.7 NATO Bombing of Belgrade, 1999

In 1998, a crisis broke out in Kosovo after Slobodan Milosevic sent Serbian troops to reclaim areas of Kosovo from the Albanians. In the absence of UN approval to intervene in the crisis, a NATO operation was undertaken in Kosovo, beginning with an air campaign in 1999. Here, local people watch a burning building in New Belgrade, after it was hit by NATO air-strikes, early on April 21, 1999. NATO jets struck the 18-storey high-rise building housing offices of the ruling SPS (Socialist Party of Serbia) and three local TV and radio stations. At least three missiles hit the building known as Ušće Business Center, located across the Sava river from the heart of the capital. Local sources claim at least 20 people were believed to be inside.

Source: PA Images.

President Aristide; and Albania in 1997, when the state collapsed into chaos. There has been a growing sense around the world that the international community, represented by the United Nations and leading states, needs to prepare to intervene in failed states to prevent or ameliorate humanitarian crises, including mass starvation and genocide.

In the current era national governments believe the international community has a right – even a moral obligation – to intervene in troubled states to prevent genocide and mass killing. NATO intervention in the Balkans and the war against Serbia were defining actions. As diplomatic negotiations at the United Nations Security Council over the crisis in Kosovo unfolded in 1998, Russia refused to agree to authorization of military action in what was an internal conflict. In the absence of UN approval, an American-led NATO operation did intervene. In framing this action, UN Secretary General Kofi Annan articulated a view of the contingent nature of norms of sovereignty and non-intervention, as enshrined in the UN Charter. Strobe Talbot, an American foreign policy analyst, recounts Annan's views:

> If the behavior of a regime toward its own people is egregious, it is not just outsiders' business to object but their responsibility to step in, stop the offenses, and even change the regime. 'State frontiers', Annan said, 'should no longer be seen as a watertight protection for war criminals or mass murderers. The fact that a conflict is "internal" does not give the parties any right to disregard the most basic rules of human conduct.' He acknowledged that 'the Charter protects the sovereignty of peoples', and that it prohibits the UN from intervening 'in matters which are essentially within the domestic jurisdiction of any State'. However, he added that the principle 'was never meant as a license for governments to trample on human rights and human dignity. Sovereignty implies responsibility, not just power'. (Talbot 2008)

A year later, Annan observed that 'state sovereignty, in its most basic sense, is being redefined.' Modern states, he argued, are 'now widely understood to be instruments at the service of their people, and not vice-versa . . . When we read the Charter today, we are more than ever conscious that its aim is to protect individual human rights not to protect those who abuse them' (Talbot 2008).

This new notion that sovereignty entailed responsibilities, as well as rights and protections, reflects a gradual and evolving redefinition of the meaning of national sovereignty. The idea was further developed in one of the most important new global norms to emerge in the decades since the end of the Cold War – the norm of the Responsibility to Protect. As mentioned earlier in the chapter, this norm – sometimes called R2P – seeks to qualify and elaborate the older norm of state sovereignty. The norm indicates that states – or the governments of states – have a responsibility to protect their citizens from violence, manifest as genocide, war crimes, crimes against humanity, and ethnic cleansing. States are obligated to act to halt or prevent these mass atrocities. If a state is unable to do so – either because it is the perpetrator of the violence or it is too weak to stop the violence – the international community has an obligation to act.

The Responsibility to Protect norm is spelled out in the 2005 World Summit Outcome Document, which was ratified by the UN General Assembly:

Responsibility to protect populations from genocide, war crimes, ethnic cleansing and crimes against humanity

138 Each individual State has the responsibility to protect its populations from genocide, war crimes, ethnic cleansing and crimes against humanity. This responsibility entails the prevention of such crimes, including their incitement, through appropriate and necessary means. We accept that responsibility and will act in accordance with it. The international community should, as appropriate, encourage and help States to exercise this responsibility and support the United Nations in establishing an early warning capability.

139. The international community, through the United Nations, also has a responsibility to use appropriate diplomatic, humanitarian and other peaceful means, in accordance with Chapters VI and VIII of the Charter, to help to protect populations from genocide, war crimes, ethnic cleansing and crimes against humanity. In this context, we are prepared to take collective action, in a timely and decisive manner, through the Security Council, in accordance with the Charter, including Chapter VII, on a case-by-case basis and in cooperation with relevant regional organizations as appropriate, should peaceful means be inadequate and national authorities are manifestly failing to protect their populations from genocide, war crimes, ethnic cleansing and crimes against humanity. We stress the need for the General Assembly to continue consideration of the responsibility to protect populations from genocide, war crimes, ethnic cleansing and crimes against humanity and its implications, bearing in mind the principles of the Charter and international law. We also intend to commit ourselves, as necessary and appropriate, to helping States build capacity to protect their populations from genocide, war crimes, ethnic cleansing and crimes against humanity and to assisting those which are under stress before crises and conflicts break out.

The norm of Responsibility to Protect emerged slowly beginning in the late 1990s. The 1994 genocide in Rwanda provided a trigger for global debate about the role and responsibility of the international community in the face of mass violence in a failed state. The United Nations Secretary General, Kofi Annan, pressed global leaders to come to some agreement about when and how member states might respond to such horrific violence. In the meantime, the Canadian government established an International Commission on Intervention and State Sovereignty in 2000 to develop ideas and ultimately came forward with the norm of the Responsibility to Protect (2001). In effect, the R2P norm announces that the international community has new obligations to see that basic human rights are protected within countries, particularly when faced with mass atrocities and other acts of organized violence (Evans 2009).

A further step in the erosion of norms of state sovereignty occurred in the aftermath of September 11. The American-led intervention in Afghanistan – where outside military force was used to topple a regime that actively protected terrorist attackers – was widely seen as a legitimate act of self-defense. The outside world has a legitimate claim to what goes on within a sovereign state if that state provides a launching pad, breeding ground, or protected area for transnational violence. The Bush administration pushed the limits of this principle in its invasion of Iraq. Now, it was the anticipatory threat of a state itself, and its ambitions to gain weapons of mass destruction, that provided the justification for intervention.

This new thinking was captured at the time by an American official at the State Department, Richard Haass:

> [There is] an emerging global consensus that sovereignty is not a blank check. Rather, sovereign status is contingent on the fulfillment by each state of certain fundamental obligations, both to its own citizens and to the international community. When a regime fails to live up to these responsibilities or abuses its prerogatives, it risks forfeiting its sovereign privileges including, in the extreme, its immunity from armed intervention. (Haass 2003)

Haass argued that there are three circumstances when exceptions to the norms of non-intervention are warranted: when a state commits or fails to prevent genocide or crimes against humanity; when a state abets, supports, or harbors international terrorists or is not capable of controlling terrorists operating within its borders; and when a state, particularly one with a history of aggression and support for terrorism, takes steps, such as an attempt to acquire weapons of mass destruction, that are a clear threat to global security.

The international community is still struggling to find ways to respond to weak and failed states. Weak states have been the target of foreign aid and other forms of assistance. When states are fully collapsed and enveloped in civil war, the United Nations has occasionally authorized peacekeeping interventions. On rare occasions, such as Afghanistan, where the state is collapsed or terrorists are based within its territory, more forceful interventions have occurred.

While the international community has begun to accept these infringements on sovereignty, including large-scale military interventions, the ability of these actions to actually reverse the collapse and failure of states is more problematic. Two scholars of development have posed questions that the international community must confront:

> How does the international community face up to the realities that the system is only as strong as its weakest link and that as many as sixty states are either on

their way to ruin or have already collapsed? What can be done that has not already been tried, unsuccessfully, to rescue and rebuild failing states in Haiti, East Timor, Bosnia, Somalia, Afghanistan, Iraq, Sudan, Nepal, and so many other struggling nations? Empirical studies are depressing: Nearly 50 percent of countries that emerge from conflict revert to hostilities within ten years. Nevertheless, the international system has failed to devise mechanisms to arrest these reversions successfully. In the past twenty years, for example, $300 billion has been spent in Africa alone, yet the continent is still rife with weak and collapsed regimes – two million people a year are dying of AIDS, three thousand children die every day of malaria, and forty million receive no schooling at all. How do we redefine a sovereign state in such a way that we can objectively measure its functionality and success? By what practicable and empirical successful method can we help struggling states get back on their feet on a sustainable basis? (Ghani and Lockhart 2008)

The dramatic attacks on the World Trade Center in September 2001 triggered a worldwide debate on the sources of terrorism and the best ways that the international community can respond to this global threat. The first and most direct responses aimed at attacking the terrorist groups themselves. But the longer-term responses have attempted to address the underlying problems of weak and failed states. There are no easy solutions to the persistent inability of some countries to develop capable and stable governments that can enforce order and the rule of law. In struggling with this problem, the international community has also been debating deeper issue about the status of state sovereignty itself. If terrorists can use weak or failed states as platforms to attack other countries, the international community needs to be in a position to intervene in these countries to deter or eliminate their terrorist threats. The international community also needs to be in a position to intervene to protect the citizens of these countries from violence, violence that is sometimes committed by a despotic ruler or as an outgrowth of civil war. But the international community has not yet found consensus on when and where the norms and institutions of state sovereignty can be violated in response to internal and transnational violence and human rights abuses.

State	International	Levels of Analysis
The changing norms of state sovereignty have altered the rights and obligations of nation-states.	Many countries agree in principle, but not always in practice, on the need for international cooperation to strengthen weak states and protect individuals from mass violence.	*International Responses*

Background

Will the nation-state remain the dominant type of political actor in world politics in the coming decades? The theoretical perspectives that we have explored do not give definitive predictions. But they do identify specific challenges and struggles that nation-states face and they offer different expectations of what is to come.

Realism: Realists expect that states will remain the dominant actors in world politics. States have struggled and overcome challenges in the past, and they will in the future. Realists emphasize that sovereign states have many advantages over non-state actors. They are able to tax and mobilize resources in pursuit of their goals. States are tied to nations, and so they are able to rely on nationalism as a source of support. States are also widely seen as the most effective organization for the protection of peoples – after all, they have the army and police.

Liberalism: Liberals expect that trade and interdependence between states will grow. States will increasingly find themselves in a world where they need to cooperate with other states to achieve their goals of security and prosperity. In a world that is increasingly interdependent, states will need to make room for other types of actors – transnational groups, multinational corporations, and international institutions. States probably will not disappear, but they will increasingly need to cooperate with each other and other types of actors.

Marxism: Marxism emphasizes the role – often hidden – of the capitalist class in shaping global economics and politics. In looking into the future, Marxists will focus on the expanding power and role of international capitalism. Whether in trade or finance, these international capitalist elites will grow in influence and directly or indirectly continue to limit and constrain the ability of states to control events and challenge capitalist interests.

Constructivism: Constructivism will keep an eye on how people in societies around the world think about states. They will look for evidence of shifts in the identity and loyalty of people to the nation-state. Will other sorts of identities – to the European Union, for example – grow in salience for people within Europe? What about transnational religious identity? Constructivists will look for how people and societies construct their ideas about the state and other groupings of people.

Whither the State?

The sovereign state has always existed in an uneasy relationship with wider global historical forces. Most of the people on earth today live within sovereign nation-states. A century ago, this was not true. At the turn of the nineteenth century, a majority of the world's people lived in territories that were not sovereign, such as empires or colonial territories. Through the great dramas of the last hundred years, the Westphalian state system rose up to dominate how and where people live. So, it is a great paradox that the forces of globalization, nationalism, and self-determination have also unleashed non-state actors that threaten the sovereign control of the state. The sovereign territorial state has never been so universal as a form of politics and rule, but today it also faces challenges.

As we have seen, non-state actors wielding violence and arms have always been an aspect of world politics. States have never been able to completely gain a monopoly on the legitimate use of violence within their own territory. Pirates, war lords, and terrorists have long been part of the world scene. But forces of globalization, nationalism, and self-determination have also unleashed powerful non-state actors, such as terrorist organizations with global reach, who threaten the stability and order as it is secured by states.

The forces of globalization have made it easier for non-state actors to travel, communicate, and operate on a worldwide basis. Technological innovations in weapons – nuclear, biological, and chemical – allow these actors to potentially gain weapons of such destructive power that it is possible to imagine whole cities suffering at their violent hands. Nationalism and the search by groups for political independence are not new. Certainly, terrorism is partly driven by aspirations for religious, political, and social freedom as peoples in various parts of the world struggle to define independence in a modernizing world. Globalization and the great economic transformations of the modern world have put pressure on people to define their aspirations. The international system also puts pressure on states, including weak and failing ones, to adjust to change and cope with uncertainties. All of these 'moving parts' have created openings for non-state wielders of force and violence to make a dramatic appearance.

So what is the future of the state in the face of non-state actors? First, it does appear that non-state actors will be increasingly able to inflict harm on people. Evolving weapons and delivery technologies seem to be giving private groups this opportunity. But, these non-state actors do not seem to have the capacity to replace the state or the state system. They do not have the ability to do what territorial states can do – build political communities with institutions that tax, provide services, and offer security. Five hundred years after the rise of the modern state, no other type of political system really can compete with it. Non-state actors can do damage, but they cannot offer an alternative way of organizing society and politics. So, the real question is: how effectively can states work together to protect their borders and strengthen their neighbors? In a sense, all states are vulnerable to the weakest among them. A failed state that cannot enforce rules and order within its society is a seedbed or haven for terrorists. Increasingly, the entire world has a stake in how these weak and failing states respond. The international community will need to find ways to build and strengthen states.

Individual	🌐 **International**	*Levels of Analysis*
The relationship between individuals and nation-states has changed over the last century because of new technologies of communication, transport, and violence.	The sovereign state system today is both more universal and more challenged than in earlier historical eras.	*Future of the Nation-State*

Revisiting the Enduring Question and Looking Ahead

In this chapter, we have explored the ways in which non-state actors have harnessed violence capabilities and challenged the Westphalian system. We have seen that these dramas are not new. But, we have also seen that globalization and technological changes are making the actions of non-state wielders of violence potentially more deadly and threatening. The international community is challenged to find ways to strengthen states and police the activities of pirates, war lords, and terrorists.

We now look forward to the future and questions about the dilemmas that states face as they seek to shape the world of the twenty-first century. New issues, such as the relationship between international politics and the global environment, are looming large. In the next chapter, we examine these challenges.

Visit **www.palgrave.com/politics/Grieco** to access extra resources for this chapter, including:

- Chapter summaries to help you review the material
- Multiple choice quizzes to test your understanding
- Flashcards to test your knowledge of the key terms in this chapter
- An interactive simulation that invites you to go through the decision-making process of a world leader at a crucial political juncture
- Pivotal decisions in which you weigh up the pros and cons of complicated decisions with grave consequences
- Outside resources, including links to contemporary articles and videos, that add to what you have learned in this chapter

---

Study Questions

1. In this chapter we looked at the history and modern experience of piracy. What sort of political and geographic settings provide congenial settings for piracy and what are the 'solutions' to the problem of piracy?
2. What are some of the technological and global political developments that make terrorism increasingly dangerous?
3. What do you think are the best solutions to the problem of failed states?
4. Are states and the Westphalian state system 'winning' or 'losing' in the struggle with non-state transnational groups such as pirates and terrorists?
5. In Chapter 7 we reviewed theories that suggested nuclear weapons may be a source of stability in the international system. Does the analysis of the current chapter challenge that view; why or why not?
6. How does the international community reconcile the tensions between a state's sovereignty within its territory and the growing notion of Responsibility to Protect?

Further Reading

Naím, Moisés (2006) *Illicit: How Smugglers, Taffickers, and Copycats are Hijacking the Global Economy* (New York: Anchor Books). A lively survey of the ways in which criminal commercial groups are operating at the edges of the global economy, outside the law and the reach of the state.

Naudé, Wim, Amelia U. Santos-Paulino, and Mark McGillivray (2011) *Fragile States: Causes, Costs, and Responses* (Oxford: Oxford University Press). A thoughtful inquiry into the causes and consequences of weak and failed states, and a survey of the various ways in which the international community has responded and can respond to these trouble spots.

Nordstrom, Carolyn (2007) *Global Outlaws: Crime, Money, and Power in the Contemporary World* (Berkeley: University of California Press). The author travels through Africa, Europe, Asia, and the United States to document the operation of illegal trade in goods, such as blood diamonds, pharmaceuticals, food, and oil.

Patrick, Stewart (2011) *Weak Links: Fragile States, Global Threats, and International Security* (Oxford: Oxford University Press). Patrick explores the relationships between weak and failing states and various transnational threats and challenges – terrorism, transnational crime, weapons of mass destruction, pandemic diseases, and energy insecurity. He shows that most frequently it is the weak and poor countries that suffer the most, even while also demonstrating that often the origins of the criminal transnational activity lie in the wealthy and more stable societies.

Richardson, Louise (2006) *What Terrorists Want: Understanding the Enemy, Containing the Threat* (New York: Random House). A comprehensive survey of expert knowledge about the sources of terrorism and how to respond to it. A sensible and balanced look at various angles of this complex topic.

Wallace, William and Daphne Josselin (eds) (2002) *Non-State Actors in World Politics* (New York: Palgrave Macmillan). An excellent survey of the diverse sorts of non-state actors that are rising up within the global system. The chapters also offer reflections on how these non-state actors matter.

12

The Environment and International Relations

Enduring question: How does the natural environment influence international relations **?**

There is almost no question but that we are spewing out enough CO_2 from our automobiles, homes, and factories that we are warming the earth's atmosphere. There is growing evidence that this process of global warming may cause the Arctic ice sheets to melt and the oceans to rise and possibly overrun parts of South Asia where millions of poor people now live. Government leaders have repeatedly said that they recognize that global climate change may be a real problem, but as we will see in this chapter, the first major international climate-change agreement they crafted, the Kyoto Protocol of 1997, has had very little impact on the problem. Moreover, repeated global negotiations to produce a stronger follow-on agreement have failed, and have sometimes witnessed sharp and even acrimonious exchanges between national representatives to the negotiations. Hence, even though there seems to be a growing international consensus that climate change is a real and pressing threat, governments seem to be unable to take strong, concerted action to resolve or at least manage that problem.

If we want to understand the past, the present, or especially the future of international relations, we must understand global environmental issues. We therefore devote this chapter to answering this enduring question: How does the natural environment influence international relations?

We begin by equipping you with two analytical tools that scholars have constructed to understand problems involving the quality of the natural environment and the sustainability of the world's natural resources. These tools center on the concepts of negative externalities and the tragedy of the commons. We will see in the discussion below that negative externalities, which have to do with costs of goods not reflected in their prices, and the tragedy of the commons, which is a logic that illuminates how rational action by individuals in the face of scarcity leads to over-usage of resources, drive many of the world's environmental issues. We then discuss a range of environmental and natural-resource problems within and between countries that involve the atmosphere, the oceans, and the land, including such specific problems as global climate change and ozone depletion, fresh-water contamination, pollution of the oceans, over-exploitation of the world's fish stocks, and deforestation. Next, we look at strategies that states have developed to deal with the international aspects of environmental and natural-resource problems. These strategies include national laws, bilateral agreements, and multilateral treaties. We will see below that each of these strategies has advantages and disadvantages, and produce differing levels of success in coping with international environmental and natural-resources challenges.

Source: © Thinkstock.

Learning Objectives

By the end of this chapter, you will be able to:

→ Explain how environmental problems often include an international dimension.

→ Describe key global environmental and resource issues involving the atmosphere, the oceans, and the land.

→ Explore how governments try to address international environmental and resource problems, with a focus on unilateral, bilateral, and multilateral strategies.

→ Identify the conditions that help or hinder those efforts, including the role of the wealthy developed countries, rising powers such as China and India, and non-governmental organizations.

Chapter Contents

- Sources of Problems for the Global Environment and Natural Resources
- Challenges for the World's Environment and Natural Resources
- Management of International Environmental Problems
- Revisiting the Enduring Question and Looking Ahead
- Study Questions
- Further Reading

Sources of Problems for the Global Environment and Natural Resources

What are the causal factors that contribute to environmental and natural-resource problems within and between countries? Scholars have identified two such factors: negative externalities and the tragedy of the commons.

Negative Externalities

Externalities: The benefits and costs not reflected in a good's price, such as ideas on how to improve a product in the future (positive externality) or pollution (negative externality).

One concept that helps us identify the sources of environmental problems within and between countries is taken from the discipline of economics. That concept is termed **externalities**, which economists define as the benefits and costs not reflected in a good's price. These externalities can be positive or negative, and their effect may be felt by the consumer, the producer, or a third party.

For example, consider a laptop computer. The price you pay for a laptop *largely* reflects two separate dynamics: the costs a manufacturer has to absorb to make the laptop, and the value you assign to the laptop, measured as the goods and services you are willing to forego to buy it. However, prices never *perfectly* reflect the costs of manufacture and the benefits of owning most goods and services. When making your laptop, the manufacturer may learn how to make an even better laptop in the future or a different product, such as a tablet computer; that valuable learning is not reflected in the price for your laptop. The laptop then has a *positive* externality for the producer, or the knowledge of how to make even better products. In contrast, imagine if, when making your laptop, the manufacturer releases pollutants into streams and rivers that harm people who, not knowing the source of the pollution, are not compensated by the manufacturer. In that case, your laptop is generating *negative* externalities. The costs incurred by the injured parties are borne neither by the laptop manufacturer nor by you, the laptop consumer.

There are two serious issues that arise from negative externalities. First, it is unfair, in the example above, that people who gained nothing from the laptop you bought incur a harm – that is, experience water pollution – but are not compensated for that harm. Second, without some way to make the laptop manufacturer incorporate the costs of compensating individuals harmed by pollution or prevent pollution in the first place, the manufacturer has no incentive to stop polluting streams and rivers.

Externalities are common in any economy. They have the potential to become international issues when the negative forms of such externalities generate harmful effects that are felt by people across borders, and create a need for countries to try to mitigate those effects through international action. Thus, negative externalities are central to answering our enduring question about human-produced environmental problems and international relations.

Acid rain in North America illustrates how international negative externalities come into being and how they may elicit an international response. Many electrical utilities and industrial firms use coal or natural gas to fuel their plants. These facilities release chemical compounds (sulfur dioxide and nitrogen oxides) into the atmosphere that can be carried great distances by the winds. These compounds become acidic when they combine with rainfall or land on the earth and come into contact with water. The resulting acids can damage rivers, lakes, and forests.

◀ **Photo 12.1 Effects of Acid Rain on Forests**

Acid rain is an example of a transborder negative externality that can harm important natural resources such as forests.

Source: © mikfoto_pl – istockphoto.com.

Canadian industrial and power plants represent one source of the acid rain that is causing damage to Canada's eastern provinces. However, Canada's acid rain problems have been compounded by transborder pollution originating in the United States. Emissions of sulfur dioxide and nitrogen oxides by US factories and power-generating plants are carried by winds to eastern Canada and cause acid rain. The consequence, the Canadian government has found, is that more than one-half of the acid deposits in the eastern part of Canada are due to emissions from the United States. Thus, acid rain originating in the United States causes harm to Canadians. However, because the costs of reducing or reversing harm were for many years not reflected in the costs that US electricity producers incurred in generating electricity, producers had no incentive on their own to stop acid rain. This is an international negative externality.

Fortunately, as we will see below, in 1991 the United States and Canadian governments reached an agreement as a result of which Canadian and US manufacturers and electrical utilities have had to make investments to curtail acid rain-producing emissions. The firms and utilities, in turn, have passed on those costs to consumers. Cooperation between the governments of Canada and the United States caused producers and consumers to face up to the true costs of their choices. As a result, there has been some success in changing those choices and reducing acid rain.

The Tragedy of the Commons

Another key dynamic that causes many international environmental and natural-resource problems is the **tragedy of the commons**, which is a process by which agents (which could be persons, households, firms, or countries) that rationally pursue their self-interest in exploiting a limited natural resource in an uncoordinated manner might eventually, through no particular actor's fault, over-use and exhaust the resource. This term was introduced in 1968 by American ecologist Garrett Hardin in an influential article on the human dynamics that can result in environmental decay or the depletion of important natural resources.

To see how humans can create such problems, Hardin invited readers to consider a hypothetical case of cattle herders and a piece of pastureland held in common by

Tragedy of the commons: A situation in which individual actors acting in their own rational self-interest combine to create a situation catastrophic to all of the individuals.

► Photo 12.2
Deforestation

Many tropical forests are being cleared to make way for large-scale agriculture or for pasturelands for cattle or other livestock.

Source: © Phototreat – istockphoto.com.

the herders. If the local human population supplied by the herders remains low and stable, the demand for meat remains limited, and the pastureland remains sufficient to maintain the cattle. If the local population grows, so does the demand for meat. Each herder is tempted to add one more head of cattle to their herd. In doing so, the herder would enjoy all the additional profit from selling that extra head of cattle, while not incurring the full cost of doing so, in terms of stressing the common pastureland. Those costs would be shared, knowingly or not, with the other herders. In these circumstances, Hardin pointed out, all the herders would be tempted to add additional heads of cattle. Doing so would soon cause the common pastureland to be depleted and destroyed, and the herders and the community that depended on them for food would face dire consequences.

Hardin emphasized that this process is a tragedy exactly in the sense that the bad outcome, the destruction of the commons and the resulting harm to the community, does not come about because people are stupid or evil or in any way intend or want the outcome to occur. Instead, in a manner similar to what we saw in Chapter 5 when we discussed the Prisoner's Dilemma and the outbreak of war, so too a tragedy of the commons results from the interaction of rational individuals pursuing their own interests and the circumstances in which they find themselves. Those circumstances in the case of a tragedy of the commons consist of a growing population (which creates an incentive for the herders to do things that place stress on resources), finite resources used in common (the pastureland is only so big and has a fixed 'carrying capacity' in terms of cattle it can support), and, perhaps most important, the absence of a governing authority (that can regulate how the common pastureland is employed).

The tragedy-of-the-commons dynamic identified by Hardin drives a number of problems relating to the international environment and global resources (Barkin and Shambaugh 1999), and is another main mechanism, in response to our enduring question, that links the natural environment to international relations. For example, fishing enterprises and their home countries still treat the oceans as an ungoverned commons with unlimited supplies of fish. Yet, as demand for fish has surged in recent decades – in part as a function of world population growth, growing personal incomes, and an increased

The Tragedy of the Commons and Deforestation of Tropical Forests

Theory: *The Tragedy of the Commons*

According to American ecologist Garrett Hardin, rational users of natural resources, in the face of growing demand for those resources or goods derived from them, and in the absence of some governmental authority that regulates their behavior, may over-utilize those resources to the point of exhaustion.

Practice: *Global Deforestation*

Deforestation has become a serious problem in the tropical regions of the world. Forest land decreased in Africa during the 1990s and early 2000s at such a pace that, as the Food and Agriculture Organization has reported, 'Africa lost more than 9 percent of its forest area.' Meanwhile, forests in South America, particularly in the Amazon River Basin, were lost at an annual rate of about 0.46 percent per year during the decade of the 1990s; that loss-rate accelerated to about 0.51 percent per year between 2000 and 2005. Such deforestation has many causes, and among those reasons, as anticipated by Hardin, is the increase in global demand for timber products and local demand for land that can be used for grazing or farming.

Source: United Nations Food and Agriculture Organization, *State of the World's Forests 2007* (Rome: FAO, 2007), pp. viii–ix.

awareness of the health benefits of eating fish – fishing enterprises have over-harvested fish to the degree that many species face collapse, as we will see in more detail below.

Global deforestation represents another example of the operation of the tragedy of the commons. Around the world, as we explore in Box 12.1, the extensive, widespread clearing of tropical forests is resulting in the depletion of this world resource, even though no person, logging firm, or government of a forest-rich country wants such harmful levels of deforestation. Instead, just as with Hardin's theoretical example of herders and common grazing lands, and the real-world problem of over-fishing, it is the combination of economic self-interests of the individuals and firms clearing the land, and under-regulation by national governments, that drives over-harvesting, especially in tropical regions of the world.

Knowledge of the ideas surrounding negative externalities and tragedies of the commons will often help you answer our enduring question about the environment and international relations. Negative externalities and tragedies of the commons are behind many of the world's most pressing international environmental challenges. We now turn our attention to an identification and exploration of some of them.

Individual	State	International
Individuals making rational decisions about productive activities that utilize scarce natural resources can bring about tragedies of the commons.	Firms often benefit from positive externalities and, unless constrained by governmental interventions, are sometimes able to avoid incorporating into the prices for their goods the emanation of negative externalities.	Transborder pollution is sometimes characterized by international negative externalities.

Levels of Analysis

Negative Externalities and the Tragedy of the Commons

Challenges for the World's Environment and Natural Resources

The world faces a host of environmental challenges that center on the atmosphere, water and water-based resources, and the use of the land. We will in this section examine two key environmental problems relating to the atmosphere: global climate change and ozone depletion. We will then explore two environmental challenges that center on the oceans: fresh-water contamination within countries and the possible mismanagement of global marine-life resources. Finally, we will examine the land-based problem of tropical deforestation.

Problems with the Atmosphere

Global climate change and ozone depletion can each have important deleterious consequences for human life, and climate change might even affect the risk of future conflicts within and between countries. They are both important to understand because, as we will see in a subsequent section, while governments around the world have devised what appears to be a strong multilateral agreement to contain the problem of ozone depletion, governments have not succeeded in putting into place an efficacious global approach to the problem of climate change. But, before we discuss the different political trajectories concerning the international management of these two problems, let us first attain a firm grasp of their respective technical characteristics.

▶ **Map 12.1 Possible Sign of Global Warming: Retreat of Arctic Summer Ice, 2012**

This map indicates that the extent of the area of the Arctic Ocean that was covered by ice in September 2012 was much less than the average area covered by summer ice between 1980 and 2000.

The white section represents the area that was ice-covered in September 2012 compared to the average area that was covered in ice between 1980 and 2000.

Source: Fetterer, F., K. Knowles, W. Meier, and M. Savoie (2002, updated daily) 'Sea Ice Index' (Boulder, Colorado USA: National Snow and Ice Data Center, digital media).

- - - - Median ice edge

◀ **Figure 12.1**
**Increasing
Concentration of CO$_2$
in the Atmosphere,
1958–2013**

Since 1958, the Mauna
Loa Observatory in
Hawaii has undertaken
the longest continuous
measurement of
carbon dioxide con-
centrations in the
atmosphere. As can be
observed in the figure,
there has been a
remarkably steady
annual increase in
atmospheric carbon
dioxide concentrations.

Source: Scripps
Institution of
Oceanography, Scripps
CO$_2$ Program.

Climate Change

The world is becoming warmer. There are vivid signs around us, such as the dramatic
reduction in sea ice in the Arctic (see Map 12.1). Credible studies suggest that the
average daily temperature on the earth has risen by about 1.4 degrees Fahrenheit since
1900, with the bulk of that increase occurring during just the past thirty years
(National Academies 2008). There is a substantial likelihood that average daily temperatures around the earth may increase by at least two degrees Fahrenheit and
perhaps a good deal more by the early years of the next century.

Emissions of carbon dioxide (CO$_2$) (see Figure 12.1), nitrous oxide, methane, and
a variety of fluorinated gases contribute to global warming. These materials are called
greenhouse gases because, just as the window panes of a greenhouse trap the sun's
heat, these gases trap some of the infrared heat produced by the sun's warming of the
earth that would otherwise escape back into outer space, thus producing global
warming. Humans produce greenhouse emissions mostly by their use of petroleum-
based products and natural gas for cars, trucks, trains, and jet aircraft, and their use
of oil, gas, and coal for electricity generating plants and other industrial facilities.
Hence, global warming is an international negative externality arising from the economic activities of human beings.

If left unchecked, global climate change will change the earth and harm a large
portion of the world's population. Some nations in relatively northern latitudes might
benefit from global warming: for example, more Canadian lands will become agri-
culturally productive. Yet, snowpack levels in the US western mountain ranges may
decline, and this could have 'adverse impacts on fish populations, hydropower, water
recreation, and water availability for agricultural, industrial, and residential use'
(National Academies 2008: 17).

The most devastating consequences of global climate change will probably take
place in the developing world. For example, as illustrated in Map 12.2, the already
flood-prone country of Bangladesh might lose a part of its land mass, causing the dis-

Greenhouse gases: Certain
gases, such as carbon
dioxide, that accumulate in
the atmosphere and trap
some of the infrared heat
produced by the sun's
warming of the earth that
would otherwise escape
back into outer space.

0 1 2 3   5   8   12   20   35   60 80

Height Above Sea Level (m)

▲ **Map 12.2 Exposure of Bangladesh to Risk of Rising Seas**

A great deal of the landmass of the South Asian country of Bangladesh is close to sea level. If global warming led to rising sea levels, many Bengalis would be forced from their homes, and significant portions of farm land would be lost, causing severe hardship in an already poor country.

Intergovernmental Panel on Climate Change (IPCC): A panel established by the UN in 1988 that studies climate change and informs the world of its effects.

placement of millions of people. Moreover, the **Intergovernmental Panel on Climate Change** (IPCC), established in 1988 by the United Nations, has estimated that if climate change continues unabated, large parts of Africa will experience severe droughts more frequently. Consequently, warns the IPCC (2007: 50), 'agricultural production, including access to food, in many African countries is projected to be severely compromised.'

As noted above, global climate change is a marked example of negative externalities. Global warming may cause Bangladesh to lose a part of its coastal landmass, and African farmers to experience frequent crop-destroying droughts. These hard-hit areas may experience in turn large refugee flows, resource disputes, and civil disorder with international implications. However, it is *not* the residents of Bangladesh or Africa who burn fossil fuels to such a degree that the earth's temperatures have been escalating. Instead, residents in the United States, the nations of Western Europe, and China are the major emitters. Hence, while the industrial and industrializing countries are the source of the problem, many of the most harmful effects are being externalized to people in other parts of the world.

Moreover, global warming is a clear instance of the relevance of our enduring question, that is, it shows vividly how an environmental problem consisting of negative externalities is an international problem. This is because there is basically nothing that the government of Bangladesh and those of the countries in Africa can do by themselves to reverse global warming. Unless the United States and the countries of Western Europe, as well as rising powers such as China, India and Brazil, control their greenhouse emissions, the residents of other (usually very poor) nations are going to suffer serious costs from global warming.

Important political and ethical issues are raised by global climate change. Developed and developing countries, we will see in the next main section, are trying to devise a new legally binding international agreement that would require countries to reduce their CO_2 emissions. Leaders disagree as to which countries have been and are now most responsible for CO_2 emissions and, therefore, should do the most to curtail them. This conflict of interest is crystallized by the information presented in Figure 12.2, which provides data on emissions from the wealthy industrialized countries, that is, the state members of the Organization for Economic Cooperation and Development (OECD); the developing countries, that is, the non-OECD countries; the particular cases of the United States and Japan as representatives of the OECD group; and three key developing countries, China, India, and Brazil.

Developed countries such as the United States want to begin with the current CO_2 levels and prevent future increases in emissions that might tip the balance toward serious global problems as described above. In framing the question this way, developed countries can focus on trends that are captured in Panels A and B of Figure 12.2, which suggest that developed-country annual CO_2 emissions are likely to level off or

Panel A: Growing Importance of Non-OECD countries as Source of Total Global CO_2 Emissions, 1990–2040

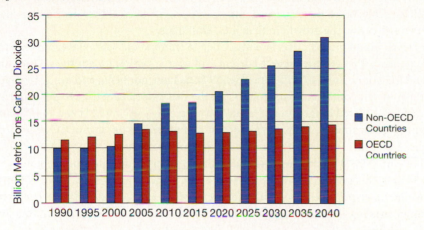

◀ **Figure 12.2**
Responsibility for Addressing the Problem of Global Warming: Developed and Developing Countries and CO_2 Emissions

The data in Panel A and B suggest that developing countries are projected to be the source of most of the growth in total global CO_2 emissions during the next two decades. The growing importance of India, Brazil, and especially China as developing-country CO_2 emitters during that period is illuminated in Panel B. However, the data in Panel C suggest that, during the next two decades, the United States will remain the world's largest CO_2 emitter on a per capita basis, and the United States and Japan will be more responsible for CO_2 emissions than China, Brazil, and India.

Sources: Data from US Energy Information Administration (EIA).

Panel B: Projected Annual Growth in CO_2 Emissions, 2010–2040 (percent per year)

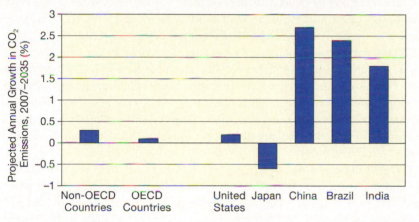

Panel C: Continuing Importance of Industrial Countries as Source of Per Capita CO_2 Emissions

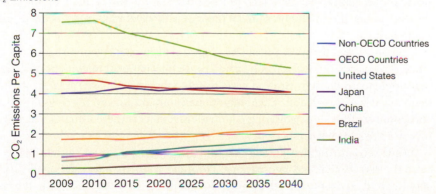

actually decrease, while those of developing countries, including China, Brazil, and India, are projected to increase and in the case of China to do so dramatically. Looking at these projections, developed-country governments believe that developing countries must curtail the growth in their CO_2 emissions.

Developing-country governments prefer to think about CO_2 emissions in terms of countries that are the biggest current and future per capita emitters. Using that standard, countries like India, Brazil, and China have not been, and are not going to be, significant contributors to global CO_2; the real culprits are the OECD countries, as can be observed in the cases of Japan and especially the United States. Developing-country governments, focusing on current and projected per capita CO_2 emissions, believe that it is the responsibility of the developed countries to do more to curtail those emissions. Developing countries also believe that since most of the build-up in CO_2 up to this point in history has been caused by wealthy nations, those countries now have a responsibility to reduce their emissions and, beyond that, to give developing countries the technology and financial resources needed to switch to a low-carbon future.

Finally, in Chapter 5 we discussed the ways in which competition between individuals, groups, or countries over scarce resources – for example, water, arable land, and diamonds – can contribute to the onset of interstate or civil wars. There has been informed speculation (Homer-Dixon 2007; Podesta and Ogden 2008) that international climate change, by way of its capacity to reduce arable lands, for example, might become a new and powerful animator of civil wars in developing countries, with an associated increase in the risk that such civil wars might spill over into neighboring countries or attract international military interventions. To the extent that there is a link between climate change, greater scarcity of resources, and war, this link highlights how, returning to our enduring question, environmental conditions can powerfully affect international relations.

How might this occur? We saw in Chapter 5 in the case of the civil war in Darfur how drought can instigate resource disputes between herders and farmers over water and land. If these disputes are reinforced by ethnic divisions, escalation of land and water disputes to full-scale civil war is possible. Given that global warming might increase the incidence of droughts in Africa, Asia, and Latin America, it is reasonable to speculate that there will be an increased risk of civil violence resulting from competition over scarce water and land in those parts of the world. If civil wars were to develop, as one did in Darfur, some of these new internal wars might bring external interventions.

There may be other ways global warming could spur societal unrest and civil violence. For example, global warming could cause international migrations of refugees that originate in drought-stricken parts of sub-Saharan and eastern Africa, or from flooded parts of Bangladesh. Such migrations could induce severe economic, social, and political stress in neighboring countries that receive these refugees, causing an increased risk of civil conflict.

Environmental determinism: The view that changes in the environment like climate change **necessarily** and **automatically** will cause human beings and human communities to react in a particular manner.

While recognizing that possible causal pathways *might* cause climate change to raise the risk of civil and international conflicts, scholars have cautioned that we should avoid **environmental determinism**, that is, the view that changes in the environment like climate change *necessarily* and *automatically* will cause human beings and human communities to react in a particular manner (Salehyan 2008; Buhaug *et al.* 2008). According to this line of thinking, global warming is likely to cause environmental stress for massive numbers of people in the years ahead. However, whether that stress translates into civil conflict will depend on the answers to a host of additional questions. Will the governments of the affected peoples be able to respond with policies that mitigate some of the economic and social dislocations arising from global climate change? Even more important, will the richer countries of the world provide poorer governments with assistance to deal with the consequences of global warming?

Domestic and international politics, as well as nature, will determine whether global climate change becomes a more serious problem. At present it does not appear that global climate change by itself is a spur to domestic or interstate conflict, but this risk is something worthy of continuing attention.

Ozone Depletion

Between the mid-1970s and the mid-1980s, scientists determined that the ozone layer in the earth's upper stratosphere was diminishing, and had reached such low concentrations over Antarctica that an 'ozone hole' was developing. Scientists also determined that human pollution of the atmosphere or emissions of chemicals, particularly chlorofluorocarbons (CFCs), were the cause of ozone depletion. CFCs served as propellants in aerosol cans and fire extinguishers, and as a key ingredient of refrigerants used in air conditioners. Finally, scientists ascertained that depletion of the ozone layer represented a serious environmental problem. The ozone layer shields the earth from the sun's ultraviolet radiation. As the ozone layer diminishes, ultraviolet radiation hitting the earth's surface greatly increases, contributing to health problems such as skin cancer, eye cataracts, and impairment of human immune systems; harming crops on land; and potentially damaging ocean-based plant life important to the maintenance of fish stocks.

The ozone layer is a type of global common whose presence protects all humans and other forms of life on earth. The degradation of that layer was an instance of a tragedy of the commons: no one consumer, business enterprise, or national government wanted ozone depletion, but the rational commercial and policy decisions of all these actors regarding air conditioning and other products were leading inexorably to the depletion of the ozone layer. Fortunately, as we will discuss in the next main section, while governments have made only limited progress to date in managing the problem of global climate change, the international community reached and has implemented a multilateral agreement that may in time reverse the depletion of the ozone layer.

Damage to the World's Water Resources

Global economic development and population increases have put increasing pressure on fresh-water resources, the health of our oceans, and the bounty of marine life. Oil spills, dangerous run-offs of chemicals and fertilizers, global climate change, and over-harvesting by the fishing industry all constitute threats to the world's water resources.

Contamination of the World's Fresh-Water Resources

As more countries develop economically, they increasingly utilize fresh water for industrial processes, commercial purposes, and residential uses. At present, about one-third of the world's renewable fresh-water supplies are now being utilized by human beings (Schwarzenbach *et al.* 2010). This intensive use of fresh-water resources is creating the risk of a contraction in drinking water, especially in developing countries.

Chlorofluorocarbons (CFCs): A chemical commonly used in propellants in aerosol cans and fire extinguishers, and as a key ingredient of refrigerants used in air conditioners. CFCs were a primary cause of the hole in the ozone layer, and have been outlawed by international multilateral agreements.

▶ Photo 12.3 Water Pollution, The River Ganges, India

Water pollution is becoming increasingly severe in a number of countries. This is a photo of the River Ganges, in India.

Source: © szefei – istockphoto.com.

For example, in many parts of China and India, heavy usage of fresh-water aquifers is leading to increased salt concentrations in fresh-water supplies, which leads to impaired drinking water levels and reduced crop yields. Gold-mining operations that employ mercury and produce cyanide as a waste material are making their way, and may be creating health problems, in such countries as Brazil, Indonesia, Tanzania, and Vietnam. Around the world, pesticides are used to protect commercial agricultural crops and residential gardens; eventually, some of these pesticides reach fresh-water streams, rivers, fresh-water fishing areas, and even the drinking supplies of large human populations.

International trade may create risks to fresh-water supplies. Toxic waste materials are often exported; if not disposed of properly in receiving countries they can ultimately contaminate the latter's fresh-water supplies. One concern often expressed in the 1990s was that as richer countries imposed more stringent governmental regulations on companies regarding the disposal of dangerous industrial waste, more would show up in poorer countries that needed export revenues and often had less stringent disposal policies. However, richer countries actually import more hazardous waste products than they export. This finding suggests that all countries are facing the resulting risks to their fresh-water supplies (Baggs 2009).

Oil Pollution in the Oceans

In April 2010, a catastrophic explosion destroyed the Deepwater Horizon drilling rig off the coast of Louisiana in the Gulf of Mexico, which was being operated on behalf of the British oil giant BP. The explosion killed eleven oil-rig workers and produced a rupture in the oil wellhead on the sea floor. Before the wellhead was capped in mid-July, some 5 million barrels of oil were released into the Gulf. The damage caused by this environmental disaster to fishing stocks, coastal wildlife, marshlands, and beaches along the coasts of Louisiana, Mississippi, Alabama, and Florida will not be fully understood or calculated for years to come.

Another source of ocean pollution stems from accidents by oil tankers. Overall, there were more than 1,700 such accidents between 1970 and 2008. These oil spills

◀ Map 12.3 Gulf of Mexico Oil Spill, 2010

The April–July 2010 oil spill in the Gulf of Mexico produced the largest accidental discharge of oil into water in history, causing environmental damage across four American states.

resulted in the release of about 5.7 million tons of oil into the oceans, with some reaching adjacent coastal shorelines. Most accidents involve the discharge of relatively small amounts of oil, but some have produced huge oil spills. Scholars have not been able to estimate the damage these oil spills have done to the environment, wildlife, and fish stocks. However, we do know that enormous resources are often required to clean beaches and adjacent wetlands after an oil spill. For example, the cost of the clean-up for the Exxon Valdese oil spill of 1989 was about $250 million; for the BP oil spill of 2010 the cost will likely be in the tens of billions of dollars.

Threats to Marine Life

In 2011, according to the United Nations Food and Agriculture Organization (UNFAO 2012: 3), humans harvested approximately 154 million tons of fish. About 85 percent of the harvested fish was used directly as food for humans, with the remainder used as feed for livestock and aquaculture. While aquaculture itself generates a great deal of the fish – roughly 40 percent of the total in 2011 – traditional fishing still accounts for the majority of marine life harvesting.

The problem is that, as we discussed in the first main section, a severe tragedy of the commons may be unfolding in regard to commercial fishing on the high seas. Humans, not out of malice or irrationality, are over-harvesting a number of marine species. As we discuss in Box 12.2, scientific studies suggest that in the past, humans over-harvested in a sporadic manner, but more recent over-harvesting may be sufficiently engrained and widespread that we are simultaneously putting at risk a large number of the world's marine species that are important for human consumption.

The dire projection discussed in Box 12.2 is based on the premise that the global community will do nothing to reverse current trends towards the exhaustion of marine species. The projection may well prove to be overly pessimistic, especially if, as in the case of the ozone layer, governments take positive action to reverse the tragedy of the commons we see developing at present in world fisheries.

Still, as we can see in Figure 12.3, trends in global fish utilization, as reported by the FAO, have not been promising. We see in that figure that about 10 percent of the world's most important varieties of fish were being over-exploited in 1979 – that is,

From Sporadic Over-Fishing to Possible Collapse of Vital Marine Life

Then: *Over-harvesting*

According to recent scholarship conducted by the History of Marine Populations at the University of New Hampshire, humans may have started to harvest ocean-based marine life to a significant degree approximately 1,000 years ago, in part because they had by that time begun to over-harvest freshwater fish. Major innovations in sixteenth- and seventeenth-century ship design and fishing techniques, including the employment of nets cast by pairs of ships, led to major increases in fish hauls and problems of over-harvesting specific fish species. For example, while fishing fleets harvested roughly 70,000 tons of cod annually from the Gulf of Maine in the 1860s, today, even with more advanced fishing technologies, they are able to harvest cod in the range of 3,000 tons per year.

Now: *Possible Crisis Point*

Growing demand for fish and the absence of effective international regulation are driving over-harvesting of many fish species. It is possible that once a marine species reaches about 10 percent of its historical levels, it has only a small chance of rebounding. As Figure 12.3 shows, approximately 30 percent of marine-life species *have already reached* the 10 percent crisis point. If current trends continue, by the middle of the current century it is possible that essentially all species of marine life important to human sustenance will hit the 10 percent crisis point.

Sources: Alexander Doyle, 'Europeans Over-Fishing Began 1000 Years Ago: Report', Reuters, May 24, 2009; and Boris Worm *et al.*, 'Impacts of Biodiversity Loss on Ocean Ecosystem Services', *Science* 314 (November 2006), p. 788. For a good overview of the findings of this study, see Cornelia Dean, 'Study Sees "Global Collapse" of Fish Species', *New York Times*, November 3, 2006.

actual catches were less than what would be the case were over-fishing not depleting those types of fish. By 2009 some 30 percent of the key fish stocks were being over-exploited. In addition, by 2009 more than half of the world's fish stocks were being exploited at maximum sustainable levels, that is, catches could not grow without depleting stocks and future catches. There is then not much room for additional growth in annual harvesting of important global fish stocks as we move into the future, without risking future harvests. Other dynamics may be reducing commercial fish stocks, including accidental and intentional oil pollution, run-offs of dangerous substances such as chemicals and fertilizers, and global climate change. However, the main problem is a tragedy of the commons: the world is over-harvesting fish.

Two additional issues relating to marine life have been important international problems for many years. First, there is the continuing issue of the commercial hunting of whales for the purpose of consumption of whale meat (Andresen 2002). Humans have brought many species of whales to the point of extinction. Governments, working through the International Whaling Commission (IWC), therefore agreed in 1982 to ban commercial whale harvesting. However, utilizing provisions of the whaling moratorium agreement that envisioned very limited whale harvesting for non-commercial purposes, such as scientific studies, fishing enterprises from Norway, Iceland, and Japan have continued to kill a significant number of whales each year. Norwegian whalers, for example, kill approximately 1,000 Minke whales per year.

◀ **Figure 12.3**
Utilization of World Marine Fish Stocks, 1974–2009

We can see from the figure that the percentage of over-exploited fish varieties around the world has steadily increased during the past thirty-five years, and almost 60 percent of the varieties of fish are already being harvested at the maximum level possible without jeopardizing future harvests of those types of fish.

Source: Food and Agriculture Organization of the United Nations, 2012, *The State of World Fisheries and Aquaculture*, http://www.fao.org/docrep/016/i2727e/i2727e.pdf. Reproduced with permission.

Norway and Japan have both also been criticized for the methods they employ in killing whales, namely grenade-tipped harpoons and rifles.

The second international marine life issue concerns dolphins. For many years, dolphins were being killed in the Eastern Tropical Pacific region, off the coasts of California, western Mexico, and western Central America, not because they are valued as food, but as collateral damage arising from fishing techniques aimed at tuna. For unknown reasons, tuna and dolphins in the Eastern Pacific congregate together, and fishing crews can sight dolphins from great distances. In these circumstances, unless constrained, fishing crews would sight dolphins, deploy large nets that surround both the tuna and the dolphins, and kill and dump the dolphins while retaining the tuna catch. Fortunately, as a result of US governmental actions, American consumer activism, and international accords, fishing fleets now largely use 'dolphin-safe' harvesting techniques for tuna; the killing of dolphins has decreased from several hundred thousand per year in the 1960s to roughly three thousand per year.

Damage to the Land

Deforestation is the clearing or over-harvesting of forests. This problem is particularly acute in the tropics, where some of the world's most important forest resources are located, as seen in Map 12.4.

Deforestation, as we discussed at the outset of this chapter, is a stark instance of the tragedy of the commons. No person, firm, or government wants to over-harvest the world's forests. However, strong commercial demand for timber products as well as lands that can be used for grazing or farming, combined with weak government conservation efforts by individual countries as well as the international community, have resulted in over-harvesting of important forest stocks around the world.

◀ **Photo 12.4**
Norwegian Minke Whale Hunting

In the North Sea in July 1994, the Norwegian whaling ship Senet kills and brings on board a Minke whale. The photo was taken by Greenpeace.

Source: Morgan/Greenpeace.

Deforestation: The clearing or over-harvesting of forests, an especially acute problem in the tropics.

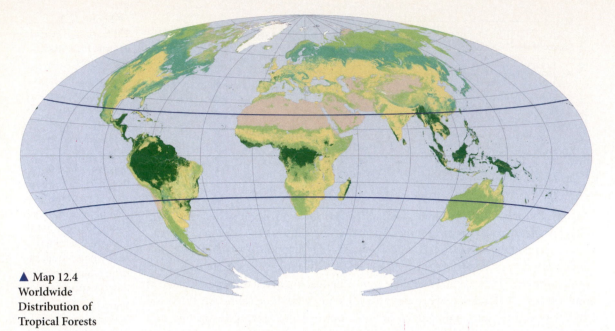

**▲ Map 12.4
Worldwide
Distribution of
Tropical Forests**

This map shows the location of tropical forests around the world. Notice the particularly heavy concentration in the Amazon region of South America, central sub-Saharan Africa, and the Indonesian Archipelago.

Source: NASA Earth Observatory Image by Robert Simmon, based on Moderate Resolution Imaging Spectroradiometer Land Cover Classification data.

Biodiversity: (1) The variety of forms of life on earth, including different species of plants, animals, marine life, insects, and microorganisms (such as bacteria), or (2) variability within species, such as different types of corn, cattle, or bees. The maintenance of a diverse biological world ensures that humans will have many different sources of building supplies, clothing, food, and medicine.

Good intentions can also have unexpected consequences. For example, the United States, Brazil, and several countries in Western Europe have sought to encourage, subsidize, or even require the use of ethanol or biodiesel in automobiles, trucks, and buses as a way of reducing their dependence on oil. The problem is that vast tracts of forest in developing countries such as Brazil, Indonesia, and Malaysia have been cleared in recent years so land could be used to raise corn that has been used to produce ethanol, palm oil trees that can be used to produce biodiesel fuel, or soybeans to fill world demand as US farmers have shifted out of soybeans and into corn. The loss of these forests, and their capacity to absorb carbon, is more harmful to the earth than any gain that might be achieved by substituting traditional gasoline with ethanol or biodiesel (Borrell 2009).

Consequences of Deforestation: Contribution to Global Climate Change

Tropical deforestation poses two serious risks to the global environment. First, fire is often used to clear forests; this clearing technique contributes to global warming. During the 1990s, tropical deforestation accounted for roughly 20 percent of all greenhouse emissions released by humans into the atmosphere. If current rates of deforestation continue until the year 2100, the amount of carbon released into the atmosphere would be equal to the total carbon released since the beginning of the utilization of fossil fuels.

Consequences of Deforestation: the Issue of Biodiversity

The second problem arising from deforestation relates to **biodiversity**. Biodiversity refers both to the variety of forms of life on earth, including different species of plants, animals, marine life, insects, and microorganisms (such as bacteria), and to variability within species, such as different types of corn, cattle, or bees. The maintenance of a diverse biological world ensures that humans will have many different sources of building supplies, clothing, food, and medicine.

Governments recognize the importance of biodiversity, and have sought to preserve it, by way of an international agreement, the Convention on Biological Diversity of 1992. Deforestation may be an especially serious challenge to biodiversity. As a report from the international secretariat responsible for implementation of the convention has noted, 'forests are home to much of the known terrestrial biodiversity' (UN 2000: 5). So, as we lose the world's forests, we also lose a major repository of the world's biodiversity. As a result, we may be putting our food supplies and ability to identify new medicines at risk.

We see from the discussion above that, in response to our enduring question, there are many specific international challenges regarding natural resources and the environment. How, then, do governments try to address these challenges? How, in other words, do international environmental issues prompt national and international action? We address that question in the next section.

Convention on Biological Diversity: An international agreement aiming to protect and preserve biodiversity, passed in 1992.

Individual	👥 State	🌐 International
Preferences of individuals for commercial products, such as gasoline, timber, or fish, can contribute to negative externalities or tragedies of the commons that end in international environmental problems.	Firms can often generate international environmental problems such as over-harvesting of fisheries or timber resources.	Many global resources, such as the earth's ozone layer and a great deal of the world's fisheries, are controlled by no single government, and this complicates the process of addressing threats to those resources.

Levels of Analysis
Environmental and Resource Challenges

Management of International Environmental Problems

Governments have pursued three basic strategies to address international environment problems: unilateral policies, bilateral agreements, and multilateral accords through international organizations. As we will see below, and in response to our enduring question, these strategies illuminate how international environmental problems spark national and international actions.

We will also observe that whether these efforts succeed or not depends on the interplay of five factors. First, in accord with constructivist theories, we will see that NGOs (non-governmental organizations) play a vital role in the international environmental domain (Betsill and Corell 2001). In particular, we will see that NGOs often help raise awareness of international environmental issues, press for national and international policy responses, and object to and put a public spotlight on governments that are not carrying out their commitments to improve the world's environment. Another important ingredient for successful international cooperation on the environment, one that is also emphasized in constructivist theory, is the creation of a consensus among policy leaders that the existence of an environmental problem is underpinned by solid scientific data (Haas 2004). Third, efforts by developed nations to consider the special needs of developing countries are essential in obtaining the support of these key actors on the environment. We will see that, in accord with liberal theories, international institutions have played a positive role in helping developing countries as the latter grapple with international environmental issues and the possibilities for mutually beneficial cooperation to address those problems. Fourth, there is the issue of cost: the greater the economic sacrifice that governments and societies need to incur in order to solve an international environmental problem, the less likely they will be to pursue that solution. Finally, and in accord with expectations of realist theory, international environmental cooperation, we will see below, requires the active support of major countries, and in particular, the United States.

Unilateral Responses

An important example of a purely national effort to remedy an international resource problem involved the United States and the killing of dolphins by tuna fishing fleets operating in the Eastern Pacific Ocean. In 1972, the US Congress passed the Marine Mammal Preservation Act (MMPA), which limits the number of dolphins that US tuna fleets could kill annually as a result of harvesting tuna. However, by the early 1980s, it was clear that implementation of the law was weak; foreign fleets not covered by MMPA were not using dolphin-safe fishing techniques. A wide range of NGOs, including Greenpeace, the Environmental Defense Fund, and the Earth Island Institute, began a national campaign to raise public awareness of the issue, including a boycott of canned tuna and demonstrations at corporate stockholders' meetings. In addition, NGOs launched a federal lawsuit to force the US government to implement the Marine Act more vigorously, pressed the government to exclude foreign-harvested tuna not caught with dolphin-safe techniques from the US market, and pressured the Heinz Corporation, parent company of the largest tuna canner StarKist, to only sell tuna it could certify had been harvested in dolphin-safe nets.

Eventually, the activists were successful. In 1990, the major tuna canners promised to market only tuna harvested with dolphin-safe nets, and the US government embargoed the importation of Mexican tuna since their fishing fleets were not meeting that standard. Mexico challenged the United States on this embargo in the General Agreement on Tariffs and Trade (GATT), received a ruling in its favor and against the United States, but elected not to press the matter (Wapner 1995). This effort by a variety of globally minded NGOs to prod the US government to take actions to protect dolphins resulted in a decrease in dolphin kills from perhaps 500,000 per year at the beginning of the 1970s to less than 20,000 by the end of that decade, and, in the wake of an international agreement in 1999 to limit dolphin kills, a subsequent decrease to about 3,000 per year (US National Oceanic and Atmospheric Administration undated).

Bilateral Efforts

Faced with clear evidence that acid rain constituted a threat to the United States and Canada, in 1990 the US Congress amended the Clean Air Act of 1963, and mandated limits on emissions by American power plants of sulfur dioxide and nitrous oxides. The following year, the United States and Canada signed the US–Canada Air Quality Agreement. As we noted above, this bilateral agreement has been important in bringing the problem of acid rain under greater control. Under the terms of the agreement, the two countries committed to reduce acid rain precursors, pursue joint projects to address the problem, and meet annually to assess progress. Between 1990 and 2010, total US emissions of nitrogen oxides dropped by about one-half, and between 1990 and 2005 (the last year of documented data), emissions of sulfur dioxide fell by about one-third (US Environmental Protection Agency 2012; US Environmental Protection Agency undated).

Multilateral Approaches

As we noted above, a major example of successful multilateral cooperation on the environment has centered on the issue of ozone depletion. This success was directly related to the negotiation, widespread acceptance, and high level of compliance with the 1987 Montreal Protocol on Substances that Deplete the Ozone Layer (Haas 1992; Sunstein 2007). The Protocol, named for the Canadian city in which the last negotiations occurred and the Protocol was signed, now has more than 180 members, and effectively bans the use of chlorofluorocarbons. In accord with the requirements of the Protocol, worldwide CFC use has declined by 95 percent and ozone levels are expected to return to normal by 2050.

The Montreal Protocol came into being, in part, because there was a significant community of scientists around the world who agreed there were grounds for concern that the ozone layer was being depleted due to the introduction of CFCs and other chemicals into the atmosphere. These scientists, as anticipated in constructivist theory, helped create an international consensus that something had to be done about CFCs. In addition, the government negotiators who worked to forge an agreement in this area recognized that developing countries would have a hard time making the transition away from CFCs. They agreed that the developing countries would have a grace period before reducing their use, and they allocated $400 million to facilitate the transition.

Finally, reflecting ideas in realist theory, the United States used its economic power to facilitate the bringing of CFCs under international control. The American public became concerned about ozone depletion during the first half of the 1970s, and the US Environmental Protection Agency (EPA) banned most uses of CFCs as aerosol-

Clean Air Act: A US Congressional Act originally passed in 1963 and amended in 1990 to mandate limits on emissions by American power plants of sulfur dioxide and nitrous oxides.

US–Canada Air Quality Agreement: A 1991 agreement between the US and Canada designed to curb the negative effects of acid rain between the countries.

Montreal Protocol on Substances that Deplete the Ozone Layer: An international agreement passed in 1987 that has successfully combatted the depletion of the ozone layer by banning CFCs. Ozone layers are expected to return to normal by 2050.

can propellants in 1978. When, in 1986 and 1987, it appeared that international negotiations to ban CFCs were stalled, the Reagan administration advised its international negotiating partners that if they did not reach an agreement on a CFC ban, the United States would unilaterally ban such products from entering the US market. This threat of unilateral action prompted the completion of the Montreal Protocol in 1987.

International institutions have played an important role in providing assistance to developing countries to meet international environmental obligations, and therefore, in accord with liberal expectations, these institutions have made it more likely that developing countries are willing to accept such obligations, and comply with them. Developed countries provide this assistance through the Global Environmental Facility (GEF). The GEF began as a World Bank pilot project in 1991 and was formally established in 1994. It is located at the World Bank in Washington DC, and is jointly managed by the World Bank, the United Nations Development Program (UNDP), and the United Nations Environment Program (UNEP). The GEF provides grants to developing countries to help them meet international legal obligations in four areas: climate change, desertification, international water pollution, and biodiversity.

Since 1991, the GEF has directly provided about $8 billion in grants to developing countries for environmental projects, and attracted more than $30 billion in co-financing by national governments, NGOs, and private firms. This funding has had moderate success in the areas of biodiversity and water pollution, but been less effective in helping developing countries with climate change (Clemencon 2006).

The World Bank also provides its own funding for environmental projects in developing countries. However, there has been controversy as to whether Bank loans have had, on balance, a positive or a negative impact on the environment in developing countries. During the 1980s, NGOs were especially outraged by a $450 million World Bank loan for the Polonoroeste project, a network of roads and rural development in the Brazilian state of Rondonia. Instead of helping local inhabitants, the project led to large-scale deforestation and serious health problems for the people living in the region. There is also concern whether recent efforts to integrate environmental concerns into loan-making decisions have been sufficient to make the Bank more responsive to ecological issues in its lending operations (Gutner 2005).

Governments have used a variety of strategies, with some success, to confront the international dimensions of acid rain, ozone depletion, and intentional oil discharge. They have been less successful with issues such as whaling, forest depletion, and, especially, climate change. The Kyoto Protocol serves as an example of an unsuccessful multilateral approach.

The Kyoto Protocol was negotiated in 1997, in large measure due to the leadership of the countries of the European Union as well as the European Commission. The Protocol came into effect in 2005, and by 2013 had more than 191 signatories. It was built on the Framework Convention on Climate Change of 1992, which had only committed countries to the general goal of reducing greenhouse emissions. The Kyoto Protocol established specific targets: total worldwide emissions by 2012 were to be reduced by 5 percent compared to levels observed in 1990, and most developed-country participants who signed the Protocol were to meet specific percentage targets for the reduction of their greenhouse emission by 2012.

The Kyoto Protocol has not had a great deal of success in reducing global greenhouse emissions, which as noted above continue to grow at an alarming rate. There are several reasons why the Protocol has had only a modest impact. First, developing

Global Environmental Facility (GEF): A program managed by the World Bank and the UN that provides grants to developing countries to help them meet international legal obligations in four areas: climate change, desertification, international water pollution, and biodiversity.

Kyoto Protocol: A multilateral agreement negotiated in 1997 to reduce the total emissions of signing states. The Protocol came into effect in 2005 but was ultimately unsuccessful in curbing emissions.

Compliance with the Kyoto Protocol

Aspiration

The Kyoto Protocol committed countries to cut their emissions of greenhouse gases. Different countries had different targets assigned to them in terms of percentage cuts in emissions compared to their respective emission levels in 1990, but they averaged about 5 percent.

Reality

Figure 12.4 depicts the extent to which countries met or failed to meet their respective Kyoto targets as of 2010. Countries highlighted in red failed to meet their commitments; countries highlighted in blue exceeded their commitments. The score for each country is the absolute value of the difference between its 2012 Kyoto goal and its performance as of 2010 in cutting emissions relative to the base year of 1990. If a country was supposed to cut its emissions between 1990 and 2012 by 5 percent, but by 2010 had actually increased its emissions by 5 percent, then its score in terms of falling short in cutting emissions relative to 1990 levels was 10 percentage points. If a country was supposed to reduce its emissions by 5 percent by 2012, but by 2010 had cut its emissions by 15 percent, then its score in terms of exceeding its Kyoto commitment was 10 percentage points. As can be seen in the figure, by 2010 it was clear that countries such as Canada and Australia were not meeting their Kyoto goals, and Canada actually withdrew from the Protocol in December 2012. In contrast, by 2010 Britain, Germany, France, and especially Sweden had already met and exceeded their 2012 targets. Notice that the countries that exceeded their Kyoto targets the most are Russia and several former Soviet bloc countries; the reason is that the economies of these countries collapsed during the 1990s, and those economies, and thus their emissions of greenhouse gases, have taken years to recover.

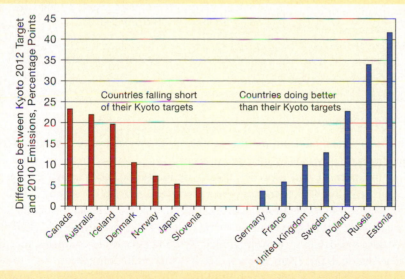

▲ **Figure 12.4 Meeting Kyoto Protocol Commitments to Cut Greenhouse Gases**

Source: Duncan Clark, 'Has the Kyoto Protocol Made Any Difference to Carbon Emissions?', *Guardian*, November 26, 2012. Copyright Guardian News & Media Ltd 2012.

The United States, India, and Greenhouse Gas Emissions

Background

During a visit to India in July 2009, Secretary of State Hillary Clinton and US special negotiator on climate change Todd Stern met with Indian Environment Minister Shri Jairam Ramesh at a new energy-efficient Indian office building outside New Delhi. The event was supposed to highlight Indian-American mutual interests in dealing with global warming, but the Secretary and the Minister actually aired sharp differences on what commitments India and other major developing countries should make in a post-Kyoto greenhouse emissions agreement. The Minister distributed a note to the media that summarized his opening comments at a meeting with the Secretary, and a US news reporter who was allowed to attend the meeting took notes on the discussion between the Minister and the Secretary.

At the Meeting

Indian Environment Minister Ramesh

India's position on the ongoing climate change agreement negotiations is clear, credible and consistent . . . Even with 8–9 percent GDP growth every year for the next decade or two, our per capita emissions will be well below that of developed country averages . . . There is simply no case for the pressure that we, who have among the lowest emissions per capita, face to actually reduce emissions . . . if this pressure was not enough, we also face the threat of carbon tariffs on our exports to countries such as yours...Apart from vastly greater financial flows from the developed world, we see a critical role for international technology cooperation in enabling countries like India to adapt to climate change.

Source: Government of India, Press Information Bureau, 'India Seeks Cooperation from America in Research Projects', July 19, 2009, emphasis added.

Secretary of State Clinton

Clinton responded that she 'completely' understood India's argument about per capita emissions, according to the notes of a US reporter permitted to observe the discussion. 'On one level, it's a fair argument', she said, but she argued that the per capita argument 'loses force' as developing countries rapidly become the biggest emitters.

Indian Environment Minister Ramesh

Ramesh replied that India's position on per capita emissions is 'not a debating strategy' because it is enshrined in international agreements. 'We look upon you suspiciously because you have not fulfilled what [developed countries] pledged to fulfill,' he said, calling it a 'crisis of credibility.'

Source: Glenn Kessler, 'Clinton, Indian Minister Clash Over Emissions Reduction Pact', *Washington Post*, July 20, 2009.

countries are exempted from the Protocol's requirement that greenhouse emissions be cut by specific amounts by specific dates, but, as we discussed in the previous main section, India, Brazil, and, especially, China are major sources of emissions. Second, as we can see in Box 12.3, there has been a great deal of variability among developed-country signatories to the Protocol in meeting their commitments to cut emissions. As we can see in the Box, Britain, Germany, France, and especially Sweden had made great strides by 2010 toward meeting their Kyoto targets; other countries, including Canada, Australia, and Spain, had attained less success in doing so.

Finally, the United States, which until recently was the world's largest source of greenhouse gases (it has been surpassed by China), did not ratify the Kyoto Protocol. Vice-President Al Gore signed the Protocol on behalf of the United States in November 1997, but President Bill Clinton, knowing the US Senate was adamantly opposed to the agreement, never submitted the Protocol to the Senate for ratification.

At the News Conference

Secretary of State Clinton

I want to make two points as clearly as I can.

First, the United States does not and will not do anything that would limit India's economic progress . . . But we also believe that there is a way to eradicate poverty and develop sustainably that will lower significantly the carbon footprint of the energy that is produced and consumed to fuel that growth.

And secondly, we in the United States, under the Obama administration, are recognizing our responsibility and taking action . . .

But it is essential for major developing countries like India to also lead, because over 80 percent of the growth in future emissions will be from developing countries.

Now, China is, by far, the largest emitter in the world right now, and certainly the largest among developing countries. But India's own greenhouse gas pollution is projected to grow by about 50 percent between now and 2030. So, climate change would not be solved even if developed countries stopped emitting greenhouse gas emissions today, unless action is taken across the world. So we have to work together. And I was very heartened, and I agree with the minister's comment that we must achieve an agreement in Copenhagen that is equal to the task.

Indian Environment Minister Ramesh

All I can say is that India already has a national action plan of climate change which was unveiled last year. And that action plan is overwhelmingly oriented towards programs and projects that will enable India to adapt to the effects of climate change. But it also has very specific and very pointed policies oriented towards mitigating emissions.

India has been saying that its primary focus will be adaptation. But there are specific areas where we are already in a policy framework [inaudible] mitigation, which means actual reduction of emissions.

So, whether that will convert into legally binding emission [inaudible] is the real question. And India's position is – I would like to make it clear that India's position is that we are simply not in a position to take on legally binding emission reduction targets . . . Now, this does not mean that we are oblivious of our responsibilities for ensuring that [inaudible] the incremental addition to greenhouse gases that both special envoy Stern, and Madame Secretary of State spoke about. We are fully conscious of that. Energy efficiency is a very fundamental driver of our economic strategy.

Sources: US Department of State, 'Remarks Following ITC Green Building Tour and Discussion', India, July 19, 2009; and David Gollus, 'US, India Clash Over Climate Change Remedies', *VOA News.com*, July 19, 2009.

Later, in March 2001, President George W. Bush announced that the United States would not complete the ratification process for the agreement.

For many years governments have been trying to negotiate an accord that would replace Kyoto with a new international agreement on global warming, but these efforts have so far proved unsuccessful. This effort to find a replacement for Kyoto commenced formally in the Danish capital of Copenhagen in December 2009, with crucial preparatory talks held during the spring and summer of that year. Those negotiations were nearly a complete failure, with key countries such as India and China working hard to stop efforts by the United States and other rich countries to move toward binding targets on all major countries to cap national emissions of carbon gases. Subsequent multilateral talks in 2010 in Cancun, Mexico, and in 2011 in Durban, South Africa, witnessed sharp disagreements between the United States and China. Talks in 2012 in Doha, Qatar, and then in Warsaw in 2013, were less acrimo-

Developed and developing countries have been unable to reach a comprehensive agreement to reduce greenhouse emissions and thus avert a host of national and transborder environmental problems that would be due to (and may already be resulting from) global climate change. What are the chances that countries will reach such an accord?

Realism: A realist would suggest that the chances a climate change agreement will be reached will depend on at least three factors: first, the chances of success depend on the degree to which countries would suffer from not reaching an agreement; second, countries will need to be assured that some countries do not benefit more from the agreement than do other, and therefore there will need to be in the agreement a balanced sharing both of gains and costs; and third, success will in all likelihood require the leadership of the most powerful developed and developing countries, such as the United States and the EU countries on the one hand and India and especially China on the other.

Constructivism: A constructivist would largely agree with the points made by the realist, and especially about the need for state leaders and policy officials to believe that they have a national interest in attaining a climate change agreement. However, a constructivist would suggest that more is needed. Leaders and officials of different countries must share common understandings about what causes climate change, namely, greenhouse gas emissions, and they must share common ideas about what are effective ways to reduce such emissions, namely, jointly agreed limits by governments, rather than, for example, allowing market forces to induce firms and households to reduce emissions. Perhaps most important, leaders and officials in developed countries must share with counterparts in developing countries the view that the wealthy countries have a responsibility to help developing nations bear the costs that they will need to incur to reduce their emissions.

Liberalism: A liberal would mostly agree with the points made by the realist and constructivist colleagues. However, the liberal would argue that there is a higher likelihood that leaders and officials from developed and developing countries would understand their common interest in addressing the problem of climate change, and the special responsibilities that developed countries have toward developing countries in dealing with this problem, if the main countries on both sides were robust, deeply rooted democracies. This would increase the chances that governments in the talks would trust each other's intentions to reach an accord as well as to comply with it, and to avoid seeking relative gains from the agreement. Truly democratic developing countries, the liberal would also suggest, would be more likely to make effective use of externally provided resources to make the necessary changes to their economies to be in compliance with a climate change agreement, and this would enhance the chances that the developed countries would be willing to provide such resources.

nious but also produced little headway in reaching an international accord on climate change.

It is possible to look to the future and see what an agreement on climate change would need to include if it is to be more effective than the Kyoto Protocol. It seems likely that it will need specific emission-reduction targets for all developed countries, including the United States. Important developing countries such as India, China, and Brazil will also need to accept emission-reduction goals, although these might not be binding. There remain sharp differences in perspectives between developed and developing countries on this matter, which we highlight in Box 12.4.

An agreement will also need to deal with the problem of deforestation by fire, given the large contribution by such fires to global greenhouse emissions. Developing countries need to be offered greater financial assistance to help them meet their emission-reduction goals, and indeed some progress was made on this particular issue during the 2013 climate agreement talks in Warsaw.

It is difficult to estimate the likelihood that the major developed and developing countries will reach a comprehensive climate-change agreement in time to avert serious global environmental damage. We can however consider how different theoretical perspectives in the field of international relations would try to assess the chances of success in the negotiations: we do this in Box 12.5.

In sum, states employ unilateral, bilateral, and multilateral strategies to address the harm that humans cause to natural resources and the environment. Those strategies as well as their interaction and success or failure are becoming an important substantive feature of international relations, and they rightly command the interest of students and scholars of international affairs.

Individual	State	International
Individuals, such as NGO activists and scientists, have played important roles in pressing governments to recognize and address international environmental problems.	The important role of the US Congress and courts in advancing US environmental policy has spurred the US government on occasion to be more active in seeking international solutions to global environmental and natural-resource problems.	The United States and governments of EU countries have been central to the success or failure of international efforts to address such environmental problems as North American acid rain, ozone depletion, and global climate change.
	NGOs are especially able to exercise influence in raising consciousness about international environmental problems in democratic countries as Japan, the United States, and in Western Europe.	Future progress on addressing the problem of global climate change has been hampered to date by a conflict of interest between already industrialized countries like the United States, Japan, and members of the EU, on the one hand, and still-industrializing countries such as China, India, and Brazil.

Levels of Analysis

Management of International Environmental Problems

Revisiting the Enduring Question and Looking Ahead

We began this chapter with a question: how do international environmental problems influence international relations? We have seen, in response to that question, how international environmental and natural-resource problems for many years have been an important element of world affairs. If we think about the issues of water pollution or fisheries management or deforestation or especially global climate change, we can see how the natural environment will continue to influence global affairs in the years ahead.

Environmental issues highlight how difficult it is for states to be successful in pursuing their international interests exclusively through their own efforts. Instead, states must work together to address mutual environmental challenges. In some instances, such as in the cases of ozone depletion, governments have achieved substantial success in crafting an international arrangement aimed at alleviating global environmental problems. However, in other areas, including deforestation, global fisheries, and most notably global climate change, governments have yet to construct effective international responses to pressing problems relating to the environment and natural resources. Will citizens and their governments have the foresight to realize that they are facing global environmental tragedies of the commons? Can governments of developing countries accept limits on emissions of greenhouse gases even if this means an abatement of national economic growth? Above all, can governments of wealthy countries make or encourage the domestic investments needed to create new, more efficient transportation and power-generating technologies and provide the financial and technological resources that developing-country partners will need to bring global warming under control? How these questions are addressed will have a large, lasting impact on the fate of the earth and the future of international relations for many decades to come.

What else will be important for the future of international relations? In the next and final chapter, we revisit our Enduring Questions and examine five possible models of the future international system.

Visit **www.palgrave.com/politics/Grieco** to access extra resources for this chapter, including:

- Chapter summaries to help you review the material
- Multiple choice quizzes to test your understanding
- Flashcards to test your knowledge of the key terms in this chapter
- An interactive simulation that invites you to go through the decision-making process of a world leader at a crucial political juncture
- Pivotal decisions in which you weigh up the pros and cons of complicated decisions with grave consequences
- Outside resources, including links to contemporary articles and videos, that add to what you have learned in this chapter

Study Questions

1. In the text we discussed over-harvesting of fish and deforestation as important international examples of the tragedy of the commons; can you think of another example?
2. What is the role of the United States in the contemporary world both as a producer of international environmental problems and a supplier of international action to address those problems?
3. What do you think is the likelihood that global climate change will be managed at the international level during the next twenty-five years?
4. There has been stalemate between major wealthy states like the US and developing countries like China and India on forging a new international agreement on CO_2 and other greenhouse gas emissions that might be related to global climate change. What proposal would you make to break the deadlock, given their positions on this matter?
5. What are the benefits and costs of using different strategies – unilateral, bilateral, or multilateral – to address an environmental problem of interest to you?

Further Reading

Haas, Peter (1990) *Saving the Mediterranean: the Politics of International Environmental Cooperation* (New York: Columbia University Press). Haas with this book was the pathfinder for the field of international relations on the issue of the international environment, and in this work and in later works he deployed constructivist theory to help explain variation in international cooperation on environmental issues, and in so doing also contributed to that theoretical perspective.

Hardin, Garrett (1968) 'Tragedy of the Commons', *Science* 162 (3589): 1243–8. This essay showed how many environmental problems are tragedies of the commons, has had enormous influence in political science, economics, and legal studies, and is essential reading for students of international environmental problems.

Homer-Dixon, Thomas (1999) *Environment, Scarcity, and Violence* (Princeton: Princeton University Press). This book provides the most persuasive argument that environmental problems that ultimately produce scarcities of important resources, such as forests, water, and arable land, can generate serious social stresses within countries and thereby contribute to the onset of violence, even civil wars, in those countries.

Edward L. Miles, Arild Underdal, Steinar Andresen, Jorgen Wettestad, Jon Skjaerseth, and Elaine Carlin (eds) (2002) *Environmental Regime Effectiveness: Confronting Theory with Evidence* (Cambridge: MIT Press). This edited volume addresses two fundamentally important questions: how do we measure variation in the effectiveness of different international agreements on the environment, and what accounts for that variation?

13

Facing the Future: Six Visions of an Emerging International Order

Enduring question: Will the international system undergo fundamental change in the future

As we look ahead to the next decade, will the international system undergo some type of fundamental change? Although the future is impossible to predict, the different assumptions scholars make about state behavior and the dynamics of international relations lead them to very different expectations about how world politics will turn out in the years ahead.

The durability and character of the Westphalian international system is an enduring question for students of international relations. In this text, we have provided a broad perspective by looking at the history of international relations and how it has been understood by liberal, realist, constructivist, Marxist, and feminist thinkers. We have also focused on international issues and challenges that make up the politics of the contemporary era. This final chapter builds on what has already been presented and prompts you to look into the future of international relations through six possible models of the emerging international system. No one can know for certain which of these models, if any, is most likely to characterize international relations in the years ahead. Nevertheless, we believe that defining and evaluating alternative visions of the future can be a valuable analytical exercise. The six models are based on different assumptions about what matters in international politics. In some models, the nation-state remains a key actor; international relations revolve around militarized great-power dynamics. In other models, economic power is far more valuable than military, or the nation-state is no longer the central focal point. Some models anticipate a world of greater cooperation; others see enhanced conflict. A critical examination of different models of the future forces us to examine our own assumptions about what is fundamental and what transitory in world politics. This concluding chapter provides an exercise to reinforce the central theme of the book – the effort to focus on and understand the enduring questions and features of international relations across time and space.

The six competing models are: a world of geo-economic competition; a return to multipolarity; a return to bipolarity; the emergence of a democratic peace; the clash of civilizations; and the global fracture of the international system. We examine the logic and core assumptions of each model and defend its plausibility. We describe the key features of a future world in terms of each model. We also provide a critical assessment of each, pointing to trends or evidence that reinforce the likelihood of the model and raising a set of critical questions that any proponent of each model would be forced to address. No model is completely right or wrong, but each may prove to be useful as an analytical device to enhance our understanding of what matters most in international relations and whether the international system as we know it is undergoing fundamental change.

Source: © dmitryelogin – istockphoto.com.

Learning Objectives

By the end of this chapter, you will be able to:

→ Evaluate critical influences on international politics in the years ahead.

→ Recognize the reasons why some scholars believe economic power will become more important than military power.

→ Identify trends that indicate whether the international system will swing to a multipolar or bipolar political structure.

→ Compare and contrast world political theories that transcend the concept of the traditional nation-state, such as democratic peace and clash of civilizations models.

→ Understand why some scholars believe the nation-state will be of declining significance in the years ahead.

→ Analyze the importance of enduring questions in predicting future influences on international relations.

Chapter Contents

- Model 1: A World of Geo-Economic Competition
- Model 2: A Return to a Multipolar Balance-of-Power System
- Model 3: A New Bipolarity
- Model 4: A Democratic Peace
- Model 5: A Clash of Civilizations
- Model 6: Global Fracture: Pre-modern, Modern, and Post-Modern Zones
- Looking Back: A Reminder to Focus on Enduring Questions

► Map 13.1 The Soviet Union and Eastern Europe during the Cold War

During the Cold War, the Soviet Union was a vast multinational state that included diverse nations including Russians, Estonians, Latvians, Ukrainians, Georgians, and Armenians among others. The Soviet Union dominated the Warsaw Pact alliance that included European countries east of the Iron Curtain depicted here.

Legend:
- Eastern Bloc
- Western Bloc
- Iron Curtain

Model 1: A World of Geo-Economic Competition

Any student with an appreciation of the history of international relations should be deeply impressed by how the Cold War ended. For over four decades, the United States and Soviet Union competed with each other as dominant powers in the international arena. Their competition not only ended abruptly in 1989–90, it ended *peacefully*.

This fact is remarkable in historical context. Struggles between rising and declining great powers have usually ended in great wars, such as the Peloponnesian War between a rising Athens and declining Sparta, the Napoleonic Wars of the early nineteenth century, and the two World Wars of the first half of the twentieth century. But the collapse of the Soviet Union turned out differently. In a remarkably short time, the Soviets lost control of their key satellite states in Eastern Europe. Then the Soviet Union itself broke apart into more than a dozen new sovereign states. The complete collapse of the power, influence, and prestige of a superpower took place without inciting a larger systemic war. Indeed, the Soviet empire collapsed without a single shot being fired across the highly militarized East–West front that characterized world politics for decades.

Map legend:
1 Albania 2009
2 Bosnia and Herzegovina
3 Croatia 2009
4 Macedonia
5 Slovenia 2004
6 Montenegro
7 Serbia
8 Kosovo

NATO member

Seeking to join

USA 1949, Canada 1949

◀ Map 13.2 Russia and the Eastward Expansion of NATO

The former Eastern European members of the Warsaw Pact – Poland, Hungary, Czechoslovakia, Bulgaria, Romania, and East Germany – are now all part of NATO, along with Latvia, Lithuania and Estonia, countries that were formerly part of the Soviet Union itself.

There are multiple explanations for this remarkably peaceful outcome. We review, in Box 13.1, how constructivists, liberals, and realists might explain the end of the Cold War. The model we focus on in this section, however, draws insights from several theoretical traditions. In accounting for the peaceful end of the Cold War, proponents of the geo-economic model would point to what they view as an increasingly powerful trend in the international system – the *declining utility of military force* in relations among great powers. The United States and Soviet Union were formidable nuclear powers; any war between them carried the risk of escalation that would result in the all-out destruction of both societies and, most likely, the international system itself. Nuclear weapons are so powerful that even a modest arsenal carries great destructive potential. In a nuclear age, great powers can no longer initiate wars against their rivals to overpower, conquer, or dominate (Mueller 1989). From this perspective, the total wars of the twentieth century, requiring societal mobilization and protracted fighting among great powers over many years, are a thing of the past. The Soviet Union, unlike the great powers that preceded it, simply did not have a viable global military option to shore up the shaky foundations of its empire and arrest its decline. The United States and NATO, in turn, had no incentive to conquer, occupy, and administer the vast territories of its collapsing enemy.

Characteristics of Geo-Economic Competition

The geo-economic model presumes that great-power war is a thing of the past. But does the end of great-power war necessarily mean the end of great-power competi-

Economic security: The ability to maintain prosperity in a world of scarcity.

Competing economic blocs: Groups of states in economic competition organized around the economies and currencies of major economic powers.

tion? For proponents of the geo-economic model, the answer is no. In the emerging international system, great-power competition simply changes form. Traditional military competition is replaced by economic competition – a 'struggle for the world product,' in the words of former German Chancellor Helmut Schmidt. States that used to see territorial acquisition or protection from conquest by other great powers as the primary concern of security policy now focus on a struggle to capture export markets, raw materials, and the highest value-added jobs for their people (Helleiner and Pickel 2005). In this new world, economic security, or the ability to maintain prosperity in a world of scarcity, replaces military security as the key nation-state objective. Governments that primarily mobilized resources for military competition will emphasize economic competition. Recall our discussion of economic nationalism in Chapter 9; the geo-economic model elaborates that perspective as the central feature of international relations. In theoretical terms we might describe this model as 'economic realism' in that the basic dynamic is state competition, but the competition is in the economic arena.

What are the central features of world geo-economic competition? The most prominent would feature the development of competing economic blocs, with groups of states organized around the economies and currencies of major economic powers. In a fully formed geo-economic world, we should anticipate the consolidation of a North American bloc organized around the United States economy and use of the dollar as a reserve and exchange currency. A European bloc would center on core members of the European Union and increased reliance on the euro as a key currency. The American economist Lester Thurow, whose 1992 book *Head to Head* helped articulate the geo-economic model, pointed to the natural competitive advantages enjoyed by a European bloc with a well-educated work force, German standards of productivity, French and Italian design contributions, and British and Swiss banking experience (Thurow 1992). In East Asia, there might be one bloc or two, depending on the willingness and capacity of Japan to organize its economic relations to either compete with, or depend on, a rising China.

According to the geo-economic model, each bloc would look to spread its influence into nearby regions. Because of geography and history, the United States would want to make sure Latin America was incorporated into its sphere of economic influence. European Union members would take a similar approach to central European countries and, perhaps, former colonies in North Africa. States in Southeast Asia would be the logical zone of dependence for a bloc organized by China or Japan. Other regions, particularly those with rich resources, would be 'up for grabs.' For example, the energy resources of the Middle East and mineral resources of sub-Saharan Africa would naturally attract the attention of each of the competing blocs.

Russia is an interesting case; as described in Chapter 10, its future great-power potential is constrained by the narrow, raw material base of its economy. A resurgent Russia with ample currency reserves could aspire to be an economic competitor in its own right, while a declining or unstable Russia would become the object of competition among more powerful economic blocs for its natural resources.

Leading governments in each of the competing blocs would look to form close working relationships with key firms in leading sectors, such as banking, communications, information technology, and transportation, perhaps by cultivating national

The end of the Cold War was one of the most important international events of the twentieth century. Not surprisingly, scholars working within different theoretical traditions have developed different explanations for that outcome.

Constructivism: Constructivists might make a two-part argument for why the Cold War ended. First, ideas matter. Once the Cold War became entrenched, many scholars and political leaders came to treat the US–Soviet conflict as a necessary and enduring feature of the international landscape. They believed that the future would resemble the past. For constructivists that view is an example of how decision makers and analysts can become trapped by their own self-reinforcing assumptions. What if, instead, policy makers and scholars envisioned a different international reality, one in which East and West were not locked in immutable conflict? Second, constructivists would point to great leaders as carriers of new ideas, that is, as people with the willingness and ability to bring about significant international change. Mikhail Gorbachev was one such leader; he explicitly referred to new ideas and new thinking as he positioned the Soviet Union to make an historic accommodation with the West, one that involved reconsidering whether the Soviet Union needed to maintain an empire in Eastern Europe and the developing world in order to be secure. Leaders in Germany and the United States proved receptive to this radical thinking of the international context and joined Gorbachev as partners in the remaking of international order.

Liberalism: Liberal theorists focus on the role of social forces that gradually eroded the seemingly secure foundation of the Cold War. Global interdependence involved the movement of goods, people, and ideas across borders. This process eventually influenced the Soviet elite, a significant fraction of which came to believe, alongside Gorbachev, that the economic costs of sitting outside of the liberal world economy no longer justified the Soviet Union's traditional emphasis on military competition in preparation for military conflict with the West. At the same time, transnational coalitions formed across East and West to draw attention to the dangers of nuclear war. Scientists, doctors, clergy, and ordinary citizens pressured governments on either side of the East–West divide to scale back risky military competition. In short, the mechanism for change consisted of societal pressures that gained a receptive hearing among government leaders in the Soviet Union, Europe, and the United States.

Realism: Realists view the end of the Cold War as a function of the shifting balance of power between East and West in general and between the Soviet Union and United States in particular. The centrally planned economies of the East simply could not keep pace with the more dynamic, productive, and technologically innovative economies of the West. Economic power is the foundation of military power, and Gorbachev recognized what other Soviet leaders had refused to accept, namely that over the long run the Soviet Union would not be able to keep up its side of the East–West military competition. Gorbachev's Soviet Union faced a painful set of choices. It could try to keep racing with the West and bankrupt its economy, it could initiate a military conflict that risked the destruction of the planet, or it could try to scale back its international commitments and reach an accommodation with the West that would allow breathing space to reform its struggling economy. Gorbachev chose the latter course and could not control the consequences it unleashed. For realists, the end of the Cold War is a story of power asymmetry – two sides were racing and one realized it could no longer keep up.

champions, which, as we discussed in Chapter 10, are companies explicitly supported by their governments to compete in key areas of the world economy. A good example of a national champion is Airbus, a European consortium that has worked closely with European governments to mobilize resources and develop the scale of operations necessary to compete on a global scale with the American firm Boeing (a beneficiary of American defense contracts) in the production of civilian aircraft. Close

► **Map 13.3 Regional Economic Blocs: NAFTA, European Union, and APEC**

Regionalism characterizes, in different ways, economic relations in North America, Europe, and East Asia. The North American Free Trade Agreement (NAFTA) governs trade relations among the United States, Canada, and Mexico. The European Union has created a single integrated market among 28 European states, with 18 of them sharing a common currency, the euro. APEC (Asia-Pacific Economic Cooperation) is a looser grouping of states bordering the Pacific Ocean, with its 21 members seeking to reduce barriers to trade and promote economic cooperation.

NAFTA

Member countries

European Union

APEC

relations with governments serve the profit and market share interests of national champion firms, and their success helps governments serve national economic interests as well.

International Trends

It is not difficult to point to trends or evidence in support of the emergence of a geo-economic model. The 1990s witnessed the rise of economic integration within the three major regions of international economic activity. The United States, Canada and Mexico forged the North American Free Trade Agreement (NAFTA) to oversee and regulate the continued integration of their neighboring economies. The United States also sought to spread regional integration southward, initiating free trade agreements (FTAs) with Chile in 2003, Peru in 2006, and six Central American nations (the Dominican Republic, Costa Rica, El Salvador, Honduras, Guatemala, and Nicaragua) in 2004. In 2012, the United States concluded free trade agreements with Colombia and Panama.

European integration proceeded even more rapidly and deeply. The core states of the European Union not only consolidated a single integrated market for goods and services, but surrendered national currencies in favor of the euro. Economic integration in East Asia was strengthened with the creation of APEC (Asia-Pacific Economic Cooperation) in 1989 and the development of ASEAN plus Three (the ten members of the Association of South-East Asian Nations plus Japan, China and South Korea) during the late 1990s. In line with the expectations of the geo-economic model, regional economic agreements rose sharply after the end of the Cold War (see Figure 13.1). At the same time, trade negotiations at the global level almost slowed to a standstill. As we discussed in Chapter 8, the Uruguay Round of multilateral negotiations, which created

▼ Figure 13.1
Evolution of Regional Trade Agreements (RTAs), 1948—2014

The figure shows all Regional Trade Agreements notified to the GATT/WTO since 1948. Note that the trend line moves sharply upward beginning in the early 1990s. This reflects the spread of regional agreements as it became increasingly difficult for states to conclude comprehensive global trade negotiations.

Source: World Trade Organization.

Chinese foreign direct investment (Millions of US dollars)

	2003	2004	2005	2006	2007	2008	2009	2010	2011	2012
Asia	1,491	2 985	4,351	7,541	16,174	42,834	39,978	43,962	44,800	61,182
Africa	75	317	392	520	1,574	5,491	1,439	2,112	3,173	2,517

▲ **Figure 13.2 Chinese FDI flows to Asia and Africa, 2003–12**

According to secret memos published on WikiLeaks, US diplomats expressed concerns about China's growing role in Africa. The cables between Washington and the US Embassy in Nigeria describe China as 'aggressive and pernicious,' and 'in Africa primarily for China.' American officials noted that if China were to begin military co-operation with African countries, train armies, or sign military base agreements, American uneasiness with Chinese activities in Africa would grow exponentially.

Source: UNCTAD FDI/TNC database, based on data from the Ministry of Commerce (MOFCOM).

the WTO in 1995, took nearly ten years to complete. The Doha Development Round began in 2001 and took thirteen years to produce, at Bali, Indonesia in December 2013, an initial and rather modest agreement to reduce global trade barriers.

Competition for natural resources among leading states has been intensifying as well. One could plausibly view the post-Cold War wars in Iraq in 1990–91 and 2002–3 as efforts by the United States to assure that the Gulf oil reserves remain in friendly hands (Clark 2005). As its economy has grown rapidly, China has stepped up efforts to consolidate political relations with important suppliers of energy and other raw materials in Central Asia and Africa. As Figure 13.2 shows, Chinese foreign direct investment in Asian and African countries has increased significantly since 2003.

Relations between business and government in both Europe and Japan have typically been marked by close cooperation in pursuit of national development goals. As we saw in Chapter 10, a similar model has characterized China's export-led growth strategy since 1978. The global financial and economic crises that began in 2008 only reinforced these trends, creating incentives for governments to step into their national economies to rescue ailing firms and save jobs for their populations. Even the United States, the rhetorical champion of the free market, found its government making major investments in the financial and automotive sectors, including costly rescues of the insurance firm American International Group (AIG) and the automotive giant General Motors.

Contrary Evidence and Questions

The geo-economic model is certainly plausible. But what contrary evidence might its proponents have overlooked? First, this model, which depicts businesses in different regions working with their respective governments to conquer world markets, must come to terms with the operations of modern transnational corporations. Liberal international relations theorists believe that, in an era of globalization, companies such as US-based Nike and General Electric, Europe-based Phillips and Siemens, and Asia-based Sony and Toyota have cross-regional identities and interests. They have established operations and are players in all major regions of the world, not just their home countries or regions. As global players with global interests, most big firms do not simply 'line up' politically with their primary home governments in order to do economic battle with other business/government clusters. How could the Japanese electronics giant Fujitsu view the US or European governments as adversaries when it has merged its European operations with the German electronics national champion Siemens, has its European headquarters in Amsterdam, and operates facilities in twenty US states with a North American headquarters in Sunnyvale, California? Regional economic conflicts actually work against the economic interests of transnational firms that have set up global production and supply networks (Brooks 2005).

This leads to a second important observation. International economic relations are more 'positive sum,' in which economic cooperation can create increasing prosperity for all regions, than 'zero sum,' in which one region gains at the expense of others. If everyone can win from increasing the overall size of the economic pie, then the incentives for geo-economic mobilization and competition diminish for governments as well as firms.

Third, it is important to ask whether regional economic blocs are more open or closed. The more open regional economic arrangements are, the more difficult it is to depict them as self-contained competitive units. To date, contemporary regionalism is more open than closed. For example, Malaysia led an effort as the Cold War ended to create an East Asian economic bloc that would exclude the United States and other non-Asian players. US and Japanese policy makers resisted this vision, and the entity that eventually emerged, APEC, was trans-Pacific rather than exclusively East Asian and included not only the United States but Mexico and Canada as well. Although the United States is not a member of the EU, it has supported European economic integration on the condition that the EU remains open to global trade and investment. For the most part it has. NAFTA hardly constitutes an exclusionary bloc, as numerous European and Asia-based firms operate in one NAFTA country, thereby gaining access to the others. Regionalism has progressed, and stands alongside globalism as a key feature of the international economic landscape. But today's regions are considerably different from the more exclusionary competitive blocs of the 1930s.

State	International	Levels of Analysis
In the geo-economic model, states and their national firms work together and share a common understanding of the national interest.	Although competition among nation-states remains the central feature of international relations in this model, the form it takes changes from military to economic.	*The Geo-Economic Model*

Model 2: A Return to Multipolarity

Instead of geo-economic competition, some scholars believe that international relations will return to a more traditional international order, one that entails a multipolar distribution of international power. This view is prominent among scholars who work within the realist school of thought (Layne 2006; Mearsheimer 2001). Many realists believe that we have been living in a multipolar international distribution of power for some years, indeed, that unipolarity was an illusion. Others find that while the United States was a disproportionately powerful and influential state for a decade or so after the Soviet Union collapsed, the world has now swiftly moved and continues to move to a multipolar international structure.

Proponents of the view that world politics is multipolar or is moving toward multipolarity, in contrast to the geo-economic proponents, presume that military competition among nation-states will continue to matter significantly as the defining feature of international politics. Even if great powers are not prone to fight all-out wars with each other, they must still be prepared to fight more limited conflicts and

Regional Economic Blocs

Then: *Regional Blocs during the 1930s*

During the Great Depression of the 1930s, the global multilateral trading system was essentially replaced by a set of regional economic blocs. As world economic activity retracted, great powers responded by turning inward or strengthening regional economic arrangements that gave them special access to the resources and markets of associated countries.

Japan, for example, proclaimed the Greater East Asian Co-Prosperity Sphere, comprising Japan, China, and parts of Southeast Asia, with the intention of creating a self-sufficient political and economic bloc of Asian nations free from Western influence. Similarly, Nazi Germany organized regional trade and financial arrangements with its eastern and central European neighbors, and used those arrangements to help finance its rearmament strategy free of the constraints imposed by Western powers after World War I. Great Britain created a currency area, based on its pound sterling, that included its colonies and protectorates. It forced those weaker countries to grant Great Britain preferential trade relations, while Britain raised its tariffs in trade with countries outside of the sterling area. The Soviet Union, under the leadership of Stalin, turned almost completely away from the world economy and relied on internal resources for economic development. The United States, as a result of the Smoot-Hawley tariff of the 1930s, sharply curtailed its participation in world trade.

In general, the regional economic blocs of the 1930s were insulated from each other, and were used by great powers to mobilize the resources they felt would be needed as the world moved from one world war to the next.

Now: *Regional Blocs after the Cold War*

Today, regional blocs are once again a prominent feature of the world economy. The United States, Canada and Mexico have formed a regional economic bloc called NAFTA. European countries have deepened their economic integration through the European Union, and share a common currency. In East Asia, a regional grouping called APEC serves as an umbrella for organizing the trade and financial relations of countries in Asia and the Pacific region.

use military force as a coercive instrument to advance their interests. From this perspective, a nation-state can only acquire great power by developing and mobilizing formidable military as well as economic capabilities.

Realists who believe we live in multipolarity and anticipate that multipolarity will be more manifestly a force in world affairs also believe that the central dynamic in international relations is the balance of power. The natural state of international affairs features multiple great powers engaged in an ongoing balancing game. The long era of international relations dominated by Europe, from 1648 to 1945, was the *normal* state of the world in international affairs, in which multiple great powers competed for primacy and security. The world of 1945 to 1990, with only two superpowers balancing each other, was an exceptional era; the era since 1990, with only one apparent superpower, has been even more exceptional. However, the proponents of multipolarity believe that, eventually, the world will revert, and perhaps has already reverted,

This time, however, regional blocs are far less insulated and exclusionary. The United States has a regional arrangement with its immediate neighbors, but also trades and invests extensively with the rest of the world. APEC is designed according to the idea of *open regionalism*; instead of trying to exclude, for example, the United States, it is actually a member of APEC. Today, transnational companies based in one country or region operate simultaneously across multiple regions. Economic regions sit alongside the multilateral trading system, rather than serving as an alternative to it.

Table 13.1 shows that between 1962 and 1994, intraregional trade increased as a percentage of total trade for the European Union, NAFTA, the countries of Mercosur, and the countries of East Asia.* Yet, it also suggests that *intra*regional trade did not replace *inter*regional trade. Trade among the three NAFTA countries, for example, accounted for less than half of their total trade in 1994. Africa, interestingly, has very little intraregional trade, and its portion of intraregional trade did not change significantly from 1962 to 1994.

▼ Table 13.1 Intraregional Trade as a Share of Total Trade of Each Region, 1962–94

Region	1962	1975	1985	1994
East Asia	0.33	0.31	0.38	0.50
EU-15	0.56	0.54	0.60	0.64
NAFTA	0.36	0.38	0.40	0.43
Mercosur	0.06	0.07	0.07	0.19
Africa	0.04	0.03	0.04	0.03

Source: Jeffrey A. Frankel (1997) *Regional Trading Blocs in the World Economic System* (Washington, DC: Institute for International Economics), p. 22.

---

* NAFTA countries are United States, Canada, and Mexico. European Union includes Belgium, Luxembourg, Denmark, France, Germany, Greece, Ireland, Italy, Netherlands, Portugal, Spain, United Kingdom, Austria, Finland, and Sweden. Mercosur includes Argentina, Brazil, Paraguay, and Uruguay. East Asia includes China, Hong Kong, Japan, South Korea, Taiwan, and Brunei, Indonesia, Malaysia, Philippines, Singapore and Thailand.

to its more natural state of multiple great powers that engage in balancing through both internal efforts, such as fortifying their military and technological capabilities, and traditional balance-of-power external strategies that rely on diplomacy and alliances. With the United States having been involved in long and costly engagements in Afghanistan and Iraq, stymied by Pakistan and North Korea, fundamentally conflicted about China, unable to stop Russian re-assertion of influence over its closest neighbors, and struggling to reduce massive economic deficits, the transition to multipolarity may be currently reordering international order.

Characteristics of Multipolarity

What would be the key features of a twenty-first century multipolar system? World politics would be dominated by three or more great powers that would engage in complex combinations of peace and hostility, or cooperation and competition. These countries would include the United States, China, probably Russia, and Germany and Japan on regional security and economic matters, as well as some global issues (Kupchan 2012). These are the countries that possess the lion's share of global material capabilities (military, economic, and scientific), and are able, in differing degrees, to project military power beyond their respective territories. Each of these great powers also has the societal capacity and administrative machinery to conduct foreign policy.

Flexible alliances, in which countries form temporary pacts and shift from one partner to the other depending on the circumstances, are a hallmark of international politics in the context of multipolarity. A premium is placed on diplomacy, and alliances take on greater importance when there are a handful of competing great powers. During the bipolar years, enduring or **fixed alliances**, in which countries remained allied with the same partners over long periods of time, took shape in NATO and the Warsaw Pact. In a new multipolar world, the famous assertion of Lord Palmerston, a British Liberal statesman and Prime Minister from 1855–58 and 1859–65, that Britain had 'no permanent friends and no permanent enemies, only permanent interests' would more likely apply to the foreign policies of the great powers. In a multipolar world, China and Russia might ally to contain the United States in some circumstances, but Japan and Russia might form an alliance against China. In some instances, such as combating global terrorism, Germany would work closely with the United States, but resist US admonishments to get tougher on Russia, a key energy supplier for Germany. Great powers might fight limited wars against each other in order to defend smaller allies, maintain access to resources, or establish dominance in a particular region. An all-out great-power war might be considered unlikely, not because of polarity dynamics, but because of nuclear weapons.

International Trends

One could point to mounting evidence for the re-emergence of multipolarity. Not long after the Cold War ended, many states, including allies of the United States, expressed anxiety about life in a unipolar world. Government officials from Russia, France, India, and China expressed the fear that even if the United States fully intended to act in a benign manner, it might be tempted by its extraordinary power advantage to remake the world to suit its preferences and, in the process, threaten the interests or security of others (Jervis 2009). After the terrorist attacks of September 11, 2001, when the United States under President George W. Bush singled out Iran, Iraq, and North Korea as an 'axis of evil', challenged the world to be 'for or against' the United States, and undertook what many viewed as an aggressive and discretionary war in Iraq, these fears seemed confirmed.

Governments alarmed by the great disparity in power between the United States and everyone else initially had limited options. It would be too costly for any state to undertake a full-scale effort to balance US power and too provocative for any group of states to form a balancing alliance against the United States. Instead, governments have come to rely on what political scientists now call soft balancing – steps to constrain or hobble the United States that fall well short of the significant mobilization of military power in opposition to the United States or the formation of anti-US security alliances. Examples of soft balancing include opposing US initiatives in the UN Security Council, refusing to go along with US sanctions against what it considers to be rogue states, seeking alternatives to the dollar as a reserve or exchange currency, and mobilizing diplomatic opposition to US intervention abroad. Another form of

Flexible alliances: Temporary alliances in which states form pacts but shift from one partner to the other depending on the circumstances.

Fixed alliances: Alliances in which countries remained allied with the same partners over long periods of time.

Axis of Evil: A term coined by US President George W. Bush to refer to Iran, Iraq, and North Korea, states which he deemed to pose the greatest threat to US and global security.

Soft balancing: Steps to constrain or hobble a great power (such as the United States today) that fall well short of the significant mobilization of military power in opposition to that power or the formation of security alliances united against the power.

◀ **Photo 13.1 Leaders Pose at an SCO Summit, 2012**

Leaders of China, Russia and four Central Asian nations (Uzbekistan, Tajikistan, Kazakhstan, and Kyrgystan) pose for photos at Beijing's Great Hall of the People on June 6, 2012, prior to a meeting of the Shanghai Cooperation Organization.

Source: PA Images.

soft balancing is the formation of international agreements that are not explicitly anti-American but might be useful in countering US initiatives. The Shanghai Cooperation Organization (SCO), an agreement among Russia, China, and the central Asian states of Uzbekistan, Tajikistan, Kazakhstan, and Kyrgyzstan, was formed in 2001 to enhance the security of member states against threats of terrorism and ethnic conflict. Although the SCO proclaims that it is not an alliance directed against any state, member states and observers have used it as a platform to criticize the United States and US policies. The United States applied for SCO observer status in 2005, but its application was politely rejected. In the late 2000s, expressing preferences expressed at SCO summits, the governments of Kyrgyzstan and Uzbekistan evicted the United States from military bases in their territory used to pursue the war on terrorism.

Multipolarity was building by the end of the Bush era in 2008. The fact that the United States could not pacify Iraq and Afghanistan raised doubts about the utility of its extraordinary military power. The global financial crisis of 2008–10, with roots in the US banking sector, raised doubts about the durability and desirability of the American economic model. Meanwhile, China's economic and military power continued to grow steadily and Russia, flush with cash from rising oil and gas prices, began to reassert its influence globally and regionally. In 2008, Russia invaded neighboring Georgia, while China enhanced its prestige by hosting the summer Olympic Games. As suggested in Chapter 10, President Bush's presence at the games in Beijing during Russia's invasion seemed to symbolize that America was a spectator at both events.

Contrary Evidence and Questions

Is a return to the classic multipolarity of the nineteenth and early twentieth century just around the corner? Foremost, it depends on whether multiple nation-states have the capability and determination to achieve great-power status. In terms of cumulative

Shanghai Cooperation Organization (SCO): An agreement among Russia, China, and the central Asian states of Uzbekistan, Tajikistan, Kazakhstan, and Kyrgyzstan formed in 2001 to enhance the security of member states against threats of terrorism and ethnic conflict.

The Future of NATO under Multipolarity

Theory: *Realists versus Liberals on the Purpose of Alliances*

Realists believe that alliances are instruments of convenience that are adopted and maintained by states when it is in their security interests to do so. Alliances come and go; states have permanent interests, but no permanent friends in an anarchic international system.

Liberals generally agree that states form alliances for multiple strategic purposes. But liberals also strongly believe in the importance of regime type and, in particular, the distinctive relations among nation-states that are democracies.

Practice: *Realists versus Liberals on Why the NATO Alliance Persists*

From the realist perspective, there is nothing special or extraordinary about the NATO alliance among the United States, Canada, and the countries of Europe. NATO was formed for the purpose of containing the Soviet Union. It has outlived the Soviet Union because the United States, the dominant player in the alliance, continues to find NATO useful as an instrument to project power in post-Cold War Europe. But, if one or more European states emerged as peer competitors in a multipolar system, most realists assume NATO would wither away. One of the most prominent realists in international relations, Kenneth Waltz, predicted in 1993 that the world would quickly revert to multipolarity, and argued that, in a multipolar world, even if we could not predict NATO's precise demise, its years would be numbered.

For liberals, the ties that bind democracies are stronger than mere strategic convenience. The democracies of the United States and Europe are especially closely linked because they share a common heritage and civilization, political tradition, and beliefs in the rule of law and the rights of the individual.

From this perspective, NATO is truly a special alliance. Liberals expect that even if Europe collectively, or individual European states, emerged as peer competitors to the United States, some form of the trans-Atlantic alliance would remain intact. Multipolarity would not mean the end of the security community of democratic nations, even if it brought other key changes to international politics. Liberals are not surprised by the persistence of NATO after the Cold War because they believe it rests on shared political characteristics rather than the temporary convergence of strategic interests.

economic and military capabilities, the world remains rather lopsided, despite the foreign policy and economic difficulties experienced by the United States in the latter 2000s. Other candidates have some distance to travel before joining the great-power club as full members. Japan is a formidable economic power with technologically advanced, though limited, military capabilities. But, as a result of domestic politics, Japan lacks nuclear weapons capabilities and, more importantly, the political will to distance itself from dependence on the United States. Russia can exercise influence against weaker neighbors, but the ability to project power and influence beyond its neighborhood is questionable. Its economy, as seen in Chapter 10, has more of the dependent, raw material-producing character of a developing country than the more diversified and technologically advanced character of a contemporary great power. China and India have great potential but are essentially great power 'works in progress,' with large populations, developing economies, and an array of challenges to political stability. China, having begun to translate its remarkable economic success into greater military and diplomatic clout, is further along the great-power road than India. Germany is a powerful state in Europe, and the central leader of the European Union. However the EU, relative to its overall capability, is a weak actor in world affairs; German leadership of that organization does not readily translate into global influence. Achieving great-power status is not impossible for these states, but remains a challenge, regardless of whether the United States seems on the verge of empire, as in 2000, trapped by its own mistakes, as in 2008, or seemingly in retreat, as in 2013–14.

Let us assume that multiple great powers do arise within the next decade. There is still the interesting question of whether twenty-first-century multipolarity would operate in the same fashion as it did in the nineteenth century. First, to what extent would alliances truly be flexible? The United States has longstanding alliance ties to the states of Europe and Japan. These countries are not just allies, but democratic allies. How strong are those binding ties? How likely is it that the United States and Europe or Japan might find they are on opposite sides of a serious political or military conflict in a multipolar world? That question forces us to directly examine our assumptions about what is of primary analytic importance in international relations – the anarchy of the international system as emphasized by realists, or the importance of common political systems as emphasized by liberal thinkers. It is possible, as we discuss in Model 4, A Democratic Peace, to conceive of a cooperative or harmonious multipolarity populated by democratic great powers.

Second, in what ways might nuclear weapons complicate the workings of multipolarity? In the classic nineteenth-century version, great powers fought frequent small wars against each other to maintain the balance of power and prevent any single state from achieving dominant status. But the Cold War demonstrated that nuclear great powers are cautious about fighting any kind of direct war with each other, for fear that conventional conflict might escalate to the nuclear level. Perhaps nuclear-armed, multipolar great powers would fight by proxy, as the Soviet Union and United States did in Korea and Vietnam during the Cold War. Or perhaps they wouldn't fight at all, lending credence to the geo-economic model discussed in Model 1, or the democratic peace model to be discussed in Model 4.

State	**International**
Countries with the potential to emerge as great powers in a multipolar world would need to develop both economic and military capabilities.	Because they make different assumptions about what matters in international relations, realists and liberals differ over the extent to which a future multipolar world would be conflict-prone or peaceful.

Levels of Analysis
A Return to Multipolarity

Model 3: A New Bipolarity

Rather than multiple great powers arising, it is possible that only one will emerge to challenge the dominant position of the United States. In this view, the era of 1945 to 1990 has become the *normal* state of international affairs. Great powers need to be superpowers; they need to be of continental size, with large populations and global reach. Very few nation-states can attain superpower status. In the coming years, the most likely candidate to join the United States in that exclusive club is China. Proponents of a new bipolarity expect the rise of China to eventually cause the United States and China to clash geopolitically in a manner similar to the great struggle of the Cold War (Friedberg 2011).

It is not difficult to imagine the origins of a new Cold War. Consider, for example, the possibility that the United States needs a central external enemy to create purpose in its foreign policy. In terms of material capability, the United States became a great power in the first half of the twentieth century. But it only *acted* as a great power when faced with a significant external threat. The United States entered World War II to defeat Nazi Germany and global fascism, and fought the Cold War to defeat the Soviet Union and global communism. But when the Cold War ended, US foreign policy seemed to drift without a clear purpose. For a while it seemed that Japan might present itself as an economic enemy but, by the mid-1990s, the threat from Japan was replaced by concern over China's rising power. The first major foreign policy conflict of the George W. Bush administration involved China. In April 2001, an American intelligence-gathering aircraft collided in midair with a Chinese fighter that got too close, and the US plane was forced to make an emergency landing on Chinese soil. A diplomatic stand-off ensued (and was eventually resolved) when the Chinese government refused to allow the United States to reclaim its aircraft for several days.

The terrorist attacks of September 11, 2001 abruptly shifted the focus from China to the Middle East. Al Qaeda and the Taliban regime in Afghanistan that provided sanctuary became the new central enemies of the United States, and the fight against global terrorism became the new central purpose of US foreign policy. Like the Cold War, the war on terrorism has been bipartisan, with broad public support. Presidents George W. Bush and Barack Obama disagreed about most things, but agreed on the need to conduct the war on terrorism. Like their Cold War predecessors, they have disagreed on the means to conduct foreign policy, but not its broad purpose.

The United States has had the luxury of focusing on terrorism as a central threat; after the Cold War, the more traditional threat of competing great powers did not exist on a large scale. Proponents of the new bipolarity, however, believe this situation will eventually change, and a great power challenger will become the central US focus. China is the logical candidate. It combines many typical great power attributes – large size, rapid economic growth, modernizing military capabilities, and foreign policy ambitions. China has a long history of being the dominant power in East Asia, and Chinese leaders carry the historical baggage of resentment against Western powers for frustrating China's global great-power ambitions. Now that China has emerged intact from the tumultuous early decades of its communist revolution, and sustained rapid economic growth and development over three decades, it is ready to reassume the mantle of great-power status (Goldstein 2005). In 2012, China's new leader, Xi Jinping, played into this view by proclaiming that the Chinese dream was the 'great revival of the Chinese nation' (*The Economist* 2013).

US–China relations have been generally positive since the two countries opened diplomatic engagement in 1971. But it is not hard to imagine a downward, action-reaction spiral. The more China grows, the more anxiety it creates among US officials, and the more Chinese leaders become emboldened to seek status and influence commensurate with their capabilities. China and the United States have different social and political systems and define human rights differently. Many Americans are crit-

◀ Photo 13.2
Taiwanese Protesters in 2010

Anti-China demonstrators hold placards as they march in a street in Taipei, Taiwan on Saturday, June 26, 2010, denouncing the Economic Cooperation Framework Agreement (ECFA) planned with China that they say will undermine the island's self-rule and its economy.

Source: PA Images.

ical of Chinese labor policies, environmental policies, and repression of religious freedom. Many Chinese view US criticisms as arrogant, hypocritical, and an unwelcome intrusion upon their sovereignty. One obvious flashpoint that could spark a more rapid downward spiral is Taiwan. China considers the small island adjacent to its mainland a renegade province that is rightfully part of China. For the United States, the nationalist regime governing Taiwan is a long-standing ally that stood side by side with America in the long struggle against global communism. America's diplomatic approach to Taiwan is a pragmatic one; it seeks to deter China from attacking Taiwan, while deterring Taiwan from provoking China by asserting its independence. This delicate strategy of double deterrence has worked, but is no guarantee against China or Taiwan initiating a conflict with the potential to draw in the United States.

Characteristics of a New Bipolarity

What might be the central features of a new bipolarity? China and the United States would face off in a replay of the Cold War. Each would be the central focus of the other's foreign policy. At both the government and societal levels, the United States would view China as its principal geopolitical competitor and potential adversary. China would view the United States in a similar fashion. As the rising challenger, Beijing would also try to offer some type of ideological alternative to an international system dominated politically, economically, and in terms of values by the United States.

In this bipolar context, the United States and China would try to enlist the support of other states, either informally or in formal alliances. The precise coalitions would depend on how political and economic relationships played out over time. America's long-standing alliances with the European Union and Japan might remain intact, forcing China to cultivate new partners in Russia, Southeast Asia, and Africa. South Korea (or perhaps a unified Korea?) might be caught between its modern, postwar allegiance to the United States and its historical role as a dependent client state in a

Chinese sphere of influence. The energy reserves of the Middle East and the Gulf, coupled with the energy needs of the two superpowers, might lead that region to remain an arena for geopolitical competition and conflict. Regardless of the particular diplomatic and alliance configurations, the main feature of the new bipolarity would be US–China suspicion and hostility organized around competing coalitions. The competition would likely begin in East Asia, with China struggling to assert its regional hegemony, and the United States seeking to maintain its postwar status as an onshore balancer or 'resident power,' as Defense Department officials liked to assert during the Bush and Obama administrations. But competition would take place globally as well.

International Trends

To be sure, the emergence of a full-blown bipolar competition is not yet apparent. During the decade of the 2000s, US–China relations proved, for the most part, cooperative. The United States sought a partnership with China and enlisted its support in the US-initiated war on terrorism, nuclear non-proliferation efforts, and after the great financial crisis of 2008–10 to help stabilize and grow the global economy. China, for its part, acted as a patient challenger. It characterized its foreign policy strategy as peaceful rise, meaning that it sought to develop economic capability and political influence without threatening or provoking regional neighbors or the broader global community. During its more vulnerable phase of great-power emergence, Chinese officials were understandably relieved to have the United States focus its hostility elsewhere, at non-state actors and so-called rogue states.

▲ Photo 13.3 Energy resources of the Middle East

The Middle East has long been a key source of energy for the global economy. The major regional exporters of Middle Eastern oil in 2010 were Saudi Arabia (37%), Qatar (14%) and Iran (13%).

Source: PA Images.

Beneath the surface of cooperation, however, were signs that each side was quietly preparing for the possibility of future geopolitical competition. During the years the United States focused on shooting wars in the Gulf and Southwest Asia, it also put the elements of a future China containment strategy into place. It reinvigorated and expanded its Cold War security alliances in East Asia, particularly with Japan, Australia, and selected Southeast Asian countries. During the 2000s, the Pentagon began publicizing an annual report on Chinese military capabilities, highlighting new and potentially disturbing developments. This was a direct echo of the Cold War – the 1980s annual publication *Soviet Military Power* was replaced 20 years later by a very similar annual titled *Chinese Military Power* (US Department of Defense 2012). In domestic politics, American business, with considerable stakes in China's market and source of supply, emerged as a strong advocate for continued US–China cooperation. However, other groups on the right and left of the political spectrum remained more ambivalent and could be mobilized into a possible anti-China coalition. These included advocates of human rights, environmental protection, religious freedom, and American workers displaced by imports from China's low-cost producers.

For its part, China coupled its patient challenger approach with subtle yet clear signs that it expected to exert greater influence regionally and globally to support its interests and acknowledge the higher international status to which it had become entitled. Chinese leaders directed a combination of military intimidation and economic cooperation at Taiwan, suggesting its willingness to use sticks and carrots to ensure that the renegade province was eventually brought back into the fold. At the outset of the 2000s, China seemed willing to find cooperative diplomatic solutions to claims it and several countries, including Vietnam, the Philippines, and Indonesia, had made to a group of small islands known as the Spratlys, which may have substantial oil reserves. By the end of the decade, China returned to the more belligerent stance on the Spratlys that it had displayed in the 1990s. It accused its main regional rival, Japan, of failing to make amends for its aggressive imperial history, and Chinese ships confronted their Japanese counterparts in several scuffles in waters patrolled by the two navies. China sent diplomatic missions and economic aid to countries in the Middle East and Africa that could supply raw materials and offer secure sources of oil and natural gas. It defied the United States by engaging the Sudanese government at the same time as US officials sought to isolate that government for human rights abuses. China accumulated hundreds of billions of dollars in its central bank and, during the financial crisis, raised doubts about the future desirability of a US-centered international monetary system by calling for alternatives to the dollar as the world's reserve currency. The financial crisis also provided the opportunity for China to display the advantages of its own economic model of state capitalism which, as discussed in Chapter 10, combines centralized political control with a decentralized economic system. Some analysts have labeled this successful set-up the Beijing Consensus, and juxtaposed it to the Washington Consensus of across-the-board-liberalization long touted by the United States.

Contrary Evidence and Questions

It is certainly plausible to imagine a new bipolar era, but how likely is it? Two important caveats are worth considering. First, China is growing rapidly but is not necessarily on a linear path to superpower status. The challenges facing China that could jeopardize its steady rise are formidable. These include the need to maintain extraordinarily high levels of growth, not just for economic reasons, but to ensure social stability and political legitimacy. If China's growth slows significantly, it will swell social discontent by being unable to absorb hundreds of thousands of new entrants to the labor force each year. A growth slowdown would also call into question the legitimacy, or right to rule, of the one-party state. The legitimacy of the Communist Party depends less on ideological appeal and more on its ability to 'deliver the goods' to a growing Chinese population with higher and higher expectations. The growing disparity between China's rich and poor adds to social and political tensions. China's environmental problems – one consequence of rapid, coal-based economic growth – are increasingly severe (Economy 2007). In several decades it must also confront the demographic challenge of a large, aging population for which the state must provide. In short, we should neither presume China's rise will be uncomplicated nor treat it as a foregone conclusion.

Second, assuming China does continue to rise and emerge as a peer competitor to the United States, will the resulting bipolar structure necessarily generate the hostility of the Cold War? The Soviet Union and the United States were not only politically hostile to each other, but largely *independent* of each other economically. China and the United States are economically interdependent in finance, trade, and investment. Economic interdependence makes it difficult for the two sides to isolate each other politically. Would American business, for example, support economic warfare against China? Would any American government jeopardize an arrangement in which China's central bank finances American fiscal and budget deficits by holding (as of mid-2009) almost $1 trillion in US financial assets? Economic interdependence also complicates the formation of rival political blocs. Would Japan or Thailand, with strong security ties to the United States and strong economic ties to China, be eager to choose sides and line up on one side or the other of the bipolar divide? A future US–China bipolarity would be more complicated than the Cold War when economic, political, and ideological differences reinforced each other across the great geopolitical divide.

Levels of Analysis
A New Bipolarity

👥 State	🌐 International
China's continued rise to great power status depends vitally on domestic economic and political developments.	Liberal thinkers believe that China and the United States may co-exist peacefully in a multipolar world, especially if China becomes a democracy.
	Economic interdependence makes the emerging US–China great-power relationship very different from that between the Soviet Union and United States during the Cold War.

Model 4: A Democratic Peace

The multipolar and bipolar models essentially take a realist view of international politics. They see the international arena as one of competition and conflict and view nation-states, especially great powers, as the central players in world politics. However, the democratic peace model reflects liberal and constructivist approaches to international relations. It focuses inside nation-states and the attributes of their domestic political systems as the key drivers of international behavior and outcomes. Proponents of a democratic peace are more optimistic than their realist counterparts. Instead of viewing international politics as an endless cycle of conflict and competition, they emphasize the potential for progress. Relations among states can improve over time and become more peaceful as states become more democratic (Russett 2001).

Characteristics of Democratic Peace

The democratic peace model of future international order rests on two key premises. The first is that the democratic form of government will continue to spread. This spread is inevitable because advocates see democracy as the wave of the future; it defeated its most formidable twentieth-century competitors, including fascism and communism, and displays resilience for the long haul not shared by other political forms (Fukuyama 1992). Sir Winston Churchill once famously remarked that 'democracy is the worst form of government except for all the others that have been tried.' The collapse of the Soviet empire provided additional impetus to the theory of inevitability for democracy. The lesson of those revolutionary events seemed to be that ordinary people could only be held down for so long; given a taste of freedom, they will embrace it wholeheartedly and make the democratic project their own.

The second critical premise, as discussed in Chapters 5 and 6, is that democracies do not fight wars *with each other*. Democratic states may be as war-prone as any other type of state. Since 1900, for example, both democratic Great Britain and non-democratic Russia have each engaged frequently in interstate wars. However, proponents of democratic peace hold that in relations with each other, democracies will be more restrained and pacific. Democracies do not fight each other because of political structure and political norms.

The argument that democratic political structures have a constraining effect on war goes back as far as German philosopher Immanuel Kant's famous 1795 essay, 'Perpetual Peace.' Kant reasoned that ordinary citizens had little interest in war because they actually had to fight it, pay for it, and 'painfully repair the devastation war leaves behind' (Kant [1795] 2009). This basic idea has been carried forward by contemporary democratic peace proponents, including Professors Bruce Russett and Michael Doyle, who suggest that war might be in the material or prestige interest of dictators or unelected elites, but in democratic political systems the natural pacific interests of the people serve as a constraint on the realization of those aspirations (Doyle 2011). Democratic peace proponents expect democracies to go to war when attacked or provoked by other states. But, in general, for democracies to fight requires the broad mobilization of public support, rather than simply the capricious desire of a particular leader. In relations among democracies, this structural inhibition is mutually reinforcing. Political scientists also argue that because democracies are open political systems, their intentions are more transparent and their commitments to abide by agreements are more credible. Therefore, it is easier for democracies to reach deals with each other as alternatives to war, and stick with them.

Recall from our discussion in Chapters 5 and 6 that the war-inhibiting effects of democratic political structures are reinforced by the effects of democratic norms. Some theorists argue that a democratic culture within a nation-state creates habits of negotiation, compromise, and consensus building. Democratic states carry these habits into foreign policy and are more inclined than authoritarian states to search for solutions to disagreements short of war. Others point out that democracy encourages a tolerance for individual differences, rather than an expectation of conformity to the beliefs of a group. The experience of democracy leads individuals to appreciate the point of view of others and be less inclined to perceive irreconcilable differences. Democratic peoples might perceive an authoritarian government as an enemy, yet have a harder time thinking in those terms about a government selected by its own population.

If we combine these two central claims – the inevitable spread of democracy, and the scarcity of war among democracies – we are left with a powerfully optimistic vision of future world order. As more and more countries become democratic, military conflict among states will become less and less prevalent. An expanding world of democratic states would enable the international system to approximate a security community – a grouping of political actors within which the resort to war as an instrument of statecraft has become highly unlikely, if not impossible. Political scientists frequently refer to the member states of the contemporary European Union as a security community. War between Germany and France, possible throughout most of European history, has become virtually unthinkable today as these two stable democracies find their political and economic decision-making increasingly intertwined.

The pacific effects of democracy are reinforced by other structures and relationships that go hand in hand with it. Democratic countries are typically eager to embed their political relationships within international institutions that establish common norms and expectations for nation-state behavior. The rule of law in politics within democratic nation-states is thereby reinforced and reflected by the rule of law among democratic nation-states acting in the international arena. Also, most democratic nation-states are simultaneously capitalist nation-states and, liberal theorists believe, free trade among them further reinforces the democratic peace. The *New York Times* columnist and best-selling author Thomas Friedman popularized this argument with the much-celebrated McDonald's (or Golden Arches) theory of war (Friedman 1999). He observed that no two countries, each of which had a McDonald's restaurant on its territory, ever went to war with each other. The underlying logic was that if a country reached the point at which its middle class was sufficiently large and well-developed to attract the McDonald's chain, that country probably also had the other social, political, and economic attributes that make war among capitalist democracies unlikely. Skeptics search for the Golden Arches in warring capitals and are quick to point to the relatively small number of disconfirming examples, such as the India–Pakistan war of 1999 or the war between Russia and neighboring Georgia in 2008.

International Trends

The democratic peace model is certainly plausible in theory – is there sufficient supportive evidence to make it viable as a future global order? Once again, we can take each of the two central arguments in turn. As we saw in Chapters 5 and 6, the empirical evidence for the proposition that 'democracies do not fight wars with each other' is robust. Numerous statistical analyses have demonstrated remarkably strong correlations between democratic political systems and peaceful relations. This correlation, according to political scientist Jack Levy, is 'as close as anything we have to an empirical law in international relations' (Levy 1988). There is no major exception, no obvious war between democracies to which we can point. Critics of the robust correlation between democracy and peace typically comb through history for a possible exception here or there, and the ensuing debates usually hinge on differing definitions of 'democracy'. For example, was the Spanish–American War of 1898 a war between democracies, or was Spain not technically a democracy because its competing parties alternated in power not by election but by prior political arrangement? Was the 2006 war between Israel and Lebanon a democratic war, or should it be coded differently because Lebanon, despite having what the international community judged a fair election in 2005, could hardly be considered a stable democracy over time? It is important to recognize that, from a statistical perspective, even a handful of exceptions would not necessarily invalidate the empirical regularity of the correlation between democracy and the absence of war.

What of the other premise – democracy's inevitable spread around the world? This proposition has appeared increasingly plausible over the past several decades as the democratic form of government has spread among nation-states in different regions of the world. In Latin America during the 1980s, military rule gave way to elections and the restoration of civilian rule in Peru, Argentina, Brazil, and Uruguay. In Central Europe, the monopoly of the Communist Party collapsed at the end of the 1980s and opposition parties were legalized in Poland, Bulgaria, Czechoslovakia, Hungary, Romania, and in the Soviet Union. Authoritarian capitalism gave way to democratic capitalism in the Philippines in 1986 and the Republic of Korea in 1987. South Africa threw off the apartheid regime and held multiracial elections in 1994. A Freedom House survey in 1987 found that 66 out of 167 countries could reasonably be characterized as electoral democracies. Some 20 years later, in 2008, they found 121 electoral democracies out of 193 countries. Of those 193 countries, 90 were considered 'free,' 60 considered 'partly free,' and 43 'not free' (Freedom House 2008).

Contrary Evidence and Questions

Advocates of democratic peace as a model of future global order must address three key challenges. The first concerns democracy's ability to continue to spread. Today, Russia and China represent prominent examples of major powers bucking the democratic trend. These large players are not simply authoritarian by default; their rulers believe that authoritarian regimes hold significant advantages over democracy, and they have managed to persuade or coerce sufficient portions of their populations to accept (or at least tolerate) that view. During the 1990s, it appeared that Russia and China might conform to democracy, but by 2014 that outcome appeared less certain.

Revolutionary upheaval against authoritarian regimes does not necessarily imply that democracy will result. In 2011, most of the world welcomed what became known as the Arab Spring. The Arab Spring began in Tunisia in December 2010, when a young man without a job burned himself to death in protest when police prevented him from selling vegetables on the street. Protests against authoritarian governments spread like wildfire across the region in 2011. The Tunisian leader was toppled and mass demonstrations in Egypt led to the resignation of President Hosni Mubarak after 30 years in power. Violent protest spread to Yemen, Bahrain, Libya, and Syria. With the assistance of NATO countries, Libyan rebels brought down the regime of long-

Revolutionary Upheaval in the Middle East

Aspiration

On June 20, 2005, US Secretary of State Condoleezza Rice gave a provocative speech in Egypt, at the American University of Cairo. She stated:

> We should all look to a future when every government respects the will of its citizens – because the ideal of democracy is universal. For 60 years, my country, the United States, pursued stability at the expense of democracy in this region here in the Middle East – and we achieved neither. Now, we are taking a different course. We are supporting the democratic aspirations of all people...Throughout the Middle East, the fear of free choices can no longer justify the denial of liberty. It is time to abandon the excuses that are made to avoid the hard work of democracy... Liberty is the universal longing of every soul, and democracy is the ideal path for every nation.

The Bush administration hoped that by invading Iraq and overthrowing Saddam Hussein in 2003, they would spread democracy not only to Iraq but elsewhere in the Middle East. Secretary of State Rice made clear that the United States intended to help that process along by promoting democracy whenever possible. In 2011, President Barack Obama welcomed the Arab Spring and called for a genuine transition to democracy in Egypt, meaningful reform in Bahrain, and a more representative government in Iran.

Reality

Reality is more complicated. A popular uprising against authoritarianism may or may not lead to democracy. Iran's revolution in 1979 has led, over three decades, to the consolidation of an Islamist regime hostile both to democracy and to the United States. Although post-Mubarak Egypt does not seem headed in that direction, its democratic future is clouded by a likely power struggle among various groups including the traditionally powerful military and an emerging Islamist group, the Muslim Brotherhood. By 2014, the military was back in full control. In Syria, as of 2011 and 2012, the uprising associated with the Arab Spring led not to democracy but to increased bloodshed as radical elements in the government and opposition strengthened and clashed, forcing moderate political voices to the sidelines.

The United States has also learned to be careful for what it wishes. In the Palestinian territories, the Islamist group Hamas, whose charter proclaims the goal of eliminating Israel, won parliamentary elections in 2006 that were held at the insistence of Secretary Rice. In Lebanon, Hezbollah, which the United States has designated as a terrorist organization, has gained considerable influence through democratic processes beginning in 2009.

To the extent democracy emerges in the Middle East, it may result at least in the short term in a loss of US influence. American behavior in the region has been unpopular since the United States has long been associated with the repressive regimes that popular protesters are determined to unseat. It is unlikely that new democracies in the Middle East will be immediately friendly to the United States and its allies. Over time, however, and to the extent the logic of the democratic peace holds, these new democracies and the world's most powerful one may come to find common ground.

standing dictator Muammar al-Gaddafi. As of 2013, revolution in Syria resulted in a long and bloody civil war – including the use of chemical weapons against rebel forces by a regime desperate to retain power – rather than a transition to democracy.

The Arab Spring holds great promise for democracy in a region where dictators have long repressed their populations politically and economically, often with the support of the United States. The US administration of Barack Obama quickly embraced the upheaval as good for democracy, the United States, and the world. As Box 13.4 explains, however, the Arab Spring represents a complicated set of political developments that guarantees neither democracy nor continued American influence in a key region of the world.

We should also bear in mind that the democratic process is not irreversible. Zimbabwe held multiracial elections upon gaining independence in 1980, but by 1987 had reverted to authoritarianism. Pakistan held elections in 1988 but found its nascent democracy replaced by military rule a decade later. In Venezuela, Hugo Chavez was initially elected in 1998 yet, over the next ten years, found ways to sidetrack his country's two-party system and concentrate power in his own hands. In 2009, Venezuelans approved a referendum lifting presidential term limits, making it possible for Chavez to maintain power indefinitely. Chavez died in March 2013, and six weeks later his handpicked successor won a six-year-term in a close and controversial election. The Venezuelan example also reminds us that not all democracies are the same. The Freedom House survey of 2008, for example, qualified 121 countries as electoral democracies, but also found that 32 of them did not provide minimal or systematic protection for basic civil liberties. In its 2010 report, *Freedom in the World 2010: Global Erosion of Freedom*, Freedom House found that declines in liberty took place in forty countries while gains in liberty took place in only sixteen (*The Economist*, 2010).

Second, even though mature democracies may not fight each other, the *transition* to democracy may be a rocky and dangerous one. Ed Mansfield and Jack Snyder show that countries in the transition phase from non-democracy to democracy actually become more war-prone and do fight democratic states (Mansfield and Snyder 1995). Their research suggests that countries making the biggest leap, from total autocracy to mass democracy, were about twice as likely as states that remained autocratic to fight wars in the decade after democratization. This argument has important policy implications. To the extent it is correct, global efforts to make the world safer – for example, by coaxing China, Russia, and Middle Eastern states into democratic transitions – could actually prove counter-productive and lead to a more dangerous world of international conflict.

Third, some critics argue that the true test of democratic peace is yet to come. In historical terms, the prevalence of democracy is a relatively recent development. Much of the statistical data in support of the democratic peace hypothesis reflects conditions under which most states were not democracies, or democratic states were allied in conflicts against non-democratic adversaries, such as the decades the democratic states of NATO banded together against the non-democratic Soviet Union. A much harder but more meaningful test of the democratic peace model will take place if and when more democratic states displace non-democratic ones.

To appreciate this logic, consider two thought experiments. Let's say that China emerges as a peer competitor to the United States in a bipolar system and, in the process, transforms itself into a mass democracy. Will relations between a democratic great-power China and United States be more cooperative or conflictual? Liberal theorists would predict cooperation on the basis of compatible regime types. Realists would expect that the United States and even a democratic China with equivalent capabilities would have plenty of grounds for conflict.

Another thought experiment would take this model's logic to its extreme and imagine a world composed exclusively of mature democratic states. Would war be eliminated in such a world? The logic of the democratic peace suggests the answer is yes; to accept that answer requires you to believe that regime type outweighs all other causes of war discussed in Chapter 5. Realists are skeptical that a world of democracies would be a peaceful one; liberals and constructivists tend to be more hopeful.

Levels of Analysis
The Democratic
Peace

 State

Over the long sweep of history, more and more countries have become democratic. For any particular country, democracy is neither inevitable nor irreversible.

Model 5: A Clash of Civilizations

Clash of civilizations: The idea that international conflict in the future will be characterized not by inter-state conflict but rather by conflict between civilizations, a loose term that seems to incorporate religious, cultural, ethnic and, to some extent, linguistic similarity.

End of history: The end of ideological conflict and the victory of liberal values.

Our fifth model is similar to democratic peace in that it focuses our attention on features of world politics that transcend the traditional nation-state. But it paints a very different and far more pessimistic picture. The idea of a clash of civilizations was first popularized in a 1993 article by the American political scientist Samuel Huntington (Huntington 1993, 1996). Writing shortly after the end of the Cold War, Huntington was reacting to what he perceived as the misplaced euphoria of Western triumph, particularly the expectation that the defeat of the Soviet Union meant the end of the great battles over ideas in world politics. Rather than the end of history, or the end of ideological conflict and the victory of liberal values, Huntington prophesied the continuation of history, though not necessarily in the same political form.

Characteristics of a Clash of Civilizations

The clash of civilizations model begins with the premise that modern world politics has always been, and will continue to be, characterized by some form of inter-group conflict. From the founding of the Westphalian system in 1648 until the outbreak of the Napoleonic Wars in 1799, that conflict was centered in Europe and took place among the monarchs and princes who controlled European territory and populations. From 1800 until the end of the Cold War in 1990, the main combatants were modern nation-states, which first appeared in Europe and spread globally. After 1990, nation-states are still relevant but the battle has shifted to *civilizations*. According to Huntington, civilization is a loose term that seems to incorporate religious, cultural, ethnic and, to some extent, linguistic similarity. A civilization might share the same territory with a particular nation-state, but is often spread across multiple nation-states. It is also possible for one nation-state to be divided among different civilizations. In Ukraine, for example, Orthodox Slavic culture dominates the eastern part of the country and European-oriented Catholics dominate the western part. Huntington asserted that 'the fault lines between civilizations will be the battle lines of the future.' For Huntington, nation-states may still be the agents of conflict, but the driving forces of conflict and, thus, world politics are civilizations.

Which major civilizations are in possible conflict? Huntington identified Sino-centric, Western, Muslim, Hindu, Orthodox Christian, and sub-Saharan African. The Sino-centric civilization includes China, present day North and South Korea, Vietnam, Singapore, Taiwan, possibly Japan, and the Chinese diaspora found in various Southeast Asian countries. Western civilization spreads geographically across North America, western and central Europe, and Australia. Latin America should be considered part of Western civilization, though it might evolve into a more distinct civilization at some point. Muslim civilization dominates the Middle East, the Gulf region, and Northern Africa, and spreads further east into Pakistan, Malaysia, and Indonesia. Hindu civilization is primarily centered among the majority population in India, although Huntington characterizes India (like Ukraine) as a 'cleft' country; alongside the Hindu majority lies a significant minority that identifies with Muslim civilization. Orthodox or eastern Christian civilization includes Russia, part of Ukraine, other parts of the former Soviet Union such as Moldova and Belarus, Bulgaria, Greece, and, after the break-up of Yugoslavia, Serbia. Sub-Saharan African civilization includes most nation-states in the eastern, central, and southern part of the continent.

The reasons that Huntington and his supporters might expect civilizations to clash rather than cooperate with each other are not hard to fathom. Different civilizations have different, deeply held values. Western civilization embraces individualism and social equality, while Sino-centric civilization focuses on the importance of the group and social hierarchy. Western and Muslim civilizations differ on the role and education of woman and the desirability (or threat) of modernity.

Conflict is likely because civilizations believe, not only in their values, but in the universality of their values. The Western insistence that liberal democracy and human rights are universal values that must be embraced by all often infuriates members of other civilizations. In both Muslim and Western worlds, missionary religions send forth adherents seeking to convert others to their cause. Huntington points out that Islam and Christianity are 'all or nothing' religions that encourage their faithful to believe theirs is the one true faith.

Clash, rather than cooperation, is also predicted in the Marxist idea of the law of uneven development. The Sino-centric world is enjoying rapid economic growth and an increase in international political influence and prestige. China's increase in power will tempt it to reassert its traditional cultural role as leader of a hierarchical political order in East Asia. Its desire for cultural and political leadership in that region could easily lead to conflict with the United States, which has strong economic and security interests there, and is determined to remain a resident great power in East Asia. In the Islamic world, there is uneven development of a different sort. The explosion of population in the Middle East and elsewhere, coupled with slower economic growth, fuels instability within that civilization and brings it into conflict with others. Huntington speculates on a possible alliance between Islamic and Sino-centric civilizations since both have grievances against the populations in dominant Western civilization that have written the rules of the contemporary global system and enjoy much of its benefits.

International Trends

Conflicts since the end of the Cold War lend a degree of plausibility to Huntington's gloomy vision. The break-up of the former Yugoslavia during the 1990s led to bloody struggle among Western-oriented Croatia, Orthodox Christian Serbia, and Muslim-dominated Bosnia. The Serbs practiced ethnic cleansing against the Bosnian Muslims, as the discussion in Chapter 1 of the tragedy in Srebrenica demonstrated. Russia's war against the breakaway Muslim province of Chechnya was especially brutal, as were Chechnya's reprisals against Russians. India and Pakistan, now both nuclear-armed, came close to war several times during the 1990s over Kashmir, a territory ruled by India but populated by Muslims sympathetic to Pakistan.

The most dramatic piece of evidence, of course, occurred on September 11, 2001. The terrorist attacks were framed in cultural or civilization terms; the target was not simply the United States but all of Western culture, with its emphasis on consumer capitalism and secular modernity. The United States responded forcefully. Although Bush administration officials repeatedly emphasized that the West was not at war with Islam, proponents of the Huntington thesis have been quick to point out that the principal targets of US counter-terrorism efforts have been Islamic fundamentalist non-state actors and Islamic fundamentalism regimes (such as the Taliban in Afghanistan) that have supported them. Subsequent terrorist attacks in London and Madrid, and even cultural conflicts such as the Danish cartoon crisis, have lent further credence to this view. In September 2005, a Danish newspaper published twelve editorial cartoons depicting the Islamic prophet Muhammad in disrespectful attire or situations (wearing devil horns or shown with a bomb in his turban). Protests across the Muslim world escalated into violence, including the burning of Danish embassies in Syria and Iran and death threats against the cartoonist and others. Over 100 people died in various countries as security forces tried to restore order. Supporters of the cartoons defended them as legitimate exercises of free speech in a free country, and pointed out that the newspapers in question often published satirical material about other religions. Critics viewed the cartoons as racist, anti-Islam, and an echo of past Western imperialism.

Contrary Evidence and Questions

Proponents of the clash of civilizations model must address some critical questions about the plausibility of their future vision. First, to what extent do cultures or civilizations form coherent or functional political units? One might reasonably point to the long-standing political, economic, and security links in the West between the European Union and United States as an example of a politically functional civilization across nation-state lines. But in other presumed civilizations, political relations are ambiguous at best. The Sino-centric world includes China and Vietnam, countries that are long historical adversaries who fought a war as recently as 1979. Japan might have cultural similarities to China but for sixty years it has been politically allied with the West; its current relationship with China is characterized more by geopolitical suspicion that cultural harmony. It is difficult to conceive of China (including US ally Taiwan), the Koreas (North and South), Vietnam, and Japan as somehow forming a viable political unit under the rubric of a common civilization.

The same might be said of the eastern Orthodox world. Cultural and religious similarities do not translate easily or necessarily into significant political cohesion. Greece, Bulgaria, and Romania are eastern in Huntington's civilization typology but are politically and economically allied with the West through NATO and the European Union. In the Middle East, despite centuries of perceived oppression at the hands of the West, no charismatic leader or leaders have emerged to craft a pan-Islamic movement that

Below, Samuel Huntington makes the analytical point that future conflict is likely to develop along cultural or 'civilizational' lines. Edward Said finds that argument overly simplified and likely to confuse more than clarify. Barack Obama, seeking to chart a new course in US relations with the Muslim world, emphasizes that different cultures must look for common interests rather than emphasizing their differences.

Samuel Huntington, Harvard Professor of Political Science:

It is my hypothesis that the fundamental source of conflict in this new world will not be primarily ideological or primarily economic. The great divisions among humankind and the dominating source of conflict will be cultural. Nation states will remain the most powerful actors in world affairs, but the principal conflicts of global politics will occur between nations and groups of different civilizations. The fault lines between civilizations will be the battle lines of the future. (*Foreign Affairs*, Summer 1993)

Edward W. Said, Columbia University Professor of English and Comparative Literature

This is the problem with unedifying labels like Islam and the West: They mislead and confuse the mind, which is trying to make sense of a disorderly reality that won't be pigeonholed or strapped down as easily as all that...These are tense times, but it is better to think in terms of powerful and powerless communities, the secular politics of reason and ignorance, and universal principles of justice and injustice, than to wander off in search of vast abstractions that may give momentary satisfaction but little self-knowledge or informed analysis. The 'Clash of Civilizations' thesis is a gimmick like 'The War of the Worlds', better for reinforcing defensive self-pride than for critical understanding of the bewildering interdependence of our time. (*The Nation*, October 4, 2001)

President Barack Obama

I have come here to seek a new beginning between the United States and Muslims around the world; one based upon mutual interest and mutual respect; and one based upon the truth that America and Islam are not exclusive, and need not be in competition. Instead, they overlap, and share common principles – principles of justice and progress; tolerance and the dignity of all human beings.

I do so recognizing that change cannot happen overnight. No single speech can eradicate years of mistrust, nor can I answer in the time that I have all the complex questions that brought us to this point. But I am convinced that in order to move forward, we must say openly the things we hold in our hearts, and that too often are said only behind closed doors. There must be a sustained effort to listen to each other; to learn from each other; to respect one another; and to seek common ground... I know there are many – Muslim and non-Muslim – who question whether we can forge this new beginning. Some are eager to stoke the flames of division, and to stand in the way of progress. Some suggest that it isn't worth the effort – that we are fated to disagree, and civilizations are doomed to clash. Many more are simply skeptical that real change can occur. There is so much fear, so much mistrust. But if we choose to be bound by the past, we will never move forward. And I want to particularly say this to young people of every faith, in every country – you, more than anyone, have the ability to remake this world.

('A New Beginning', Remarks in Cairo, Egypt, June 4, 2009)

transcends the interests of particular nation-states. Countries of the Middle East and the Gulf region share Islam as a religion but are ethnically fragmented, with Arabs, Turks, Palestinians, and others having competing political orientations. Being part of the same civilization did not prevent Iran and Iraq from fighting a brutal and bloody war between 1980 and 1988. Some countries and non-state actors within the Muslim civilization regard Israel as a mortal enemy and refuse to acknowledge its right to exist. Others, such as Egypt, have made peace with Israel. Saddam Hussein's quest to unify the Arab civilization against the West was met by resistance from fellow Arab states such as Saudi Arabia. The United States may be fighting some Muslims in the war on terrorism, but it has defended others – the Bosnian Muslims under attack from Serbia and Croatia, and Albanians in Kosovo under attack from Serbia – in prior conflicts. Civilizations do not necessarily form political units and cultural affinities do not always dictate political behavior among nation-states.

Second, even if we accept the utility of 'civilization' as an organizing concept, must relations among civilizations be characterized by conflict? There are numerous examples of cross-civilization cooperation in world politics. Furthermore, some extreme groups resist modernization precisely because one of the consequences is the transmission of different values, integration of various cultures, and the softening of stark distinctions across civilizations. Seventy years ago, the United States and Japan were mortal adversaries and culturally alien to each other. Today they are long-standing allies whose cultures and foreign policies have become increasingly intertwined. Americans can experience baseball in Tokyo just as Japanese can enjoy sushi in almost every American city.

The clash of civilizations is a provocative vision that has generated widespread criticism in the scholarly community. Some argue that economic opportunities and environmental challenges create more cohesion, rather than conflicts, across civilizational divides. Others point to global trends in favor of secularism, and still others observe that the majority of conflicts in the world today occur between members, either within or across nation-states, of the same civilization (Gurr 1994). Finally, some analysts have worried that Huntington's thesis could create a self-fulfilling prophecy. To stipulate a clash of civilizations as the defining feature of international relations reinforces the views of the most anti-Western extremists in the Middle East and the most xenophobic nationalists in Western Europe and the United States. By stressing differences among cultures, rather than interactions and reciprocal influences, Huntington's thesis risks an ominous replay of the Cold War.

Levels of Analysis
The Clash of
Civilizations

 State

The clash of civilizations model posits that allegiance to the nation-state will be less powerful in the future than allegiance to cross-national cultures or civilizations.

Model 6: Global Fracture: Pre-Modern, Modern, and Post-Modern Zones

Global fracture: A model of the future international system in which sovereign states give way to various 'zones' with differing characteristics.

Our final model questions whether it still makes analytical sense to discuss a single, coherent international system of sovereign nation-states. Proponents of the **global fracture** model view the sovereign nation-state as under attack from above and below. Supranational institutions, such as the European Union, are gaining more political authority as states pool their sovereignty or cede it to transnational authorities. At the same time, as discussed in Chapter 11, local actors including tribes, drug cartels, and terrorist groups have challenged the authority of central governments and have even established control over territories, populations, and the provision of services. In some parts of the world, the nation-state is alive and well. But in others it no longer dominates other political forms.

State success, as well as state failure, might help to account for the demise of the traditional nation-state. In some parts of the world, such as Western Europe, sovereign states have been so successful in providing security and prosperity to their people, or in resolving differences with their neighbors, that they are no longer needed to take on the functions they have traditionally performed. But in other parts of the world, such as parts of central Africa, sovereign states have failed. Their inability to provide people with security and a functioning economy, or even basic life necessities, have led other actors to take matters into their own hands. Significant variation in the role, capacity, and necessity of the modern nation-state means that we live in a fractured world, no longer usefully characterized in terms of a single integrated state system.

Characteristics of Global Fracture

Versions of the global fracture thesis have been put forth by various authors since the end of the Cold War. In 1993, Max Singer and Aaron Wildavsky argued that the traditional ways of understanding international politics needed to be replaced by new thinking:

> The key to understanding the new world order is to separate the world into two parts. One part is zones of peace, wealth, and democracy. The other part is zones of turmoil, war, and development. There are useful things to say about the zones of peace; and there are useful things to say about the zones of turmoil; but if you try to talk about the world as a whole all you can get is falsehoods or platitudes. (Singer and Wildavsky 1993: 3)

Along similar lines, in 2003 Robert Cooper, a former foreign policy advisor to British Prime Minister Tony Blair, published *The Breaking of Nations* (Cooper 2003). Cooper also sees the new world order as transcending the traditional Westphalian system of interacting, sovereign nation-states. He criticizes realists for assuming that all states objectively pursue determined interests and seek to accumulate power. Cooper suggests instead that some states can radically change their interests and identities, while others are simply incapable of purposive action because they lack organizational capacity or legitimacy. Cooper's model is representative of the global fracture vision of the emerging world order.

Cooper argues that three different political forms co-exist uneasily in what used to be an integrated international system. He describes pre-modern, modern, and post-modern worlds. The **pre-modern world** is a haven of lawlessness where states have either failed completely or cannot wield authority over sub-national actors who control territory, command the allegiance of parts of the population, and may even control their own private or local armies. One example is Somalia, which has struggled for two decades to establish some degree of political centralization and stability. The United States briefly engaged in Somalia in 1992–93, but backed away when it became clear that its nation-building efforts faced resistance from autonomous tribal warlords. In 2000, the United Nations recognized a Transitional Federal Government as the ruling body for the entire nation-state. But that government proved unable to control even the capital city, Mogadishu, much less outlying regions. A new president was chosen by the Somali parliament in 2004, but the election and legislative session had

Pre-modern world: A haven of lawlessness where states have either failed completely or cannot wield authority over sub-national actors who control territory, command the allegiance of parts of the population, and may even control their own private or local armies. The pre-modern world is one zone in a potential model of global fracture.

► **Photo 13.5 Women in Somalia**

Women from southern Somalia holding babies stand in a line to receive aid at a refugee camp in Dadaab, Somalia, August 15, 2011. Thousands of people arrived in Dadaab seeking assistance due to lack of water and food. The worst drought in the Horn of Africa sparked a severe food crisis and high malnutrition rates, with parts of Kenya and Somalia experiencing pre-famine conditions, according to the United Nations.

Source: © sadikgulec – istockphoto.com.

to be held in neighboring Kenya because Mogadishu was under siege. In 2006, the Islamic Courts Union, a group with significant influence across southern Somalia seeking to introduce Islamic law to the country, gained control of the capital but not necessarily the country. Over two dozen militia groups run by tribal war lords have set up semi-functional governments in different parts of the country and engage in military conflicts with each other. Since 1991, there have been over a dozen efforts, none ultimately successful, at national reconciliation.

Cooper's modern world reflects the familiar system of Westphalian nation-states. Sovereign governments control their countries internally and mobilize resources to pursue national interests. They engage in diplomacy, play balance-of-power politics, form alliances, and threaten or reassure their neighbors as part of efforts to enhance their influence, extract resources, or secure borders. Contemporary Syria *prior* to the upheavals of the Arab Spring typified Cooper's modern world. Its ruling Ba'ath party administered an authoritarian government that used external threats to justify tight control over its population and resources. Syria fought wars with Israel in 1967 and 1973 and has been unable to reach a peace settlement with the country it considers its principal regional adversary. It has long been a power broker in the neighboring Lebanon, and Syrian troops have remained there for several decades as a counter to Israel (Israeli and Syrian forces clashed in Lebanon in 1982), and as a means to exercise influence over Lebanon itself, which was part of Syria until 1926. Syria wishes to work with other Arab states against Israel, but also tries to prevent any particular Arab state from getting strong enough to dominate Syria. Despite the fact that Syria and Iraq were both ruled by Ba'ath parties during the era of Saddam Hussein, Syria's fear of Iraq's power led it to back Iran in the 1980s Iran–Iraq War and to back the US-led coalition that ousted Iraq from Kuwait in 1991. But Syria opposed US efforts in 2002–03 to oust Saddam Hussein from power and occupy Iraq itself.

◀ **Map 13.4 Syria and its Neighbors**

Syria has long been a quintessential 'modern' state in Cooper's terms. It has fought wars with Israel, occupied Lebanon, and worked with Iran to undermine US influence it its region. The Syrian regime maintained order through repression at home until 2011, when the Arab Spring spread to its people and the regime found itself struggling to control a mobilized population demanding political freedoms.

Until the Arab Spring, Syrian foreign policy echoed that of an eighteenth- or nineteenth-century European power seeking to make its way in an anarchical state system. But since 2011, Syria has faced a different problem – the breakdown of its central governing authority and a civil war pitting the regime against an opposition willing to risk extreme violence in an effort to overthrow it. In Cooper's terms, Syria as of 2013 had moved from the modern to the pre-modern world. Time will tell whether Syria will re-emerge as a possibly reconfigured modern state, or will be mired in the ongoing instability more characteristic of the pre-modern world.

According to Cooper, much of Europe itself is no longer part of the modern world that European states created back in 1648. The core states of the European Union constitute a **post-modern world**. They have willingly relinquished some of the key attributes of the traditional, sovereign nation-state. Contemporary Germany, for example, does not look much like the country that unified in 1870, enhanced its power through a careful balance-of-power strategy, and mobilized its resources to fight two world wars in an effort to dominate the politics of its continent. Germany today has merged much of its economic and foreign policies with those of its traditional adversary, France, and other neighboring countries. It has ceded much of its sovereign authority to the collective EU enterprise. It gave up its national currency, the Deutschmark, in favor of a common European currency. Even after reunification in 1990–91, Germany has proved more interested in enhancing the prosperity and welfare of its citizens than mobilizing resources to enhance its influence, prestige, and grandeur on the world stage. It is a 'civilian' great power, bound tightly to its neighbors and enmeshed in complicated layers of supranational decision-making.

Post-modern world: States that have given up their sovereignty in favor of larger, civilian-led cooperative unions (such as the EU). The post-modern world is one zone in a potential model of global fracture.

International Trends

The global fracture models of Cooper and others clearly illustrate the divergent political units of the current and emerging international system. We can point to ample evidence for the existence of pre-modern, modern, and post-modern politics that cut across traditional nation-state boundaries. Parts of South America are pre-modern as governments struggle to harness drug cartels that control their own military forces and administer large areas of cocaine-producing territory, simultaneously protecting and exploiting the peasants who work the land. The arc of instability stretching across the Middle East, North Africa, and Southwest Asia contains failed states such as Yemen, weakly centralized states such as Lebanon and Afghanistan, and states unable to control large and remote parts of their own territory, such as Pakistan and, as of 2014, Iraq and Syria. Much of the US war against Al Qaeda has taken place in the 'no man's land' on the mountainous Afghanistan–Pakistan border, under no real control by either central government. Examples of modern nation-states abound. One could point to Iran, Israel, and Saudi Arabia in the Middle East, emerging great powers China, India and Brazil, and former great powers seeking to recover their status such as Russia. The European Union, comprising the area that used to be the core of the sovereign nation-state system, is the most prominent example of post-modernism. It is a highly developed, institutionalized, and legitimate system for nation-states to interfere at all levels in the affairs of their neighbors, from foreign and financial policy all the way down to the ingredients that are acceptable in the production of cheese and beer.

Contrary Evidence and Questions

Global fracture offers a plausible snapshot of the contemporary world. Yet does it capture the essence of international politics more effectively than the other models? One key challenge for its proponents is to establish the nature of interaction – or lack of interaction – among the three different political forms. The model of a fractured international system would be especially powerful if the pre-modern, modern, and post-modern worlds formed self-contained sub-systems of limited interaction with each other. In that circumstance the global fracture model would resemble, as discussed in Chapter 2, a pre-Westphalian world in which the key units were isolated from each other rather than integrated into a single system. However, Cooper's three worlds seem drawn together in many ways. The chaos and instability of the pre-modern world spills over into the modern and post-modern worlds (Kaplan 2012). Refugees from pre-modern war zones in Africa and the Middle East cross borders and make their way to Europe and North America. Genocide and famine in the pre-modern world are often too horrible in humanitarian terms for governments and people in the post-modern world to ignore; recall from Chapter 11 the discussion of how the international community has taken on a 'responsibility to protect' civilians in crisis around the (usually pre-modern) world. Aggrieved groups in the pre-modern world threatened by 'post-modernity' can lash out using weapons of the weak – terrorism and weapons of mass destruction. There is also a strong historical connection. It is arguable that the modern world helped to create the instability of the pre-modern; great powers of an earlier era drew arbitrary colonial borders that created conflicts across ethnic and tribal lines that remain unresolved.

Other connections across worlds may be less obvious, yet no less important. To what extent is the security of the post-modern world a function of protection by modern states using very modern means? The post-modern, civilian power zones enjoyed by the European Union and Japan developed under the security umbrella provided during the Cold War by the United States. Particularly in Japan, that security umbrella remains in place. In the absence of a secure environment provided by others, it is possible that today's post-modern world might be forced to return to the modern one. Absent a US security guarantee, and facing nuclear-armed neighbors, Japan might be forced to reconsider its identity as a civilian great power. European states, facing a resurgent Russia not balanced by the United States, might have to rethink their long-standing preference for consumer, rather than military spending. In other words, the 'post-modernity' of Japan and the European countries may be a reflection, not necessarily guaranteed over time, of American power and protection.

This leads to another challenge for Cooper's global fracture model – how does the United States fit in? American society is decidedly post-modern: consumer-oriented, technologically advanced, and, in relative terms, living in prosperity and peace (which is why the September 11 terrorist attack was so shocking). Yet the American government is decidedly modern. It mobilizes and projects military power around the world. It plays balance-of-power politics in every key region. It initiates wars against modern states like Iraq and pre-modern ones like Afghanistan. The United States, arguably the single most influential actor in international relations, uneasily straddles the modern/post-modern divide. The fact that it cannot be easily categorized forces us to consider the usefulness of the distinction itself.

State	International
The global fracture model reminds us that both failed states such as Somalia and supra-national institutions such as the EU pose challenges to the primacy of the Westphalian nation-state.	Global fracture takes us back to a pre-Westphalian world characterized by the lack of an integrated international system.

Levels of Analysis
Global Fracture

Looking Back: A Reminder to Focus on Enduring Questions

Our survey of six different visions of the emerging international order should make one thing clear – there is no obvious winner. No doubt, some students will be uncomfortable with the gloomy pessimism of the clash of civilizations, the seemingly naïve optimism of the democratic peace, or the frustrating continuity of a multipolar or bipolar balance-of-power politics. Nonetheless, the debate is a useful one because it helps us map the overall terrain and contemplate what types of changes are plausible in world politics. It also forces us to reflect on our assumptions about what matters most in international relations. The six models, taken together, also illuminate two central questions about the future.

First, will the sovereign nation-state remain the central actor in world politics? No model predicts the disappearance of the nation-state, but they do divide on the question of whether it will continue to be the key driver of cooperation and conflict. The first three models place their bets in different ways on the continued primacy of the nation-state. The latter three give more weight to either political units or processes that cross nation-state boundaries, or particular features of certain nation-states (for example, democracy) in answering the question of what will likely matter most in future world politics.

Second, how much will military power continue to matter? No model believes the military factor will be completely eliminated from global politics but, again, a clear divide is evident. The bipolar, multipolar, and clash-of-civilizations models expect that political actors will prepare for and, in all likelihood, engage in military competition and conflict as a key feature in their international relationships. For different reasons, the geo-economic and democratic peace models downplay the importance of military power and point instead to fundamental changes in how future states will interact.

These two questions take us back to where we began, with a focus on the enduring questions of international relations. Our approach in this book has tried to encourage students to step away from the immediate politics of the moment and appreciate the knotty problems that have long engaged scholars and practitioners of world politics. On the hardest questions of our discipline, there are no easy answers. That makes it all the more essential to identify and struggle with these questions, understand how and why they have been answered in the past, develop your own answers, and learn to defend them logically through evidence drawn from the rich past and fascinating present of the international system.

Visit **www.palgrave.com/politics/Grieco** to access extra resources for this chapter, including:

• Chapter summaries to help you review the material
• Multiple choice quizzes to test your understanding
• Flashcards to test your knowledge of the key terms in this chapter
• Outside resources, including links to contemporary articles and videos, that add to what you have learned in this chapter

Study Questions

1. Which vision of a future international order do you find most compelling, and why? Which do you find least compelling and why?
2. What features are most important in distinguishing the multipolar balance-of-power model from the democratic peace model?
3. Is the clash of civilizations a realist model? Why or why not?
4. Do you believe a world of democratic states would be a more peaceful world than the current international order? Why or why not?
5. Consider an unrealistic thought experiment: If the United States disappeared from the international system tomorrow, which model of international order would likely emerge as the dominant one, and why?
6. From the perspective of China, is a bipolar world in which they are one of two dominant powers preferable to a multipolar world in which they are one of five major powers? What about from the perspective of a non-major power, for example, Vietnam?

Further Reading

Cooper, Robert (2003) *The Breaking of Nations* (New York: Grove/Atlantic). This is a provocative book by a British and European Union diplomat and former advisor to British Prime Minister Tony Blair. Cooper lays out a vision of a fractured world consisting of modern, pre-modern and post-modern zones co-existing uneasily with each other.

Kupchan, Charles (2012) *No One's World: The West, the Rising Rest, and the Coming Global Turn* (New York: Oxford University Press). Kupchan emphasizes that Western values are not universal, and the 'Western' international order is giving way to one in which no particular set of values will dominate. The previously dominant players in North America and Western Europe will need to accommodate a variety of actors with different interests and ideals.

Mueller, John (1989) *Retreat from Doomsday: The Obsolescence of Major War* (New York: Basic Books). Mueller's argument, partly constructivist and partly liberal, is that in modern times war has fallen out of fashion – following in the footsteps of previously robust social practices such as slavery or settling personal differences by dueling.

Ohmae, Kenichi *The End of the Nation-State: The Rise of Regional Economies* (New York: Free Press, 1996). A Japanese commentator argues that the forces of economic globalization have undermined the role and effectiveness of the nation-state. Economic power in this new world is held in regions rather than by governments.

Rifkin, Jeremy *The Empathetic Civilization: The Race to Global Consciousness in a World of Crisis* (New York: Penguin, 2009). Rifkin takes a 'first-level' approach to future world order. He draws on biology and cognitive neuroscience to suggest human beings are fundamentally empathetic rather than aggressive. He re-interprets modern international and economic history from this perspective.

Zakaria, Fareed *The Post-American World* (New York: Norton, 2009). Zakaria is the host of CNN's *Fareed Zakaria GPS* and a well-known international commentator. His book focuses on the diffusion of international power and the 'rise of the rest' including China, India, South Africa and Brazil. He provides advice to the United States on how to navigate an emerging and more multipolar global order.

Glossary

Absolute advantage: A situation in which one country has a productive advantage over another in two (or more) goods, but trade can still be mutually beneficial due to the principle of **comparative advantage**.

Absolute gains: An important element of economic liberalism, absolute gains is the idea that economic interactions create only winners, even if some gain more than others. Contrasts with **relative gains**.

Alliances: coalitions of states formed for mutual protection.

Ambassadors: Official representatives of a state's government representing that state diplomatically in another state.

Anarchists: Late nineteenth-century Russian terrorists who used assassination by bomb as a means to incite popular revolt against the state.

Anarchy: The fact that in international relations there is no centralized authority, no government of the whole world to adjudicate disputes among states and protect weak ones from strong ones.

Anti-dumping duties: Tariffs that offset the price cuts offered by foreign suppliers below what they charge in their own markets (**dumping**).

Anti-dumping: A type of policy designed to prevent **dumping** by other states. Permitted by international law, **anti-dumping** policies constitute one sort of **non-tariff barrier (NTB)**.

Appeasement: An effort by one state to reduce conflict with another by accommodating the demands of the latter.

Arab Spring: Near-simultaneous eruptions of revolutions in North Africa and the Middle East that began in 2011.

ASEAN Free Trade Agreement (AFTA): A trade agreement formed between ASEAN members with the initial goal of eliminating tariffs between the six original members.

Asian Tigers: Originally Taiwan, South Korea, Singapore, and Hong Kong, countries that achieved rapid growth rates using a strategy of **export-led growth**, causing many Asian countries to follow in their path. Now many rapidly growing Asian countries are considered 'tigers.'

Assured destruction: The ability and will to inflict unacceptable damage on an adversary – even after the adversary hits first with its best nuclear attack. Also known as **second-strike capability**.

Austerity: A policy by which governments raise interest rates or reduce government spending in an effort to discourage consumption and investment at home and, in so doing, reduce inflation and inflationary pressures.

Autarky: The separation of a country from the world economy in an effort to protect its economy from the effects of the global market.

Authoritarian capitalist model: An economic model in which a state employs a capitalist model but maintains control over the key economic actors. Unlike in a liberal model, the state is hands-on to the extent of owning and controlling the major firms.

Axis of Evil: A term coined by US President George W. Bush to refer to Iran, Iraq, and North Korea, states which he deemed to pose the greatest threat to US and global security.

Balance of payments: A summary of the international transactions of a state's residents, including individuals, households, private enterprises, and the government, with residents in the rest of the world during some fixed period of time, usually a quarter (three months) or a year.

Balance of power: Any situation in which a rough equality of power exists between the major states in the international system at a given moment in time. Balance of power is thought by many scholars to be an important condition for peace.

Bandwagoning: When smaller, weaker states ally with a larger, powerful state for protection. Contrasts with **balancing behaviour**.

Bank deposits and lending: One sort of investment transaction involving multiple currencies, in which banks headquartered in one country might extend loans to a foreign individual or enterprise.

Battle of Britain: A campaign of air attacks starting in June 1940 by Germany against Britain intended to compel Britain, at the time the only remaining German opponent, to surrender. British air defenses held.

Battle of Stalingrad: A battle between September 1942 and February 1943 in which Soviet forces destroyed a massive German army. It was a major turning point of World War II's European Theater.

Beggar-thy-neighbor policies: Policies designed to shift the negative consequences of the global economic downturn onto a state's neighbors, pursued by many countries during the Great Depression.

Beijing Consensus: The idea that, for some poor countries, development can be best attained in a world of economic turbulence by following the Chinese model of systematic government controls on the pace of trade integration, capital inflows and outflows, the movement of labor within the country, and the external value of the national currency.

Berlin Conference: A conference that brought together European leaders in 1878 to solve disputes over the division of Africa into colonies. The conference was sponsored by Otto von Bismarck in an attempt to stabilize European affairs in a manner favorable to Germany.

Berlin Wall: The wall that divided Soviet East Berlin from American, French, and British West Berlin during the Cold War, until its fall in 1989.

Bilateral diplomacy: The process by which representatives of two governments meet and discuss matters of common concern.

Biodiversity: (1) The variety of forms of life on earth, including different species of plants, animals, marine life, insects, and microorganisms (such as bacteria), or (2) variability within species, such as different types of corn, cattle, or bees. The maintenance of a diverse biological world ensures that humans will have many different sources of building supplies, clothing, food, and medicine.

Biological weapons: A category of WMD that kills people by spreading bacteria or viruses.

Bipolarity: In an international system, the characteristic of being driven by the existence of and competition between two especially powerful states.

Blast effect: The immediate explosive effect of a nuclear weapon. Can be powerful enough to level all buildings in a several-mile radius and to produce destructive winds of between 100 and 200 miles per hour.

Blitzkrieg: Lightning war, used by Germany to conquer westward at the beginning of World War II.

Bretton Woods system: The international system created in 1944 to encourage progressive trade liberalization and stable monetary relations between all the countries of the world. Although initial membership was fairly low due to Cold War tensions, membership in the resulting organizations steadily increased to include the vast majority of the world's countries. The **ITO**, **GATT**, **IMF**, and **World Bank** were all created as a result of the Bretton Woods system.

BRICS: Brazil, Russia, India, China, and South Africa. These five rapidly developing countries have the collective potential, within several decades, to overtake the combined economic weight of the industrial world.

Brinksmanship: A political tactic in which a country goes to the brink of war to convince an adversary they are willing to fight even though they would prefer not to.

Bureaucratic politics: A possible influence on a country's strategy characterized by national leaders and their subordinates engaging in foreign policy debates, building coalitions, and generally seeking to influence each other.

Chemical weapons: A category of WMD that uses manufactured chemicals to kill people.

Chlorofluorocarbons (CFCs): A chemical commonly used in propellants in aerosol cans and fire extinguishers, and as a key ingredient of refrigerants used in air conditioners. CFCs were a primary cause of the hole in the ozone layer, and have been outlawed by international agreements.

Civil defense: Defenses, such as fallout shelters, designed to protect civilians in case of a nuclear strike from an adversary.

Civil war: A sustained clash between forces that are controlled by the national government and forces that are controlled by an organized opposition group within the country.

Clash of Civilizations: The idea that international conflict in the future will be characterized not by interstate conflict but rather by conflict between *civilizations*, a loose term that incorporates religious, cultural, ethnic and, to some extent, linguistic similarity.

Class conflict: Conflict between the capitalist owners of wealth and industrial production and the workers they employ. Class conflict is driven by antagonistic economic interests and, according to Marxism, will increasingly define the relations between workers and capitalists.

Clean Air Act: A US Congressional Act originally passed in 1963 in response to the danger of acid rain in the US and Eastern Canada and amended in 1990 to mandate limits on emissions by American power plants of sulfur dioxide and nitrous oxides.

Coercive diplomacy: aggressive actions short of the immediate large-scale use of military force (such as moving an aircraft carrier closer to the shores of another country) designed to convince a country to rethink some behavior.

Cold War: Period from the mid-1940s to the late 1980s in which there was high tension and risk of war between the United States and the Soviet Union

Collective security: Security provided by the members of an international cooperative institution in which, if any state threatened or actually used military force illegally against a member state, the other members pledged to form an overwhelming coalition to defeat the aggressor.

Colonies: Areas conquered by a colonizing power over which the colonizer has political and economic control. Colonizers exploit colonized lands and peoples through trade or settlement for economic and political gain.

Commercial liberalism: The idea that market society and economic interdependence tend to have a *pacifying* impact on relations among states. As the economic relations between two states increase, the interests of these states in stable and continuous relations grow.

Commitment problem: A state's fear that any diplomatic agreement it reaches with an adversary to stave off a war might be violated at some point in the future when that adversary is in a position to be more deadly and demanding. The commitment problem arises due to the anarchic nature of the international system.

Comparative advantage: One country has a **comparative advantage** over another in the production of a good if, in order to make one more unit of that good, it has to forego less of another good.

Competing economic blocs: Groups of states in economic competition organized around the economies and currencies of major economic powers.

Conditionality: An **IMF** practice in which the **IMF** would lend foreign currency to a state running a deficit to allow that state to buy its own currency on international markets and, as a condition for receiving the loan, the **IMF** could prescribe policies for the receiving country to enact in its domestic economy to help solve economic issues and avoid future problems.

Contagion: The spread to neighboring countries of an internal war in one country, often caused by rebels seeking shelter in a neighboring country and beginning conflict there. Contagion can also refer to the spread of a financial crisis from one country to another.

Containment: A strategy by which one state employs diplomacy, economic assistance, and militay power to counter and check what it believes are efforts by an adversary state to extend its global aphere of influence.

Convention on Biological Diversity: An international agreement aiming to protect and preserve biodiversity, passed in 1992.

Convention to Prevent Pollution from Ships (MARPOL): A 1973 agreement that was the culmination of numerous international efforts, spearheaded by the United States, to reduce pollution from oil tankers.

Convertible currency: A currency that can be exchanged at market price for the currency of another country.

Cosmopolitanism: The tendency of peoples in different countries to embrace each other as fellow global citizens. Cosmopolitanism can be contrasted with nationalism.

Covert operations: Activities that a government directs against the interests of another government or non-state actor in such a way that the foreign targets and others are kept from knowing that the initiating government is responsible for the activities. Covert operations are a form of coercive diplomacy.

Crisis diplomacy: Emergency diplomacy in a crisis situation, designed to defuse tension between relevant states and decrease the likelihood of conflict.

Cruise missiles: Missiles, capable of being launched from land, air, or sea, that can travel below radar detection and guide themselves around obstacles to deliver the warhead they carry.

Currency market intervention: The purchase or sale of currency by a government in international markets to maintain a constant exchange rate between that government's currency and another currency.

Currency union: A group of countries in which each has given up its respective national currency in favor of a common currency.

Current account: The current account consists of the country's balance of trade in goods and services (the value of exports minus the value of imports), plus its income receipts such as the receipt of earnings from past investments abroad or the payment of such earnings to foreigners, and other transfers such as remittances that workers send out of the country or local residents receive from abroad.

Cyber-warfare: The use of the internet and related technologies by governments to damage or disrupt the activities or systems of an adversary or a private entity of value to an adversary.

Dawes Plan: US-mediated 1924 plan named for author Charles Dawes to end the Ruhr crisis. The plan called for France to leave the Ruhr, Germany's reparations payments to be reduced, and private international banks to lend Germany money to use for the payments.

Decolonization: The process by which imperial powers relinquished their overseas holdings leading to an upswell in the number of independent nations around the world. In the years following World War II, decolonization swept the globe.

Deforestation: The clearing or over-harvesting of forests, an especially acute problem in the tropics.

Demand curve: A demand curve specifies the quantity of a good that consumers wish to purchase at different prices. Along with **supply curves**, demand curves can show the likely price of goods, including currencies, in international markets.

Democratic peace theory: The theory that democracies are unusually peaceful toward each other. Democracies, or republics, are understood as states that have elected governments, a free press, private property, and the rule of law.

Demography: The makeup of a state's population. This includes population size as well as the balance between young and old, working-age and retired, etc. A state's demography is an important element in determining its capabilities relative to another state.

Dependencia: A school of thought that argues that international economic linkages hinder development in developing countries. Proponents of *dependencia* argue that the connections between developing countries and wealthy countries are designed for the benefit of the wealthy countries (often former colonial powers) and the people in the developing country who benefit are in the small elite that promotes the international linkages.

Détente: A relaxing of tension in the middle of the Cold War in which economic interdependence began to develop between East and West and global trade increased.

Deterrence: Using the threat of retaliation to protect oneself from an attack. Nuclear states use the threat of nuclear retaliation to deter other states from attacking them.

Devaluation: A downward change in the *official* price of the currency often undertaken to more accurately reflect its market value.

Developed countries: Wealthy countries with advanced economies.

Developing countries: Poor countries with small economies whose residents have not, on average, attained the living standards typically enjoyed on average by residents of wealthy countries.

Diplomacy: The process by which representatives of two or more governments meet and discuss matters of common concern.

Diplomatic immunity: The privileges and immunities granted by a host country to foreign ambassadors and embassy staff, exempting them from the full force of local laws.

Dirty Bomb: A device that, without the profound power of a nuclear explosion (and its attendant heat and blast effects), disperses some type of radioactive material.

Dissatisfied states: States who feel that their influence, status, and material benefits should be higher than what they are actually achieving.

Dollarization: A monetary policy in which a country substitutes a foreign currency for its own in its home market. Historically the US dollar has been the most commonly substituted foreign currency.

Dumping: The sale of goods by producers in a foreign market at prices that are lower than what those producers charge in their home market. Producers might engage in dumping to gain market share in the targeted foreign markets, drive out local producers in those markets, and, having done so, then increase prices and obtain very high profits.

Dynastic states: States ruled by 'imperial dynasties' or 'dynastic families', in which members of a given extended family, over a number of generations, maintain power within a state or empire.

Economic development: The attainment by a poorer country of an increase in its rate of growth of GDP per capita.

Economic incentives: An instrument of persuasion in foreign policy. Economic incentives are basically carrots: country A promises some economic gain to B, and delivers it if B does what A wants it to do.

Economic sanctions: An instrument of coercion in foreign policy. Economic sanctions are basically sticks: A threatens B with some form of economic loss if B does something A does not want it to do, or fails to do something A wants it to do.

Economic security: The ability to maintain prosperity in a world of scarcity.

Economic warfare: Aggressive economic actions by a state intended to damage another state economically.

Empires: Political entities that contain a substantial geographical space, often many different peoples, and over which a single powerful ruler governs.

Enduring questions: Questions which have engaged and challenged generations of international relations scholars and students – unresolved questions that have stood the test of time. This book is organized around these questions.

End of History: The end of ideological conflict and the victory of liberal values.

Environmental determinism: The view that changes in the environment like climate change *necessarily* and *automatically* will cause human beings and human communities to react in a particular manner.

Ethnic cleansing: Sustained, organized violence perpetrated against a particular ethnic group with the goal of eradication of that group.

Euro: the common currency of the **Euro zone**.

Euro zone: The world's most prominent **currency union**, consisting of eighteen countries in Europe all using the Euro as a national currency.

European Union: A group of 28 European countries that abide by common laws and practices.

Exchange rate: The amount of one currency that must be offered to purchase one unit of a foreign currency.

Export-led growth (ELG): A strategy that argues that international economic linkages are good for developing countries because the international economy presents important opportunities for development. The strategy entails switching preference for government credit and foreign currency from firms producing for local markets to firms producing for export markets.

Extended deterrence: The threat by one country to use its nuclear forces to protect other countries.

External balancing: The process by which states enter into security alliances with other states to balance the power of a particularly strong state or coalition of states.

Externalities: The benefits and costs not reflected in a good's price, such as ideas on how to improve a product in the future (positive externality) or pollution (negative externality).

Extra-state war: A violent clash – resulting in at least 1,000 combat deaths – between the national government of a recognized state and an entity that is not an internationally recognized state, or a non-state actor located in a foreign state.

Failed states: States that lack the basic institutions and capacities of government – taxing, policing, upholding the rule of law, protecting property, providing public roads and services, and maintaining control over territory.

Fallout effect: The tertiary effect of a nuclear explosion. Because nuclear weapons cause dirt and air particles to become radioactive, an explosion can expose people hundreds of miles from the blast site to fatal cancers over time. This exposure to radiation is the fallout effect, and affects a much wider range than the blast or thermal effects.

Feudalism: A system in which individuals act as 'vassals' and receive land in exchange for swearing loyalty to specific high-ranking leaders (e.g., counts, dukes) and, at the apex of the system, the king.

First-strike capability: The negation of another country's **second-strike capability**. A state has first-strike capability if it has sufficient nuclear capability to eliminate an adversary's capacity to respond to a preliminary strike.

Fission: An atom-splitting chain reaction that is central to the working of a nuclear weapon.

Fixed (or pegged) exchange-rate system: A system in which a currency trades at a government-specified rate against a particular currency or a group of currencies, and the government intervenes in the foreign exchange market or takes monetary or fiscal policy measures to keep those rates in place.

Fixed alliances: Alliances in which countries remained allied with the same partners over long periods of time.

Fixed capital: The value of assets a company utilizes in an ongoing way in the production of a good or service.

Flexible (or floating) exchange-rate system: A system in which a government allows supply and demand in foreign exchange markets to determine the exchange rate of its national currency.

Flexible alliances: Temporary alliances in which states form pacts but shift from one partner to the other depending on the circumstances.

Foreign affairs media: Those individuals and organizations who report or common foreign developments in print, on television, over radio, and through the internet.

Foreign direct investment (FDI): (1) One sort of investment transaction involving multiple currencies in which residents in one country – most typically multinational enterprises – may establish wholly-owned foreign subsidiaries, or buy enough shares of a foreign firm to control the operations of that firm, or (2) when an enterprise (usually an MNE) in one country moves capital to another country with the intention of establishing an on-going business presence.

Foreign exchange market: The marketplace (important locations are in London, New York, Frankfurt, and Tokyo) in which individuals, firms, and even governments sell and buy foreign currencies.

Framing: The process by which media participants select or present particular elements of a news story in such a way as to influence the opinions of recipients of the story.

Free Trade Agreement (FTA): An agreement between two or more states to eliminate tariffs, preferences, and import quotas on all (or most) goods between those states.

Functionalism: The liberal idea that institutions are tools that allow states to develop more efficient and durable forms of cooperation.

Garrison state: A highly militarized state in which the government controls economic, social, and political life in order to maximize military power.

General Agreement on Tariffs and Trade (GATT): When the ambitious **ITO** fell through, **GATT** represented an initial, less ambitious attempt by the United States and other Western countries to lower their respective tariff rates on a wide variety of goods and to establish a first set of rules to resolve trade disputes among nations (finalized in 1947).

General war: A war that involves many or all of the most powerful states in a particular historical era. Synonymous with **major war**.

Geo-economic competition: A situation in which traditional military competition is replaced by economic competition – a 'struggle for the world product' – and international dominance is measured by economic security.

Glasnost: An increase in political openness in the USSR led by Mikhail Gorbachev between 1985 and 1989 designed to keep the Soviet Union internationally competitive. However, providing Soviet states with political openness gave them the strength and motivation to rebel against Soviet rule, and the process ended up aiding in the collapse of the Soviet Union. See *Perestroika.*

Global civil society: The realm of private activity that lies outside the political system, where religious, ethnic, and civic groups flourish. Civil society exists within countries but it also operates between countries, often manifest in transnational groups and associations. Global civil society is, in effect, the sum total of these transnational groups and activities.

Global Environmental Facility (GEF): A program managed by the World Bank and the UN that provides grants to developing countries to help them meet international legal obligations in four areas: climate change, desertification, international water pollution, and biodiversity.

Global fracture: A model of the future international system in which sovereign states give way to various 'zones' with differing characteristics.

Globalization: The ongoing process of international economic and technological integration, made possible by advances in transportation and communication.

Good governance: A country with good governance at home typically possesses transparent and consistent political and legal systems, combats official corruption, and protects property. These factors encourage individuals to save, make investments, and pursue technological innovations that promote economic growth.

Government procurement: The purchase by government agencies of goods and services from private suppliers. Because national governments spend so much money every year, government choices in how to purchase such goods and services can have a major impact on international trade. Thus, government procurement constitutes a possible **non-tariff barrier (NTB)**.

Great Depression: An international economic disaster precipitated by the 1929 crash of the US stock market. The disaster blocked Europe's path to economic recovery and political reconciliation.

Greed: A person's intense desire to possess goods or money. On the individual level of analysis, a primary mechanism that increases the likelihood of internal war.

Greenhouse gases: Certain gases, such as carbon dioxide, that accumulate in the atmosphere and trap some of the infrared heat produced by the sun's warming of the earth that would otherwise escape back into outer space.

Grievance: A person's belief that he or she is being victimized by or excluded from important institutions in a country. On the individual level of analysis, a primary mechanism that increases the likelihood of internal war.

Gross fixed capital formation: The total increase in fixed capital that occurs in a country or in the world during a given period of time, usually a year.

Group of 20 (G-20): A broader group of states, including the G-8 members along with newly rising economic powers like China and India, oil producers like Saudi Arabia, and middle powers such as Australia, Turkey, and Argentina, which has replaced the **G-8** in international economic decision-making.

Group of 7 (G-7): The group of seven countries (United States, United Kingdom, France, Germany, Japan, Italy and Canada) that governed international economic relations after the collapse of the Bretton Woods system by coordinating their exchange rates and their domestic monetary and fiscal policies.

Group of 77 (G-77): Spawned by UNCTAD, the Group of 77 is a loose coalition (now grown to some 130 countries) of developing states that seeks to further the economic interests of its members through collective diplomacy at the UN.

Group of 8 (G-8): The **Group of 7 (G-7)** plus Russia. In the aftermath of the Cold War, Russia was added for political and symbolic reasons.

Groupthink: The idea that a psychological need on the part of individuals to be accepted and liked by their work colleagues can lead national leaders and especially their advisors to make serious errors of analysis and judgment in the midst of a foreign policy crisis.

Hegemonic war: A war the outcome of which determines which states will have predominant influence in the international system in the coming years or even decades.

Hegemony: The dominance of one state over other states. Many scholars believe that a hegemonic international system is most prone to peace.

Human development: A process of enlarging people's choices and giving them a means to lead lives that they value. Measurements of human development include such factors as life expectancy, income, and education.

Idealism: The notion that ideas matter in international relations.

Imperialism: A state strategy in which one country conquers foreign lands to turn them into colonies.

Import quotas: Government-imposed numerical limits on how much of a particular good or service may be imported during some period of time, usually one year. Import quotas are a form of **non-tariff barrier (NTB)**.

Import-substituting industrialization (ISI): A national development strategy that seeks to minimize international economic linkages in favor of focusing on domestic production. High tariffs and other similar measures encourage the local economy to forego imported goods in favor of goods produced locally by **national champions**.

Incentives: Rewards of some form offered by one state to another designed to influence the foreign policy of the recipient. Incentives are a form of persuasion.

Individual level of analysis: A level of analysis focusing on the impact of individual decision makers (like presidents and their main advisors) on international relations and foreign policy.

Infant-industry protection: A policy in which imports of a certain type of good are restricted (in theory temporarily) to allow for the development of the capacity to produce that good domestically.

Inflationary expectations: The belief on the part of individuals, firms, unions, and other economic agents that price increases are always just around the corner.

Institutional constraints: The constitutional or customary checks within a country that impede, slow, or limit the capacity of a leader unilaterally to undertake some action.

Inter-communal wars: A war in which members of different religious communities in a country become embroiled in large-scale organized violence.

Intercontinental ballistic missile (ICBM): Missile that in under an hour can travel thousands of miles through outer space and release multiple nuclear warheads, each carrying a payload of several hundred kilotons and independently guided to explode within several hundred feet of their respective targets.

Interest: Some condition of the world sufficiently important that a state is willing to pay meaningful costs to attain or maintain it.

Interest group: Individuals or organizations that share a common set of political concerns and band together in an association to persuade leaders and the public to pursue, support, or accept policies that are in accord with the preferences of the association.

Intergovernmental Panel on Climate Change (IPCC): A panel established by the UN in 1988 that studies climate change and informs the world of its effects.

Internal balancing: The process by which states muster their own power to balance rival states by mobilizing their economy and increasing their defense capabilities.

Internal war: Any war within a state, contrasted with war between two or more states.

International bank loans: A kind of international private capital flow in which banks in one country supply loans to individuals in another country.

International bonds: A kind of international private capital flow in which individuals or firms in one country buy bonds originating in another country.

International commodity agreement: An agreement, generally sought by developing countries exporting a particular commodity, on the supply and price of that commodity. The goal is not to maximize prices but rather to establish an acceptable, consistent price that the developing country can rely on.

International commodity cartels: Groupings of developing-country governments that try to control the supply of a raw material or agricultural product on world markets in order to drive up prices and maximize revenues.

International customary law: The accumulation of principles and norms that states have put forward over the centuries and which have come to be widely seen as legitimate and authoritative, enshrining basic ideas about international organization and the standing of states and reflecting basic principles such as sovereignty, recognition, freedom of the seas, international responsibility, and self-defense.

International financial flows: The movement of capital – sometimes in the form of actual cash, but usually as a result of electronic transfers – from private or governmental individuals or organizations inside one country to private or governmental individuals or organizations inside another country. These flows consist of both **private** and **official financial flows.**

International governmental organizations (IGOs): Organizations that states join to further their political or economic interests.

International law: The body of rules, norms, and standards that states have crafted over time that give those states and other actors rights and obligations in their interactions with one another.

International level of analysis: A level of analysis focusing on the international system

International Monetary Fund (IMF): An international institution created in 1946 to facilitate and reinforce the exchange-rate system created in the aftermath of World War II. The IMF remains one of the world's most important international economic institutions.

International order: The method by which the world's states organize themselves such that state leaders can develop somewhat stable expectations about the behavior of other states. War, peace, cooperation, and international institutions like the UN are all aspects of international order.

International Political Economy (IPE): The subfield of international relations that seeks to understand how politics and economics interact and shape one another in the international domain.

International portfolio investments: A type of international private capital flow in which an investor in one country buys shares (but not enough to have any management say) in a firm located in another country.

International relations: The field concerned with the political, economic, social, and cultural relations between two countries or among many countries, and those relations involving other important actors such as multinational corporations or international organizations.

International system: States and non-state actors, taken collectively, co-existing and interacting at some point in history.

International Trade Organization (ITO): An ambitious scheme for global trade management proposed in 1947. The ITO eventually failed because the United States refused to support it, and was largely replaced by the less ambitious **GATT**.

Internationalism: A strategy in which a state is fully engaged with other states through institutionalized arrangements directed at maintaining world security and promoting global economic prosperity.

Internationalization of civil war: The process by which, during a civil war, one or more foreign states intervenes and supports one or another of the warring sides, possibly by introducing combat forces, but does not take over the bulk of the fighting.

Interstate war: When two or more national governments direct military forces against each other in organized, sustained, and oftentimes deadly clashes.

Intra-firm trade: The cross-country movement of different components that are put together at one or more final assembly plants in one or more countries.

Invisible hand: A term coined by Adam Smith to describe the uncoordinated behavior of individuals and firms acting in their own selfish interest in the marketplace.

Iron Curtain: A term coined by British leader Winston Churchill to capture the profound political and human divisions separating the western and eastern parts of Europe.

Iron Rice Bowl: A guarantee from the government of Communist China of job security and access to basic necessities for Chinese citizens.

Isolationism: A strategy in which a state avoids engaging with other states through any sort of international institutions or agreements and focuses solely on itself and its domestic politics.

Janjaweed: Local Arab militias in Sudan allied with the central government in Khartoum against the Sudanese Liberation Movement/Army and the Justice and Equality Movement in the Sudanese civil war.

Kellogg-Briand Pact: A 1928 international pact outlawing war, authored by US Secretary of State Frank Kellogg and French Foreign Minister Aristide Briande.

Kyoto Protocol: A multilateral agreement negotiated in 1997 to reduce the total emissions of signing states. The Protocol came into effect in 2005 but was ultimately unsuccessful in curbing emissions.

League of Nations: An international body established by the Treaty of Versailles at the end of World War I and designed to provide states with an ongoing international legal and institutional framework to solve their disputes and avoid war.

Legitimacy: A sense of rightness and acceptance of a state's authority by other states.

Levels of analysis: Different ways of looking for answers to questions in international relations, generally grouped into the individual, state, and international levels.

Limited war: Smaller war in which major powers avoid fighting each other directly, contrasted with **general** or **major war**.

Lobbying: Meeting and speaking with members of legislatures and officials in executive departments in an attempt to influence policy. Interest groups often engage in lobbying.

Locarno Accords: In a step toward European political reconciliation after World War I, Germany accepted its borders with France and Belgium, Britain and Italy promised to guarantee Germany's compliance with those commitments, and

Germany promised to resolve border disputes with Poland and Czechoslovakia via arbitration rather than force.

Long Telegram: Written by US diplomat George Kennan from Moscow in 1946, the Long Telegram argued that the Soviet Union could not be treated as a cooperative partner.

Lootable wealth: Natural resources that can be readily acquired, transported, and sold for cash. In some countries, **greed** and lootable wealth combine to make internal conflict more likely.

Major war: A war that involves many or all of the most powerful states in a particular historical era. Synonymous with **general war**.

Manhattan Project: The secret project that brought together expert scientists to build a super weapon, culminating in the creation of the first atomic bomb. The Manhattan Project was begun by the United States around the time it entered World War II.

Marine Mammal Preservation Act (MMPA): A US law passed in 1972 which set limits on the number of dolphins that US tuna fleets could kill annually as a result of harvesting tuna. The law proved ineffective as implementation was weak and international parties were not answerable to US law.

Marshall Plan: A plan developed by Secretary of State George Marshall to counteract Soviet influence in Europe by providing economic aid to help European nations rebuild after World War II.

Meiji Restoration: The leaders of a modernizing element of the Japanese nobility who, beginning with the rise of Emperor Meiji in 1868, set Japan on a course of selective adaptation of Western science, education, and industrial technology for the purposes of strengthening Japan economically and militarily.

Mercantilism: A doctrine that states that military power is the central goal of states, such power rests on financial wealth, and the financial wealth of the world is a fixed quantity. Thus, the best way to gain wealth and thereby power is to pursue export surpluses, often through imperialism.

Mercosur: A free trade agreement (the 'common market of the south' or Mercado Común del Sur) formed in 1991 between Argentina, Brazil, Paraguay, and Uruguay; Chile and Bolivia were added later in the decade.

Militarized interstate dispute: An instance in which a state threatens to use force against another state, mobilizes or moves military forces against the other in a threatening manner, or two states engage in military clashes at a level of severity below full-scale war.

Military force: A form of coercive diplomacy in which a state actively uses its military to influence another state's foreign policy.

Military-industrial complex: The combination of a large military bureaucracy and a powerful network of defense industry firms, united to obtain a disproportionate and overly powerful influence over national security policy (generally applied to the United States).

Millennium Development Goals (MDGs): A series of goals agreed upon by world leaders at the UN in September 2000, include cutting extreme poverty by one-half, achieving universal primary education and gender equality at all levels of education, reducing the mortality rate of children under five and new mothers by two-thirds, and cutting the incidence of AIDs/HIV, malaria, tuberculosis, and other diseases.

Mode of production: The basic organization of the economy – the way in which people relate to one another and to the material world

Modernization: The idea that mankind is constantly inventing, innovating, improving, and creating, and that process itself.

Montreal Protocol on Substances that Deplete the Ozone Layer: An international agreement passed in 1987 that has successfully combatted the depletion of the ozone layer by banning **CFCs**. Ozone layers are expected to return to normal by 2050.

Moral hazard: When an individual or some other actor believes they can take very great risks because, if things go badly, someone else will pay for the consequences of the risky behavior. Some accuse the **IMF** of encouraging moral hazard.

Multilateral diplomacy: The process by which representatives of more than two governments meet and discuss matters of common concern.

Multinational enterprise (MNE): A firm that has its headquarters in one country and ongoing business operations in one or (more typically) several other countries.

Munich Analogy: A reference, sometimes invoked by political leaders, to the 1938 transfer of a part of Czechoslovakia to Nazi Germany by Western European democratic leaders. It is generally invoked as a criticism of policy or strategy that resembles appeasement.

Mutual Assured Destruction (MAD): (1) A situation in which two adversaries each possess **assured destruction** capability, meaning that a nuclear conflict would likely inflict **unacceptable damage** on both countries. (2) A theory favored by many Cold War policymakers. This theory argues that a state should want **second-strike capability** but not **first-strike capability**.

Nation: Collections of people who share a common culture, history, or language.

National champion: In a state pursuing a strategy of **ISI**, firms the government believe could do the best job of producing the substituted industrial goods.

National interest: An interest of a country as a whole.

National leaders: Individuals who hold executive offices as a result of which they are entitled to make foreign policy and military decisions on behalf of their countries.

National treatment: A clause in the EEC that allows American-based companies operating within EEC member countries to be treated legally as the same as European companies.

Nationalism: A term that describes an intense political identity a people share, or a sense of collective fate as a political community.

Nation-state: A political unit inhabited by people sharing common culture, history, or language.

Nazi–Soviet Non-Aggression Pact: A pact signed between Nazi Germany and Soviet Russia in 1939 in which the two countries agreed not to attack each other and to jointly attack Poland, dividing the country between them. The pact came as a blow to Britain and France, who had sought to enlist the Soviet Union as an ally against Germany.

Non-Aligned Movement: A movement founded in 1955 to create a pathway by which member states could remain aloof from the confrontations of the Cold War. The NAM now includes over 100 countries, representing over one-half of the world's population.

Non-state actor: Actors others than states that operate within or across state borders with important consequences for international relations.

Non-tariff barrier (NTB): Policies, such as anti-dumping duties, import quotas, or controlled government procurement, by which a state can control imports and import prices without imposing tariffs.

Normative change: The idea that as global learning and international socialization occur, ideas about what is or is not acceptable or 'normal' change. As normative change occurs, it can impact international relations.

Normative constraints: The beliefs, values, and attitudes that inform and shape the behavior of leaders.

North American Free Trade Agreement (NAFTA): A free trade agreement among the United States, Canada, and Mexico, signed in the early 1990s.

North Atlantic Treaty Organization (NATO): A defense pact formed in 1949 between the US, Britain, and several other western European states. It has since expanded and is still very active today.

Nuclear club: The group of states believed to possess nuclear weapons.

Nuclear freeze: A plan that would stop an arms race in its place by simply preventing two adversaries from developing or deploying any new warheads or delivery systems.

Nuclear trip wire: The practice of placing one country's military forces within the borders of an allied country to assure that, if the ally is attacked, the former country will become directly involved in the conflict and thus be more likely to maintain its commitment to respond to the attack with nuclear weapons if necessary. This practice enhances the credibility of **extended deterrence**.

Nuclear Utilization Theory (NUTS): Contrary to **MAD** proponents, many Cold War policy makers followed this strategy, which argues that the United States should do everything it can to be prepared to fight a nuclear war. Then, in the case of a Soviet strike, the US would be prepared to respond with full force *and* protect its civilians.

Nuclear winter: A situation, feared by many scientists in the 1980s, in which the smoke and soot resulting from numerous nuclear explosions blocked out the sunlight from the earth's surface for extended periods of time.

Objective: A state's goal in IR, generally the attainment or maintenance of some interest.

Official Development Assistance (ODA): The provision by a donor government to a developing country of grants or loans with highly favorable repayment terms (for example, 50 years to repay, at 1 percent interest).

Official financial flows: International financial flows that originate with governmental entities.

Oil curse: Over-reliance on the proceeds from oil sales in some countries of the Middle East and Latin America has been associated with autocratic rule, large gaps in the distribution of income and wealth, and a failure to move beyond oil to a more diversified set of economic activities. Thus, developing countries that rely on the export of natural resources must be wary of being trapped by this 'curse.'

OPEC (Organization of Petroleum Exporting Countries): A cartel of the world's oil-producing states. By working together to control oil supply and prices, OPEC can wield considerable political clout in the international system.

Opium Wars: Two wars, fought in 1839–42 and 1856–60, in which the British defeated the Chinese. The result was the opening of China to British (and eventually American) trading communities and the weakening of China as a world power.

Opportunity cost: The cost of producing more of a certain good in foregone production of another good. Opportunity costs are crucial in considering comparative advantage and the possibility for mutual gains from trade.

Peace movements: Popular movements by a state's citizens protesting wars and pushing for peace.

Peaceful change: The problem of how the international system copes with the relative transition among rising and declining great powers.

Peace of Westphalia of 1648: The treaty that ended the Thirty Years War. The treaty divided Europe into sovereign states independent of higher authorities, giving rise to the state system that characterizes the international order today.

Peacekeeping: UN operations in which UN-sponsored troops are deployed in countries in the aftermath of war or civil violence to keep the warring groups apart and enforce the peace settlement.

Peacemaking: UN action before war breaks out designed to prevent two states from going to war with each other by brokering peaceful settlements. Contrasts with **peacekeeping**, which occurs in the aftermath of war.

Perestroika: The Russian name for Mikhail Gorbachev's plan to reform and restructure the Soviet economic system during the 1980s.

Pirates: Non-state gangs who commit robbery or criminal violence on the high seas.

Plutonium: Along with **uranium**, one of the two materials that can be used to create a nuclear weapon. Rarely found in nature, plutonium is found as a byproduct when energy is generated by a nuclear power plant, and must then be extracted and reprocessed to become weapons grade.

Policy instrument: A tool used by a state's government to attain its interests. Policy instruments come in many forms, divided into **persuasive** and **coercive** forms.

Pollution haven: Countries that have low standards or lax enforcement of their environmental rules and regulations, which may attract foreign companies.

Portfolio investment: One sort of investment transaction involving multiple currencies in which residents in one country – individuals, mutual funds acting on behalf of individuals, or firms acting on their own – may purchase foreign securities such as bonds, or purchase equities of foreign firms in amounts that do not confer managerial control.

Positive illusions: The idea that what we think we can accomplish is often greater than what we would expect to achieve if we had a truly accurate picture of our capabilities.

Post-modern world: States that have given up their sovereignty in favor of larger, civilian-led cooperative unions (such as the EU). The post-modern world is one zone in a potential model of global fracture.

Poverty trap: When a country is so poor that most of its national resources must be used to satisfy the immediate day-to-day needs of the population, with insufficient resources left for savings or investment.

Power balancing: Efforts by states to protect themselves in a dangerous world by arraying power against power, consisting of both **internal balancing** and **external balancing**.

Power transitions: When the relative power of two (or more) states changes, often due to technological innovations and uneven economic growth.

Pre-modern world: A haven of lawlessness where states have either failed completely or cannot wield authority over sub-national actors who control territory, command the allegiance of parts of the population, and may even control their own private or local armies. The pre-modern world is one zone in a potential model of global fracture.

Price inflation: A situation in which too much money is chasing too few goods, pushing up prices of goods and services.

Prisoner's dilemma: A helpful analytical device from game theory used to model certain instances of state behavior. For a discussion of the prisoner's dilemma, see Chapter 5.

Private financial flows: International financial flows that originate with non-governmental entities, such as individuals, private charities, or private firms such as banks or multinational corporations.

Private information problem: The tendency of states to overstate their resolve and capabilities during a diplomatic or military crisis because there is no international authority to force states to reveal their true preferences, intentions, and capabilities. This tendency can make a diplomatic solution more difficult to obtain and war more likely.

Privateers: Privately owned ships hired by European governments, primarily in the seventeenth century, to attack and harass Spanish ships in the Caribbean. In addition to taking half of the spoils, European governments benefited from not having to build larger navies to deal with Spanish dominance.

Privatization of war: The idea that the states no longer have a monopoly on the effective use of violence. As technology advances, private parties have greater and greater capacities to wage war and engage in violence.

Production possibilities frontier (PPF): A graphical representation of the different combinations of goods that a country may produce during some period of time with the resources it has in its possession.

Propaganda: The selective use of information, and at times misinformation, in order to advance a state's interests.

Protectionism: Any of a number of policies in which a country puts restrictions on incoming goods in an effort to protect the domestic economy.

Proxy wars: Military conflicts of the Cold War in which the US and USSR never directly engaged each other, but instead backed opposing sides of smaller conflicts in an effort to gain influence throughout the world.

Purchasing power parity (PPP): A measure economists use to compare the value of a similar basket of goods across countries with different living standards and exchange rates.

Race to the bottom: A situation in which two or more countries put into place progressively lower policy rules and standards regarding the environment and worker rights out of a fear of losing, and perhaps out of greed for attracting, foreign investments from multinational enterprises.

Rally 'round the flag effect: A commonly observed boost in the popularity of a leader due to external conflicts or war.

Regional blocs: Groups of smaller countries dominated by great powers, put in place by those great powers to help their domestic economies in the face of the Great Depression.

Reinsurance Treaty: A secret 1887 treaty between Germany and Russia in which the two nations promised not to be dragged into war against each other by their respective allies, Austria and France.

Relations of production: The system by which the people in a productive system are related, or the relations between those people. According to Marxism, these relations are shaped by the mode of production. In a capitalist industrial mode, the relations of production will be characterized by class conflict.

Relative gains: (1)The gains a state makes *relative* to other states, as opposed to **absolute gains**, which are simply the total materials gains made by a state, relative gains focus on the gains one state makes compared to a rival. Realists emphasize the importance of relative gains. (2) An important element of economic nationalism, relative gains is the idea that some gain more than others in economic interactions, and those who gain less lose out, even if they have positive absolute gains.

Responsibility to Protect: An international norm that says that if a particular state is inflicting harm or violence on its own citizens or if it is unable to protect its own citizens from harm or violence, the international community has the right – indeed the obligation – to act.

Revolution: According to Marxism, in any instance of class conflict a breakpoint is eventually reached when the workers take control from the capitalist owners. Revolution is the dominant mode of political change in the Marxist school.

Rhineland Crisis: In March 1936, in clear violation of the Versailles settlement, Hitler ordered troops to reoccupy the Rhineland. Britain and France consulted and decided to do nothing, allowing Hitler to continue to bully Europe.

Ruhr Crisis: When Germany failed to meet its reparations payments in 1923, France occupied Germany's Ruhr valley. Germans replied with work stoppages, the German government paid its workers simply by printing more paper money, hyperinflation ensued.

Rum Triangle: A trans-Atlantic trading triangle active in the seventeenth and eighteenth centuries between Europe, West Africa, and the Americas. The Rum Triangle was the result of European imperialism, and the exploitation of West African and Native American populations by the imperialists was catastrophic to those populations (and highly beneficial to the imperialists).

Schlieffen Plan: A German military plan believed by the Germans to be foolproof in which German forces stand on the defense against Russian forces, undertake a massive sweep through Belgium and France and, after outflanking and destroying French forces, then turn east and destroy the Russian army. The plan was not foolproof; hubris about the ease of military victory was a major cause of World War 1.

Scramble for Africa: The carving up of Africa by colonial powers after 1870.

Secessionist civil war: A civil war in which the rebel group seeks to bring about the breaking away of a part of the territory of a country to form a new, separate state.

Second-strike capability: The ability and will to inflict unacceptable damage on an adversary – even after the adversary hits first with its best nuclear attack. Also known as **assured destruction**.

Security dilemma: A security dilemma exists between states when one state seeks to ensure its survivability in the international system by acquiring military power but, in doing so, triggers insecurity in another state, leading it to try to protect itself by acquiring military power – thus making both states less secure than when they started.

Self-determination: The idea that every people should determine and manage their own political systems. Self-determination was a popular idea among colonized people fighting for independence and decolonization.

Sensitivity: A state is sensitive to another state's actions if those actions can temporarily hamper a state until it finds a replacement for the good or service from another location.

Shanghai Cooperation Organization (SCO): An agreement among Russia, China, and the central Asian states of Uzbekistan, Tajikistan, Kazakhstan, and Kyrgyzstan formed in 2001 to enhance the security of member states against threats of terrorism and ethnic conflict.

Six-Party Talks: Diplomatic talks between North Korea, South Korea, the United States, China, Russia, and Japan intended to convince North Korea to suspend its nuclear program in exchange for normalized relations with the rest of the world.

Smoot–Hawley Tariff: A 1930 US law that raised tariffs to high levels in an attempt to protect the US economy. The act had disastrous consequences and contributed to the Great Depression in the United States, and globally.

Socioeconomic classes: Groupings of peoples based on their relationship to the economy.

Soft balancing: Steps to constrain or hobble a great power that fall well short of the significant mobilization of military power in opposition to that power or the formation of security alliances united against the power.

Sovereignty: The effective and recognized capacity to govern residents within a given territory and an ability to establish relationships with governments that control other states.

Sphere of influence: A geographic-political space, consisting of one or more countries, whose foreign and domestic policies and political institutions are greatly influenced by an external power.

Stabilization program: Essentially a contract between the **IMF** and a country receiving an emergency short-term loan stipulating what the country will do to ensure that its short-term foreign exchange shortfall does not become permanent.

State level of analysis: A level of analysis focusing on the particular political or economic characteristics of countries or states.

State system: A group of competing states

State: A political entity with two key features: a piece of territory with reasonably well-defined borders, and political authorities who enjoy **sovereignty.**

State-owned enterprises (SOEs): Companies owned directly by the government of a state. These are generally found in **authoritarian capitalist models**.

Strategic culture: Strategic culture refers to assumptions about the nature of the global system – for example, which states are friends and enemies – and strategies of action that are shared by government elites.

Strategy: The overarching connection of means to an end for a state. A strategy aims at a policy objective, and outlines what policy instruments will be used to attain that objective.

Submarine-Launched Ballistic Missile (SLBM): Missile that can produce much the same effect as an **intercontinental ballistic missile (ICBM)** from a platform deep beneath the ocean's surface.

Superpowers: Especially powerful states with disproportionate influence in an international system.

Supply curve: A curve specifying how much of a good producers are willing to offer at different prices. Along with **demand curves**, supply curves can show the likely price of goods, including currencies, in international markets.

Tariff: A tax collected by the government on goods coming into the country.

Terms of trade: The rate at which goods will be exchanged between two states.

Theory: A group of ideas intended to explain some empirical phenomenon.

Thermal effect: The secondary effect of a nuclear explosion, in which the heat waves from the explosion can cause third-degree burns up to five miles from the detonation site.

Thermonuclear bomb: A type of nuclear weapon, even more powerful than a conventional nuclear weapon, that relies on the power of a contained fission explosion to trigger the fusing of hydrogen particles, a process that yields even greater amounts of destructive energy than a fission reaction alone. Also known as a **fusion** bomb.

Third World: Poorer states, weaker than super powers or mid-level powers, largely in Africa, Asia, and Latin America. During the Cold War, the US and USSR competed for influence in the Third World to avoid a domino effect of poorer states falling one by one to the other side.

Tied aid: A practice in which donor governments require that the funds they give to a recipient country must be used to purchase goods and services provided by firms from the donor country.

Total war: War in which belligerent states mobilize all resources and target civilians as part of their war strategy.

Tragedy of the commons: A situation in which individual actors acting in their own rational self-interest combine to create a situation catastrophic to all of the individuals.

Transnational business: Businesses that operate across state lines. This tendency enriches capitalists and impoverishes workers.

Transnationalism: The tendency of groups within countries to build cooperative associations with groups in other countries.

Triple Alliance: A military alliance finalized in 1882 between Germany, Austria-Hungary, and Italy.

Triple Entente: A military alliance finalized in 1907 between France, Britain, and Russia, forming the other pole (countering the Triple Alliance) that divided early-twentieth century Europe.

Treaty: A formal agreement between two or more states designed to settle a dispute or set down guidelines for future action.

Truman Doctrine: The declaration by Harry Truman that US assistance would be given to 'free peoples everywhere facing external aggression or internal subversion.' Truman declared this pledge in response to perceived Soviet designs on Greece and Turkey.

UN Conference on Trade and Development (UNCTAD): Formed in 1964, UNCTAD is a body that aims to highlight the special problems of developing countries in the world economy.

US–Canada Air Quality Agreement: A 1991 agreement between the US and Canada designed to curb the negative effects of acid rain between the countries.

Unacceptable damage: The level of damage that a state is absolutely unwilling to sustain. During the Cold War, a nuclear conflict was held off by each adversary's knowledge that a nuclear retaliation from the other state would likely cause unacceptable damage.

Unipolarity: In an international system, the characteristic of being driven by the existence of a single especially powerful state wielding disproportionate power.

Uranium: Along with **plutonium**, one of two materials that can be used to create a nuclear weapon. Unlike plutonium, uranium can be found in nature, but is not suitable in that form (U-238) for nuclear weapon use. It needs to be *highly enriched* in a sophisticated technical facility to produce the concentrated uranium (U-235) that can sustain a chain reaction.

Utility: Well-being attained by an individual through the consumption of goods and services. That individuals seeks and attain utility through financial transactions is a critical assumption for economists.

Voluntary export restraint (VER): A restraint on exported goods that a country agrees to, technically 'voluntarily' but likely as a result of pressure from a trading partner.

Vulnerability: A state is vulnerable to another state's actions if it is unable to compensate effectively for losses caused by the other state's actions.

War lords: Private authority figures who control their own local armies or militias.

Warsaw Pact: An alliance between the Soviet Union and several mid-level powers in Europe during the Cold War. The Warsaw Pact formed a Soviet sphere of influence in much the same way that NATO formed an American one.

Washington Consensus: A group of controversial US-backed policies (smaller state sectors, privatized markets, and liberalized trade and financial sectors) set forth by the IMF as the necessary path to prosperity from the 1980s until the Great Recession of 2008, when the Consensus began to be widely questioned.

Weak states: States with functioning central governments but only weak control over their territory and borders.

Weimar Republic: Republic formed by democratically elected German delegates in the aftermath of World War I to replace the old imperial system.

Westphalian state system: A state system in which each state is sovereign, with no higher authority, that has characterized the international system since 1648.

Worker productivity: The amount of output any worker can produce in a fixed period of time.

World Bank: The International Bank for Reconstruction and Development. Initially created to provide loans to countries to help them with economic recovery from World War II, today the World Bank finances and manages projects – for example, the construction of a dam, the development of a communications grid, the building of highways – to foster the economic growth of developing countries.

World Trade Organization (WTO): The successor to the **GATT**. The great majority of the world's countries are WTO members, and the WTO contains a more developed mechanism for resolving trade disputes among countries than was available under the GATT.

Zone of peace: The number of democratic countries and the geographic space they possess within which states do not want to use military force or believe it will be used against them, in keeping with the **Democratic Peace Theory**.

References

Acemoglu, Daron and James Robinson (2012) *Why Nations Fail: The Origins of Power, Prosperity, and Poverty.* New York: Crown Business.

Acemoglu, Daron, Simon Johnson, and James Robinson (2002) 'Reversal of Fortune: Geography and Institutions in the Making of the Modern World Income Distribution,' *Quarterly Journal of Economics* 117 (4): 1231–94.

Acheson, Dean (1945) 'Bretton Woods: A Monetary Basis for Trade,' Address before Economic Club of New York, April 16.

Allison, Graham (1971) *Essence of Decision.* Boston: Little, Brown.

Allison, Graham (2004) *Nuclear Terrorism: The Ultimate Preventable Catastrophe.* New York: Times Books.

Allison, Graham and Philip Zelikow (1999) *Essence of Decision: Explaining the Cuban Missile Crisis,* Second Edition. New York: Longman.

Amery, Hussein (1997) 'Water Security as a Factor in Arab-Israeli Wars and Emerging Peace,' *Studies in Conflict & Terrorism* 20 (1): 95–104.

Anderson, Perry (1962) 'Portugal and the End of Ultra-Colonialism 2,' *New Left Review* 1 (12): 88–123.

Andresen, Steinar (2002) 'The International Whaling Commission (IWC): More Failure than Success.' In Edward L. Miles, Arild Underdal, Steinar Andresen, Jorgen Wettestad, Jon Skjaerseth, and Elaine Carlin (eds) *Environmental Regime Effectiveness: Confronting Theory with Evidence.* Cambridge: MIT Press, pp. 379–403.

Art, Robert J. and Patrick Cronin (eds) (2003) *The United States and Coercive Diplomacy.* Washington, DC: United States Institute of Peace.

Baggs, Jen (2009) 'International Trade in Hazardous Waste,' *Review of International Economics,* 17 (1): 1–16.

Baker III, James A. (1995) *The Politics of Diplomacy: Revolution, War, & Peace, 1989-1992,* p. 350. New York: Putnam.

Baldwin, David (ed.) (1993) *Neorealism and Neoliberalism: The Contemporary Debate.* New York: Columbia University Press.

Barkin, J. and George E. Shambaugh (1999) 'Hypotheses on the International Politics of Common Pool Resources.' In Barkin and Shambaugh (eds) *Anarchy and the Environment: The International Relations of Common Pool Resources.* Albany: SUNY Press, pp. 1–21.

BBC News (2013) 'Timeline: Seige of Srebrenica,' accessed at http://www.bbc.co.uk/news/have_your_say/.

Bell, P.M. H. (2007) *The Origins of the Second World War in Europe.* Third Edition, Harlow: Pearson.

Berinsky, Adam J. and Donald R. Kinder (2006) 'Making Sense of Issues Through Media Frames: Understanding the Kosovo Crisis,' *Journal of Politics* 68: 640–56.

Betsill, Michele and Elisabeth Corell (2001) 'NGO Infuence in International Environmental Negotiations: A Framework for Analysis,' *Global Environmental Politics* 1 (4): 65–85.

Bevin, Ernest (1948) Speech before House of Commons, col. 407–8, January 22.

Black, Jeremy (2010) *A History of Diplomacy,* pp. 17, 19. London: Reaktion Books.

Blainey, Geoffrey (1988) *The Causes of War*, Third Edition. New York: Free Press.

Blanchard, Jean Marc F. and Norrin M. Ripsman (1996/97), 'Commercial Liberalism Under Fire: Evidence from 1914 and 1936,' *Security Studies* 6 (2): 4–50.

Borrell, Brendan (2009) 'Biofuel Showdown: Should Domestic Ethanol Producers Pay for Deforestation Abroad?' *Scientific American.com*, available at http://www.scientificamerican.com/article.cfm?id=biofuel-showdown.

Bradsher, Keith (2010) 'Amid Tension, China Blocks Vital Exports to Japan,' *New York Times*, September 23.

Braithwaite, Alex (2010) 'Resisting Infection: How State Capacity Conditions Conflict Contagion,' *Journal of Peace Research* 47 (3): 311–19.

Bremmer, Ian (2010) *The End of the Free Market: Who Wins the War Between States and Corporations?* New York: Viking Press.

Brodie, Bernard (1946) *The Absolute Weapon.* New York: Harcourt Brace.

Brooks, Stephen G. (2005) *Producing Security: Multinational Corporations, Globalization, and the Changing Calculus of Conflict.* Princeton: Princeton University Press.

Brown, Chris (2002) *Sovereignty, Rights and Justice: International Political Theory Today*, p. 35. Cambridge: Polity Press.

Brzezinski, Zbigniew (1986) *Game Plan: A Geostrategic Framework for the Conduct of the US-Soviet Contest.* Boston: Atlantic Monthly Press.

Buckley, Chris (2010) 'China Military Paper Spells Out Nuclear Arms Stance.' *Reuters*, April 22, 2010, accessed at www.reuters.com/article/2010/04/22.

Bueno de Mesquita, Bruce, Alastair Smith, Randolph Siverson, and James Morrow (2003) *The Logic of Political Survival.* Cambridge: MIT Press.

Buhaug, Halvard and Kristian Gleditsch (2008) 'Contagion or Confusion? Why Conflicts Cluster in Space,' *International Studies Quarterly* 52 (2): 215–33.

Buhaug, Halvard, Nils Gleditsch and Ole Theisen (2008) 'Implications of Climate Change for Armed Conflict,' prepared for the World Bank Group, available at http://siteresources.worldbank.org/INTRANETSOCIALDEVELOPMENT/Resources/SDCCWorkingPaper_Conflict.pdf.

Bull, Hedley (1977) *The Anarchical Society: A Study of Order in World Politics.* New York: Columbia University Press.

Bull, Hedley and Adam Watson (eds) (1985) *The Expansion of International Society.* Oxford: Oxford University Press.

Burr, William (ed.) (2007) *The Atomic Bomb and the End of World War II: A Collection of Primary Sources.* National Security Archive Electronic Briefing Book No. 162, April 27, 2007, accessed at www.gwu.edu/nsarchive.

Bush, George W. (2003) 'Bush: Leave Iraq within 48 Hours,' March 17, available at http://www.cnn.com/2003/WORLD/meast/03/17/sprj.irq.bush.transcript/.

Bush, George W. (2003) Address before the United Nations General Assembly, September 23, available at http://www.whitehouse.gov/news/releases/2003/09/20030923-4.html.

Bush, President George W. (January 20, 2005) *Second Inaugural Address.*

Bussmann, Margrit (2010) 'Foreign Direct Investment and Militarized International Conflict,' *Journal of Peace Research* 47 (2): 143–53.

Buzan, Barry (2004) *From International to World Society?* Cambridge: Cambridge University Press.

Cali, Basik (2010) *International Law for International Relations.* Oxford: Oxford University Press.

Canadian Broadcasting Company (1969) 'Trudeau's Washington Press Club Speech.' CBC Digital Archives, March 29, 1969.

Caprioli, Mary and Mark Boyer (2001) 'Gender, Violence, and International Crisis,' *Journal of Conflict Resolution* 45 (4): 503–18.

Cardoso, Fernando and Enzo Faletto (1979) *Dependency and Development in Latin America.* Berkeley: University of California Press.

Carr, Edward Hallett (1939) *The Twenty Years' Crisis, 1919–1939: An Introduction to the Study of International Relations.* London: Macmillan.

Cederman , Lars-Erik, Andreas Wimmer, and Brian Min (2010) 'Why Do Ethnic Groups Rebel? New Data and Analysis,' *World Politics* 62 (1): 87–119.

Cheney, Dick (2002) 'Vice President Cheney's Speech to the Veterans of Foreign Wars' (August 26), available at http://www.newamericancentury.org/iraq-082602.htm.

Cheng, Li, (2012) 'Opportunity Lost? Inside China's Leadership Transition,' *Foreign Policy*, November 16, 2012.

Chiozza, Giacomo and Hein Goemans (2011) *Leaders and International Conflict.* Cambridge: Cambridge University Press.

Clark, William (2005) *Petrodollar Warfare: Oil, Iraq, and the Future of the Dollar.* Gabriola Island, Canada: New Society Publishers.

Claude Jr, Inis L. (1956) *From Swords into Ploughshares: The Problems and Process of International Organization.* New York: Random House.

Clemencon, Raymond (2006) 'What Future for the Global Environmental Facility,' *Journal of Environment and Development* 15 (1): 50–74.

Clinton, President Bill (1994) State of the Union Address, January 25.

Colgan, Jeffrey (2013) *Petro-Aggression: When Oil Causes War.* Cambridge: Cambridge University Press.

Collier, Paul (2007) *The Bottom Billion: Why the Poorest Countries Are Failing and What Can be Done About It.* Oxford: Oxford University Press.

Collier, Paul, Anke Hoeffler, and Dominic Rohner (2009) 'Beyond Greed and Grievance: Feasibility and Civil War,' *Oxford Economic Papers* 61 (1):1–27.

Cooley, John (1984) 'The War Over Water,' *Foreign Policy*, 54 (Spring):3–26.

Cooper, Robert (2003) *The Breaking of Nations: Order and Chaos in the 21st Century*. New York: Atlantic Monthly Press.

Cox, Robert and Timothy J. Sinclair (1996) *Approaches to World Order*. Cambridge: Cambridge University Press.

Cox, Robert W. (1987) *Production Power and World Order: Social Forces in the Making of History*. New York: Columbia University Press.

Crowley, Roger (2005) *1453: The Holy War for Constantinople and the Clash of Islam and the West*. New York: Hyperion.

Crowley, Roger (2008) *Empire of the Sea: The Siege of Malta, the Battle of Lepanto, and the Contest for the Center of the World*. New York: Random House.

Dao, James, and Dalia Sussman (2011) 'For Obama, Big Rise in Poll Numbers after Bin Laden Raid.' *New York Times*, May 4.

Dehio, Ludwig (1962) *The Precarious Balance: Four Centuries of the European Power Struggle*. New York: Knopf.

Diamond, Jared (1999) *Guns, Germs, and Steel: The Fates of Human Societies*. New York: W.W. Norton.

Dos Santos, Theotonio (1970) 'The Structure of Dependence,' *American Economic Review* 60 (2): 231–6.

Downes, Alexander (2008) *Targeting Civilians in War*. Ithaca: Cornell University Press.

Doyle, Michael (1997) *Ways of War, Ways of Peace: Realism, Liberalism, Socialism*. New York: Norton.

Doyle, Michael (2011). *Liberal Peace: Selected Essays*. New York: Routledge.

Drezner, Daniel (2009) 'Bad Debts: Assessing China's Financial Influence in Great Power Politics,' *International Security* 34 (2): 7–45.

Dunbabin, John (2008) *The Cold War: The Great Powers and their Allies*, Second Edition. Harlow: Pearson.

Dunne, Timothy (1998) *Inventing International Society: A History of the English School*. New York: Palgrave Macmillan.

Dyson, Freeman (1985) 'On Russians and their Views of Nuclear Strategy.' In Charles Kegley and Eugene Wittkopf *The Nuclear Reader*. New York: St. Martin's Press.

Earle, Edward Mead (1971) 'Adam Smith, Alexander Hamilton, Friedrich List: The Economic Foundations of Military Power.' In Edward Mead Earle, *Makers of Modern Strategy*. Princeton: Princeton University Press.

Easterly, William (2002) *The Elusive Quest for Growth: Economists' Adventures and Misadventures in the Tropics*. Cambridge: MIT Press.

Easterly, William (2006) *The White Man's Burden: Why the West's Efforts to Aid the Rest Have Done So Much Ill and So Little Good*. New York: Penguin.

Easterly, William (2007) 'The Ideology of Development,' *Foreign Policy*, No. 161: 30–35.

Economist, The (2010) 'Democracy's Decline,' January 16.

Economist, The (2012) 'Roiling the Waters: Tensions Rise Between China and Vietnam in the South China Sea.' July 7.

Economist, The (2013) 'Chasing the Chinese Dream,' May 4.

Economy, Elizabeth (2007) 'The Great Leap Backward?' *Foreign Affairs* September–October.

Eichengreen, Barry, and David Leblang (2008) 'Democracy and Globalization,' *Economics and Politics* 20 (3): 289–334.

Eisenhower, Dwight (1961) 'Military-Industrial Complex Speech,' available at http://coursesa.matrix.msu.edu/~hst306/documents/indust.html.

Elshtain, Jean Bethke (1987) *Women and War.* New York: Basic Books.

Englebert, Pierre, Stacy Tarango, and Matthew Carter (2002) 'Dismemberment and Suffocation. A Contribution to the Debate on African Boundaries,' *Comparative Political Studies* 35 (10): 1093–118.

English, Robert (2005) 'The Sociology of New Thinking: Elites, Identity Change and the End of the Cold War,' *Journal of Cold War Studies* 7: 43–80.

Enloe, Cynthia (2000) *Bananas, Beaches, Bases: Making Feminist Sense of International Politics.* Berkeley: University of California Press, updated edition.

Entman, Robert (2004) *Projections of Power: Framing News, Public Opinion, and US Foreign Policy.* Chicago: University of Chicago Press.

Eskeland, Gunnar, and Ann Harrison (2003) 'Moving to Greener Pastures? Multinationals and the Pollution Haven Hypothesis,' *Journal of Development Economics* 70 (1): 1– 23.

Evans, Gareth (2009) *The Responsibility to Protect: Ending Mass Atrocity Crimes Once and For All.* Washington: The Brookings Institution Press.

Evans, Peter (2000) 'Fighting Marginalization with Transnational Networks: Counter-Hegemonic Globalization,' *Contemporary Sociology* 29 (1): 230–41.

E-World (1997) 'Albert Einstein's Letters to Franklin Delano Roosevelt.' Accessed at www.hypertextbook.com/eworld.

Fairbanks, John K. (1992) *China: A New History,* with Merle Goldman, enlarged edition. Cambridge: Harvard University Press.

Fearon, James (1995) 'Rationalist Explanations for War,' *International Organization* 49 (3): 379–414.

Fearon, James, and David Laitin (2003) 'Ethnicity, Insurgency, and Civil War,' *American Political Science Review* 97 (1): 75–90.

Feis, Herbert (1970) *From Trust to Terror: The Onset of the Cold War.* New York: W.W. Norton.

Ferguson, Niall (2004) *Empire: The Rise and Demise of the British World Order and the Lessons for Global Power.* New York: Basic Books.

Ferguson, Niall (2006) *The War of the World: Twentieth Century Conflict and the Descent of the West.* New York: Penguin.

Fiske, Susan and Shelley Taylor (1984) *Social Cognition.* Reading, MA: Addison-Wesley.

Fortna, Virginia Page (2008) *Does Peacekeeping Work? Shaping Belligerents' Choices after Civil War.* Princeton: Princeton University Press.

Frank, Andre (1966) 'The Development of Underdevelopment,' *Monthly* Review 18: 17–31.

Freedman, Lawrence (2004) *Deterrence*. New York: Polity Press.

Freedom House (2008) *Freedom in the World, 2008: The Annual Survey of Political Rights and Civil Liberties*. New York: Rowman & Littlefield.

Friedberg, Aaron (2000) *In the Shadow of the Garrison State: America's Anti-Statism and its Cold War Grand Strategy*. Princeton: Princeton University Press.

Friedberg, Aaron (2011) *A Contest for Supremacy: China, America, and the Struggle for Mastery in Asia*. New York: Norton.

Frieden, Jeffry (2006) *Global Capitalism: Its Fall and Rise in the Twentieth Century*. New York: W.W. Norton.

Friedman, Thomas (1999) *The Lexus and the Olive Tree*. New York: Anchor Books.

Fukuyama, Francis (1992) *The End of History and the Last Man*. New York: Avon Books.

Fukuyama, Francis (1998) 'Women and the Evolution of World Politics,' *Foreign Affairs* 77 (5): 24–40.

Gaddis, John Lewis (2006) *The Cold War: A New History*. New York: Penguin.

Gallagher, Mary (2002) '"Reform and Openness": Why China's Economic Reforms Have Delayed Democracy,' *World Politics* 54 (3): 338–72.

Gartzke, Erik (2007) 'The Capitalist Peace,' *American Journal of Political Science* 51 (1): 166–91.

Gartzke, Erik and Quan Li (2003) 'War, Peace, and the Invisible Hand: Positive Political Externalities of Economic Globalization,' *International Studies Quarterly* 47 (4): 561–86.

Gause, Gregory (2001) 'Iraq and the Gulf War: Decision-Making in Baghdad,' *Columbia International Affairs Online* October 1, 2001.

Gelpi, Christopher, Peter Feaver, and Jason Reifler (2009) *Paying the Human Costs of War: American Public Opinion and Casualties in Military Conflicts*. Princeton: Princeton University Press.

George, Alexander and Robert Keohane (1980) 'The Concept of National Interest: Uses and Limitations.' In Alexander George (ed.) *Presidential Decision-Making in Foreign Policy: The Effective Use of Information and Advice*. Boulder: Westview Press.

German Marshall Fund of the United States (2013) *Transatlantic Trends: Key Findings 2013*.

Gettleman, Jeffrey (2012) 'US Swoops in to Free 2 from Pirates in Somali Raid,' *New York Times*, January 25.

Ghani, Ashraf and Clare Lockhart (2008) *Fixing Failed States: A Framework for Rebuilding a Fractured World*, p. 22. New York: Oxford University Press.

Ghosn, Faten, Glenn Palmer, and Stuart Bremer (2004) 'The MID3 Data Set, 1993–2001: Procedures, Coding Rules, and Description,' *Conflict Management and Peace Science* 21 (2): 133–54.

Gibbon, Edward (1996) *The History of the Decline and Fall of the Roman Empire*. London: Penguin.

Gilbert, Christopher (2004) 'International Commodity Agreements as Internationally Sanctioned Cartels.' In Peter Grossman (ed.), *How Cartels Endure and How They Fail: Studies in Industrial Collusion*. Cheltenham: Edward Elgar, pp. 224–52.

Gill, Stephen (1992) *American Hegemony and the Trilateral Commission.* Cambridge: Cambridge University Press.

Gilpin, Robert G. (1975) *U.S. Power and the Multinational Corporation: The Political Economy of Foreign Direct Investment*, Chapter 1. New York: Basic Books.

Gilpin, Robert G. (1981) *War and Change in World Politics.* Cambridge: Cambridge University Press.

Gilpin, Robert (1987) *The Political Economy of International Relations.* Princeton: Princeton University Press.

Gilpin, Robert (2001) *Global Political Economy: Understanding the International Economic Order.* Princeton: Princeton University Press.

Gleditsch, Nils Petter, Kathryn Furlong, Havard Hegre, Bethany Lacina, and Taylor Owen (2006) 'Conflicts over Shared Rivers: Resource Scarcity or Fuzzy Boundaries?' *Political Geography* 25 (4): 361–82.

GlobalSecurity.org (undated) 'US Casualties in Iraq,' available at http://www.globalsecurity.org/military/ops/iraq_casualties.html.

Goldstein, Avery (2005) *Rising to the Challenge: China's Grand Strategy and International Security.* Stanford: Stanford University Press.

Goldstein, Joshua S. (2001) *War and Gender: How Gender Shapes the War System and Vice Versa*, Chapter 3. New York: Cambridge University Press.

Gorgemans, Andre (2008) 'Addressing Child Labor: An Industry Approach,' posted August 1, 2008 on America.gov and available at http://www.america.gov/st/hr-english/2008/August/20080818091032SrenoD0.390423.html.

Graham, Edward (2000) *Fighting the Wrong Enemy: Antiglobal Activists and Multinational Enterprises.* Washington: Institute for International Economics.

Gray, Colin (1979) '"Nuclear Strategy: The Case for a Theory of Victory,' *International Security* Vol. 4 (Summer).

Guardian (2012) 'German tax collectors volunteer for Greek Duty,' February 26.

Guardian (2013) 'Syria Crisis: David Cameron Still Wants "Robust" Response.' August 30.

Gurr, Ted Robert (1994) 'Peoples Against the State: Ethnopolitical Conflict and the Changing World System,' *International Studies Quarterly* 38.

Gutner, Tamar (2005) 'World Bank Environmental Reform: Revisiting Lessons from Agency Theory,' *International Organization* 59 (3): 773–83.

Haas, Peter (1992) 'Banning Chlorofluorocarbons: Epistemic Community Efforts to Protect Stratospheric Ozone,' *International Organization* 46 (1): 187–224.

Haas, Peter (2004) 'When Does Power Listen to Truth? A Constructivist Approach to the Policy Process,' *Journal of European Public Policy* 11 (4): 569–92.

Haass, Richard (2003) 'Sovereignty: Existing Rights, Evolving Responsibilities,' lecture at Georgetown University, January 14.

Haass, Richard (2008) 'The Age of Nonpolarity: What will Follow US Dominance,' *Foreign Affairs*, May–June.

Haggard, Stephan (1990) *Pathways From the Periphery: The Politics of Growth in the Newly-Industrializing Countries.* Ithaca, NY: Cornell University Press.

Haggard, Stephan (2000) *The Political Economy of the Asian Financial Crisis.* Washington, DC: Institute for International Economics.

Hahn, Juergen (2012) 'Ship Piracy Evolve in East, West Africa,' *Breakbulk Magazine,* May 14. http://www.breakbulk.com/commentary/ship-piracy-evolves-east-west-africa

Halle, Louis (1991) *The Cold War as History.* New York: Harper Perennial.

Hampton, Mary N. (1996) *The Wilsonian Impulse: US Foreign Policy, the Alliance, and the Reunification of Germany.* New York: Praeger Publishers.

Hampton, Mary N.(1995) 'NATO at the Creation: US Foreign Policy, West Germany, and the Wilsonian Impulse,' *Security Studies*, 4 (3): 610–56.

Hardin, Garrett (1968) 'Tragedy of the Commons,' *Science* 162 (3589): 1243–8.

Harmon, Chris (2009) *Zombie Capitalism: Global Crisis and the Return of Marx.* London: Bookmarks.

Harnden, Toby (2011) 'U.S. Secretly Shifts Armed Drones to Fight Terrorists in Pakistan,' *The Telegraph*, July 7.

Hassner, Pierre (1993) 'Beyond Nationalism and Internationalism: Ethnicity and World Order,' in Michael Brown (ed.) *Ethnic Conflict and International Security,* pp. 125–41. Princeton, Princeton University Press.

Helleiner, Eric and Andreas Pickel (eds) (2005) *Economic Nationalism in a Globalizing World.* Ithaca: Cornell University Press.

Henley Visa Restriction Index for 2012. Accessed at http://news.visato.com/visit-visa-2/henley-visa-restriction-index-for-top-100-countries-in-2012/20120905.

Herz, John (1950) 'Idealist Internationalism and the Security Dilemma,' *World Politics* 2 (2): 157–80.

Hirschman, Albert (1980) *National Power and the Structure of Foreign Trade.* Berkeley: University of California Press.

Holsti, Kalevi J. (1991) *Peace and War: Armed Conflicts and International Order, 1648-1989*, p. 25. New York: Cambridge University Press.

Holsti, Ole (1972) *Crisis, Escalation, War.* Montreal: McGill-Queen's.

Holsti, Ole (2004) *Public Opinion and American Foreign Policy.* Ann Arbor: University of Michigan Press.

Homer-Dixon, Thomas (2007) 'Terror in the Forecast,' *New York Times*, April 24, available at http://www.nytimes.com/2007/04/24/opinion/24homer-dixon.html.

Hsu, Spencer (2006) 'Katrina Report Spreads Blame.' *Washington Post,* February 12, 2006.

Hudson, Valerie, Mary Caprioli, Bonnie Ballif-Spanvill, Rose McDermott, and Chad Emmett (2008/2009) 'The Heart of the Matter: the Security of Women and the Security of States,' *International Security* 33 (3): 7–40.

Hufbauer, Gary Clyde, Jeffrey J. Schott, Kimberly Ann Elliott, and Barbara Oegg (2007) *Economic Sanctions Reconsidered,* Third Edition. Washington: Peterson Institute for International Economics.

Hull, Cordell (1938) 'The Outlook for the Trade Agreements Program,' speech delivered before the 25th National Foreign Trade Convention, New York City, November 1, 1938.

Human Security Report (2011) *Human Security Report 2009/10: The Causes of Peace and the Shrinking Costs of War.* New York: Oxford University Press

Hunt, Swanee (2007) 'Let Women Rule,' *Foreign Affairs* 86 (3): 109–20.

Huntington, Samuel (1993) 'The Clash of Civilizations?' *Foreign Affairs* Summer.

Huntington, Samuel (1996) *The Clash of Civilizations and the Remaking of World Order.* New York: Touchstone.

Hurwitz, Jon and Mark Peffley (1987) 'The Means and Ends of Foreign Policy as Determinants of Presidential Support,' *American Journal of Political Science* 31.

Ikenberry, G. John (2001) *After Victory: Institutions, Strategic Restraint, and the Rebuilding of Order After Major War.* Princeton: Princeton University Press.

Ikenberry, G. John (2001) *After Victory: Institutions, Strategic Restraint, and the Rebuilding of Order After Major Wars.* Princeton: Princeton University Press.

Intergovernmental Panel on Climate Change (2007) *Climate Change 2007: Synthesis Report,* available at http://www.ipcc.ch/pdf/assessment-report/ar4/syr/ar4_syr.pdf.

International Monetary Fund (2011) *Articles of Agreement.* Washington: IMF, available at http://www.imf.org/External/Pubs/FT/AA/pdf/aa.pdf.

Iriye, Akira (1987) *The Origins of the Second World War in Asia and the Pacific.* Harlow: Pearson.

Jackson, Patrick Thaddeus (2003), 'Defending the West: Occidentalism and the Formation of NATO,' *The Journal of Political Philosophy* 11 (3): 241.

Jackson, Patrick Thaddeus (2006) *Civilizing the Enemy: German Reconstruction and the Invention of the West.* Ann Arbor: University of Michigan Press.

Janis, Irving (1982) *Groupthink: Psychological Studies of Policy Decisions and Fiascoes.* Boston: Houghton Mifflin Company.

Jentleson, Bruce W. (2010) *American Foreign Policy: The Dynamics of Choice in the 21st Century.* Fourth edition, New York: Norton.

Jervis, Robert (1978) 'Cooperation Under the Security Dilemma,' *World Politics* 30: 167–214.

Jervis, Robert (1984) *The Illogic of American Nuclear Strategy.* Ithaca: Cornell University Press.

Jervis, Robert (1985) 'The Madness beyond MAD.' In Charles Kegley and Eugene Wittkopf, *The Nuclear Reader.* New York: St. Martin's Press.

Jervis, Robert (1988) 'War and Misperception,' *Journal of Interdisciplinary History* 18 (4): 675–700.

Jervis, Robert (1989a) *Pyschology and Deterrence.* Baltimore: Johns Hopkins University Press.

Jervis, Robert (1989b) *The Meaning of the Nuclear Revolution*. Ithaca: Cornell University Press.

Jervis, Robert (2001) 'Was the Cold War a Security Dilemma?' *Journal of Cold War Studies*, 3 (1): 36–60.

Jervis, Robert (2006) 'Understanding Beliefs,' *Political Psychology* 27: 641–63.

Jervis, Robert (2009) 'Unipolarity: A Structural Perspective,' *World Politics* 61 (1).

Johnson, Dominic (2004) *Overconfidence and War: The Havoc and Glory of Positive Illusions*. Cambridge: Harvard University Press.

Johnson, Dominic D.P. (2006) 'Overconfidence in Wargames: Experimental Evidence on Expectations, Aggression, Gender and Testosterone,' *Proceedings of the Royal Society* 273: 2512–20.

Johnson, Dominic, Rose McDermott, Emily Barrett, Jonathan Cowden, Richard Wrangham, Matthew McIntyre, and Stephen Rosen (2006) 'Overconfidence in Wargames: Experimental Evidence on Expectations, Aggression, Gender and Testosterone,' *Proceedings of the Royal Society* 273 (1600): 2513–20.

Johnson, Lyndon Baines (1965) 'Statement by President Johnson at White House News Conference on July 28, 1965: We Will Stand in Viet-Nam,' Department of State *Bulletin*, August 16, available at http://www.mtholyoke.edu/acad/intrel/pentagon4/ps2.htm.

Johnson, Simon and James Kwak (2010) *13 Bankers: The Wall Street Takeover and the Next Financial Crisis*. New York: Pantheon Books.

Johnston, Alastair I. (1995) *Cultural Realism: Strategic Culture and Grand Strategy in Chinese History*. Princeton: Princeton University Press.

Johnston, Alistair Iain (2008) *Social States: China in International Institutions, 1980-2000*. Princeton: Princeton University Press.

Joll, James and Gordon Martel (2007) *The Origins of the First World War*, Third Edition. Harlow: Pearson.

Jones, Eric (2003) *The European Miracle: Environments, Economics, and Geopolitics in the History of Europe and Asia* , Third Edition, Cambridge: Cambridge University Press.

Junhao, Hong (2005) 'The Internet and China's Foreign Policy Making: The Impact of Online Public Opinions as a New Societal Force.' In Yufan, Hao and Su Lin (eds) *Chinese Foreign Policy Making: Societal Forces and Chinese Foreign Policy*. Aldershot: Ashgate Press.

Kaiser, David (2000) *Politics and War: European Conflict from Philip II to Hitler*. Cambridge: Harvard University Press.

Kalyvas, Stathis and Laia Balcells (2010) 'International System and Technologies of Rebellion: How the End of the Cold War Shaped Internal Conflict,' *American Political Science Review* 104 (3): 415–29.

Kalyvas, Stathis and Matthew Kocher (2009) 'The Dynamics of Violence in Vietnam: An Analysis of the Hamlet Evaluation System,' *Journal of Peace Research* 46 (3): 335–55.

Kamen, Henry (2004) *Empire: How Spain Became a World Power, 1492–1763*. New York: Perennial.

Kan, Shirley (2007) *China/Taiwan: Evolution of the 'One China' Policy - Key Statements from Washington, Beijing, and Taipei* (CRS Report for Congress), available at http://www.fas.org/sgp/crs/row/RL30341.pdf.

Kang, David (2010) *East Asia Before the West: Five Centuries of Trade and Tribute*. New York: Columbia University Press.

Kant, Immanuel ([1795] 2009) *Perpetual Peace*. Rockville, MD: Wildside Press.

Kaplan, Robert (2012) *The Revenge of Geography: What the Map Tells Us about Coming Conflicts and the Battle Against Fate*. New York: Random House.

Kaufman, Chaim (1994) 'Out of the Lab and into the Archives: A Method for Testing Psychological Explanations of Political Decision Making,' *International Studies Quarterly* 38 (4): 557–86.

Keck, Margaret E. and Kathryn Sikkink (1998) *Activists Beyond Borders: Advocacy Networks in International Politics*. Ithaca: Cornell University Press.

Keeny, Spurgeon and Wolfgang Panofsky (1981–82) 'Nuclear Weapons in the 1980s: MAD vs. NUTS,' *Foreign Affairs* 60, No. 2 (Winter).

Kegley, Charles and Gregory Raymond (1994) *A Multipolar Peace? Great Power Politics in the Twenty-First Century*. New York: St. Martin's Press.

Kellenberg, Derek (2009) 'An Empirical Investigation of the Pollution Haven Effect with Strategic Environment and Trade Policy,' *Journal of International Economics* 78 (2): 242–55.

Kemp, R. Scott (2012) 'Cyberweapons: Bold Steps in a Digital Darkness?' *Bulletin of the Atomic Scientists*, June 7, 2012, accessed at http:/thebulletin.org/web-edition.

Kennedy, Paul (1987) *The Rise and Fall of the Great Powers*, Chapter 3. New York: Random House.

Keohane, Robert (1984) *After Hegemony*. Princeton: Princeton University Press.

Keohane, Robert (1989) 'International Relations Theory: Contributions of a Feminist Standpoint,' *Millennium – Journal of International Studies*: 245–53.

Keohane, Robert and Joseph Nye (1977) *Power and Interdependence*. Boston: Little, Brown.

Keylor, William (2011) *The Twentieth Century World and Beyond: An International History Since 1900*. Sixth Edition, Oxford: Oxford University Press.

Kindleberger, Charles (1973) *The World in Depression, 1929-1939*. Berkeley: University of California Press.

Kindleberger, Charles P. (1973) *The World in Depression, 1929-1939*. Berkeley: University of California Press, esp. p. 247.

Kirshner, Jon (2007) *Appeasing the Bankers: Financial Caution of the Road to War*. Princeton: Princeton University Press.

Kline, Harvey R. (2003) 'Colombia: Lawlessness, Drug Trafficking, and Carving Up the State,' in Robert I. Rotberg (ed.) *State Failure and State Weakness in a Time of Terror*, pp. 167–9. Washington: Brookings Institution Press.

Klotz, Audie (1995) *Norms in International Relations: The Struggle Against Apartheid*. Ithaca: Cornell University Press.

Knock, Thomas (1995) *To End all Wars: Woodrow Wilson and the Quest for a New World Order* (Princeton: Princeton University Press).

Kohli, Atul (2009) 'Nationalist versus Dependent Capitalist Development: Alternative Pathways of Asia and Latin America in a Globalized World,' *Studies of Comparative International Development*, 44 (4): 386–410.

Kolko, Gabriel, and Joyce Kolko (1972) *The Limits of Power: The World and United States Foreign Policy 1945-1954.* New York: Harper & Row.

Kramer, Roderick (1998) 'Revisiting the Bay of Pigs and Vietnam Decisions 25 Years Later: How Well Has the Groupthink Hypothesis Stood the Test of Time?' *Organizational Behavior and Human Decision Processes* 73 (2/3): 236–71.

Krasner, Stephen D. (1978) *Defending the National Interest: Raw Materials Investments and US Foreign Policy.* Princeton: Princeton University Press.

Krueger, Anne (1975) *The Benefits and Costs of Import Substitution in India: A Microeconomic Study.* Minneapolis: University of Minnesota Press.

Krushelnysky, Askold (2013) 'The End of Ukraine's Balancing Act,' *Foreign Policy,* February 7, 2013.

Kupchan, Charles (2012). *No One's World: The West, the Rising Rest, and the Coming Global Turn.* Oxford: Oxford University Press.

LaFeber, Walter (2006) *America, Russia and the Cold War 1945-2006*, Tenth Edition. New York: McGraw-Hill.

Lasswell, Harold (1941) 'The Garrison State,' *American Journal of Sociology* 46 (4): 455–68.

Layne, Christopher (2006) *The Peace of Illusions: American Grand Strategy from 1940 to the Present.* Ithaca: Cornell University Press.

Leahy, William (1950) *I was There: The Personal Story of the Chief of Staff to Presidents Roosevelt and Truman.* New York: McGraw-Hill.

Lebow, Richard Ned and Thomas Risse-Kappen (eds) (1995), *International Relations Theory and the End of the Cold War.* New York: Columbia University Press.

Lee, Hoon and Sara McLaughlin Mitchell (2012) 'Foreign Direct Investment and Territorial Disputes,' *Journal of Conflict Resolution* 56 (4): 675–703.

Legro, Jeffrey W. (2000) 'Whence American Internationalism,' *International Organization* 54: 253–89.

Leng, Russell (2004) 'Escalation: Competing Perspectives and Empirical Evidence,' *International Studies Review* 6 (4): 51–64.

Leng, Russell (2005) 'Realpolitik and Learning in the India-Pakistan Rivalry.' In T.V. Paul (ed.) *The India-Pakistan Conflict: An Enduring Rivalry*. Cambridge: Cambridge University Press, pp. 103–28.

Lenin, Vladimir (1917) *Imperialism: The Highest Stage of Capitalism.* Russian Republic: Zhizn' i znanie.

Lenin, Vladimir I. (1916) *Imperialism: The Highest Stage of Capitalism.* New York: International Publishers.

Levy, Jack (1988) 'Domestic Politics and War,' *Journal of Interdisciplinary History* 18.

Levy, Jack (1994) 'Learning and Foreign Policy: Sweeping a Conceptual Minefield,' *International Organization* 48: 279–312.

Levy, Jack, and William Thompson (2011) *The Arc of War: Origins, Escalation, and Transformation*. Chicago: University of Chicago Press.

Lewis, Michael (2010) *The Big Short: Inside the Doomsday Machine*. New York: Norton.

Li, Xiaoying and Xiaming Liu (2005) 'Foreign Direct Investment and Economic Growth: An Increasingly Endogenous Relationship,' *World Development* 33 (3): 393–407.

Liberman, Peter (1996) *Does Conquest Pay? The Exploitation of Occupied Societies*. Princeton: Princeton University Press.

Lieber, Keir and Daryl Press (2006) 'The Rise of US Nuclear Primacy,' *Foreign Affairs* (March–April).

Lipson, Charles (2003) *Reliable Partners: How Democracies Have Made a Separate Peace*. Princeton: Princeton University Press.

Lobell, Steven (2007) 'The Second Face of Security: Britain's "Smart" Appeasement Policy Towards Japan and Germany,' *International Relations of the Asia-Pacific*, 7 (1): 73–98.

Locke, Richard, Matthew Amengual, and Akshay Mangla (2009) 'Virtue out of Necessity? Compliance, Commitment, and the Improvement of Labor Conditions in Global Supply Chains,' *Politics & Society* 37 (3): 319–51.

Maddison, Angus (2006) *The World Economy: A Millennial Perspective*. Paris: Organisation for Economic Co-operation and Development.

Malinak, Daniel (2008) 'Women in International Relations,' *Politics & Gender* 4 (1): 122.

Mansfield, Edward and Jack Snyder (1995) 'Democratization and War,' *Foreign Affairs* May–June.

Mansfield, Edward D. (1994) *Power, Trade and War*. Princeton: Princeton University Press.

Maoz, Zeev (1989) 'Joining the Club of Nations: Political Development and International Conflict, 1816-1976,' *International Studies Quarterly* 33 (2): 199–231.

Marshall, George (1948) 'Congressional testimony on the European Recovery Program,' *Department of State Bulletin* 71.

Mastanduno, Michael (1992) *Economic Containment: CoCom and the Politics of East-West Trade*. Ithaca: Cornell University Press.

Mastanduno, Michael (1999) 'Economic Statecraft, Interdependence, and National Security: Agendas for Research,' *Security Studies* 9 (1–2): 218–316.

Mastanduno, Michael (2011) 'Economic Statecraft.' In Steve Smith, Amelia Hadfield, and Tim Dunne (eds) *Foreign Policy: Theory, Actors, Cases*. Oxford: Oxford University Press.

Mastanduno, Michael, David Lake, and G. John Ikenberry (1989) 'Toward a Realist Theory of State Action,' *International Studies Quarterly* 33: 457–74.

Mattingly, Garrett (1988) *Renaissance Diplomacy*. New York: Dover Publications, Inc.

Maxfield, Sylvia (1998) 'Understanding the Political Implications of Financial Internationalization in Emerging Market Countries,' *World Development* 26 (7): 1201–19.

Maxfield, Sylvia (2000) 'Comparing East Asia and Latin America: Capital Mobility and Democratic Stability,' *Journal of Democracy* 11(4): 95–106.

Mazower, Mark (1998) *Dark Continent: Europe's Twentieth Century*. New York: Vintage Books.

McDermott, Rose, Dustin Tingley, Jonathan Cowden, Giovanni Frazzetto, and Dominic Johnson (2009) 'Monoamine Oxidase A Gene (MAOA) Predicts Behavioral Aggression Following Provocation,' *Proceedings of the National Academy of Sciences* 106 (7): 2118–23.

McDonald, Mark (2011) 'North Korea Suggests Libya Should Have Kept Nuclear Weapons Program.' *New York Times,* March 24, 2011.

McFaul, Michael and Kathryn Stoner-Weiss (2008) 'The Myth of the Authoritarian Model,' *Foreign Affairs*, 87 (1): 68–84.

McMillan, Susan M. (1997) 'Interdependence and Conflict,' *Mershon International Studies Review* 41 (1): 33–58.

McNeill, William (1965) *The Rise of the West: A History of the Human Community*. Chicago: University of Chicago Press.

Mearsheimer, John (2001) *The Tragedy of Great Power Politics*. New York: Norton.

Mearsheimer, John and Stephen Walt (2007) *The Israel Lobby and US Foreign Policy*. New York: Farrar, Straus & Giroux.

Meltzer, Allan (2000) 'Statement of Allan H. Meltzer on the Report of the International Financial Institution Advisory Commission,' Senate Committee on Banking, Housing, and Urban Affairs, available at http://www.gsia.cmu.edu/afs/andrew/gsia/meltzer/.

Milbank, Dana (2005) 'Intelligence Design and the Architecture of War,' *Washington Post*, December 8, available at http://www.washingtonpost.com/wp-dyn/content/article/2005/12/07/AR2005120702224.html.

Miller, Steven, Sean Lynn-Jones, and Stephen Van Evera (eds) (1991) *Military Strategy and the Origins of the First World War*, Revised and Expanded Edition. Princeton: Princeton University Press.

Morgenthau, Hans J. (1967) *Politics Among Nations*, Fourth Edition, p. 26. New York: Knopf.

Morgenthau, Hans (1985) *Politics Among Nations: The Struggle for Power and Peace*, sixth edition. New York: Knopf.

Mosley, Layna, and Saika Uno (2007) 'Globalization and Collective Labor: Racing to the Bottom or Climbing to the Top? Economic Globalization and Collective Labor Rights,' *Comparative Political Studies* 40 (8): 923–48.

Mueller, John (1973) *War, Presidents, and Public Opinion*. New York: Wiley.

Mueller, John (1989) *The Obsolescence of Major War*. New York: Basic Books.

Mueller, John (2009) 'War Has Almost Ceased to Exist: An Assessment,' *Political Science Quarterly* 124: 297–321.

Naim, Mosies (2005) *Illicit: How Smugglers, Traffickers, and Copycats are Hijacking the Global Economy,* pp. 69, 78–9. New York: Anchor Books.

National Academies of Science (2008) *Understanding and Responding to Climate Change: Highlights of National Academies Reports,* available at http://dels.nas.edu/dels/rpt_briefs/climate_change_2008_final.pdf.

National Resources Defense Council (2002) 'The Consequences of a Nuclear War between India and Pakistan.' June 4, 2002, accessed at www.ndrc.org/nuclear/southasia.asp.

Natsios, Andrew and Michael Abramowitz (2011) 'Sudan's Secession Crisis,' *Foreign Affairs.*

NBC (2003) *Meet the Press,* 'Interview with Vice-President Dick Cheney,' Transcript for March 16, 2003, available at https://www.mtholyoke.edu/acad/intrel/bush/cheneymeetthepress.html.

Neff, Stephen (1990) *Friends but No Allies: Economic Liberalism and the Law of Nations.* New York: Columbia University Press.

Neumayer, Eric and Indra De Soysa (2006) 'Globalization and the Right to Free Association and Collective Bargaining: An Empirical Analysis,' *World Development* 34 (1): 31–49.

Neustadt, Richard (1976) *Presidential Power: The Politics of Leadership, with Reflections on Johnson and Nixon.* New York: John Wiley.

Newnham, Randall (2002) *Deutsche-Mark Diplomacy: Positive Economic Sanctions in German-Russian Relations.* University Park: Penn State University Press.

Nexon, Daniel H. (2009) *The Struggle for Power in Early Modern Europe,* p. 6. Princeton: Princeton University Press.

Nicolson, Harold (1963) *Diplomacy,* pp. 3–4. Oxford: Oxford University Press.

Office of Technology Assessment, US Congress (1979) *The Effects of Nuclear War.* Washington, DC: Government Printing Office.

Olearchyk, Roman and Neil Buckley (2010) 'Russia–Ukraine Gas Peace Threatens to Unravel,' *Financial Times,* September 23.

Oneal, John R. and Bruce Russett (1997) 'The Classic Liberals Were Right: Democracy, Interdependence, and Conflict, 1950-1985,' *International Studies Quarterly* 41 (2): 267–94.

Organization for Economic Cooperation and Development (2012) 'Looking to 2060: Long-Term Global Growth Prospects,' *OECD Economic Policy Papers No. 3.*

Overy, R. J. (2008) *The Origins of the Second World War.* Third Edition, London: Longman Press.

Owen, John (1994) 'How Liberalism Produces Democratic Peace,' *International Security* 19 (2): 87–125.

Pape, Robert (2006) *Dying to Win: The Strategic Logic of Suicide Terrorism.* New York: Random House.

Paterson, Thomas (1973) *Soviet-American Confrontation: Postwar Reconstruction and the Origins of the Cold War.* Baltimore: Johns Hopkins University Press.

Phythian, Mark (2006) 'The Perfect Intelligence Failure? US Pre-War Intelligence on Iraqi Weapons of Mass Destruction,' *Politics & Policy* 34 (2): 400–24.

Podesta, John and Peter Ogden (2008) 'The Security Implications of Climate Change,' *The Washington Quarterly* 31 (1): 115–38.

Price, Richard (1998) 'Reversing the Gun Sights: Transnational Civil Society Targets Land Mines,' *International Organization*. 52: 613–44.

Record, Jeffrey (2002) *Making War, Thinking History: Munich, Vietnam, and Presidential Uses of Force from Korea to Kosovo.* Annapolis: US Naval Institute Press.

Rhodes, Richard (1986) *The Making of the Atomic Bomb.* New York: Simon & Schuster.

Rice, Condoleezza (2006) '*Transformational Diplomacy*,' speech at Georgetown University, January 18.

Richardson, Louise (2007) *What Terrorists Want: Understanding the Enemy, Containing the Threat,* p. 4. New York: Random House.

Ripsman, Norrin, and Jack Levy (2008) 'Wishful Thinking or Buying Time? The Logic of British Appeasement in the 1930s,' *International Security* 33 (2): 148–81.

Roberts, J.M., and O.A. Westad (2013) *The Penguin History of the World*, Sixth Edition. Harmondsworth: Penguin.

Rohde, David (1997) *Endgame: The Betrayal and Fall of Srebrenica, Europe's Worst Massacre Since World War II.* New York: Farrar, Straus, & Giroux.

Rosecrance, Richard (1999) *Rise of the Virtual State: Wealth and Power in the Coming Century.* New York: Basic Books.

Rosen, Stephen (2005) *War and Human Nature.* Princeton: Princeton University Press.

Rotberg, Robert I. (2003) 'Failed States, Collapsed States, Weak States: Causes and Indicators,' in Rotberg (ed.) *State Failure and State Weakness in a Time of Terror*, p. 5. Washington, DC: The Brookings Institution.

Rothwell, Donald R. and Tim Stephens (2010) *The International Law of the Sea.* Oxford: Hart Publishing.

Rudra, Nita (2005) 'Globalization and the Strengthening of Democracy in the Developing World,' *American Journal of Political Science* 49 (4): 704–30.

Ruggie, John (1982) 'International Regimes, Transactions, and Change: Embedded Liberalism in the Postwar Economic Order,' *International Organization* 36 (2): 379–415.

Russett, Bruce (1993) *Grasping the Democratic Peace.* New Haven: Yale University Press.

Russett, Bruce (1993) *Grasping the Democratic Peace: Principles for a Post-Cold War World.* Princeton: Princeton University Press.

Russett, Bruce (2001) *Grasping the Democratic Peace: Principles for a Post-Cold War World.* Princeton: Princeton University Press.

Rutland, Peter (2006) 'Russia's Economic Role in Asia: Toward Deeper Integration.' In Ashley Tellis and Michael Wills *Strategic Asia 2006-07: Trade, Interdependence and Security.* Seattle: National Bureau of Asian Research, pp. 173–202.

Sachs, Jeffrey (2005a) *The End of Poverty: Economic Possibilities for Our Time*. New York: Penguin.

Sachs, Jeffrey (2005b) *Investing in Development: A Practical Plan to Achieve the Millennium Development Goals*. New York: UN Development Program, available at available at http://www.unmillenniumproject.org/reports/fullreport.htm.

Sagan, Scott (1988) 'The Origins of the Pacific War,' *Journal of Interdisciplinary History*, 18 (4): 893–922.

Sagan, Scott (1994) 'From Deterrence to Coercion: The Road to Pearl Harbor.' In Alexander George and William Simons (eds), *Limits of Coercive Diplomacy*, Second Edition, pp. 57–90. Boulder: Westview Press.

Sagan, Scott and Kenneth Waltz (2002) *The Spread of Nuclear Weapons: A Debate Renewed*, Second Edition. New York: Norton.

Sagan, Scott, Kenneth Waltz, and Richard. Betts (2007) 'A Nuclear Iran: Promoting Stability or Courting Disaster,' *Journal of International Affairs* 60 (2): 135–50.

Salehyan, Idean (2008) 'From Climate Change to Conflict? No Consensus Yet,' *Journal of Peace Research* 45 (3): 315–26.

Sanger, David E. (1999) 'A Deal That America Just Can't Refuse,' *New York Times*, November 16.

Sarkees, Meredith Reid, and Frank Wayman (2010) *Resort to War: A Data Guide to Inter-State, Extra-State, Intra-state, and Non-State Wars, 1816-2007*. Washington: CQ Press.

Saunders, Elizabeth (2009) 'Transformative Choices: Leaders and the Origins of Intervention Strategy,' *International Security* 34: 119–61.

Schlesinger, Arthur (1967) 'Origins of the Cold War,' *Foreign Affairs*, 46 (1): 22–52.

Schmitt, Eric and Mark Mazzetti (2011) 'Pakistan Arrests CIA Informants in Bin Laden Raid.' *New York Times,* June 14, 2011.

Schwartz, Stephen (1998) *Atomic Audit: The Costs and Consequences of US Nuclear Weapons Since 1940*. Washington: The Brookings Institution.

Schwarzenbach, Rene, Thomas Egli, Thomas B. Hofstetter, Urs von Gunten, and Bernhard Wehrli (2010) 'Global Water Pollution and Human Health,' *Annual Review of Environment and Resources* 35: 109–36.

Senese, Paul and John Vasquez (2005) 'Assessing the Steps to War,' *British Journal of Political Science* 35 (4): 607–34.

Sharma, Dinesh (2011) *Barack Obama in Hawaii and Indonesia: The Making of a Global President*. Santa Barbara: Praeger Publishers.

Shih, Victor (2008) *Factions and Finance in China: Elite Conflict and Inflation*. Cambridge: Cambridge University Press.

Shultz, George, *et al.* (2007) 'A World Without Nuclear Weapons,' *Wall Street Journal,* January 4.

Singer, J. David (1961) 'The Levels-of-Analysis Problem in International Relations,' *World Politics* 14 (October): 77–92.

Singer, Max and Aaron Wildavsky (1993) *The Real World Order: Zones of Peace, Zones of Conflict. London:* Chatham House.

Skocpol, Theda (1974) *States and Social Revolutions: A Comparative Analysis of France, Russia, and China.* Cambridge: Cambridge University Press.

Smith, Adam ([1776] 1937) *Wealth of Nations,* edited by Edwin Cannan, p. 456. New York: The Modern Library.

Smith, Adam ([1776] 1977) *The Wealth of Nations.* New York: Oxford University Press.

Snyder, Jack (1991) *Myths of Empire: Domestic Politics and International Ambition.* Ithaca: Cornell University Press.

Snyder, Timothy (2010) *Bloodlands: Europe Between Hitler and Stalin.* New York: Basic Books.

Sobel, Richard (2001) *The Impact of Public Opinion on U.S. Foreign Policy Since Vietnam: Constraining the Colossus.* New York: Oxford University Press.

Spruyt, Hendrik (2005) *Ending Empire: Contested Sovereignty and Territorial Partition.* Ithaca: Cornell University Press.

Stein, Janice Gross (1994) 'Political Learning by Doing: Gorbachev as Uncommitted Thinker and Motivated Learner,' *International Organization* 48: 155–83.

Steiner, Zara (2005) *The Lights That Failed: European International History 1919–1933.* Oxford: Oxford University Press.

Stiglitz, Joseph E. (2002) *Globalization and Its Discontents.* New York: Norton.

Stimson, Henry (1947) 'The Decision to Use the Atomic Bomb,' *Harper's Magazine* February 1947, p. 97–107.

Straus, Scott (2005) 'Darfur and the Genocide Debate,' *Foreign Affairs,* 84 (1): 123–33.

Sunstein, Cass (2007) 'Montreal vs. Kyoto: a Tale of Two Protocols,' *Harvard International Environmental Law Review* 31 (1): 1–65.

Tadec, Boris (2010) 'An Apology for Srebrenica.' *Wall Street Journal,* April 16, p. A17.

Talbot, Strobe (2008) *The Great Experiment: The Story of Ancient Empires, Modern States, and the Quest for a Global Nation,* p. 313. New York: Simon & Schuster.

Tannenwald, Nina (2008) *The Nuclear Taboo: The United States and the Non-Use of Nuclear Weapons since 1945.* Cambridge: Cambridge University Press.

Taylor, Jeffrey (2001) 'Russia is Finished,' *The Atlantic Monthly,* 287 (5): 35–49.

Thucydides (1954) *The Peloponnesian War,* Book V, Chapter 89.

Thucydides (1954, translated by Rex Warner) *The Peloponnesian War.* Harmondsworth: Penguin, p. 48.

Thurow, Lester (1992) *Head to Head: The Coming Battle Among Japan, Europe, and America.* New York: Warner Books.

Tickner, J. Ann (1997) 'You Just Don't Understand: Troubled Engagements Between Feminists and IR Theorists,' *International Studies Quarterly* 41: 621.

Tickner, J. Ann (1999) 'Why Women Can't Rule the World: International Politics According to Francis Fukuyama,' *International Studies Review* 1 (3).

Ticktin, Hillel (2011) *Marxism and the Global Financial Crisis.* New York: Routledge.

Tilly, Charles, (ed.) (1975) *The Formation of National States in Western Europe.* Princeton: Princeton University Press.

Tilly, Charles (1985) 'War Making and State Making as Organized Crime.' In Peter B. Evans, Dietrich Rueschemeyer, and Theda Skocpol (eds) *Bringing the State Back In.* New York: Cambridge University Press.

Tilly, Charles (1990) *Coercion, Capital, and European States, AD 900–1900.* Cambridge: Blackwell.

Tow, William, (ed.) (2009) *Security Politics in the Asia Pacific: A Regional-Global Nexus?* Cambridge: Cambridge University Press.

United Nations (2000) *Sustaining Life: How the Convention on Biological Diversity Promotes Nature and Human Well-Being* , available at http://www.cbd.int/doc/publications/cbd-sustain-en.pdf.

United Nations, Food and Agriculture Organization (2012) *The State of World Fisheries and Aquaculture: 2012,* available at http://www.fao.org/docrep/016/i2727e/i2727e00.htm.

US Department of Defense (1977) *Protection in the Nuclear Age.* Defense Civil Preparedness Agency, H-20, February 1977.

US Department of Defense (2010) *Nuclear Posture Review Report.* Washington, accessed at www.defense.gov/npr/docs/2010.

US Department of Defense (2012) *Military and Security Developments Involving the People's Republic of China, 2012.* Annual Report to Congress, Washington.

US Environmental Protection Agency (2012) 'Nitrogen Dioxide: National Trends in Nitrogen Dioxide Levels,' available at http://www.epa.gov/airtrends/nitrogen.html.

US Environmental Protection Agency (undated) 'Sulfur Dioxide Emissions' available at http://cfpub.epa.gov/eroe/index.cfm?fuseaction=detail.viewInd&lv=list.listByAlpha&r=219694&subtop=341.

US National Oceanic and Atmospheric Administration, Fisheries Service (undated) 'The Tuna-Dolphin Issue,' available at http://swfsc.noaa.gov/textblock.aspx?Division=PRD&ParentMenuId=228&id=1408.

Valentino, Benjamin, Paul Huth, and Dylan Balch-Lindsay (2004) '"Draining the Sea": Mass Killing and Guerrilla Warfare,' *International Organization* 58 (2): 375–407.

Walt, Stephen (1996) *Revolution and War.* Ithaca: Cornell University Press.

Walt, Stephen (2000) 'Rush to Failure: The Flawed Politics and Policies of Missile Defense,' *Harvard Magazine* (May–June 2000).

Waltz, Kenneth N. (1959) *Man, the State, and War: A Theoretical Analysis.* New York: Columbia University Press.

Waltz, Kenneth (1979) *Theory of International Politics.* Reading: Addison-Wesley.

Waltz, Kenneth (1993) 'The Emerging Structure of International Politics,' *International Security* 18 (2): 44–79.

Wang, Miao (2009) 'Manufacturing FDI and Economic Growth: Evidence from Asian Economies,' *Applied Economics* 41 (8): 991–1002.

Wapner, Paul (1995) 'Politics Beyond the State: Environmental Activism and World Civic Politics,' *World Politics* 47 (3): 311–40.

Ward, Curtis A. (2003) 'Building Capacity to Combat International Terrorism: The Role of the United Nations,' *Journal of Conflict and Security Law*, 289–305.

Weber, Max (1970) 'Politics as a Vocation.' In H.H. Gerth and C. Wright Mills (eds) *From Max Weber: Essays in Sociology.* London: Routledge, p. 78.

Weinstein, Jeremy (2005) 'Resources and the Information Problem in Rebel Recruitment,' *Journal of Conflict Resolution* 49 (4): 598–624.

Wendt, Alexander (1999) *Social Theory of International Politics.* New York: Cambridge University Press.

Westad, Odd Arne (2005) *The Global Cold War.* Cambridge: Cambridge University Press.

White House (2002), *The National Security Strategy of the United States of America*, Preface and p. 1.

Wilson, Woodrow (1917), Address to the Senate, January 22.

Winer, Jonathan M. (2003) 'The Growing Role of International Institutions in Counterterrorism and Law Enforcement,' Roundtable on Old Rules, New Threats (Council on Foreign Relations/American Society for International Law), November 5.

Wohlforth, William (1999) 'The Stability of a Unipolar World,' *International Security* 21.

World Bank (1998) *Assessing Aid: What Works, What Doesn't, and Why.* Washington: available at http://www.worldbank.org/research/aid/.

World Bank (2013a) *South Africa Overview*, available http://www.worldbank.org/en/country/southafrica/overview.

World Bank (2013b) *World Databank: World Development Indicators.* Washington: available at http://databank.worldbank.org/ddp/home.do?Step=12&id=4&CNO=2.

World Economic Forum (2013) *Global Gender Gap Report 2013*, accessed at www.weforum.org/issues/global-gender-gap.

Wright, Robert (2006) 'Will Globalization Make Hatred More Lethal?' *The Wilson Quarterly*, pp. 35–6.

Xin-An, Lu (2005) 'Ministry of Foreign Affairs in the Age of the Internet.' In Yufan, Hao and Su Lin (eds) *Chinese Foreign Policy Making: Societal Forces and Chinese Foreign Policy.* Aldershot: Ashgate Press.

Xing, Y. and N. Detert (2010) 'How the iPhone Widens the United States Trade Deficit with the People's Republic of China,' *ADBI Working Paper No. 257.* Tokyo: Asian Development Bank Institute.

Zartman, William (1995) 'Introduction: Posing the Problem of State Collapse.' In William Zartman (ed.) *Collapsed States: The Disintegration and Restoration of Legitimate Authority*, p. 5. Boulder: Lynne Rienner.

Index

absolute advantage 250
absolute gains 293, 306–7
Abyssinia 190–1
Acheson, D. 75, 198
acid rain 390–1, 407
actors 100–1
Afghanistan 94, 111–12, 141
    weak/failed state 366, 367–9
Africa 66
    foreign aid and development in 337, 338
    present day 19
    scramble for 18
agriculture
    and development 324–6
    protectionism 308
aid, foreign 334, 335, 336–9, 340–1
airport body scanners 361
Al Qaeda 4, 111–12, 141, 368–9, 372–3, 373–4, 379
alliances 43–4, 75, 431
    fixed and flexible 428
Allison, G. 112–13, 241
ambassadors 178, 179–80
Americas, the
    empires in 15, 35, 36
    European subjugation 39–41
anarchists 372
anarchy 10, 72
    constructivism 93–4
    underlying causes of war 160–2
Angell, N. 197
Annan, K. 380–1, 382
anocratic states 84
anthrax 235
anti-dumping 255–6
anti-dumping duties 255
apartheid 130–1, 350
appeasement 48
Arab Spring 65, 439, 440
Arctic summer ice 394, 395
Argentina 318
arms control 220–2
ASEAN plus Three 422
Asia–Pacific Economic Cooperation (APEC) 422, 423, 425, 427
Asian Tigers 330
aspiration–reality connection 3, 16, 23–4, 55, 87, 103, 155, 191, 218–19, 262, 308, 340, 363, 409, 440

assured destruction 213–17
    see also mutual assured destruction
Atlantic Agreement 336
atmosphere, problems of 394–9
    climate change 394, 395–9, 404, 407–13
    ozone depletion 399, 407–8
Aum Shinrikyo 235
Auschwitz 147
austerity 263, 280–1
Austria 148
autarky 248, 251–2
authoritarian capitalism 350
authoritarian regimes 114, 439
autocratic states 84, 114
autonomy, national 269–70, 300–6
axis of evil 429
Aztec Empire 35, 36, 39

Baker, J. 182
balance of payments 260
balance of power 74–5, 176–7
bandwagoning 184
Bangladesh 395–6
banks
    bankers' influence on foreign policy 126
    international bank loans 258, 333–4, 335
Baruch Plan 234
Battle of Britain 50
Battle of Stalingrad 50
battlefield fatalities 144–5, 146, 166
Bay of Pigs 153, 154
beggar-thy-neighbour policies 47
Beijing Consensus 330
Beijing Olympic Games 298
Berlin Conference 43
Berlin Wall 5–6, 61
Bevin, E. 200
bilateral environmental agreements 407
Bin Laden, Osama 110, 111, 369
biodiversity 404–5
Biological and Toxic Weapons Convention (BWC) 238
biological weapons 235–9
bipolarity 54, 416
    new 432–6
Bismarck, O. von 43–4
Blitzkrieg 50

bonds, international 333, 334, 335
Borsellino, P. 359
Bosnia 22–3
Brazil 347–8
Bretton Woods Conference 198, 274, 277
Bretton Woods system 272, 277, 278
BRICS 342–51
brinksmanship 56, 57
British Empire 39–40
Bull, H. 78
bureaucratic politics 114–17
Bush, G.H.W. 49, 113, 201
Bush, G.W. 201, 308, 368
    administration and terrorism 375–6, 379

Cambodian Civil War 166, 167
Canada–US Air Quality Agreement 391, 407
capitalism 86–92, 157, 296
capitalist class 88, 89
carbon dioxide 395
    emissions 396–8
Cardoso, F.H. 330, 331
Caribbean piracy 362–3
central planning 348–9
centralized states 297–8
Chamberlain, N. 191
Chechnya 366, 367
chemical weapons 235–9
Chemical Weapons Convention (CWC) 237
Cheney, D. 148–9
child labor 336
child soldiers 164
China 34, 75, 76, 150
    Beijing Olympics 298
    centralized state 298
    coercive diplomacy 111, 112
    dollar/renminbi exchange rate 263–4
    and East Asia 304
    East China Sea 301, 302
    emerging great power 343–5
    foreign policy 116–17
    and Google 291
    and international institutions 311, 312
    new bipolarity model 432–6
    Opium Wars 41

China (*continued*)
outward FDI 422, 425
Politburo Standing Committee 117, 118
power balancing 184
rare earth mineral exports 305
rise of and peace 201–2
South China Sea 8, 9, 111, 112
US dependence on for finance 302–3
US foreign policy toward 75, 107, 108
chlorofluorocarbons (CFCs) 399
Churchill, W.S. 52, 53, 55
civil defense 217, 218–19
civil wars 164–5
climate change and 398–9
civilian deaths in war 145–7, 166
clash of civilizations 442–6
characteristics 442–3
contrary evidence and questions 444–6
international trends 443–4
class conflict 88–9
Claude, I. 189
Clausewitz, C. von 213
Clean Air Act 407
cleavages 26–8
climate change 394, 395–9, 404
multilateral approaches 407–13
Clinton, B. 202
Clinton, H. 98, 108, 410–11
closed regional blocs 425, 426
codes of conduct 336
coercive diplomacy 111
coercive policy instruments 109–12
Cold War 27, 51–8, 140, 142, 419, 432
end of 61–3, 418, 421
and internal wars 170–1
as an international order 55–7
nuclear strategies during 213–14, 216
origins 52–5
peace movement 203
collective security 46
international law and institutions 189–93
Colombia 370–1
colonialism 18, 19
and failure to develop as legacy of 323–4
and internal war 170
colonies 39, 323
commercial liberalism 82–3
commitment problem 161
commodity cartels 328
communism 89
communist revolution 92
Community of Democracies 201
comparative advantage 249–51

competing economic blocs 418–27
competition 73–4
Concert of Europe 39
conditionality 278, 280–1
conflict *see* war
connections 16–24
constructivism 17, 92–5, 100–1
assumptions 93
BRICS 343
China and international institutions 312
and climate change agreement 412
economic sanctions against South Africa 130–1
end of the Cold War 421
future of the nation-state 385
G-20 282
groupthink and the Bay of Pigs 154
propositions 93–5
states' desire for nuclear weapons 229
consumption 248–9
trade and gains in 252–3
contagion 163
Convention on Biological Diversity 405
convertible currencies 290
Cooper, R. 447–8
Correlates of War (COW) project 141, 142, 143, 165
cosmopolitanism 85
counter-terrorism regime 378
covert operations 110–11
crisis escalation 152–3
cruise missiles 210
Cuban Missile Crisis 56, 57
currency market interventions 260
currency unions 261–2
current account 260–1
cyber-warfare 241–2
Czechoslovakia 191

Darfur War 168–9
Dawes Plan 47
decentralized states 297–8
decolonization 58–9
deforestation 392, 393, 403–5
demand curves 258–60
democracy
inhibition of war 437–8
MNEs, human rights and 270–1
spread of 436–7, 438–9
US and support for during the Cold War 55
democratic countries 84, 114
possible international community of 199–202

democratic peace 10, 83
characteristics 436–8
contrary evidence and questions 439–41
international trends 438–9
model of future international order 436–41
thesis 157–60, 199–202
democratization 270–1, 441
Deng Xiaoping 129
dependence 300–6
dependencia theory 323–4
détente 64
deterrence 213–19, 228–30
devaluation 278
developed countries 26–7
developing countries 26–7, 318–53
emerging great powers 342–51
growth experiences of groups of 321–2
IMF lending to 339–41
international relations and challenges to 323–6
market-accepting trade strategies 329–30, 331
market-controlling trade strategies 327–9
seeking a better deal in trade negotiations 330–2
development 318–53
difficulties in 324–6
economic 124–5, 320–1
international finance as path to 332–41
international trade as path to 326–32
strategies and emerging great powers 342–51
dictators 47–8
diplomacy 107–9
and promotion of peace 178–82
diplomatic immunity 180
dirty bomb 241
disarmament 230–1, 233, 234
dispute settlement 275
dissatisfied states 27–8
Doha Development Round 276, 346
dollar 278–9, 314
exchange rate with the renminbi 263–4
dollarization 262
dolphins 403, 406–7
domestic economic systems 10, 81, 157
domestic institutions 114–17
political 157–60
domestic law 185
domestic political regimes 114, 148, 149

changes in and shifts in foreign policy 129–31
domestic politics 114–17
  societal actors and 108, 118–23
drug cartels 370–1
dumping 255
Dutch East India Company 288
dynastic states 34, 35, 72

East Asia 66, 304
East China Sea 301, 302
East–West division 27
Easterly, W. 337, 338
economic development 320–1
  relative level of 124–5
economic growth
  experiences of groups of developing countries 321–2
  liberalism and shared benefits of 87
  promoting national growth 299–300
economic incentives 109
economic interdependence 82–3, 196–9, 436
economic liberalism 292–3
economic nationalism 294
economic policy 127
economic sanctions 109–10
  against South Africa 130–1
economic security 418–19
economic self-sufficiency 325
economic systems 10, 81, 157
Eisenhower, D.D. 159
elections 118–19
elites 93
Elshtain, J.B. 97
embassies 180, 181
emerging great powers 14, 342–51
empires 34–6, 72
end of history 442
enduring questions 12–16
energy 314–15, 422
  conflicts over 147–9
  interstate dependence 300–1, 302
English School 77–8
Enloe, C. 96
environment 27, 388–415
  land degradation 392, 393, 403–5
  management of environmental problems 406–13
  MNEs and 269–70
  problems in the atmosphere 394–9, 404, 407–13
  sources of problems 390–3
  water resource problems 392–3, 399–403
environmental determinism 398

ethnic cleansing 150
ethnic identity 149–50, 168
euro 4, 5, 260, 280
euro zone 261–2
Europe
  in 1500 35
  economic integration 198
  gas pipelines 301
  imperialism 39–43
  state system emerges 36–9
European Court of Justice 195
European Economic Community (EEC) 266–7
European Union (EU) 4, 5, 65–6, 280, 422, 423
  and international peace 193–5
  member states 80
exchange-rate systems 258–65, 277–80
exchange rates 258, 259
executive branch 117–18
export-led growth (ELG) 329–30, 331
exports 268
  as a percentage of GDP 289
extended deterrence 227
external balancing 182–4
external shocks 133
externalities 390–1
extra-state wars 141
  incidence 144, 145
  lethality 145, 146

failed state index 366
failed states 61, 299, 358
  challenges to state sovereignty 360–1, 364–71
  global responses to 379–83
  strengthening 378–9
'Failure of Initiative, A' 219
fallout effect 210, 211
feminism 96–9, 100–1, 156
  assumptions 96
  groupthink and the Bay of Pigs 154
  propositions 97–9
feudalism 36
finance capitalism 89–90
financial crises
  global financial crisis of 2008 290, 296, 314
  risk of 335
first-strike capabilities 214–15
fish stocks 392–3, 401–2, 403
fixed alliances 428
fixed capital 267
fixed (pegged) exchange-rate systems 258, 260–5
  benefits and problems 263–5
flexible alliances 428

flexible (floating) exchange-rate systems 258–60
Ford Motor Company 265, 266
foreign affairs media 119–20, 124, 125
foreign aid 334, 335, 336–9, 340–1
foreign direct investment (FDI) 257–8, 267–8, 333–4, 335–6
foreign exchange market 258
foreign policy 91, 104–36
  analysis and study of international relations 106–7
  individual level of analysis 113–14, 127–9
  interests 107, 108
  international level of analysis 123–6, 132–3
  sources 112–26
  sources of change in 127–33
  state level of analysis 114–23, 129–32
  strategy 107–12
Fortna, V.P. 193
Framework Convention on Climate Change 408
framing 120
France 4–5, 148
Franco–Ottoman military alliance 37, 38
free trade agreements (FTAs) 276, 422
fresh-water supplies 399–400
Friedman, T. 438
Fukuyama, F. 99
functionalism 84
fusion bombs 208

gains from trade 251–3, 306–7
Ganges River 400
gangs 359
garrison state 159
gender
  bias 96–9
  and positive illusions 156
  see also feminism
General Agreement on Tariffs and Trade (GATT) 273–4, 275
general wars 140
genocide 145–7, 166, 167
geo-economic competition 418–27
  characteristics 418–22
  contrary evidence and questions 424–6
  international trends 422–4
geography 124
Germany 4–5, 303–4
  political regime change and shifts in foreign policy 129–31
  post-modern world 448–9
  postwar occupation zones 52

Germany (*continued*)
  rise of Hitler   47–8
  Wars of German Unification   183
  Weimar Republic   46–7
  World War I   43–5
  World War II   49–50
Ghani, A.   382–3
glasnost   62
global capitalism   86–92
global civil society   94–5, 202–4
Global Environmental Facility (GEF)   408
global financial crisis of 2008   290, 296, 314
global fracture   446–51
  characteristics of   446–9
  contrary evidence and questions   450–1
  international trends   449–50
global governance   281–3
global warming   *see* climate change
globalization   15–16, 66–7, 87, 198
  and its challenge   314–16
  Marxism and   92
  two great eras of   288–92
Golan Heights   149
good governance   323
Google   291
Gorbachev, M.   62, 63–4, 128, 129
governance
  good   323
  international institutions   281–3
  world trends in   84
government
  managing domestic and international relations   297–9
  preparing for nuclear war   217–19
government procurement   256
Great Depression   47, 48, 296
great-power centrism   25–6
great powers   54
  emerging   14, 342–51
  and the world economy   310–13
Greece   280, 299
  Peloponnesian War   12, 13, 14, 21–2
greed   168
greenhouse gases   395
  emissions   408–13
grievance   168
gross domestic product (GDP)   268, 320
  per capita   320, 321–2
  shares of world GDP   345
gross fixed capital formation   267–8
Group of 7 (G-7)   283
Group of 8 (G-8)   283
Group of 20 (G-20)   281, 282, 283, 315
Group of 77 (G-77)   60, 330–2

groups   80
groupthink   153, 154
Gulf of Mexico oil spill   400, 401
Gulf Wars
  First   113, 115, 181–2, 238, 239
  Second   148–9, 155, 203

Haass, R.   382
Hamilton, A.   294, 324, 325
Han Empire   177
Hardin, G.   391–2
hegemonic wars   140
hegemony   90, 177
Hindu civilization   442
Hiroshima   50–1, 208
Hirschman, A.   303
historical materialism   87
history   101
  end of   442
Hitler, A.   11, 47–8, 49
Holocaust   145–6
Holsti, O.   152
Hong Kong   277
Hull, C.   196, 197, 311
human development   320
Human Development Index (HDI)   320
human rights   108, 270–1
humanitarian interventions   94, 164, 379–83
Huntington, S.   442, 443, 445
Hurricane Katrina   218–19
Hussein, Saddam   113, 115

idealism   93
identities   93, 95
  ethnic identity   149–50, 168
imperial preference system   272
imperialism   17–19
  European   39–43
implosion bomb   224
import quotas   257
import-substituting industrialization (ISI)   327
Incan Empire   35, 36, 39
incentives   109
independence movements   366
India   34
  emerging great power   345–7
  European subjugation   39–41
  greenhouse gas emissions   410–11
individual level of analysis   9, 10
  and internal war   168–9
  sources of foreign policy   113–14
  sources of foreign policy change   127–9
  underlying causes of war   151–6
individuals, liberalism and   80
industrial revolution   87

infant-industry protection   253–4, 255
inflationary expectations   263
institutional constraints   158
inter-communal wars   165
intercontinental ballistic missiles (ICBMs)   210
interdependence, economic   82–3, 196–9, 436
interest groups   120–3, 256
interests   8, 93
  foreign policy   107, 108
Intergovernmental Panel on Climate Change (IPCC)   396
internal balancing   182–4
internal wars   163–71
  causes of   168–71
  and international peace and security   163–4
  types and trends   164–7
International Atomic Energy Agency (IAEA)   230, 231
international bank loans   258, 333–4, 335
international bonds   333, 334, 335
international commodity agreements (ICAs)   328–9
international commodity cartels   328
international conventions on terrorism   377
International Criminal Court (ICC)   186
international customary law   184, 186
international economic institutions   272–84
  finance   277–81
  governance   281–3
  trade   272–7
international economics   246–85
  MNEs   265–71
  trade theory and policy   246, 248–57
international finance and money   257–65
  exchange-rate systems   258–65, 277–80
  international institutions   277–81
  as path to development   332–41
international financial flows   332–41
  opportunities and challenges for developing countries   335–41
  types and magnitudes   332–5
international governmental organizations (IGOs)   6
international institutions   84–5
  China and   311, 312
  economic *see* international economic institutions
  as a mechanism for peace   185–95

international law 84–5
  as a mechanism for peace 185–95
international level of analysis 10
  and internal war 169–71
  sources of foreign policy 123–6
  sources of foreign policy change
    132–3
  underlying causes of war 160–2
International Monetary Fund (IMF)
    277–81
  lending to developing countries
    339–41
international order 39
  Cold War as 55–7
  contemporary 65–7
international organizations 179
international political economy (IPE)
    15–16
international portfolio investment 258,
    332, 334, 335
international relations 2–30
  basic concepts 6–8
  connecting aspiration and reality 16,
    23–4
  connecting past and present 16, 20–3
  connecting theory and practice 16–20
  enduring questions 12–16
  levels of analysis 8–12
  multiple perspectives 24–8
  part of everyday life 4–6
  recognizing cleavages in the
    international system 26–8
  recognizing great-power centrism
    25–6
  study of and foreign policy analysis
    106–7
international society 77–8
international system 10, 32–69
  cleavages within 26–8
  Cold War 51–8
  contemporary 65–7
  decolonization 58–9
  end of the Cold War and collapse of the
    Soviet Union 61–4
  European pursuit of foreign empire
    39–43
  formation from 1500 to 1900 36–43
  influencing the overall political
    orientation of 311–12
  interwar period 46–8
  models of see models of the emerging
    international system
  Non-Aligned Movement 59–60
  Third-World pressure for a new
    international economic order 59–
    61
  Western European state system 36–9

Westphalian state system 37–8,
    358–60
  the world in 1500 34–6
  World War I 43–6
  World War II 49–51
international trade see trade
International Trade Organization (ITO)
    272–3
internationalism 128
internationalization of civil wars 166–7
interstate wars 140–1
  incidence 142–3
  and internal wars 169–70
  lethality 144–7
intra-firm trade 268
intraregional trade 427
invisible hand 293
Iran 111, 215
  nuclear program 225–6
Iran–Iraq War 1980–88 236
Iraq 115
  First Gulf War 113, 115, 181–2, 238,
    239
  Second Gulf War 148–9, 155, 203
Irish Republican Army (IRA) 373
iron rice bowl 345
isolationism 127
Israel 215, 233
Italy 190–1

Janjaweed 168
Japan 34, 66
  East China Sea 301, 302
  and European imperialism 41
  invasion of Manchuria 190
  Meiji Restoration 41
  protection of rice farming 256
  US nuclear attacks in World War II
    50–1, 208, 209
  US oil embargo 158
Jervis, R. 216, 218
Johnson, D. 156
Johnson, L.B. 49

Kant, I. 83, 199–200, 437
Kashirskoye Shosse apartment bombing
    367
Kashmir 181
Keck, M. 132
Kellogg–Briand Pact 47
Kennedy, J.F. 153
Keynes, J.M. 274
Khan, Abdul Qadeer 226
Kindleberger, C. 312–13
Kindleberger spiral of declining world
    trade 272, 273
Kissinger, H. 233, 234

Kline, H.F. 371
Korea, North 180–1, 227, 228, 231, 232
Korea, South 300, 318
Kosovo 120, 380
Krueger, A.O. 255
Kyoto Protocol 106, 408–11

land degradation 392, 393, 403–5
landmines 132
Latin America 66
Law of the Sea Treaty 187–8
leadership
  and the liberal world economy
    312–13
  national leaders see national leaders
League of Nations 46, 189–91
Leahy, W.D. 209
learning 94, 95
  by national leaders and changes in
    foreign policy 127–9
legislative branch 117–18
legitimacy 188
Lenin, V.I. 17–19, 89–90, 295
levels of analysis 9–12
liberalism 17, 79–86, 87, 100–1
  assumptions 79–82
  BRICS 343
  China and international institutions
    312
  and climate change agreement 412
  economic 292–3
  end of the Cold War 420
  future of the nation-state 385
  future of NATO under multipolarity
    431
  G-20 282
  propositions 82–6
  role of the UN 194
  states' desire for nuclear weapons 229
Libya 227, 228
life expectancy 321
limited wars 140
loans
  international bank loans 258, 333–4,
    335
  from official creditors 334–5
lobbying 122
Locarno Accords 47
Lockhart, C. 382–3
Long Telegram 52
lootable wealth 168
Lula, President 348

Mafia 359
major wars 140
male-oriented assumptions 97–8
Manchuria 190

Manhattan Project 208
Mansfield, E. 441
manufacturing 324–6
Mao Zedong 129
marine life 392–3, 401–3
Marine Mammal Preservation Act
    (MMPA) 406–7
market-accepting trade strategies
    329–30, 331
market-controlling trade strategies
    327–9
market–state relationships 292–309
    managing domestic and international
        relations 298–9
    philosophies 292–6
    promoting national economic growth
        299–300
    protecting autonomy 300–6
    pursuing relative and absolute gains
        306–7
    state building, war and markets 307–9
Marshall, G. 200
Marshall Islands 210
Marshall Plan 53
Marxism 17, 86–92, 100–1
    assumptions 88–90
    economic sanctions against South
        Africa 131
    future of the nation-state 385
    propositions 90–2
    states and markets 295–6
Mayan Empire 35
McDonald's theory of war 438
Mearsheimer, J. 202
media 119–20, 124, 125
Meiji Restoration 41
Melos 21–2
mercantilism 39, 248
Mercosur 276
Middle East 215, 422, 444
    Arab Spring 65, 439, 440
militarized international disputes (MIDs)
    141
    incidence 143–4
military action
    against terrorists 377
    humanitarian interventions 94, 164,
        379–83
    pre-emptive 233
    see also war
military force 46, 111–12
military-industrial complex 159
Millennium Development Goals 339
misperceptions 152–3
missile defense 214, 232–3
Missile Technology Control Regime 232
mode of production 88

models of the emerging international
    system 416–53
    clash of civilizations 442–6
    democratic peace 436–41
    geo-economic competition 418–27
    global fracture 446–51
    new bipolarity 432–6
    return to multipolarity 426–32
modern world 447–8, 449, 450
modernization 79–80
Montreal Protocol on Substances that
    Deplete the Ozone Layer 407–8
moral hazard 340
Morgenthau, H. 26
motivated biases 152–3
multilateral environmental efforts
    407–13
multinational enterprises (MNEs) 91,
    265–72, 424
    characteristics 265–7
    and development 335–6
    domestic political consequences
        270–1
    importance to the world economy
        267–8
    and international peace 272
    and national autonomy 269–70
    political issues 268–72
multiple perspectives 24–8
multipolarity 425–31
    characteristics of 428
    contrary evidence and questions
        430–1
    international trends 428–30
Mumbai 346
Munich Analogy 48, 49
Muslim civilization 442, 443–4
Mussolini, B. 47
mutual assured destruction (MAD) 56,
    214–23

Nagasaki 51, 208
Nasser, G. 60
nation-states 7
    see also states
national autonomy 269–70, 300–6
national champions 327
national leaders 6–7
    learning and changes in foreign policy
        127–9
    over-optimism 155–6
    sources of foreign policy 113–14,
        115
    turnover 129
national perspective 25
National Resources Defense Council
    211

national treatment 266–7
national wealth 310
nationalism 59, 77, 78
    economic 294
nations 7
Nazi–Soviet Non-Aggression Pact 49
negative externalities 390–1
Nehru, J. 60, 324, 325
Nestlé Corporation 265, 266
new bipolarity 432–6
    characteristics of 433–4
    contrary evidence and questions
        435–6
    international trends 434–5
New International Economic Order
    (NIEO) 60–1, 332
news media 119–20, 124, 125
Nexon, D. 366
Nixon shock 279
Nkrumah, President 60
Non-Aligned Movement 59–60
non-combatant deaths 145–7, 166
non-governmental organizations (NGOs)
    179
    and changes in foreign policy 131–2
    and the environment 406–7
    peace movements and global civil
        society 202–4
non-state actors 7–8, 356–87
    challenges to state sovereignty 360–77
    international responses to 377–83
non-tariff barriers (NTBs) 254–7, 274
normative change 95
normative constraints 159
North American Free Trade Agreement
    (NAFTA) 276, 422, 423, 425
North Atlantic Treaty Organization
    (NATO) 5, 53, 55, 75
    eastward expansion 420
    future of under multipolarity 431
    humanitarian intervention 94
    intervention in Kosovo 120, 380
North Korea 180–1, 227, 228, 231, 232
nuclear accidents 230
nuclear blast effect 210
nuclear club 211–12
nuclear freeze 220
Nuclear Non-Proliferation Treaty (NPT)
    230–2
Nuclear Security Project 233, 234
Nuclear Suppliers' Group (NSG) 232
Nuclear Utilization Theorists (NUTS)
    217–19
nuclear weapons 14–15, 208–35, 418,
    431
    arms control 220–2
    assured destruction 213–17

compared with chemical and biological weapons 238–9
current capabilities 212, 222–3
deterrence 213–17, 228–30
government preparations to fight nuclear war 217–19
mutual assured destruction 56, 214–23
obtaining nuclear capability 224–6
proliferation 223–35
states' reasons for wanting 226–8, 229
terrorism and 240–1
US nuclear attacks on Japan 50–1, 208, 209
nuclear winter 211
Nunn, S. 233, 234
Nunn–Lugar program 232
Nuremberg Trials 82

Obama, G. 121, 123, 368, 445
objectives 9
ocean pollution 400–1
Office of Technology Assessment (OTA) 210–11
official creditors, loans from 334–5
official development assistance (ODA) 334, 335, 336–9, 340–1
official financial flows 332–3, 334–5
oil
exports 109–10
pollution in the oceans 400–1
production and reserves 328
open regional blocs 425, 426–7
Opium Wars 41
opportunity cost 248–9
Organization of Petroleum Exporting Countries (OPEC) 60, 328, 329
Organization for the Prohibition of Chemical Weapons (OPCW) 237
organized crime 359
Orthodox Christian civilization 442, 444
Ottoman Empire 35, 41
over-fishing 392–3, 401–2, 403
over-optimism 155–6
ozone depletion 399, 407–8

Pakistan 233
Panasonic Washing Machine Company 267
Pape, R. 379
Partial Test Ban Treaty 220
past–present connections 16, 20–3
Pax Romana 176, 177
peace 174–205
democratic see democratic peace
internal wars and 163–4

international distribution of power 176–7
international law and institutions 185–95
MNEs and 271
state strategies for achieving 178–84
transnational mechanisms 196–204
peace movements 202–4
Peace of Westphalia 37–8, 178–9
peaceful change 76
peacekeeping operations 192–3
peacemaking 192
Peloponnesian War 12, 13, 14, 21–2
perestroika 62
Perry, W. 233, 234
personal envoys 180
persuasion, instruments of 107–9
Pipes, R. 216
piracy/pirates 362–4, 365
plutonium 224
policy disagreements 149
policy instruments 9
political institutions, domestic 157–60
political psychology 113–14
political regimes see domestic political regimes
pollution havens 269–70
portfolio investment 258, 332, 334, 335
positive externalities 390
positive illusions 155, 156
post-modern world 448–9, 449–50
poverty trap 337–9
power
balance of 74–5, 176–7
changes in relative power 133
international distribution of 176–7
power balancing 182–4
power transitions 76–7
Prebisch, R. 327
pre-emptive military action 232
pre-modern world 447, 449, 450
price inflation 263
Prisoner's Dilemma 161–2
private financial flows 332–4
private information problem 160–1
privateers 363
privatization of war 374–6
production 88, 248–9
production possibilities frontier (PPF) 248–9
progress 81–2
propaganda 110
'Protection in the Nuclear Age' 218–19
protectionism 253–7
proxy wars 56
public opinion 118–19
Pugwash Conferences 203

purchasing power parity (PPP) 344
Putin, V. 349, 350

race to the bottom 269
rally 'round the flag effect 119
Ramesh, S.J. 410–11
rare earth minerals 305
rationality of states 72–3
raw materials 324–6
Reagan, R. 63, 64, 234
realism 17, 72–9, 100–1, 151
assumptions 72–4
BRICS 343
China and international institutions 312
and climate change agreement 412
economic sanctions against South Africa 130
end of the Cold War 420
English School 77–8
future of the nation-state 385
future of NATO under multipolarity 431
G-20 282
international law and institutions 187
propositions 74–7
role of the UN 194
states' desire for nuclear weapons 229
regime change 129–31
regional blocs 272, 418–27
regional level of analysis 11
regional trade agreements (RTAs) 422, 424
Reinsurance Treaty 44
relations of production 88
relative capabilities 125–6
relative gains 75–6, 294, 306–7
relative level of economic development 124–5
relative power, changes in 133
renminbi/dollar exchange rate 263–4
resource curse 326
resource scarcity 147
Responsibility to Protect (R2P) 361, 381–2
revolution 89, 92
Arab Spring 65, 439, 440
Reykjavik Summit 234
Rhineland Crisis 48
Ricardo, D. 248, 293
Rice, C. 116, 378, 440
Rodrik, D. 81
Roman Empire 176, 177
Romney, M. 121
Roosevelt, F.D. 53, 127–8
Rosecrance, R. 271
Ruhr Crisis 46

rum triangle trade 40–1, 42
Rumsfeld, D. 116
Russia 66, 301, 420
    Chechnya secession movement 366, 367
    emerging great power 348–50
    Ukraine's energy dependence on 300–1, 302
    see also Soviet Union
Rwanda 166, 167

Sachs, J. 337–9
Sagan, S. 228–30
Said, E.W. 445
sarin 235
Schlieffen Plan 44, 45
Schuman, R. 198
scramble for Africa 18
secessionist civil wars 164–5
second-strike capabilities 214–15
security 73
    collective 46, 189–93
    economic 418–19
    internal wars and 163–4
    post-modern world 450
    tightening against terrorism 378
security dilemmas 74–5, 76
    thesis of the Cold War 54
self-determination 52, 59
sensitivity 302
September 11 terrorist attacks 4, 371–2, 373, 443
Serbia 44, 120
    nationalist rally 78
Shanghai Cooperation Organization (SCO) 429
Shultz, G. 233, 234
Sikkink, K. 132
Singer, M. 446–7
Sino-centric civilization 442, 443, 444
Six-Party Talks 181, 232
Smith, A. 82, 83, 87, 196, 248, 292–3
Smoot-Hawley Tariff 20, 47
Snyder, J. 73, 441
social change 64
socialization 94, 95
societal actors 118–23
society of states 77–8
socioeconomic classes 88
soft balancing 429
Somalia 447, 448
    piracy 363, 364, 365
South Africa
    economic sanctions against 130–1
    emerging great power 350–1
South China Sea 8, 9, 111, 112
South Korea 300, 318

Southeast Asia 76
sovereignty 7, 356–87
    challenges to 360–77
    theory and practice 375
    Westphalian system and 358–60
Soviet Union 418, 419
    and the Cold War 52–3, 54, 55–7
    Cold War nuclear strategy 213–14, 216
    collapse of 61–4
    economic reform 61–2
    see also Russia
specialization 251–2, 256
sphere of influence 53–4
Spratlys, the 435
Srebrenica 22–3, 24
stabilization programs 339–40
Stalin, J. 47, 52, 53, 54
state building 307–9
state level of analysis 10
    and internal war 169
    sources of foreign policy 114–23
    sources of foreign policy change 129–32
    underlying causes of war 157–60
state-owned enterprises (SOEs) 344
states 7
    English School and society of 77–8
    future for 384–5
    and the global capitalist system 90–1
    global system of *see* international system
    rationality of 72–3
    realism and 72–3
    reasons for desiring nuclear weapons 226–8, 229
    relationship to markets *see* market–state relationships
    sovereignty *see* sovereignty
    strategies for achieving peace 178–84
status 226–7
Stimson, H. 209
Strait of Hormuz 109, 110
Strategic Arms Limitation Treaties (SALT) 220
Strategic Arms Reduction Treaties (START) 220–2
strategic culture 94, 95
strategies 9
    development 342–51
    foreign policy 107–12
stress 152
Stuxnet 241
submarine-launched ballistic missiles (SLBMs) 210
Sub-Saharan Africa 35, 334, 335
    European subjugation 39–41

Sub-Saharan African civilization 442
Sudan 369–70
Sudetenland 48
Sukarno, President 60
superpowers 54
    see also great powers
supply curves 258–60
Syria 117–18, 124, 236–7, 447–8, 449
system of states *see* international system

Taiwan 150, 151, 300, 433
Talbot, S. 380
Taliban 111–12, 141, 368–9
Tannenwald, N. 213
tariffs 254, 273–4
Taylor, C. 82, 164
technology
    challenges to state sovereignty 360, 361, 362
    and the privatization of war 374–6
terms of trade 252
territory
    conflicts of interest over 150–1
    sovereign states and control of 360–1
terrorism 432, 443–4
    challenges to state sovereignty 361, 371–4
    international responses 377–9
    September 11 attacks 4, 371–2, 373, 443
    war on 4, 377, 443
    WMD and 240–2
theories of international relations 9, 70–103
    comparing traditions 99–101
    connections between theory and practice 16–20
    constructivism 92–5, 100–1
    English School 77–8
    feminism 96–9, 100–1
    liberalism 79–86, 87, 100–1
    Marxism 86–92, 100–1
    realism 72–9, 100–1
thermal effect 210, 211
thermonuclear bombs 208–9
Third World 56, 58–61
    pressure for a new international economic order 60–1
    see also developing countries; development
Thirty Years War 37
Thucydides 12, 14, 21–2
Tickner, A. 97, 99
tied aid 337
Tito, President 60
Tokyo Round 274

trade   20, 26, 246, 248–57
   comparative advantage   249–51
   free in principle, not practice   308
   gains from   251–3, 306–7
   international institutions   272–7
   as path to development   326–32
   and promotion of peace   196–9
   protectionism   253–7
   pursuing relative and absolute gains
     306–7
   rum triangle   40–1, 42
trade negotiations   330–2, 422
tragedy of the commons   391–3
transition to democracy   270–1, 441
transnational business   91
transnational peace mechanisms
   196–204
   economic interdependence   196–9
   international community of democratic
     nations   199–202
   peace movements and global civil
     society   202–4
transnationalism   85
treaties   186–8
Treaty of Westphalia   37–8, 178–9
trench warfare   45
Trinity test   208
Triple Alliance   43–4
Triple Entente   44
tropical deforestation   392, 393, 403–5
Truman, H.S.   122–3
Truman Doctrine   53, 55
tuna fishing   403, 406–7

Ukraine   121–2
   energy dependence on Russia   300–1,
     302
unacceptable damage   214
under-representation of women   98–9
unilateral environmental efforts
   406–7
unipolarity   65
unitary-actor assumption   158
United Nations (UN)   51
   and failed states   379–81
   and international peace   191–3, 194
   Security Council   7, 56–7, 109, 188,
     192, 193
United Nations Conference on Trade and
   Development (UNCTAD)   60
United States (US)
   and acid rain in Canada   391
   Clean Air Act   407
   and the Cold War   53–4, 55–7
   Cold War nuclear strategy   213–14,
     216
   decentralized state   298

democracies and international peace
   200–1
dependence on China for finance
   302–3
First Gulf War   113, 115, 181–2, 238,
   239
foreign policy toward China   75, 107,
   108
in global fracture model   450–1
India and greenhouse gas emissions
   410–11
and the Kyoto Protocol   410–11
Marine Mammal Preservation Act
   406–7
new bipolarity model   432–6
nuclear attacks on Japan   50–1, 208,
   209
nuclear deal with India   346
oil embargo against Japan   158
role in ending the Cold War and Soviet
   collapse   63–4
Second Gulf War   148–9, 155, 203
Smoot-Hawley Tariff   20, 47
support for democracy during the Cold
   War   55
unipolarity   65
US–Canada Air Quality Agreement
   391, 407
Vietnam War   20, 23, 203
war on terrorism   4, 377, 443
and the world economy   278–9,
   310–13
unmanned drones   61, 362
uranium   224
Uruguay Round   274
utility   248

Versailles Treaty   45–6
Vietnam War   20, 203
   Memorial   23
voluntary export restraints (VERs)
   257
vulnerability   302

Waltz, K.   125, 160, 173, 228, 431
war   10–11, 73–4, 138–73
   between countries   140–7
   diplomacy and averting   180–2
   immediate causes   147–51
   individual level of analysis   151–6,
     168–9
   inhibited by democracy   437–8
   internal wars   163–71
   international level of analysis   160–2,
     169–71
   privatization of   374–6
   state building, markets and   307–9

state level of analysis   157–60, 169
   underlying causes   151–62
war crimes   82, 163–4
war lords   359, 364–71
war on terrorism   4, 377, 443
war zones (combat zones)   124, 125
Warsaw Pact   55
Washington Consensus   81, 281
water resources   399–403
   contamination of fresh-water supplies
     399–400
   oil pollution in the oceans   400–1
   threats to marine life   392–3, 401–3
weak states   360–1, 364–71
   strengthening   378–9
   see also failed states
weapons of mass destruction (WMD)
   206–43, 374–6, 377
   chemical and biological weapons
     235–9
   cyber-warfare   241
   nuclear weapons   see nuclear weapons
   and terrorism   240–2
Weimar Republic   46–7
Western civilization   442, 443
Western Front   45
Westphalian state system   37–8,
   358–60
whale hunting   402–3
Wildavsky, A.   446–7
William II of Germany   44
Williams, J.   132
Wilson, W.   122, 189, 190, 200
women, under-representation of   98–9
worker productivity   326
workers' rights   269–70
World Bank   277, 408
world economy
   contemporary   314–16
   great powers and   310–13
   importance of MNEs to   267–8
   institutions   272–84
   see also international economics
World Trade Organization (WTO)   201,
   273, 275, 276–7, 315, 332
World War I   43–6, 201
World War II   49–51, 310–11
   genocide   145–7
   US nuclear attacks on Japan   50–1,
     208, 209
Wright, R.   379

Yalta Conference   53
Yemen   375

Zedillo, E.   255
zone of peace   199